HUMAN BEHAVIOR AT WORK: ORGANIZATIONAL BEHAVIOR

McGRAW-HILL SERIES IN MANAGEMENT
Fred Luthans and Keith Davis, Consulting Editors

As an additional learning tool, McGraw-Hill also publishes a study guide to supplement your understanding of this textbook. Here is the information your bookstore manager will need to order it for you: 15569-0 STUDY GUIDE TO ACCOMPANY HUMAN BEHAVIOR AT WORK, 7/e

HUMAN BEHAVIOR AT WORK: ORGANIZATIONAL BEHAVIOR

Seventh Edition

KEITH DAVIS, Ph.D.
Arizona State University

JOHN W. NEWSTROM, Ph.D.
University of Minnesota, Duluth

McGraw-Hill Book Company
New York   St. Louis   San Francisco   Auckland
Bogotá   Hamburg   Johannesburg   London   Madrid
Mexico   Montreal   New Delhi   Panama   Paris
São Paulo   Singapore   Sydney   Tokyo   Toronto

HUMAN BEHAVIOR AT WORK: Organizational Behavior

Copyright © 1985, 1981, 1977, 1972 by McGraw-Hill, Inc. All rights reserved. Formerly published under the title of *Human Relations at Work: The Dynamics of Organizational Behavior,* copyright © 1967, 1962, 1957 by McGraw-Hill, Inc. All rights reserved. Printed in the United States of America. Except as permitted under the United States Copyright Act of 1976, no part of this publication may be reproduced or distributed in any form or by any means, or stored in a data base or retrieval system, without the prior written permission of the publisher.

This book was set in Times Roman by Black Dot, Inc. (ECU).
The editors were John R. Meyer and Laura D. Warner;
the designer was Robin Hessel;
the production supervisor was Phil Galea.
New drawings were done by Fine Line Illustrations, Inc.
Von Hoffmann Press, Inc., was printer and binder.

1 2 3 4 5 6 7 8 9 0 V N H V N H 8 9 8 7 6 5 4

ISBN 0-07-015566-6

Library of Congress Cataloging in Publication Data

Davis, Keith, date
    Human behavior at work.

    (McGraw-Hill series in management)
    Bibliography: p.
    Includes indexes.
    1. Organizational behavior.   2. Industrial sociology.
I. Newstrom, John W.   II. Title.   III. Series
HD58.7.D36   1985   658.3   84-15480
ISBN 0-07-015566-6

ABOUT THE AUTHORS

KEITH DAVIS is Professor Emeritus of Management in the College of Business Administration at Arizona State University. He is the author of prominent books on management and a consulting editor for approximately eighty books in the McGraw-Hill Book Company's Series in Management. He is a Fellow in both the Academy of Management and the International Academy of Management. Prior to entering the teaching field, Davis was a personnel specialist in industry and a personnel manager in government.

Davis received his Ph.D. from Ohio State University and has taught at the University of Texas and Indiana University. His fields of work are organizational behavior, personnel management, and social issues in management. He has been visiting professor at a number of universities, including the University of Western Australia and the University of Central Florida. In addition, he has served as consultant to a number of business and government organizations, including Mobil Oil Company, Texaco, the U.S. Internal Revenue Service, and the state of Hawaii.

Davis is a former president of the Academy of Management, and he received the National Human Relations Award from the Society for Advancement of Management. He also has been a National Beta Gamma Sigma Distinguished Scholar. He is an Accredited Senior Professional in Human Resources.

Two other popular books by Davis are (with William B. Werther) *Personnel Management and Human Resources* (2d ed., 1985) and (with William C. Frederick) *Business and Society* (5th ed., 1984), both published by McGraw-Hill Book Company. He also has contributed chapters to over 100 other books, and he is the author of over 150 articles in journals such as *Harvard Business Review, Academy of Management Journal, Management International*, and *California Management Review*. Four of his books have been translated into other languages.

JOHN W. NEWSTROM is Professor of Management and Industrial Relations in the School of Business and Economics at the University of Minnesota, Duluth. He previously taught at Arizona State University after receiving his Ph.D. from the University of Minnesota. His fields of interest are in management development, performance appraisal, alternative work schedules, management by objectives, and group dynamics.

Newstrom is a former chairperson of the Management Education and Development Division of the Academy of Management, and is on the board of directors for the American Society for Training and Development. He has served on the editorial review boards for the *Academy of Management Review, Academy of Management Journal, Journal of Management Development,* and *Personnel Administrator.* He also has been a training consultant to numerous organizations, including the Bureau of Indian Affairs, Blandin Paper Company, Diamond Tool, and Minnesota Power.

Newstrom is the coauthor (with Keith Davis) of *Organizational Behavior: Readings and Exercises* (7th ed., 1985) and (with Edward E. Scannell) of *More Games Trainers Play* (1983). He also has prepared two other books published by McGraw-Hill Book Company, and he is the author of over fifty articles in journals such as *Personnel Psychology, Journal of Management, Journal of Occupational Behaviour,* and *Academy of Management Journal.*

**To our mothers,
and to the memory
of our fathers**

———————————

CONTENTS

PART 4
ORGANIZATIONAL ENVIRONMENT

**PART 5
SOCIAL ENVIRONMENT**

PART 6
COMMUNICATION AND COUNSELING

PART 7
CONCLUSION

PREFACE

This book is about people at work in all kinds of organizations and how they may be motivated to work together more productively. This subject is called organizational behavior, human relations, or human behavior at work, and it is an integration of social sciences as they affect people at work. A subject so vast can be merely introduced in the space of one book. Management, labor, and others can take justifiable credit for advances in the field of organizational behavior during this century, but much improvement still lies ahead. Perhaps this book can suggest directions toward further progress.

All people who work in organizations should find this book helpful in understanding and guiding the behavior of others. It is designed for use in university courses, management development programs, advanced supervisory training, adult education classes, and management self-study. Earlier editions have been used worldwide; and international editions include one published in Japan for the Asian market, an edition in India, and translations into three other languages.

The book has been tested on the firing line in university classrooms and in organizations for more than twenty-five years, and many ideas offered by users of earlier editions have been incorporated into this new one. We actively invite comments from both faculty and students to help us make the book even more useful. We listen, and we care. In response to recommendations by readers, we have expanded features such as figures and examples from actual practice to illustrate ideas. We emphasize content and substance, and the seventh edition has been upgraded by thorough citations to recent research.

In order to produce a book that is both teachable and readable, we have tried to present material in an organized fashion that will enable readers to integrate the various parts of this discipline into a whole philosophy of organizational behavior. Where appropriate, we have included different viewpoints to encourage readers to do their own thinking on a subject, but we have attempted to screen out trivial issues and passing fads.

One of the most notable features of this book is its careful blending of theory with practice, so that basic theories come to life in a realistic context. Readers learn that concepts and models will apply in the real world and will help to build better organizations and a better society. The ideas and skills they learn in an organizational behavior course can help them cope better with life.

Another popular feature, widely recognized, is the hundreds of examples of real organizational situations. They illustrate how actual organizations operate and how people act in specific situations. The majority of major concepts in this book are illustrated with one or more of these examples.

A feature liked by both faculty and students is the book's readability. Following the concepts of both Flesch and Gunning, we have maintained a moderate vocabulary level and a readable style. Variety enhances the readability by inclusion of the many change-of-pace examples mentioned earlier.

Other features of the book include:

1 A framework of four models of organizational behavior extending throughout the book

2 Broad coverage of employee communication, much of it based on the authors' own research

3 Extensive discussion of organizational climate and quality of work life (QWL)

4 A strong section on motivational theories and their application to reward systems in organizations

5 General freedom from a sexist vocabulary and content

6 Several longer cases, appropriate for written and group assignments, at the end of the text material

New or expanded features in the seventh edition include:

1 A revised structure, placing the chapter on climate earlier, and the discussion of informal organization immediately following the condensed material on organization structure

2 A new emphasis on the role of organizational behavior in contributing to productivity

3 New coverage of Theory Z

4 Introduction of attribution theory, and expanded treatment of the expectancy model of motivation

5 Expanded coverage of employee stress, including burnout

6 Completely revised chapters on appraising and rewarding performance; interpersonal and group dynamics; and structure, technology, and people

7 The addition of margin notes to highlight key concepts, expansion of the Table of Contents, and inclusion of a comprehensive glossary of terms at the end of the book

8 Expanded treatment of the post-industrial labor force, as well as the limitations of organizational behavior

9 New coverage of socialization, employee turnover, robotics, employee ownership plans, social cues, ecological control, and networks

Learning aids

Major features included in each chapter are chapter objectives, introductory quotations and incidents, a chapter summary, terms and concepts for review, true case incidents for analysis in terms of chapter ideas, and a thorough and up-to-date set of references that provide a rich source of additional information for the interested reader. There are also numerous discussion questions, many of which require thought, encourage insight, or invite students to analyze their own experiences in terms of the ideas in the chapter. Other questions suggest appropriate group projects. A number of experiential exercises are also included for classroom use.

Instructional aids

Since this book has been used in classrooms for six editions, several classroom-proven instructional aids have been developed and refined over the years.

1 *Readings and experiential exercises.* The seventh edition of *Organizational Behavior: Readings and Exercises,* by Keith Davis and John W. Newstrom, has over seventy readings from a rich variety of sources to give students a broader view of organizational behavior. There are also several experiential exercises designed to allow students to compare their own thoughts with those of other classmates in the application of organizational behavior ideas.

2 *Study guide.* The study guide, by Jon L. Pierce and John W. Newstrom, provides a valuable tool to help students learn and assess their progress as they work through the text. It includes a brief chapter summary and objectives, plus a variety of multiple-choice, true-false, matching, and essay questions arranged in assignments for each chapter.

3 *Test bank.* There is an extensive test bank to help instructors prepare examinations. It is available through McGraw-Hill Book Company.

4 *Instructor's manual.* The instructor's manual, prepared by Fred Brandt, contains sample course assignment sheets, various types of questions for each chapter, notes on the incidents and end-of-text cases, and sample examinations. In addition, there is a film and videotape list for each chapter.

5 *Transparency masters.* A full set of transparency masters is supplied for each chapter with the instructor's manual.

Acknowledgments

Many scholars, managers, and students have contributed ideas to this book, and we wish to express our appreciation for their aid. In a sense, it is their book, for we are only the agents who prepared it. We are especially grateful for able reviews of portions of the book by Carmen Caruana, St. John's University; William M. Dickson, Green River Community College; Jon English, George Mason University; Bruce D. Evans, The University of Dallas; Joseph Foerst, Georgia State University; Ronald E. Guitarr, Northeastern University; Gerald D. McCarthy, Purdue University; Charles Noty, Roosevelt University; and Gene Schneider, Austin Community College. We also appreciate the help of many McGraw-Hill employees who worked with the book, especially John Meyer, Kathi Benson, and Laura Warner.

Keith Davis
John W. Newstrom

PART

1

FUNDAMENTALS OF ORGANIZATIONAL BEHAVIOR

CHAPTER

1

WORKING WITH PEOPLE

The human being is the center and yardstick of everything.
Ernesto Imbassahy de Mello[1]

If you dig very deeply into any problem, you will get "people."
J. Watson Wilson[2]

CHAPTER OBJECTIVES

TO UNDERSTAND:
The meaning of organizational behavior
Some of the elements with which it is concerned
High points in its early history
Basic concepts of organizational behavior
Holistic organizational behavior

Organizations are social systems. If one wishes to work in them or to manage them, it is necessary to understand how they operate. Organizations combine science and people—technology and humanity. Technology is difficult enough by itself, but when you add people you get an immensely complex social system that almost defies understanding. However, society must understand organizations and use them well because they are necessary to achieve the benefits of civilization. They are necessary for world peace, successful school systems, and other desirable goals that people seek. Modern society depends on organizations for its survival.

Human behavior in organizations is rather unpredictable as we now see it. It is unpredictable because it arises from people's deep-seated needs and value systems. However, it can be partially understood in terms of the frameworks of behavioral science, management, and other disciplines; and that is the objective of this book. There are no simple, cookbook formulas for working with people. There is no perfect solution to organizational problems. All that can be done is to increase our understanding and skills so that human relationships at work can be upgraded. The goals are challenging and worthwhile.

No simple formulas

We can work effectively with people if we are prepared to think about them in human terms. Consider the following situation in which a manager's motivation was increased after years of passive, minimum performance.

John Perkins, age about fifty, worked as assistant manager of a branch bank in a large banking system. He had been an assistant manager for eleven years. His work was so mediocre that no branch manager wanted him. Usually his current manager would arrange to move him out of the way by transferring him to a new branch that was opening; so John worked in eight branches in eleven years. When he became assistant manager at his ninth branch, his manager soon learned of his record. Although tempted to transfer John, the manager decided to try to motivate him. The manager learned that John had no economic needs because he had a comfortable inheritance and owned several apartment houses. His wife managed the apartments. His two children were college graduates and had good incomes. John was contented.

The manager made little headway with John and twice considered discharging him. Occasionally John developed a drive for a few weeks, but then he lapsed into his old ways again. After a careful analysis of John's situation, the manager concluded that although John's needs for tangible goods were satisfied, he might respond to more recognition; so the manager started working in that direction. For example, on the branch's first birthday the manager held a party for all employees before the bank opened. He had a caterer prepare a large cake and write on top an important financial ratio that was under John's jurisdiction and was favorable at the moment. John was emotionally inspired by the recognition and the ''kidding'' that his associates gave him about the ratio. His behavior substantially changed thereafter, and with further recognition he improved to become a successful manager of another branch within two years. In this instance John's performance was improved because his manager carefully analyzed the situation and used behavioral skills, such as recognition, to achieve a result beneficial to both parties. That is the essence of organizational behavior.

Definition

Organizational behavior is the study and application of knowledge about how people act within organizations. It is a human tool for human benefit. It applies broadly to the behavior of people in all types of organizations, such as business, government, schools, and service organizations. Wherever organizations are, there is a need to understand organizational behavior.[3]

The key elements in organizational behavior are people, structure, technology, and the environment in which the organization operates. When people join together in an organization to accomplish an objective, some kind of structure is required. People also use technology to help get the job done, so there is an interaction of people, structure, and technology, as shown in Figure 1-1. In addition, these elements are influenced by the external environment, and they influence it. Each of the four elements of organizational behavior will be considered briefly.

Key elements

People   People make up the internal social system of the organization. They consist of individuals and groups, and large groups as well as small ones. There are unofficial, informal groups and more official, formal ones. Groups are dynamic. They form, change, and disband. The human organization today is not the same as it was yesterday, or the day before. People are the living, thinking, feeling beings who created the organization to achieve their objectives. Organizations exist to serve people, rather than people existing to serve organizations.

Structure   Structure defines the official relationships of people in organizations. Different jobs are required to accomplish all of an organization's activities. There are managers and employees, accountants and assemblers. These people have to be related in some structural way so that their work can be effective. These relationships create complex problems of cooperation, negotiation, and decision making.

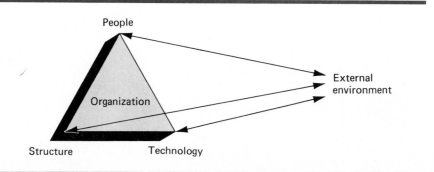

People

External
environment

Organization

Structure   Technology

Figure 1-1
Key elements in
organizational
behavior

Technology   Technology provides the resources with which people work and affects the tasks that they perform. They cannot accomplish much with their bare hands, so they build buildings, design machines, create work processes, and assemble resources. The technology that results has a significant influence on working relationships. An assembly line is not the same as a research laboratory, and a steel mill does not have the same working conditions as a hospital. The great benefit of technology is that it allows people to do more and better work, but it also restricts people in various ways. It has costs as well as benefits.

Environment   All organizations operate within an external environment.[4] A single organization does not exist alone. It is part of a larger system that contains many other elements, such as government, the family, and other organizations. All of these mutually influence each other in a complex system that becomes the lifestyle of a group of people. Individual organizations, such as a factory or a school, cannot escape being influenced by this external environment. It influences the attitudes of people, affects working conditions, and provides competition for resources and power. It must be considered in the study of human behavior in organizations.

The administrative point of view

All people in organizations are concerned with improving organizational behavior. The clerk, the machinist, and the manager all work with people and thereby influence the behavioral quality of life in an organization. Managers, however, tend to have a larger responsibility, because they are the ones who make decisions affecting many people throughout an organization, and most of their daily activities are people-related. Managers represent the *administrative system,* or management system, and their role is to use organizational behavior to improve people-organization relationships, as shown in Figure

Figure 1-2
The administrative
system in
organizational
behavior

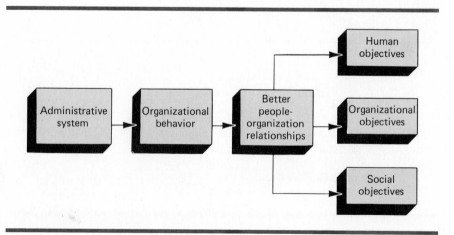

1-2. Managers try to build a climate in which people are motivated, work together productively, and become more effective persons.

When organizational behavior is applied successfully, it becomes a *triple reward system* in which human, organizational, and social objectives are met. People find more satisfaction in work when there is cooperation and teamwork. They are learning, growing, and contributing. The organization also is more successful, because it operates more effectively. Quality is better and costs are less. Perhaps the greatest beneficiary of the triple reward system is society itself, because it has better products and services, better citizens, and a climate of cooperation and progress. There is a three-party win-win-win result in which there are no losers.

Triple reward system

HISTORICAL DEVELOPMENT OF ORGANIZATIONAL BEHAVIOR

Historical origins

Although human relationships have existed since the beginning of time, the art and science of trying to deal with them in complex organizations is relatively new. In the early days people worked alone or in such small groups that their work relationships were easily handled. It has been popular to assume that under these conditions people worked in a Utopia of happiness and fulfillment, but this assumption is largely a nostalgic reinterpretation of history. Actual conditions were brutal and backbreaking. People worked from dawn until dusk under intolerable conditions of disease, filth, danger, and scarcity of resources. They had to work this way to survive, so they had little time to improve job satisfactions.

Then came the industrial revolution. In the beginning the condition of people did not improve, but at least the seed was planted for potential improvement. Industry created a surplus of goods and knowledge that eventually gave workers increased wages, shorter hours, and more work satisfaction. In this new industrial environment Robert Owen, a young Welsh factory owner, about the year 1800, was one of the first to emphasize human needs of employees. He refused to employ young children. He taught his workers cleanliness and temperance and improved their working conditions. This could hardly be called modern organizational behavior, but it was a beginning. He was called "the real father" of personnel administration by an early writer.[5]

Robert Owen

Andrew Ure incorporated human factors into his *The Philosophy of Manufactures,* published in 1835.[6] He recognized the mechanical and commercial parts of manufacturing, but he also added a third factor, which was the human factor. He provided workers with hot tea, medical treatment, "a fan apparatus" for ventilation, and sickness payments. The ideas of Owen and Ure were accepted slowly or not at all, and they often deteriorated into a paternalistic, do-good approach rather than a genuine recognition of the importance of people at work.

Andrew Ure

Early development

Frederick W. Taylor

Interest in people at work was awakened by Frederick W. Taylor in the United States in the early 1900s. He is often called "the father of scientific management," and the changes he brought to management paved the way for later development of organizational behavior. His work eventually led to improved recognition and productivity for industrial workers. He pointed out that just as there was a best machine for a job, so were there best ways for people to do their jobs. To be sure, the goal was still technical efficiency, but at least management was awakened to the importance of one of its neglected resources.

Taylor's major work was published in 1911.[7] During that decade interest in human conditions at work was accelerated by World War I. The National Personnel Association was formed, and later, in 1923, it became the American Management Association, carrying the subtitle "Devoted Exclusively to the Consideration of the Human Factor in Commerce and Industry." During this period Whiting Williams was studying workers while working with them, and in 1920 he published a significant interpretation of his experiences, *What's on the Worker's Mind.*[8]

Mayo and Roethlisberger

*Development
of research*

In the 1920s and 1930s Elton Mayo and F. J. Roethlisberger at Harvard University gave academic stature to the study of human behavior at work. They applied keen insight, straight thinking, and sociological backgrounds to industrial experiments at the Western Electric Company, Hawthorne Plant. The result was the concept that an organization is a social system and the worker is indeed the most important element in it.[9] Their experiments showed that the worker is not a simple tool but a complex personality interacting in a group situation that often is difficult to understand.

To Taylor and his contemporaries, human problems stood in the way of production and so should be minimized. To Mayo, human problems became a broad new field of study and an opportunity for progress. He is recognized as *Human relations* the father of what was then called *human relations* and later became known as *organizational behavior.* Taylor increased production by rationalizing it. Mayo and his followers sought to increase production by humanizing it.

The Mayo-Roethlisberger research has been strongly criticized as being inadequately controlled and interpreted,[10] but its basic ideas, such as a social system within the work environment, have stood the test of time. The important point is that it was substantial research about human behavior at work, and its influence was widespread.

In the 1940s and 1950s other major research projects developed in a number of organizations, including the Research Center for Group Dynamics, University of Michigan (especially leadership and motivation); Personnel Research Board, Ohio State University (leadership and motivation); Tavistock Institute of Human Relations in London (various subjects); and the National Training Laboratories in Bethel, Maine (group dynamics). As the

Figure 1-3
The cooperative approach can be overdone.
Source: *United Features Syndicate, copyright © 1956. Used with permission.*

results of this research began to filter into the business and academic communities, it stimulated new interest in the behavior of people at work. An "age of human relations" had begun.

A fad

The new emphasis on people at work was a result of trends that had been developing over a long period of time. It helped bring human values back into balance with other values at work. The unfortunate part of the situation, however, was that human relations grew so fast that much faddism and shallowness developed. Some practitioners began to emphasize the big smile, "being nice to people," and "keep 'em happy," while subtly trying to manipulate employees. This approach is illustrated by the cartoon in Figure 1-3. One humorist observed, "We have moved from the 'invisible hand' of Adam Smith's economics to the 'glad hand' of human relations." These practices led to well-deserved criticisms.[11]

The term "human relations" gradually lost favor, although it continues to be used—especially at the operating level—because of its appropriateness. An example is the statement "The supervisor is effective with human relations." As the field became more mature and research-based, the new term that arose to describe it was "organizational behavior."[12]

FUNDAMENTAL CONCEPTS

Every field of social science (or even physical science) has a philosophical foundation of basic concepts that guide its development. In accounting, for example, a fundamental concept is that "for every debit there will be a credit." The entire system of double-entry accounting was built on this philosophy when it replaced single-entry bookkeeping many years ago. In physics, a basic philosophy is that elements of nature are uniform. The law of gravity operates uniformly in Tokyo and London, and an atom of hydrogen is identical in Moscow and Washington, D.C. But the same cannot be said for people.

As shown in Figure 1-4, organizational behavior deals with a set of fundamental concepts revolving around the nature of people and organizations. A summary of these ideas follows, and they are developed further in later chapters.[13]

The nature of people
* Individual differences
* A whole person
* Motivated behavior
* Value of the person (human dignity)

Figure 1-4
Fundamental
concepts of
organizational
behavior

The nature of organizations
* Social systems
* Mutual interest

Result   Holistic organizational behavior

The nature of people

With regard to people, there are four basic assumptions: individual differences, a whole person, motivated behavior, and value of the person (human dignity).

Individual differences   People have much in common (they become excited, or they are grieved by the loss of a loved one), but each person in the world is also individually different. On the hills of Greenland lie billions of tiny snowflakes; yet we are reasonably sure that each is different. On the planet Earth are billions of complex people who are likewise all different (and we expect that all who follow will be different)! Each one is different from all others, probably in millions of ways, just as each of their fingerprints is different, as far as we know. And these differences are usually substantial rather than meaningless. Think, for example, of a person's billion brain cells and the billions of possible combinations of connections and bits of experience that could be stored therein. All people are different. This is a fact supported by science.

     The idea of individual differences comes originally from psychology. From the day of birth, each person is unique, and individual experiences after birth tend to make people even more different. Individual differences mean that management can get the greatest motivation among employees by treating them differently. If it were not for individual differences, some standard, across-the-board way of dealing with employees could be adopted, and minimum judgment would be required thereafter. Individual differences require that justice and rightness with employees shall be individual, not

Law of Individual Differences

statistical. This belief that each person is different from all others is typically called the *Law of Individual Differences*.[14]

A whole person   Although some organizations may wish they could employ only a person's skill or brain, all that they can employ is a whole person, rather than certain separate characteristics. Different human traits may be separately studied, but in the final analysis they are all part of one system making up a whole person. Skill does not exist apart from background or knowledge. Home life is not totally separable from work life, and emotional conditions are not separate from physical conditions. People function as total human beings.

For example, a supervisor wanted Margaret Townsend to work overtime Wednesday night on a rush report. Townsend had the necessary knowledge and skill for the job. She also wanted the overtime pay. However, from her point of view a social obligation made it impossible for her to work that night. The date was her tenth wedding anniversary, and an anniversary party was scheduled with a few friends at her house. This anniversary was important to her, so her supervisor had to consider her needs as a whole person, not just a worker.

When management practices organizational behavior, it is trying to develop a better employee, but also it wants to develop a better *person* in terms of growth and fulfillment. Research suggests that jobs do shape people somewhat as they perform them, so management needs to be concerned about its effect on the whole person.[15] Employees belong to many organizations other than their employer, and they play many roles outside the firm. If the whole person can be improved, then benefits will extend beyond the firm into the larger society in which each employee lives.

Better person

Motivated behavior From psychology we learn that normal behavior has certain causes. These may relate to a person's needs and/or the consequences that result from acts. In the case of needs, people are motivated not by what we think they ought to have but by what they themselves want. To an outside observer a person's needs may be unrealistic, but they are still controlling. This fact leaves management with two basic ways to motivate people. It can show them how certain actions will increase their need fulfillment, or it can threaten decreased need fulfillment if they follow an undesirable course of action. Clearly a path toward increased need fulfillment is the better approach.

Motivation is essential to the operation of organizations. No matter how much machinery and equipment an organization has, these things cannot be put to use until they are released and guided by people who have been motivated.

Think for a minute in terms of a steam locomotive sitting in a railroad station. All the rails and equipment are in order; the schedule and routes are prepared; the objective is set; tickets are sold; and the passengers are on board. No matter how well all this preliminary work has been done, the train cannot move an inch toward the next station until the steam is usefully released—that is, until the motive power is supplied. Similarly, in an organization motivation turns on the power to keep the organization going.

Value of the person (human dignity) This concept is of a different order from the other three because it is more an ethical philosophy than a scientific conclusion. It confirms that people are to be treated differently from other factors of production because they are of a higher order in the universe. It recognizes that because people are of a higher order, they want to be treated with respect and dignity—and should be treated this way. Every job, however simple, entitles the people who do it to proper respect and recognition of their unique aspirations and abilities. The concept of human dignity rejects the old idea of using employees as economic tools.

Ethics

Ethical philosophy is reflected in the conscience of humankind confirmed by the experience of people in all ages.[16] It has to do with the consequences of our acts to ourselves and to others. It recognizes that life has an overall purpose and accepts the inner integrity of each individual. Since organizational behavior always involves people, ethical philosophy is involved in one way or another in each action. Human decisions cannot, and should not, be made apart from values.

The nature of organizations

With regard to organizations, the key assumptions are that they are social systems and that they are formed on the basis of mutual interest.

Social systems   From sociology we learn that organizations are social systems; consequently, activities therein are governed by social laws as well as psychological laws. Just as people have psychological needs, they also have social roles and status. Their behavior is influenced by their group as well as by their individual drives. In fact, two types of social systems exist side by side in organizations. One is the formal (official) social system, and the other is the informal social system.

The existence of a social system implies that the organizational environment is one of dynamic change, rather than a static set of relations as pictured on an organization chart. All parts of the system are interdependent and subject to influence by any other part. Everything is related to everything else.

> The effects of the broader social system can be seen in the experience of a supervisor, Glenda Ortiz. Ortiz disciplined an employee for a safety violation. The action was within the rules and considered routine by Ortiz. However, the local union already was upset because of what it considered to be unfair discipline for safety violations in another branch of the company. It wanted to show sympathy for its fellow members in the other branch, and it also wanted to show management that it would not accept similar treatment in this branch. In addition, the union president, Jimmie Swallen, was running for reelection, and he wanted to show members that he was protecting their interests.
>
> The union encouraged the employee to file a grievance about Ortiz's action, and the simple disciplinary matter became a complex labor relations problem that consumed the time of many people.

The idea of a social system provides a framework for analyzing organizational behavior issues. It helps make organizational behavior problems understandable and manageable.

Superordinate goal

Mutual interest   Mutual interest is represented by the statement "Organizations need people, and people also need organizations." Organizations have a human purpose. They are formed and maintained on the basis of some mutuality of interest among their participants. People see organizations as a

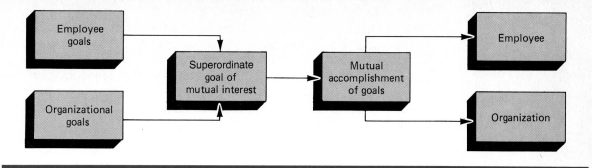

Figure 1-5
Mutual interest
provides a
superordinate goal
for employees and
the organization.

means to help them reach their goals, while organizations need people to help reach organizational objectives. If mutuality is lacking, it makes no sense to try to assemble a group and develop cooperation, because there is no common base on which to build. As shown in Figure 1-5, mutual interest provides a superordinate goal that integrates the efforts of individuals and groups. The result is that they are encouraged to attack organizational problems rather than each other!

Holistic organizational behavior

When the six fundamental concepts of organizational behavior are considered together, they provide a holistic concept of the subject. *Holistic organizational behavior* interprets people-organization relationships in terms of the whole person, whole group, whole organization, and whole social system. It takes an across-the-board view of people in organizations in an effort to understand as many as possible of the factors that influence their behavior. Issues are analyzed in terms of the total situation affecting them rather than in terms of an isolated event or problem.

> The holistic concept is illustrated by the story of John Perkins, bank manager, at the beginning of this chapter. Perkins's problems could not be understood in terms of the job he currently held. His manager had to examine his job history, career needs, investments outside the bank, children's status, and other factors. In this way Perkins could be helped to become effective again. This was holistic organizational behavior.

BASIC APPROACHES OF THIS BOOK

An interdisciplinary approach

As shown in Figure 1-6, organizational behavior is interdisciplinary. It integrates social sciences and other disciplines that can contribute to the subject. It applies from these disciplines any ideas that will improve the

Figure 1-6
Basic approaches of the book

Interdisciplinary An integration of many disciplines
Human resources (supportive) Support of employee growth and development for effectiveness
Contingency Allowance for different behaviors required by different environments for effectiveness
Productivity A ratio that compares units of output with units of input
Systems Interaction of all parts of an organization in a complex relationship

relationships between people and organizations. Its interdisciplinary nature is similar to that of medicine, which applies physical, biological, and social sciences into a workable medical practice.

The interest of various social sciences in people is sometimes expressed by the general term "behavioral science," which represents the systematized body of knowledge pertaining to why and how people behave as they do. This book especially seeks to integrate behavioral science with formal organizations. It has been said that the formal organization view sees "organizations without people," while behaviorists speak of "people without organizations." However, organizations must have people, and people working toward goals must have organizations; so it is desirable to treat the two as a working unit.

A human resources (supportive) approach

The human resources approach is developmental. It is concerned with the growth and development of people toward higher levels of competency, creativity, and fulfillment, because people are the central resource in any organization and any society. The nature of the human resources approach can be understood by comparing it with the traditional management approach in the early 1900s. In the traditional approach, managers decided what should be done and then closely controlled employees to ensure task performance. Management was directive and controlling.

The human resources approach, on the other hand, is supportive. It helps employees become better, more responsible persons, and then it tries to create a climate in which they may contribute to the limits of their improved abilities.[17] It is assumed that expanded capabilities and opportunities for people will lead directly to improvements in operating effectiveness. Work satisfaction also will be a direct result when employees make fuller use of their abilities. Essentially, the human resources approach means that better people achieve better results. It is somewhat illustrated by this ancient proverb:

Give a person a fish, and you feed that person for a day;
Teach a person to fish, and you feed that person for life.

Supportive approach

Another name for the human resources approach is the *supportive* approach, because the manager's role changes from control of employees to support of their growth and performance. The supportive model of organizational behavior is discussed in a later chapter.

A contingency approach

Traditional management relied on principles to provide a "one best way" of managing. There was a correct way to organize, to delegate, and to divide work. The correct way applied regardless of the type of organization or situation involved. Management principles were considered to be universal. As the field of organizational behavior developed, many of its followers also supported the concept of universality. Behavioral ideas were supposed to apply in any type of situation. For example, employee-oriented leadership should consistently be better than task-oriented leadership, whatever the circumstances. An occasional exception might be admitted, but the ideas were more or less universal.

The more accepted view is that there are few across-the-board concepts that apply in all instances. Situations are much more complex than first perceived, and the different variables may require different behavioral approaches. The result is *contingency approach to organizational behavior,* which means that different environments require different behavioral practices for effectiveness.[18]

No one best way

No longer is there a one best way. Each situation must be analyzed carefully to determine the significant variables that exist in order to establish the kinds of practices that will be more effective. The strength of the contingency approach is that it encourages analysis of each situation prior to action while at the same time discouraging habitual practice based on universal assumptions about people. The contingency approach also is more interdisciplinary, more system-oriented, and more research-oriented than the traditional approach. Thus it helps to use in the most appropriate manner all the current knowledge about organizations. It also is called the situational approach, because appropriate action depends on situational variables.

A productivity approach

Most organizations have an objective of productivity, so this idea is a common thread woven through organizational behavior.[19] *Productivity* is a ratio that compares units of output with units of input. If more outputs can be produced from the same amount of inputs, productivity is improved. Or if fewer inputs can be used to produce the same amount of outputs, productivity has increased. The idea of productivity does not imply that one should produce more output; rather, it is a measure of how efficiently one produces whatever output is desired. Consequently, better productivity is a valuable measure of how well resources are used in society. It means that less is consumed to produce each unit of output. There is less waste and better conservation of resources.

Productivity

Productivity often is measured in terms of economic inputs and outputs, but human and social inputs and outputs also are important. For example, if better organizational behavior can improve job satisfaction, a human output or benefit occurs. In the same manner, when employee development programs lead to a by-product of better citizens in a community, a valuable social

Multiple inputs and outputs

output occurs. Organizational behavior decisions typically involve human, social, and/or economic issues, so productivity usually is a significant part of them and will be discussed throughout this book.

A systems approach

Conceptually a system implies that there are a multitude of variables in organizations and that each of them affects all the others in a complex relationship. An event that appears to affect one individual or one department actually may have significant influences elsewhere in the organization. This means that managers in taking actions must look beyond the immediate situation in order to determine effects on the larger system.

Cost-benefit analysis

Often negative effects as well as positive effects result from a behavioral action, so it is necessary to make a *cost-benefit analysis* to determine whether an action will produce a net positive or a net negative effect. No longer is it sufficient to look at benefits, because there may be costs in other parts of the system. This is illustrated in the following experience of a supervisor:

> In the upholstery department of a furniture factory, a supervisor refused to allow an employee to take leave without pay to attend the funeral of a second cousin in a city 200 miles away. The employee claimed that special family relationships with this cousin required her attendance and took two days off without permission. When she returned, the supervisor disciplined her by giving her one day off without pay. Employees in other departments heard about the incident, and they felt that the discipline was unfair; so all plant employees walked off the job in a wildcat strike, threatening to remain off the job until the supervisor withdrew her penalty. The supervisor had failed to realize that actions in her department could have effects beyond that department in the larger factory system.

The systems approach applies especially to the social system discussed in Chapter 3.

SUMMARY

Organizational behavior is the study and application of knowledge about how people act in organizations. Key elements are people, structure, technology, and the external environment. From the administrative point of view, managers apply organizational behavior to build a climate in which people are motivated to work together and to become more effective persons. The result should be a triple reward system in which human, organizational, and social objectives are met.

From the 1930s to the 1960s organizational behavior was more commonly known as human relations, following the research of Mayo and Roethlisberger that began in the 1920s at the Western Electric Company. Fundamental philosophical concepts of organizational behavior relate to the nature of people (individual differences, a whole person, motivated behavior, and value of the person) and to the nature of organizations (social systems and mutual interest). The result is a holistic concept of organizational behavior. Understanding is aided by the use of interdisciplinary, human resources, contingency, productivity, and systems approaches.

TERMS AND CONCEPTS FOR REVIEW

Organizational behavior

Key elements in organizational behavior

Triple reward system

Frederick W. Taylor

Elton Mayo and F. J. Roethlisberger

Fundamental concepts of organizational behavior

Law of Individual Differences

Holistic organizational behavior

Basic approaches of this book

Productivity

REVIEW QUESTIONS

1 Define organizational behavior and state its key elements.

2 Assume that a friend of yours states, "Organizational behavior is selfish and manipulative, because it serves only management interests." How would you respond to your friend?

3 Trace the early history of human relations and organizational behavior.

4 Comment on the statement "Organizations need people, and people also need organizations."

5 Discuss the fundamental concepts that form the foundation of organizational behavior. Is any one concept more important than the others?

6 Select one of your work associates or friends and discuss the qualities that make that person individually different from you.

7 Discuss the social system in an organization where you have worked. How did that social system affect your job?

8 Discuss the idea of holistic organizational behavior. Can it be of practical help to supervisors in real situations? How?

INCIDENT

The Transferred Sales Representative

Harold Burns served as district sales representative for an appliance firm. His district covered the central part of a Midwestern state, and it included about 100 retail outlets. He had been with the company twenty years and in his present job and location for five years. During this time he met his district sales quota each year.

One day Burns learned through local friends that the wife of a sales representative in another district was in town to try to rent a house. She told the real estate agency that her family would be moving there in a few days because her husband was replacing Burns. When Burns heard this, he refused to believe it.

Two days later, on January 28, he received an airmail letter, postmarked the previous day, from the Regional Sales Manager. The letter read:

Dear Harold:

Because of personnel vacancies we are requesting that you move to the Gunning District, effective February 1. Mr. George Dowd from the Parsons District will replace you. Will you please see that your inventory and property are properly transferred to him?

I know that you will like your new district. Congratulations!

Sincerely yours,

(Signature)

In the same mail he received his twenty-year service pin. The accompanying letter from the Regional Sales Manager read:

Dear Harold:

I am happy to enclose your twenty-year service pin. You have a long and excellent record with the company. We are honored to give you this recognition, and I hope you will wear it proudly.

Our company is proud to have many long-service employees. We want you to know that we take a personal interest in your welfare because people like you are the backbone of our company.

Sincerely yours,

(Signature)

Harold Burns checked his quarterly sales bulletin and found that sales for the Gunning District were running 10 percent below those in his present district.

QUESTIONS

1 Comment on the events in this case as they relate to organizational behavior.

2 Was a human resources approach to Burns applied in this instance? Discuss.

REFERENCES

1 Ernesto Imbassahy de Mello, "To Dignify the Human Being," *The Rotarian,* July 1975, p. 16.

2 J. Watson Wilson, "The Growth of a Company: A Psychological Case Study," *Advanced Management Journal,* January 1966, p. 43. Entire quotation italicized in the original.

3 For additional discussion, see L. L. Cummings, "Toward Organizational Behavior," *Academy of Management Review,* January 1978, pp. 90–98.

4 For further discussion of the external social system, see Keith Davis and William C. Frederick, *Business and Society,* 5th ed., New York: McGraw-Hill Book Company, 1984.

5 Lee K. Frankel and Alexander Fleisher, *The Human Factor in Industry,* New York: The Macmillan Company, 1920, p. 8; and Frank Podmore, *Robert Owen,* New York: Augustus M. Kelly, 1968.

6 Andrew Ure, *The Philosophy of Manufactures,* London: Charles Knight, 1835.

7 Frederick W. Taylor, *The Principles of Scientific Management,* New York: Harper & Brothers, 1911. Most of Taylor's insights are supported as being valid in Edwin A. Locke, "The Ideas of Frederick W. Taylor: An Evaluation," *Academy of Management Review,* January 1982, pp. 14–24.

8 Whiting Williams, *What's on the Worker's Mind,* New York: Charles Scribner's Sons, 1920; and Whiting Williams, *Mainsprings of Men,* New York: Charles Scribner's Sons, 1925. More recent, similar studies are Studs Terkel, *Working: People Talk about What They Do All Day and How They Feel about What They Do,* New York: Pantheon Books, a division of Random House, 1974; and Robert Schrank, *Ten Thousand Working Days,* Cambridge, Mass.: The MIT Press, 1978.

9 Elton Mayo, *The Human Problems of an Industrial Civilization,* Cambridge, Mass.: Harvard University Press, 1933; F. J. Roethlisberger and W. J. Dickson, *Management and the Worker,* Cambridge, Mass.: Harvard University Press, 1939; and F. J. Roethlisberger, *The Elusive Phenomena: An Autobiographical Account of My Work in the Field of Organizational Behavior at the Harvard Business School,* Cambridge, Mass.: Harvard University Press, 1977. The symposium on the fiftieth anniversary of the Western Electric Company, Hawthorne Studies, is reported in Eugene Louis Cass and Frederick G. Zimmer (eds.), *Man and Work in Society,* New York: Van Nostrand Reinhold Company, 1975. Recollections of the participants are reported in Ronald G. Greenwood, Alfred A. Bolton, and Regina A. Greenwood, "Hawthorne a Half Century Later: Relay Assembly Participants Remember," *Journal of Management,* Fall–Winter 1983, pp. 217–231. The earliest general textbook on human relations was Burleigh B. Gardner and David G. Moore, *Human Relations in Industry,* Chicago: Irwin, 1945.

10 For example, see Alex Carey, "The Hawthorne Studies: A Radical Criticism," *American Sociological Review,* June 1967, pp. 403–416; and Richard Herbert Franke and James D. Kaul, "The Hawthorne Experiments: First Statistical Interpretations," *American Sociological Review,* October 1978, pp. 623–643.

11 An example of criticism is Malcolm P. McNair, "Thinking Ahead," *Harvard Business Review,* March–April 1957, pp. 15ff.

12 For a discussion of organizational behavior in the 1980s, see a special section on the subject by a variety of authors in *Decision Sciences,* July 1981, pp. 365–398.

13 For ideas about current concepts and research in organizational behavior, see Barry M. Staw and L. L. Cummings (eds.), *Research in Organizational Behavior,* Greenwich, Conn.: JAI Press, vol. 1, 1979; vol. 2, 1980; vol. 3, 1981; vol. 4, 1982; and vol. 5, 1983. Order of editors varies with each volume.

14 Erwin S. Stanton, *Reality-Centered People Management,* New York: AMACOM, 1982, pp. 30–35.

15 Melvin L. Kohn and Carmi Schooler, "Occupational Experience and Psychological Functioning: An Assessment of Reciprocal Effects," *American Sociological Review,* February 1973, pp. 97–118.

16 One author argues that ethics is the basis for participative management. See Marshall Sashkin, "Participative Management Is an Ethical Imperative," *Organizational Dynamics,* Spring 1984, pp. 4–22. Other examples are Manuel G. Velasquez, *Business Ethics,* Englewood Cliffs, N.J.: Prentice-Hall, 1982; and Thomas Donaldson and Patricia H. Werhane (eds.), *Ethical Issues in Business,* Englewood Cliffs, N.J.: Prentice-Hall, 1979.

17 Early emphasis on the human resources approach to organizational behavior was provided in Raymond E. Miles, "Human Relations or Human Resources?" *Harvard Business Review,* July–August 1965, pp. 148–163; it was later presented in his book *Theories of Management: Implications for Organizational Behavior and Development,* New York: McGraw-Hill Book Company, 1975.

18 For example, see Fiedler's contingency model of leadership in Chapter 8. An early book on contingency management is Don Hellriegel and John W. Slocum, Jr., *Management: Contingency Approaches,* 2d ed., Reading, Mass.: Addison-Wesley, 1978.

19 For discussion and examples in both the public and private sectors of the economy, see Robert Zager and Michael P. Rosow, *The Innovative Organization: Productivity Programs in Action,* Elmsford, N.Y.: Pergamon Press, 1982; Robert R. Blake and Jane Srygley Mouton, *Productivity: The Human Side,* New York: AMACOM, 1981; Ira. B. Gregerman, *Knowledge Worker Productivity,* New York: AMACOM, 1981; John Greiner and others, *Productivity and Motivation: A Review of State and Local Government Initiatives,* Washington: The Urban Institute Press, 1981, which includes an extensive bibliography on productivity and motivation in both the public and private sectors of the economy; and William B. Werther, Jr., "Out of the Productivity Box," *Business Horizons,* September–October, 1982, pp. 51–59. For a productivity model, see Jon English and Anthony R. Marchione, "Productivity: A New Perspective," *California Management Review,* January 1983, pp. 57–66.

FOR ADDITIONAL READING

Cass, Eugene L., and Frederick G. Zimmer (eds.), *Man and Work in Society,* New York: Van Nostrand Reinhold, 1975.

Gregerman, Ira B., *Knowledge Worker Productivity,* New York: AMACOM, 1981.

Karlins, Marvin, *The Human Use of Human Resources,* New York: McGraw-Hill Book Company, 1981.

Mayo, Elton, *The Human Problems of an Industrial Civilization,* Cambridge, Mass.: Harvard University Press, 1933.

Roethlisberger, F. J., *The Elusive Phenomena: An Autobiographical Account of My Work in the Field of Organizational Behavior at the Harvard Business School,* Cambridge, Mass.: Harvard University Press, 1977.

Roethlisberger, F. J., and W. J. Dickson, *Management and the Worker,* Cambridge, Mass.: Harvard University Press, 1939.

Schrank, Robert, *Ten Thousand Working Days,* Cambridge, Mass.: The MIT Press, 1978.

Staw, Barry M., and L. L. Cummings (eds.), *Research in Organizational Behavior,* Greenwich, Conn.: JAI Press, vol. 1, 1979; vol. 2, 1980; vol. 3, 1981; vol. 4, 1982; vol. 5, 1983. Order of editors varies with each volume.

2

CLIMATE AND MODELS OF ORGANIZATIONAL BEHAVIOR

Men employees are given one evening a week for courting and two if they go to prayer meeting. After 14 hours in the store, the leisure hours should be spent mostly in reading.[1]

Most large corporations have little sense of their social personality.

Marshall McLuhan and Bruce Powers[2]

CHAPTER OBJECTIVES

TO UNDERSTAND:
Organizational climate and its effects
How climate is developed and measured
Allocative and incremental values
An organizational behavior system
Models of organizational behavior
Trends in the models of organizational behavior
Theory Z systems

If you board an airplane in Chicago on a cold winter day and fly to the warm sea breezes of Miami, the differences in geographical climate will be apparent. There are similar differences in organizational climate. The introductory quotation and the factory rules of Amasa Whitney in Figure 2-1 indicate that organizations have undergone tremendous changes during the

Figure 2-1
Factory rules
in 1830
Source: *Samuel H. Adams,* Sunrise to Sunset, *New York: Random House, Inc.,* 1950.

RULES & REGULATIONS
To Be Observed By All Persons
Employed In The Factory Of
A M A S A W H I T N E Y

FIRST : The Mill will be put into operation 10 minutes before sunrise at all seasons of the year. The gate will be shut 10 minutes past sunset from the 20th of March to the 20th of September, at 30 minutes past 8 from the 20th of September to the 20th of March. Saturdays at sunset.

SECOND : It will be required of every person employed, that they be in the room in which they are employed, at the time mentioned above for the mill to be in operation.

THIRD : Hands are not allowed to leave the factory in working hours without the consent of their Overseer. If they do, they will be liable to have their time set off.

FOURTH : Anyone who by negligence or misconduct causes damage to the machinery, or impedes the progress of the work, will be liable to make good the damage for the same.

FIFTH : Anyone employed for a certain length of time, will be expected to make up their lost time, if required, before they will be entitled to their pay.

SIXTH : Any person employed for no certain length of time, will be required to give at least 4 weeks notice of their intention to leave (sickness excepted) or forfeit 4 weeks pay, unless by particular agreement.

SEVENTH : Anyone wishing to be absent any length of time, must get permisison of the Overseer.

EIGHTH : All who have leave of absence for any length of time will be expected to return in that time; and, in case they do not return in that time and do not give satisfactory reason, they will be liable to forfeit one week's work or less, if they commence work again. If they

do not, they will be considered as one who leaves without giving any notice.

NINTH : Anything tending to impede the progress of manufacturing in working hours, such as unnecessary conversation, reading, eating fruit, &c.&c., must be avoided.

TENTH : While I shall endeavor to employ a judicious Overseer, the help will follow his direction in all cases.

ELEVENTH : No smoking will be allowed in the factory, as it is considered very unsafe, and particularly specified in the Insurance.

TWELFTH : In order to forward the work, job hands will follow the above regulations as well as those otherwise employed.

THIRTEENTH : It is intended that the bell be rung 5 minutes before the gate is hoisted, so that all persons may be ready to start their machines precisely at the time mentioned.

FOURTEENTH : All persons who cause damage to the machinery, break glass out of the windows, &c., will immediately inform the Overseer of the same.

FIFTEENTH : The hands will take breakfast, from the 1st of November to the last of March, before going to work—they will take supper from the 1st of May to the last of August, 30 minutes past 5 o'clock P.M.—from the 20th of September to the 20th of March between sundown and dark—25 minutes will be allowed for breakfast, 30 minutes for dinner, and 25 minutes for supper, and no more from the time the gate is shut till started again.

SIXTEENTH : The hands will leave the Factory so that the doors may be fastened within 10 minutes from the time of leaving off work.
 AMASA WHITNEY
Winchendon, Mass. July 5, 1830.

last 150 years. Employers in early days had no systematic program for managing their employees, but their existing rules still created an evident organizational climate for them. The old rules, measured by today's practices, are quaint and "out of this world." But before being critical of them, we should consider whether someday, a hundred years from now, people will look back upon present-day factory rules and consider them equally quaint. This is the price—and the reward—of progress. One wonders what would be the reaction of employees today if their employer instructed them to spend their leisure hours in reading or attending prayer meeting.

Amasa Whitney's reference to employees as "hands" was a natural outgrowth of the concept that the employer purchased the commodity of labor—that is, the skill of the *hands* of employees. The words by which one refers to employees (such as "hands"), the attitudes of top management, company policies, and other direct and indirect evidence all combine to establish the organizational climate in each institution.

This chapter builds on fundamental concepts presented in Chapter 1 by showing how all behavioral factors can be combined to develop an effective organizational climate. We discuss the elements of climate, an organizational behavior system, and alternative models of organizational behavior.

ORGANIZATIONAL CLIMATE

Organizational climate is the human environment within which an organization's employees do their work. It may refer to the environment within a department, a major company unit such as a branch plant, or an entire organization.[3] We cannot see climate or touch it, but it is there. Like the air in a room, it surrounds and affects everything that happens in an organization. In turn, climate is affected by almost everything that occurs in an organization. It is a dynamic systems concept.

Organizations, like fingerprints and snowflakes, are always unique. Each has its own culture, traditions, and methods of action which, in their totality, constitute its climate.[4] Some organizations are bustling and efficient; others are easygoing. Some are quite human; others are hard and cold. An organization tends to attract and keep people who fit its climate, so that its patterns are to some extent perpetuated. Just as people may choose to move to a certain geographic climate of sea, mountains, or desert, they also will choose the organizational climate they prefer.

Climates are different.

> A certain manufacturing company serves as an illustration. Its management stresses seniority, centralized control, and cautious decision making. It has difficulty attracting and retaining young college graduates with promotion potential. What else could be expected? People of this background do not fit the company's pattern of living—its climate.

Climate can influence motivation, performance, and job satisfaction. It does this by creating employee expectations about what consequences will follow from different actions. Employees expect certain rewards, satisfactions, and frustrations on the basis of their perception of the organization's climate. The way in which these expectations lead to motivation will be explained in the chapters on motivation and satisfaction.

A sound climate is a long-run proposition. Managers need to take an assets approach to climate, meaning that they take the long-run view of climate as an organizational asset. Unwise discipline and putting pressures on people may temporarily get better performance, but at the cost of the asset called climate. Such an organization eventually will suffer from depleted assets.

Incremental values

The human values that compose climate are quite different from economic values in an organization. Economics deals with the allocation of scarce resources. If you have automobile A, I cannot have it; if you have budget B, those funds are not available to my department. Economic values are, therefore, mostly *allocative,* but human values are mostly *incremental.* They are self-generated, being created within individuals and groups as a result of their attitudes and lifestyles.

> The difference between allocative and incremental values is illustrated by a dollar bill and an idea. If Mary has dollar bill L95484272A and she gives it to you, you have it and she does not. Either you or she can have it, but not both of you. However, if you have an idea and give it to her, both of you have it. What was one unit becomes two units; and though she has it, she took nothing of like kind away from you. You can give the idea away fifty times, but you do not lose it. All you do is spread it.

*Human values
are incremental.*

Human values, such as fulfillment and growth, are mostly of this incremental type. In order to build job satisfaction in employee A, it is not necessary to take it from employee B. In order to build satisfaction in department C, one does not have to take it from department D. Likewise, a climate of human dignity can be built without taking it from anywhere else.

There are exceptions to the incremental nature of climate because many events in an organization are allocative. In the main, however, organizational climate is incremental. For example, there is enough job satisfaction for everybody. In fact, some organizations have achieved high cooperation and job satisfaction for nearly every member, as indicated in the following example.

> Tandem Computers Inc. is a microcomputer company with 100 percent annual growth of revenues, attaining its success through a unique "fail-safe" computer, no direct early competition, and a people-oriented management philosophy.[5] Featuring complete informality, peer pressure, open communications, flexible hours, and stock options for every employee, the company has been able to attract excellent people and retain them (the turnover rate is one-third of the industry average). Employees, who also receive a six-week sabbatical leave with full pay every four years, clearly enjoy the benefits of Tandem's organizational climate.

Elements of a favorable climate

Climate can range along a continuum from favorable to neutral to unfavorable. Both employers and employees want a more favorable climate because of its benefits, such as better performance and job satisfaction.

Several typical elements that contribute to a favorable climate are shown in Figure 2-2.[6] Employees feel that the climate is favorable when they are doing something useful that provides a sense of personal worth. They frequently want challenging work that is intrinsically satisfying. Many employees also want responsibility and the opportunity to succeed. They want to be listened to and treated as if they have value as individuals. They want to feel that the organization really cares about their needs and problems.

What climate do employees want?

> One firm went out of its way to help an employee with home problems. Sara Burney was the sole support of her teenage diabetic son, who was confined to their home because he had to take four large doses of insulin daily. The doses were difficult to regulate, and he had been in the hospital on several occasions with insulin reactions. One day when she returned from work she found him in an insulin coma, and he did not regain consciousness until the next day in the hospital.
>
> When Burney returned to work the second day, she was prepared to resign in order to remain at home to care for her son; but she found that company management was working on a plan to allow her to do her work at home. Her job was working with customer orders, using an electronic display terminal. Management arranged for one of the terminals to be moved to her home, and cables were run from the factory to her home so that the equipment would be connected directly with factory records. An employee in the department brings work to her each morning, so that now she does not have to leave her home. The company's genuine concern for her well-being not only retained a valued employee but provided concrete evidence of a favorable climate to other employees throughout the firm.

Measuring climate

Several instruments have been developed to measure a firm's organizational climate.[7] The instruments typically identify a number of elements of climate, and employees rate these elements on numerical scales. The scores are then combined and interpreted for management.

Employees assess climate.

> One researcher, Rensis Likert, developed a classic instrument that focuses on the management style used.[8] The Likert survey covers these factors: leadership, motivation, communication, interaction-influence, decision making, goal setting, and

• Quality of leadership	• Fair rewards
• Amount of trust	• Reasonable job pressures
• Communication, upward and downward	• Opportunity
• Feeling of useful work	• Reasonable controls, structure, and bureaucracy
• Responsibility	• Employee involvement; participation

Figure 2-2
Typical elements that contribute to a favorable climate

control. Respondents are given a continuum of choices for each item to indicate whether, in their view, the organization tends to have an autocratic, highly structured climate or a more participative, human-oriented one. Steps along the continuum are called Systems 1, 2, 3, and 4, referring to different systems of management. Likert concludes that the more human-oriented climate produces both a higher level of performance and greater job satisfaction.

Climate profile charts

How are profile charts used?

Firms that measure their climate often chart it on *climate profile charts,* as shown in Figure 2-3, in order to provide visual evidence of the strong and weak elements in their climate.[9] The charts become a basis for discussing and analyzing a firm's climate so that plans for improving it may be developed.

For example, the firm shown in the profile chart found that it especially was weak in decision making and goal setting. After analysis of causes and possible remedies, it developed a three-year plan to make major improvements in these two areas. It also planned moderate improvements in motivation and communication. It projected only gradual improvement in leadership, because management believed it would take longer than three years to train and develop its leadership.

Climate is a systems concept that reflects the entire lifestyle of an organization. When that lifestyle can be improved, measurable gains in performance are likely to occur.

Delta Air Lines provides a strong model in the transportation industry for the beneficial effects of managing its organizational climate. It emphasizes planning (a fifteen-year time horizon), motivation (generous benefits and high job security),

Figure 2-3
General climate profile chart for a company, using the Likert elements

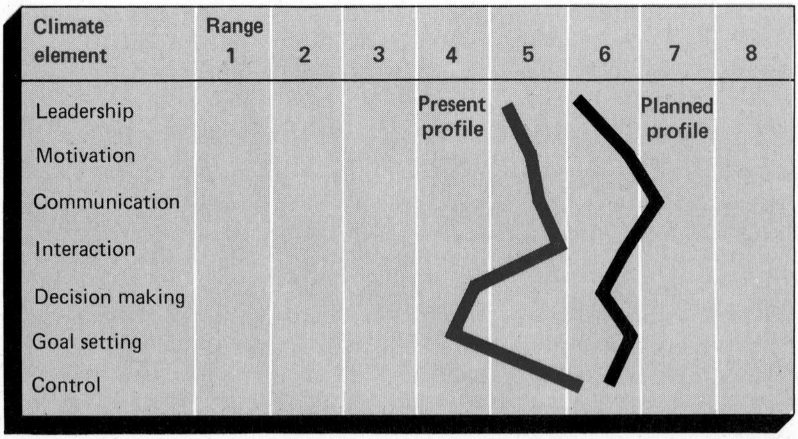

Note: Each of the major elements has subelements that are measured to give more details about it.

decision making (by consensus), leadership (teamwork), and open communications (top managers meet periodically with employee groups). The results of these conscious efforts include a loyal work force, the absence of restrictive work rules, an enviable productivity record, and the world's most profitable airline.[10]

CHAPTER 2:
CLIMATE AND
MODELS OF
ORGANIZATIONAL
BEHAVIOR

27

AN ORGANIZATIONAL BEHAVIOR SYSTEM

The climate of each firm is developed and communicated through an organizational behavior system, as shown in Figure 2-4. Major elements of this system are described below and presented in detail throughout the book.

Elements of the system

The climate of an organization has its basis in the philosophy and goals of those who join together to create it. The philosophy of organizational behavior held by a manager derives from both fact and value premises. *Fact premises* represent our view of how the world behaves, and are drawn from behavioral science study and personal experiences. Accordingly, you would not jump from a ten-story building, because you believe gravity will pull you downward and crush you against the ground. *Value premises,* on the other hand, represent our view of the desirability of certain goals.[11] If you were so unhappy that you wanted to die, you might then choose to jump off the ten-story building. You still accept the fact premise of gravity, but your value premises have changed. As this illustration shows, value premises are variable and therefore under our control.

Fact premises

Value premises

People also bring their psychological, social, and economic goals with them to an organization, which they express individually and collectively. All these different interests come together in a working social system.

The philosophy and goals of people are implemented by leadership (discussed in Part Three) working through formal and informal organizations (discussed in Part Four). Formal and informal organizations provide the structure to bind the institution together into a working team.

Each organization is affected by the other institutions it comes in contact with, which constitute its social environment. In Figure 2-4, these institutions are shown as separate from the employing institution but may be very much involved with it through laws and contracts. For example, union Local 3146 represents workers in companies A, B, and C. It is a separate legal organization but is very much involved in each of the three companies. This social environment is discussed primarily in Part Five.

All organizations influence their members by means of a control system that reflects a combination of the forces of formal organizations, informal organizations, and social environment. This combination is made possible by communication (described in Part Six) and is reflected in the organization's motivation and reward system (Part Two).

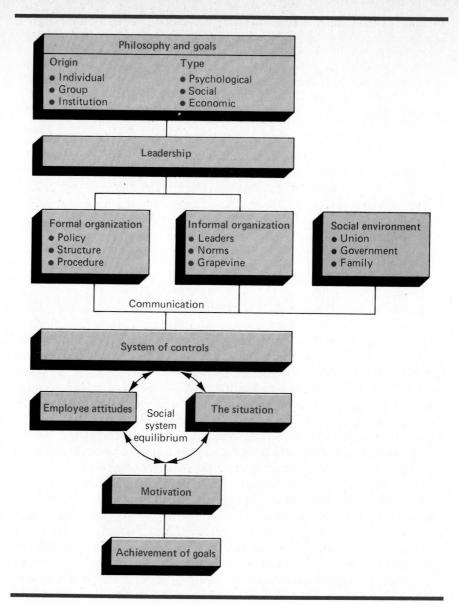

Figure 2-4
An organizational
behavior system

The social system at work

The system of controls in an organization interacts with employee attitudes and with situational factors to produce a specific motivation for each employee at a certain time. If any one of the three—controls, attitudes, or situations—is changed, the motivation will be different. The relationship is a contingency one. For example, if a control is tightened but attitudes and the situation remain the same, motivation will change and produce different results.

CHAPTER 2:
CLIMATE AND
MODELS OF
ORGANIZATIONAL
BEHAVIOR

29

The Johnson Company decided to tighten controls because it was having cost overruns on certain contracts. It wanted more and better employee performance. However, the employees felt strongly about freedom on the job, and they reacted to the controls by producing less, not more. Management had failed to deal with the whole system.

The result of an effective organizational behavior system is productive motivation. This kind of motivation should get above-average performance out of average people. It develops problem solvers instead of problem makers. It builds two-way relationships, meaning that manager and employee are jointly influencing each other and jointly benefiting. This is power with people rather than power over them. There is no one-way manipulation of one party by the other. People are treated like people, nothing more and nothing less.

MODELS OF ORGANIZATIONAL BEHAVIOR

Organizations differ in the quality of organizational behavior that they develop. These differences are substantially caused by different *models of organizational behavior* that dominate management's thought in each organization. The model that a manager holds usually begins with certain assumptions about people and leads to certain interpretations of events. Underlying theory, therefore, is an unconscious but powerful guide to managerial behavior. Managers tend to act as they think. Eventually this means that the underlying model that prevails in an organization's management (especially in the firm's chief executive officer) determines the climate in that firm. For this reason, models of organizational behavior are highly significant.

Why are models important?

We highlight in this chapter a discussion of the following four models: autocratic, custodial, supportive, and collegial. (Earlier models, such as those of feudalism and slavery, are bypassed.) These four models are summarized in Figure 2-5. In the order mentioned, they represent an approximate historical evolution in management practice during the last 100 years or more. One model tends to dominate a particular time in history, but at the same time each of the other models is practiced by some organizations.

Just as organizations differ among themselves, so practices may vary within the departments or branches of one organization. The production department may work within a custodial model while the supportive model is being tried in the research department. And, of course, the practices of individual managers may differ from their organization's prevailing model because of their personal preferences or different conditions in their department. The point is that no one model of organizational behavior is sufficient to describe all that happens in an organization, but it can help distinguish one way of life from another.

	AUTOCRATIC	**CUSTODIAL**	**SUPPORTIVE**	**COLLEGIAL**
Basis of model	Power	Economic resources	Leadership	Partnership
Managerial orientation	Authority	Money	Support	Teamwork
Employee orientation	Obedience	Security and benefits	Job performance	Responsibility
Employee psychological result	Dependence on boss	Dependence on organization	Participation	Self-discipline
Employee needs met	Subsistence	Security	Status and recognition	Self-actualization
Performance result	Minimum	Passive co-operation	Awakened drives	Moderate enthusiasm

Figure 2-5
Four models of
organizational
behavior

The autocratic model

The autocratic model has its roots deep in history, and certainly it became the prevailing model of the industrial revolution. As shown in Figure 2-5, it depends on *power*. Those who are in command must have the power to demand, "You do this—or else," meaning that an employee who does not follow orders will be penalized.

Power and authority are used.

In an autocratic environment the managerial orientation is formal, official *authority*. This authority is delegated by right of command over the people to whom it applies. Management believes that it knows what is best and that the employee's obligation is to follow orders. It assumes that employees have to be persuaded and pushed into performance, and this is management's task. Management does the thinking; the employees obey the orders. This conventional view of management leads to tight control of employees at work.

Under autocratic conditions the employee orientation is *obedience* to a boss, not a manager. The psychological result for employees is *dependence* on their boss, whose power to hire, fire, and "perspire" them is almost absolute. The boss pays minimum wages because *minimum performance* is given by employees. They give minimum performance—sometimes reluctantly—because they must satisfy *subsistence* needs for themselves and their families. Some employees give higher performance because of internal achievement drives, because they personally like their boss, because the boss is "a natural-born leader," or because of some other factor; but most of them give only minimum performance.

Autocratic model works.

The autocratic model is a useful way to accomplish work. It is not a complete failure. The picture of the autocratic model just presented has been an extreme one, but actually the model exists in all shades of gray from rather dark to rather light. This view of work built great railroad systems, operated giant steel mills, and produced the dynamic industrial civilization that developed in the United States. It does get results, but usually only moderate results. *Its principal weakness is its high human costs.*

The fundamental question we ask of the autocratic model must be: Is there a better way? Now that we have brought organizational conditions this far along, can we build on what we have in order to move one step higher up the ladder of progress?

The custodial model

As managers began to study their employees, they soon recognized that although autocratically managed employees did not talk back to their boss, they certainly "thought back." There were many things they wanted to say, and sometimes they did say them when they quit or lost their tempers! Employees were filled with insecurity, frustrations, and aggressions toward their boss. Since they could not vent these feelings directly, sometimes they went home and vented them on their families and neighbors; so the entire community might suffer from this relationship.

It seemed rather obvious to progressive employers that there ought to be some way to develop better employee satisfactions and security. If the insecurities, frustrations, and aggressions of employees could be dispelled, they might feel more like working. In any case, they would have a better quality of work life.

To satisfy the security needs of employees, a number of companies began welfare programs in the 1890s and 1900s. In their worst form these welfare programs later became known as paternalism. In the 1930s welfare programs evolved into a variety of fringe benefits to provide employee security. Employers—and unions and government—began caring for the security needs of workers. They were applying a custodial model of organizational behavior.

As shown in Figure 2-5, a successful custodial approach depends on *economic resources*. If an organization does not have the wealth to provide pensions and pay other benefits, it cannot follow a custodial approach. The resulting managerial orientation is toward *money* to pay wages and benefits. Since employees' physical needs are already reasonably met, the employer looks to *security* needs as a motivating force.

The custodial approach leads to employee *dependence on the organization.* Rather than being dependent on their boss for their weekly bread, employees now depend on organizations for their security and welfare. Perhaps more accurately stated, an organizational dependence is added to a reduced personal dependence on the boss. If employees have ten years of seniority under the union contract and a good pension program, they cannot afford to quit even if the grass looks greener somewhere else!

Employees become dependent.

Employees working in a custodial environment become psychologically preoccupied with their economic rewards and benefits. As a result of their treatment, they are well maintained, happy, and contented, but they are not strongly motivated, so they give only *passive cooperation*. The result is that they do not produce much more vigorously than under the old autocratic approach.

The custodial model is described in its extreme in order to show its emphasis on material rewards, security, and organizational dependence. In actual practice, the model has various shades of gray from dark to light. Its great benefit is that it brings security and satisfaction to workers, but it does have substantial flaws. The most evident flaw is that most employees are not producing anywhere near their capacities, nor are they motivated to grow to the greater capacities of which they are capable. Though employees are happy, most of them really do not feel fulfilled or motivated. In confirmation of this condition, a series of studies at the University of Michigan in the 1940s and 1950s reported that "the happy employee is not necessarily the most productive employee."[12] Consequently, managers and academic leaders started to ask again, "Is there a better way?"

The search for a better way is not a condemnation of the custodial model as a whole but rather a condemnation of the assumption that this is "the final answer"—the one best way to motivate employees. The error in reasoning occurs when people perceive the custodial model as so desirable that there is no need to build on it toward something better. A reasonable amount of the custodial model is desirable to provide security. It is the foundation for growth to the next step.

The supportive model

The supportive model of organizational behavior had its origins in the "principle of supportive relationships" as stated by Rensis Likert, who said, *"The leadership and other processes of the organization must be such as to ensure a maximum probability that in all interactions and all relationships with the organization each member will, in the light of his background, values, and expectations, view the experience as supportive and one which builds and maintains his sense of personal worth and importance."*[13] It is similar to the human resources approach to people mentioned in Chapter 1.

The supportive model depends on *leadership* instead of power or money. Through leadership, management provides a climate to help employees grow and accomplish in the interests of the organization the things of which they are capable. The leader assumes that workers are not by nature passive and resistant to organizational needs but that they are made so by an inadequately supportive climate at work. They will take responsibility, develop a drive to contribute, and improve themselves if management will give them a chance. Management's orientation, therefore, is to *support* the employee's *job performance,* rather than simply supporting employee benefit payments as in the custodial approach.

Employees are supported.

Since management supports employees in their work, the psychological result is a feeling of *participation* and task involvement in the organization. They may say "we" instead of "they" when referring to their organization. They are more strongly motivated than by earlier models because their status and recognition needs are better met. Thus they have *awakened drives* for work.

Supportive behavior is not the kind of behavior that requires money. Rather, it is a part of management's lifestyle at work, reflected in the way that it deals with other people. The manager's role is one of helping employees solve their problems and accomplish their work. Following is an example of a supportive approach.

Juanita Salinas, a young divorcee with one child, had a record of frequent tardiness as an assembler in an electronics plant. Her supervisor, Helen Ferguson, scolded her several times about her tardiness, and each time Salinas improved for two or three weeks but then lapsed back into her normal habit pattern. At about this time Ferguson attended a company training program for supervisors, so she decided to try the supportive approach with Salinas.

The next time Salinas was tardy, Ferguson approached her with concern about what might have caused her tardiness. Rather than scolding her, Ferguson showed a genuine interest in Salinas's problems, asking, "How can I help?" and "Is there anything we can do at the company?" When the discussion focused on delays in getting the child ready for school early in the morning, Ferguson arranged for Salinas to talk with other mothers of children in the department. When Salinas talked about the distance she had to walk to catch a bus, Ferguson worked with the personnel department to get her into a dependable car pool.

Although the new car pool undoubtedly helped, an important point was that Salinas seemed to appreciate the recognition and concern that was expressed, so she was more motivated to come to work on time. She also was more cooperative and interested in her job. It was evident that the supportive approach influenced Salinas's behavior. An important by-product was that Ferguson's job became easier because of Salinas's better performance.

Supportive approaches work well with both employees and managers. One study of 200 clerical workers, for example, reported that employees with high job satisfaction had supportive supervisors.[14] Another study of 200 managerial and professional employees reported that supportive supervision was correlated with organizational effectiveness and job satisfaction.[15] An additional study reported that supportive managers usually encouraged high motivation among their subordinate managers. Among those managers who were low in motivation, only 8 percent had supportive managers.[16]

The supportive model has been widely accepted by managers in the United States, particularly at the higher organizational levels. One survey of middle managers reported that 90 percent agreed with many of the basic ideas of a supportive approach to organizational behavior.[17] However, their agreement with supportive ideas does not mean that they practice these ideas regularly. The step from theory to practice is a difficult one.

Are managers supportive?

The supportive model tends to be especially effective in affluent nations with a complex technology because it appeals to a wide array of employee needs. It may have less application in less developed nations, because their employees' current needs and social conditions are different.

The collegial model

A useful extension of the supportive model is the collegial model. The term "collegial" relates to a body of persons having a common purpose. It is a team concept. The collegial model especially is useful in research laboratories and similar work environments, and gradually it is evolving into other work situations as well.

The collegial model is less useful on assembly lines, because the rigid work environment makes it difficult to develop there. A contingency relationship exists in which the collegial model tends to be more useful with unprogrammed work, an intellectual environment, and considerable job freedom. In other environments management often finds that other models may be more successful.

As shown in Figure 2-5, the collegial model depends on management's building a feeling of *partnership* with employees. The result is that employees feel needed and useful. They feel that managers are contributing also, so it is easy to accept and respect their roles in the organization. Managers are seen as joint contributors rather than as bosses.

Teamwork is required. The managerial orientation is toward *teamwork*. Management is the coach that builds a better team. The employee response to this situation is *responsibility*. For example, employees produce quality work not because management tells them to do so or because the inspector will catch them if they do not, but because they feel inside themselves an obligation to provide others with high quality. They also feel an obligation to uphold quality standards that will bring credit to their jobs and company.

The psychological result of the collegial approach for the employee is *self-discipline*. Feeling responsible, employees discipline themselves for performance on the team in the same way that the members of a football team discipline themselves to training standards and the rules of the game. In this kind of environment employees normally feel some degree of fulfillment, worthwhile contribution, and *self-actualization,* even though the amount may be modest in some situations. This self-actualization will lead to *moderate enthusiasm* in performance.

The collegial model tends to produce improved results in situations where it is appropriate. One study covered scientists in three large research laboratories. Laboratories A and B were operated in a relatively traditional hierarchical manner. Laboratory C was operated in a more open, participative, collegial manner. There were four measures of performance: esteem of fellow scientists, contribution to knowledge, sense of personal achievement, and contribution to management objectives. All four were higher in Laboratory C, and the first three were significantly higher.[18]

Changing use of the models

Several conclusions may be drawn about the models of organizational behavior. The first is that our use of these models tends to change gradually. As our understanding of human behavior increases or as new social conditions develop, we move to new models. It is a mistake to assume that one particular model is a "best" model that will endure for the long run. This mistake was made by some managers about both the autocratic model and the custodial model, with the result that they became psychologically locked into these models and had difficulty altering their practices when conditions demanded it. Eventually the supportive model may also fall to limited use. There is no one permanently "best" model, because what is best is contingent on what is known about human behavior in whatever environment exists at that time.

The primary challenge for management is to identify the model it is actually using and then assess its current effectiveness. Some observers suggest that this self-examination is a difficult task for managers, who tend to profess publicly one model (e.g., the supportive or collegial) yet practice another.[19] In effect, a manager has two key tasks—to acquire a new set of values as models evolve and to learn and apply the behavioral skills that are consistent with those values.

> The challenge of changing the values and behaviors of intact management teams has been successfully addressed by the Norwegian Center for Organizational Learning in Oslo.[20] The fifteen top managers from a single institution experience an intense week-long simulation of a relevant organizational crisis (e.g., an oil spill in the North Sea). Through continual questioning and feedback, the managers discover how their colleagues perceive their behavior and its consequences. The rich data provided to them create a potent stimulus for reexamination and change of their underlying model.

Can managers change?

Relation of models to human needs

A second conclusion is that the four models discussed in this chapter are closely related to human needs. New models have been developed to serve the different needs that became important at the time. For example, the custodial model is directed toward the satisfaction of employees' security needs. It moves one step above the autocratic model, which reasonably serves subsistence needs but does not meet needs for security. Similarly the supportive model is an effort to meet employees' other needs, such as affiliation and esteem, which the custodial model is unable to serve.

A number of people have assumed that emphasis on one model of organizational behavior is an automatic rejection of other models, but comparison suggests that *each model is built upon the accomplishments of the other.* For example, adoption of a supportive approach does not mean abandonment of custodial practices that serve necessary employee security needs. What it does mean is that custodial practices are given secondary emphasis, because employees have progressed to a condition in which newer needs dominate. In other words, the supportive model is the appropriate model to use because subsistence and security needs are already reasonably met by a suitable structure and security system. If a misdirected modern manager should abandon these basic organizational needs, the system would

Effect of satisfied needs

move back quickly to seek structure and security in order to satisfy these
needs for its people.

Tendency toward more democratic models

A third conclusion is that the trend toward more democratic models will
probably continue. Despite rapid advances in computers and management
information systems, top managers of giant, complex organizations cannot be
authoritarian in the traditional sense and be effective.[21] Because they cannot
know all that is happening in their organization, they must learn to depend on
other centers of power nearer to operating problems. In addition, many
employees are not readily motivated toward creative and intellectual duties
by the autocratic model. Only the newer models can offer the satisfaction of
their needs for esteem, autonomy, and self-actualization.

Contingent use of all models

A fourth conclusion is that, though one model may be most used at any point
in time, some appropriate uses will remain for other models. Knowledge and
skills vary among managers. Role expectations of employees differ, depending upon cultural history. Policies and ways of life vary among organizations.
Perhaps more important, task conditions are different. Some jobs may
require routine, low-skilled, highly programmed work that will be mostly
determined by higher authority and will provide mostly material rewards and
security (autocratic and custodial conditions). Other jobs will be unprogrammed and intellectual, requiring teamwork and self-motivation. They
generally respond best to supportive and collegial approaches. Therefore,
probably all four models will continue to be used, but the more advanced
models will have growing use as progress is made.

A hybrid model: Theory Z

Theory Z

An integrative model of organizational behavior, proposed by William
Ouchi, provides a useful example of the way in which behavioral prescriptions
for management must be woven together with the organization's environment.[22] The *Theory Z* model adapts the elements of effective Japanese
management systems to U.S. culture. The distinguishing features of Theory Z
companies are listed in Figure 2-6, and these are believed to foster close,
cooperative, trusting relationships with workers, managers, and other groups.
The central notion is the creation of an industrial team and a stable and
cohesive work environment where employee needs for affiliation, independence, and control are met. The first step in this direction is to create and
publicize a humanistic statement of corporate philosophy.

Theory Z reflects several points made in the preceding section regarding
models of organizational behavior. On the positive side, it does not attempt

- Lifetime employment
- Nonspecialized careers
- Individual responsibility
- Concern for the total person
- Control systems that are less formal
- Consensus decision making
- Slower rates of promotion

Figure 2·6
Typical features of Theory Z organizations

to transplant Japanese ideas without first adapting them to U.S. culture. As a hybrid model, Theory Z is based on shared concern for multiple employee needs, and clearly typifies the democratic trend by accenting the use of consensus-oriented decision processes. Further, there is some evidence that Theory Z firms are productive, and many corporate giants (such as Eli Lilly, Rockwell International, and Dayton-Hudson) claim to hold Theory Z values.[23]

A Theory Z approach was given credit for the sharply improved performance of a public agency in a large metropolitan area.[24] A new management team and a cross section of labor representatives composed a labor-management committee. They sought out and solved operating problems, opened up communications with workers by making frequent visits to field locations, and trained workers to increase their ability to provide useful input to the decision process. The spectacular results included a two-year cost savings of $16.5 million, an output index that rose from 53.3 to 82.1 percent, and a shortfall service-level index that fell from 27 to 0 percent. This provides encouraging evidence that current climate models can be applied in public organizations as well as private firms.

Early criticisms of Theory Z have been frequent, and time is required to check their validity. Some critics suggest that Theory Z is merely an extension of earlier theories that were less popular.[25] Others conclude that no research data exists to confirm the greater productivity of Theory Z firms.[26] Most damaging, perhaps, is the suggestion that Theory Z fails to provide useful criteria for helping managers decide when to use it.[27] Despite these comments, Theory Z has at least served to stimulate many U.S. managers to examine the nature and effects of their organizational climate.

Attacks on Theory Z

SUMMARY

Organizational climate represents an organization's way of life. It can have a major influence on employee motivation, performance, and job satisfaction. Climate is derived from an organizational behavior system that includes philosophy and goals, leadership, formal and informal organization, and the social environment. These items join in a system of controls that interacts with personal attitudes and situational factors to produce motivation in employees.

Four models of organizational behavior are the autocratic, custodial, supportive, and collegial models. The supportive and collegial models are more consistent with contemporary employee needs and, therefore, provide a superior organizational climate. Theory Z is a supportive model that blends elements of successful Japanese practice with American culture. It focuses heavily on a humanistic philosophy, trust, and consensus decisions but is still in an experimental stage. The role of culture in social systems will be explored in Chapter 3.

TERMS AND CONCEPTS FOR REVIEW

Organizational climate	Autocratic model
Allocative values	Custodial model
Incremental values	Supportive model
Climate profile charts	Collegial model
Organizational behavior system	Theory Z

REVIEW QUESTIONS

1 What is organizational climate? Discuss its importance in an organization.

2 Distinguish between allocative and incremental values.

3 Discuss the climate at the organization where you now work or most recently worked. What model of organizational behavior does (did) your supervisor follow? Is (Was) the supervisor's model the same as top management's model?

4 In the job that you discussed in question 3, what are (were) the two most important elements contributing to a favorable climate? What are (were) the two most important ones contributing to an unfavorable climate? Discuss.

5 Prepare a climate profile chart for the job discussed in questions 3 and 4. Use the seven Likert elements. For comparison, also chart the profile of the climate you would like to have.

6 Interview two friends in different jobs; use the seven elements on the Likert scale as the basis for your questions. Then prepare a climate profile chart showing the profile of each element. Discuss the similarities and differences in climate between the two jobs.

7 Discuss similarities and differences among the four models of organizational behavior.

8 What model of organizational behavior would be best in the following situations? Assume a "present state of the art" in which you must use the kinds of employees and supervisors now available in the labor market.
   a Telephone operators in a large-city dial-system office
   b Accountants with a small certified professional accounting firm

c Food servers in a local restaurant of a prominent fast-food hamburger chain

d Salesclerks in a large department store

e Circus laborers temporarily employed to work the week that the circus is in the city

9 Discuss why the supportive and collegial models of organizational behavior are especially appropriate for use in more affluent nations.

10 Discuss trends in the models of organizational behavior as they have developed over a period of time. Especially discuss why the trends are moving in the directions that they are.

11 Theory Z was presented as a hybrid model of organizational behavior. Identify the ways in which it appears to draw from each of the other models presented.

INCIDENT

The New Plant Manager

Toby Butterfield worked his way upward in the Montclair Company until he became assistant plant manager in the Illinois plant. Finally his opportunity for a promotion came. The Houston plant was having difficulty meeting its budget and production quotas, so he was promoted to plant manager and transferred to the Houston plant with instructions to "straighten it out."

Butterfield was ambitious and somewhat power-oriented. He believed that the best way to solve problems was to take control, make decisions, and use his authority to carry out his decisions. After preliminary study, he issued orders for each department to cut its budget 5 percent. A week later he instructed all departments to increase production 10 percent by the following month. He required several new reports and kept a close watch on operations. At the end of the second month he dismissed three supervisors who had failed to meet their production quotas. Five other supervisors resigned. Butterfield insisted that all rules and budgets should be followed and he allowed no exceptions.

Butterfield's efforts produced remarkable results. Productivity quickly exceeded standard by 7 percent, and within five months the plant was within budget. His record was so outstanding that he was promoted to the New York home office near the end of his second year. Within a month after he left, productivity in the Houston plant collapsed to 15 percent below standard, and the budget again was in trouble.

QUESTIONS

1 Discuss the model of organizational behavior Butterfield used and the kind of organizational climate he created.

2 Discuss why productivity dropped when Butterfield left the Houston plant.

3 If you were Butterfield's New York manager, what would you tell him about his approach? How might he respond?

EXPERIENTIAL EXERCISE

The Rapid Corporation

The Rapid Corporation is a refrigeration service organization in a large city. It has about seventy employees, mostly refrigeration service representatives. For many years the company's policies have been dominated by its president and principal owner, Otto Blumberg, who takes pride in being a "self-made man."

Recently Otto and his office manager attended an organizational behavior seminar in which the value of a written corporate philosophy for employees was discussed. Both men agreed to draft one and compare their efforts.

1 Divide the class into two types of groups. One set of groups should draft policy statements for the Rapid Corporation based on the autocratic model; the other groups should create comparable statements of philosophy using the supportive model as a basis.

2 Ask representatives of each group (autocratic and supportive) to read their statements to the class. Discuss their major differences. Have the class debate the usefulness of policy statements for guiding the organizational climate in a firm of this type.

REFERENCES

1 "Store Rules" of a Chicago department store about 1850, *Advanced Management,* March 1954, p. 19.

2 Marshall McLuhan and Bruce Powers, "Ma Bell Minus the Nantucket Gam: Or the Impact of High-Speed Data Transmission," *Journal of Communication,* Summer 1981, p. 191.

3 A comprehensive discussion of organizational climate is R. H. George Field and Michael A. Abelson, "Climate: A Reconceptualization and Proposed Model," *Human Relations,* March 1982, pp. 181–201. See also H. Russell Johnston, "A New Conceptualization of Source of Organizational Climate," *Administrative Science Quarterly,* March 1976, pp. 95–103; and Benjamin Schneider and Arnon E. Reichers, "On the Etiology of Climates," *Personnel Psychology,* Spring 1983, pp. 19–39.

4 An argument for the unique climate to be found in public-sector organizations is Joseph W. Whorton and John A. Worthley, "A Perspective on the Challenge of Public Management: Environmental Paradox and Organizational Culture," *Academy of Management Review,* July 1981, pp. 357–361.

5 "What Makes Tandem Run," *Business Week,* July 14, 1980, pp. 73–74.

6 Examples are reported in Paul M. Muchinsky, "Organizational Communication: Relationships to Organizational Climate and Job Satisfaction," *Academy of Management Journal,* December 1977, pp. 592–607.

7 Examples are John W. Hall, "A Comparison of Halpin and Croft's Organizational Climates and Likert and Likert's Organizational Systems," *Administrative Science Quarterly,* December 1972, pp. 586–590; Robert J. House and John R. Rizzo, "Toward the Measure of Organizational Practices: Scale Development and Validation," *Journal of Applied Psychology,* October 1972, pp. 388–396; and Paul M. Muchinsky, "An Assessment of the Litwin and Stringer Organizational Climate

Questionnaire: An Empirical and Theoretical Extension of the Sims and La-Follette Study," *Personnel Psychology,* Autumn 1976, pp. 371–392.

8 Rensis Likert, *The Human Organization: Its Management and Value,* New York: McGraw-Hill Book Company, 1967, pp. 3–12; and Rensis Likert, "Management Styles and the Human Component," *Management Review,* October 1977, pp. 23ff.

9 Benjamin Schneider, "The Service Organization: Climate Is Crucial," *Organizational Dynamics,* Autumn 1980, pp. 52–65; and Lee Ginsburg, "Strategic Planning for Work Climate Modification," *Personnel,* November–December 1978, pp. 10–20. Another approach to profiling climate is to compare the individual's perception with the average assessment of it, as done in William F. Joyce and John M. Slocum, "Climate Discrepancy: Refining the Concepts of Psychological and Organizational Climate," *Human Relations,* November 1982, pp. 951–972.

10 "Delta: The World's Most Profitable Airline," *Business Week,* Aug. 31, 1981, pp. 68–72.

11 Howard Schwartz and Stanley M. Davis, "Matching Corporate Culture and Business Strategy," *Organizational Dynamics,* Summer 1981, pp. 30–48.

12 An example of this early research is a study of the Prudential Insurance Company in Daniel Katz, Nathan Maccoby, and Nancy C. Morse, *Productivity, Supervision and Morale in an Office Situation,* Part 1, Ann Arbor, Mich.: Institute for Social Research, University of Michigan, 1950. The conclusion about job satisfaction and productivity is reported on page 63.

13 Rensis Likert, *New Patterns of Management,* New York: McGraw-Hill Book Company, 1961, pp. 102–103. Italics in original.

14 Byron G. Fiman, "An Investigation of the Relationships among Supervisory Attitudes, Behaviors, and Outputs: An Examination of McGregor's Theory Y," *Personnel Psychology,* Spring 1973, pp. 95–105.

15 Robert J. House and John R. Rizzo, "Role Conflict and Organizational Behavior," *Organizational Behavior and Human Performance,* June 1972, pp. 467–505.

16 M. Scott Myers, "Conditions for Manager Motivation," *Harvard Business Review,* January–February 1966, p. 61, covering 1344 managers at Texas Instruments, Inc.

17 Joel K. Leidecker and James L. Hall, "The Impact of Management Development Programs on Attitude Formation," *Personnel Journal,* July 1974, pp. 507–512.

18 Frank Harrison, "The Management of Scientists: Determinants of Perceived Role Performance," *Academy of Management Journal,* June 1974, pp. 234–241.

19 Chris Argyris, "The Executive Mind and Double-Loop Learning," *Organizational Dynamics,* Autumn 1982, pp. 4–22.

20 Kjell R. Knudsen, "Management Subcultures: Research and Change," *Journal of Management Development,* 1:4, 1982, pp. 11–26.

21 "Some Chief Executives Bypass, and Irk, Staffs in Getting Information," *Wall Street Journal* (Midwest edition), Jan. 12, 1983, pp. 1, 24.

22 William Ouchi, *Theory Z: How American Business Can Meet the Japanese Challenge,* Reading, Mass.: Addison-Wesley Publishing Company, 1982.

23 William Ouchi and J. B. Johnson, "Types of Organizational Control and their Relationship to Emotional Well Being," *Administrative Science Quarterly,* June 1978, pp. 293–317. See also Ouchi, op. cit.

24 Ronald Contino and Robert M. Lorusso, "The Theory Z Turnaround of a Public Agency," *Public Administration Review,* January–February 1982, pp. 66–71.

25 David Hunt and Donald Bolon, "The Development and Application of Theory Z's," in Dennis F. Ray (ed.), *Contribution of Theory and Research to the Practice of Management,* Mississippi State, Miss.: Southern Management Association, 1982, pp. 340–342.

26 Jeremiah J. Sullivan, "A Critique of Theory Z," *Academy of Management Review,* January 1983, pp. 132–142.

27 Edgar H. Schein, "Does Japanese Management Style Have a Message for American Managers?" *Sloan Management Review,* Fall 1982, pp. 55–68.

FOR ADDITIONAL READING

Deal, Terrence E., and Allan A. Kennedy, *Corporate Cultures: The Rites and Rituals of Corporate Life,* Reading, Mass.: Addison-Wesley Publishing Company, 1982.

Hofstede, G., *Culture's Consequences: International Differences in Work-Related Values,* Beverly Hills, Calif.: Sage Publications, 1980.

Joyce, William F., and John W. Slocum, "Climates in Organizations," in Steve Kerr (ed.), *Organizational Behavior,* San Francisco: Grid Publishing Co., 1979.

Litwin, George H., and R. A. Stringer, *Motivation and Organizational Climate,* Boston: Harvard University Press, 1968.

Ouchi, William, *Theory Z: How American Business Can Meet the Japanese Challenge,* Reading, Mass.: Addison-Wesley Publishing Company, 1981.

Pascale, Richard T., and Anthony G. Athos, *The Art of Japanese Management: Applications for American Executives,* New York: Simon & Schuster, Inc., 1981.

Taguiri, Renato, and George H. Litwin (eds.), *Organizational Climate: Explorations of a Concept,* Boston: Harvard University Press, 1968.

SOCIAL SYSTEMS

Organizations can be observed as a series of patterned interactions among actors.

J. Eugene Haas and Thomas E. Drabek[1]

CHAPTER OBJECTIVES

TO UNDERSTAND:
The operation of a social system
The psychological contract
Culture and cultural change
The work ethic
The social responsibility of organizations
Role and role conflict in organizations
Status and status symbols

Stanley Pedalino graduated from the university in the top 10 percent of his graduating class. He decided that he needed some manual labor experience before entering his chosen profession of marketing, so he went to work as a construction laborer for a year. He found that his college education was not valued by his fellow construction workers. Many of them looked down on college types, and some of them inquired what "a college dude" like Pedalino was doing working as a construction laborer. A year later, when Pedalino joined the market research staff of a national firm, he found that his education was favorably received. Unlike the construction crew, the research staff respected education and even encouraged pursuit of a master's degree.

Pedalino never stopped to analyze the situation, but he had experienced two social systems, and they had a significant influence on many parts of his job. Similarly, many college students have held a variety of part-time jobs and encountered different social systems in each organization. These systems determine the attitudes and values surrounding each job and influence the way that people work together. In this chapter we examine ideas about a social system, such as social equilibrium, culture, the work ethic, role, and status.

UNDERSTANDING A SOCIAL SYSTEM

A *social system* is a complex set of human relationships interacting in many ways. Possible interactions are as limitless as the stars in the universe. Each small group is a subsystem within larger groups that are subsystems of even larger groups, and so on, until the world's population is included. Within a single organization, the social system is all the people in it as they relate to each other and to the outside world.

Complexity of human relationships

The complex interactions in a system of this type may be illustrated by a chart, as shown in Figure 3-1.[2] The figure shows a box frame with objects A through E fastened to it by elastic bands 1 through 6. The objects are fastened to each other by bands 7 through 12. Suppose that elastic band 6 is moved toward corner *a*. In this instance, all five of the objects will be affected rather than just object E. They will move in location, and the tension on the bands will change. Consider object A. It will be affected by path 6–7, by path 6–11–12, and by path 6–11–10–9–8. At the same time, all the other objects will be affected by various paths interacting together. If any other elastic band is moved, all the other objects will be affected each time. This physical example illustrates the mutual interdependence of all parts of a social system. Simply stated, a change in one part of a system affects all other parts. Further, the system must monitor its environment and be ready to react to it.

Social equilibrium

A system is said to be in *social equilibrium* when there is a dynamic working balance among its interdependent parts. Equilibrium is a dynamic concept, not a static one. Despite constant movement in every organization, the

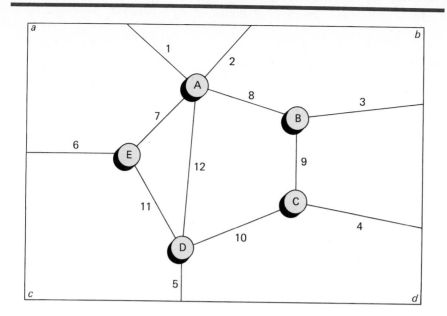

Figure 3-1
Illustration of
interdependence in
a social system

system's working balance is retained. The system is like a sea in which there is continuous motion, but the sea's basic character changes very little.

When minor changes occur in a social system, they are absorbed by adjustments within the system and equilibrium is retained. On the other hand, many changes or a series of rapid changes may throw an organization out of balance, seriously reducing its vigor until it can reach a new equilibrium. In a sense, when it is in disequilibrium, its parts are working against one another instead of in harmony. Here is an example:

*Tendency of change
to cause
disequilibrium*

> In a South American factory, accidents were high. The six native jefes, or supervisors, were not following management's instructions for accident prevention. They seemed agreeable but failed to "get the message" of accident prevention; consequently their employees were careless too. This was disequilibrium, with groups working at cross-purposes.
>
> Finally, management had three-dimensional faces of the six jefes molded and colored, with the idea that each week these faces would be arranged into a "totem pole" in the order of the weekly safety rank of each department. No jefe wanted to be low on the safety totem pole; so the accident problem was quickly corrected.

Functional and dysfunctional actions

A change such as the factory totem pole is considered *functional* when it is favorable for the system. When a change creates unfavorable effects (such as a productivity decline) for the system, it is *dysfunctional*. A major management task is to appraise both actual and proposed changes in the social system

The effects of change

to determine their possible functional or dysfunctional effects, so that appropriate responses can be made.

For example, American business has been sharply criticized for investing too little in human resources development. Instead, managers have emphasized the attainment of short-term profits.[3] In essence, decisions that appear to be functional for an organization in the short run may undermine its capacity to survive and prosper in the long run.

Psychological and economic contracts

Psychological contract

When employees join an organization, they make an unwritten psychological contract with it, although generally they are not conscious of doing so. As shown in Figure 3-2, this contract is in addition to the economic contract for wages, hours, and working conditions. The *psychological contract* defines the conditions of each employee's psychological involvement with the system. Employees agree to give a certain amount of work and loyalty, but in return they demand more than economic rewards from the system. They seek security, treatment as human beings, rewarding relationships with people, and support in fulfilling expectations.

If the organization honors only the economic contract and not the psychological contract, employees tend to have low job satisfaction and performance because their expectations are not met. On the other hand, if both their psychological and economic expectations are met, they tend to be satisfied, stay with the organization, and become high performers.

Figure 3-2
The psychological
contract and the
economic contract

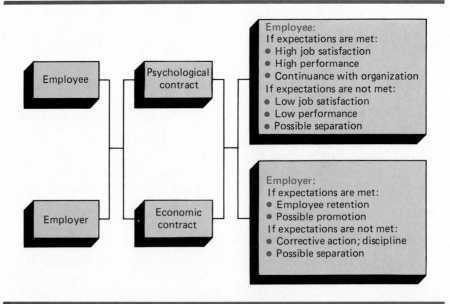

For example, one study covered clerks in a Midwestern retail firm.[4] Data about job expectations were collected at the time the clerks were hired. After they had been on the job a month, they completed forms telling how well their jobs were meeting their expectations. At the same time, supervisors rated the clerks' performance. The results showed that those who felt that their psychological contract was being reasonably met tended to have higher job satisfaction. Even more important, their ratings showed higher job performance.

As shown in Figure 3-2, an employer responds in a similar way to the economic and psychological contract that it sees. It expects responses such as high performance and cooperation. When these results occur, an employee is retained and may earn a promotion. However, if cooperation and performance do not meet expectations, corrective action and even separation may occur.

Equity

Employees are concerned with the fairness of rewards that they receive from their organization. This issue of fairness applies to all types of rewards—psychological, social, and economic—and it makes the contracting process discussed above much more complex. *Equity theory* describes employee feelings and reactions to the reward system. The theory states that employees tend to judge fairness by comparing their inputs and rewards on the job with those of other relevant people.[5]

How employees judge equity

Three combinations can occur. If employees feel overrewarded, they may be inclined to increase their own contributions or, possibly, discount the value of the rewards they receive. If employees perceive equity, they will continue to contribute at about the same level. Frequently, however, some workers feel that they have been inadequately rewarded. When this happens, they may quit, lower the quantity or quality of their work, or simply experience lower levels of satisfaction. They are reacting to inequity by bringing their inputs into balance with their outputs.

For example, a guest at a resort hotel left her camera at the information counter while she went shopping for the afternoon. The clerk placed the camera under the counter for safekeeping.

When the guest returned, her camera was missing. The clerk called the manager, who investigated the situation and eventually gave the guest a $275 credit for the value of the camera. The manager determined that twenty-seven employees had access to the camera's storage place during the time that it was supposed to be there. He then applied a $10 payroll deduction to each of them to pay for the camera, although he stated that he would return the charge if the thief confessed and paid the $275.

The affected employees were angry and upset. They felt that they were being treated unfairly because they had not taken the camera but were being required to pay for someone else's theft. Most of them resented the fact that their honesty had been questioned. Three employees resigned because of the incident, and two others said they would leave as soon as they could find other jobs. Dissatisfaction and antimanagement attitudes increased, and performance declined. As stated by one of the employees, "If they are going to give us shabby treatment, then that's what we will give their guests."

CULTURE

Impact of culture

Whenever people act in accordance with the expectations of others, their behavior is social, as in the case of an employee we will call Maria. Like all other workers, Maria grows to be an adult in a *culture,* which is her environment of human-created beliefs, customs, knowledge, and practices. Culture is the conventional behavior of her society, and it influences all her actions even though it seldom enters her conscious thoughts. Maria drives to work on the right or left side of the road, depending on the culture of her society, but she seldom consciously stops to think of this. The car she drives, the drama she attends, and the organization that employs her are evidence of her culture. Some of the important ways in which culture affects work are discussed in the following paragraphs.

Cultural change

People learn to depend on their culture. It gives them stability and security, because they can understand what is happening in their community and know how to respond. However, two types of change may confront employees. One involves a move to a new location and its culture, the other a gradual change in their existing environment. Employees need to learn to adapt to both situations in order to avoid possible negative consequences.

What is cultural shock?

New culture Companies frequently transfer employees between different cities for new job assignments. The employees who move to new job locations often experience various degrees of *cultural shock,* which is a feeling of confusion, insecurity, and anxiety caused by a strange new environment. They are concerned about not knowing how to act and about losing their self-confidence when the wrong responses are made.

A cultural change does not have to be dramatic to cause some degree of shock. For example, when an employee moves from a small town to the Boston or Chicago home office, both the employee and family are likely to suffer cultural shock. A similar shock may occur when a Boston or Chicago employee is transferred to a small town in an isolated rural area. The whole family may not know what to do with their time or how to act and dress.

Cultural shock is even greater when there is a move from one nation to another, especially if the language is different. For unprepared employees, the environment can appear to be chaos. They become disoriented, retreat into isolation, and want to return home on the next airplane. But a different culture is not behavioral chaos; it is a systematic structure of behavioral patterns, probably as systematic as the culture in the employee's home country. It can be understood if employees have receptive attitudes. But it is different, and these differences are a strain on newcomers regardless of their adaptability. Sometimes the strain is likely to be so great that an employee should not make the move.

> **For example, some of the important issues an employee faces when moving to a different nation are the opportunity to initiate contact with the supervisor, different patterns of working hours, and the expected pace of work. One employee from France who was transferred to the United States had to break the habit of shaking hands with everyone else in the office (twenty people!) at the beginning and end of each day.**[6]

Cultural evolution A second type of cultural change occurs when the environment around an employee evolves to a different form. Even though employees have remained in the same location, the new culture may have dramatic effects on them. Examples of such changes are evolving moral values, technological advances, or changes in the composition of the work force. Alert employees will monitor these changes and attempt to adapt to the emerging culture around them.

> **An example of evolutionary change is the trend toward a service economy in the United States. The majority of labor hours are now employed in service industries, such as retailing, banking, insurance, and education. The United States was the first major country to shift from an agricultural to an industrial base and on to a service economy in just one century. The computer revolution of the 1980s is magnifying the pace of this change and increasing the difficulties of employee adjustment to cultural change.**

Another recent example of cultural evolution has been the rapid emergence of *dual-career couples,* in which each spouse has a separate career. As a result, both the couple and the employer are required to cope with new conditions. On the favorable side, employers have a larger labor market to draw from and a greater selection of skills available to them. On the unfavorable side, 20 percent of organizations report that dual-career couples create problems for them.[7] Geographical transfers of an employee are especially difficult. Since both spouses hold jobs, one may want to make the transfer while the other does not. Consequently, dual-career couples often are reluctant to accept a transfer.

Effects of dual-career couples

> **An encouraging trend reported in one survey of 1000 firms is that 25 percent of them said they provide job assistance to spouses. These programs, called *transplacement,* provide services such as placement aid for the spouse, job counseling, tips on preparation of personal data sheets for seeking employment, and occasionally hiring the spouse into the company.**[8] **Under these conditions, the dual-career couple generally is more willing to accept the transfer.**

The work ethic

For many years the culture of much of the Western world has emphasized work as a desirable and fulfilling activity. This attitude also is strong in parts of Asia, such as Japan. The result is a *work ethic* for many people, meaning that they view work as a central life interest and a desirable goal in life. They

Work as a desirable life goal

tend to like work and derive satisfaction from it. They usually have a stronger commitment to the organization and its goals than do other employees.[9] These characteristics of the work ethic make it appealing to employers.

Origins of the work ethic   The work ethic has its origins in both religious and secular values. The Calvinists during the Protestant Reformation, and later the Puritans in the United States, strongly supported the work ethic. Because of its religious origins, it has been called the Protestant ethic, although it is held by people of various religions. The religious view of the work ethic is that work is an act of service to God and to other people because it builds a better society to help fulfill God's plan. Human talents have been given to people by their Maker for the purpose of use, so hard work and lack of waste become moral obligations. Studies in various organizations confirm that employees who have the work ethic usually feel a moral commitment about the ethic rather than viewing it as a rational, businesslike choice.[10]

Secular origins   The secular origins of the work ethic probably arose from the hard necessities of pioneer life. People had to work hard to stay alive, and therefore they found reason to glorify work. It was a central fact of their environment. It also was the only way they could possibly improve their standard of living, so they viewed it as a desired ideal whereby each generation could contribute something to the generations that were to follow.

> The existence of a strong work ethic is shown in the surprising response of some million-dollar lottery winners when they are asked about their future job plans. "Of course I'll keep on working," they state. "My job is very important to me."

Trends in the work ethic   The work ethic often is a subject of controversy. Some observers claim it is healthy, some contend that it is declining, and others suggest that it is dead or should be laid to rest.[11] The available research indicates that there are wide variations across groups. The proportion of employees with a work ethic varies sharply among sample groups, depending on factors such as personal background, type of work, and geographical location. The ratio of employees in different jobs who report that work is a central life interest may range from 15 to 85 percent.

Decline of the work ethic   In addition to differences among groups, the general level of the work ethic also has declined gradually since the 1930s. The decline is mostly evident in the different attitudes between younger and older workers. Predictably, since their backgrounds differ sharply, younger employees are not as supportive of the work ethic. This is shown in studies such as the following.

> College students are surveyed annually by the research firm of Yankelovich, Skelly, and White, Inc. In the mid-1960s over 70 percent believed that "hard work always pays off." A decade later, only 40 percent held that view.[12] What will the figure be in 1990 or 2000?

Dramatic social changes in the latter half of the twentieth century have brought about the work ethic's decline. Competing social values have emerged, such as a leisure ethic, desire for closer personal relationships, and a belief in being entitled to rewards without work. In addition, changes in social policy and tax laws have reduced incentives to work and occasionally even penalized hard work and success. These represent additional illustrations of complex social relationships in action, and they show how an employee's work ethic is contingent on situational factors.

> **An example is the underground coal mining industry. Interviews with managers reveal that miners are productive when three conditions exist: a feeling of certainty at work, some competition between crews or shifts, and conditions that seem to make time pass quickly.[13] When management creates these conditions, the workers mine coal safely and continuously. This study suggests that the work ethic will emerge if a proper social context is created.**

Managing the work ethic

Social responsibility

From the 1950s through the 1970s, new cultural values arose out of an awareness of the interdependence of organizations, society, and the environment. People began to realize that organizational actions passed costs to the external society along with their benefits, and there was a strong drive to improve this cost-benefit relationship. In this way, society could receive additional net benefits from organizations, and these benefits would be more fairly distributed.

These new values generally go by the name of social responsibility, social responsiveness, or social involvement. *Social responsibility* is the recognition that organizations have significant influence on the social system and that this influence must be properly considered and balanced in all organizational actions. It simply means that organizations must function as part of a larger social system because they are, in fact, a part of that system.[14]

There is strong evidence that businesses are becoming more socially involved. One example is corporate gifts to community organizations (such as the American Red Cross, Public Broadcasting Service, Boy Scouts, colleges and universities, and the Salvation Army), which average over $2.5 billion annually.[15] In addition to money these gifts include services and products, such as a food producer's donation of canned goods to communities with high unemployment rates.

Social responsibility in action

These social values apply to all organizations, whether they are involved in business, labor, government, or some other activity. Each affects society in both positive and negative ways. For example, the employment policy of a construction company may discriminate against women, handicapped employees, or other groups. The labor union strike of the municipal transit agency may inconvenience thousands of commuters, reduce attendance at schools, increase consumption of scarce energy, and so on. And when a naval ship dumps its wastes into the sea, marine life may be harmed. The essential philosophy of social responsibility is that "We are all part of one social system, and we all live together on one planet. We must act according to those facts."

Historical development In the past most firms tried to be socially responsible by providing fair pay, fringe benefits, and working conditions. However, there were gaps that needed to be corrected, such as inadequate facilities for handicapped people. In addition, there were major oversights in relation to the external environment, such as poor environmental protection and unconsidered secondary effects on society. Managers needed to take a larger view. They had fallen out of step with new expectations, so large gaps developed between actual and expected outcomes.

A narrow view of responsibility

Figure 3-3 presents a chart of a chemical company's responsiveness to the social system. It was meeting expectations reasonably well in pay, fringe benefits, and working conditions. It was showing social responsibility.

On the other hand, it was being less responsive in some other areas, because large gaps existed between social expectations and company practices. For example, its employment practices had some elements of discrimination, even though much improvement had been made. Consumer protection in the use of its products had been largely ignored, and it was polluting the environment unnecessarily in a number of ways. Its community relations also were poorly developed. It needs to take major action to be more socially responsive.

Socioeconomic model of responsiveness

A socioeconomic model Most organizations in the past, whether they were business or government, made their decisions on the basis of economic and technical values. The new emphasis on social responsiveness has led to a *socioeconomic model of decision making* in which social costs and benefits are considered along with the traditional economic and technical values in decision making. Organizations are developing a broader outlook of the

Figure 3-3
Comparison of
social expectations
and social
responsiveness for
a chemical company

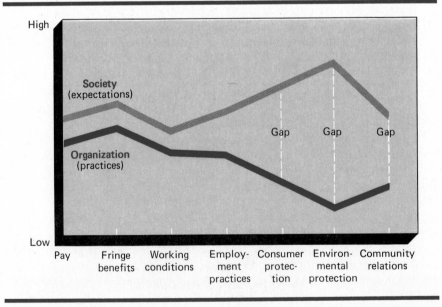

social system and its interdependence. They are learning to be more human and to operate more in harmony with the earth's environment. They are being socially responsive.

The effect on leaders of business, labor unions, and government has been to require their retraining to operate with a more holistic view of organizational behavior and other areas of management. Executives are increasingly aware that it is not enough for them to be sensitive to environmental forces. They must balance "the traditional economic/technical considerations with the non-economic interests of constituents, external as well as internal to the company."[16]

ROLE

A *role* is the pattern of actions expected of a person in activities involving others. Role reflects a person's position in the social system, with its accompanying rights and obligations, power and responsibility. In order to be able to interact with each other, people need some way to anticipate others' behavior. Role performs this function in the social system.

Roles define expected behaviors.

A person has roles both on the job and away from it, as shown in Figure 3-4. One person performs the occupational role of worker, the family role of parent, the social role of club president, and many others. In those various roles, a person is both buyer and seller, supervisor and subordinate, and giver and seeker of advice. Each role calls for different types of behavior. Within

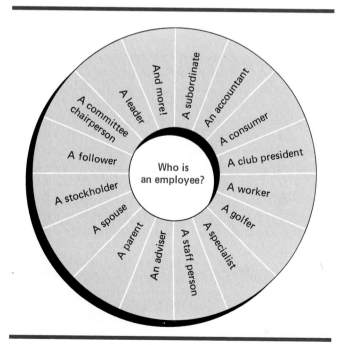

Figure 3-4
Each employee performs many roles.

the work environment alone, a worker may have more than one role, such as a worker in group A, a subordinate to supervisor B, a machinist, a member of a union, and a representative on the safety committee.

Socialization

Organizations socialize employees.

Where do employees obtain information regarding their work-related roles? In addition to formal methods like job descriptions and orientation sessions, socialization is a powerful mechanism. *Socialization* is the process by which organizations shape the attitudes, thoughts, and behavior of employees. It occurs when an employee encounters others at work and watches, questions, or is advised by them on acceptable patterns of behavior.[17]

Mentors are role models.

A special form of socialization occurs when one employee "adopts" and guides another. This is called *mentoring.* The mentor is often older, upwardly mobile, respected by peers, and willing to commit time and energy to assist a newer worker move up the corporate ladder.[18] In effect, the mentor serves as a role model to help the new employee gain valuable data on roles to play and roles to avoid. Sometimes the relationship fails, as in the following example.

In an office, Kenneth Benton, an older employee, tried to play the role of adviser and helper with a new employee, Ben Grossman. Grossman misinterpreted Benton's initiatives and felt that he was being "bossed" by someone who had no right to give him orders. Rebuffed as a mentor, Benton later refused to share his insights with Grossman, even when asked.

Role perceptions

Activities of managers and workers alike are guided by their *role perceptions,* that is, how they think they are supposed to act in their own roles and how others should act in their roles. Since managers perform many different roles, they must be highly adaptive in order to change from one role to another quickly. Supervisors especially need to change roles rapidly as they work with subordinates and superiors and with technical and nontechnical activities.

Multiple role perceptions

When two people such as a manager and an employee interact, each one needs to understand at least three role perceptions, as shown in Figure 3-5.[19] For a manager, the three roles are as follows (three similar roles exist for the employee): First there is the manager's role as required by the job being performed. Then there is the role of the employee being contacted. Finally there is the manager's role as seen by the employee. Obviously one cannot meet the needs of others unless one can perceive what they expect.

Role conflict

When others have different perceptions or expectations of a person's role, that person tends to experience *role conflict,* because it is difficult to meet one set of expectations without rejecting another. A company president faced role

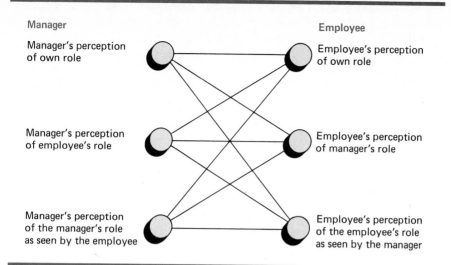

Manager

Manager's perception
of own role

Manager's perception
of employee's role

Manager's perception
of the manager's role
as seen by the employee

Employee

Employee's perception
of own role

Employee's perception
of manager's role

Employee's perception
of the employee's role
as seen by the manager

Figure 3-5
The complex web of
manager-employee
role perceptions

conflict, for example, when she learned that both the controller and the personnel director wanted her to allocate the new organizational planning function to their departments.

Role conflict at work is fairly common. A national sample of wage and salary workers reported that 48 percent experienced role conflict from time to time and 15 percent said that role conflict was a frequent and serious problem.[20] Role conflict was most difficult for employees with many job contacts outside the organization, that is, with boundary roles. They found that their external roles placed different demands on their jobs than their internal roles, so role conflict resulted. When people were classified according to the number of their outside job contacts, those with few contacts had the least role conflict and those with frequent contacts had the most conflict.

Role conflict is common.

Role ambiguity

When roles are inadequately defined or are substantially unknown, *role ambiguity* exists, because people are not sure how they should act in situations of this type. When role conflict and ambiguity exist, there usually is a decline in job satisfaction and organizational commitment.[21] On the other hand, employees tend to be more satisfied with their jobs when their roles are clearly defined by job descriptions and statements of performance expectations. A better understanding of roles helps people know what others expect of them and how they should act. If any role misunderstanding exists when people interact, then problems are likely to occur.

Role ambiguity causes problems.

For example, a factory employee, Bryce Bailey, was a union steward. He came to his supervisor, Shelly Parrish, for guidance on a work problem. Parrish thought Bailey was approaching in his role as union steward and was trying to challenge her authority. Because of the misunderstood roles, the two people were not able to communicate, and the problem remained unsolved.

STATUS

Status is the social rank of a person in a group. It is a mark of the amount of recognition, honor, and acceptance given to a person. Within groups, differences in status apparently have been recognized ever since civilization began. Wherever people gather into groups, status distinctions are likely to arise, because they enable people to affirm the different characteristics and abilities of group members.

Individuals are bound together in *status systems,* or *status hierarchies,* which define their rank relative to others in the group. If they become seriously upset over their status, they are said to feel *status anxiety.*

Status is important.

Loss of status, sometimes called "losing face," is a serious event for a typical person. People, therefore, become quite responsible in order to protect and develop their status. One of management's pioneers, Chester Barnard, stated, "The desire for improvement of status and especially the desire to protect status appears to be the basis of a sense of general responsibility."[22]

Since status is important to people, they will work hard to earn it. If it can be tied to actions that further the company's goals, then employees are strongly motivated to support their company.

A laundry manager formerly gave negative attention and reprimands (low status) to workers whom he found idle, even when they had finished their work and were waiting for more from another operator. He wanted them to help other operators, but he found that his approach simply caused them to work more slowly. Upon reexamining his approach, he decided to try to build the status of his "idle" employees who finished their work ahead of others.

He visited with them in a friendly way as he walked through his shop. He permitted them to go to any other work station to talk and visit or to get soft drinks for themselves or others. The slow workers began to work faster to achieve this status, and the fast workers improved in order to preserve their relative position. As the fast workers visited other work stations, they developed friendships and did much informal training and helping of the slow workers. The manager later commented, "I am amazed by the changed attitudes of the workers and their increased productivity."

Status relationships

High-status people within a group usually have more power and influence than those with low status. They also receive more privileges from their group and tend to participate more in group activities. They interact more with their peers than with those of lower rank. Basically, high status gives people an opportunity to play a more important role in an organization. As a result, lower-status members tend to feel isolated from the mainstream and to show more stress symptoms than higher-ranked members.[23]

In a work organization, status provides a system by which people can relate to each other as they work. Without it, they would tend to be confused and spend much of their time trying to learn how to work together. Though status can be abused, normally it is beneficial because it helps people cooperate with one another.

Sources of status

The sources of status are numberless, but in a typical work situation several sources are easily identified. As shown in Figure 3-6, education and job level are two important sources of higher status. A person's abilities, job skills, and type of work also are major sources of status.

Where do we get status?

Other sources of status are amount of pay, seniority, and age. Pay gives economic recognition and an opportunity to have more of the amenities of life, such as travel. Seniority and age often earn for their holder certain privileges, such as first choice of vacation dates. Method of pay (hourly versus salary) and working conditions also provide important status distinctions, such as distinguishing blue-collar and white-collar work.

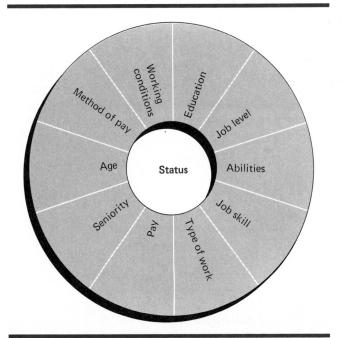

Figure 3-6
Major sources of status on the job

For example, the Eaton Corporation, a manufacturing company, uses pay and working conditions to give white-collar status to blue-collar workers in some of its plants, and improved performance has resulted.[24] Regular shop workers receive a salary and no longer have to punch time clocks. Their salary continues while they are sick, just as it would for a manager. Supervisors are trained to be helpful and supportive, much like those in a well-run office.

The result of these efforts toward improving status is that workers are more self-disciplined and productive. Since they like their jobs better, absences are 3 percent or less, compared with 6 to 12 percent in other plants. Turnover has been reduced to 4 percent compared with as high as 60 percent in other plants. However, the new approach makes the supervisor's job more difficult, and the company admits that some employees take advantage of the new policies.

Status symbols

Status symbols are everywhere.

The status system reaches its ultimate end with *status symbols.* These are the visible, external things that attach to a person or workplace and serve as evidence of social rank. They exist in the office, shop, warehouse, refinery, or wherever work groups congregate. They are most in evidence among different levels of managers, because each successive level usually has the authority to provide itself with surroundings just a little different from those of people lower in the structure.

As shown in Figure 3-7, there are a variety of symbols of status, depending on what employees feel is important. For example, in one office the type of wastebasket is a mark of distinction. In another, significant symbols are type of desk and telephones. In the executive offices, such items of rank as rugs, bookcases, curtains, and pictures on the wall are important.

Another symbol of much significance is a corner office, because these offices are larger and have windows on two sides. There may even be distinctions between an office with windows and one with no windows. Outside the office, the truck driver who operates the newest or largest truck has a symbol of status.

The clothes people wear at work are also symbols of status. A coat and tie implies higher status than slacks and a sport shirt in most situations. For an airline pilot, the uniform is a symbol of status. The job title, such as senior pilot or captain, also is important.

Figure 3-7
Typical symbols
of status

- *Furniture,* such as a large executive desk
- *Interior decorations,* such as rugs, paintings, and draperies
- *Location of workplace,* such as a corner office
- *Facilities at workplace,* such as a computer terminal or desk water bottle
- *Quality and newness of equipment used,* such as a new truck
- *Type of clothes normally worn,* including uniforms
- *Privileges given,* such as a club membership or personal use of a company automobile
- *Job titles,* such as vice president
- *Employees assigned,* such as a private secretary

All this concern for symbols of status may seem amusing, but status symbols are a serious matter. They may endanger job satisfaction because employees who do not have a certain symbol and think they should can become gloomy and nervous. When, for example, an employee gives unreasonable attention to status symbols, there is evidence of status anxiety, and this requires management attention.

Many organizations have a policy that persons of equal rank in the same department should receive approximately equal status symbols. There may be some variation between departments, such as production and sales, because the work is different and rank is not directly comparable. In any case, managers need to face the fact that status differences exist and must be managed successfully. Managers have the power to influence and control status relationships somewhat. The organization gives some status, and it can take some away!

Significance of status

Status is significant to organizational behavior in several ways. It often is the source of employee problems and conflicts that management needs to solve. It influences the kinds of transfers an employee will take. It helps determine who will be informal leader of a group, and it definitely serves to motivate those seeking to advance in the organization. Some people are status seekers, wanting a job of high status regardless of its other conditions. These people can be encouraged to qualify themselves for high-status jobs so that they will feel rewarded.

Status influences behavior.

> By contrast, those persons who already have high economic status are unlikely to flaunt it. A poll of chief executives of small, medium, and large firms showed that most do not have chauffeurs, private planes, tailor-made suits, bodyguards, or long vacations.[25] Their office status does not carry much weight at home, either. They often shop at discount stores, help with grocery shopping, and do home chores.

Having status in one context clearly does not imply that the same person will have it in another situation. It must be earned or acquired there too.

SUMMARY

When people join a work group, they become part of that organization's social system. It is the medium by which they relate to the world of work. The variables in an organizational system operate in a degree of working balance called social equilibrium. Individuals make a psychological contract to define their personal relationship with the system.

The environment that people develop for their society is their culture, and a major change in culture can lead to cultural shock. Important cultural influences include the work ethic, different attitudes in the labor force, and social responsibility.

Role is the pattern of action expected of a person in activities involving others. Related ideas are socialization, role perception, role conflict, and role ambiguity. Status is the social rank of a person in a group, and it leads to status systems, status anxiety, and status symbols. Status symbols are sought as if they were magical herbs because they may bring status to their possessors.

TERMS AND CONCEPTS FOR REVIEW

Social equilibrium	Social responsibility
Functional and dysfunctional effects	Role
	Socialization
Psychological contract	Role conflict
Equity	Role ambiguity
Culture	Status
Cultural shock	Status anxiety
Dual-career couples	Status symbols
The work ethic	

REVIEW QUESTIONS

1 What psychological contract do you feel is present in this course? Describe its key features.

2 Think of a time when you felt a lack of equity in a situation. Describe what you did and how your actions corresponded with equity theory.

3 Discuss a time when you experienced cultural shock. Perhaps it was a situation in which you did not know how to behave or you were surprised by the behavior of others. How did you react? How do you wish you had reacted?

4 A management specialist recently commented about the work ethic, "You can discover if you personally have a work ethic if you ask yourself this question: Do I think more about the amount of salary that I make than I do about the quality of the product I make?" Comment.

5 What is social responsibility? Does it apply to people as well as institutions? Describe three acts of social responsibility that you have performed in the last month.

6 Reflect back on your first few days in college. In what ways were you socialized? Did you resist, or did you accept the process?

7 What are role conflict and ambiguity? Describe a situation in which you have experienced one of these.

8 Interview an office manager to determine what the manager believes to be the five principal status symbols in the office.

Liberty Construction Company

Liberty Construction Company is a small company in Colorado. Over half its revenue is derived from the installation of underground water and power lines, so much of its work is seasonal and there is high turnover among its employees.

Michael Federico, a college student, had been employed by Liberty as a backhoe operator for the last three summers. On his return to work for the fourth summer, Federico was assigned the second newest of the company's five backhoes. The owner reasoned that Federico had nine months of work seniority, so according to strict seniority he should have the second backhoe. This action required the present operator of the backhoe, Pedro Alvarez, a regular employee who had been with the company seven months, to be reassigned to an older machine. Alvarez was strongly dissatisfied with this; he felt that as a regular employee he should have retained the newer machine instead of having to give it to a temporary employee. The other employees soon fell into two camps, one supporting Alvarez and one supporting Federico. Job conflicts arose, and each group seemed to delight in causing work problems for the other group. In less than a month Alvarez left the company.

QUESTION

Discuss this case in terms of the social system, equilibrium, the psychological contract, role, status, and status symbols.

The Green Corporation

Jerry Blue is supervisor of purchasing for the Green Corporation, a manufacturer of a consumer product in a town of 5000 people. The company employs 350 people. Reporting to Blue is one buyer, John James. James is an ambitious young community college graduate who is very intent on opportunity and advancement. His abilities have been recognized by higher management, and he is being considered for two different higher positions that may open within the next year. Blue, who is older and has only one year of college, is content in his present position.

James has a clerk-typist named Barbara Smith reporting to him. Recently Barbara Smith and her husband bought a new home on the same block in which the Blues live. Since they are neighbors, the Smiths have become close social friends of the Blue family.

As a result of this close friendship, Barbara Smith recently has been going to Jerry Blue to get answers to her work problems rather than to her immediate supervisor, John James. James feels bypassed in the chain of command, but he has said nothing to Blue or Smith about this. No one at the company knew about the problem until James's wife telephoned the personnel manager, explaining that James is so upset about the problem that he has had to seek medical attention.

QUESTIONS

1 Using the point of view of social systems, analyze the causes of this developing problem.

2 You are Jerry Blue, and the personnel manager has just told you about the telephone call. What will you do?

REFERENCES

1 Eugene Haas and Thomas E. Drabek, *Complex Organizations: A Sociological Perspective,* New York: The Macmillan Company, 1973, p. 8.

2 This manner of conceptualizing the social system was first discovered by the authors in Lawrence J. Henderson, *Pareto's General Sociology: A Physiologist's Interpretation,* Cambridge, Mass.: Harvard University Press, 1935.

3 Robert H. Hayes and David A. Garvin, "Managing as if Tomorrow Mattered," *Harvard Business Review,* May–June, 1982, pp. 70–79.

4 James D. Portwood and Edwin L. Miller, "Evaluating the Psychological Contract: Its Implications for Employee Job Satisfaction and Work Behavior," in Robert L. Taylor and others (eds.), *Academy of Management Proceedings,* 1975, Mississippi State, Miss.: Academy of Management, 1976, pp. 109–113.

5 For details of equity theory, see Richard M. Steers and Lyman W. Porter, *Motivation and Work Behavior,* 2d ed., New York: McGraw-Hill Book Company, 1979, Chap. 3, "Equity Theory," pp. 104–146, which includes material by J. Stacy Adams, who developed the equity framework. Equity exists when the following formula is in balance as shown. If either side is greater, then there is inequity.

$$\frac{\text{Person's outcomes}}{\text{Person's inputs}} = \frac{\text{Other's outcomes}}{\text{Other's inputs}}$$

6 Rae Andre, "Managing the Visiting Employee in the United States," *Personnel Administrator,* July 1982, pp. 45–49. Other examples of cultural differences and shock are reported in Pershing P. Stahlman, "Working Abroad: Some Problems and Pitfalls," *Personnel Administrator,* August 1979, pp. 27–30.

7 Richard E. Kopelman, Lyn Rosensweig, and Lauren H. Lally, "Dual-Career Couples: The Organizational Response," *Personnel Administrator,* September 1982, pp. 73–78. See also Francine Hall and Douglas Hall, "Dual Careers—How Do Couples and Companies Cope with Problems," *Organizational Dynamics,* Spring 1978, pp. 57–77.

8 Karen E. Debats, "The Current State of Corporate Relocation," *Personnel Journal,* September 1982, pp. 664–670.

9 Robert Dubin, Joseph E. Champoux, and Lyman W. Porter, "Central Life Interests and Organizational Commitment of Blue-Collar and Clerical Workers," *Administrative Science Quarterly,* September 1975, pp. 411–421. This article provides references to many other studies.

10 Aryeh Kidron, "Work Values and Organizational Commitment," *Academy of Management Journal,* June 1978, pp. 239–247.

11 For a positive view, see Michael Maccoby, "Leadership in a Changing Work Environment," in *Personnel Management—Policies and Practices Report,* Bulletin I, Section 2, Englewood Cliffs, N.J.: Prentice-Hall, Inc., June 22, 1981, pp. i–ii. A critical perspective is provided in Alan L. Porter, "The Work Ethic—An Idea Whose Time Has Gone?" *Business,* January–February 1981, pp. 15–22.

12 Daniel Yankelovich, "New Rules in American Life: Searching for Self-Fulfillment in a World Turned Upside Down," *Psychology Today,* April 1981, pp. 35ff.

13 Richard L. Hannah, "The Work Ethic of Coal Miners," *Personnel Journal,* October 1982, pp. 746ff.

14 A book devoted to this subject is Keith Davis and William C. Frederick, *Business and Society,* 5th ed., New York: McGraw-Hill Book Company, 1984.

15 Melanie Lawrence, "Social Responsibility: How Companies Become Involved in Their Communities," *Personnel Journal,* July 1982, pp. 502–510.

16 George A. Steiner, "The New Class of Chief Executive Officer," *Long Range Planning,* 14:4, 1981, p. 13.

17 Daniel C. Feldman, "The Multiple Socialization of Organization Members," *Academy of Management Review,* April 1981, pp. 309–318; and Gareth R. Jones, "Psychological Orientation and the Process of Organizational Socialization: An Interactionist Perspective," *Academy of Management Review,* July 1983, pp. 464–475.

18 Penny George and Jean Kummerow, "Mentoring for Career Women," *Training,* February 1981, pp. 44–49.

19 A special case of multiple role perceptions and how to handle them is provided in John W. Newstrom and Melissa S. Leifer, "Triple Perceptions of the Trainer: Strategies for Change," *Training and Development Journal,* November 1982, pp. 90–96.

20 Robert L. Kahn and others, *Organizational Stress: Studies in Role Conflict and Ambiguity,* New York: John Wiley & Sons, Inc., 1964, pp. 56, 99–124; and John J. Parkington and Benjamin Schneider, "Some Correlates of Experienced Job Stress: A Boundary Role Study," *Academy of Management Journal,* June 1979, pp. 270–281.

21 Arthur G. Bedeian and Achilles A. Armenakis, "A Path-Analytic Study of the Consequences of Role Conflict and Ambiguity," *Academy of Management Journal,* June 1981, pp. 417–424; see also R. Stephen Wunder, Thomas W. Dougherty, and M. Ann Welsh, "A Causal Model of Role Stress and Employee Turnover," in Kae H. Chung (ed.), *Academy of Management Proceedings,* 1982, Mississippi State, Miss.: Academy of Management, pp. 297–301.

22 Chester I. Barnard, "Functions and Pathology of Status Systems in Formal Organizations," in William F. Whyte (ed.), *Industry and Society,* New York: McGraw-Hill Book Company, 1946, p. 69.

23 Alan Mazur, "A Cross-Species Comparison of Status in Small Established Groups," *American Sociological Review,* October 1973, pp. 513–514.

24 "Where White-Collar Status Boosts Productivity," *Business Week,* May 23, 1977, pp. 80–85.

25 Frank Allen, "Most Bosses Shun Symbols of Status, Help Take Care of Household Tasks," *Wall Street Journal,* Oct. 23, 1981, p. 29.

FOR ADDITIONAL READING

Cherrington, David J., *The Work Ethic: Working Values and Values That Work,* New York: AMACOM, 1980.

Hoffman, Michael W., and Thomas J. Wyly (eds.), *The Work Ethic in Business: Proceedings of the Third National Conference on Business Ethics,* Cambridge, Mass.: Oelgeschlager, Gunn, and Hain, Publishers, Inc., 1981.

London, Manuel, and Stephen A. Stumpf, *Managing Careers,* Reading, Mass.: Addison-Wesley Publishing Co., 1982.

McLuhan, Marshall, *Culture Is Our Business,* New York: McGraw-Hill Book Company, 1970.

Parsons, Talcott, *Social Structure and Personality,* New York: Free Press of Glencoe, 1964.

Ritti, R. Richard, and G. Ray Funkhouser, *The Ropes to Skip and the Ropes to Know: Studies in Organizational Behavior,* 2d ed., Columbus, Ohio: Grid Publishing Co., 1982.

Sheehy, Gail, *Pathfinders,* New York: William Morrow and Company, Inc., 1981.

Yankelovich, Daniel, *New Rules: Searching for Self-Fulfillment in a World Turned Upside Down,* New York: Random House, Inc., 1981.

PART

2

MOTIVATION AND REWARD SYSTEMS

CHAPTER

4

MAINSPRINGS OF MOTIVATION

Motivation says do this because it's very meaningful for me to do it.

Frederick Herzberg[1]

If you are like a wheelbarrow, going no farther than you are pushed, then do not apply for work here.

Sign at factory employment gate many years ago

CHAPTER OBJECTIVES

TO UNDERSTAND:
Types of needs
How needs affect action
Maslow's priority of needs
Motivational and maintenance factors
Intrinsic and extrinsic motivators
Behavior modification
Types of reinforcement methods

Assume that an employee called Mary Smith works as a computer programmer in a government office or in a business. Mary, an individual, enters the organization, an operating social system. She brings to her job certain needs that in her environment are translated into wants. Perhaps she wants to learn and advance, hoping someday to become a systems manager, or perhaps she wants security and good working conditions. Within this situation the organization tries to provide a climate wherein Mary is motivated in a way that serves her and its interests.

In a way, this whole book is about Mary's situation; however, it is first necessary to discuss certain foundations of motivation, and this is the purpose of the next two chapters.

HUMAN NEEDS

When a machine malfunctions, people recognize that it needs something. Assume that a machine will not grind a piece of metal to a close enough tolerance. Perhaps it needs oil. Or maybe a nut is loose. First the operator tries to find the trouble. Then the operator asks the supervisor for help. Finally the supervisor calls a maintenance mechanic or an engineer, and so on, until the cause of the problem is found and the machine is put back into working order.

All the people who tried to find the causes of the breakdown did so (or should have done so) in an analytical manner based upon their knowledge of the operations and needs of the machine. It would be wasteful to tighten nuts and oil gears haphazardly in the hope that the trouble could be found. Such action might aggravate the malfunction.

Suppose that the machine operator "malfunctions" by talking back to the supervisor in a way that borders on insubordination. The supervisor may want to reprimand the operator without analyzing the situation, but this is no better than haphazard machine repair. Like the machine, the operator who malfunctions does so because of definite causes that may be related to needs. In order for improvement to occur, the operator requires skilled and professional care just as the machine does. If we treated (maintained) people as well as we do expensive machines, we would have more satisfied and productive workers.

Managers also require care to keep them motivated. Managerial malfunctions and problems are sometimes so serious that managers become ineffective in motivating their employees and are replaced.[2]

A model of motivation

Although a few human activities occur without motivation, nearly all conscious behavior is motivated, or caused. It requires no motivation to grow hair, but getting a haircut does. Eventually, anyone will fall asleep without motivation (although parents with young children may doubt this), but going to bed is a conscious act requiring motivation. Management's job is to identify and activate employee motives toward task performance.

Motives are perceived as expressions of a person's needs; hence they are personal and internal. *Incentives,* on the other hand, are external to the person. They are made part of the work environment by management in order to encourage workers to perform tasks. For example, management offers salespeople a bonus as an incentive to encourage higher sales and also satisfy the salesperson's need for recognition and status.

Motives and incentives

Diagramed very simply, the relation of needs to performance is summarized in the model of motivation in Figure 4-1.[3] Needs create tensions that are modified by one's environment to cause certain wants. Employees then examine the positive and negative incentives that are available to them and determine which ones will best satisfy their wants. Based on their appraisal of the total situation, they are motivated to take actions that satisfy their needs. To illustrate, the need for food produces a tension of hunger. Since environment affects one's appetite for particular types of food, a South Seas native may want roast fish, while a Colorado rancher wants broiled steak. Both persons will be motivated to take action, but they will seek different foods in different ways.

Types of needs

There are various ways to classify needs. A simple one is (1) basic physical needs, called *primary* needs, and (2) social and psychological needs, called *secondary* needs. The physical needs include food, water, sex, sleep, air, and a reasonably comfortable temperature. These needs arise from the basic requirements of life and are important for survival of the human race. They are, therefore, virtually universal among people, but they vary in intensity from one person to another. For example, a child needs much more sleep than an older person.

Primary needs

Needs also are conditioned by social practice. If it is customary to eat three

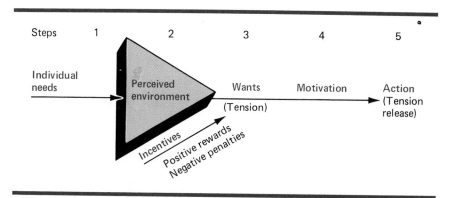

Figure 4-1
A model of
motivation

Secondary needs

meals a day, then a person tends to become hungry for three, even though two might be adequate. If a coffee hour is introduced in the morning, then that becomes a habit of appetite satisfaction as well as a social need.

Secondary needs are more vague because they represent needs of the mind and spirit rather than of the physical body. Many of these needs are developed as one matures. Examples are rivalry, self-esteem, sense of duty, self-assertion, giving, belonging, and receiving affection. The secondary needs are the ones that complicate the motivational efforts of managers. Nearly any action that management takes will affect secondary needs; *therefore, management planning should consider the effect of any proposed action on the secondary needs of employees.*

Variations in needs

Secondary needs vary among people much more than primary needs. They even exist as opposites in two different persons. One person has a need for self-assertion and is aggressive with people. A second person, on the other hand, seeks to be submissive and to yield to others' aggressions. Needs also change according to time and circumstance.

Analysis of behavior would be simple if a person's actions at a given time were the result of one need and one alone, but this is seldom the case. Needs of all types and intensities influence one another so that a worker's motivation at any single time is a combination of many different forces. Furthermore, some needs are so hidden that a person cannot recognize them. This fact alone makes motivation difficult. For example, dissatisfied workers often say that their dissatisfaction is caused by something easy to identify, such as low wages, but their real problem is something else. Consequently, even when management pays their wage request, they remain dissatisfied.

In summary, secondary needs:

- Are strongly conditioned by experience
- Vary in type and intensity among people
- Are subject to change within any individual
- Work in groups rather than alone
- Are often hidden from conscious recognition
- Are vague feelings instead of specific physical needs
- Influence behavior (It is said that "we are logical only to the extent that our feelings let us be.")

MASLOW'S HIERARCHY OF NEEDS

Psychologists recognize that needs have a certain priority. As the primary needs are satisfied, a person seeks to fulfill the secondary higher-level needs. A need hierarchy of five levels by A. H. Maslow, as shown in Figure 4-2, has gained wide attention.[4] The five levels are:

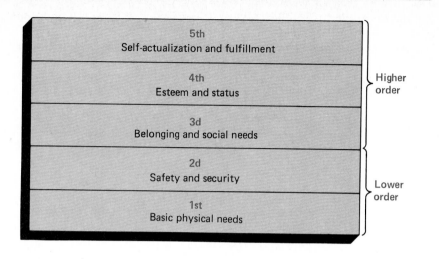

Figure 4-2
Hierarchy of human
needs according to
Maslow

1 Basic physical needs

2 Safety and security

3 Belonging and social needs

4 Esteem and status

5 Self-actualization and fulfillment

Need levels 1 and 2 are typically called *lower-order needs,* and levels 3, 4, and 5 are called *higher-order needs.*

Lower-order needs

The first-level needs involve basic survival. In the typical work situation they rarely dominate because they are reasonably well satisfied. Only an occasional experience, such as two days without sleep or a crumb in one's windpipe, reminds one of the essential nature of basic body needs. *Physical needs*

People must labor to satisfy their physiological needs, but when these are satisfied to some degree they wish to satisfy other needs. The need level that next tends to dominate is safety and security. It works somewhat as follows. *Security needs* Having met their basic physical needs today, people want some assurance that these needs will be met tomorrow and thereafter. Accordingly they build walls around primitive cities, build granaries for food storage, or establish pension programs. They want bodily safety as well as economic security. Security essentially assures that primary needs will be met tomorrow and for as long thereafter as possible. In reality, then, second-level needs relate to those at the first level.

Because of individual differences, people seek different amounts of security, but virtually all people have some need for security. People also vary in the ways in which they try to provide their security, as illustrated by the approaches of two sales representatives in a computer office.

> One employee tried to obtain his security by spending extra hours writing long reports on the analog control line to ensure that he would be considered so expert in this field that the company could not do without him. The other employee reacted differently, going to school at night to learn about digital theory and application, which was a new product area with the company. She felt that she could best be secure by becoming knowledgeable in the new control equipment. Thus two people reacted differently under the same circumstances and in relation to the same needs.

Higher-order needs

Social needs
According to Maslow, there are three levels of higher-order needs. Third-level needs concern belonging and social involvement. Some people say that these needs should be met mostly off the job; however, one-third to one-half of an employee's waking hours are spent at work. People work in a social environment, and some of their social needs must be met there as well as away from work.

Esteem needs
The needs at the fourth level include those for esteem and status. We need to have, to receive, and to give these sentiments. We need to feel inside ourselves that we are worthy, to feel also that others think we are worthy (status), and to believe that they likewise are worthy. This need is especially recognized in the philosophy of "value of the person" presented in Chapter 1. It is an important need in developed nations perhaps because the first three Maslow needs are already partly satisfied.

Self-actualization needs
The basic fifth-level need is self-actualization, which means becoming all that one is capable of becoming. This need is less apparent than others because many people have not emphasized it. They are still busy with third- and fourth-level needs. Though self-actualization dominates few people, it influences nearly all people. They choose occupations that they like, and they get certain satisfactions from accomplishing their tasks. To the degree that this fifth-level need can be emphasized, people will find their work a challenge and an inner satisfaction, as illustrated by the following incident.

> Jim Whittaker was the first American to climb Mount Everest (May 1, 1963). This was a dangerous undertaking (one climber was killed) and an exhausting one (returning by the South Summit he could only take one step every five minutes when the oxygen supply became exhausted). He was asked why he dared the dangers of a climb to the top of Everest. His simple, straight answer came quickly, "Because it was there!" To him it was a challenge—something to do for self-actualization.
>
> However, a challenge remained. Whittaker later led a team that included the first two Americans to conquer K2, the second highest mountain in the world.

Needs continually change.
It cannot be assumed that when the labor force reaches the fifth need level there is no room for further progress. Level 5 is a broad classification of needs, and it would be possible to reclassify it into five more steps for improvement. Needs can never be fully satisfied. People are beings who perpetually want. The sports figure who makes $1 million has achieved all

that was wanted when earnings were only a few thousand, but now this person's wants have increased to $2 million or $5 million. The conclusion that we must reach is that *need satisfaction is a continuous problem for organizations*. It cannot be permanently solved by satisfying a particular need today.

Interpreting the hierarchy of needs

The Maslow hierarchy has many limitations, and it has been difficult to verify with research. Some critics say that it is mostly a philosophical framework to describe typical attitudes of U.S. workers. After a thorough study, one critic concluded, "The evidence and argument of this examination indicate that the need satisfaction model must be seriously reexamined, and does not warrant the unquestioning acceptance it has attained in organizational psychology literature."[5]

In spite of its limitations, the need-hierarchy model presents some sound ideas for helping managers motivate employees. A study by Porter and others reaches the following general conclusions.[6]

> There is strong evidence to support the view that unless the existence [basic physical] needs are satisfied none of the higher-order needs will come into play. There is also some evidence that unless security needs are satisfied, people will not be concerned with higher-order needs. There is, however, little evidence to support the view that a hierarchy exists once one moves above the security level.

People will require organizations to change their ways of operation to meet changes in human needs. Most organizational practices were established at a time when lower-order needs were dominant, so some of these practices will be outmoded as the need distribution changes. This condition supports a contingency approach to organizational behavior because choice of what is a "better" practice becomes somewhat contingent on employees' needs.

What the need-hierarchy model essentially says is that gratified needs are not as strongly motivating as unmet needs. That is, *employees are more enthusiastically motivated by what they are seeking than by what they already have.* They may react protectively to try to keep what they already have, but they move forward with enthusiasm only when they are seeking something else. In harsher terms, people work for bread alone only when they have no bread.

HERZBERG'S TWO-FACTOR MODEL

On the basis of research with engineers and accountants, Frederick Herzberg developed a two-factor model of motivation in the 1950s.[7] He asked his subjects to think of a time when they felt especially good about their jobs and a time when they felt especially bad about their jobs. He also asked them to describe the conditions that led to those feelings. Herzberg found that employees named different types of conditions for good and bad feelings. That is, if a feeling of achievement led to a good feeling, the lack of achievement was rarely given as cause for bad feelings. Instead, some other factor such as company policy was given as a cause of bad feelings.

Herzberg concluded that two separate factors influenced motivation. Prior to that time people assumed that motivation and lack of motivation were merely opposites of one factor on a continuum. Herzberg upset the traditional view by stating that certain job factors primarily dissatisfy employees when the conditions are absent. However, as shown in Figure 4-3, their presence generally brings employees to a satisfied neutral state. The factors are not strongly motivating. These potent dissatisfiers are called *hygiene factors,* or *Maintenance factors* *maintenance factors,* because they are necessary to maintain a reasonable level of satisfaction in employees.

Other job conditions operate primarily to build motivation, but their absence rarely is strongly dissatisfying. These conditions are known as *Motivational factors* *motivational factors,* motivators, or satisfiers. For many years managers had been wondering why their fancy personnel policies and fringe benefits were not increasing employee motivation. The idea of separate motivational and maintenance factors helped answer their question, because fringe benefits and personnel policies were primarily maintenance factors according to Herzberg.

The Herzberg model outlines a general tendency only. Maintenance factors may be motivators to some people who want these rewards. Conversely, some motivators may be only maintenance factors to other people. As with most other human situations, there is only a tendency toward one direction or the other. There is no absolute distinction; neither factor is wholly one-dimensional in its influence.

Job content and context

Figure 4-4 shows the Herzberg factors. Motivational factors such as achievement and responsibility mostly are related directly to the job itself, the employee's performance, and the recognition and growth that are secured from it. Motivators mostly are job-centered; they relate to *job content.*

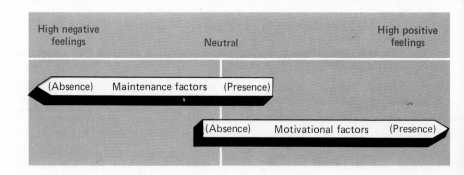

Figure 4-3
Maintenance and
motivational factors

High negative feelings   Neutral   High positive feelings

(Absence)   Maintenance factors   (Presence)

(Absence)   Motivational factors   (Presence)

MAINTENANCE FACTORS	**MOTIVATIONAL FACTORS**
Dissatisfiers	Satisfiers
Hygiene factors	Motivators
Job context	Job content
Extrinsic factors	Intrinsic factors
Examples	**Examples**
Company policy and administration	Achievement
Quality of supervision	Recognition
Relations with supervisors	Advancement
Peer relations	Work itself
Relations with subordinates	Possibility of growth
Pay	Responsibility
Job security	
Working conditions	
Status	

Figure 4-4
Herzberg's
classification of
maintenance and
motivational factors

On the other hand, maintenance factors are mainly related to *job context,* because they are more related to the environment surrounding the job. This difference between job content and job context is a significant one. It shows that employees primarily are motivated strongly by what they do for themselves. When they take responsibility or gain recognition through their own behavior, they are strongly motivated. If these conclusions are correct, then management's role is to provide a supportive environment for employee performance. Management helps rather than bosses.

Intrinsic and extrinsic factors

The difference between job content and job context is similar to the difference between intrinsic and extrinsic motivators in psychology. *Intrinsic motivators* are internal rewards that a person feels when performing a job, so there is a direct connection between work and rewards. An employee in this situation is self-motivated. *Extrinsic motivators* are external rewards that occur apart from work, providing no direct satisfaction at the time the work is performed. Examples are retirement plans, health insurance, and vacations.

Prior to Herzberg's research, managers centered their attention on extrinsic maintenance factors, often with poor results. Now that they have a better understanding of the difference between the two factors, they are giving more emphasis to the intrinsic ones because this approach often leads to better results for the employee, the organization, and society.

Interpretations of the two-factor model

The two-factor model is both supported and rejected by other analysts of motivation. Supporters show wide application of the model in the United States and other nations. It especially tends to apply to managerial, professional, and upper-level white-collar employees.[8]

Most critics of the model reject the idea of two separate factors affecting motivation. They believe that motivation is based on one factor along a continuum, rather than two factors. Other critics say that the model does not give enough emphasis to the motivating qualities of pay, status, and relations with others, which the model identifies as maintenance factors.[9]

Criticisms

Critics of the model state that it is easiest to get results favorable to the model by using the Herzberg method. A number of other research methods have failed to produce similar results.[10] Critics say that the model is "method-bound," which gives it limited usefulness. They say that when the Herzberg method is used and people are asked to report favorable job situations, their egos lead them to report things that *they* have done. When unfavorable situations are requested, then their egos lead them to report things that *others* have done, such as improper treatment from a supervisor. The result is an appearance of two factors where in reality there is only one.

Despite the criticism, this model remains useful because of its distinction between factors that motivate employees and factors that primarily help maintain employees in a ready condition to be motivated. Important developments from the two-factor idea are job enrichment and the quality of work life. Because of their importance, they are discussed separately in a later chapter.

Comparison of the Herzberg and Maslow models

Although the Herzberg and Maslow models are somewhat similar, as shown in Figure 4-5, there are important contrasts. Maslow centers on needs of the psychological person, while Herzberg focuses on job conditions for need satisfaction. The Herzberg model says that in modern society, many workers have satisfied their lower-order needs, so that they are now motivated mainly by higher-order needs. The lower-order needs are no longer strong, driving forces for an employee. Rather, they merely ensure *maintenance* at the current level of progress.

BEHAVIOR MODIFICATION

Cognitive theories

The models of motivation that have been discussed up to this point are known as *cognitive theories of motivation* because they are based on thinking and feeling (i.e., cognition). They relate to the person's inner self and how that person views the world. For example, in Maslow's need hierarchy, a person's internal state of needs determines behavior.

The major difficulty with cognitive models of motivation is that they are not subject to precise scientific measurement and observation. It is impossible, for example, to measure a person's esteem needs at any given time. For this reason it is argued that more attention should be given to models that are more subject to scientific treatment. The principal model of this type is *behavior modification,* as evolved from the work of B. F. Skinner.[11] Its application in organizations may be called *organizational behavior modification,* or O.B. Mod.[12]

O.B. Mod

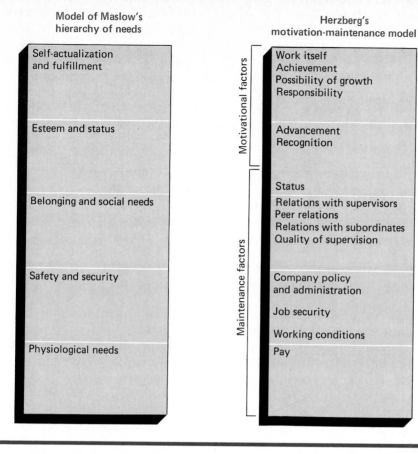

Figure 4-5
A comparison of
Maslow's and
Herzberg's models

Behavior modification is based on the idea that *behavior depends on its consequences;* therefore, it is possible to control a number of employee behaviors by manipulating their consequences. This model is developed from learning theory. While cognitive theories argue that internal needs lead to behavior, behavior modification states that external consequences tend to determine behavior. The differences between the two approaches are substantial.

Various forms of behavior modification have been used in a number of companies, such as Frito-Lay, Weyerhaeuser, and B. F. Goodrich. Key terms that apply to behavior modification are summarized in Figure 4-6.

Operant conditioning

Behavior modification is achieved through *operant conditioning,* which is any type of reinforcement to modify behavior by its consequences. If the consequences of a certain behavior are favorable to an employee, the

KEY TERM	DEFINITION
Operant conditioning	Any type of reinforcement to modify behavior by its consequences
Law of Effect	Tendency of a person to repeat behavior that is accompanied by favorable consequences and not to repeat behavior that is accompanied by unfavorable consequences
Positive reinforcement	A favorable consequence that accompanies behavior and encourages repetition of the behavior
Negative reinforcement	Removal of an unfavorable consequence that accompanies behavior
Shaping	Successive reinforcements as behavior comes closer to the desired behavior
Punishment	An unfavorable consequence that accompanies behavior and discourages repetition of the behavior
Extinction	No significant consequence accompanying behavior
Reinforcement schedule	Frequency with which reinforcement accompanies a desired behavior

Figure 4-6
Key terms used
in behavior
modification

tendency to repeat the behavior is strengthened. Conversely, if the consequences are unfavorable, the tendency to repeat the behavior is weakened. In this manner operant conditioning occurs. There is reinforcement to encourage desirable future behaviors and to discourage undesirable ones.

Law of Effect

The *Law of Effect* from learning theory explains the idea of operant conditioning. The law states that a person tends to repeat behavior that is accompanied by favorable consequences (reinforcement) and tends *not* to repeat behavior that is accompanied by unfavorable consequences. Assume, for example, that an employee found that helping a trainee learn the job produced favorable consequences. The behavior would tend to be repeated with the next trainee. But if a helping effort produced only conflict and problems, then the employee would tend not to help the next trainee.

Positive and negative reinforcement

Positive reinforcement

Behavior primarily is encouraged through positive reinforcement. *Positive reinforcement* provides a favorable consequence that encourages repetition of a behavior. An employee, for example, may find that when high-quality work is done, the supervisor gives a reward of recognition. Since the employee likes recognition, behavior is reinforced, and the employee tends to want to do high-quality work again. The reinforcement always is contingent on the employee's correct behavior.

An example of positive reinforcement is the experience of Emery Air Freight with its containerized shipping operations.[13] The company's practice is to consolidate small packages into large containers in order to reduce handling and shipping costs. The standard is for 90 percent of small packages to be shipped in large containers, but an

audit at various locations showed that actual use was about 45 percent. Further study
showed that workers were properly trained and reasonably cooperative, but they
were not motivated to meet the standard.

To improve performance, management applied a program of positive reinforcement. It trained supervisors to give daily performance feedback, recognition, and other rewards. In the first test office, performance went to 95 percent the first day. As the program was applied in other offices, their performance also went to 90 percent or better, most of them increasing to standard within a single day. The effective results continued for the four years covered in the study. The regular feedback and recognition gave workers consequences that strongly influenced their behavior. In this instance positive reinforcement scored a notable success.

Negative reinforcement occurs when behavior is accompanied by removal of an unfavorable consequence; therefore, it is not the same as punishment, which normally adds something unfavorable. Consistent with the Law of Effect, behavior responsible for the removal of something unfavorable is repeated when that unfavorable state is again encountered. An example of negative reinforcement is the experience of a jet aircraft mechanic who learned that if she wore noise suppressors over her ears, she could prevent discomfort from the jet engine noise; this reinforcement encouraged her to wear the proper noise equipment.

*Negative
reinforcement*

Shaping

Shaping occurs when reinforcements are successively given as one comes closer to the desired behavior. Even though the correct behavior does not occur, it is encouraged by giving reinforcement for behavior in the desired direction. Shaping is especially useful for teaching complex tasks.

An illustration of shaping is the training procedure used by a supervisor in a retail store. The store was so small that it had no centralized training program for sales clerks, so all sales training was a responsibility of the supervisor. In the beginning a new sales clerk did not know how to deal with customers effectively, so the supervisor explained the proper sales procedure. The supervisor observed the clerk's behavior, and from time to time when the clerk showed improved behavior in some part of the procedure, the supervisor expressed approval and encouraged the employee. This was favorable recognition for the employee, so it helped shape behavior in the correct direction.

Punishment and extinction

Punishment occurs when *an unfavorable* consequence accompanies and discourages a certain behavior. Although punishment may be necessary to discourage an undesirable behavior, it has certain limitations.[14] A major one is that punishment only *discourages* an undesirable behavior; it does not encourage any kind of desirable behavior. Further, since the punisher is also the person who offers reinforcement at other times, the two roles become confused, which may reduce the punisher's effectiveness when offering future reinforcements. Also, people who are punished may become confused about what specific part of their behavior is being punished, so it is possible that some desirable behaviors may be discouraged.

Extinction

Extinction occurs when there are no significant consequences for a behavior. Learned behavior needs to be reinforced in order to occur in the future. If no reinforcement occurs, the behavior tends to be extinguished through lack of reinforcement. In one instance an employee made three suggestions to her supervisor over a period of several weeks. The supervisor did not reject the suggestions or accept them or do anything else. The suggestions just disappeared in the bureaucratic maze. Needless to say, the employee's suggestion-making behavior was extinguished by these consequences. In this case the supervisor probably did not intend to cause the extinction, but in other cases extinction is used as a conscious strategy. Then alternative responses that are desired can be reinforced to change behavior.

Schedules of reinforcement

Reinforcement may be either continuous or partial, as shown in Figure 4-7.

Continuous reinforcement

Continuous reinforcement occurs when a reinforcer accompanies each correct behavior by an employee. In some instances, this level of reinforcement may be desirable to encourage quick learning, but in the typical work situation it usually is not possible to reward an employee for every correct behavior. An example of continuous reinforcement is payment of employees for each acceptable item that they produce.

Partial reinforcement

Partial reinforcement occurs when only some of the correct behaviors are reinforced. Learning is slower with partial reinforcement than with continuous reinforcement. However, a unique feature of partial reinforcement is that learning tends to be retained longer when it is secured under conditions of partial reinforcement.[15]

Figure 4-7
Types of reinforcement schedules

Reinforcement schedule	Example
1 *Continuous.* Reinforcement accompanying each correct behavior	A piece rate of 10 cents is paid for each acceptable piece produced.
2 *Partial.* Reinforcement following only some of the correct behaviors	
a *Time intervals*	
• *Fixed interval.* Reinforcement after a certain period of time	A paycheck arrives every two weeks.
• *Variable interval.* Reinforcement after a variety of time periods	The safety department makes safety checks of every department four times a year on a random basis.
b *Ratio*	
• *Fixed ratio.* Reinforcement after a certain number of correct responses	Sales employees are given a bonus after every fifth automobile sold.
• *Variable ratio.* Reinforcement after a variable number of correct responses	There is a lottery for employees who have not been absent during the week.

There are four types of partial-reinforcement schedules: fixed-interval, variable-interval, fixed-ratio, and variable-ratio schedules. These offer a variety of reinforcement approaches.

Fixed interval   A fixed-interval schedule provides a reinforcement after a certain period of time. A typical example is a paycheck that arrives every two weeks. Except in very unusual circumstances, employees can depend on the check arriving on a certain day every two weeks.

Another example comes from the experience of Western Air Lines.[16] It had five telephone reservation offices with over 1500 employees and it needed to motivate those employees to encourage callers to make actual flight reservations. The company chose a fixed-interval reinforcement along with supervisory improvements. It kept records of the percentage of callers who made flight reservations and then fed back this information daily to each employee. The results were excellent. The ratio of reservations to calls increased from only 1 in 4 to 1 in 2.

Variable interval   Variable-interval schedules give reinforcement after a variety of time periods. Usually the variations are grouped around some target, or average, period of reinforcement. An example is one company's policy of making safety inspections of every department four times a year in order to encourage compliance with safety regulations. The inspections are made on a random basis, so the intervals between them vary.

Fixed ratio   Fixed-ratio schedules occur when there is reinforcement after a certain number of correct responses. An example is payment of sales bonuses after a certain number of large items (such as automobiles) are sold. In one automobile agency, sales personnel are given a bonus after every fifth car sold. This bonus is an encouragement to sell more cars, especially when employees reach a point where they already have sold three or four and need only two or one more to earn the bonus.

Variable ratio   A variable-ratio schedule is a reinforcement after a variable number of correct responses, such as reinforcement after 19, 15, 12, 24, and 17 responses. This type of reinforcement schedule provokes much interest and is preferred by employees for some tasks.[17] It tends to be the most powerful of all the reinforcement schedules. An interesting fact is that slot machines and a number of other gambling devices operate on a variable-ratio schedule, so gamblers experienced the power of this reinforcement schedule before it was isolated and studied by behavioral scientists.

Variable-ratio reinforcement has been used successfully to reduce absenteeism and tardiness. One project applied a lottery incentive system to 215 hourly employees in a manufacturing and distribution facility.[18] Each day all employees who came to work on time were allowed to choose a card from a deck of playing cards. At the end of the week any employee who was on time every day had a normal poker hand of five cards. The highest hand won $20, and eight winners were allowed in the whole group. After this program was initiated, absenteeism dropped 18 percent.

A hospital used a similar lottery for nurses who were not absent during each three-week period. Employees responded to the lottery by reducing absences significantly.[19]

Criticisms of behavior modification

Does O.B. Mod manipulate people?

Behavior modification has been criticized regarding its philosophy and methods.[20] Critics state that it is an inherently autocratic method of management, because behavioral consequences are controlled in such a way that people find themselves forced to change their behavior. Thus behavior modification manipulates people and is inconsistent with humanistic models (for example, Maslow's need hierarchy), which assume that people are autonomous and self-actualizing, being motivated by their own internal needs. Behavior modification, on the other hand, assumes that the causes of behavior are largely outside the person and are in the environment. The image of self-actualizing people is rejected, and the question arises: Who will control the controllers?

Other critics say that behavior modification insults people's intelligence. They are treated like rats in a training box when in fact they are intelligent, self-controlled people who are capable of making their own choices.

Application of behavior modification

The major benefit of behavior modification is that it allows more scientific analysis than cognitive models by focusing on specific consequences instead of intangible, internal human needs. It is, however, often difficult to apply. To start the process, it is necessary to identify behaviors that need to be modified and then to determine what stimuli lead to them and how they are being reinforced at present. Next, the work environment is studied to develop a realistic intervention strategy that encourages or discourages the behaviors. Performance feedback and recognition are often parts of this strategy, because they tend to be strong reinforcements.[21] General guidelines for an intervention strategy are shown in Figure 4-8. When properly applied, they can lead to substantial improvements.

Collins Food International used behavior modification with clerical employees in its accounting department.[22] One of the items selected for modification was billing error

Figure 4-8
General guidelines for applying behavior modification

- Identify exact behavior to be modified.
- Use positive reinforcement whenever possible.
- Use punishment only in unusual circumstances and for specific behaviors.
- Ignore minor undesirable behavior to allow its extinction.
- Use shaping procedures to develop correct complex behavior.
- Minimize the time between the correct response and reinforcement.
- Provide reinforcement frequently.

rates. Management measured existing error rates and then met with employees to discuss and set goals for improvement. It also praised employees for reduction of errors, and it reported error results to them regularly. Employees in the accounts payable department responded by reducing error rates from more than 8 percent to less than 0.2 percent.

Behavior modification also worked well in hospital jobs such as admitting patients, keeping medical records, and billing patients. For example, average time used to admit a patient was reduced from 44 to 14 minutes, and clerical costs per admission dropped from $15.05 to $11.73.[23]

Behavior modification works best when specific behaviors can be identified so that specific reinforcements can be applied to them. Examples are absences, tardiness, and error rates. When the job is more complex, behavior modification has more limitations. For example, it is difficult to identify specific behaviors in the job of a corporate lawyer and reinforce them. For its flight attendants, Western Air Lines wanted to use behavior modification, but was unable to do so. It could not find a simple output measure to quantify. As stated by one manager, "How do you quantify what a flight attendant does?"

Contingency application

SUMMARY

When people join an organization, they bring with them certain needs that affect their on-the-job performance. Some of these needs are physical; others are related to psychological and social values. The latter are much more difficult to determine and satisfy, and they vary greatly from one person to another. Maslow has developed a hierarchy of needs that relates motivation to a person's priority of needs. Herzberg, on the other hand, has developed a two-factor model based on maintenance and motivational factors. Important motivational factors are the work itself, achievement, growth, responsibility, advancement, and recognition. These are primarily intrinsic motivators rather than extrinsic ones. The Maslow and Herzberg models both focus on needs, but they do so from somewhat different points of view. Each has significant limitations.

Behavior modification states that a number of employee behaviors can be controlled by manipulating their consequences, and this is a more precise, scientific approach in many motivational situations than focusing on a person's needs. Applied through operant conditioning, its various approaches include positive and negative reinforcement, shaping, and extinction. Punishment normally is not used. Reinforcement can be continuous or partial. Criticisms of behavior modification are that it manipulates people and does not apply very well in complex work environments.

TERMS AND CONCEPTS FOR REVIEW

Needs

Maslow's hierarchy of needs

Lower-order and higher-order needs

Herzberg's two-factor model

Motivational and maintenance factors

Job content and job context

Intrinsic and extrinsic motivators   Positive reinforcement
Cognitive theories of motivation   Negative reinforcement
Behavior modification   Shaping
OB Mod   Punishment
Law of Effect   Extinction

REVIEW QUESTIONS

1 Think of someone who, in the past, did an excellent job of motivating you. Describe how this was done. Which of the following approaches, if any, did this person use?
   a Lower-order or higher-order needs?
   b Maintenance or motivational factors, and which one or ones?
   c Behavior modification?

2 In your role as a student, do you feel that you are motivated more by Maslow's lower-order or higher-order needs? Explain.

3 Which one Herzberg factor in the two-factor model is most motivating to you at the present time? Explain. Is this a motivational or a maintenance factor?

4 It has been said that the difference between extrinsic and intrinsic motivation is similar to the difference between things of the pocketbook and things of the spirit. Do you agree? Discuss.

5 Compare the Maslow and Herzberg models with regard to their similarities and differences.

6 Discuss how behavior modification operates to motivate people. Why is it still important to understand people's needs when using this approach?

7 What are the differences between negative reinforcement and punishment?

8 Discuss various forms of gambling, such as bingo and blackjack, and the type of reinforcement schedule each uses. Then identify two work situations in which the same reinforcement schedule could be used.

9 Discuss the statement "Behavior modification is unacceptable because it manipulates people."

INCIDENTS

The Piano Builder[24]

Waverly Bird builds pianos from scratch. He is a piano consultant to a piano manufacturer. He is on call and works about one week a month, including some travel to solve problems of customers. He also rebuilds about a dozen grand pianos every year for special customers; but, according to Bird, the most satisfying part of his life is his hobby of building pianos from the beginning. "It's the part that keeps a man alive," he says. The challenge of the work is what lures Bird onward. He derives satisfaction from precision and quality, and he comments, "Details make the difference. When you cut a little corner here and a little corner there, you've cut a big hole. A piano is like the human body; all the parts are important."

Bird has a substantial challenge in making a whole piano. His work requires skills in cabinetmaking, metalworking, and engineering, with knowledge of acoustics and a keen ear for music. It requires great precision, because a tiny misalignment would ruin a piano's tune. It also requires versatility, ranging from a keyboard that is balanced to respond to the touch of a finger all the way to the pinblock that must withstand up to 20 tons of pressure. Bird had to make many of his own piano construction tools.

Bird has built forty pianos in his thirty-four-year career. Though construction takes nearly a year, he sells his pianos at the modest price of a commercial piano. He is seeking not money but challenge and satisfaction. He says, "The whole business is a series of closed doors. You learn one thing, and there's another closed door waiting to be opened." Bird says his big dream is to build a grand piano; "It is the one thing I haven't done yet and want to do."

QUESTION
Discuss the nature of Bird's motivation in building pianos. Discuss whether an organization could build the same motivation in most of its employees.

Westside Department Store
Westside Department Store has a number of drivers who operate its delivery trucks. At the end of the day the drivers are required to complete a delivery report that takes 5 to 10 minutes. Preparation of this report has been a frequent source of conflict between management and the drivers. Drivers often fail to complete the report properly or delay completing it, which causes their supervisor to criticize and/or threaten them. The supervisor believes there must be a better way to motivate drivers to prepare reports properly, but he is not sure what approach to take.

QUESTION
Recommend to the supervisor a motivational model that might improve the drivers' behavior. Explain how it will apply to them.

REFERENCES

1 Frederick Herzberg, "Managers or Animal Trainers?" *Management Review,* July 1971, p. 9. The words "for me" are italicized in the original.

2 Ellen Joy Bernstein, "Employee Attitude Surveys: Perception vs. Reality," *Personnel Journal,* April 1981, pp. 300–305.

3 For a summary of different models of motivation and selected motivational issues, see Terence R. Mitchell, "Motivation: New Directions for Theory, Research, and Practice," *Academy of Management Review,* January 1982, pp. 80–88; and James L. Perry and Lyman W. Porter, "Factors Affecting the Context for Motivation in Public Organizations," *Academy of Management Review,* January 1982, pp. 89–98.

4 A. H. Maslow, "A Theory of Human Motivation," *Psychological Review*, vol. 50, 1943, pp. 370–396; and A. H. Maslow, *Motivation and Personality*, New York: Harper & Row, Publishers, Inc., 1954. See also A. H. Maslow, *The Farther Reaches of Human Nature*, New York: The Viking Press, Inc., 1971.

5 Gerald R. Salancik and Jeffrey Pfeffer, "An Examination of Need-Satisfaction Models of Job Attitudes," *Administrative Science Quarterly*, September 1977, p. 453.

6 Lyman W. Porter, Edward E. Lawler III, and J. Richard Hackman, *Behavior in Organizations*, New York: McGraw-Hill Book Company, 1975, p. 43.

7 Frederick Herzberg, Bernard Mausner, and Barbara Snyderman, *The Motivation to Work*, New York: John Wiley & Sons, Inc., 1959; Frederick Herzberg, *Work and the Nature of Man*, Cleveland: The World Publishing Company, 1966; and Frederick Herzberg, *The Managerial Choice: To Be Efficient or to Be Human*, rev. ed., Salt Lake City: Olympus, 1982.

8 For support of the two-factor model with professional workers in Australia, see Gregory C. Murphy and Barry J. Fraser, "Intuitive-Theoretical Scales of Content and Context Satisfaction," *Personnel Psychology*, Autumn 1978, pp. 485–494. For support of the theory in Zambia, see Peter D. Machungwa and Neal Schmitt, "Work Motivation in a Developing Country," *Journal of Applied Psychology*, February 1983, pp. 31–42.

9 A sample criticism is Martin G. Evans, "Herzberg's Two-Factor Theory of Motivation: Some Problems and a Suggested Test," *Personnel Journal*, January 1970, pp. 32–35. See also Valerie M. Bockman, "The Herzberg Controversy," *Personnel Psychology*, Summer 1971, pp. 155–189. This article reports the first ten years of research on the model.

10 Examples of research projects that failed to support the Herzberg model when they used a different research method are Edwin A. Locke and Roman J. Whiting, "Sources of Satisfaction and Dissatisfaction among Solid Waste Management Employees," *Journal of Applied Psychology*, April 1974, pp. 145–156; and D. A. Ondrack, "Defense Mechanisms and the Herzberg Theory: An Alternate Test," *Academy of Management Journal*, March 1974, pp. 79–89.

11 B. F. Skinner, *Science and Human Behavior*, New York: The Macmillan Company (The Free Press), 1953; and B. F. Skinner, *Contingencies of Reinforcement*, New York: Appleton-Century-Crofts, Inc., 1969.

12 Fred Luthans, "Organizational Behavior Modification," in Stephen R. Michael and others (eds.), *Techniques of Organizational Change*, New York: McGraw-Hill Book Company, 1981, pp. 47–88; and Fred Luthans and Robert Kreitner, *Organizational Behavior Modification and Beyond: An Operant and Social Learning Approach*, Glenview, Ill.: Scott, Foresman and Company, 1984. Behavior modification is compared with cognitive theories in Donald B. Fedor and Gerald R. Ferris, "Integrating OB Mod with Cognitive Approaches to Motivation," *Academy of Management Review*, January 1981, pp. 115–125.

13 "At Emery Air Freight: Positive Reinforcement Boosts Performance," *Organizational Dynamics*, Winter 1973, pp. 41–50. For a program that emphasizes recognition as a reinforcer, see David J. Cherrington and B. Jackson Wixom, Jr., "Recognition Is Still a Top Motivator," *Personnel Administrator*, May 1983, pp. 87–91.

14 For a discussion of punishment's limitations in an actual organizational setting, see Philip M. Podsakoff, William D. Todor, and Richard Skov, "Effects of Leader

Contingent and Noncontingent Reward and Punishment Behaviors on Subordinate Performance and Satisfaction," *Academy of Management Journal,* December 1982, pp. 810–821.

15 W. Clay Hamner, "Reinforcement Theory and Contingency Management in Organizational Settings," in Henry L. Tosi and W. Clay Hamner (eds.), *Organizational Behavior and Management: A Contingency Approach,* Chicago: St. Clair Press, 1974, p. 100.

16 "Productivity Gains from a Pat on the Back," *Business Week,* Jan. 23, 1978, pp. 56–62.

17 Gary P. Latham and Dennis L. Dossett, "Designing Incentive Plans for Unionized Employees: A Comparison of Continuous and Variable Reinforcement Schedules," *Personnel Psychology,* Spring 1978, pp. 47–61. See also Lise M. Saari and Gary P. Latham, "Employee Reactions to Continuous and Variable Ratio Reinforcement Schedules Involving a Monetary Incentive," *Journal of Applied Psychology,* August 1982, pp. 506–508.

18 Ed Pedalino and Victor U. Gamboa, "Behavior Modification and Absenteeism: Intervention in One Industrial Setting," *Journal of Applied Psychology,* December 1974, pp. 694–698.

19 Tedd A. Stephens and Wayne A. Burroughs, "An Application of Operant Conditioning to Absenteeism in a Hospital Setting," *Journal of Applied Psychology,* August 1978, pp. 518–521.

20 An example of criticism and reply is Edwin A. Locke, "The Myths of Behavior Mod in Organizations," *Academy of Management Review,* October 1977, pp. 543–553; and Jerry L. Gray, "The Myths of the Myths about Behavior Mod in Organizations: A Reply to Locke's Criticisms of Behavior Modification," *Academy of Management Review,* January 1979, pp. 121–129 (and Locke's reply in the same issue, pp. 131–136). The authors provide references to other criticisms and support.

21 Judith L. Komaki, Robert L. Collins, and Pat Penn, "The Role of Performance Antecedents and Consequences in Work Motivation," *Journal of Applied Psychology,* June 1982, pp. 334–340.

22 "Productivity Gains from a Pat on the Back," op. cit., pp. 56–62. Books discussing how to apply behavior modification include Thomas K. Connellan, *How to Improve Human Performance: Behaviorism in Business and Industry,* New York: Harper & Row, Publishers, Incorporated, 1978; and Lawrence M. Miller, *Behavior Management: The New Science of Managing People at Work,* New York: John Wiley & Sons, Inc., 1978. The success of behavior modification in an entire company of fifty employees making waterbed liners is reported in Fred Luthans and Jason Schweizer, "How Behavior Modification Techniques Can Improve Total Organizational Performance," *Management Review,* September 1979, pp. 43–50.

23 Charles A. Snyder and Fred Luthans, "Using OB Mod to Increase Hospital Productivity," *Personnel Administrator,* August 1982, pp. 67–73. For another application of OB Mod, see Fred Luthans, Walter S. Maciag, and Stuart A. Rosenkrantz, "O.B. Mod.: Meeting the Productivity Challenge with Human Resources Management," *Personnel,* March–April 1983, pp. 28–36. For a discussion of how some companies use both needs and reinforcement to motivate their employees, see Thomas J. Peters and Robert H. Waterman, Jr., "How the Best-Run Companies Turn So-So Performers into Big Winners," *Management Review,* November–December 1982, pp. 8–16.

24 Developed from an article by Liz Roman Gallese, "Stephen Jellen Builds Pianos Not for Money but for Satisfaction," *Wall Street Journal* (Pacific Coast Edition), Sept. 6, 1973, pp. 1, 12.

FOR ADDITIONAL READING

Frederiksen, Lee W. (ed.), *Handbook of Organizational Behavior Management*, New York: John Wiley & Sons, Inc., 1982.

Herzberg, Frederick, *The Managerial Choice: To Be Efficient or to Be Human*, rev. ed., Salt Lake City: Olympus, 1982.

Herzberg, Frederick, Bernard Mausner, and Barbara Snyderman, *The Motivation to Work*, New York: John Wiley & Sons, Inc., 1959.

Karlins, Marvin, *The Human Use of Human Resources*, New York: McGraw-Hill Book Company, 1981.

Leavitt, Harold J., *Managerial Psychology*, 4th ed., Chicago: University of Chicago Press, 1978.

Luthans, Fred, and Robert Kreitner, *Organizational Behavior Modification and Beyond: An Operant and Social Learning Approach*, Glenview, Ill.: Scott, Foresman and Company, 1984.

Maslow, A. H., *Motivation and Personality*, New York: Harper & Row, Publishers, Incorporated, 1954.

Miller, Lawrence M., *Behavior Management: The New Science of Managing People at Work*, New York: John Wiley & Sons, Inc., 1978.

O'Brien, Richard M., Alyce M. Dickenson, and Michael P. Rosow (eds.), *Industrial Behavior Modification: A Management Handbook*, Elmsford, N.Y.: Pergamon Press, 1982.

Rosenbaum, Bernard L., *How to Motivate Today's Workers: Motivational Models for Managers and Supervisors*, New York: McGraw-Hill Book Company, 1982.

Skinner, B. F., *Science and Human Behavior*, New York: The Macmillan Company (The Free Press), 1953.

Steers, Richard M., and Lyman W. Porter, *Motivation and Work Behavior*, 3d ed., New York: McGraw-Hill Book Company, 1983.

MOTIVATING EMPLOYEES

We believe in the principle that hard work, high productivity is something to be proud of.

Intel Corporation[1]

I think I am doing all right, because the boss hasn't criticized me in two or three months.

A factory worker

CHAPTER OBJECTIVES

TO UNDERSTAND:
Major motivational patterns
The expectancy model of motivation
How employees perceive their needs
The process of attribution
The relationship among motivational models

Marsha Donner, a skilled advertising specialist, worked on special projects in the advertising office of a large department store chain. On one occasion her manager assigned her Project Symposium, which would require about one-third of her time for the next six months or so. The project required her to work with various business and service organizations in the region served by the department store. Donner felt that she was qualified to handle Project Symposium, and she thought that the project would prove interesting; but she really was not enthusiastic about it. She felt that it would interfere with some of her other duties that were more important.

Donner's supervisor recognized her attitude and on various occasions discussed the project with her, hoping to motivate her. After several discussions he felt that he was making no progress, but one day he remarked to Donner, "Marsha, do you realize that Project Symposium will help you meet most community leaders in this region? You know, your acquaintance with these people will help you with Project Mainstream if we ever decide to go with it." Donner had developed the unique idea of Project Mainstream, and she strongly wanted it to be approved. When she saw that her work with Project Symposium might help her with Project Mainstream, she immediately became motivated on Symposium. She worked hard at it for the next eight months, and both she and her supervisor were pleased with the results.

The situation with Marsha Donner concerns a problem of motivation. Although Donner was cooperative and interested in her work, she really was not motivated until her supervisor explained the connection between her present work and a future challenging project that she wanted. She became motivated when she perceived that her work was connected with something important *to her*. This relationship is the essence of motivation. *Motivated employees are those who see their work as helping them accomplish their important goals.* In this chapter we discuss some contemporary motivational approaches, including drives, expectancy, attribution, and macromotivation.

MOTIVATIONAL PATTERNS

Each person tends to develop certain motivational patterns as a product of the cultural environment in which that person lives. These patterns are the attitudes that affect the way people view their jobs and approach their lives.

Four patterns of motivation

Four motivational patterns especially significant are achievement, affiliation, competence, and power, as shown in Figure 5-1.

Much of the interest in these patterns of motivation was generated by the research of David C. McClelland of Harvard University.[2] His studies reveal that people's motivational patterns reflect the cultural environment in which

Figure 5-1
Motivational patterns

Achievement A drive to overcome challenges, advance, and grow
Affiliation A drive to relate to people effectively
Competence A drive to do high-quality work
Power A drive to influence people and situations

they grow up—their family, school, church, and books. In most nations, one or two of the motivational patterns tend to be strong among the workers because they have grown up with similar backgrounds.

Achievement motivation

Achievement motivation is a drive some people have to overcome challenges and obstacles in the pursuit of goals. An individual with this drive wishes to develop and grow, and advance up the ladder of success. Accomplishment is important for its own sake, not for the rewards that accompany it.

A number of characteristics define achievement-oriented employees. They work harder when they perceive that they will receive personal credit for their efforts, when there is only moderate risk of failure, and when they receive specific feedback about their past performance. As managers, they tend to trust their subordinates, share and receive ideas openly, set higher goals, and expect that their employees will also be oriented toward achievement.[3]

Characteristics of achievers

Here is an example of achievement motivation in practice. During a heavy snowstorm, the president and vice presidents of one company reached their offices on time, but a number of lower managers were late or absent. The top executives undoubtedly were there because they felt an inner drive and sense of responsibility, factors that helped them climb to top leadership. On the other hand, some of the lower managers apparently lacked this inner drive and felt no strong compulsion to brave blizzard conditions to get to work.

Affiliation motivation

Affiliation motivation is a drive to relate to people on a social basis. Comparisons of achievement-motivated employees with affiliation-motivated employees will illustrate how the two patterns influence behavior. Achievement-oriented people work harder when their supervisor provides a detailed evaluation of their work behavior. But persons with affiliation motives work better when they are complimented for their favorable attitudes and cooperation. Achievement-motivated people select assistants who are technically capable, with little regard for personal feelings about them; however, those who are affiliation-motivated tend to select friends to surround them. They receive inner satisfactions from being with friends, and they want the job freedom to develop these relationships.

Comparing achievement and affiliation drives

One study covered over 400 industrial workers and supervisors.[4] It reported that both achievers and affiliators disliked structured tasks and wanted more job autonomy. Their reasons for doing so differed, however.

The achievement-oriented workers disliked the structured tasks because their jobs had less challenge and opportunity for making decisions. By contrast, the affiliation-oriented workers disliked a structured task because it restricted their freedom to make contacts with friends and mix socially on the job.

Competence motivation

Competence motivation is a drive to do high-quality work. Competence-motivated employees seek job mastery, develop problem-solving skills, and strive to be innovative. Most important, they profit from their experiences.[5] In general, they tend to perform good work because of the inner satisfaction they feel from doing it and the esteem they gain from others.

The competence motive in Japan

The competence motive is a cornerstone of the Japanese value system.[6] There, managers expect employees to be concerned with quality, and discussions in employee meetings often revolve around quality issues. This attitude is reflected in the automobiles they produce, where the recall rate is sharply less than that for most American vehicles.

Competence-motivated people also expect high-quality work from their associates and may become impatient if those working with them do poor work. In fact, their drive for good work may be so great that they tend to overlook the importance of human relationships on the job or the need to maintain reasonable levels of output.

For example, Joleen is a commercial artist who feels good about herself and receives respect from others when she creates an excellent design. However, she infuriates her supervisor when she misses her deadlines and she antagonizes her coworkers when she fails to socialize with them. Clearly, her competence drive is stronger than her affiliation need.

Power motivation

Power motivation is a drive to influence people and change situations. Power-motivated people wish to create an impact on their organizations and are willing to take risks to do so. Once this power is obtained, it may be used either constructively or destructively.

Institutional vs. personal power

Power-motivated people make excellent managers if their drives are for institutional power instead of personal power. Institutional power is the need to influence others' behavior for the good of the whole organization. In other words, these people seek power through legitimate means, rise to leadership positions through successful performance, and therefore are accepted by others. However, if an employee's drives are toward personal power, that person tends to be an unsuccessful organizational leader.

Knowledge of motivational patterns helps managers understand the work attitudes of each employee. They can then deal with employees differently according to the strongest motivational pattern in each. For example, an achievement-motivated employee can be assigned a job, accompanied by an explanation of its challenges. A competence-motivated employee could be assigned a similar job with emphasis on its requirements for high-quality work. In this way, the supervisor communicates with each employee according to that particular person's needs. As one employee said, "My supervisor talks to me in my language."

A widely accepted approach to motivation is the *expectancy model,* also known as *expectancy theory,* that was developed by Victor H. Vroom and has been expanded and refined by Porter and Lawler and others.[7] Vroom explains that motivation is a product of three factors: how much one wants a reward (valence), one's estimate of the probability that effort will result in successful performance (expectancy), and one's estimate that performance will result in receiving the reward (instrumentality). This relationship is stated in the following formula:

$$V \times E \times I = M$$

Valence $\times$ expectancy $\times$ instrumentality = motivation

Valence

Valence refers to the strength of a person's preference for receiving a reward. It is an expression of the amount of one's desire for a goal. For example, if an employee strongly wants a promotion, then promotion has high valence for that employee. Valence for a reward is unique to each employee, is conditioned by experience, and may vary substantially over a period of time as old needs become satisfied and new ones emerge.

Reward preference

The relative valence that workers attach to rewards is influenced by conditions such as age, education, and type of work. A young worker is likely to give less emphasis to a retirement plan than an older worker. Similarly, a young college graduate may have stronger desire for career advancement than an older factory worker with less education. Further, when economic conditions change, employees may also change their preferences for various rewards.

On the other hand, when the labor force is considered as a whole, employee needs in the United States have remained reasonably consistent for several decades. In spite of changes in lifestyles, family income, and other factors, workers tend to value highly the same benefits that their counterparts did twenty or thirty years before.

The experience of Minnesota Gas Company illustrates this consistency. For thirty years, all job applicants completed a "Job Preferences" blank in which they ranked ten job factors according to the valence of each. Since all applicants completed the form, the resulting data provide a cross section of worker wants in a single community for a thirty-year period. The results showed that the rank order of items remained remarkably stable for the period, with an accent on security, desirable type of work, advancement, and a desirable company.[8]

Since people may have positive or negative preferences for an outcome, valence may be negative as well as positive. When a person prefers not attaining an outcome compared with attaining it, valence is a negative figure. If a person is indifferent to an outcome, the valence is 0. The total range is from −1 to +1, as shown in Figure 5-2.

Can valence be negative?

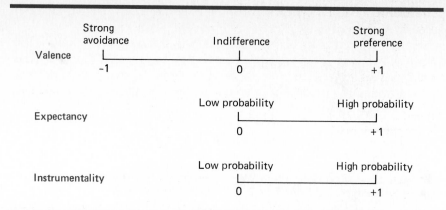

Figure 5-2
Range of valence,
expectancy, and
instrumentality

Some employees will find intrinsic valence in the work itself, particularly if they have a strong work ethic or competence motivation. They derive satisfaction directly from their work through a sense of completion, of doing a task right, or of creating something. In this instance, outcomes are largely within the employee's own control and less subject to management's reward system.

Expectancy

Expectancy is the strength of belief that work-related effort will result in completion of a task. For example, a person selling magazine subscriptions door to door may know from experience that the volume of sales is directly related to the number of sales calls made. Expectancies are stated as probabilities—the employee's estimate of the degree to which performance will be determined by the amount of effort expended. Since expectancy is an association between effort and performance, its value may range from 0 to 1. If an employee sees no chance that effort will lead to the desired perform-ance, the expectancy is 0. At the other extreme, if the employee is highly confident that the task will be completed, the expectancy has a value of 1. Normally, employee estimates of expectancy lie somewhere between these two extremes.

*Effort→performance
probability*

Instrumentality

Instrumentality represents the employee's belief that a reward will be received once the task is accomplished. Here the employee makes another subjective judgment about the probability that the organization values the performance and will administer rewards on a contingent basis. The value of instrumentali-ty also ranges from 0 to 1. If an employee sees that promotions are based on

*Performance→reward
probability*

performance data, instrumentality will be rated high. However, if the basis for such decisions is unclear, a low estimate will be made.

CHAPTER 5:
MOTIVATING
EMPLOYEES

95

How the model works

The product of valence, expectancy, and instrumentality is *motivation*.[9] It is defined as the strength of the drive toward an action. Here is an example of the expectancy model in operation.

> Marty Fulmer, age thirty-one, works as a welder in a large factory. Fulmer has very strong desires (high valence) to be in white-collar work instead of his present job, which he no longer enjoys.
>
> Fulmer recognizes that good welding will result in high performance appraisals by his supervisor (high expectancy). However, all white-collar jobs in the plant require a college degree, and Fulmer has only a high school diploma. Because of this barrier, Fulmer's instrumentality estimate is low. Being a good welder will not result in promotion to the desired position. Despite his strong desire for something, he sees no viable way to achieve it and, therefore, is not motivated to perform his job better.

The three factors in the expectancy model may exist in an infinite number of combinations, as illustrated in Figure 5-3. The combination that produces the strongest motivation is high positive valence, high expectancy, and high instrumentality. If any of the elements are low, then motivation will be moderate, at best. If all three factors are low, weak motivation will result.

All factors should be high.

A special case occurs when valence is negative. For example, some employees would prefer not to be promoted because of the stress, loss of overtime pay, or additional responsibilities they would bear. Where promotion has a negative valence, the employee will try to avoid earning it. The strength of avoidance behavior depends not only on the negative valence but on the expectancy and instrumentality factors as well.

Through experience, people learn to place a different value on the rewards available to them and also on the varying levels of rewards offered.[10] They also develop expectancy and instrumentality estimates through direct experi-

Valence	Expectancy	Instrumentality	Motivation
High pos.	High	High	Strong motivation
High pos.	High	Low	Moderate motivation
High pos.	Low	High	Moderate motivation
High pos.	Low	Low	Weak motivation
High neg.	High	High	Strong avoidance
High neg.	High	Low	Moderate avoidance
High neg.	Low	High	Moderate avoidance
High neg.	Low	Low	Weak avoidance

Figure 5-3
Some combinations of valence, expectancy, and instrumentality

ences and observations. As a consequence, employees perform a type of cost-benefit analysis for their own behavior at work. If the estimated benefit is worth the cost, then employees are likely to apply more effort.

Employee perceptions are important.

The role of perception   Reaction to rewards is filtered by *perception,* which is an individual's own view of the world. People perceive their environment in an organized framework that they have built out of their own experiences and values. Their own problems, interests, and backgrounds control their perception of each situation. Essentially, each individual is saying, "I behave according to the facts as I see them, not as you see them. My needs and wants are paramount, not yours. I act on the basis of my perception of myself and the world in which I live. I react not to an objective world, but to a world seen in terms of my own beliefs and values."

Since perceptions are strongly influenced by personal values, managers cannot motivate merely by making rational statements about the intended value of rewards or their likelihood of being received. People insist on acting like human beings rather than rational machines. We must accept them as the emotional beings they are and motivate them in their individual ways. We cannot easily persuade them to adopt the motivational patterns we want them to have. We always motivate people in terms of *their needs,* not ours.

Different perceptions   Since perception is an individual experience, there can be two or more views of the same situation. As shown in the cartoon in Figure 5-4, two people may view the depth of the snow in two different ways. Snow depth is an objective fact that can be measured, but most human situations are complex and not measurable. This fact makes motivation especially difficult unless we try to understand the perceptions of other people. The results of our attempts are sometimes startling, as illustrated here.

> One of the authors was surveying employee reactions to a new work schedule that gave workers wide latitude in setting their daily hours. Most responses to a question regarding their new flexibility were highly positive. One woman, however, reported that she had *no* flexibility. When asked to explain her curious response, she stated that she had to be home at 3:20 p.m. every day to welcome her children home from school. Consequently, she perceived that the new system offered no flexibility, and indeed it did not—for her.

Perceptual set

One of the characteristics of perception is *perceptual set;* that is, people tend to perceive what they expect to perceive. If a new employee is told the supervisor is friendly, the employee will be more likely to see a friendly supervisor and to respond in a friendly way. For this reason perceptual set sometimes can cause us to misread a situation and only "see" what we expect to see.

> One supervisor's experience shows the tricks that perception can play. One of his machinists strongly wanted three days of vacation in order to go deer hunting. Since the department was so rushed that it was working overtime every Saturday, the supervisor would not give him time off. The machinist also had a record of tardiness.

THE FAMILY CIRCUS®   By Bil Keane

Copyright 1979
The Register and Tribune
Syndicate, Inc.

"This is nothing. When I was your age we had
snow that came all the way up to here on me."

Figure 5-4
Two perceptions of
the same situation
From The Family Circus
*by Bil Keane. Reprinted
courtesy of the Register
and Tribune Syndicate,
Inc.*

One morning he was thirty minutes late. The harassed supervisor, without giving much thought to his words, threatened the employee with three days off without pay if he were tardy again that month.

Guess who was tardy the next morning. You are correct. The machinist perceived the "threat" as an opportunity to go on his desired deer hunt. The supervisor saw no other choice than to give the machinist a disciplinary penalty of three days without pay. In this way, management policies were upheld and the machinist reached his goal of deer hunting, but the needed work was not done.

The impact of uncertainty   If we accept the expectancy model, it follows that in order to motivate a person we can pursue two paths. First, we can recognize and attempt to affect the employee's perception of the rewards—the valence and probability of receipt. Second, we can work to strengthen both the actual value of the rewards and the connections between effort and performance as well as performance and rewards.

The connection between effort and ultimate reward is often uncertain. There are so many causes and effects in a situation that rarely can an employee be sure that a desired reward will follow a given action. In addition, there are both primary and secondary outcomes. The *primary outcomes* result directly from an action. Then the *secondary outcomes* follow from the

*Primary and
secondary outcomes*

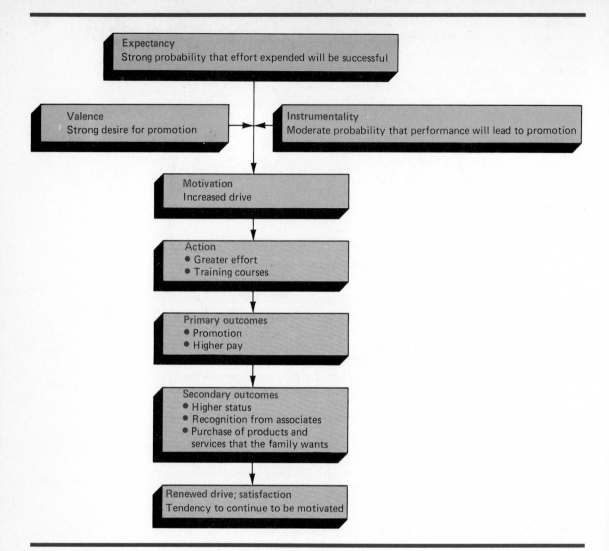

Figure 5-5
Operation of the
expectancy model

primary ones. For example, as shown in Figure 5-5, an employee secures more training and eventually earns the primary outcome of a promotion and the pay that goes with it. Then secondary outcomes follow. The promotion brings more status and recognition from associates. The higher pay allows the employee and family to purchase more products that they want. The result is a complex and variable series of outcomes from almost any major action.

Another cause of outcome uncertainty is that many outcomes are controlled by others and the employee cannot be sure how they will act. In the case of the employee who is seeking a promotion, both the promotion and the higher pay are given by management, and the higher status is given by one's associates. This second-party relationship often creates great uncertainty.

Since the expectancy model depends on the employee's view of the relationship between effort, performance, and rewards, often a simple, straightforward incentive is more motivating than a complex one. The complex one may involve so much uncertainty that the employee does not sufficiently connect the desired work behavior with a valued reward. The simple incentive, on the other hand, offers a practical course of action that the employee can picture and understand; therefore, it carries higher values for expectancy and instrumentality.

Appraising the expectancy model

Perhaps the greatest value obtained from the expectancy model is that it forces managers to examine closely the process through which motivation occurs. It also encourages them to design a motivational climate that will increase the probability of appropriate employee behavior. Three questions remain to be examined, however.

First, has the model been validated by research evidence? Although it does not explain all that happens in any situation, studies show that it does apply in many settings.

Expectancy issues

> For example, one test of the model in two different companies found that it applied in one of them but was not effective in the other because of certain special conditions.[11] A study of 138 incentive workers in a steel fabricating plant showed that the expectancy model did apply, but the variances explained by parts of the model were low.[12] Another study covered seventy-six women employees performing office work in a telephone company. The results clearly supported the general model and the linkages that it predicts.[13]
>
> The model has some application in other nations. One study of insurance sales representatives in Japan found that the model applied in approximately the same way as it does in the United States.[14]

Second, can valence, expectancy, and instrumentality be measured? A number of approaches have been used to assess them in research studies, but relatively few attempts have been made to measure the factors in work settings.

> One research study examined the rewards that salespeople value and found that a two-step procedure was a useful method for assessing valence.[15] Respondents first ranked the rewards offered from 1 to 12, then valued them all on thermometer scales (with the best anchored at 100 points). Compared to two other methods, this technique required the least time and was the most acceptable to the respondents.

A third question asks whether the model is complete in its present form. Recent indications are that some additional factors must be added to better explain employee behavior. Organizational commitment, for example, is also a function of employee beliefs in future payoffs, fulfillment of a debt to the organization, strong identification with the employer, and a lack of job alternatives resulting in limited mobility.[16] Other authors suggest that the high

Additions to the model

energy levels of some employees predispose them to be unusually productive or that their strong beliefs in the morality of an activity override expectancy considerations alone.[17]

The expectancy model has been shown to be closely related to behavior modification, as well as a number of other important managerial practices.[18] Path-goal leadership, management by objectives, and goal setting are among these and will be discussed in Chapter 8.

THE ATTRIBUTION PROCESS

A recent addition to the motivational literature is attribution theory. *Attribution* is the process by which people interpret the causes of their own and others' behavior. It stems from the work of Fritz Heider and has been expanded and refined by others.[19] Its value lies in the belief that if we can understand how people assign causes to what they see, we will then be able to predict their future behavior more accurately.

Two basic distinctions underlie the approach, as shown in Figure 5-6. The first is whether people tend to point toward the environment or personal characteristics as causal factors for their performance. The second requires an assessment as to whether those factors are perceived to be relatively stable or dynamic. The combination of those two assessments results in four different

Four general attributions

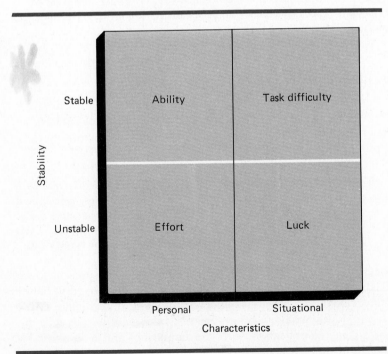

Figure 5-6
Situations leading to
different attributions

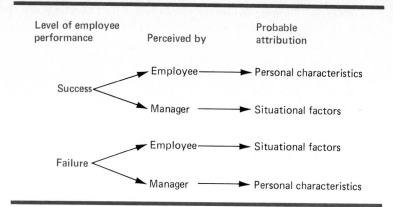

Figure 5-7
Different attributions
of an employee's
behavior

potential explanations for an employee's performance on a task—ability, effort, difficulty of the task, or luck.[20]

> For example, after each professional football game, the head coach sits down with the assistant coaches and grades each player's performance. After doing so, the coach must also determine whether it was the result of superior/inferior ability, greater/lesser effort, an experienced/inexperienced opponent, or good/bad luck. Since these are subjective assessments, we are interested in what affects the choice of explanations.

One important factor is whether we are evaluating our own behavior or interpreting another's. In general, people tend to overestimate the influence of personal traits when judging others while attributing their own behavior to situational factors. These judgments, however, are modified by whether or not the behavior observed was productive or unproductive in attaining the desired goal. These elements are combined in Figure 5-7, which indicates that the attributional tendency contrasts sharply, depending on the situation.

> These perceptual differences accent the existing viewpoints of managers and employees. Consider again the case of Marsha Donner at the beginning of this chapter. At the conclusion of the project, she might appraise her work as successful, see it as consistent with her overall work performance, and conclude that she has exceptional ability (thus reinforcing her competence drive). Her manager may be equally satisfied with the quality of Project Symposium, agree that it reflects her usual level of performance, but conclude that the tasks assigned to her have been too easy (and thus not praise her). What will happen to her future motivation?

The attributional model can be easily integrated with our earlier discussion of other motivational approaches. For example, achievement-oriented persons may claim that their accomplishments are the direct result of their high level of effort expended. Competence-driven individuals are more likely to believe that they have a high level of general ability.

Integrating the models

In conjunction with the expectancy model, an employee who fails on a task may feel that the environment precludes success and, therefore, may reduce the level of future effort. Users of behavior modification are cautioned to consider carefully their response to an employee's successful performance. A manager may assume it was due to luck or an easy task and withhold appropriate recognition. The employee, who believes that success was due to ability or effort, may experience a decline in motivation for the lack of reward.

Managers might benefit from greater awareness of their own attributional process and how it affects their behavior toward employees. They should be especially cautious about falling into a self-confirming cycle of observing an employee's behavior, attributing a simple cause and responding, and then obtaining a continued (undesirable) behavior. Employee behavior is also partly determined by the task, social context, and environment, as outlined in Chapter 1.[21]

INTERPRETING MOTIVATIONAL MODELS

Several motivational models have been presented in this chapter and earlier ones. These include Maslow's need hierarchy, Herzberg's motivational and maintenance factors, Skinner's behavior modification, McClelland's achievement motivation, Vroom's expectancy model, and the attribution process. All the models have strengths and weaknesses, advocates and critics. No model is perfect, but all of them add something to our understanding of the motivational process. Other models are being developed, and attempts are being made to integrate existing approaches.

Cognitive models dominate thinking about motivation. People have internal needs and are consciously aware of them. Managers motivate people by providing a work situation that satisfies their inner needs while achieving organizational objectives. The models have similarities in that they all recognize human needs, but they differ in their approaches, interpretations, and emphases.

Contingent use of motivational models

The cognitive models are likely to continue dominating organizational practice for some time, as indicated by the recent attention to the attribution model. They are most consistent with our supportive and holistic view of people. However, behavior modification also has some usefulness, especially in stable situations with minimum complexity, where there appears to be a direct connection between behavior and its consequences. In more complex, dynamic situations, cognitive models will be used more often. In other words, the motivational model used must be adapted to the situation.

Micromotivation

Type A motivation

The emphasis of the last two chapters has been on motivation on the job and within the firm. This kind of motivation is called *micromotivation,* or type A motivation. It focuses on motivation within one individual organization. The idea is to change conditions within the firm in order to increase employee productivity, that is, to motivate employees better. However, we cannot ignore the fact that firms employ whole people who live and play away from their work. They bring to the job many attitudes that are conditioned by their environment, and these attitudes influence their job performance.

Macromotivation

The area of interest that focuses on environmental conditions outside the firm that influence job performance is called *macromotivation,* or type B motivation.[22] This external environment may have a major influence on performance. For example, does society support work, or does it emphasize leisure as a primary value? Does it perceive factory workers as alienated moneygrubbers or as major contributors to society? Does it tax the added money one earns from a promotion, thus restricting its use? All these environmental conditions affect the rewards one derives from work.

Type B motivation

Consider how macromotivation applies to the expectancy model. Employees usually seek primary outcomes in order to reach secondary outcomes, such as social esteem and the purchase of products and services. These secondary outcomes are frequently controlled by the macromotivational environment, not by the firm. If the tax system penalizes with a higher tax rate the employees who earn a raise in pay, then expectancy for reward from the raise is reduced.

Other models of motivation apply in a similar way. Using the earlier example of the higher tax rate following a raise, the behavior modification model predicts that reinforcement for better performance is reduced. In other instances society may not penalize workers, but it fails to reward them by giving recognition or esteem for their efforts. In that case, there is no reinforcement and the behavior is extinguished.

Similarly, in Maslow's need hierarchy, major needs in advanced nations are social and esteem needs. If the social environment fails to give these rewards to employees who are the high performers in the system, then their needs are not met and they try to satisfy them through other behavior.

Since there are two environments (inside and outside the firm) that affect motivation, both need to be improved for high motivation. If job conditions are unrewarding, motivation is likely to be weak no matter how supportive the external environment is. However, the reverse also applies. If environmental conditions do not support better job performance, motivation tends to be weak, even when conditions on the job are favorable. Management cannot alone solve motivation problems. It must have society's support.

SUMMARY

Two different models of motivation are the expectancy model and the attribution process. The expectancy model states that motivation is a product of how much one wants something and the probabilities that effort will lead to task accomplishment and reward. The formula is valence × expectancy ×

instrumentality = motivation. Valence is the strength of a person's preference for an outcome. Expectancy is the strength of belief that one's effort will be successful in accomplishing a task. Instrumentality is the strength of belief that successful performance will be followed by a reward.

The attribution process examines the way people interpret the causes of behavior. Attributions differ, depending on who is making the judgment and whether the behavior was successful or not. Four general attributions are made. Ability and effort are personal factors, while two situational explanations involve the difficulty of the task and luck.

Cognitive models that focus on internal states dominate thinking about motivation, but behavior modification, discussed in Chapter 4, also is useful. Most attention has been given to type A motivation (micromotivation), but in order to build a complete motivational environment, increased emphasis must be given to type B motivation (macromotivation).

TERMS AND CONCEPTS FOR REVIEW

Achievement motive	Expectancy
Affiliation motive	Instrumentality
Competence motive	Attribution
Power motive	Micromotivation (type A)
The expectancy model	Macromotivation (type B)
Valence	

REVIEW QUESTIONS

1 Consider the four motivational patterns. What is one possible disadvantage associated with a strong drive for each?

2 How could you discover which motivational patterns are strongest in your employees? Do you think you could change them? How?

3 Can the expectancy model be applied to your own personal motivation? Discuss.

4 How would you use the expectancy model in the following situations?
  a You want two employees to switch their vacations from the summer to the spring so that job needs will be filled suitably during the summer.
  b You believe that one of your employees has excellent potential for promotion and want to encourage her to prepare for it.
  c You have a sprained ankle and want a friend to walk to a fast-food restaurant and get you a hamburger.

5 Name two outcomes in your job or classroom that have negative valence for you personally. How would knowledge of these help someone who is trying to motivate you?

6 Think of one success and one failure experience in your life. Did your attribution of the causes on those occasions match the prediction of the attribution model? Explain.

7 Would an achievement-oriented manager be likely to attribute failure of an employee to different causes than an affiliation-oriented manager? Discuss.

8 What are the similarities and differences between the expectancy model and behavior modification?

9 Which of the motivational models will be most widely used during the next twenty years? How do they relate to type B motivation?

INCIDENT

Jacob Arnold

Jacob Arnold is an engineer in a large design engineering office. Jacob comes from a rural background, and his family had a low income and stern rules. In order to earn his college degree, he had to work, and he paid most of his own expenses.

Jacob is an intelligent and capable worker. His main fault is that he does not want to take risks. He hesitates to make decisions for himself, often bringing petty and routine problems to his supervisor or to other engineers for a decision. Whenever he does a design job, he brings it in rough draft to his supervisor for approval before he finalizes it.

Since Jacob is a capable person, his supervisor wants to motivate him to be more independent in his work. The supervisor believes that this approach will improve Jacob's performance, relieve the supervisor from extra routine, and give Jacob more self-confidence. However, the supervisor is not sure how to go about motivating Jacob to improve his performance.

QUESTION
In the role of supervisor, plan how you will motivate Jacob. Give reasons.

EXPERIENTIAL EXERCISE

Personal Motivational Patterns

Working individually, students should rate (from a low of 1 to a high of 10) the strength of their own achievement, affiliation, competence, and power drives. Divide the class into four groups, one for each motivational pattern, and assign the high scorers to each. The task of each group is to develop a list of three assets and three liabilities that a person dominated by that pattern might bring to the organization. Ask for a brief report from each group, and then solicit reactions from the others.

REFERENCES

1 This statement is part of the Intel corporate philosophy, as reported in William Ouchi, *Theory Z: How American Business Can Meet the Japanese Challenge,* Reading, Mass.: Addison-Wesley Publishing Company, 1981, p. 253.

2 The original work on achievement motivation is David C. McClelland, *The Achieving Society,* New York: D. Van Nostrand Company, 1961. A recent study showing that high achievement need correlates with managerial success at AT&T is

David C. McClelland and Richard E. Boyatzis, "Leadership Motive Pattern and Long-Term Success in Management," *Journal of Applied Psychology,* December 1982, pp. 737–743.

3 Robert K. Glasgow, "High Achievers Are Made, Not Born," *Data Forum,* 1:1, 1900, pp. 7–8; and Tamao Matsui, Akinori Okada, and Takashi Kakuyama, "Influence of Achievement Need on Goal Setting, Performance, and Feedback Effectiveness," *Journal of Applied Psychology,* October 1982, pp. 645–648.

4 John E. Stinson and Thomas W. Johnson, "Tasks, Individual Differences, and Job Satisfaction," *Industrial Relations,* October 1977, pp. 315–322.

5 Jay Hall, *The Competence Process,* The Woodlands, Texas: Teleometrics International, 1980.

6 William B. Werther, Jr., "Productivity Improvement through People," *Arizona Business,* February 1981, pp. 14–19. For a comparable attempt to capitalize on the competence motive in the U.S. auto industry, see Jeremy Main, "Ford's Drive for Quality," *Fortune,* Apr. 18, 1983, pp. 62–64ff.

7 Victor H. Vroom, *Work and Motivation,* New York: John Wiley & Sons, Inc., 1964; Lyman W. Porter and Edward E. Lawler III, *Managerial Attitudes and Performance,* Homewood, Ill.: The Dorsey Press and Richard D. Irwin, Inc., 1968.

8 Clifford E. Jurgensen, "Job Preferences (What Makes a Job Good or Bad?)" *Journal of Applied Psychology,* June 1978, pp. 267–276.

9 Hugh J. Arnold, "A Test of the Validity of the Multiplicative Hypothesis of Expectancy-Valence Theories of Work Motivation," *Academy of Management Journal,* March 1981, pp. 128–141.

10 Gilbert A. Churchill and Anthony Pecotich, "Determining the Rewards Salespeople Value: A Comparison of Methods," *Decision Sciences,* July 1981, pp. 456–470. Research also shows that expectancy theory is effective for predicting the occupational choices of individuals; see John P. Wanous, Thomas L. Keon, and Janina C. Latack, "Expectancy Theory and Occupational/Organizational Choices: A Review and Test," *Organizational Behavior and Human Performance,* August 1983, pp. 66–86.

11 H. Peter Dachler and William H. Mobley, "Construct Validation of an Instrumentality-Expectancy-Task-Goal Model of Motivation: Some Theoretical Boundary Conditions," *Journal of Applied Psychology,* December 1973, pp. 397–418. Thirty-one early studies of the model are reported in Robert J. House, H. Jack Shapiro, and Mahmoud A. Wahba, "Expectancy Theory as a Predictor of Work Behavior and Attitude: A Re-evaluation of Empirical Evidence," *Decision Sciences,* December 1974, pp. 54–77.

12 John E. Sheridan, John W. Slocum, Jr., and Byung Min, "Motivational Determinants of Job Performance," *Journal of Applied Psychology,* February 1975, pp. 119–121.

13 Gerald A. Kesselman, Eileen L. Hagen, and Robert J. Wherry, Sr., "A Factor Analytic Test of the Porter-Lawler Expectancy Model of Work Motivation," *Personnel Psychology,* Winter 1974, pp. 569–579.

14 Tamao Matsui and Toshitake Terai, "A Cross-cultural Study of the Validity of the Expectancy Theory of Work Motivation," *Journal of Applied Psychology,* April 1975, pp. 263–265.

15 G. Churchill, op. cit., pp. 456–470.

16 Richard W. Scholl, "Differentiating Organizational Commitment from Expectancy as a Motivating Force," *Academy of Management Review,* October 1981, pp. 589–599.

17 Lawrence R. Walker and Kenneth W. Thomas, "Beyond Expectancy Theory: An Integrative Motivational Model from Health Care," *Academy of Management Review,* April 1982, pp. 187–194.

18 Terence R. Mitchell, "Motivation: New Directions for Theory, Research, and Practice," *Academy of Management Review,* January 1982, pp. 80–88.

19 The attribution process was first presented in Fritz Heider, *The Psychology of Interpersonal Relations,* New York: John Wiley & Sons, Inc., 1958. It was elaborated in H. H. Kelley, "The Processes of Causal Attribution," *American Psychologist,* 1973, pp. 107–128.

20 Attribution research is summarized in Jean M. Bartunek, "Why Did You Do That? Attribution Theory in Organizations," *Business Horizons,* September–October 1981, pp. 66–71. The classification of four causal types was extended to organizational contexts in Joseph F. Porac, Gail Nottenburg, and James Eggert, "On Extending Weiner's Attributional Model to Organizational Contexts," *Journal of Applied Psychology,* February 1981, pp. 124–126; another application is James R. Bettman and Barton A. Weitz, "Attributions in the Board Room: Causal Reasoning in Corporate Annual Reports," *Administrative Science Quarterly,* June 1983, pp. 165–183.

21 Terence R. Mitchell, "Attributions and Actions: A Note of Caution," *Journal of Management,* Spring 1982, pp. 65–74.

22 For an example, see George F. Dreher, "The Impact of Extra-Work Variables on Behavior in Work Environments," *Academy of Management Review,* April 1982, pp. 300–304.

FOR ADDITIONAL READING

Boyatzis, Richard E., *The Competent Manager,* New York: John Wiley & Sons, Inc., 1982.

Deci, Edward L., *Intrinsic Motivation,* New York: Plenum Press, 1976.

Harvey, John H., William J. Ickes, and Robert F. Kidd, *New Directions in Attribution Research,* New York: Halsted Press, 1976.

Lawler III, Edward E., *Motivation in Work Organizations,* Monterey, Calif.: Brooks/Cole Publishing Co., 1973.

McClelland, David C., *The Achieving Society,* New York: D. Van Nostrand Company, 1961.

Miner, John B., *Theories of Organizational Behavior,* Hinsdale, Ill.: The Dryden Press, 1980.

Patchen, Martin, *Participation, Achievement, and Involvement on the Job,* Englewood Cliffs, N.J.: Prentice-Hall, Inc., 1970.

Vroom, Victor H., *Work and Motivation,* New York: John Wiley & Sons, Inc., 1964.

Weiner, B., *Achievement Motivation and Attribution Theory,* Morristown, N.J.: General Learning Press, 1974.

JOB SATISFACTION

Job satisfaction does seem to reduce absence, turnover, and perhaps accident rates.

Robert L. Kahn[1]

You can draw much more objective conclusions if you stick to descriptive, observable evidence.

Robert J. Wherry[2]

CHAPTER OBJECTIVES

TO UNDERSTAND:
The nature of job satisfaction
The relationship between performance and job satisfaction
Some consequences of dissatisfaction
Characteristics of a satisfied employee
Benefits of studying job satisfaction
Design and use of job satisfaction surveys

O ne of the surest symptoms of deteriorating conditions in an organization is low job satisfaction. In its more sinister forms it is behind wildcat strikes, work slowdowns, absences, and employee turnover. It also may be a part of grievances, low performance, poor product quality, employee theft, disciplinary problems, and other difficulties. The costs associated with job dissatisfaction may be astronomical, as shown in this illustration.

> **General Motors Corporation reports that its rate of casual absenteeism—failure of employees to report to work as scheduled—is 5 percent.**[3] **This translates into 25,000 employees absent each day, and 50 million hours lost each year. The total annual cost to the company is a staggering $1 billion.**

High job satisfaction, on the other hand, is desired by management because it tends to be connected with the positive outcomes that managers want. High job satisfaction is one hallmark of a well-managed organization and is fundamentally the result of effective behavioral management. It is a measure of the continuing process of building a supportive human climate in an organization. Discussion in this chapter concerns the nature and outcomes of job satisfaction, ways to secure information about it, and how to use this information effectively.

THE NATURE OF JOB SATISFACTION

What is job satisfaction?

Job satisfaction is a set of favorable or unfavorable feelings with which employees view their work.[4] There is an important difference between these feelings and two other elements of employee attitudes. Job satisfaction is a feeling of relative pleasure or pain ("I enjoy having a variety of tasks to do") that differs from objective thoughts ("My work is complex") and behavioral intentions ("I plan to quit this job in three months"). Together, the three parts of attitudes help managers understand employee reactions to their jobs and predict the effect on future behavior.

Job satisfaction is a feeling.

What is the source of job satisfaction? When employees join an organization, they bring with them a set of wants, needs, desires, and past experiences that combine to form job expectations. Job satisfaction expresses the amount of agreement between one's emerging expectations and the rewards that the job provides, so it also relates closely to equity theory, the psychological contract, and motivation as discussed in earlier chapters.

Job satisfaction typically refers to the attitudes of a single employee. For example, an administrator might conclude that "Antonio Ortega seems very pleased with his recent promotion." Job satisfaction also may refer to the general level of attitudes within a group, as in "The job satisfaction of the Tool and Die Department is at an all-time high." In addition, the term *morale* often refers to group attitudes.

Morale

Job satisfaction has many dimensions. It may represent an overall attitude, or it can apply to parts of an individual's job. For example, although Antonio

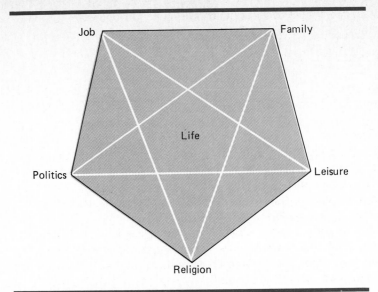

Figure 6-1
Some related
elements of life
satisfaction

Ortega's general job satisfaction may be high and he likes his promotion, he may be dissatisfied with his vacation schedule. Job satisfaction studies often focus on these parts and divide the elements into those that are directly

Content and context   related to job content (the nature of the task that Antonio performs) and job context (Antonio's feelings about his task environment—the supervisor, coworkers, and organization.)

As a set of feelings, job satisfaction is dynamic. Managers cannot establish the conditions leading to high satisfaction now and then neglect it for several years. It can decline as quickly as it developed—usually more quickly—so it requires managerial attention week after week, month after month, year after year.

Job satisfaction is part of life satisfaction. The nature of one's environment off the job influences one's feelings on the job. Similarly, since a job is an important part of life, job satisfaction influences one's general life satisfac-

Spillover effect   tion.[5] The result is that there is a spillover effect that occurs in both directions between job and life satisfaction. Consequently, managers may need to monitor not only the job and immediate work environment but also their employees' attitudes toward other parts of life, as shown in Figure 6-1.

Importance of job satisfaction

Should managers study the job satisfaction of their employees and seek to improve it where appropriate? Aside from a desire to apply the "golden rule" or build a better organization or society, the answer revolves around three critical questions.

- Are substantial numbers of workers dissatisfied?
- Is job dissatisfaction related to detrimental behaviors?
- Are those behaviors costly to the organization?

Level of job satisfaction Long-term nationwide studies indicate that general job satisfaction has been relatively high and stable in the United States.[6] Beginning largely in the 1970s, however, many social changes were occurring that led to widespread allegations that job satisfaction was falling substantially. Worker expectations dramatically increased. The complexion of the labor force changed as more young people, females, and minorities sought work. Despite rising expectations of the work force, the quality of management practices also improved, so that some studies show that more than 80 percent of the work force still reports job satisfaction.[7]

Satisfaction reported by most workers

Even though the proportion of dissatisfied employees is modest, it represents millions of workers, so there is much room for improvement. In addition, there are millions of workers who are dissatisfied with some specific part of their job, such as working conditions, even though their general job satisfaction is high. This creates one persuasive argument for managers to study job satisfaction.

Job satisfaction and performance Some managers may assume that high satisfaction always leads to high employee performance, but this assumption is not correct. Satisfied workers may be high, average, or even low producers, and they will tend to continue the level of performance that previously brought them satisfaction. The satisfaction-performance relationship is more complex than the simple path of "satisfaction leads to performance."

A complex relationship

> Fran Tarkenton, the successful football quarterback, states that the Minnesota Vikings often lost their games when he became overly satisfied. Satisfaction led him to be complacent and play carelessly, so his team was defeated. On the other hand, when he was dissatisfied with his own contributions and felt a strong need to win, he was more strongly motivated and sought to perform better.[8] Here, *dissatisfaction* may have led to better performance!

A more accurate portrait of the relationship is that high performance contributes to high job satisfaction, as shown in Figure 6-2.[9] The sequence is that better performance typically leads to higher economic, sociological, and psychological rewards. If these rewards are seen as fair and equitable, then improved satisfaction develops because employees feel that they are receiving rewards in proportion to their performance. On the other hand, if rewards are seen as inadequate for one's level of performance, dissatisfaction tends to arise. In either case, one's level of satisfaction leads to either greater or lesser commitment which then affects effort and eventually performance. The result is a continuously operating *performance-satisfaction-effort loop*. Three examples of negative employee behaviors that flow from dissatisfaction will be discussed.

Importance of equitable rewards

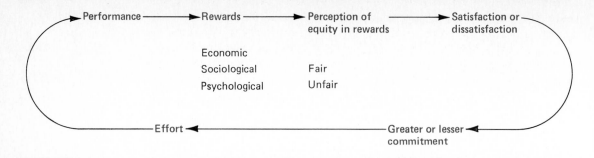

Figure 6-2
The performance-
satisfaction-effort
loop

Turnover   As might be expected, higher job satisfaction is associated with lower employee turnover, which is the proportion of employees leaving an organization.[10] More satisfied employees are likely to stay with their employer longer. Similarly, as shown in Figure 6-3, those employees who have lower satisfaction usually have higher rates of turnover. They are more likely to seek greener pastures elsewhere and leave their employers, while their more satisfied associates remain.

Who tends to leave?

Research studies have sought to identify the factors contributing to high turnover.[11] In addition to employee dissatisfaction, workers who are young, have limited job tenure, lack commitment to the organization, and perceive their jobs to be insecure tend to search for alternative jobs. Surprisingly, many employees quit their jobs in spite of knowing that there are only limited employment opportunities for them elsewhere.

Figure 6-3
Relationship of job
satisfaction to
turnover and
absences

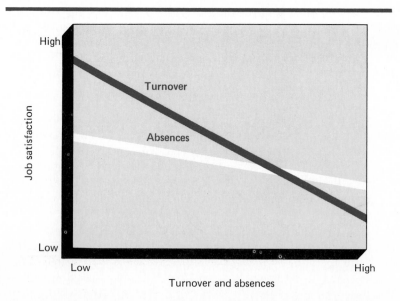

Employee turnover is costly, especially when the turnover rate in some industries like electronics reaches 35 percent annually.[12] In addition to the direct and indirect costs to the organization of replacing workers, the employees who remain may suffer decreased satisfaction from the loss of valued coworkers and the disruption of established social patterns. Equally important to consider are the benefits that may arise, such as more opportunities for internal promotion and the infusion of expertise from newly hired employees.[13]

Merrill Lynch used a matrix similar to Figure 6-4 to initiate a program which lowered their broker turnover rate from 8 percent above the industry average to 11 percent below the average.[14] They developed a compensation program focused on retaining the more desirable employees while also recognizing that some turnover is not only acceptable but desirable. By doing this, they reduced the number of brokers that otherwise would have become a costly statistic in cell C of the matrix.

Desirability of some turnover

Absences   Figure 6-3 shows that those employees who have less satisfaction tend to be absent more often.[15] As shown by the steepness of the lines in the figure, job satisfaction may not have quite as strong an influence on absences as it does on turnover, because some absences are valid. Dissatisfied employees do not necessarily plan to be absent, but they find it easier to respond to the opportunities to do so. Those discretionary absences may be lessened by providing various incentives to attend, such as the O.B. Mod lotteries discussed in Chapter 4.

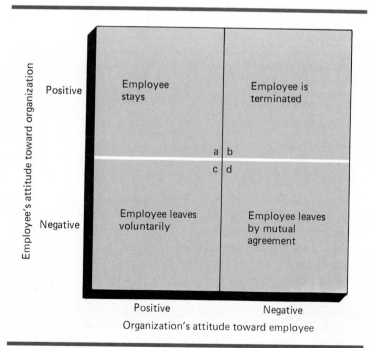

Figure 6-4
Four products of employee-organization attitudes

*Why do some
employees steal?*

Theft   Although there are many causes of employee theft, some employees steal because they are frustrated by the impersonal treatment that they receive from their organization. In their own minds, employees may justify this extraordinary behavior as a way of gaining revenge for what they consider ill treatment at the hands of a supervisor. Some estimates of the direct cost of employee theft place it at over $30 billion annually, with up to half the employees involved in the activity.[16] Tighter corporate controls and threats of punishment do not always solve problems like these, since they are directed at the symptoms and not at the underlying causes such as severe dissatisfaction.

Profile of satisfied workers

*Correlates of
satisfaction*

Job satisfaction is related to a number of variables that allow managers to predict which groups are more likely to exhibit the problem behaviors associated with dissatisfaction. Some of these variables describe the employee, others the job environment.

Age   As workers grow older, they tend to be slightly more satisfied with their jobs.[17] There are a number of reasons, such as lowered expectations and better adjustment to their work situation because of experience with it. Younger workers, on the other hand, tend to be less satisfied because of higher expectations, less adjustment, and other causes. There are exceptions, but the general trend is for higher job satisfaction with advancing age. This general relationship is shown in Figure 6-5. The trend applies to managers as well as workers.

For example, one study of nearly 4000 managers showed a steadily rising job satisfaction index with advancing age.[18] The age groups and satisfaction indexes are as follows:

- Under 30 years   3.41
- 30 to 40 years   3.42
- 41 to 55 years   3.57
- Over 55 years   3.63

Occupational level   Figure 6-5 also shows that people with higher-level occupations tend to be more satisfied with their jobs.[19] They usually are better-paid and have better working conditions, and their jobs make fuller use of their abilities; therefore they have good reason to be more satisfied. The result is that managers and professionals usually are more satisfied than skilled workers, who tend to be more satisfied than semiskilled and unskilled workers. The steepness of the lines in the figure indicates that occupation is more strongly related to job satisfaction than age. Those who work at high occupational levels are considerably more satisfied than unskilled workers.

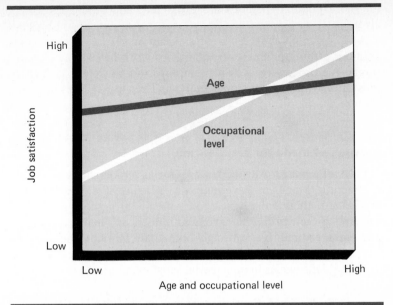

Figure 6-5
Relationship of
job satisfaction
to age and
occupational level

Organizational size Organizational size often is inversely related to job satisfaction. The term "organization size" refers to the size of an operating unit, such as a branch plant, rather than that of an entire corporation or governmental unit.

As organizations grow larger, there is some evidence that job satisfaction tends to decline moderately unless corrective action is taken to offset the trend.[20] Without corrective action, large organizations tend to overwhelm people and disrupt supportive processes, such as communication, coordination, and participation. Because decision-making power is so far removed, employees begin to feel that they are losing control over the events that affect them. The work environment also loses elements of personal closeness, friendship, and small-group teamwork that are important to the satisfaction of many people.[21]

The size-satisfaction tendency can be overcome by corrective action to maintain the human responsiveness the firm had when it was smaller. Large firms do not automatically have low satisfaction among their employees. It develops when firms become careless and lose their human responsiveness.

STUDYING JOB SATISFACTION

Management needs job satisfaction information in order to make sound decisions, both in preventing and solving employee problems. This section discusses the types of benefits that management can gain and the conditions under which a study of job satisfaction will be most likely to succeed. Some of the more popular methods are explained, and guidelines for their use are given.

A typical method used is a job satisfaction survey, also known as a morale, opinion, attitude, climate, or quality-of-work-life survey. A *job satisfaction survey* is a procedure by which employees report their feelings toward their jobs and work environment. Individual responses are then combined and analyzed.

Surveys of manager satisfaction

Surveys of manager satisfaction are just as important as surveys of employee satisfaction. Managers have human needs, just like other people. If they are dissatisfied, their unhappiness can spread throughout a whole department because of their broad management influence. Their feelings also may filter into their communities through both their families and their many public contacts outside the company. Job satisfaction surveys are necessary to diagnose deficiencies in managerial satisfaction and to take corrective action.

Sears, Roebuck and Company surveyed its managers and found that they were dissatisfied with the firm's relocation policies, since these led to frequent moves.[22] They felt that relocation had a negative impact on their families and cost them extra money. Perhaps more important, they felt that many moves were unnecessary for their career development.

As a result of the survey, Sears revised its relocation policies. It upgraded relocation payments to provide adequate financial protection, and it reduced the frequency of moves. Instead of sending managers to another city for career development, it rotated people across jobs in one store or among the stores in one metropolitan area. In this way the managers were not required to move from their present homes or to relocate their families. If spouses were working, they were able to retain their jobs in the same community.

Benefits of job satisfaction study

Job satisfaction surveys can produce positive, neutral, or negative results. If properly planned and administered, they will usually produce a number of important benefits, such as the following.

General job satisfaction   One benefit of surveys is that they give management an indication of general levels of satisfaction in a company. Surveys also indicate specific areas of satisfaction or dissatisfaction (as with employee services) and particular groups of employees (as in the tool department or among those over the age of forty). In other words, a survey tells how employees feel about their jobs, what parts of their jobs these feelings are focused on, which departments are particularly affected, and whose feelings are involved (for example, supervisors, employees, or staff specialists). The survey is a powerful diagnostic instrument for assessing employee problems.

In one company, for example, major changes were made in human resources policies, and the company wanted to check on employee reaction to the changes. Another company had recently doubled its work force, and it wished to determine how well new employees were being integrated into the firm.

Communication   Another benefit is the valuable communication brought by a job satisfaction survey. Communication flows in all directions as people plan the survey, take it, and discuss its results. Upward communication is especially fruitful when employees are encouraged to comment about what is on their minds instead of merely answering questions about topics important to management.

Improved attitudes   One benefit, often unexpected, is improved attitudes. For some, the survey is a safety valve, an emotional release, a chance to get things off their chests. For others, the survey is a tangible expression of management's interest in employee welfare, which gives employees a reason to feel better toward management.

Aaron Goldberg had strong feelings about how management could improve its ways of working with people. He felt that some changes were needed. For more than a year he had been waiting for the right opportunity to express his viewpoints, but the opportunity never seemed to develop. His ideas were bottled up within him, and he was beginning to feel agitated. At about this time management took a job satisfaction survey that included generous space for employee comments. Aaron filled out the comments pages and then felt much better because finally he had a chance to give management his ideas.

Training needs   Job satisfaction surveys are a useful way to determine certain training needs. Usually employees are given an opportunity to report how well they feel their supervisor performs certain parts of the job, such as delegating work and giving adequate job instructions. Since employees experience these supervisory acts, their perceptions may provide useful data about the training needs of their supervisors.

Union benefits   Surveys may also bring benefits to unions. As explained by one union officer, both management and union often argue about what the employees want, but neither really knows. The job satisfaction survey is one way to find out. Unions rarely oppose surveys, and occasionally they give them support when they know that the union will share the data.

Planning and monitoring changes   Alert managers are aware of the need to assess employee reactions to major changes in policies and programs. Advance surveys are useful for identifying problems that may arise, comparing the response to several alternatives, and encouraging managers to modify their original plans. Follow-up surveys allow management to evaluate the actual response to a change and study its success or failure.

For example, numerous firms have explored the move of their corporate headquarters from northern locations to the sun belt. Others, like Union Carbide, have relocated from the urban environments of New York City to rural settings in Connecticut.[23] In these decisions, survey input from employees helped the architect design a functional building and allowed employees to select interior furnishings that matched their tastes.

Ideal survey conditions

Desired prerequisites Surveys are most likely to produce some of the benefits reviewed above when the following conditions are met:

- Top management actively supports the survey.
- Employees are fully involved in planning the survey.
- A clear objective exists for conducting the survey.
- The study is designed and administered consistent with standards for sound research.
- Management is capable and willing to take follow-up action.
- Both the results and action plans are communicated to employees.

Use of existing job satisfaction information

Before they conduct formal job satisfaction surveys, managers might examine two other methods for learning about current employee feelings—daily contacts and existing data. These approaches recognize that formal job satisfaction surveys are similar to an annual accounting audit in the sense that *Daily contacts* both are merely periodic activities; yet there is a day-by-day need to monitor job satisfaction just as there is a regular need to keep up with the financial accounts.

Management stays in touch with the level of employee satisfaction primarily through face-to-face contact and communication. This is a practical and timely method of determining the job satisfaction level of individuals, but there are also a number of other satisfaction indicators already available *Existing data* in an organization. As shown in Figure 6-6, examples include absences, grievances, and exit interviews. This information is usually collected separately for other purposes, but it readily can be assembled into a monthly report that gives management insights into the general level of satisfaction among employees.

Some of the items in Figure 6-6 are behavioral indicators of job satisfaction, such as turnover, absenteeism, and tardiness, while others, such as medical and training records, only provide indirect clues that something may be wrong. Carefully interpreted, they form a substantial body of knowledge about worker satisfaction in an organization. Their chief advantages are that in most cases they are already available, many of them provide quantifiable data, and they are a good measure of trends over a period of time.

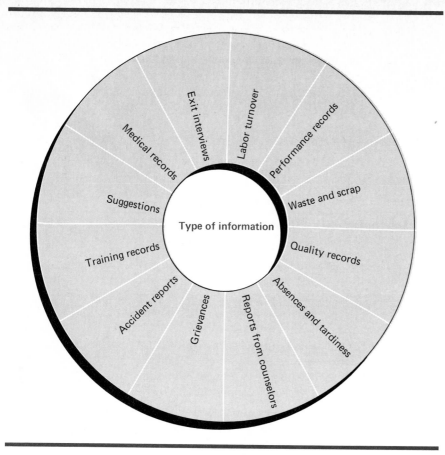

Figure 6-6
Examples of
job satisfaction
information
frequently available
in organizations

Types of survey questions

Studies of job satisfaction typically gather data either by survey question-naires or by interviews. Whichever method is used, careful attention should be paid to the form of question asked and the nature of the response allowed. *Objective surveys* present both questions and a choice of answers in such a way that employees simply select and mark the answers that best represent their own feelings. *Descriptive surveys* present questions on a variety of topics but let employees answer in their own words. The typical survey form uses both objective and descriptive approaches.

Objective surveys There are various kinds of objective surveys, but a hallmark of each is the high degree of structure in the response categories.[24] One popular type (for example, the Index of Organizational Reactions) uses multiple-choice questions. Here respondents read all the answers to each question and then mark the response that comes closest to their own feelings. Other surveys use questions with "true or false" or "agree or disagree"

*Providing
structured responses*

answers. The frequently used Job Descriptive Index provides respondents with a set of statements (e.g., "my work is routine") and asks them to indicate whether the term describes their work situation by checking either "Yes," "No," or "?" ("I can't decide") responses. Somewhat more flexible are the surveys that present a statement and request employees to respond by checking a numerical scale to indicate their degree of agreement or disagreement, as shown here.

My feeling of security in my job (circle one number):

How much is there now?   (min.) 1   2   3   4   5 (max.)

Because of concern over the meaning that employees may attach to only numbers in a response scale, instruments like the Minnesota Satisfaction Questionnaire provide brief descriptions for each number on the scale—for example, 1 = not satisfied, 2 = slightly satisfied, 3 = satisfied, 4 = very satisfied, and 5 = extremely satisfied. These aid employees in selecting their responses and help management interpret the data.

The chief advantage of objective surveys is that they are easy to administer and to analyze statistically. Much of the tabulation and analysis can be performed by computers, which minimizes clerical time, costs, and errors when large numbers of employees are surveyed. The chief defect of objective surveys is that management or a survey consultant writes all the structured responses available to employees, none of which may be viewed as an accurate expression of their real feelings. In other words, the objective approach really does not give employees a full opportunity to express themselves.

Descriptive surveys   In contrast to objective surveys, descriptive surveys seek responses from employees in their own words. This unstructured approach permits employees to express their feelings, thoughts, and intentions fully.

Seeking personal feelings

These more personal comments usually make a strong impression on management, especially if large numbers of employees agree and state their feelings in powerful language. For example, managers may not be too impressed if they discover that thirty-nine employees think the sick-leave plan is poor, but how would they react to thirty-nine comments similar to the following: "Our sick-leave plan stinks! You don't let us carry over unused leave more than two years, so I have no protection for serious illness that causes me to be absent more than a month." Now management may be more inclined to listen, and respond.

Figure 6-7 shows two types of descriptive surveys. The directed question focuses employee attention on a specific part of the job and asks questions about it. This approach permits depth analysis of satisfaction with a specific job condition. On the other hand, the undirected question asks for general comments about the job. In this way management learns about the topics that currently are troubling employees and seem important to them.

A survey that uses personal interviews to gather data is by its nature more descriptive than objective. A suitable interview usually takes from one to two

Directed question

What do you think of the company's pension program? _____

_____

_____

Undirected question

What are the three things you like most about your job?

1 _____

2 _____

3 _____

Figure 6-7
Types of descriptive
survey questions on
job satisfaction

hours for each interviewee; hence it is both time-consuming and expensive. In order to ensure that the same material is covered in a consistent manner with each employee, each interviewer is carefully trained and follows a standardized interviewer's guide that tells what material to cover and how to phrase questions.

Survey design and administration

Job satisfaction survey procedures are more complicated than they appear to be at first glance.[25] It seems simple enough to go to employees, get their responses, and then interpret them, but experience shows that careless errors in survey design can seriously limit the usefulness of a survey. Reliability and validity are two elements that serve as the backbone of any effective study. *Reliability* is the capacity of a survey instrument to produce consistent results, regardless of who administers it. If an instrument is reliable, we can be confident that any difference found between two groups is real, and not the product of ambiguous questions or widely varying administrative procedures.

Reliability

In addition to reliability, studies of job satisfaction need to be *valid,* or measure what they claim to measure. The difference between reliability and validity becomes clear when we attempt to use a wooden yardstick to measure metric distances. In this case, the yardstick is consistently accurate at what it does (it is reliable), but it is invalid since it measures the wrong thing. Obviously, we need to seek to improve *both* the reliability and validity of our measures of job satisfaction. This task is easier with objective surveys but much more difficult with the qualitative nature of descriptive surveys.

Validity

Many critical issues arise in the process of question construction and survey administration. As shown in Figure 6-8, particular attention needs to be given to sample selection, maintenance of anonymity for employees, the use of norms in interpreting data, the voluntary participation of employees, and other factors.[26] Response rates can be raised by requiring that surveys be returned in a short period of time. The tendency of employees to respond in a socially desirable fashion (for example, overestimating the importance of a challenging job) can be controlled. Norms from comparable organizations can be useful to interpret response patterns. Although no attempt is made

Socially desirable responses

- Should participation be voluntary or mandated?
- Should a sample be used, or the total population?
- Should responses be signed or anonymous?
- Should norms be used for comparison, or not?
- Should the forms be returned to the supervisor or to an independent consulting firm?
- Should the survey be designed and conducted by internal staff or by external consultants?
- Should a deadline be stated for return of the surveys, or should no date be set?
- Should a standardized instrument be used, or should one be created for this situation?
- How should feedback be given to employees?

Figure 6-8
Some issues in
survey design and
administration

here to cover the many details and pitfalls in survey procedures, the following description of one organization's survey provides an overview.

> Management decided it needed more information about employee attitudes and called a consultant, who developed—with management's assistance—a set of objectives and written policies for the survey. These were approved by an executive committee with the company president in attendance. At this time they selected the questionnaire method and decided to survey all managers and workers. Then the consultant, the personnel director, and a personnel specialist planned the details. In addition, the president appointed a committee of seven middle managers to help draft questions for the survey. The consultant guided the committee and served as chairperson. The committee also approved an official announcement of the survey (six weeks before it was given) and aided in informal publicity for the event.
>
> The consultant made the survey on three consecutive days. Somewhat different questionnaires were used for office, managerial, and production employees. Each questionnaire took about forty-five minutes to complete, so a new group of employees was surveyed every hour in a large conference room. The personnel director introduced the consultant and left the room, after which the consultant explained the survey and administered it. Employees placed responses in a locked ballot box.
>
> After the survey was completed, the consultant quickly prepared a full report for management and a condensed report for employees. The consultant also advised the executive committee as it planned its program of action on the survey.

USING SURVEY INFORMATION

Once job satisfaction information has been collected, the big question remaining is: What does all this mean in terms of my organization and my employees? Although gathering this information is chiefly a matter of technique, use of the resulting data requires skilled management judgment. It is the final important step in a job satisfaction survey. When appropriate action is taken, results can be excellent.

> In one survey at a General Electric Company branch, more than half the employees reported that they were unhappy with two areas: (1) the information they received and (2) opportunities for promotion.[27]

As a result of the survey, management began to hold regular monthly meetings with employees, brought in qualified people to answer difficult questions, and started a newsletter. Management gave special emphasis to information about opportunities for advancement.

CHAPTER 6: JOB SATISFACTION

123

When a survey was made a year later, the number of employees who felt they lacked information had dropped to zero! Even though opportunities for promotion were limited, employees who were unhappy about them dropped to 20 percent. Management explained that at least employees understood the situation, and "that made the difference."

Survey feedback

The first step in using job satisfaction information is to communicate it to all managers so that they can understand it and prepare to use it. This is known as *survey feedback*.[28] Managers will be the ones to make any changes suggested by the data, so they want to see the evidence in order to make their own judgments. The recommendations of job satisfaction specialists are helpful, but managers must make the final decisions.

Managers require evidence.

Comparative data   In larger organizations, comparisons among departments are an effective way to encourage managers to sit up and take note of satisfaction data. Just as a lagging baseball team makes every effort to pass other teams in its league, managers whose departments do not show high job satisfaction will be spurred to improve their employees' attitudes by the time the next study is made. Comparisons of this type must be handled with skill so that the lower performers will not feel intimidated.

Survey data spur competition.

If there is a chance of hurt feelings or personality clashes, it is wise to designate each department with a letter such as *A* or *B*. Departmental managers are told privately which letter represents their own department. They then can compare their score with other departmental scores, but they cannot identify which score belongs to which department. Scores, however, must not be overemphasized in a way that makes "score-happy" managers. The real goal is to encourage desirable behavioral changes in managers, and a single score can only partially represent the complexity of the total situation. The score is not a goal but a tool for making comparisons.

There are a number of useful comparisons besides departmental ones, as shown in Figure 6-9.

• Departments, divisions, branches	• Sex
• Age	• Work shift
• Seniority	• Building where work is performed
• Marital status	• General type of work done, such as professional, clerical, and production
• Formal education	
• Company training received	• Trends over time

Figure 6-9
Types of comparisons often made with job satisfaction information

For example, comparisons according to age groups may reveal a trend toward more satisfaction for older employees, as discussed earlier in this chapter. However, if the survey reports that younger workers are more satisfied, it suggests that conditions for older employees are atypical and perhaps unsatisfactory. In this instance, management needs to investigate and, if appropriate, take corrective action.

If earlier surveys have been made, trends over time can be plotted. More elaborate statistical comparisons and correlations can be made if the evidence looks promising. For example, do those who say their supervisor is a good manager say also that they have more pride in their organization as a place in which to work? Ultimately, all the questions and job satisfaction categories can be compared with each other in a search for meaningful relationships.

The managers' interests in job satisfaction statistics are heightened by asking them to predict their subordinates' attitudes toward various items and then to compare their predictions with actual survey results. Wherever their prediction misses its mark, they are forced to ask themselves why they misjudged this condition. Even if a prediction is accurate, it may still encourage soul-searching. Consider the case of a department head who predicted his employees would report dissatisfaction with grievance handling. They did report dissatisfaction, which forced him to ask: "If I knew about this condition before the survey—and apparently I did—why didn't I do something about it?"

Employee comments   As mentioned earlier, employee comments are very useful. This information often makes a greater impression on management than scores, statistics, and charts do. In terms of communication, this gets through to them because it is more personal.

Some comments are about very minor conditions, but these conditions do annoy someone and are therefore worthy of management's sincere attention. It is a mistake to correct only the big problems shown in a survey while ignoring many minor conditions that will add up to big problems.

In a marketing department survey, the comments of several field sales representatives showed negative attitudes toward the sales paperwork required of them. Although the subject appeared to be minor, management redesigned the paperwork so that it was reduced by about 30 percent. The bottom-line results were more sales calls each week and 8 percent higher unit sales with the same sales force. This change helped the salespeople earn more commissions and helped management reduce its costs, so both parties benefited.

Administrative follow-up

Committee work   One way to get managers to introduce change in their departments following a survey is to set up working committees whose responsibility is to review the survey data and develop plans for corrective action.

In one company, for example, the president appointed a special executive committee to follow up a survey and recommend changes. Then the general manager appointed supervisory committees in each department to discuss how the survey applied to local departmental problems. The supervisory committees worked out their own solutions on departmental matters, but if their proposed action affected other departments, it had to be forwarded to the executive committee for approval.

The personnel director chaired each committee, which usually met monthly. At each meeting, a separate part of the survey was discussed in some depth. Meetings continued for more than a year, assuring an extended follow-up of the information uncovered by the survey. This long-run approach kept executives thinking about the survey and gave it time to soak in.

Committees recommend action.

The long-run approach to using job satisfaction information is important. Too many employers make the mistake of giving a survey immense publicity and interest for a few weeks and then forgetting about it until another survey is run. They shoot the works, giving their surveys all the fanfare of a Mardi Gras—but when Mardi Gras has passed, they return to their old way of living.

Feedback to employees When corrective action is taken as the result of a survey, details of what was done should be shared with employees as soon as possible. Only in this way will the people who participated feel that management listened to them and took action on the basis of their ideas. This also assures employees that their ideas really were wanted—and are wanted still. In fact, good publicity to managers and employees is essential from start to finish in a job satisfaction study in order to explain what the study intends to accomplish, to report the information gathered, and to announce what corrective action has been taken.

Feedback and action are required.

One thing is sure: if a job satisfaction survey is made, management should be prepared to take action on the results. Employees feel that if they co-operate in stating their feelings, management should try to make some of the improvements they suggest. A sure way to close off future expressions of employee opinion is to fail to take action on opinions already given. It should be remembered that management asked employees for their ideas, so employees are justified in feeling that action will be taken on at least some of them.

SUMMARY

Job dissatisfaction often leads to absenteeism, turnover, and theft; so employers want to develop satisfaction among their employees. The vast majority of workers in the United States report that they are satisfied with their jobs, although perhaps dissatisfied with specific elements of them. High performance and equitable rewards encourage high satisfaction through a performance-satisfaction-effort loop.

Higher job satisfaction usually is associated with lower turnover, fewer absences, older employees, and higher occupational levels. Larger organizations tend to have employees with slightly lower levels of satisfaction unless vigorous attempts are made to build high satisfaction.

Useful job satisfaction information is obtained by using questionnaires and interviews, as well as by examining existing personnel data. Information is communicated to managers through survey feedback that uses summary data, makes relevant comparisons, and reports actual employee comments. Follow-up is accomplished by committees to assure employees that appropriate action is taken after a survey. Ultimately, job satisfaction information is most useful if it influences managers to improve their performance.

TERMS AND CONCEPTS FOR REVIEW

Job satisfaction

Performance-satisfaction-effort loop

Job satisfaction survey

Objective survey

Descriptive survey

Reliability

Validity

Survey feedback

REVIEW QUESTIONS

1 What is job satisfaction? Why is it important? Do you think modern managers overemphasize or underemphasize it?

2 Assume that a survey of the twenty employees in your department found that 90 percent of them were basically satisfied with their jobs. What are the implications?

3 What is the relationship between satisfaction and performance?

4 Think of a job you have held. List the areas of your job in which you were most satisfied and those that satisfied you least. Note in each case the degree to which management had some control over the item mentioned.

5 Prepare a series of directed and undirected questions, and interview three friends to determine their areas of job satisfaction and dissatisfaction. Discuss the results.

6 Select an industry (e.g., financial institutions or hospitals), and contact three organizations within it to learn their absenteeism and turnover rates. What have they done to reduce them or hold them down?

7 Construct a short questionnaire using objective questions, and survey a small work team about their job satisfaction. Tabulate and interpret your results.

8 Prepare a plan for using the data from a job satisfaction survey in an insurance office to provide feedback to managers and employees.

9 Contact a local fast-food restaurant, and ask the manager to estimate the proportion of turnover that can be attributed to effective employees leaving of their own choice. What suggestions could you make to reduce the problem?

Barry Niland

Barry Niland, supervisor of a small sales department, noticed that one of his industrial sales representatives, Henry Hunter, appeared to have low job satisfaction. Among other signs of low satisfaction, his sales had declined in the last six months, although most other sales representatives regularly were exceeding their quotas. Niland decided to try to boost his sales representative's satisfaction by reminding him of the many opportunities for satisfaction in a sales job.

Niland explained his actions as follows:

I pointed out that in his customer's eyes he alone is the company. He has the opportunity to help his customer. He has the opportunity to show his ability and knowledge to many types of people. He has the opportunity through his own efforts to help many types of people. He has the opportunity to support the people who make our products, to reward the stockholders, and to control his financial return through his own know-how. He has the opportunity of testing his creative ideas, with immediate feedback about their value. He has the opportunity to meet constantly changing conditions, so there is no boredom in his job. There is no quicker way to achieve personal satisfaction than sales work.

QUESTION

Comment on Niland's approach in dealing with his sales representative.

EXPERIENTIAL EXERCISE

Job Satisfaction in the Classroom

The discussion of job satisfaction that was presented in this chapter can also be related to the college classroom.

1 Working individually, class members should rate their overall satisfaction with the course on a scale of 1 to 10 (1 = low, 10 = high).

2 Ask the instructor to predict the overall average rating of the class.

3 Compute the average of all ratings obtained in step 1.

4 Working in small groups of four or five persons, discuss the reasons for the overall level of job satisfaction in the class, the relative accuracy of the instructor's prediction, and a realistic action plan for improving the level of job satisfaction.

5 Discuss the probable reliability and validity of the data gathered in steps 1 and 2 above.

REFERENCES

1 Robert L. Kahn, "The Work Module: A Tonic for Lunchpail Lassitude," *Psychology Today*, February 1973, p. 94.

2 C. J. Bartlett, "Robert J. Wherry, Sr. Biography," *Personnel Psychology*, Autumn 1982, p. 517.

3 Clarence R. Deitsch and David A. Dilts, "Getting Absent Workers Back on the Job: The Case of General Motors," *Business Horizons,* September–October 1981, pp. 52–58.

4 A general discussion of job satisfaction is presented in Michael M. Gruneberg, *Job Satisfaction,* New York: John Wiley & Sons, Inc., 1976. Nine definitions of general job satisfaction are reviewed in John P. Wanous and Edward E. Lawler III, "Measurement and Meaning of Job Satisfaction," *Journal of Applied Psychology,* April 1972, pp. 95–105.

5 Neal Schmitt and Arthur G. Bedeian, "A Comparison of LISREL and Two-Stage Least Squares Analysis of a Hypothesized Life–Job Satisfaction Reciprocal Relationship," *Journal of Applied Psychology,* December 1982, pp. 806–817.

6 Stable job satisfaction is reported in Charles N. Weaver, "Job Satisfaction in the United States in the 1970s," *Journal of Applied Psychology,* June 1980, pp. 364–367; and Dennis W. Organ, "Inferences about Trends in Labor Force Satisfaction: Causal-Correlational Analysis," *Academy of Management Journal,* December 1977, pp. 510–519. Declining job satisfaction is reported in M. R. Cooper and others, "Changing Employee Values: Deepening Discontent?" *Harvard Business Review,* January–February 1979, pp. 117–125.

7 Robert P. Quinn and Graham L. Staines, *The 1977 Quality of Employment Survey,* Ann Arbor, Mich.: Survey Research Center, Institute for Social Research, The University of Michigan, 1979, p. 210.

8 Fran Tarkenton, "Job Satisfaction: The Popular Myth, the Unpopular Reality," *Sky,* August 1979, pp. 34–35.

9 Edward E. Lawler III and Lyman W. Porter, "The Effect of Performance on Job Satisfaction," *Industrial Relations,* October 1967, pp. 20–28; Rabi S. Bhagat, "Conditions under Which Stronger Job Performance–Job Satisfaction Relationships May Be Observed: A Closer Look at Two Situational Contingencies," *Academy of Management Journal,* December 1982, pp. 772–789; and John W. Bardo and Robert H. Ross, "The Satisfaction of Industrial Workers as Predictors of Production, Turnover, and Absenteeism," *The Journal of Social Psychology,* October 1982, pp. 29–38.

10 R. M. Steers and R. T. Mowday, "Employee Turnover and Post-decision Accommodation Processes," in L. L. Cummings and B. M. Staw (eds.), *Research in Organizational Behavior* (vol. 3), Greenwich, Conn.: JAI Press, 1981; James L. Price and Charles W. Mueller, "A Causal Model of Turnover for Nurses," *Academy of Management Journal,* September 1981, pp. 543–565; and Peter W. Hom, Ralph Katerberg, Jr., and Charles L. Hulin, "Comparative Examination of Three Approaches to the Prediction of Turnover," *Journal of Applied Psychology,* June 1979, pp. 280–290.

11 Hugh J. Arnold and Daniel C. Feldman, "A Multivariate Analysis of the Determinants of Job Turnover," *Journal of Applied Psychology,* June 1982, pp. 350–360; an interesting model is presented in John E. Sheridan and Michael A. Abelson, "Cusp Catastrophe Model of Employee Turnover," *Academy of Management Journal,* September 1983, pp. 418–436.

12 Thomas E. Hall, "How to Estimate Employee Turnover Costs," *Personnel,* July–August 1981, pp. 43–52.

13 The economic benefits of turnover are presented in Dan R. Dalton and William Todor, "Turnover: A Lucrative Hard Dollar Phenomenon," *Academy of Management Review,* April 1982, pp. 212–218. A balanced review of positive and negative

consequences to the individual and organization appears in William H. Mobley, "Some Unanswered Questions in Turnover and Withdrawal Research," *Academy of Management Review,* January 1982, pp. 111–116.

14 Allen C. Bluedorn, "Managing Turnover Strategically," *Business Horizons,* March–April, 1982, pp. 6–12; Dan R. Dalton, William D. Todor, and David M. Krackhardt, "Turnover Overstated: The Functional Taxonomy," *Academy of Management Review,* January 1982, pp. 117–123; also see John W. Seybolt, "Dealing with Premature Employee Turnover," *California Management Review,* Spring 1983, pp. 107–117.

15 Mixed results appear in Tove Helland Hammer, Jacqueline C. Landau, and Robert N. Stern, "Absenteeism When Workers Have a Voice: The Case of Employee Ownership," *Journal of Applied Psychology,* October 1981, pp. 561–573. Favorable outcomes appear in Richard M. Steers and Susan R. Rhodes, "Major Influences on Employee Attendance: A Process Model," *Journal of Applied Psychology,* August 1978, pp. 391–407, while a contrary opinion is reported in Nigel Nicholson, Colin A. Brown, and J. K. Chadwick-Jones, "Absence from Work and Job Satisfaction," *Journal of Applied Psychology,* December 1976, pp. 728–737.

16 Richard J. Tersine and Roberta S. Russell, "Internal Theft: The Multi-Billion-Dollar Disappearing Act," *Business Horizons,* November–December 1981, pp. 11–20.

17 Norval D. Glenn, Patricia Taylor, and Charles N. Weaver, "Age and Job Satisfaction among Males and Females: A Multivariate, Multisurvey Study," *Journal of Applied Psychology,* April 1977, pp. 189–193.

18 Frank J. Smith, Kenneth D. Scott, and Charles L. Hulin, "Trends in Job-Related Attitudes of Managerial and Professional Employees," *Academy of Management Journal,* September 1977, pp. 454–460.

19 U.S. Department of Labor, *Job Satisfaction: Is There a Trend?* 1974, pp. 9–10: and Kahn, op. cit., pp. 39, 94.

20 Lyman W. Porter, Edward E. Lawler III, and J. Richard Hackman, *Behavior in Organizations,* New York: McGraw-Hill Book Company, 1975, pp. 248–252.

21 There is some evidence that employee perceptions of openness decline as organizational size increases. See Fredric M. Jablin, "Formal Structural Characteristics of Organizations and Superior-Subordinate Communication," *Human Communication Research,* Summer 1982, pp. 338–347.

22 Frank J. Smith and Lyman W. Porter, "What Do Executives Think about Their Organizations?" *AMA Management Digest,* July 1978, pp. 10–15.

23 Walter McQuade, "Union Carbide Takes to the Woods," *Fortune,* Dec. 13, 1982, pp. 164ff.

24 The Index of Organizational Reactions is described in F. J. Smith and L. W. Porter, "What do Executives Really Think about Their Organizations?" *Organizational Dynamics,* Autumn 1977, pp. 68–80. The Job Descriptive Index is reported in P. C. Smith, L. M. Kendall, and C. L. Hulin, *The Measurement of Satisfaction in Work and Retirement,* Chicago: Rand McNally & Company, 1969. The scale shown in the color example on page 120 is adapted from Lyman W. Porter, "A Study of Perceived Need Satisfactions in Bottom and Middle Management," *Journal of Applied Psychology,* January 1961, pp. 1–10. The Minnesota Satisfaction Questionnaire is presented in D. J. Weiss, R. V. Dawis, G. W. England, and L. H. Lofquist, *Manual for the Minnesota Satisfaction Questionnaire, Minnesota Studies*

in Vocational Rehabilitation: XXII, University of Minnesota Industrial Relations Center, Work Adjustment Project, 1967.

25 For a more complete discussion, see Randall B. Dunham and Frank J. Smith, *Organizational Surveys: An Internal Assessment of Organizational Health,* Glenview, Ill.: Scott, Foresman & Company, 1979; and William J. Rothwell, "Conducting an Employee Attitude Survey," *Personnel Journal,* April 1983, pp. 308–311.

26 Dennis I. Dosset, Gary P. Latham, and Lise M. Saari, "The Impact of Goal Setting on Survey Returns," *Academy of Management Journal,* September 1980, pp. 561–567; Hugh J. Arnold and Daniel C. Feldman, "Social Desirability Response Bias in Self-Report Choice Situations," *Academy of Management Journal,* June 1981, pp. 377–385; and Daniel C. Ganster, Harry W. Hennessey, and Fred Luthans, "Social Desirability Response Effects: Three Alternative Models," *Academy of Management Journal,* June 1983, pp. 321–331. For an opposing view on norms, see Michael R. Cooper, "Warning: Traditional Employee Attitude Surveys Don't Work," *Management Review,* August 1982, pp. 56–57.

27 "A Productive Way to Vent Employee Gripes," *Business Week,* Oct. 16, 1978, pp. 168–171.

28 For an expanded discussion, see Mitchell Lee Marks, "Conducting an Employee Attitude Survey," *Personnel Journal,* September 1982, pp. 684–691; and William E. Dodd and Michael L. Pesci, "Managing Morale through Survey Feedback," *Business Horizons,* June 1977, pp. 36–45.

FOR ADDITIONAL READING

Campbell, John P., Richard L. Daft, and Charles L. Hulin, *What to Study: Generating and Developing Research Questions,* Beverly Hills, Calif.: Sage Publications, Inc., 1982.

Chadwick-Jones, J. K., Nigel Nicholson, and Colin Brown, *Social Psychology of Absenteeism,* New York: Praeger Publishers, 1982.

Dunham, Randall B., and Frank J. Smith, *Organizational Surveys: An Internal Assessment of Organizational Health,* Glenview, Ill.: Scott, Foresman and Company, 1979.

Hakel, Milton D., Melvin Sorcher, Michael Beer, and Joseph L. Moses, *Making It Happen: Designing Research with Implementation in Mind,* Beverly Hills, Calif.: Sage Publications, Inc., 1982.

Mobley, William H., *Employee Turnover: Causes, Consequences, and Control,* Reading, Mass.: Addison-Wesley Publishing Company, Inc., 1982.

Mowday, Richard T., Lyman W. Porter, and Richard M. Steers, *Employee-Organization Linkages: The Psychology of Commitment, Absenteeism, and Turnover,* New York: Academic Press, 1982.

CHAPTER

7

APPRAISING AND REWARDING PERFORMANCE

While management and economists have overestimated the importance of pay, psychologists have underestimated it.

Bernard M. Bass[1]

Management has the obligation to employees to first and foremost provide them the opportunity to earn according to their productivity.

Nucor Corporation policy statement[2]

CHAPTER OBJECTIVES

TO UNDERSTAND:
Money as an economic and social medium of exchange
The expectancy and equity models applied to pay
Behavioral considerations in performance appraisal
Incentive measures that link pay with performance
Uses of profit sharing and production sharing
Elements of a complete pay program

For twenty-four years Mark McCann worked as bank teller in a small town. He was the senior person among three tellers, and on rare occasions when both bank officers were away, he was left in charge of the bank. In his community he was a respected citizen. He belonged to a downtown business club and was an elder in his church. Recently he confided to a trusted friend, "I'm looking for another job—just anything to get away from *that bank*." Further questioning revealed that he had been quite satisfied with his job and was still satisfied except for one event. Because of a local labor shortage, one teller's position went unfilled for three months. Finally the bank, in desperation, recruited a young, untrained college man from another city. In order to get him the bank paid him a monthly salary $25 higher than Mark received. Mark suddenly felt bypassed and forgotten. His whole world had come tumbling down the day he learned of the new teller's rate. He felt that his community social standing had collapsed and that his self-image was destroyed. The employee he was *training* was earning $25 more!

This case illustrates how economic rewards are important to employees and how pay relationships carry immense social value. Management has not always recognized their social importance to workers. In the nineteenth and early twentieth centuries employees were supposed to want primarily money; therefore, money was believed to produce direct motivation—the more money offered, the more motivation. Roethlisberger and his followers successfully buried this idea by showing that economic rewards operated through the attitudes of workers in the social system to produce an *indirect* incentive.

In this chapter we discuss the complex relationship between economic reward systems and organizational behavior. More details about these systems will be found in books about compensation and human resource management; only their significant behavioral aspects are examined here. The focus of this chapter is on money as a means of rewarding employees, expectancy and equity theory applied to pay, cost-reward break-even analysis, and behavioral considerations in performance appraisal. Then we discuss incentive pay, where each worker's pay varies in relation to employee or organizational performance. Finally, we show how incentives are combined with other parts of wage administration to build a complete pay program that encourages motivation.

MONEY AS A MEANS OF REWARDING EMPLOYEES

It is evident that money is important to employees for a number of reasons. Certainly money is valuable because of the goods and services that it will purchase. This is its economic value as a medium of exchange for allocation of economic resources; however, money also is a *social medium of exchange*. All of us have seen its importance as a status symbol for those who have it and can thus save it, spend it conspicuously, or give it generously. Money has status value, when it is being received and when it is being spent. It represents to employees what their employer thinks of them. It is also an indication of one

Money has social value.

employee's relative status compared with that of other employees. It has about as many values as it has possessors.[3] Here is an example of how people respond differently to it.

CHAPTER 7: APPRAISING AND REWARDING PERFORMANCE   **133**

A manager gave two field sales representatives the same increase in pay because each had done a good job. One sales representative was highly pleased with this recognition. She felt she was respected and rewarded because the raise placed her in a higher income bracket. The other sales representative was angered because he knew the raise amounted to the minimum standard available; so he considered it an insult rather than an adequate reward for the outstanding job he felt he was doing. He felt that he was not properly recognized, and he saw this small raise as a serious blow to his own esteem and self-respect. This same raise also affected the security of the two employees in a different manner. The first employee now felt she had obtained more security, but the second employee felt that his security was in jeopardy.

Application of the expectancy model

One useful way to think about money as a reward is to apply it to the expectancy model, discussed in Chapter 5. Expectancy theory states that valence × expectancy × instrumentality = motivation. This means that if money is to act as a strong motivator, an employee must want more of it (valence), believe that effort will be successful (expectancy), and trust that the monetary reward will follow better performance (instrumentality).

Valence of money is not easily influenced by management. It is contingent upon an employee's personal values and the macromotivational environment. For example, if an employee has an independent income, a small increase in pay may have little valence. The same conclusion applies to an employee who cherishes other values and only desires a subsistence income. Similarly, the value of money to people in an affluent society tends to decline, since money tends to satisfy lower-order needs more directly than higher-order needs. However, since money has many social meanings to people, employees may seek it for its social value even when its economic value has low valence. This means that most employees do respond to money as a reward.

With regard to instrumentality, many employees are not sure that additional performance will lead to additional pay. They see some employees deliver minimum performance, yet receive almost the same pay increases as high performers. They often see promotions based more on seniority than performance. Instrumentality is an area where management has much opportunity for positive action, because it can change substantially the connection between increased performance and reward.

Application of equity theory

Equity theory, discussed in Chapter 3, also applies to monetary rewards.[4] Equity relates to the fairness of management's reward system. It concerns how near rewards are to what employees think they should receive on the basis of their inputs. Employees consider all types of input as shown in Figure

Are the rewards fair?

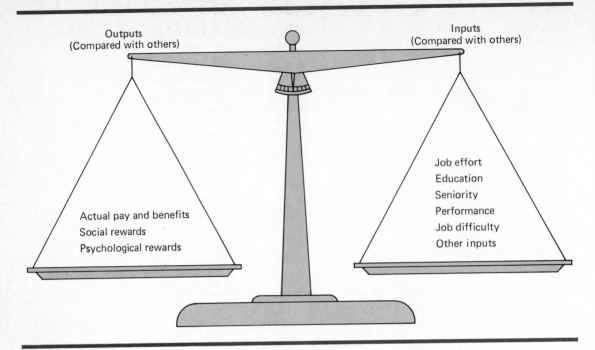

Figure 7-1
Key factors in
equity assessment

7-1. Then they compare their outcomes with the outcomes of others. Questions such as the following are asked:

- Are my rewards fair compared with the rewards of others doing the same or similar work?

- Are my rewards fair in relation to employees doing different work in my organization?

- Are my rewards fair in relation to those received by others in my community and my society?

Fairness of rewards may even be judged in comparison to relatively arbitrary criteria like age, as this example shows.

> Irene Nickerson is a supervisor in a large public utility. For several years, her friends told her she could consider herself successful when her salary (in thousands of dollars) surpassed her age. One year, at age 34, she received a substantial salary increase that placed her income at $33,865. She was incensed for weeks afterward! For an extra $136, the company could have matched her equity expectations and produced a motivated employee.

Equity has various bases.   Pay was a symbolic scorecard by which Nickerson compared her outputs with her inputs. Another feature of equity perceptions is the tendency of employees to shift the basis to the standard that is most favorable for them.

Recent college graduates often inflate the value of their education, whereas employees with longer service favor seniority. One nationwide study of workers reported that they chose middle managers as their comparison group, and this resulted in feelings of inequity.[5] Since most people tend to have high opinions of themselves, they often find it rather easy to conclude that pay inequities exist. For organizational rewards to be fair, employees must see a rough balance between their *perception* of their worth to the organization and their *actual place* in that reward structure.

Extrinsic and intrinsic rewards

Money is essentially an extrinsic reward rather than an intrinsic one, so it has all the limitations of extrinsic benefits. No matter how closely management attaches pay to performance, pay is still something that originates outside the job. As shown by Herzberg and others, intrinsic job rewards tend to be more motivating. For example, the personal satisfaction of a job well done is a powerful motivator to many people. Economic rewards, therefore, have their limitations. They cannot provide all the needed rewards for a psychologically healthy person.

An important task for management is how to integrate extrinsic and intrinsic rewards successfully. Employees differ in the amount of intrinsic and extrinsic rewards that they want, and jobs and organizational conditions also differ. These conditions suggest that what is needed is a contingency approach to rewards that considers needs of workers, type of job, organizational environment, and the fact that some of the most important rewards are in the form of fringe benefits and allowances. These rewards often are more valuable to employees because they have more psychological and social meaning. Special benefits may be evidence of recognition, status, or other important social values.

Both types are needed.

A community hospital had a nursing director in charge of 200 nurses. Her work was outstanding, but she did not desire further promotion into nonnursing administrative work. She was earning the top rate provided in the salary plan for her job, so it would be difficult to provide more salary. However, management wanted to reward her in some way and encourage her continued growth. Knowing of her interest in professional conventions and travel, management arranged for her to be the hospital's representative to two international nursing and medical conferences in other nations during a period of three years. The nursing director appreciated this recognition, and so did other employees in the hospital. Motivation and job attitudes were improved.

Cost-reward break-even analysis

It is evident that many complex issues determine how employees will respond to economic rewards. There is no simple answer for the employer or the employee. The employee's solution to this complex problem is a rough type of *cost-reward break-even analysis,* in which the employee identifies and com-

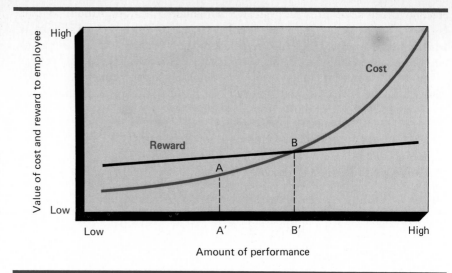

Figure 7-2
Cost of performance
in relation to reward
for an employee.
Employee's
performance will
tend to be in the
area of *A'B'*.

pares personal costs and rewards to determine the point at which they are approximately equal, as shown in Figure 7-2.[6] Employees consider all the costs of higher performance, such as more effort. Then they compare these costs with probable rewards, both intrinsic and extrinsic. Both costs and rewards always are valued *from the individual employee's point of view.* Management can provide the rewards, but the individual employee determines their value.

Perception is critical.

The break-even point of costs and rewards is the point at which costs and rewards are equal for a certain level of performance, as shown by point *B* on the chart. Employee performance tends to be near the break-even point but below it, because typically the employee does not try to be so precise as to maximize the cost-reward relationship. Rather, the employee tries for a satisfactory relationship in which rewards are relatively favorable in relation to costs. Performance tends to be somewhere along the line *A'B'*.

In Figure 7-2 employee costs are shown rising more steeply near the highest level of performance to represent the additional difficulty that maximum effort and concentration require. Each employee's line will have a different shape, representing individual values. The reward line is shown as a straight line, such as that provided by a piece rate, but in most instances it rises only in steps after a certain amount of performance improvement occurs. If the reward line can be made to rise more steeply by means of larger rewards, then the break-even point will be at a higher level of performance.

Compliance with law

In addition to understanding the effects of expectancy, equity, and break-even models, compensation management is also complicated by the need to comply with all relevant laws.[7] A variety of laws affecting organizational behavior, such as those that apply to equal employment opportunity, will be discussed in Chapter 18. Basically, the law states that reward systems must be designed so that equal jobs receive equal pay.

ORGANIZATIONAL BEHAVIOR AND PERFORMANCE APPRAISAL

Performance appraisal plays a key role in reward systems. It is the process of evaluating the performance of employees. As shown in Figure 7-3, appraisal is necessary in order to (1) allocate resources in a dynamic environment, (2) reward employees, (3) give employees feedback about their work, (4) maintain fair relationships within groups, (5) coach and develop employees, and (6) comply with regulations. Appraisal systems, therefore, are necessary for proper management and for employee development.

Reasons for employee appraisal

The first recorded appraisal system in industry was Robert Owen's use of character books and blocks in his New Lanark cotton mills in Scotland around 1800. The character books recorded each worker's daily reports. The character blocks were colored differently on each side to represent an evaluation of the worker ranging from bad to good, and they were displayed at each employee's workplace. Owen was quite impressed by the way the blocks improved worker behavior.[8]

The social environment surrounding organizations has changed considera-

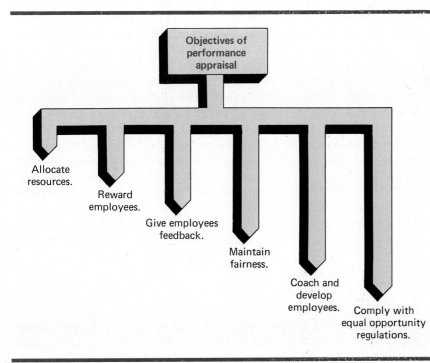

Figure 7-3
Objectives of performance appraisal

Objectives of performance appraisal

Allocate resources.

Reward employees.

Give employees feedback.

Maintain fairness.

Coach and develop employees.

Comply with equal opportunity regulations.

Figure 7-4
Necessary criteria
to assure equal
employment
opportunity in
performance
appraisal

The performance appraisal system—
• Is an organizational necessity.
• Is based on well-defined, objective criteria.
• Is based on careful job analysis.
• Uses only job-related criteria.
• Is supported by adequate studies of its reliability and validity.
• Is applied by trained, qualified raters.
• Is applied objectively throughout the organization.
• Can be shown to be nondiscriminatory as defined by law.

bly since Owen developed his system. Federal and state laws have added to the complexity and difficulty of appraisal plans. For example, as shown in Figure 7-4, criteria for compliance with equal employment laws are stringent.[9] Management needs to design and operate its appraisal systems carefully in order to comply with these laws.

Appraisal philosophy

A generation ago, appraisal programs tended to emphasize employee traits, deficiencies, and abilities, but modern appraisal philosophy emphasizes present performance and future goals. Modern philosophy also stresses employee participation in mutually setting goals with the supervisor. Thus the hallmarks of modern appraisal philosophy are (1) performance orientation, (2) focus on goals or objectives, and (3) mutual goal setting between supervisor and employee.

Mutual goal setting

The underlying philosophy behind mutual setting of goals is that people will work harder for goals or objectives that they have participated in setting. The assumption is that people want to satisfy some of their needs through work and that they will do so if management will provide them with a supportive environment. Among their desires are to perform a worthwhile task, share in a group effort, share in setting their objectives, share in the rewards of their efforts, and continue personal growth. Mutual setting of objectives helps accomplish these needs. For example, employees who participate in goal setting for performance appraisal also show significantly better performance.[10] As the saying goes, "If you know where you want to go, you are more likely to get there."

The appraisal interview

The appraisal interview is a highly sensitive and difficult human relationship. Although it often is seen as affecting only the person appraised, it also has a significant influence on the appraiser.[11] One of its benefits is to encourage managers to do more analytical and constructive thinking about their employees. The requirement of an interview encourages managers to be more specific about each employee's capabilities and to perceive that each is different and must be treated that way.

Managers sometimes fail in an appraisal interview when they save up a list of employee shortcomings and unload the whole list during the interview. Being presented with a whole list of shortcomings at one time is too much for employees. It overwhelms them and causes defensive reactions. Employees need feedback about weaknesses, but these can be discussed more as needs for development in order to meet objectives.[12]

Role of the appraiser

A review of the research shows that successful performance appraisals are most likely to occur when the appraiser (1) is knowledgeable about the employee's job and performance, (2) provides support, acceptance, and praise, and (3) encourages self-review and participation. However, these studies also suggest that the approach taken by the appraiser should be contingent on several employee and job factors. For example, a problem employee may need frequent reviews until performance rises to acceptable levels. Greater participation may be more appropriate when the employee is knowledgeable, has a strong independence need, and has demonstrated acceptable performance in the past.[13]

Appraisal systems provide an assessment or rating of employee contributions to job-related objectives. However, since the rating received only acts as a source of feedback and psychic reward, economic incentives are then needed to obtain employee motivation.

ECONOMIC INCENTIVE SYSTEMS

An *economic incentive system* of some type could be applied to almost any job. The basic idea of them all is to vary an employee's pay in proportion to some criterion of individual, group, or organizational performance. These criteria could include employee production, company profit, units shipped, or the ratio of labor cost to sales prices. Payment may be immediate or may be delayed, as in a profit-sharing plan.

Our discussion of economic incentives focuses on their behavioral implications. We do not attempt to discuss all types of incentives or all details about them. The ones selected for presentation are wage incentives, which are a widely used individual incentive, and profit sharing and production sharing, which are popular group incentives. Finally, we show how incentives are combined with other parts of wage administration to make a complete pay program.

Although most of our discussion is on long-run incentive programs, it should be recognized that temporary incentives also have a role to play in compensation. Sometimes they provide just the right amount of added motivation to cause a desired increase in performance. Here is an example:

A manufacturer of specialized business equipment experienced a substantial decline in sales for one of its models. The decline was so severe that it had scheduled a one-month closing of this model's production line during the Christmas season. At the sales manager's suggestion, the company offered to give its salespeople a new $10 bill for each item of this model sold during the month of December. The offer was made in the context of an extra Christmas bonus opportunity. The response was so great that the production line was kept operating, and some salespeople earned over $4000 in bonus money paid in $10 bills. A $4000 bonus amounted to 10 to 20 percent of a typical salesperson's annual income.

Incentives linking pay with performance

There are several broad types of incentives that link pay with performance. Major ones are shown in Figure 7-5. Perhaps the most popular measure is for the amount of output to determine pay, as illustrated by a sales commission or a *piece rate*. It provides a simple, direct connection between performance and reward. Those workers who produce more are rewarded more. Often pay is determined by a combination quantity-quality measure in order to assure that *Piece rate*   a high quality of product or service is maintained. For example, a piece rate usually is paid only for those pieces that meet quality standards.

In other instances an incentive bonus is given only to those employees who reach established goals. For example, a bonus might be given for selling fifteen automobiles during a month, but there would be no bonus for selling only fourteen. Rewards also may be given on the basis of profit success, as in a profit-sharing plan. Another measure is to link pay with cost efficiency. An example is production sharing, discussed later in this chapter. Regardless of the type of incentive that is used, its objective is to link a portion of a worker's pay to some measure of employee or organizational performance.

Potential advantages

Incentives provide several potential employee advantages. A major advantage is that they increase employee beliefs (instrumentality) that reward will *Improved motivation*   follow high performance. If we assume that money has valence to an employee, then motivation should increase.

Incentives also appear favorable from the point of view of equity theory. Those who perform better are rewarded more. This kind of input-output balance is perceived by many people to be equitable. Further, if more pay is a

	INCENTIVE MEASURE	EXAMPLE
Figure 7-5 Major incentive measures to link pay with performance	**Amount of output**	Piece rate: sales commission
	Quality of output	Piece rate only for pieces meeting the standard; commission only for sales that are without bad debts
	Success in reaching goals	Bonus for selling fifteen automobiles (but not fourteen)
	Amount of profit	Profit sharing
	Cost efficiency	Production sharing

valued reward, then incentive systems are favorable from the point of view of behavior modification. They provide a desirable consequence (pay) that should reinforce behavior. Rewards, such as sales commissions, often are rather immediate and frequent, which is consistent with the philosophy of behavior modification.

Another advantage from the employee's point of view is that incentives are comparatively objective. They can be computed from the number of pieces, dollars, or similar objective criteria. Compared with a supervisor's subjective performance ratings, the objective approach tends to have higher acceptance by employees.

Potential difficulties

With so many favorable conditions supporting incentives, it seems that workers would welcome almost any incentive because of the rewards it could bring. However, there are difficulties that tend to offset some of the potential advantages. Potential equity is offset by other developments that are perceived as inequities. In behavior modification terms, there are unfavorable consequences that exist alongside the favorable consequences of more pay, so they tend to reduce the potential advantages of incentive pay. When workers make their cost-reward break-even analysis, they find that costs have risen along with rewards. The result may be that the break-even point has changed very little, if at all. The extra problems caused by the incentive may offset much of the economic gain expected. For example, new employees may have difficulty learning the system; other employees with declining energy may experience a decrease in total pay; and some unions may resist the incentive idea. The key thought is that *incentive systems produce both positive and negative employee consequences.* Both must be evaluated in determining the desirability of an incentive system. Economic consequences are likely to be positive, but the direction of psychological and social consequences is less certain.

USE OF WAGE INCENTIVES

More pay for more production

Basically, *wage incentives* provide more pay for more production.[14] The main reason for use of wage incentives is clear; they nearly always increase productivity while decreasing unit labor costs. Workers under normal conditions without wage incentives have the capacity to produce more, and wage incentives are one way to release that potential. The increased productivity often is substantial.

Lincoln Electric Company pioneered the development of individual wage incentives over fifty years ago. The company states that worker efficiency makes stable employment possible, so it has not had a layoff in over thirty years. Factory employees typically double their annual pay with the year-end bonus based on their productivity. Despite the pressure to be productive, employee turnover is only 6 percent a year, which is one-sixth the rate for comparable firms.[15]

*Advantage of
simple systems*

In order to be successful, a wage incentive needs to be simple enough for employees to have a strong belief that reward will follow performance. If the plan is so complex that workers have difficulty relating performance to reward, then higher motivation is less likely to develop.

An incentive that is operating successfully can bring psychological as well as economic rewards. There is satisfaction from a job well done. Self-image may improve because of feelings of competence. There is also the feeling that one is helping to fulfill social needs by means of higher output in relation to inputs. Some incentives may encourage high group cohesion and teamwork because of the need for employees to work together to earn the incentive rewards. Teamwork of this type is described by one researcher as follows:[16]

> On a more anecdotal level, I should just like to refer to the most highly motivated, most productive and perhaps proudest work group I have ever observed. For many years, I have been engaged in organizational field work, and some years ago I studied several hundred work groups in a wide variety of industrial settings. One in particular sticks in my memory because both the workers themselves and their managers confirmed their extraordinary morale and productivity. They were a five man metal bending crew making the frame for folding chairs. Each did a short cycle, repetitive, manual job involving one of the bending and spot welding operations and then passed the part on to a colleague who did a similar, but slightly different bend and weld. The frame was completed in what must have been no more than a minute or two, and to the naked, neophyte eye it looked as though the metal just flowed among these ten hands. They earned more incentive pay and were faster and higher paid than any team in the factory. Everyone knew their reputation, and they would work like proverbial greased lightning for perhaps an hour and then take whatever break they felt like because they were always ahead of the standard. They were so independent and so perfect a physical team that they insisted on having a veto over any changes in team membership should there be illness or turnover.
>
> No job interest or complexity or ego challenge here, just a good old fashioned, cohesive work group that had gotten a great piece rate for itself.

Difficulties with wage incentives

Production wage incentives furnish an example of the kinds of difficulties that may develop with many incentive plans, despite their potential benefits. Management's job is to try to prevent or reduce the problems while increasing benefits, so that the incentive plan works more effectively.

*Disruption of
social systems*

The basic human difficulty with wage incentives of this type is that disruptions in the social system may lead to feelings of inequity and dissatisfaction. At times these disruptions are severe enough to make incentive workers less satisfied with their pay than workers who are paid an hourly wage, even though the incentive workers are earning more.

For any wage incentive plan to be successful, it needs to be coordinated carefully with the whole operating system. If there are long periods when employees must wait for work to arrive at their workplace, then the incentive loses its punch. If the incentive is likely to replace workers, then management needs to plan for their use elsewhere so that employee security is not threatened. If work methods are erratic, then they must be standardized so that a fair rate of reward can be established. This is a complex process leading to many difficulties.

1 Wage incentives normally require establishment of performance standards. *Rate setting* is the process of determining the standard output for each job, which becomes the fair day's work for the operator. Rate setters are often resented not only because subjective judgment is involved but also because they are believed to be a cause of change and more difficult standards.

Rate setting

2 Wage incentives may make the supervisor's job more complex. Supervisors must be familiar with the system, so that they can explain it to employees. Paperwork increases, resulting in greater chance of error and more employee dissatisfaction. Relationships are compounded, and supervisors are required to resolve different expectations from higher management, rate setters, workers, and unions.

3 A thorny problem with production wage incentives is *loose rates*. A rate is loose when employees are able to reach standard output with less-than-normal effort. When management adjusts the rate to a higher standard, employees predictably experience a feeling of inequity.

Loose rates

4 Wage incentives may cause disharmony between incentive workers and hourly workers. When the two groups perform work in a sequence, hourly workers may feel discriminated against because they earn less. If the incentive workers increase output, hourly workers further along the process must work faster to prevent a bottleneck. The incentive workers earn more for their increased output, but the hourly workers do not.

Hourly workers who precede incentive workers in the production process can on occasion "take it easy" and produce less with no cut in pay. But the incentive worker's income is cut when less work is available. The same problem occurs if an hourly worker is absent and reduces the flow of material to incentive workers. Conflicts of this type are so difficult to resolve that it is best for management not to mix the two groups in any closely integrated production sequence.

5 Another difficulty with wage incentives is that they may result in *output restriction,* by which workers limit their production and thus defeat the purpose of the incentive. This phenomenon is caused by several factors— group insecurities that the production standard will be raised, resistance to change by the informal social organization, and the fact that people are not comfortable working always at full capacity.

Output restriction

Although restriction of work tends to be more evident in factory incentive plans, it also exists in sales work. This is illustrated by the following situation involving salespeople on commission.

Industrial equipment salespeople in one company received a substantial salary plus a commission of 1 percent on sales until a total commission of $20,000 was earned. Any

commission thereafter was at 0.25 percent. Each salesperson had an annual quota, but annual sales often varied as much as 100 percent because of the nature of the product. Some salespeople worked only until their quota was earned and then held back, because (1) they were afraid their quota might be raised the next year and they did not want the strain of trying to make a difficult quota or (2) they objected to the commission reduction from 1 to 0.25 percent which occurred at about the same time their quota was reached. Others sold a little more than their quota, because they "wanted to look good on the record" regardless of commission rate; but then they held back because they feared the company would split their territory if sales became too high. Other salespeople tried to sell all they could all the time, regardless of incentive factors.

USE OF PROFIT AND PRODUCTION SHARING

Profit sharing

Profit sharing is a system that distributes to employees some portion of the profits of business, either immediately following the fiscal year or deferred until a later date. It was first tried in industry at the beginning of the industrial revolution, but did not become popular until after World War II. The growth of profit sharing has been encouraged by federal tax laws that allow employee income taxes to be deferred on funds in profit-sharing pension plans.

The role of profit sharing is to develop mutual interest and cooperation among employees, management, and stockholders. As early as 1832, Charles Babbage wrote:

> It would be of great importance, if, in every large establishment, the modes of paying the different persons employed could be so arranged, that each should derive advantage from the success of the whole, and that the profits of the individuals should advance as the factory itself produced profit, without the necessity of making any change in the wages agreed upon. This is by no means easy to effect, particularly amongst that class whose daily labour procures for them their daily meal.[17]

Mutual interest is emphasized. Basic pay rates, performance pay increases, and most incentive systems recognize individual differences, while profit sharing recognizes mutual interests. Employees become interested in the economic success of their employer when they see that their own rewards are affected by it. Greater institutional teamwork tends to develop.

Young organizations working on the fringes of science have found that profit sharing especially is useful to give them the vigor to forge ahead of competitors. If they are successful, the rewards are great, and this possibility builds strong motivation and mutual interest among their employees.

For example, the president of a young computer company in Massachusetts became concerned about the lack of cooperation that developed as his company grew larger. He commented, "Different departments were becoming like little kingdoms. People were becoming more concerned over their own little department, its growth and problems, than they were about the company."[18]

In order to encourage more cooperation, the president made an unusual and substantial offer to his employees. He said that if they would double sales and earnings during the following year, he would give all of them a free one-week trip to London or Disney World. They met their goal satisfactorily, so he shut down the plant and gave them their free one-week trip. Employees traveled as a group, and each received full pay, most trip expenses, and $100 spending money. Family members or guests could accompany an employee at cost.

Employees liked the award, so the following year the president offered a trip to Rome for another doubling of sales and earnings. Employees again met their goal.

In general, profit sharing tends to work better for fast-growing, profitable organizations in which there are opportunities for substantial employee rewards. It is less likely to be useful in stable and declining organizations with low profit margins and intense competition. Profit sharing also is more applicable to managers and high-level professional people, because their decisions are more likely to have a significant effect on their firm's profits. Operating workers, on the other hand, have more difficulty connecting their isolated actions with their firm's profitability, so profit sharing has less appeal to them.

Some difficulties with profit sharing

Even in those situations where profit sharing seems appropriate, some general disadvantages are relevant:

1 Profits are not directly related to an employee's effort on the job. Poor market conditions may nullify an employee's hard work. *Indirect relationship*

2 The lengthy time interval that employees must wait for their reward diminishes its impact. *Delay*

3 Since profits are somewhat unpredictable, total worker income may vary from year to year. Some workers may prefer the security of a more stable wage or salary. *Lack of predictability*

The social aspects of profit sharing are just as significant as its economic and tax aspects, if not more so. For profit sharing to develop a genuine community of interest, workers need to understand how it works and feel a sense of fairness in its provisions. If they do not, they may resent it, as in the following situation:

Marvin Schmidt, an idealistic owner of a small retail store, employed twenty-five people. He had worked hard to pyramid his meager investment into a prosperous store in the short period of seven years. Much of his success resulted from loyal, cooperative employees who had worked for him several years. He recognized their contributions and wanted to give them extra rewards, but he always had been short of capital.

Finally he had a very prosperous year, so he decided to begin a cash profit-sharing plan to be given as a bonus at Christmas. The generous bonus amounted to 30 percent of each person's pay for the year. It was announced and given as a surprise with the weekly paycheck immediately preceding Christmas. Not one employee thanked him, and most of his employees were cool and uncooperative thereafter. He eventually learned that they felt if he could give that large a bonus, he must have been unjustly exploiting them for years, even though they admitted they had been receiving more than the prevailing wage.

The union view

Just as workers sometimes dislike profit sharing, many unions and their leaders are suspicious of it. Union opposition arises basically because unions have very little control of the factors influencing profit, with the exception of labor costs. They also fear that it will undermine union loyalty, collective bargaining, and organizing campaigns. Profit sharing varies wage earnings from company to company, a fact that may conflict with union goals to establish uniform nationwide rates for their members. There is, however, nothing in profit sharing contrary to union objectives for advancing workers' welfare. Many profit-sharing companies have unions representing their workers, and practical-minded local unions do not oppose it as long as it works.

Production-sharing plans

Another useful group incentive is production sharing. A well-known example is the Scanlon plan. It was developed by Joseph N. Scanlon at a small steel company in 1938, and it has been copied by a number of other organizations.[19]

Scanlon plan

A *production-sharing plan,* usually called a *Scanlon plan,* is an incentive program that pays employees for improvements in labor costs that are better than standard. It allocates to labor a standard labor cost based on experience and analysis, such as 42 percent of the total product cost or the total sales value of production. As labor works more efficiently to reduce that percentage cost, the value of the savings is shared with workers. The share usually is in proportion to actual earnings of each employee during the period. It is paid monthly or quarterly regardless of a firm's profit or loss. Figure 7-6 summarizes how the production-sharing bonus is calculated.

The Scanlon plan is as much concerned with organizational behavior activities as it is with pay.[20] It establishes active, cooperative participation

Figure 7-6
Summary of
calculations for
monthly
production-sharing
(Scanlon plan)
bonus

Monthly bonus calculation	
Net sales for month	$11,500,000
Inventory increase	300,000
Sales value of production	$11,800,000
Standard payroll costs (42 percent of sales value)	$ 4,956,000
Less actual payroll	4,031,000
Production-sharing bonus	$ 925,000
Bonus as percentage of payroll (To be distributed to each participant in proportion to earnings)	18.66%

between workers and managers in order to reduce labor costs. It encourages employee suggestions, acts as a teamwork incentive, and develops improved communication. It also encourages employee development, because employees are participating and concerned with the affairs of their organization. It especially broadens the understanding of employees as they see a larger picture of the system, rather than confining their outlook to the narrow specialty of their job.

One company that implemented a Scanlon plan reported these results.[21] Over five years, the product cost was reduced by 50 percent, rejected units fell from over 9 to less than 1 percent, and the absenteeism rate declined from 3.4 to less than 1 percent. In addition, communication barriers between management and employees disappeared, and morale improved.

Key factors in the success of production-sharing plans include favorable management attitudes toward employee participation in production decisions, a corporate willingness to share benefits of production increases with employees, and production conditions in which costs can be readily computed.[22] The sharing formula is complex and difficult to administer. The style of supervision and the social organization of the work group need to be changed substantially. More two-way communication is required, and managers need to be more tolerant of criticism from employees. The amount of interaction required is so great that use of the plan may be more difficult in large organizations.

A COMPLETE PAY PROGRAM

Rating jobs, employees, and the organization

Many types of pay are required for a complete economic reward system.[23] Job analysis and wage surveys *rate jobs,* comparing one job with another according to levels of responsibility. Performance appraisal and incentives *rate employees* in their performance and give them more reward. Profit sharing *rates the organization* in terms of its general economic performance and rewards employees as partners in it. Together these three systems are the incentive foundation of a complete pay program, as roughly diagrammed in the pay pyramid in Figure 7-7. Each can contribute something to the employee's economic reward.

The three systems are complementary because each reflects a different set of factors in the total situation. Base pay motivates employees to progress to jobs of higher skills and responsibility. Performance pay is an incentive to improve performance on one's job. Profit sharing motivates toward teamwork to improve an organization's performance.

Relating pay to objectives

Other payments, primarily nonincentive in nature, are added to the incentive foundation. Seniority pay adjustments are made to reward workers for extended service and to encourage them to remain with their employer, as

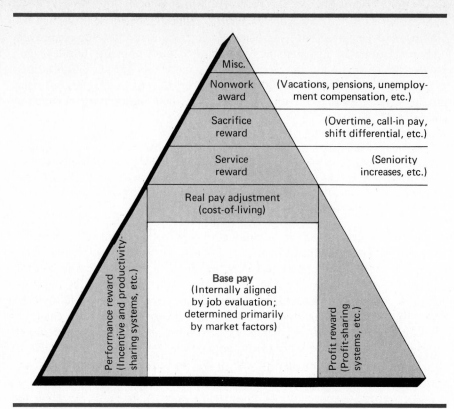

Figure 7-7
The pay pyramid:
the makeup of
a complete pay
program (read
from bottom)

is humorously shown in Figure 7-8. If an employer asks workers to sacrifice by working overtime, working on their day off, or working at undesirable hours, the workers may be paid extra for this inconvenience. Other payments are given for periods when an employee does not work, such as vacations, holidays, jury service, and layoffs subject to guaranteed pay.[24]

The additions to the incentive foundation of the pay pyramid have little direct incentive value because they do not increase according to improved job performance. Some of these additions may result in indirect incentive through better attitudes. Other additions, such as seniority pay, actually may decrease worker incentive. It is clear that not one but many factors enter into computation of a worker's paycheck. Some of these factors are related less to incentive than they are to such broad objectives as security, equity, and social justice. An effective program of economic rewards is a balance of most of these factors. In this way a variety of employee needs are served.

Flexible benefits

The particular combination of economic rewards that an employer uses is contingent on the needs of employees, type of work, and organizational environment. In order to serve employee needs in a better way, some

"I'M IN THE WRONG JOB, AND THE WRONG PROFESSION; WITH THE WRONG COMPANY... BUT I'VE GOT SENIORITY!"

Figure 7-8
Seniority sometimes imprisons an employee in a poor work situation.
Source: *The Register and Tribune Syndicate. Used with permission.*

Cafeteria programs

organizations provide *flexible benefit programs,* also called *cafeteria benefit programs,* because they allow employees to select their individual combination of benefits as they would select food in a cafeteria. Each employee receives a certain total economic allowance for a job, and then—within a range of choices available—the employee selects a preferred combination of individually priced economic rewards that use the allowed total.[25]

> For example, a young employee with several dependents may choose to divert some benefit money from the retirement plan into larger amounts of life insurance and expanded medical and dental coverage. A single person nearing retirement may reduce life insurance while accenting contributions to the pension plan and specialized items, such as optical care and financial counseling. The capacity of these cafeteria programs to meet individual needs was demonstrated at American Can Company. There, a survey showed that 92 percent of the employees with a flexible program thought they had substantially improved their benefits by having the proper mix of items.[26]

SUMMARY

Economic rewards provide social as well as economic value. According to the expectancy model, money will be a motivator if employees want more of it and believe that greater effort and better performance will bring more. Employees also assess the perceived equity of rewards, balancing their inputs and outputs in relation to others. Considering all factors, employees perform a rough cost-reward break-even analysis and work somewhat near but below the break-even point.

Performance appraisal provides a systematic basis for distribution of economic rewards. Modern appraisal philosophy focuses on performance, objectives, and mutual goal setting.

Incentive rewards provide different amounts of pay in relation to some measure of performance. They tend to increase employee expectations that rewards will follow performance. The result is that they nearly always bring more productivity, but they also tend to produce offsetting negative consequences. Wage incentives reward greater output by individuals or groups, while profit sharing emphasizes mutual interest with the employer to build a successful organization. Production sharing emphasizes reduction of labor costs.

Since employees have different needs to be served, many types of pay are required for a complete economic reward system. In some organizations, flexible benefit programs allow employees to select individual combinations of economic rewards. The four chapters in Part Two have attempted to show that economic rewards must be combined with social and psychological rewards to make a complete reward system for an organization.

TERMS AND CONCEPTS FOR REVIEW

Money as a social medium of exchange

Expectancy model applied to pay

Equity theory applied to pay

Cost-reward break-even analysis

Performance appraisal

Economic incentive systems

Wage incentives

Rate setter

Loose rates

Profit sharing

Production sharing

Scanlon plan

Complete pay program

Flexible benefit program

REVIEW QUESTIONS

1 Explain how money can be both an economic and a social medium of exchange. As a student, how do you use money as a social medium of exchange?

2 Think of a job that you formerly had or now have.
   a Discuss specifically how the expectancy model applied (applies) to your pay.
   b Discuss how you felt (feel) about the equity of your pay and why you felt (feel) that way.
   c Develop and explain a cost-reward break-even chart for your pay and effort.

3 Explain some of the behavioral benefits of modern performance appraisal systems compared with more traditional appraisal programs.

4 What are the major measures used to link pay with production? Which

ones, if any, were used in the last job you had? Discuss the effectiveness of the measure or measures used.

5 Discuss some of the advantages and difficulties linked with incentive rewards.

6 Would you use profit sharing, production sharing, or wage incentives in any of the following jobs? Discuss your choice in each instance.
a Employees in a small, fast-growing computer company
b Teacher in a public school
c Clerks processing insurance claims in an insurance office
d Automobile repair mechanic in a small repair shop
e Farm worker picking peaches
f Production worker in a shoe factory making men's shoes

7 Form into small groups, each led by a member who has worked for a sales commission. Discuss how the commission related to both equity theory and expectancy theory, and report highlights of your discussion to your entire classroom group.

8 Have you ever participated in restriction of output (a) in a job and/or (b) in an academic course? Discuss why you did it and what its consequences were.

9 Discuss the different types of pay that make a complete pay program and what purposes each of them serves.

10 During your first ten years after leaving college, would you want a flexible benefit program in your employment? Discuss why.

INCIDENT

The New Performance-Rating Program

Miles Johnson is supervisor of a district sales office in a town of about one-half million persons. Several months ago Johnson studied various articles and pamphlets about performance rating in order to determine if he could improve the rating plan that he had for his salespeople. On the basis of his reading, he did develop a new rating plan that has been in effect for six months. Recently he made the following statement about his new plan.

The new plan definitely has increased morale and productivity of my employees. Formerly I ranked my people strictly on dollar volume. The highest producer was number one, and so on down the line. The ranking was posted on the bulletin board so that each salesperson knew the ranking of all other salespeople. The purpose was to increase competition, and it did accomplish this goal, but it did not tell the whole story about their performance. For example, the top producer in sales was also the worst in delinquent accounts receivable. Some of the lower producers in sales were better in sales discount expense than some of their higher-producing colleagues. I now have a performance appraisal that recognizes a person's rank in each of ten important categories of the total job, and this new approach has given my organization a tremendous boost. My people now work for achievement of the whole job, rather than for the one measure of sales volume.

QUESTIONS

1 Has Johnson improved his performance-rating program? Explain how in terms of expectancy theory, equity theory, and other variables.

2 Can you recommend further improvements for Johnson? If so, explain them.

EXPERIENTIAL EXERCISE

Performance Appraisal Philosophy[27]

1 Read the following set of statements about people and indicate your degree of agreement/disagreement on the rating scales.

2 Meet in small discussion groups, tabulate the responses to each question, and explore possible reasons for any significant disagreements in the ratings.

3 In your group, develop alternative statements for any items you do not support at present. Explain how your new statements reflect your knowledge of human behavior gained through reading Chapters 1 to 7.

		STRONGLY AGREE				STRONGLY DISAGREE
A	Most people don't like to get negative feedback.	1	2	3	4	5
B	Most people don't wish to develop themselves beyond their current levels.	1	2	3	4	5
C	Appraisal is ineffective, as it does not improve employee performance.	1	2	3	4	5
D	Most employees prefer the status quo rather than acquiring new skills.	1	2	3	4	5
E	Most employees don't care about the organization's success unless it affects their own pay.	1	2	3	4	5

REFERENCES

1 Bernard M. Bass, *Organizational Psychology,* Boston: Allyn and Bacon, Inc., 1965, p. 76.

2 John Savage, "Incentive Programs at Nucor Corporation Boost Productivity," *Personnel Administrator,* August 1981, p. 33.

3 For a general overview of wage administration, see Thomas Patten, Jr., *Pay: Employee Compensation and Incentive Plans,* Riverside, N.J.: The Free Press, 1977.

4 For general discussions related to equity and pay, see R. P. Vecchio, "An Individual-Differences Interpretation of the Conflicting Predictions Generated by Equity Theory and Expectancy Theory," *Journal of Applied Psychology,* August 1981, pp.470–481; and Michael R. Carrell and John E. Dittrich, "Equity Theory: The Recent Literature, Methodological Considerations, and New Directions," *Academy of Management Review,* April 1978, pp. 202–210.

5 Joanne Martin, "The Fairness of Earnings Differentials: An Experimental Study of the Perceptions of Blue-Collar Workers," *The Journal of Human Resources,* Winter 1982, pp. 110–122.

6 A related discussion is Philip C. Grant, "Explaining Motivation Phenomena with the Effort–Net Return Model," *Nevada Review of Business & Economics,* Spring, 1982, pp. 29–32.

7 Paul S. Greenlaw and John P. Kohl, "The EEOC's New Equal Pay Act Guidelines," *Personnel Journal,* July 1982, pp. 517–521.

8 Robert Owen, *The Life of Robert Owen,* New York: Alfred A. Knopf, Inc., 1920, pp. 111–112 (from the original published in 1857).

9 The figure is adapted from data in Samuel T. Beacham, "Managing Compensation and Performance Appraisal under the Age Act," *Management Review,* January 1979, pp. 51–54; and Dena B. Schneider, "The Impact of EEO Legislation on Performance Appraisals," *Personnel,* July–August 1978, pp. 24–34. Support appears in William H. Holley and Hubert S. Feild, "Will Your Performance Appraisal System Hold Up in Court?" *Personnel,* January–February 1982, pp. 59–64; and Giovanni B. Giglioni and others, "Performance Appraisal: Here Comes the Judge," *California Management Review,* Winter 1981, pp. 14–23.

10 Gary P. Latham, Terence R. Mitchell, and Dennis L. Dossett, "Importance of Participative Goal Setting and Anticipated Rewards on Goal Difficulty and Job Performance," *Journal of Applied Psychology,* April 1978, pp. 163–171; and Robert L. Dipboye and Rene de Pontbriand, "Correlates of Employee Reactions to Performance Appraisals and Appraisal Systems," *Journal of Applied Psychology,* April 1981, pp. 248–251.

11 For example, acting as an appraiser can lower the satisfaction of managers. See Cynthia D. Fisher and Joe Thomas, "The Other Face of Performance Appraisal," *Human Resource Management,* Spring 1982, pp. 24–26.

12 A classic argument for developmental appraisals is Norman R. F. Maier, *The Appraisal Interview: Three Basic Approaches,* rev. ed., La Jolla, Calif.: University Associates, 1976.

13 Douglas Cederblom, "The Performance Appraisal Interview: A Review, Implications, and Suggestions," *Academy of Management Review,* April 1982, pp. 219–227. See also Robert L. Taylor and Robert A. Zawacki, "Trends in Performance Appraisal: Guidelines for Managers," *Personnel Administrator,* March 1984, pp. 71–80.

14 Guidelines for developing an incentive program are in Bernard Dwortzan, "The ABCs of Incentive Programs," *Personnel Journal,* June 1982, pp. 436–442. The declining use of incentive pay is discussed in Edward E. Lawler, "What Ever Happened to Incentive Pay?" *New Management,* 1:4, 1984, pp. 37–41.

15 William Baldwin, "This Is the Answer," *Forbes,* July 5, 1982, pp. 50ff.

16 Leonard R. Sayles, "Job Enrichment: Little That's New—and Right for the Wrong Reasons," in Gerald G. Somers (ed.), *Proceedings of the Twenty-Sixth Annual Winter Meeting,* Madison, Wis.: Industrial Relations Research Association, 1974, p. 207. Reprinted with permission.

17 Charles Babbage, *On the Economy of Machinery and Manufactures,* London: Charles Knight, 1832, p. 177.

18 Stephen Solomon, "How a Whole Company Earned Itself a Roman Holiday," *Fortune,* Jan. 15, 1979, pp. 80–83.

19 See, for example, Judith Ramquist, "SMR Forum: Labor-Management Cooperation—The Scanlon Plan at Work," *Sloan Management Review,* Spring 1982, pp. 49–55; and "Incentive Program: Key Role in Turnaround," *Management Review,* August 1983, pp. 43–44.

20 For a discussion of the analogous group reward plans in Japan, see Jon P. Alston, "Awarding Bonuses the Japanese Way," *Business Horizons,* September–October 1982, pp. 46–50.

21 Linda S. Tyler and Bob Fisher, "The Scanlon Concept: A Philosophy As Much As a System," *Personnel Administrator,* July 1983, pp. 33–37.

22 K. Dow Scott and Timothy Cotter, "The Team that Works Together, Earns Together," *Personnel Journal,* March 1984, pp. 59ff; James W. Driscoll, "Working Creatively with a Union: Lessons from the Scanlon Plan," *Organizational Dynamics,* Summer 1979, pp. 61–80; and J. Kenneth White, "The Scanlon Plan: Causes and Correlates of Success," *Academy of Management Journal,* June 1979, pp. 292–312.

23 John D. McMillan and Valerie C. Williams, "The Elements of Effective Salary Administration Programs," *Personnel Journal,* November 1982, pp. 832–838.

24 Time off without pay to relieve stress and pursue leisure activities is also valued by some employees and is a unique form of reward that might be part of a total "pay" system. See J. H. Foegen, "Time-off without Pay: Value Can Exceed Cost," *Human Resource Management,* Summer 1981, pp. 10–12.

25 Albert Cole, Jr., "Flexible Benefits Are a Key to Better Employee Relations," *Personnel Journal,* January 1983, pp. 49–53; and Lawrence B. Chonko and Ricky W. Griffin, "Trade-off Analysis Finds the Best Reward Combinations," *Personnel Administrator,* May 1983, pp. 45–47ff.

26 Robert B. Cockrum, "Has the Time Come for Employee Cafeteria Plans?" *Personnel Administrator,* July 1982, pp. 66–72.

27 This exercise was developed from material in Stephen L. Cohen and Cabot L. Jaffee, "Managing Human Performance for Productivity," *Training and Development Journal,* December 1982, pp. 94–100.

FOR ADDITIONAL READING

Bernardin, H. John, and Richard W. Beatty, *Performance Appraisal,* Boston, Mass.: Kent Publishing Co., 1984.

Carroll, Stephen J., and Craig E. Schneier, *Performance Appraisal and Review Systems,* Glenview, Ill.: Scott, Foresman and Company, 1982.

Henderson, Richard I., *Compensation Management: Rewarding Performance,* Reston, Va.: Reston Publishing Co., 1979.

Latham, Gary P., and Kenneth N. Wexley, *Increasing Productivity through Performance Appraisal,* Reading, Mass.: Addison-Wesley Publishing Company, Inc., 1981.

Lawler, Edward W., III, *Pay and Organizational Effectiveness: A Psychological View,* New York: McGraw-Hill Book Company, 1971.

Moore, Brian E., and Timothy L. Ross, *The Scanlon Way to Improved Productivity: A Practical Guide,* New York: John Wiley & Sons, Inc., 1978.

Patten, Thomas H., Jr., *A Manager's Guide to Performance Appraisal,* New York: The Free Press, 1982.

Sashkin, Marshall, *Assessing Performance Appraisal,* San Diego, Calif.: University Associates, 1981.

Wallace, Marc J., Jr., and Charles H. Fay, *Compensation Theory and Practice,* Boston, Mass.: Kent Publishing Company, 1983.

LEADERSHIP AND ORGANIZATIONAL CHANGE

LEADERSHIP AND SUPERVISION

The leader *role is clearly among the most significant of all roles.*

Henry Mintzberg[1]

Leadership is still an art despite the efforts of social science researchers to make it a science.

James Owens[2]

CHAPTER OBJECTIVES

TO UNDERSTAND:
The nature of leadership
The path-goal model of leadership
Power and politics in organizations
Distinctions between Theory X and Theory Y
Different leadership styles
The contingency model of leadership
Views of the supervisor's leadership role

*Definition of
leadership*

Human beings are the most precious part of civilization. What responsibility could be more important than the leadership and development of
people, as Mintzberg notes in the opening reference? Without leadership, an
organization is only a confusion of people and machines. *Leadership* is the
process of encouraging and helping others to work enthusiastically toward
objectives. It is the human factor that binds a group together and motivates it
toward goals.

The leader's act of motivation is similar in effect to that of the secret
chemical that turns the insect pupa into a butterfly with all the beauty that was
the pupa's potential. Leadership transforms potential into reality. This was
the role played by Lee Iacocca, who provided superb leadership to guide
Chrysler Corporation out of hard times in the early 1980s. Leadership is the
ultimate act that brings to success all the potential that is in an organization
and its people. It is so important that people have been concerned about it
since the beginning of history.

In this chapter we discuss the nature of leadership—the behaviors, roles,
and skills that combine to form different leadership styles. A contingency
framework is presented to encourage managers to examine the fit between
their style and situation. We conclude with a section on supervision, since
supervisors accent somewhat different leadership roles compared with higher
managers.

THE NATURE OF LEADERSHIP

*Leadership
compared with
management*

Leadership is an important part of management but not all of it. Managers
are required to plan and organize, for example, but the primary role of a
leader is to influence others to seek defined objectives enthusiastically. This
means that strong leaders may be weak managers if their poor planning causes
their group to move in wrong directions. Though they can get their group
going, they just cannot get it going in directions that serve organizational
objectives.

Other combinations also are possible. A person can be a weak leader and
still be a relatively effective manager, especially if one happens to be
managing people who clearly understand their jobs and have strong drives to
work. This set of circumstances is less likely, and therefore we expect
excellent managers to have reasonably high leadership ability.

Leadership behavior

Formerly it was thought that personal traits were the major source of
successful leadership,[3] but more recent emphasis is on identifying leadership
behaviors. That is, successful leadership depends on appropriate behaviors,

skills, and actions, not personal traits. Leaders use three different types of skills—technical, human, and conceptual.[4] Although these skills are interrelated in practice, they can be considered separately.

Technical skill refers to a person's knowledge and ability in any type of process or technique. Examples are the skills learned by accountants, engineers, typists, and toolmakers. This skill is the distinguishing feature of job performance at the operating level, but as employees are promoted to leadership responsibilities, their technical skills become proportionately less important, as shown in Figure 8-1. They increasingly depend on the technical skills of their subordinates and in many cases have never practiced some of the technical skills that they supervise.

Three leadership skills

Human skill is the ability to work effectively with people and to build teamwork. No leader at any organizational level escapes the requirement for effective human skill. It is a major part of leadership behavior and is discussed throughout this book.

Conceptual skill is the ability to think in terms of models, frameworks, and broad relationships, such as long-range plans. It becomes increasingly important in higher managerial jobs. Conceptual skill deals with ideas, while human skill concerns people and technical skill is with things.

Analysis of leadership skills helps to explain why outstanding department heads sometimes make poor vice presidents. They may lack the proper mixture of skills required for the higher-level job, particularly additional conceptual skill.

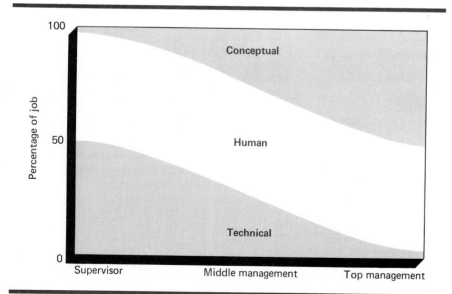

Figure 8-1
Variations in use of leadership skills at different organizational levels

Situational aspects

Successful leadership requires behavior that unites and stimulates followers toward defined objectives in specific situations. All three elements—leader, followers, and situation—are variables that affect each other in determining appropriate leadership behavior.

> **The interdependence of leader, follower, and situation is illustrated by a hard-boiled superintendent, Gregg Hicks, who still is managing the way he was twenty years ago. He thinks that leadership resides in himself alone, untouched by outside influences. He fails to realize that as his people and environment change, he needs to change his leadership. Though his style of leadership was acceptable twenty years ago, it is not acceptable today.**

It is evident that leadership is situational. In one situation, action A may be the best cluster of leadership acts, but in the next situation, action B will be best. To try to have all an organization's leaders fit a standard pattern will suppress creative differences and be inefficient as well, because many square pegs will be trying to fit into round holes. Leadership is part of a complex system, so there is no simple way to answer "What makes a leader?"

Sometimes leaders must resist the temptation to be visible in a situation. Even though good leadership involves a set of behaviors, it should not be confused with mere activity when it is not needed. Aggressiveness and constant interaction with others will not guarantee good leadership. At times the appropriate leadership action is to stay in the background keeping pressures off the group, to keep quiet so that others may talk, to be calm in times of uproar, to hesitate, and to delay decisions.

Leaders as followers

With few exceptions, leaders in organizations are also *followers*.[5] They nearly always report to someone else. Even the president reports to a board of directors. Leaders must be able to wear both hats gracefully, to be able to relate both upward and downward. They need validation from higher authority just as much as they need support from followers. In formal organizations of several levels, ability to follow is one of the first requirements for good leadership. It is the key that unlocks the door to leadership opportunities and keeps the leader in balance with the rest of the organization.

Followership skills

> **A vice president of Saga Corporation suggests that most people fail in jobs because they lack followership skills. These are behaviors that help a person to be an effective subordinate and may include avoiding competition with the leader, acting as a loyal devil's advocate, and constructively confronting the leader's ideas, values, and behavior.[6]**

What must a leader do to obtain these behaviors from employees? The next section will present a model of leadership behavior that revolves around goals and a support system for accomplishing them.

Robert House and others have developed and refined a path-goal view of leadership, which is derived from the expectancy model of motivation (see Chapter 5).[7] The *path-goal model of leadership* states that the leader's job is to create a work environment through structure, support, and rewards that helps employees reach the organization's goals. The two major roles involved are to create a goal orientation and to improve the path toward the goals so that they will be attained.

Figure 8-2 shows the path-goal process. Leaders identify employee needs, provide appropriate goals, and then connect goal accomplishment to rewards by clarifying expectancy and instrumentality relationships. Barriers to performance are removed, and guidance is provided to the employee. The result of the process is job satisfaction, acceptance of the leader, and greater motivation.

Path-goal process

Goal setting

Goal setting plays a central role in the path-goal process. It is the establishment of targets and objectives for successful performance, both long-run and short-run. It provides a measure of how well individuals and groups are meeting performance standards.

Figure 8-2
The path-goal
leadership process

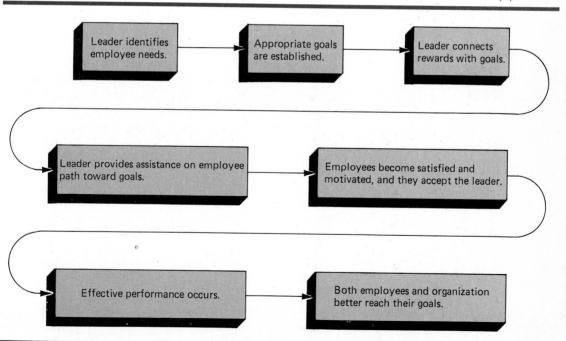

The theory underlying goal setting is that human behavior is goal-directed.[8] Group members need to feel that they have a worthwhile goal that can be reached with the resources and leadership available. Without goals, different members go in different directions. This difficulty will continue as long as there is no common understanding of the goals involved.

The goal-setting process requires at least four steps, as follows: define the goals, set specific goals, make them challenging, and give feedback about goal accomplishment.

Explain the purpose. **Goal definition** Proper goal definition requires a leader to explain the purpose behind goals and the necessity for them. Whatever the situation, people need goals that are meaningful to them in order to be fully motivated. Following is an example of how a government manager learned the hard way about the importance of goal definition.

> A federal staff executive from Washington named Bailey appeared at a large federal regional office and called a meeting of its entire accounting staff of forty employees. When Bailey was introduced by the accounting chief, he immediately launched into an explanation of certain special work that all the staff would need to do quickly on overtime. The people were antagonistic and responded coldly. (Bailey commented later, "There was so much ice in that room that it cracked.") They objected strongly and started to ridicule Washington leadership. Bailey saw he was in trouble and tried to determine what was wrong.
>
> He soon discovered that the staff did not know the purpose of the extra work. The accounting chief assumed Bailey would tell why the work was required, and Bailey assumed the staff already knew! As soon as Bailey explained why the work was needed, the group switched to an attitude of cooperation—and even enthusiasm. Bailey later reported, "That one incident taught me never to make assumptions about goals when I am motivating people."

Be specific. **Specific goals** Goals need to be as specific as possible so that employees will know when a goal is reached. It is not enough to say, "Do your best," because that kind of goal is not specific enough for most people.

> In one instance goal setting was used with logging-truck drivers to encourage them to carry loads nearer the legal capacity of their trucks.[9] Under instructions to "do your best," the drivers had been carrying about 60 percent of the legal limit. After goals were more specifically set, performance increased to slightly over 90 percent of the legal limit, and this level continued for the next twelve months. Drivers were given no extra rewards other than recognition for their higher production. Nevertheless, they seemed to feel a sense of achievement in meeting their goals and judging the loading of their trucks to the legal limit, so their performance was better.

Make it challenging. **Goal difficulty** Somewhat surprisingly, most employees work harder when they have difficult goals to accomplish rather than easy ones.[10] Hard goals present a challenge that appeals to the achievement motive within employees. To obtain commitment to difficult goals, however, managers typically invite employees to participate in the goal-setting process. In this way, employees make a conscious commitment to achieving the goal.

Feedback about progress toward goals When people have well-defined goals, then they need feedback about how well they are reaching their goals. Otherwise, they are "working in the dark" and have no way to know how successful they are. A ball team needs to know its score if the team members are to remain motivated, and the same can be said for a team on a production line or in an office. Job feedback tends to encourage better job performance, and self-generated feedback is an especially powerful motivational tool.

Provide feedback.

One study examined the performance of 209 engineers working in project teams at six different sites.[11] Engineers receiving feedback controlled costs better and had fewer overtime hours. Self-generated feedback groups were superior to those receiving external feedback as judged by cost control, quality control, and overtime. In addition, they expressed greater intrinsic satisfaction and commitment to the organization.

Path improvement

The steps surrounding goal setting represent only half of the path-goal leadership process. Leaders also need to consider some contingency factors (such as employee personality characteristics and nature of the task) before deciding how to go about smoothing the path toward a goal. A discussion of path-oriented ideas, including management by objectives, follows.

Task and psychological support Leaders provide both task and psychological support for their employees. They provide task support when they help assemble the resources, budgets, power, and other elements that are essential to get the job done. Equally important, they can remove environmental constraints that sometimes inhibit employee performance, exhibit upward influence, and provide recognition contingent upon effective effort and performance.[12] But psychological support is also needed. Leaders must stimulate people to want to do the job. The combination of task and psychological support in a leader is described by a telephone company employee as follows:[13]

> There is a supervisor here in the Western Area who is the epitome of a leader. The reason? He cares. He cares about people [psychological support] and about getting the job done right [task support]. His enthusiasm is real, not forced, and it's quite contagious. His employees want to work for him and learn from him.
>   It all stems from two basic reasons: he knows what he's talking about and he treats subordinates like they are rational human beings with the ability to do the job. And he expects them to do it. He gives them the recognition that their work is important. Therefore, people get the feeling that they are working with him to get the entire job done.

Role modeling It is said that "supervisors tend to supervise as they themselves are supervised." The same thought applies to leaders. They serve as *role models,* or examples, for their followers, who tend to act in about the same way that the leaders do. For example, if a leader is considerate and

Leaders are role models.

supportive with followers, their responses are likely to be similar. If a leader follows an opposite pattern, however, employees also may turn opposite.

> In a state tax office, a manager named Rebecca Lapp blamed either followers or superiors whenever a problem developed. She also delayed work until deadlines approached, which led to rushed work and pressure on the group. She was impatient with others. Gradually, over time, her employees developed similar behavior, so performance in the office was poor. Rebecca was not an effective leader.

Power and politics

All leaders deal with power and politics. *Power* is the ability to influence other people and events. It is the leader's stock in trade, the way that leaders extend their influence to others. It is somewhat different from authority, because authority is delegated by higher management. Power, on the other hand, is earned and gained by leaders on the basis of their personalities, activities, and the situations in which they operate.

Politics relates to the ways that leaders gain and use power. It is necessary to help a leader keep "on top of a situation" and control events toward desired objectives.[14] Politics concerns balances of power, saving face, "horse trading," "mending fences," ingenious compromises, trade-offs, and a variety of other activities. It has been a classic human activity since the beginning of civilization, so it is not unique to modern organizations. But modern organizations are a fertile place for politics to thrive. Observers have said that leaders who are otherwise capable but who lack basic political skills will have trouble rising to the top in modern organizations. In the words of one observer, political power is "one of the few mechanisms available for aligning an organization with its own reality."[15] In simple terms, political skills are essential for leaders, both for their personal success and for smoothing the path to employee performance.

Types of power

Four sources of power

Power develops in a number of ways. Following are the major types of organizational power and their sources.

Personal power Personal power—also called referent power, charismatic power, and power of personality—comes from each leader individually. It is the ability of leaders to develop followers from the strength of their own personalities. They have a personal magnetism, an air of confidence, and a belief in objectives that attracts and holds followers. People follow because they want to do so; their emotions tell them to do so. The leader senses the needs of people and promises success in reaching them. Well-known historical examples are Joan of Arc in France, Mahatma Gandhi in India, and Franklin D. Roosevelt in the United States.

Legitimate power   *Legitimate power,* also known as position power and official power, comes from higher authority. It arises from the culture of society by which power is delegated legitimately from higher established authorities to others. It gives leaders the power to control resources and to reward and punish others. People accept this power because they believe it is desirable and necessary to maintain order and discourage anarchy in a society. There is social pressure from peers and friends who accept it and expect others to accept it.

Expert power   *Expert power,* also known as the authority of knowledge, comes from specialized learning. It is power that arises from a person's knowledge of and information about a complex situation. It depends on education, training, and experience, so it is an important type of power in our modern technological society. For example, if your spouse were having an attack of some type in a hospital emergency room, you would be likely to give your attention to the physician who comes in to provide treatment rather than to the helper who is delivering fresh laundry supplies. The reason is that you expect the physician to be a capable expert in the situation.

Political power   *Political power* comes from the support of a group. It arises from a leader's ability to work with people and social systems to gain their allegiance and support. It develops in all organizations.

The types of power are developed from different sources, but they are interrelated in practice. When one power base is removed from supervisors, employees perceive that other bases of influence decline as well.[16] Other studies indicate that the use of a power base must fit its organizational context for it to be effective. Political power thrives when the organizational and technical environment is uncertain,[17] and it will now be presented in greater detail.

Tactics used to gain political power

There are a number of tactics that leaders can use to gain political power; several examples are given in Figure 8-3. Two of the most popular ones are social exchanges and alliances of various types. Social exchange implies, "If you'll do something for me, I'll do something for you." It relies on the powerful *norm of reciprocity* in society, where two people in a continuing relationship feel a strong obligation to repay their social "debts" to each other. When these trade-offs are successfully arranged, both parties get something they want. Continuing exchanges over a period of time usually lead to an alliance in which two or more persons join in a longer-term power group to get benefits that they mutually desire.

Norm of reciprocity

Another popular path toward political power is to become identified with a higher authority and/or a powerful figure in an organization. Then, as the saying goes, some of the power "rubs off" on you. Often this identification

TACTIC USED	EXAMPLE
Social exchange	In a trade-off the chief engineer helps the factory manager get a new machine approved if the manager will support an engineering project.
Alliances	The information system manager and the financial vice president join together to work for a new computer system.
Identification with higher authority	The president's personal assistant makes minor decisions for her.
Control of information	The research and development manager controls new product information needed by the marketing manager.
Selective service	The purchasing manager selectively gives faster service to more cooperative associates.
Power and status symbols	The new controller arranges to double the size of the office, decorate lavishly, and employ a personal assistant.
Power plays	Manager A arranges with the vice president to transfer part of manager B's department to A.
Networks	A young manager joins a racquetball club.

Figure 8-3
Examples of tactics used to gain political power

gains you special privileges, and in many cases you become recognized as a representative or spokesperson for the more powerful figure. Others may share problems with you, hoping that you will help them gain access to the higher figure. An example of identification is the president's personal assistant who represents the president in many contacts with others.

In one company the president's personal assistant, Howard Janus, became widely accepted as the president's representative throughout the company. He issued instructions to other managers in the name of the president, so other managers accepted them as orders. He represented the president on special assignments. He controlled access to the president, and he partly controlled the flow of information both to and from the president. He handled power effectively and gradually became a major influence in the corporation. When the president retired, the assistant became a major executive and was accepted by other managers.

Another popular way to acquire political power is to give service selectively to your supporters. For example, a purchasing manager gives faster service and "bends the rules" to help friends who support the purchasing function. Another tactic is to acquire power and status symbols that imply that you are an important person in the firm, although this can backfire if you do not have power equal to your symbols.

Some managers use the more aggressive tactic of power plays to grab power from others. This approach is risky because others may retaliate in ways that weaken the power-grabbing manager's power.

A common tactic for increasing power is to join or form interest groups that have a common objective. These networks operate on the basis of friendships and personal contacts, and may provide a meeting place for influential people.[18] A young manager who joins the chamber of commerce or a racquetball club is opening the door to new contacts that may be useful.

As illustrated by the following example, power and politics are a basic part of leadership success in an organization.

Management in a state office was considering whether to move a certain activity from one department to another. Finally the director of the entire operation decided to hold a staff meeting of all senior managers to decide where the disputed activity should be located. Prior to the meeting the manager of the department that wanted the activity prepared an elaborate and convincing report that fully supported moving the activity to her department. Meanwhile the manager of the department that might lose the activity was visiting all committee members to mend fences, make trades, and support her department's point of view.

When the committee met two weeks later, most of its members already had decided in favor of the manager who used the political approach. The convincing logic of the written report was ignored, and the committee voted to retain the activity in its present location. Political skills won the dispute.

Management by objectives

A popular approach that illustrates some aspects of path-goal leadership is *management by objectives* (MBO).[19] Generally, MBO involves a procedure similar to that shown in Figure 8-4. An employee considers job and personal goals for the next period and then prepares a list of objectives for that period.

What is MBO?

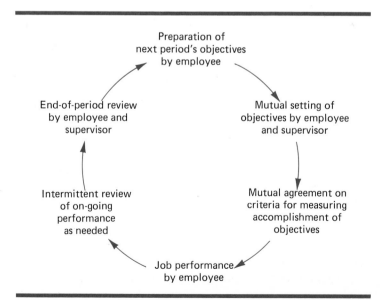

Figure 8-4
Circular process of management by objectives

Preparation of next period's objectives by employee

Mutual setting of objectives by employee and supervisor

Mutual agreement on criteria for measuring accomplishment of objectives

Job performance by employee

Intermittent review of on-going performance as needed

End-of-period review by employee and supervisor

The employee presents the list to the supervisor, and, through mutual discussion, they agree on the employee's objectives for the next year. They also reach agreement on the criteria that will be used to measure accomplishment of the objectives. Then the employee works toward performance according to the objectives established.

> One study of managers in a service organization found that the level of agreement between managers and employees on the elements of an employee's job averaged only 75 percent.[20] However, there were strong correlations between manager-employee agreement on job elements and goal attainment by employees. The implication for MBO users is obvious—goal clarification is an important early step in the process.

In order to support employee autonomy and growth, the employee is given as much freedom as possible to determine how the chosen objectives will be met. Instead of close supervision, there is intermittent review of ongoing performance as needed. In this way corrective action can be taken if performance begins to vary too far from objectives. Finally, at the end of the period, there is a more formal review and a new setting of objectives by the employee, which begins the entire process for the next period. The result is the circular, self-renewing process shown in the figure.

Suitability of MBO   MBO is especially suitable for managerial, professional, and sales people and those who work independently. For example, it can be applied to field salespersons who travel from their home locations for a week at a time. They are working independently under conditions where internal motivation is important. There also are objective criteria for measuring performance, such as amount of sales, kinds of sales, number of sales calls, and number of complaints. On the other hand, MBO is less applicable to routine worker-level jobs, such as an assembly line.

Role relationships in MBO   MBO changes the role relationships of subordinates and managers. Employees are given more responsibility for determining their own job objectives and encouraged to take new initiative to plan their methods and pace of work. Finally, they have a larger role in appraising their own performance.

The role of management also changes. After reaching consensus on the goals to be achieved, the managerial role becomes a supportive one. The dual task is to connect rewards to effort and performance and provide supportive services so that employees can better succeed.

It is difficult for both supervisors and employees to change their role relationships, so changes are likely to occur slowly. Many employees are not used to setting their own objectives, so they may proceed cautiously. Some managers may have initial difficulty learning to ask, "How can I help?" rather than saying, "Here's how you should do it." The net result is that a successful MBO program takes a long time to develop, and much training may be required.

The total pattern of leaders' actions, as perceived by their employees, is called *leadership style*. It represents their philosophy, skills, and attitudes in practice. The styles that are discussed differ on the basis of motivation, power, or orientation toward tasks and people. Although they are typically used in combination or even applied differently to various employees, they are discussed separately to highlight the contrasts among them. The impact of assumptions on leadership style is presented first.

Theory X and Theory Y

In 1957, Douglas McGregor presented a convincing argument that most management actions flow directly from whatever theory of human behavior managers hold.[21] The idea is that *management philosophy controls practice*. Management's personnel practices, decision making, operating practices, and even organizational design flow from assumptions about human behavior. The assumptions may be implicit rather than explicit, but they can be inferred from observing the kinds of actions that managers take.

Theory X is a traditional set of assumptions about people. As shown in Figure 8-5, it assumes that most people dislike work and will try to avoid it if possible. They engage in various work restrictions, have little ambition, and will avoid responsibility if at all possible. They are relatively self-centered, indifferent to organizational needs, and resistant to change. The common rewards given by organizations are not enough to overcome their dislike for

Theory X assumptions

Theory X	Theory Y
• The typical person dislikes work and will avoid it if possible.	• Work is as natural as play or rest.
• The typical person lacks responsibility, has little ambition, and seeks security above all.	• People are not inherently lazy. They have become that way as a result of experience.
• Most people must be coerced, controlled, and threatened with punishment to get them to work.	• People will exercise self-direction and self-control in the service of objectives to which they are commited.
	• People have potential. Under proper conditions they learn to accept and seek responsibility. They have imagination, ingenuity, and creativity that can be applied to work.
With these assumptions the managerial role is to coerce and control employees.	With these assumptions the managerial role is to develop the potential in employees and help them release that potential toward common objectives.

Figure 8-5
McGregor's Theory X and Theory Y, alternative assumptions about employees

work, so the only way that management can secure high employee performance is to coerce, control, and threaten them. Though managers may deny that they have this view of people, their actions strongly suggest that Theory X is their typical assumption about employees.

Theory Y assumptions

Theory Y implies a more human and supportive approach to managing people. It assumes that people are not inherently lazy. Any appearance they have of being that way is the result of their experiences with organizations; but if management will provide the proper environment to release their potential, work will become as natural to them as play or rest. They will exercise self-direction and self-control in the service of objectives to which they are committed. Management's role is to provide an environment in which the potential of people can be released at work.

McGregor's argument was that management has been ignoring the facts about people. It had been following an outmoded set of assumptions about people because it adhered to Theory X when the facts are that most people are closer to the Theory Y set of assumptions. There are important differences among people, so a few may come closer to Theory X, but nearly all employees have some Theory Y potential for growth. Therefore, McGregor argued, management needed to change to a whole new theory of working with people: Theory Y. The relationship between alternative assumptions about human behavior and leadership styles can be seen throughout the following paragraphs.

Positive and negative leaders

There are differences in the ways leaders approach people to motivate them. If the approach emphasizes rewards—economic or otherwise—the leader

Positive leadership

uses *positive leadership*. Better employee education, greater demands for independence, and other factors have made satisfactory employee motivation more dependent on positive leadership.

Negative leadership

If emphasis is placed on penalties, the leader is applying *negative leadership*. This approach can get acceptable performance in many situations, but it has high human costs. Negative leaders act domineering and superior with people. To get work done, they hold over their personnel such penalties as loss of job, reprimand in the presence of others, and a few days off without pay. They display authority in the false belief that it frightens everyone into productivity. They are bosses more than leaders.

A continuum of leadership styles exists, ranging from strongly positive to strongly negative. Almost any manager uses both styles somewhere on the continuum every day, but the dominant style sets a tone within the group. Style is related to one's model of organizational behavior. The autocratic model tends to produce a negative style; the custodial model is somewhat positive; and the supportive and collegial models are clearly positive. Positive leadership generally achieves higher job satisfaction and performance.[22]

Autocratic, participative, and free-rein leaders

The way in which a leader uses power also establishes a type of style. Each style—autocratic, participative, and free-rein—has its benefits and limitations. A leader uses all three styles over a period of time, but one style tends to be the dominant one. An illustration is a factory supervisor who is normally autocratic, but she is participative in determining vacation schedules, and she is free-rein in selecting a department representative for the safety committee.

Autocratic leaders *Autocratic leaders* centralize power and decision making in themselves, as shown in Figure 8-6. They structure the complete work situation for their employees, who do what they are told. The leaders take full authority and assume full responsibility. Autocratic leadership typically is negative, based on threats and punishment; but it can be positive, as demonstrated by the *benevolent autocrat* who chooses to give rewards to employees.

Some advantages of autocratic leadership are that it is often satisfying for the leader, permits quick decisions, allows the use of less competent subordinates, and provides security and structure for employees. The main disadvantage is that people dislike it, especially if it is extreme to the point of creating fear and frustration.

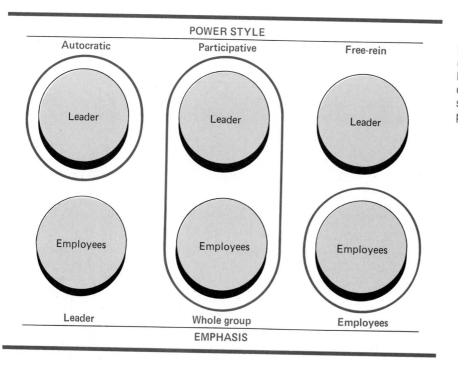

Figure 8-6
Different emphasis (shown by colored lines) results from different leadership styles in use of power

Participative leaders   *Participative leaders* decentralize authority. Participative decisions are not unilateral, as with the autocrat, because they arise from consultation with followers and participation by them. The leader and group are acting as a social unit, as illustrated in Figure 8-6. Employees are informed about conditions affecting their jobs and encouraged to express their ideas and make suggestions. The general trend is toward wider use of participative practices because they are consistent with the supportive and collegial models of organizational behavior. Because of its importance, participative management is discussed in the next chapter.

Free-rein leaders   *Free-rein leaders* avoid power and responsibility. They depend largely upon the group to establish its own goals and work out its own problems. Group members train themselves and provide their own motivation. The leader plays only a minor role. Free-rein leadership ignores the leader's contribution approximately in the same way that autocratic leadership ignores the group. It tends to permit different units of an organization to proceed at cross-purposes, and it can degenerate into chaos. For these reasons normally it is not used as a dominant style but is useful in those situations where a leader can leave a choice entirely to the group.

Leader use of consideration and structure

Employee and task orientations   Two different leadership styles with employees are *consideration* and *structure,* also known as employee orientation and task orientation. There is consistent evidence that leaders secure somewhat higher performance and job satisfaction if high consideration is their dominant leadership style. Considerate leaders are concerned about the human needs of their employees. They try to build teamwork and help employees with their problems. Structured, task-oriented leaders, on the other hand, believe that they get results by keeping people constantly busy and urging them to produce.

> The difference between the two orientations is illustrated by the reply of Paul Blumberg, a mine superintendent in a Western mining town. A clerk brought him the following news about one of his truck drivers: "John Jones just ran the truck off the road into Mile Deep Canyon." The superintendent's task-oriented reply was, "Get another truck out there right away and get that ore to the mill." (We wonder what happened to Jones.)

Consideration and structure appear to be somewhat independent of each other, so they should not necessarily be viewed as opposite ends of a continuum. A manager who becomes more considerate does not necessarily become less structured. A manager may have both orientations in varying degrees. If consideration exists alone, production may be bypassed for superficial popularity and contentment; so it appears that the most successful managers are those who combine relatively high consideration and structure, giving somewhat more emphasis to consideration.[23]

Early research on consideration and structure was done at the University of

Michigan and Ohio State University. In several types of environment, such as truck manufacturing, railroad construction, and insurance offices, the strongly considerate leader achieved somewhat higher job satisfaction and productivity. Subsequent studies confirm this general tendency and report desirable side effects, such as lower grievance rates, lower turnover, and reduced stress within the group.[24] Conversely, turnover, stress, and other problems are likely to occur if a manager is unable to develop consideration.

A contingency model of leadership

The positive, participative, considerate leader is not always the best leader. At times there are exceptions. The model that helps explain these exceptions is the *contingency* (or *situational*) *model of leadership* developed by Fiedler and associates.[25] The contingency model states that the most appropriate style of leadership depends on the situation in which the leader works. More specifically, the best leadership style depends on whether the situation is favorable, unfavorable, or in an intermediate range of favorability to the leader. As the situation varies, leadership requirements also vary.

Fiedler shows that a leader's effectiveness is determined by the interaction of employee orientation with three additional variables that relate to the followers, the task, and the organization. They are leader-member relations, task structure, and leader position power. *Leader-member relations* are determined by the manner in which the leader is accepted by the group. If, for example, there is group friction with the leader, rejection of the leader, and reluctant compliance with orders, then leader-member relations are low. *Task structure* reflects the degree to which one specific way is required to do the job. *Leader position power* describes the organizational power that goes with the position the leader occupies. Examples are power to hire and fire, status symbols, and power to give pay raises and promotions.

Three situational variables

The relationship among these variables is shown in Figure 8-7. High and low employee orientation are shown on the vertical scale. Various combinations of the other three variables are shown in the horizontal scale, arranged from leader-favorable conditions to leader-unfavorable conditions. Each dot on the chart represents the data from a specific research project. The chart clearly shows that the considerate, employee-oriented manager is most successful in situations that have intermediate favorableness to the leader (the middle of the chart). At the chart's extremes, which represent conditions either quite favorable or quite unfavorable to the leader, the structured, task-oriented leader seems to be more effective.

For example, the members of an automobile assembly-line crew have a structured task and a supervisor with strong position power. If leader-member relations are positive, the situation is favorable for task-oriented leaders who can use their strengths. Similarly, a structured leader is more effective in a position of weak power, low task structure, and poor leader-member relations. However, in intermediate conditions of favorableness, the considerate leader is the most effective; and these situations are the most common ones in work groups.

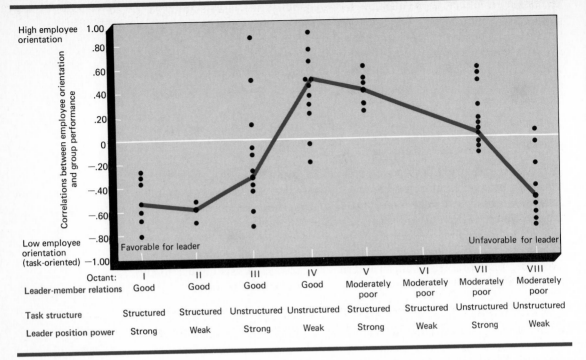

Octant:	I	II	III	IV	V	VI	VII	VIII
Leader-member relations	Good	Good	Good	Good	Moderately poor	Moderately poor	Moderately poor	Moderately poor
Task structure	Structured	Structured	Unstructured	Unstructured	Structured	Structured	Unstructured	Unstructured
Leader position power	Strong	Weak	Strong	Weak	Strong	Weak	Strong	Weak

Figure 8-7
Research showing how the contingency model of leadership applies

Adapted from A Theory of Leadership Effectiveness, *by Fred E. Fiedler, p. 146. Copyright © 1967 by McGraw-Hill Book Company. Used with permission of McGraw-Hill Book Company.*

The conclusions of the Fiedler model may be explained in the following manner. In highly unstructured situations the leader's structure and control are seen as removing undesirable ambiguity and the anxiety that results from it, so a structured approach may be preferred. In situations where the task is highly routine and the leader has good relations with the employees, they may perceive a task orientation as supportive to their job performance (clearing the path). The remaining broad middle ground requires better leader-member relations to be established, so a more considerate, employee-oriented leader is effective.

Despite criticism, the contingency model has made a major contribution to discussions on leadership style. For example, managers are encouraged to:[26]

- Examine their situation—the people, task, and organization
- Be flexible in the use of various skills within an overall style
- Consider modifying elements of their jobs to obtain a better match with their preferred style

A new direction

Are there substitutes for leadership?

A different approach to the study of leadership has been proposed by Steven Kerr and others.[27] Taking a contingency orientation, they suggest that there are some situations where *neither* a considerate nor structured leader is necessary. In effect, there may be characteristics of the task, employees, or the organization that provide *substitutes for leadership*. Some of these possibilities, such as self-management, are listed in Figure 8-8.[28] However, more research is needed before a clear pattern can emerge.

The supervisor's unique leadership role

Supervisors are leaders who occupy positions at the lowest management level in organizations. They supervise *nonmanagement employees*, while higher managers primarily supervise *other managers* below them. This means that supervisors, not managers, are the point of direct contact with most employees.

Supervisors need to be leaders just as other managers do. However, the unique organizational positions of supervisors complicates their leadership job and merits further discussion. There are five rather different views of the supervisor's job, as shown in Figure 8-9 and discussed below: key person, supervisor in the middle, marginal supervisor, another worker, and behavioral specialist.

Key person in management The traditional management view of supervisors is that they are key persons in management. They make decisions, control work, interpret policy, and generally are the key people in the process of accomplishing work. They represent management to the workers, and they also represent workers to management. Higher management knows its workers primarily through supervisors. They are an essential element because they are strategically located on the chains of authority and communication; they can block anything going upward or downward. A supervisor is like the hub of a wheel, around which everything revolves.

This key-person concept tends to prevail in management literature and speeches. Managers apparently believe it. However, surveys of supervisors show that only 40 percent feel they are a real part of company management.[29]

Five views

SOURCE	NATURE
Task	1 Intrinsic satisfaction
	2 Feedback from the task itself
	3 Routine, predictable tasks
Organization	1 Cohesive work groups
	2 Explicit plans, goals, and procedures
	3 Decentralized decision making
Employees	1 Professional orientation
	2 Ability, experience, training, and knowledge
	3 Capacity for self-management

Figure 8-8
Some potential substitutes for leadership
Adapted from Jon P. Howell and Peter Dorfman, "Substitutes for Leadership: Test of a Construct," Academy of Management Journal, *December 1981, pp. 714–728.*

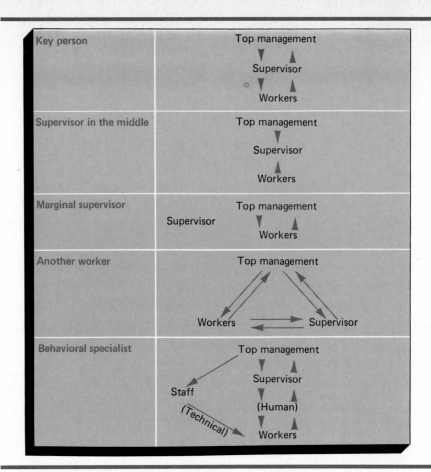

Figure 8-9
Different viewpoints
of the supervisor's
role

Supervisor in the middle According to the in-the-middle viewpoint, supervisors are pressed between opposing social forces of management and workers. Management has one set of expectations for supervisors. It wants them to prevent waste, keep employees disciplined, control production, and otherwise carry out its plans. It demands loyalty and maximum effort. Its expectations are largely technical or production-centered.

The pressures brought by workers, on the other hand, are largely matters of feeling. They want their supervisor "to be a good supervisor," to keep them out of trouble, to interpret their fears and wants to management, and to be loyal to them. In short, management expects one set of responses from the supervisor and workers expect another. The supervisor is caught between opposing forces, knowing that the expectations of both cannot be met. The result is that many supervisors find themselves in ambiguous situations in which, because of different expectations from different groups, they are not

sure of the right course of action. In-the-middle supervisors become frustrated because they are victims of the situation, not supervisors of it.

CHAPTER 8:
LEADERSHIP **177**
AND SUPERVISION

The marginal supervisor   The marginal supervisor is left out of, or is at the
margin of, the principal activities and influences that affect the department.
Unaccepted by management, ignored by the staff, and not one of the workers,
the supervisor is truly the one who walks alone. Top management has
stockholders, other managers, and staff specialists supporting it. Workers
have their union, their shop stewards, and their informal groups. But who
supports the supervisor?

Though the picture of marginal supervisors is bleak indeed, they sometimes
are found in organizations.[30] The fact that supervisors manage operating
employees instead of other managers places them in a position to feel
marginal in the beginning. In addition, various staff specialists make decisions
and issue instructions that supervisors merely transmit, if they see them at all.
Further, the supervisory role in labor relations is mostly a passive one. Others
above the supervisors conduct labor negotiations, and any labor decisions the
supervisors make are subject to review through the grievance procedure.
They feel obligated to act like managers, yet they do not receive the reward of
full participation in management. They are marginal persons.

Another worker   A fourth view of supervisors is that they remain employees
in all but title. First, they often lack authority. The center of decision making
is elsewhere, so that supervisors are only expediters who carry out decisions.
They perform operating work. They run errands, communicate, and make
records. Second, supervisors feel they are not a part of the management
group. They lack management status, and their thought patterns are much
closer to those of workers than to those of higher management. This means
that supervisors often tend to interpret management policies and actions in a
way differnet from that intended by management.

A behavioral specialist   Management in some situations looks upon the
supervisor as primarily a behavioral specialist. According to this view,
supervisors are specialists, just like most of the staff people with whom they
interact. They look after the human side of operations, and the staff handle its
technical side. Supervisors are not marginal, because they are definitely a part
of activities. Neither are they key persons; instead, they are among the many
specialists who deal with operating problems. Their specialty is human behavior. This viewpoint tends to be found in centralized, repetitive manufacturing, as on an assembly line.

Is the view of the supervisor as a behavioral specialist valid? It is partly, but
only partly. As shown in Figure 8-1 earlier in this chapter, human skills are a
significant part of every leader's job, but other skills also are needed.
Together, these skills form a balanced package. No capable supervisor is just
a specialist in one skill, such as human behavior.

What is the supervisor's leadership role?

Different parts of the supervisory job may fit all five of the viewpoints just mentioned. Supervisors are partly marginal persons, just another worker, and so on. There also are major differences among jobs such as assembly-line supervisor and supervisor of clerks in an insurance office. But there are basic similarities that permit description of the supervisor's job in general terms.

Perhaps foremost, supervisors are management people. They direct the work of others. Since supervisors are management's point of contact with workers and vice versa, they certainly are key people in management; but they also receive pressures from both sides (similar to the in-the-middle concept), and they need to be behavioral specialists in dealing with their people. These three ideas can be reconciled by considering the supervisor as *The supervisor* the *keystone,* not in management, but in the structure of the organization. As *is a keystone.* shown in Figure 8-10, the supervisor is like the keystone in an arch, the element that connects both sides and makes it possible for each to perform its function effectively. The sides are effectively joined only by using the keystone. It takes the pressures of both sides and uses them to strengthen, not weaken, the overall arch and to make success possible for the organization.

To the extent that supervisors feel marginal, they are out of the arch and unable to serve in their keystone function. To the extent that they are like

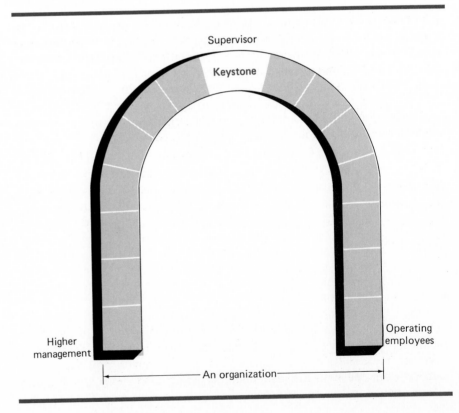

Figure 8-10
The supervisor's
keystone role in the
organizational arch

other workers, they are not in the keystone locations. The marginal-supervisor and another-worker concepts have no place in the keystone model of the supervisor's leadership role.

SUMMARY

Leadership is the process of encouraging and helping others to work enthusiastically toward objectives. It is determined primarily by one's role behavior, not by one's personal traits. Leaders' roles combine technical, human, and conceptual skills, which they apply on a situational basis. Their behavior as followers is also important to the organization.

The path-goal model of leadership accents two major roles. One is goal setting, and the other is supporting task accomplishment, where the use of power and politics become important tools. Management by objectives is a system that clarifies goals, as well as provides task and psychological support for employees.

Leaders apply different leadership styles. A positive, participative, considerate leader tends to be more effective in typical situations. However, as shown by the contingency model of leadership, a more autocratic style can be successful in situations that are either very favorable or very unfavorable to a leader.

Supervisors have somewhat different leadership roles because they are the point of direct contact with most employees. When an organization is compared to an arch, the supervisor is the keystone uniting higher management with employees.

TERMS AND CONCEPTS FOR REVIEW

Leadership

Technical, human, and conceptual skills

Path-goal leadership

Goal setting

Task and psychological support

Types of power

Politics

Management by objectives

Theory X and Theory Y

Different leadership styles

Contingency model of leadership

Substitutes for leadership

Keystone role of supervisors

REVIEW QUESTIONS

1 Think of the best leader you have ever worked with in a job, in sports, or in any other activity, and then the worst leader. Discuss the contrasting styles and skills used by the two. What caused you to select them?

2 It is said that leadership is situational and also that there may be substitutes for leadership. How can you reconcile these two statements?

3 Discuss your own experiences in a situation in which you were a leader. What leadership style did you use? Using hindsight, what would you have done differently?

4 Discuss why conceptual leadership skills become more important at higher organizational levels.

5 Discuss the relationship between the path-goal model of leadership and management by objectives.

6 Think of an organization in which you participated and discuss the power and politics in it. What types of power were used? What types of political tactics?

7 Explain how Theory X and Theory Y relate to leadership styles. Comment on the statement "Management philosophy controls practice."

8 Discuss how the contingency model of leadership applies to leadership styles.

9 Discuss the five views of the supervisor's leadership role and how these relate to the keystone concept.

INCIDENT

The Work Assignment

Effie Pardini supervised eleven accounting clerks in the budget and planning department of a large computer manufacturer. None of the clerks had accounting degrees, but all were skilled in handling records and figures. They primarily prepared budgetary plans and analyses for operating departments. Data inputs were secured from the departments and from company records. Pardini assigned projects to the clerks on the basis of their interests and skills. Some projects were more desirable than others because of prestige, challenge, the contacts required, or other factors; so there were occasional conflicts over which clerk was to receive a desirable project. One clerk who seemed especially sensitive and regularly complained about this issue was Sonia Prosser.

On one occasion Pardini received a desirable project and assigned it to a clerk by the name of Joe Madden. Prosser was particularly distressed because she felt she should have had the assignment. She was so distressed that she retaliated by gathering up her present assignment and putting it away in her desk. Then she took a book from her desk and started reading it. Since all the clerks were together in the same office, most of them observed her actions. She announced to one in a voice loud enough to be heard by others, "Nobody around here ever gives me a good assignment."

Pardini overheard Prosser's comment and looked up from her desk, noting what was happening. Pardini was angered, but she sat at her desk for five minutes wondering what to do. Meanwhile Prosser continued reading her book.

1 What leadership issues are raised by this incident?

2 Discuss what action Pardini should take. Consider politics and power, the path-goal model of leadership, and the contingency model of leadership before making your decision.

EXPERIENTIAL EXERCISE

Westgate Community Hospital

Manuel Martinez was the administrator of Westgate Community Hospital. The Controller, Sam Westin, reported to him and directed the financial affairs of the hospital. Westin's general attitude was to be a tight-fisted guardian of the dollar. He was rigid in attitude, not wanting to approve any action that was a departure from routine or a variance from policy. Martinez was the type who desired to take action, regardless of the restrictions of past practice or policy. The differing attitudes of the two men had led to conflicts in the past, and on two occasions Martinez had warned, "If you can't follow my orders, Sam, I am going to have to fire you." Westin held his ground and usually won his arguments, contending that his approach was proper accounting practice and, therefore, not subject to challenge by Martinez.

One afternoon Martinez approached Westin and commented, "Sam, here's a merit wage increase that I just put through for Clara Nesbit. She's the best floor supervisor we have, and she deserves an increase. She threatened to leave unless we raised her. I promised this on her next paycheck, so be sure to put it through at once."

Westin looked at the merit increase form and commented, "Manuel, you know I can't put this through. It is contrary to policy. She is already making the top rate allowed for her classification."

MARTINEZ: "That doesn't make any difference. Put it through. I'm the administrator of this hospital, and when I say 'do it,' then put it through."

WESTIN: "I can't do it. It's against policy."

MARTINEZ: "I'm the boss here, and I say do it."

WESTIN: "I'm not going to violate policy."

Martinez pointed his finger at Westin and talked so loudly that it attracted the attention of the others in the office: "Who's the boss here, Sam?"

WESTIN: "You are."

MARTINEZ (heatedly): "Then put through this raise."

WESTIN: "No."

A shouting match developed that diverted the attention of the whole office. Finally Martinez said, "Sam, I have had enough. You are fired."

WESTIN: "You can't fire me for that."

MARTINEZ: "I just did it. You are through."

Martinez did not retract his action. Westin was removed from the payroll and left the hospital that afternoon.

ASSIGNMENT

Divide the class into pairs of individuals. One person in each pair should assume the role of Martinez, and the other the role of Westin. Role-play the interaction over the wage increase again, but this time Martinez should consider using other leadership behaviors that would have a more productive outcome. Discuss the results in class.

REFERENCES

1 Henry Mintzberg, *The Nature of Managerial Work,* Englewood Cliffs, N.J.: Prentice-Hall, Inc., 1980, p. 61.

2 James Owens, "The Uses of Leadership Theory," *Michigan Business Review,* January 1973, p. 19.

3 For summaries of early research, see Cecil E. Goode, "Significant Research on Leadership," *Personnel,* March 1951, pp. 342–250; and Ralph M. Stogdill, "Personal Factors Associated with Leadership: A Survey of the Literature," *The Journal of Psychology,* January 1948, pp. 35–71.

4 This three-way classification was originally proposed in Robert L. Katz, "Skills of an Effective Administrator," *Harvard Business Review,* January–February 1955, pp. 33–42. See also Katz's "Retrospective Commentary," *Harvard Business Review,* September–October 1974, pp. 101–102.

5 William Litzinger and Thomas Schaefer, "Leadership through Followership," *Business Horizons,* September–October 1982, pp. 78–81; Joseph A. Steger, George E. Manners, Jr., and Thomas W. Zimmerer, "Following the Leader: How to Link Management Style to Subordinate Personalities," *Management Review,* October 1982, pp. 22–28ff. A review of research on followership is in Trudy Heller and Jon Van Til, "Leadership and Followership: Some Summary Propositions," *Journal of Applied Behavioral Science,* 18:3, 1982, pp. 405–414; a focus on the communication skills of effective subordinates is in Cal W. Downs and Charles Conrad, "Effective Subordinancy," *Journal of Business Communication,* Spring 1982, pp. 27–37.

6 Robert W. Johnston, "Leader-Follower Behavior in 3-D, Part 2," *Personnel,* September–October 1981, pp. 50–60. Other research suggests, however, that the newest generation of managers is increasingly reluctant to accept a followership role. See Ann Howard and James A. Wilson, "Leadership in a Declining Work Ethic," *California Management Review,* Summer 1982, pp. 33–46.

7 Robert J. House, "A Path Goal Theory of Leadership Effectiveness," *Administrative Science Quarterly,* September 1971, pp. 321–328. Support for the path-goal model is reported in Charles N. Greene, "Questions of Causation in the Path-Goal Theory of Leadership," *Academy of Management Journal,* March 1979, pp. 22–41.

8 A summary of several goal-setting studies is reported in Gary P. Latham and Edwin A. Locke, "Goal Setting—A Motivational Technique That Works," Autumn 1979, pp. 68–80. See a connection between goal setting and attribution in Thomas I. Chacko and James C. McElroy, "The Cognitive Component in Locke's

Theory of Goal Setting: Suggestive Evidence for a Causal Attribution Interpretation," *Academy of Management Journal*, March 1983, pp. 104–118.

9 Gary P. Latham and J. James Baldes, "The Practical Significance of Locke's Theory of Goal Setting," *Journal of Applied Psychology*, February 1975, pp. 122–124.

10 Howard Garland, "Goal Levels and Task Performance: A Compelling Replication of Some Compelling Results," *Journal of Applied Psychology*, April 1982, pp. 245–248; see also Gary P. Latham and Gary A. Yukl, "A Review of Research on the Application of Goal Setting in Organizations," *Academy of Management Journal*, December 1975, pp. 824–845.

11 John M. Ivancevich and J. Timothy McMahon, "The Effects of Goal Setting, External Feedback, and Self-Generated Feedback on Outcome Variables: A Field Experiment," *Academy of Management Journal*, June 1982, pp. 359–372.

12 J. C. Wofford, "An Integrative Theory of Motivation," *Journal of Management*, Spring 1982, pp. 27–47; and Janet Fulk and Eric R. Wendler, "Dimensionality of Leader-Subordinate Interaction: A Path-Goal Investigation," *Organizational Behavior and Human Performance*, October 1982, pp. 241–264.

13 "Mgr. Forum," *Mgr.* (American Telephone & Telegraph Company, Long Lines Division), no. 4, 1976, p. 2.

14 For other definitions, see Bronston T. Mayes and Robert W. Allen, "Toward a Definition of Organizational Politics," *Academy of Management Review*, October 1977, pp. 672–678. For a typology of legitimate and illegitimate political behavior in organizations, see Dan Farrell and James C. Petersen, "Patterns of Political Behavior in Organizations," *Academy of Management Review*, July 1982, pp. 403–412.

15 Gerald R. Salancik and Jeffrey Pfeffer, "Who Gets Power—and How They Hold On to It: A Strategic-Contingency Model of Power," *Organizational Dynamics*, Winter 1977, p. 3. See also Dean Tjosvold, "The Dynamics of Positive Power," *Training and Development Journal*, June 1984, pp. 72–76.

16 Charles N. Greene and Philip M. Podsakoff, "Effects of Withdrawal of a Performance-Contingent Reward on Supervisory Influence and Power," *Academy of Management Journal*, September 1981, pp. 527–542.

17 Ramesh K. Shukla, "Influence of Power Bases in Organizational Decision Making: A Contingency Model," *Decision Sciences*, July 1982, pp. 450–470.

18 Andrew Kakabadse, "Politics of Interpersonal Influence: Issues for the Management Development Adviser," *Journal of Management Development*, 1:3, 1982, pp. 43–53.

19 Peter F. Drucker, *The Practice of Management*, New York: Harper & Row, Publishers, Incorporated, 1954; Heinz Weihrich, "A Hierarchy and Network of Aims," *Management Review*, January 1982, pp. 47–54. A review of the research is Jack N. Kondrasuk, "Studies in MBO Effectiveness," *Academy of Management Review*, July 1981, pp. 419–430. A summary of the problem areas in MBO is in Robert C. Ford and Frank McLaughlin, "Avoiding Disappointment in MBO Programs," *Human Resource Management*, Summer–Fall 1982, pp. 44–49.

20 There is evidence that some leaders divide their employees into different groups and treat each group differently, developing a "leader-member exchange" relation between each. See George B. Graen, Robert C. Liden, and William Hoel, "Role of Leadership in the Employee Withdrawal Process," *Journal of Applied Psychology,* December 1982, pp. 868–872.

21 Theory X and Theory Y were first published in Douglas McGregor, "The Human Side of Enterprise," in *Proceedings of the Fifth Anniversary Convocation of the School of Industrial Management,* Cambridge, Mass.: Massachusetts Institute of Technology, Apr. 9, 1957.

22 Robert T. Keller and Andrew D. Szilagyi, "A Longitudinal Study of Leader Reward Behavior, Subordinate Expectancies, and Satisfaction," *Personnel Psychology,* Spring 1978, pp. 119–129. Other dimensions of positive and negative leadership are described in Arthur C. Beck and Ellis D. Hillmar, "The Power of Positive Management," *Personnel Journal,* February 1983, pp. 126–131.

23 Chester A. Schriesheim, "The Great High Consideration—High Initiating Structure Leadership Myth: Evidence on its Generalizability," *The Journal of Social Psychology,* April 1982, pp. 221–228; see also Harold J. Leavitt and Jean Lipman-Blumen, "A Case for the Relational Manager," *Organizational Dynamics,* Summer 1980, pp. 27–41.

24 Examples of early reports from each university are Daniel Katz and others, *Productivity, Supervision and Morale in an Office Situation,* Ann Arbor, Mich.: The University of Michigan Press, 1950; and E. A. Fleishman, *"Leadership Climate" and Supervisory Behavior,* Columbus, Ohio: Personnel Research Board, Ohio State University Press, 1951. The personality attributes of effective leaders (e.g., intelligence, initiative, verbal facility) were reported in Ralph M. Stogdill, *Handbook of Leadership,* New York: The Free Press, 1974.

25 Fred E. Fiedler, *A Theory of Leadership Effectiveness,* New York: McGraw-Hill Book Company, 1967; and Fred E. Fiedler and Martin M. Chemers, *Leadership and Effective Management,* Glenview, Ill.: Scott, Foresman and Company, 1974.

26 Boris Kabanoff, "A Critique of Leader Match and Its Implications for Leadership Research," *Personnel Psychology,* Winter 1981, pp. 749–764; and D. D. Warrick, "Leadership Styles and Their Consequences," *Journal of Experiential Learning and Simulation,* December 1981, pp. 155–172.

27 Steven Kerr and J. M. Jermier, "Substitutes for Leadership: Their Meaning and Measurement," *Organizational Behavior and Human Performance,* December 1978, pp. 375–403; and Peter W. Howard and William F. Joyce, "Substitutes for Leadership: A Statistical Refinement," in Kae H. Chung (ed.), *Academy of Management Proceedings* '82, Mississippi State, Miss.: Academy of Management, pp. 165–169.

28 Charles C. Manz and Henry P. Sims, Jr., "Self-Management as a Substitute for Leadership: A Social Learning Theory Perspective," *Academy of Management Review,* July 1980, pp. 361–357; and Charles C. Manz, "Improving Performance through Self-Leadership," *National Productivity Review,* Summer 1983, pp. 288–297.

29 Lester R. Bittel and Jackson E. Ramsey, "The Traditional, Limited World of Supervisors," *Harvard Business Review,* July–August 1982, pp. 26ff; and B. Sacha, "The Old Foreman Is on the Way Out, and the New One Will Be More Important," *Business Week,* 1983, pp. 74–75.

30 Rosabeth Moss Kanter, "Power Failure in Management Circuits," *Harvard Business Review,* July–August 1979, pp. 67–70. An early article on this subject is Donald E. Wray, "Marginal Men of Industry: The Foreman," *American Journal of Sociology,* January 1949, pp. 298–301.

Allen, Robert W., and Lyman W. Porter, *Organizational Influence Processes,* Glenview, Ill.: Scott, Foresman and Company, 1983.

Bennis, Warren, *More Power to You,* Garden City, N.Y.: Doubleday & Company, Inc., 1983.

Child, John, and Bruce Partridge, *Lost Managers: Supervisors in Industry and Society,* Cambridge, Mass.: Cambridge University Press, 1982.

Fiedler, Fred E., *A Theory of Leadership Effectiveness,* New York: McGraw-Hill Book Company, 1967.

Hunt, J. G., U. Sekaran, and C. A. Schriesheim (eds.), *Leadership: Beyond Establishment Views* (vol. 6 in the Leadership Symposia Series), Carbondale, Ill.: Southern Illinois University Press, 1981.

Josefowitz, Natasha, *Paths to Power: A Woman's Guide from First Job to Top Executive,* Reading, Mass.: Addison-Wesley Publishing Co., 1980.

Lassey, William R., and Marshall Sashkin, *Leadership and Social Change,* 3d ed., San Diego, Calif.: University Associates, 1983.

Locke, Edwin A., and Gary P. Latham, *Goal Setting: A Motivational Technique that Works!* Englewood Cliffs, N.J.: Prentice-Hall, Inc., 1984.

McGregor, Douglas, *The Human Side of Enterprise,* New York: McGraw-Hill Book Company, 1960.

Mintzberg, Henry, *Power In and Around Organizations,* Englewood Cliffs, N.J.: Prentice-Hall, Inc., 1983.

Shorris, Earl, *The Oppressed Middle: Politics of Middle Management, Scenes from Corporate Life,* Garden City, N.Y.: Anchor Press–Doubleday, 1981.

Stogdill, Ralph M., *Handbook of Leadership,* New York: The Free Press, 1974.

Vance, Stanley C., *Corporate Leadership: Boards, Directors, and Strategy,* New York: McGraw-Hill Book Company, 1983.

EMPLOYEE PARTICIPATION

As a rule, participative management is more likely to produce high levels of satisfaction and motivation than an authoritarian management.

Edward E. Lawler III[1]

Regardless of how well participation works, it will not solve all organizational problems.

Rosabeth Moss Kanter[2]

CHAPTER OBJECTIVES

TO UNDERSTAND:

The idea of participation
Prerequisites for participation
Benefits of participation
The participative process
Types of participative programs
Labor union involvement
Limitations of participation

A s discussed in the preceding chapter, a participative style is important for effective leadership. Participation has excellent potential for building teamwork, but it is a difficult practice and can fail if poorly applied. When participation is well done, two of its best results are acceptance of change and a commitment to goals that encourages better performance.

Observe in the experience of one company how participation improved safety. A large aircraft manufacturer employed from 5000 to 20,000 shop workers during a ten-year period. It used a safety committee system in which each department was represented on the committee by one of its workers. During these ten years not one person had a disabling injury while serving as safety committee member. When people became safety committee members, they ceased having disabling injuries! This record occurred despite the fact that there were hundreds of members during the decade, and sometimes "accident-prone" workers were appointed committee members in order to make them safety-conscious. The facts of this situation show a significant difference between committee members and nonmembers. Part of this difference surely came from the fact that the committee members were responsible, participating people with regard to safety.

Let us now discuss what participation is, the kinds of experiences we have had with it, management programs to develop it, and its ever-present limitations.

THE NATURE OF EMPLOYEE PARTICIPATION

What is participation?

Participative managers consult with their employees, bringing them in on problems and decisions so that they work together as a team. The managers are not autocrats, but neither are they free-rein managers who abandon their management responsibilities. Participative managers still retain ultimate responsibility for the operation of their units, but they have learned to share operating responsibility with those who perform the work. The result is that employees feel a sense of involvement in group goals. As shown earlier, in Figure 2-5, the "employee psychological result" of supportive management is "participation." It follows that *participation is mental and emotional involvement of persons in group situations that encourage them to contribute to group goals and share responsibility for them.* There are three important ideas in this definition—involvement, contribution, and responsibility.

Elements in participation

Mental and emotional involvement First, and probably foremost, participation means mental and emotional involvement rather than mere muscular activity. A person's *self* is involved, rather than just one's skill. This involvement is psychological rather than physical. A person who participates is *ego-involved* instead of merely *task-involved*. Some managers mistake task involvement for true participation. They go through the motions of participation, but nothing more. They hold meetings, ask opinions, and so on, but all

Ego involvement

the time it is perfectly clear to employees that their manager is an autocratic boss who wants no ideas. This is *busywork,* not participation. Employees fail to become ego-involved.

> The difference between ego-involved participation and task-involved activity is shown by a description of a part of a day for a worker named Joseph Carter. He wakens to the music of his clock-radio, interrupted occasionally by an announcer he does not know, cannot see, and cannot talk back to. After eating alone, since his family does not awake so early in the morning, his next personal interaction is with a bus driver whom he does not know and who works for some abstract transportation system that Carter does not understand and in which he has no control.
>
> At the company he shows his badge to a guard, though he does not know the guard's name and does not really care when he asks, "How are you feeling this morning?" In fact, he is irked because the guard keeps asking to see his badge, though surely after three years the guard must know he is an employee. Going into the shop, he has to stop by the personnel office to sign an insurance paper which he cannot understand and which is thrust at him by an employee who acts as if she were selling soap in a grocery store. Finally, he enters his work area to be greeted by a supervisor whose name he does know, but that is about all, because the supervisor is only in the department temporarily for training and is to be sent somewhere else soon by "somebody upstairs." And so it goes throughout the day.

Though Joseph Carter has been furiously active all day, most of this was routine, impersonal activity that was imposed on him. How much was he ego-involved in his activity? How much did he participate?

Motivation to contribute   A second important idea in participation is that it motivates people to contribute. They are given an opportunity to release their own resources of initiative and creativity toward the objectives of the organization, just as Theory Y predicts. In this way participation differs from "consent." The practice of consent uses only the creativity of the manager who brings ideas to the group for the members' consent. The consenters do not contribute; they merely approve. Participation is more than getting *Two-way* consent for something that has already been decided. It is a *two-way* social *social exchange* exchange among people, rather than a procedure for imposing ideas from above. Its great value is that it uses the creativity of all employees.

Participation especially improves motivation by helping employees understand and clarify their paths toward goals. According to the path-goal model of leadership, the improved understanding of path-goal relationships produces a higher responsibility for goal attainment. The result is improved motivation.

> For example, a stockbrokerage firm studied forty of its offices throughout the United States.[3] A stockbroker's work requires independent activities of the kind that will be affected by each individual broker's motivation. The study showed "a strikingly high" correlation between the participative offices and higher performance. Brokers in participative offices also had higher morale.

Acceptance of responsibility   A third idea in participation is that it encourages people to accept responsibility in their group's activities. It is a social process by which people become self-involved in an organization and want to see it work successfully. When they talk about their organization, they begin to say "we," not "they." When they see a job problem, it is "ours," not "theirs." Participation helps them become responsible employee-citizens rather than nonresponsible, machinelike performers.

As individuals begin to accept responsibility for group activities, they see in it a way to do what *they* want to do, that is, to get a job done for which they feel responsible. This idea of getting the group to want teamwork is a key step in developing it into a successful work unit. When people *want* to do something, they will find a way. Under these conditions employees see managers as supportive contributors to the team. Employees are ready to work actively with managers rather than reactively against them.

Responsibility builds teamwork.

Broad application

There is ample evidence to suggest that participation works in practice in a variety of jobs.[4] Employees can be involved in technical, staffing, operational, and strategic decisions. Although formal programs for participation receive the most attention, informal procedures also can be effective.[5]

> For example, an insurance sales representative, George Langdon, reported to friends that he had an outstanding new supervisor. The sales representative largely worked without supervision. He was highly skilled, possessing certificates as a Certified Life Underwriter and as a Certified Property and Casualty Underwriter. He was a member of the Million Dollar Club, meaning that he had sold over $1 million of insurance in a year. Nevertheless he was pleased because his supervisor had sought his advice about what management could do to help him perform his job better. He had worked for his organization eight years, but he said that never before had anyone sought his ideas. They were always trying to tell him what to do and urging him to do better. Now he felt he was participating.

The great benefit of participation is that it restores to people at work their birthright to be contributing members of the groups in which they work. It builds human values in organizations, because it serves employee needs for security, social interaction, esteem, and self-fulfillment. This improvement of human values at work is important for society as well as for employees.

A sharing process

Participation is a sharing process among managers and employees. Managers who encourage participation do not abandon their jobs and leave everything to employees. They merely share by getting others actively involved so that all may contribute.

When managers first consider participation, they often ask, "If by means of participation I share authority with my employees, don't I lose some of it? I can't afford to lose authority because I am responsible, and if I am responsible, I must have the authority." This is a normal worry, but it is not a justifiable one because participative managers still retain final authority. All they do is share the use of authority so that employees will become more involved in the affairs of the organization.

Increased power and influence

Strange as it may seem, participation actually may increase the power of both managers and their employees. It is evident that employees gain more power with participation, but what about managers? The autocratic view of management is that power is a fixed quantity, so someone must lose what another gains.

Participation expands influence.

However, as shown in Figure 9-1, the participative view is that power in a social system can be increased without taking it from someone else.[6] The process works like this. Managerial power depends partly on conditions such as employee trust in management, feeling of teamwork, and sense of responsibility. Participation improves these conditions. Since employees feel more cooperative and responsible, they are likely to be more responsive to managerial attempts to influence them. In a sense, what occurs is that managers make social transactions with their work groups that improve goodwill and responsibility. These conditions are similar to a savings deposit that managers can draw upon later (perhaps with interest!) when they need to apply their power.

Here is an example that shows how a manager may increase power by sharing it. The manager of a computer operation having over fifty employees felt that some changes were needed. In the beginning she tried the usual autocratic approach, aided by a consultant. Desired changes were proposed, but the employees would not accept them. Finally, the effort was abandoned.

The manager continued to think that changes were necessary, so a year later she decided to try again, using more participatory approaches. She discussed the need with her supervisors and several key employees. Then she set up committees to work on designated parts of a "self-examination study." The groups worked hard, and in a few months they submitted a capable report that recommended a number of

Figure 9-1 Two views of power and influence	**Autocratic view** Power—	**Participative view** Power—
	• Is a fixed amount.	• Is a variable amount.
	• Comes from the authority structure.	• Comes from people through both official and unofficial channels.
	• Is applied by management.	• Is applied by shared ideas and activities in a group.
	• Flows downward.	• Flows in all directions.

1 Adequate time to participate
2 Potential benefits greater than costs
3 Relevance to employee interests
4 Adequate employee abilities to deal with the subject
5 Mutual ability to communicate
6 No feeling of threat to either party
7 Within the area of job freedom

Figure 9-2
Prerequisites for participation

important changes. In this instance the members felt a sense of pride and ownership in the report. It was theirs. They had created it. The result was that they made a genuine effort to implement it. With the full support of the whole group, they made substantial changes. Participation had increased the manager's power and influence.

Prerequisites for participation

The success of participation is directly related to how well certain prerequisite conditions are met, as shown in Figure 9-2. Some of these conditions occur in the participants; some exist in their environment. They show that participation works better in some situations than in others—and in certain situations it works not at all. Major prerequisites are as follows:[7]

1 There must be time to participate before action is required. Participation is hardly appropriate in emergency situations.

2 The potential benefits of participation should be greater than its costs. For example, employees cannot spend so much time participating that they ignore their work.

3 The subject of participation must be relevant and interesting to the employees; otherwise employees will look upon it merely as busywork.

4 The participants should have the ability, such as intelligence and technical knowledge, to participate. It is hardly advisable, for example, to ask janitors in a pharmaceutical laboratory to participate in deciding which of five chemical formulas deserve research priority; but they might participate in helping resolve other problems related to their work.

5 The participants must be able mutually to communicate—to talk each other's language—in order to be able to exchange ideas.

6 Neither party should feel that its position is threatened by participation. If workers think their status will be adversely affected, they will not participate. If managers feel that their authority is threatened, they will refuse participation or will be defensive.

7 Participation for deciding a course of action in an organization can take place only within the group's area of job freedom. Some degree of restriction is required on parts of an organization in order to maintain unity for the whole. Each separate subunit cannot make decisions that violate

Area of job freedom

policy, collective-bargaining agreements, legal requirements, and similar restraints. Likewise there are restraints due to the physical environment (a flood closing the plant is an extreme example) and due to one's own limitations (such as not understanding electronics). The *area of job freedom* for any department is its area of discretion after all restraints have been applied. In no organization is there complete freedom, even for the top executive.

Within the area of job freedom, participation exists along a continuum, as shown in Figure 9-3. Within a period of time a manager will practice participation at many points along the continuum. That is, a manager may seek the group's ideas before deciding vacation schedules, but the same manager decides overtime schedules independently. Similarly, a manager may find it necessary to limit the participation used with one employee while consulting freely with another. Since a consistent approach provides employees with a predictable environment, each manager gradually becomes identified with some general style of participation as a usual practice. The popular terms designated for amounts of participation along the continuum are representative of a broad area on the continuum instead of a certain point. Several of these terms are defined later in this chapter.

Figure 9-3
Participation exists along a continuum.
Adapted from Robert Tannenbaum and Warren H. Schmidt, "How to Choose a Leadership Pattern," Harvard Business Review, *March–April 1958, p. 96.*

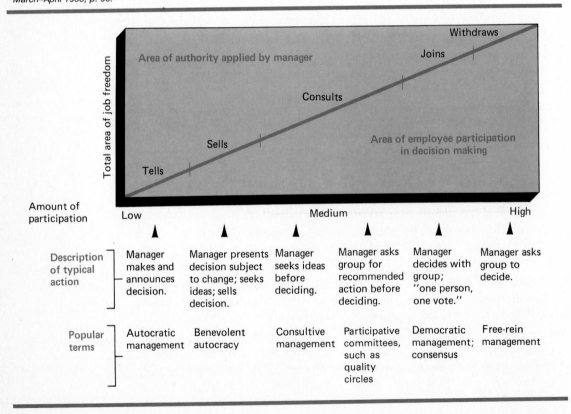

Experience with participation

CHAPTER 9:
EMPLOYEE
PARTICIPATION

193

Classic studies

Although managers have for years recognized various benefits of participation, these benefits were first experimentally suggested in classic studies in industry by Roethlisberger, Bavelas, Coch and French, and others.[8] Conducted by skilled social scientists under controlled conditions, these experiments were useful in drawing attention to the potential value of participation. Their collective results suggested the general proposition that, *especially in the introduction of changes, participation tends to improve performance and job satisfaction.*

Participation in organizations generally has been successful, although there have been problems and even failures. One insurance company, for example, found that employee decision making became too independent. Sometimes two employees were calling on the same customer. Other employees were seeking only easy accounts, leaving the hard ones for someone else. Eventually the company had to restore some controls.

One successful experiment involved 246 managerial, professional, technical, and clerical employees in a division of a utility.[9] About one-third (direct participants) actively contributed to the planning and implementation of changes in organizational goals, structure, reward systems, and decision-making procedures. The other employees (indirect participants) were recipients of the changes and learned of them through various media.

The results at eighteen months and again at three years indicate that the direct participants perceived themselves as having more influence over work decisions. They also had more favorable attitudes toward their jobs and the organization.

HOW PARTICIPATION WORKS

A simple model of the participative process is shown in Figure 9-4. It indicates that *in some situations* participation results in mental and emotional involvement that produces generally favorable outcomes for both the employees and the organization. Before we review the major types of participative programs in use today, three questions will be addressed. What are some of the benefits of participation? Do all employees desire to participate? How does the situation affect the success of participative programs?

The participative process

Benefits of participation

In various types of organizations under many different operating conditions, participation has contributed to a variety of benefits.[10] Some of these are direct and others are less tangible. Participation typically brings higher output and a better quality of output. In certain types of operations the quality improvement alone is worth the time invested in participation. Employees often make suggestions for both quality and quantity improvements. Although not all the ideas are useful, there are enough valuable ones to produce genuine long-run improvements.

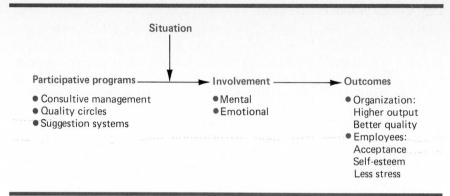

Figure 9-4
The participative
process

In one firm, for example, computer operations were running $100,000 over budget, and management sought ways to reduce this drain on resources. In the beginning, management discussed the problem in several meetings, but the managers could not agree on any major cost-saving changes. Then management sought the advice of a consultant. Although the consultant recommended some changes, they produced minor savings.

Finally one manager suggested that management should ask employees for ideas. Some managers doubted that this approach would help, but after discussion they decided to bring employees in the computer department into full participation on the program. Within thirty days the employees suggested cost-saving ideas that eventually provided about double the savings needed.

Participation tends to improve motivation because employees feel more accepted and involved in the situation. Their self-esteem, job satisfaction, and cooperation with management also may improve. The results often are reduced conflict and stress, more commitment to goals, and better acceptance of change.[11] Employees also may reduce turnover and absences, because they feel that they have a better place to work and that they are being more successful in their jobs. Finally, the act of participation by itself establishes better communication as people mutually discuss work problems.

Benefits may emerge slowly. The results clearly show that participation has broad systems effects that favorably influence a variety of organizational outputs. The benefits may not appear immediately, however. When Westinghouse Electric adopted participative management, it predicted it would take *ten years* to achieve the full effect.[12] Once the organizational climate is changed, then the system as a whole becomes more humanly effective.

Different needs for participation

It must be recognized that some employees desire more participation than others.[13] Educated and higher-level workers typically seek more participation, because they feel more prepared to make useful contributions. When they lack participation, they tend to have lower performance, less satisfaction, lower self-esteem, more stress, and other symptoms of tension and dissatisfaction. However, some other people desire a minimum of participation and are not upset because they lack it.

The difference between one's desired and actual participation gives a measure of the match between a company's practices and an individual's desires. When employees want more participation than they have, they a "participatively deprived" and there is *underparticipation*. In the opposite situation, when they have more participation than they want, they are "participatively saturated" and there is *overparticipation*.

There is evidence that where there is either underparticipation or overparticipation, people are less satisfied than those who participate in a degree that matches their needs. This relationship is shown in Figure 9-5. As participation comes closer to matching either high or low needs, satisfaction with the company goes up. Conversely, as a mismatch increases, these positive feelings decline. Participation is not something that should be applied equally to everyone. Rather, it should match their needs.

Situational influences

As with the use of many behavioral ideas, there are situational factors that influence the success of participative programs.[14] These may be found in the environment, the organization, its leadership, technology, or employees, as

Factors affecting participation

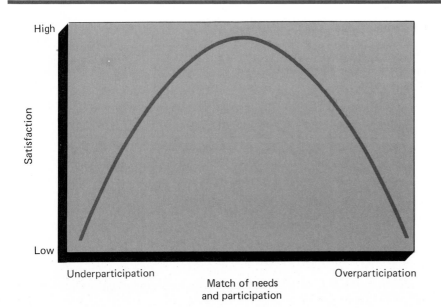

Figure 9-5
The relation of satisfaction to the match of need and actual participation

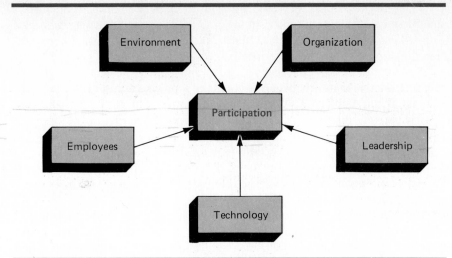

Figure 9-6
Situational
influences on the
use and success
of participation

shown in Figure 9-6. For example, national cultures and political systems vary sharply across the world, resulting in a restrictive environment for participation in a dictatorship and a more supportive one in a democracy. Organizational structures need to differ in their responses to turbulent or stable environments.

We have previously discussed (chapter 8) the impact of Theory X or Theory Y beliefs on selection of leadership style. There is also some evidence that top managers' beliefs about the nature and purpose of work affect their rationale for using participation.[15] Task characteristics should also be examined before choosing a participative program; intrinsically satisfying tasks may diminish the need for greater participation, while routine tasks may suggest that participation could produce fruitful results.

With regard to employees, their *perceptions* of the situation are important. The evidence suggests that participation will be more successful where employees feel they have a valid contribution to make, it is valued by the organization, and they will be rewarded for it. Overall, it is clear that several contingency factors play a key role in determining the effectiveness of any participative program.

PROGRAMS FOR PARTICIPATION

We can further understand how participation works if we examine selected programs to develop it, as shown in Figure 9-7. These programs usually are clusters of practices that focus on some specific area of participation, such as employee suggestions. When a company uses a sufficient number of programs to develop a general feeling of participation among its employees, it is said to

*Participative
management*

practice *participative management*.

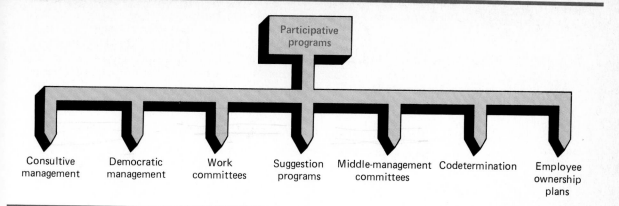

Figure 9-7
Selected types of participative programs

Consultive management

Consultive management is the kind of participation that managers can apply even though those above them do not apply it. No new policies are required, and existing authority-responsibility relationships are not affected. *Consultive management,* as the name implies, means that managers consult with their employees in order to encourage them to think about issues and contribute their own ideas before decisions are made. Managers do not consult on every issue, but they do set a climate of consultation.

Vroom model

A useful model of consultive management has been developed by Victor Vroom and others.[16] They recognized that problem-solving situations differ and, therefore, examined the nature of those differences. By classifying problems according to the importance of decision quality, employee acceptance, timing, cost factors, source of relevant data, degree of structure for the problem, and subordinate motivation, they created a decision model that suggests to managers the *degree* of consultation appropriate for each problem type. This approach has two key prerequisites: it assumes that managers can accurately classify problems and that they have the humility to be genuinely receptive to employee ideas.

Democratic management

Democratic management goes further than consultive management and refers a number of major decisions to employee groups, as shown in Figure 9-3. The main process by which democratic management occurs is group discussion, which makes full use of group ideas and group influence. In its extreme form it operates according to consensus and reflects many of the Theory Z ideas presented in Chapter 2. In the absence of clear goals, however, it is possible for managers to lose control, as illustrated here.

Group decision

One study of democratic management under operating conditions found that it did not provide adequate focus on organizational objectives. The study covered thirty-two geographically separate units of a national package delivery company. Units with democratic management were not the high-performing ones. The researchers concluded, "While this pattern of control may lead to high rank-and-file morale, it does not appear to promote basic identification with organizational objectives and practices or motivated action leading to high performance. It appears that in this organization high rank-and-file control relative to the leaders may have the effect of members' acting simply in terms of their own self-interests and not accepting the contributions of the leaders."[17]

Democratic management especially applies in voluntary social organizations, where an easy pace and natural community of interests make it easier to achieve consensus. It is more difficult to apply in hierarchical, task-oriented situations, where competition over scarce resources is likely.

Work committees

Work committees are groups of workers and their managers that are organized primarily to consider and solve job problems. Applicable to both union and nonunion organizations, they have been used for decades. Other names for work committees include labor-management committees, work-improvement task forces, quality circles, and safety committees. They have such broad usefulness that most of the employees can be involved. For example, one firm with thousands of employees reported that 83 percent of them were organized into "involvement teams" that seek ways to improve their own productivity.

Quality circles   Quality circles have expanded rapidly as an involvement technique in the United States and Europe after achieving spectacular success in Japan.[18] *Quality circles* are voluntary groups that receive training in statistical techniques and problem-solving skills and then meet to produce ideas for improving productivity and working conditions. They meet regularly—often on company time—and generate solutions for management to evaluate and implement.

> A number of firms in the aircraft and electronics industries have experimented with quality circles. Lockheed, for example, reported these results after just two years' experience.
>
> - Fifteen circles produced cost savings of $2.8 million
> - The reject rate in one operation dropped by 80 percent
> - A survey of participants indicated that 97 percent were enthusiastic about continuing the program.[19]

Quality circles succeed because they create opportunities for personal growth, achievement, and recognition. Employees are committed to the solutions they generate, because they "own" them. To remain successful, quality circles need continuous support from higher management, assurance that employee security will not be threatened, and an image as an ongoing managerial strategy to increase the organization's effectiveness.

Suggestion programs are formal plans to encourage individual employees to recommend work improvements. The programs, which typically require written input, average about 15 suggestions for every 100 employees who are covered by a suggestion system in the United States. About 25 percent of suggestions are accepted, according to the National Association of Suggestion Systems, but the rate varies from firm to firm. Figure 9-8 shows that over 70 percent of the ideas received at Northern Natural Gas Company were accepted in a recent year.

In most companies the employee whose suggestion results in a cost saving may receive a monetary award in proportion to the first year's saving, so the award can be a substantial amount of money. For example, a commercial airline pilot received an award of $45,850 for saving $458,500 in fuel costs the first year. The idea was to move cargo so as to shift the jetliner's center of gravity during flight.

Although suggestion programs provide many useful ideas, they require major effort to keep them working.[20] One difficulty is that they exist primarily by written communication, so the motivation that comes from face-to-face discussion of problems is lacking. In addition, some managers and staff specialists look upon suggestions in their area as criticisms of their own ability. Programs can also be hurt by slow response to submitted suggestions or a lack of top-management support.

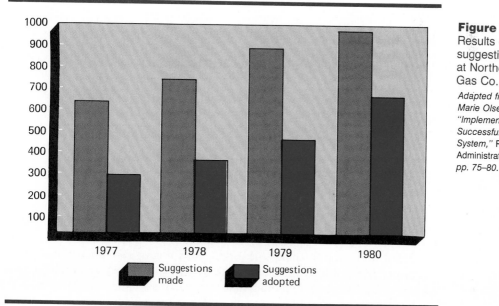

Figure 9-8
Results of a suggestion system at Northern Natural Gas Co.

Adapted from data in Marie Olsen, "Implementing a Successful Suggestion System," Personnel Administrator, May 1982, pp. 75–80.

Middle-management committees

Middle-management committees are group mechanisms to improve participation of managers below top organizational levels. They also are known as *multiple management,* a term used by McCormick and Company, a tea and spice company that developed the practice in the 1930s.[21]

Multiple management has been used successfully around the world in hundreds of companies, both unionized and nonunionized. Its central core is a junior board of directors that is given the opportunity to study any problem and to recommend courses of action. Employer information is made freely available to the board, and its meetings are unrestrained by the presence of senior executives. Members make their own bylaws and rotate their membership. The program encourages careful study of ideas before they are presented to management; therefore top management rarely vetoes a recommendation.

Multiple management has many benefits, especially for the sometimes overlooked middle managers. It is an excellent way to develop executive skills among middle managers and train them for top management. It encourages their growth and helps them develop a spirit of cooperation as they work together. It also taps their reserve of creativity, so new ideas are brought to management. The process itself encourages them to study policy issues carefully, take responsibility for their decisions, and broaden their experience. The result is a program that helps meet their desire to participate and does so in a way that benefits managers, workers, owners, and customers alike. As with any program, there have been occasional failures.

Industrial democracy

Industrial democracy is government-mandated worker participation at various levels of the organization with regard to decisions that affect workers. Occasionally the term also is applied to voluntary programs rather than mandated ones. At lower levels it is applied through *works councils,* which are similar to the work committees discussed earlier. At the top level it is called *codetermination* and typically means that workers or their representatives have rights to seats on the boards of directors of firms.[22] It was established in West Germany in the 1940s, when steel firms were required to organize boards with one-third worker representation. Since that time the practice has spread gradually to other nations in Western Europe, although the form used varies among them. The idea has not gained strong support from labor in the United States.

The basic philosophy of industrial democracy is to institutionalize worker participation in management in order to encourage cooperation rather than the traditional attitude of labor against management. This process also should build both worker and management understanding of each other's problems. Offsetting disadvantages include weakened ability of management to manage, excessive paperwork and meeting time, slower decision making, bypassing of middle management, and occasional unauthorized release or misuse of confidential information. In some situations labor-management conflict has increased rather than decreased. In many cases worker apathy is a problem; labor representatives are more interested in workplace issues than policy decisions.

Employee ownership plans

Employees have often been urged to "buy the product you make"; today, that slogan has occasionally been replaced with "buy the company you work for." *Employee ownership* of a firm emerges when employees provide the capital to purchase control of an existing operation. The stimulus often comes from threatened closings of marginally profitable plants, where workers see little hope of other employment in a devastated local economy. Employee ownership has been tried in diverse industries such as plywood, meat packing, steel, and furniture manufacturing. On the surface, these plans appear to offer the highest degree of participative decision making, as employees take control. Better management, heightened morale, and improved productivity have all been predicted to follow.

The limited evidence that is available on employee-owned firms is mixed. On the positive side, several firms and thousands of jobs have been saved, and this is a satisfactory result in view of the primary need at stake—job security for employees. On the other side, expected reductions in absenteeism have not materialized, the compensation gaps between workers and managers have widened, and labor-management cooperation has sometimes deteriorated to the point of union strikes against their own firm! Surprisingly, "the degree of day-to-day participation has been much less than in contemporary, collective forms of organizations."[23] Clearly, we have much to learn regarding the integration of employee ownership and effective management.

Does employee ownership work?

Labor union attitudes toward participation

The subject of this section is the labor union's role in management programs for participation, not those that are government-mandated. In responding to participative programs, unions make a distinction between (1) employee participation in the official role of union representative and (2) participation by an individual employee, as in a shop-safety committee. Unions are much more hesitant about the former because they are officially involved. They look more favorably upon the latter practice but still have some reservations because they fear that member loyalty to the union will be diminished.[24]

Union reaction is mixed.

Some union leaders feel that if they participate in helping management decide courses of action, the union's ability to challenge those actions is weakened. These union leaders prefer to remain aloof, having freedom to express disagreement with management and to challenge it at any time. The opposite point of view, held by other leaders, is that participation gives them an opportunity to get on the inside and to express their viewpoints *before* action is taken, which is superior to disagreement and protest *after* a decision is made. In practice most union viewpoints are somewhere between these two extremes; some types of participation are considered acceptable, but others are not.

Limitations of participation

For several pages we have been commenting favorably on participation, so it is now appropriate to put the brakes on enthusiasm and toss a few brickbats. Participation does have its costs as well as gains.[25] All the prerequisites discussed earlier are limitations to some extent, but there are others.

Technology and organizations today are so complex that specialized work roles are required, making it difficult for people to participate successfully if they are very far beyond their specialties. This means that lower-level workers can participate successfully in operating matters, but they usually have difficulty in policy matters.

Difficulties especially arise when workers make proposals in areas where they are not competent. Then, when their idea is rejected, they refuse to support whatever course of action was adopted and become alienated. A related problem is that some workers *expect* to be consulted on every issue, even those to which they cannot contribute. When they are not consulted, they become resentful and uncooperative.

Rigid expectations may result.

Another issue is an employee's right *not* to participate. There is no evidence that participation is desired by everybody. We have said only that participation is a useful means of building better relations in a group, and we also have said that people are all different. There is evidence that many individuals do not want to be bothered with participation. Shall we, regardless, push them into it merely because we think it is good for them?

A further problem is that supervisors have difficulty adjusting to participation. It tends to threaten their traditional authority. Unless higher management makes changes to give supervisors new responsibilities that use their surplus capacity, they may become dissatisfied. For example, one study of twelve companies that had increased worker participation found that supervisors were the most dissatisfied and frustrated people in the company.

Another difficulty with participation—as was the case with scientific management—is that practitioners become lost in the procedures of participation while overlooking its philosophy. The substance of participation does not automatically flow from its procedures; there is no such mechanistic connection. Procedures do not automatically lead to participation; rather, when they are used at the right time and in the right way, they make it possible for participation to develop in the minds of employees.

A serious issue with participation is that it can be used to manipulate employees. This manipulation is not necessarily by management. It may be by the union or by undercover cliques led by members skilled in group dynamics—the social engineers of consent. Too often groups are used to impose conformity on individualistic members. It is no wonder, then, that some employees prefer the open tyranny of an autocratic boss to the sometimes hidden tyranny of a group.

In spite of its numerous limitations, participation generally has achieved substantial success. It is not the answer to all organizational problems, but experience does show its general usefulness. The demand of employees to participate is not a passing fancy. It appears to be rooted deeply in the culture of free people around the world, and it is probably a basic drive in human beings. They want some control over things that affect them. Because of its significance, participation is the kind of practice to which organizational leaders need to devote long-range efforts. It affords a means of building some of the human values needed at work. It has been so successful in practice that it has become widely accepted in more advanced nations.

SUMMARY

Participation is an important contributor to organizational effectiveness. Participation is mental and emotional involvement of persons in group situations that encourage them to contribute to group goals and share responsibility for them. For employees, it is the psychological result of supportive management.

Participation is a sharing process that may increase the power of both employees and the supervisor, because power is an expandable resource. When participation's prerequisites are met, it can provide a variety of benefits for both employees and employers. Some employees desire more participation than others, so it is most effective when it reasonably matches their needs. If there is underparticipation or overparticipation, both satisfaction and performance may decline.

There are a number of participative programs that are effective. All have their benefits as well as their limitations. A program that is desirable for some employees is not necessarily good for all of them. Labor unions typically support management's participative efforts, but they are more hesitant about becoming officially involved in these efforts.

TERMS AND CONCEPTS FOR REVIEW

Participation

Prerequisites for participation

Area of job freedom

Overparticipation and underparticipation

Consultive management

Democratic management

Quality circles

Suggestion programs

Multiple management

Industrial democracy

Codetermnation

Employee ownership plans

Limitations of participation

REVIEW QUESTIONS

1 Think of your last full-time or part-time job. Discuss the amount of participation that was there. Was it more or less than you needed? What was the effect on you?

2 Ask several persons outside the class what is meant by "participation." Explain why their answers might differ.

3 How is it possible for participation to increase the power and influence of both manager and employee?

4 Discuss the prerequisites for effective participation. Do they help explain why some managers are relatively autocratic?

5 Most employees desire more participation. Managers were employees at one time. Why, then, don't these managers provide more opportunities for participation?

6 What benefits can participation provide? Compare the various programs on the basis of benefits.

7 Have you ever worked in a firm with a suggestion program? Did you or your friends use it? Discuss.

8 Appraise the comment, "Managers get enough participation. They are on the 'inside' and make all the decisions, so they certainly do not need any participative aids such as multiple management."

9 What was the area of job freedom in your last job? Was it adequate for your needs? What groups or institutions restricted this freedom? Based on your experiences and reading, do you think government controls are bringing a net increase or decrease in job freedoms? Discuss.

10 Explain the differences between:
   a Ego involvement and task involvement
   b Consultive management and democratic management
   c Codetermination and employee ownership plans

INCIDENT

Joe Adams

Joe Adams is supervisor in the final assembly department of an automobile body plant. Work in this department is not dependable, with temporary layoffs or short weeks occurring three or four times a year. The work is physically difficult, but the skill required is minimal; so most employees are high school graduates only. Some do not even have a high school education. About one-third of the work force comes from ethnic and racial minority groups. The work procedure and pace of work are tightly controlled by industrial engineers and other staff groups.

Adams attended a one-day conference of his Supervisors' Association recently and learned the many potential benefits of participation. In his own words, "This conference sold me on participation," so now he wishes to establish it in his assembly department. Management feels that conditions on an assembly line are not suitable for participation. Further, it believes that the majority of workers employed have an autocratic role expectation of supervision. In addition, management has said that the production schedule will not allow time off for participation during the workday. This means that if Adams wants to hold any meetings about participation, he will have to do so after work and on the workers' own time. Adams feels sure that his employees will not wish to remain after work on their own time, and he is not even sure that they would do so if he paid them overtime.

QUESTIONS

1 Recommend a course of action for Adams.

2 Would any ideas from the following be helpful in this case: McGregor, Herzberg, McClelland, Fiedler, models of organizational behavior, prerequisites for participation, area of job freedom, and programs for participation?

REFERENCES

1 Edward E. Lawler III, "For a More Effective Organization—Match the Job to the Man," *Organizational Dynamics,* Summer 1974, p. 27.

2 Rosabeth Moss Kanter, "Dilemmas of Managing Participation," *Organizational Dynamics,* Summer 1982, p. 23.

3 Johannes M. Pennings, "Dimensions of Organizational Influence and Their Effectiveness Correlates," *Administrative Science Quarterly,* December 1976, pp. 688–699.

4 See, for example, "The New Industrial Relations," *Business Week,* May 11, 1981, pp. 84ff.

5 John W. Dickson, "Participatory Forums and Influence," *Academy of Management Journal,* December 1982, pp. 915–920.

6 For a discussion of power and participation, see Burt K. Scanlan and Roger M. Atherton, Jr., "Participation and the Effective Use of Authority," *Personnel Journal,* September 1981, pp. 697–703; see also Marshall Sashkin, "Changing toward Participative Management Approaches: A Model and Methods," *Academy of Management Review,* July 1976, pp. 75–86.

7 See Robert Tannenbaum, Irving R. Weschler, and Fred Massarik, *Leadership and Organization: A Behavioral Science Approach,* New York: McGraw-Hill Book Company, 1961, pp. 88–100.

8 William F. Muhs, "Worker Participation in the Progressive Era: An Assessment by Harrington Emerson," *Academy of Management Review,* January 1982, pp. 99–102; F. J. Roethlisberger and W. J. Dickson, *Management and the Worker,* Cambridge, Mass.: Harvard University Press, 1939; Norman R. F. Maier, *Psychology in Industry,* Boston: Houghton Mifflin Company, 1946, pp. 264–266; Lester Coch and John R. P. French, Jr., "Overcoming Resistance to Change," *Human Relations,* 1:4, 1948, pp. 512–532.

9 Aaron J. Nurick, "Participation in Organizational Change: A Longitudinal Field Study," *Human Relations,* May 1982, pp. 413–430.

10 Examples of various types of improvements are reported in Frank J. Ruck, Jr., "A Participative Management Concept Shares Success, Responsibilities at Employee Transfer Corp.," *Personnel Administrator*, June 1982, pp. 65–71ff; Marshall Sashkin, "Participative Management Is an Ethical Imperative," *Organizational Dynamics*, Spring 1984, pp. 4–22. For a criticism contending that difficult goals alone produce effects surpassing those from participation, see Gary P. Latham, Timothy P. Steele, and Lise M. Saari, "The Effects of Participation and Goal Difficulty on Performance," *Personnel Psychology*, Autumn 1982, pp. 677–686.

11 Susan E. Jackson, "Participation in Decision Making as a Strategy for Reducing Job-Related Strain," *Journal of Applied Psychology*, February 1983, pp. 3–19.

12 Jeremy Main, "Westinghouse's Cultural Revolution," *Fortune*, June 15, 1982, pp. 74ff.

13 Jerome Rosow has reported that about 60 percent of Americans believe they have a right to participate in decisions affecting their jobs. He is interviewed in Karen E. Debats, "The Continuing Personnel Challenge," *Personnel Journal*, May 1982, pp. 332ff.

14 Peter Brownell, "Participative Management," *The Wharton Magazine*, Fall 1982, pp. 38–43.

15 John W. Dickson, "Top Managers' Beliefs and Rationales for Participation," *Human Relations*, March 1982, pp. 203–217.

16 V. H. Vroom and P. W. Yetton, *Leadership and Decision Making*, Pittsburgh: University of Pittsburgh Press, 1973, contains both the individual (consultive) model and a similar one for group decision making. For recent research on the model, see Arthur G. Jago and Victor H. Vroom, "Sex Differences in the Incidence and Evaluation of Participative Leader Behavior," *Journal of Applied Psychology*, December 1982, pp. 776–783.

17 Clagett G. Smith and Oguz N. Ari, "Organizational Control Structure and Member Consensus," *American Journal of Sociology*, May 1964, p. 638.

18 Quality circle experiences in Germany, Italy, France, and the United Kingdom are reported in Ron Collard, "Quality Circles: Developments in Europe," *Personnel Management*, November 1982, pp. 37–39; the Japanese experience is reviewed in George Munchus III, "Employer-Employee Based Quality Circles in Japan: Human Resource Policy Implications for American Firms," *Academy of Management Review*, April 1983, pp. 255–261; and an extensive review of U.S. results is H. J. Bocker and H. O. Overgaard, "Japanese Quality Circles: A Managerial Response to the Productivity Problem," *Management International Review*, 22:2, 1982, pp. 13–19.

19 E. Yager, "The Quality Circle Explosion," *Training and Development Journal*, April 1981, pp. 98–103.

20 Program problems and extensive references are reported in Lee A. Graf, "Suggestion Program Failure: Causes and Remedies," *Personnel Journal*, June 1982, pp. 450–454.

21 Charles P. McCormick, *Multiple Management*, New York: Harper & Row, Publishers, Incorporated, 1938; this is updated in "Five Decades of Participative Management," *Training and Development Journal*, July 1983, pp. 10–11. A similar idea of "core management groups" is reported in Trevor A. Wilkins, "A Participative Design for Dispersed Employees in Turbulent Environments," *Human Relations*, November 1982, pp. 1043–1058.

22 Harry R. Gudenberg, "Codetermination: Wave of the Future?" *Personnel Journal*, December 1981, pp. 969–971; Klaus Bartolke and others, "Workers' Participation and the Distribution of Control as Perceived by Members of Ten German Companies," *Administrative Science Quarterly,* September 1982, pp. 380–397; and Richard G. Nehrbass, "The Myths of Industrial Democracy," *Personnel Journal,* July 1982, pp. 486–487.

23 Michael A. Gurdon, "Is Employee Ownership the Answer to Our Economic Woes?" *Management Review,* May 1982, p. 14. An optimistic social view is Warner Woodworth, "Workers as Bosses," *Social Policy,* January–February 1981, pp. 41–45; disappointing results are reported in Richard J. Long, "Worker Ownership and Job Attitudes: A Field Study," *Industrial Relations,* Spring 1982, pp. 196–215; and Tove Helland Hammer, Jacqueline C. Landau, and Robert N. Stern, "Absenteeism When Workers Have a Voice: The Case of Employee Ownership," *Journal of Applied Psychology,* October 1981, pp. 561–573.

24 Robert S. Greenberger, "Quality Circles Grow, Stirring Union Worries," *Wall Street Journal* (Western ed.), Sept. 22, 1981, p. 25.

25 W. Mathew Juechter, "The Ups and Downs of Participative Management," *Training and Development Journal,* January 1983, pp. 92–93; and Richard E. Walton and Leonard A. Schlesinger, "Do Supervisors Thrive in Participative Work Systems?" *Organizational Dynamics,* Winter 1979, pp. 25–38.

FOR ADDITIONAL READING

Anthony, William P., *Participative Management,* Reading, Mass.: Addison-Wesley Publishing Company, Inc., 1978.

Bass, Bernard M., *Stogdill's Handbook of Leadership,* New York: Free Press, 1981.

Graham, Ben S., Jr., and Parvin S. Titus (eds.), *The Amazing Oversight: Total Participation for Productivity,* New York: AMACOM, 1979.

Inagami, Takeshi, *Labor-Management Communication at the Workshop Level,* Tokyo, Japan: Japan Institute of Labour, 1983.

Industrial Democracy in Europe (IDE) International Research Group, *Industrial Democracy in Europe,* New York: Clarendon, Oxford University Press, 1981.

Ingle, Sud, *Quality Circles Master Guide,* Englewood Cliffs, N.J.: Prentice-Hall, Inc., 1982.

Kanter, Rosabeth Moss, "Dilemmas of Participation" (chap. 9) in *The Change Masters,* New York: Simon and Schuster, 1983.

Lawler, Edward, *Productivity through Employee Involvement,* Reading, Mass.: Addison-Wesley Publishing Company, 1984.

Shrank, Robert (ed.), *Industrial Democracy at Sea,* Cambridge, Mass.: The MIT Press, 1983.

Thompson, Phillip C., *Quality Circles: How to Make them Work in America,* New York: AMACOM, 1982.

Vroom, V. H, and P. W. Yetton, *Leadership and Decision Making,* Pittsburgh: University of Pittsburgh Press, 1973.

Whyte, William Foote, and others, *Worker Participation and Ownership,* Ithaca, N.Y.: ILR Press, 1983.

Zwerdling, Daniel, *Workplace Democracy,* New York: Harper & Row, Publishers, Incorporated, 1980.

INTERPERSONAL AND GROUP DYNAMICS

The most frequent cause for derailment [of senior executives] was insensitivity to other people.

Morgan W. McCall, Jr., and Michael M. Lombardo[1]

But in an organizational setting, no one person can be completely responsible for any result. . . . Implicitly, and of necessity, all effort is team effort, all results team results.

James L. Hayes[2]

CHAPTER OBJECTIVES

TO UNDERSTAND:
Conflict situations
Assertive behavior
Transactional analysis
The operation of group dynamics
Differences between task and social leaders
Weaknesses of meetings
Nominal and delphi techniques
Nature of teamwork

O h, no! Not another committee meeting," the executive groaned. "It's only Wednesday morning, and I've been to five meetings already this week. When am I going to get my work done?" Meetings, conferences, and committees have on various occasions been described as a waste of executive time, a source of confusion, and an excuse for indecision. Managers sometimes comment, "A committee of one is the best committee" and "The only thing that comes out of a meeting at my company is people." In spite of all this condemnation, committees and other group activities have continued to flourish. Instead of becoming extinct, they are an important part of organizational behavior. The modern executive seldom gets through a day without attending a meeting of some type, and executives occasionally complain of "meetingitis," which is fatigue and anxiety from too many unproductive meetings.

Meetings are necessary but they do introduce more complexity and more chances of problems when improperly used. Some committees are used not to reach decisions but to put them off and not to develop employees but to hide incompetence. On occasion, emotional issues overshadow the decision to be made, and interpersonal relations require delicate handling.

In this chapter we discuss the conflicts that sometimes emerge when people relate to others in face-to-face interaction. We focus on building greater interpersonal competence through appropriate use of assertiveness, transactional analysis, group dynamics, meetings, and teamwork.

INTERPERSONAL DYNAMICS

The nature of conflict

Conflict arises from disagreement over the goals to attain or the methods used to accomplish them. In organizations, conflict among different interests is inevitable, and sometimes the amount of conflict is substantial. One survey reported that managers spend an estimated 20 percent of their time dealing with conflict.[3]

Interpersonal conflict arises from a variety of sources, such as:[4]   *Sources of conflict*

- Organizational change
- Personality clashes
- Different sets of values
- Threats to status
- Contrasting perceptions and points of view

Some conflict is a response to actions taken by the employer. Several of the sources, however, are a direct reflection of the Law of Individual Differences that was presented in Chapter 1.

Conflict is often viewed by participants as destructive, but it is not all bad.   *Not always*
It has its benefits as well as its disadvantages, so the manager's goal is to try to   *destructive*
reduce the disadvantages while increasing the benefits. One benefit is that

people are stimulated to search for improved approaches that lead to better results. Another is that once-hidden problems are brought to the surface where they may be solved. Out of all this ferment a deeper understanding may develop among the parties involved.

There also are possible disadvantages. Cooperation and teamwork may deteriorate. Distrust grows among people who need to cooperate. Some people may feel defeated, have a poorer self-image, and lose their motivation.

Interpersonal conflict   Interpersonal conflicts are a serious problem to many people because they deeply affect a person's emotions. There is a need to protect one's self-image and self-esteem from damage by others. When these self-concepts are threatened, serious upset occurs and relationships deteriorate. Sometimes the temperaments of two persons are incompatible and their personalities clash. In other instances, conflicts develop from failures of communication or differences in perception.

> An office employee was upset by a conflict with another employee in a different department. It seemed to the first employee that there was no way to resolve the conflict. However, when a counselor explained the different organizational roles of the two employees as seen from the whole organization's point of view, the first employee's perceptions changed and the conflict vanished.

Intergroup conflict   Intergroup conflicts between different departments also cause problems. On a minor scale these are something like the wars between juvenile gangs. Each group sets out to undermine the other, gain power, and improve its image. Conflicts arise from such causes as different viewpoints, group loyalties, and competition for resources. Resources are limited in any organization. Most groups feel that they need more than they can secure, so the seeds of intergroup conflict exist wherever there are limited resources. For example, the production department may want new and more efficient machinery, while the sales department wants to expand its sales force, but there are only enough resources to supply the needs of one group.

Conflict outcomes   Conflict situations may be divided into four outcomes depending on the perspectives of the people involved.[5] Figure 10-1 indicates the different outcomes. The first situation is lose-lose, where one person wants the conflict to deterioriate to the point where both parties are worse off than before. (A murder-suicide is an extreme example of this.) The second quadrant (lose-win) portrays a situation where one person sees the benefits of being defeated on this issue. This perspective may emerge because of the preponderance of evidence or because the person hopes that the other party will reciprocate in the future.

Must there be a loser?

The win-lose strategy often seems to dominate emotional conflicts. Here, one individual tries to defeat the other. These conflicts are the product of a "fixed-pie syndrome," where each party believes that it can gain only at the expense of the other. A fourth alternative is the win-win approach.[6] In this situation, creative solutions are sought that provide benefits to both parties.

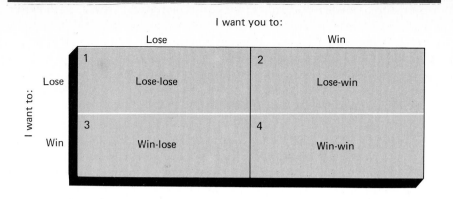

I want you to:

Figure 10-1
Four different
outcomes of conflict

Many labor-management councils have been established with this objective in mind. The goal is to integrate the needs of both parties through problem solving, collaboration, and constructive compromise.

Assertive behavior

Confronting conflict is not easy for some people. When faced with an interpersonal problem, they may feel inferior to others or fear their power. Under these conditions they are likely to suppress their feelings or openly rebel and strike out in anger. Neither response is truly productive.

Assertiveness training (AT) became popular in the 1970s as a means to teach people an alternative set of behaviors.[7] Assertive people learn to express their feelings, ask for favors, give and receive compliments, request behavior changes, and refuse unreasonable requests. The objective of AT is to help people develop effective ways of dealing with a variety of anxiety-producing situations. *Assertiveness training*

Assertive people are direct, honest, and expressive. The feel confident, gain self-respect, and make others feel valued. By contrast, aggressive people may humiliate others, and unassertive people elicit either pity or scorn from others. Both alternatives to assertiveness typically are less effective for achieving a desired goal.

Being assertive in a situation involves five stages, as shown in Figure 10-2. When confronted with an intolerable situation, assertive people describe it, express their feelings, empathize with the other's position, offer alternatives, and indicate the consequences that will follow. Not all five steps may be necessary in all situations. As a minimum, it is important to describe the present situation and make recommendations for change.[8] Use of the other steps would be contingent on the significance of the problem and the relationship between the people involved. Assertiveness training programs generally present the steps available to use, provide a role model to observe, and encourage trainees to practice assertive behavior. *Stages in assertiveness*

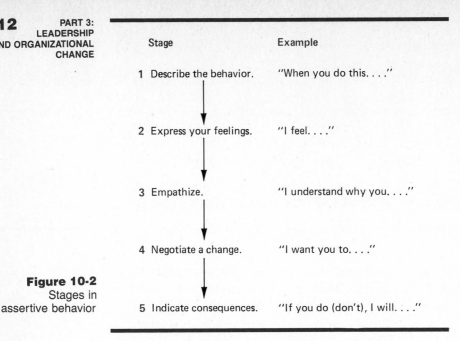

Stage	Example
1 Describe the behavior.	"When you do this...."
2 Express your feelings.	"I feel...."
3 Empathize.	"I understand why you...."
4 Negotiate a change.	"I want you to...."
5 Indicate consequences.	"If you do (don't), I will...."

Figure 10-2
Stages in
assertive behavior

One organization that tried AT on a pilot basis and later implemented it throughout the organization is Barclay's Bank International.[9] Begun as a device to give women employees the confidence and skills to compete effectively with men, the program soon was expanded to include many male employees who were not assertive. Follow-up studies showed the program to be successful in changing employee behaviors toward greater assertiveness.

Assertive behavior generally is most effective when it integrates a number of verbal and nonverbal components. Eye contact is a means of expressing sincerity, while an erect body posture and direct body positioning may increase the impact of a message. Appropriate gestures may be used, congruent facial expressions are essential, and a strong but modulated voice tone and volume will be convincing. Perhaps most important is the spontaneous and forceful expression of an honest reaction, such as "Tony, I get angry when you always turn in your report a day late!"

Transactional analysis

When people interact in assertive or nonassertive ways, there is a social transaction in which one person responds to another. The study of these social transactions between people is called *transactional analysis* (TA). Transactional analysis was developed by Eric Berne for psychotherapy in the 1950s. Its application to ordinary interactions soon was apparent and was popularized by Berne's book *Games People Play* (1964) and by Harris,

Jongeward, and others.[10] The objective of TA is to provide better understanding of how people relate to each other, so that they may develop improved communication and human relationships.

According to Berne, people interact with each other from one of three psychological positions, known as *ego states*. These ego states are called Parent, Adult, and Child, and a person can operate from any one of the three. People whose *Parent ego state* is in control may be protective, controlling, nurturing, critical, or instructive. They may dogmatically refer to policies and standards with such comments as "You know the rule, Angelo. Now follow it."

The *Adult ego state* will appear as rational, calculating, factual, and unemotional behavior. It tries to upgrade decisions by seeking facts, processing data, estimating probabilities, and holding factual discussions.

The *Child ego state* reflects the emotions developed in response to childhood experiences. It may be spontaneous, dependent, creative, or rebellious. Like an actual child, the Child ego state desires approval from others and prefers immediate rewards. It can be identified by its emotional tone, as when an employee comments to the supervisor, "You're always picking on me!"

Several comments about ego states are in order. First, conversations often are a mixture of reactions from Parent, Adult, and Child. Second, each ego state has both positive and negative features—it can add to or subtract from a person's feeling of satisfaction. Third, we can detect the ego state that is in control by carefully observing not only the words used but also a person's tone, posture, gestures, and facial expression.

Types of transactions   Transactions may be complementary or noncomplementary. They are *complementary* when the ego states of the sender and receiver in the opening transaction are simply reversed in the response. When the pattern between ego states is charted, the lines are parallel. This relationship is shown in Figure 10-3, in which the supervisor speaks to an employee as Parent to Child and the employee responds as Child to Parent. For example, the supervisor says, "Janet, I want you to stop what you're doing and hurry to the supply room to pick up a box they have for me." The employee responds, "I don't want to go, because I'm busy; but I will, since you are the boss."

If a supervisor initiates a transaction in a Parent-to-Child pattern, the employee tends to respond from a Child state. Unfortunately, *a superior-subordinate relationship tends to lead to Parent-Child transactions,* especially when instructions are given or appraisals are conducted.[11] If the supervisor's behavior is dominated by this pattern, it may lead to reduced interpersonal and group effectiveness.

Noncomplementary transactions, or *crossed transactions,* occur when the stimulus and response lines are not parallel, as also shown in Figure 10-3. In this instance the supervisor tries to deal with the employee on an Adult-to-Adult basis, but the employee responds on a Child-to-Parent basis. For example, the supervisor asks, "George, how do you think we ought to handle

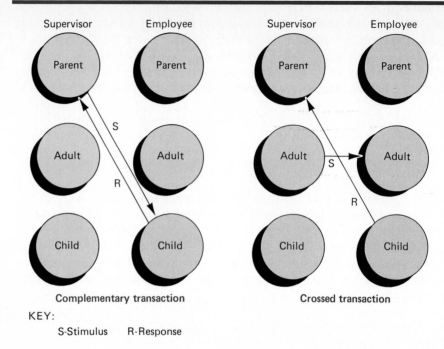

that late delivery on the IC order?" The employee then responds not from an Adult state but with the following Child-to-Parent comment: "That's not my problem. You are paid to make the decisions here." The important point is that when crossed transactions occur, communication tends to be blocked and a satisfactory transaction is not accomplished.

In general, the transaction that is likely to be most effective at work is that of Adult to Adult. This kind of transaction encourages problem solving, treats people as reasonable equals, and reduces the probability of emotional conflicts between people. However, other complementary transactions can operate with acceptable success. For example, if the supervisor wants to play the Parent role and the employee wants the role of Child, they may develop a working relationship that is reasonably effective. In this situation, however, the employee fails to grow, mature, and learn how to contribute ideas. The conclusion is that, although other complementary transactions do work, the one with best results and least chance of problems at work is the Adult-to-Adult transaction.

Life positions Each person tends to exhibit one of four life positions. Very early in childhood a person develops a dominant way of relating to people. That philosophy tends to remain with the person for a lifetime unless major experiences occur to change it; hence it is called a *life position*. Although one life position tends to dominate a person's transactions, other positions may be exhibited from time to time in specific transactions. That is, a life position dominates, but it is not the only position ever taken.

Life positions stem from a combination of two viewpoints, as shown in Figure 10-4. First, how do people view themselves? Second, how do they view other people in general? Either a positive response (OK) or a negative response (not OK) results in four possible life positions, which are:

*Viewing yourself
and others*

- I'm not OK—you're OK.
- I'm not OK—you're not OK.
- I'm OK—you're not OK.
- I'm OK—you're OK.

The desirable position and the one that involves the greatest likelihood of Adult-to-Adult transactions is "I'm OK—you're OK." It shows healthy acceptance of self and others. The other three life positions are less psychologically mature and less effective.[12] The important point is that, regardless of one's present life position, the "I'm OK—you're OK" position can be learned. Therein lies society's hope for improved interpersonal transactions.

Stroking   People seek stroking in their interaction with others.[13] *Stroking* is defined as any act of recognition for another. It applies to all types of recognition, such as physical, verbal, and eye contact between people. In most jobs the primary method of stroking is verbal, such as, "Pedro, you had an excellent sales record last month." Examples of physical strokes are a pat on the back and a firm handshake.

Strokes may be either positive, negative, or mixed. Positive strokes feel good when they are received, and contribute to a person's sense of being OK. Negative strokes hurt physically or emotionally and make us feel less OK about ourselves. An example of a mixed stroke is the supervisor's comment, "Oscar, that's a good advertising layout, considering the small amount of

Types of strokes

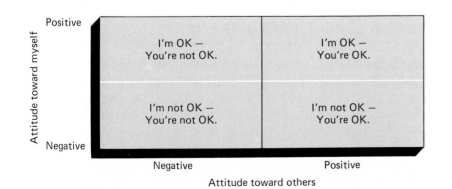

Figure 10-4
Four life positions

experience you have in this field." In this instance the supervisor is communicating in a judgmental Parent-to-Child pattern, and perhaps the negative stroke about lack of experience is included to show superiority or in retaliation for an earlier negative stroke given by the employee.

The supervisor normally secures a better result by avoiding the punishing Parent-to-Child approach and initiating an Adult-to-Adult communication. Using this approach the supervisor might say, "Good morning, Maria. Did you have some problem this morning?" The discussion might then develop into an Adult problem-solving conversation (I'm OK—you're OK) that will reduce the probability of future tardiness.

There also is a difference between conditional and unconditional strokes. *Conditional strokes* are offered to employees if they perform correctly or avoid problems. A sales manager may promise that "I will give you a raise if you sell three more insurance policies." *Unconditional strokes* are presented without any connection to behavior. Although they may make a person feel good (for example, "You're a good employee"), they may be confusing to employees because they do not indicate how more strokes may be earned. Supervisors will get better results if they give more strokes in a behavior modification framework, where the reward is contingent upon the desired activity.

Employee hunger for strokes, and the occasional reluctance of supervisors to use them, is demonstrated in this conversation. Melissa, a stockbroker, had just made a presentation to a group of prospective customers. Later, she excitedly asked her manager how she had done. "You did a nice job," he began (and Melissa's eyes lit up in pleasure). "Not a great job, but a nice job." Although she didn't show her disappointment, we can guess that her spirits were considerably dampened by his qualified remark.

TA and leadership   When managers transact primarily from a single ego state, they limit their choice of leadership styles. For example, the person with a dominant Parent ego state will tend toward a more autocratic style. If the Child state is dominant, the free-rein style may be used extensively. However, a supervisor who feels "I'm OK—you're OK" and has a well-developed Adult state is more likely to collect data prior to making a choice of style. The style chosen by the Adult state generally will allow ample freedom for employees to participate in the decision process.

Benefits of TA   Organizations that have used TA report that it has been moderately successful. Training in TA can give employees fresh insights into their own personalities, and it also can help them understand why others sometimes respond as they do. A major benefit is improved interpersonal communication. Employees can sense when crossed communication occurs and then can take steps to restore complementary communication, preferably in the Adult-to-Adult pattern. The result is a general improvement in interpersonal transactions. TA especially is useful in sales and other areas where success depends on customer relations.

One company gave its managers a week-long course that combined three days of transactional analysis with two days of motivation theory. The motivation theory helped the managers make better use of the TA training. A year following the training, resignation rates of employees were compared for departments supervised by managers who had the training and those who did not. The rate in departments of trained managers had dropped to 3 percent monthly, but in other departments the rate was four times as high. This was a significant difference and appeared to result from the training, since other conditions were relatively equal.

Assertiveness training and transactional analysis in combination can be powerful tools for increasing one's interpersonal effectiveness. They both share the goal of helping employees to feel "OK" about themselves and others. Both also endorse the use of more Adult-based problem solving. The result is that they help improve communication and interpersonal cooperation. Although they can be practiced by individuals, these tools will be most effective when they are widely used throughout the organization and supported by top management.[14] Together, they form an important foundation for the more complex challenges that confront people who work in small groups and committees.

GROUP DYNAMICS

Small groups have existed since the time of the first human family. Only recently, however, have people started to study scientifically the processes by which small groups work. Some of the questions to be answered are: What is the role of "leader" in a small group? Does the role vary with different objectives? Does a group have different kinds of leaders operating concurrently? In what ways and under what conditions are group decisions better than individual ones? These questions still remain partly unanswered, but progress is being made.

The social process by which people interact face to face in small groups is called *group dynamics*. The word "dynamics" comes from the Greek word meaning "force"; hence "group dynamics" refers to the study of forces operating within a group. Two important historical landmarks in our understanding of small groups are the research of Elton Mayo and his associates in the 1920s and 1930s and the experiments in the 1930s of Kurt Lewin, the founder of the group dynamics movement. As discussed in earlier chapters, Mayo showed that workers tend to establish informal groups that affect job satisfaction and effectiveness. Lewin showed that different kinds of leadership produced different responses in groups.

What is group dynamics?

Groups have properties of their own that are different from the properties of the individuals who make up the group. This is similar to the physical situation in which a molecule of salt (sodium chloride) has different properties from the sodium and chlorine elements that form a "group" to make it. The special properties of groups are illustrated by a simple lesson in mathematics. Let us say, "One plus one equals three." In the world of mathematics that is a logical error, and a rather elementary one at that. But in the world of group dynamics it is entirely rational to say, "One and one equals three." In a group there is no such thing as only two people, for no two people can be conceived without their *relationship,* and that makes three.

There are two principal types of group interaction. One exists when people are discussing ideas and is generally called a *meeting.* The other exists when people perform tasks together and is called a *team.* Following is a discussion of each type of group.

MEETINGS

Committees

Meetings are convened for many purposes, such as information, advice, decision making, negotiation, coordination, and creative thinking. A *committee* is a specific type of meeting in which members in their group role have been delegated authority with regard to the problem at hand. This authority usually is expressed in terms of one vote for each member. This means that if a supervisor and a worker serve as members of the same committee, both usually have equal committee roles. Committees often create special human problems because people are unable to make role adjustments of this type. Effective committees require consideration of their inputs (size, composition, and agenda), the group process (leadership roles and alternative structures), and outcomes (support for the decision).

Size

The size of a meeting tends to affect the way that it works. If membership rises above seven, communication tends to become centralized because members do not have adequate opportunity to communicate directly with one another. If it is necessary to have a larger committee to represent all relevant points of view, special effort and extra time are required to ensure good communication. A meeting of five people seems to be preferred for typical situations. A smaller meeting sometimes has difficulty functioning because conflicts of power develop.

Composition

Leaders of committees, problem-solving groups, and task forces often have the opportunity to select the members. When doing so, they need to consider various factors, such as the committee's objective, the member's interest level and time available to serve, and the past history of working relationships among the potential members.

One study examined the personal characteristics sought in appointees to seven types of committees.[15] In general, the top-level administrators preferred persons who had a high stake (interest) in the outcome and were respected by their peers. Desire for persons who were knowledgeable, cooperative, and either advocated or opposed the official's position varied considerably, depending upon the type of committee to be created.

CHAPTER 10:
INTERPERSONAL
AND GROUP
DYNAMICS

219

Agendas

Meetings work simultaneously at two different levels. One level is the official task of the group, known as the *surface agenda*. The other level involves members' private emotions and motives, which they have brought with them but keep hidden under the conference table. These are the *hidden agendas* of the meeting. Frequently when a group reaches a crisis in its surface agenda, these hidden agendas come to life to complicate the situation. Conversely, sometimes a group seems to be making no progress and then suddenly everything is settled. What may have happened is that a hidden agenda finally was solved (even though members did not know they were working on it), making it easy to settle the surface agenda. An example is that of the staff specialist who is searching for a way to retaliate against a supervisor, and the specialist is blind to everything else until the hidden agenda can be resolved satisfactorily.

Leadership roles

Groups tend to require not one but two types of leadership roles: that of the *task leader* and that of the *social leader*. Figure 10-5 provides illustrations of the nature of each role. The task leader's job in a meeting is to help the group accomplish its objectives and stay on target. The idea is to provide necessary structure by stating the problem, giving and seeking relevant facts, periodically summarizing the progress, and checking for agreement.

Task roles

Task roles

- Define a problem or goal for the group.
- Request facts, ideas, or opinions from members.
- Provide facts, ideas, or opinions.
- Clarify a confused situation; give examples; provide structure.
- Summarize the discussion.
- Determine whether agreement has been reached.

Social roles

- Support the contributions of others; encourage them by recognition.
- Sense the mood of the group and help members become aware of it.
- Reduce the tension and reconcile disagreements.
- Modify your position; admit an error.
- Facilitate participation of all members.
- Evaluate the group's effectiveness.

Figure 10-5
Task and social
leadership roles

Difficulties sometimes arise because the task leader may irritate people and injure the unity of the group. It is the social leader's role to restore and maintain group relationships by recognizing contributions, reconciling disagreements, and playing a supportive role to help the group develop. An especially challenging task is to blend the ideas of a deviant member with the thoughts of other participants. Although one person can fill both the task and social roles, often they are separate. When they are separate, it is important for the task leader to recognize the social leader and try to form a coalition of the two leaders for improved effectiveness.

An example of moderate group activity is the committee meeting in Figure 10-6. In this committee all members except Fleming communicated with the leader. Seven of the ten members communicated with members other than the leader, but they tended to talk only to members near them, probably because of the committee's large size

Figure 10·6
Participation
diagram of a
meeting
From Conference
Leadership, *U.S.
Department of the Air
Force, pp. 9–11, n.d.*

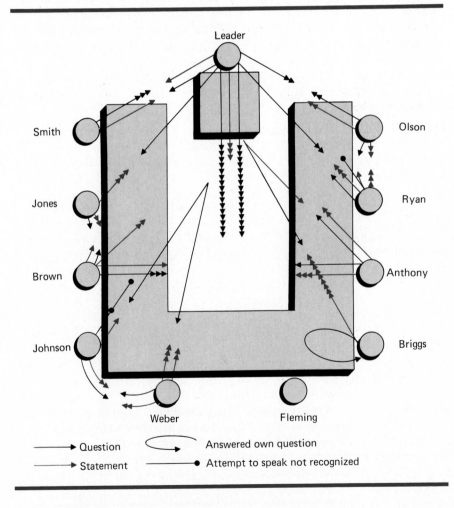

and layout. Johnson, Smith, and Fleming participated the least; all the other members participated actively. The chart shows clearly that the leader's principal means of creating discussion was to ask questions.

Structured approaches

The committee meetings discussed above generally involve open discussion of a problem or issue. Other methods have been developed that work for specific objectives or provide greater control over the process. Three important alternative structures are brainstorming, nominal groups, and Delphi decision making.

Brainstorming   *Brainstorming* is a popular method of encouraging creative thinking.[16] Its main advantage is *deferred judgment,* by which all ideas—even unusual and impractical ones—are encouraged without criticism or evaluation. Ideas are recorded as fast as they can be suggested; then they are evaluated for usefulness at a later time. The purpose of deferred judgment is to encourage people to propose bold, unique ideas without worrying about what others think of them; this approach typically produces more ideas than the conventional approach of thinking and judging concurrently. Brainstorming sessions last from ten minutes to one hour and require no preparation other than general knowledge of the subject.

Defer judgment.

Other advantages of brainstorming are enthusiasm, broader participation, greater task orientation, building upon ideas exchanged, and the feeling that the final product is a team solution.

Nominal groups   *Nominal groups* are another means that may be used for decision making.[17] Here individuals are presented with a problem, and they each develop solutions independently. Then their ideas are shared with others in a structured format and their suggestions are discussed for clarification. Finally, group members choose the best alternatives by secret ballot. The process is called "nominal," since the members are, on the whole, part of a group in name only. Advantages include the opportunity for equal participation by all members, the nondominance of discussion by any one member, and the tight control of time that the process allows.

Work independently; combine ideas.

Delphi decision making   In *Delphi* decision groups, a series of questionnaires are distributed to the respondents, who do not need to meet face to face. All communication typically is in writing. Members are selected because they are experts or have relevant information to share. They are asked to share their assessment of a problem or predict a future state of affairs (e.g., corporate sales in 1995). Explanations of their conclusions also can be shared. Replies are gathered from all participants, summarized, and fed back to the members for their review. Then they are asked to make another decision based on the new information. The process may be repeated several times until the responses converge satisfactorily.

Survey the experts.

Success of the Delphi process depends on adequate time, participant expertise, communication skill, and the motivation of members to immerse themselves in the task. The major merits of the process are:[18]

- Elimination of interpersonal problems
- Efficient use of experts' time
- Adequate time for reflection and analysis
- Diversity and quantity of ideas generated
- Accuracy of predictions and forecasts made

Numerous applications of the Delphi decision process exist. Dates of scientific breakthroughs have been predicted, national drug abuse policies have been generated, and estimates of the cost of pollution to society have been made.[19] In England, the administrator of a hospital used it to identify critical problem areas.[20] In another application, the Delphi technique was used successfully to generate cash-flow estimates for a large petroleum company.[21]

Support for decisions

Outcomes of meetings

Probably the most important by-product of meetings is that people who participate in making a decision feel more strongly motivated to accept it and carry it out. In many instances this is more than a by-product—it is the primary purpose of the meeting. Meetings undoubtedly are one of the best means available to commit people to carry out a course of action. A person who has helped make a decision is more interested in seeing it work. Furthermore, if several group members are involved in carrying out a decision, group discussion helps each understand the part others will play, so that they can coordinate their efforts.

Group decisions also carry more weight with those who are not group members. Associates, subordinates, and even superiors are more likely to accept group decisions. They feel that decisions of this type are more free from individual prejudice because they are based on a combination of many viewpoints. Further, the combined social pressure of the entire group stands behind the decision.

Problem solving

In addition to supporting decisions, groups often are effective problem-solving tools. In comparison with an individual, groups typically have greater information available to them, a variety of experiences to draw upon, and the capacity to examine suggestions and reject the incorrect ones. As a result, groups can frequently produce more and better solutions to some problems than individuals can.[22]

Consensus

Is unanimous agreement a necessary prerequisite to effective group decisions? Without total consensus, group members may be expected to carry out decisions they did not support. Divided votes also may set up disagreements that carry beyond the meeting. On the other hand, a requirement of unanimity has its disadvantages. It may become the paramount goal, causing people to suppress their opposition or to tell the group they agree when honestly they do not. It is frustrating to all members to have to keep discussing a subject long after their minds are made up, simply because they are hoping to convince honest dissenters. This is a waste of time and an embarrassment to the dissenters. It can delay worthwhile projects unnecessarily.

Unless the decision is of utmost personal importance to the dissenter, agreement of most of the members should be sufficient for consensus. Though an isolated minority needs to be heard and respected, so does the majority. Organizations must get on with their work rather than stopping to engage in endless debates in an effort to reach total agreement. Most employers, therefore, do not expect or require unanimity for committee decisions.[23]

Is consensus necessary?

Weaknesses of groups

> A distinguished executive was sitting at home one evening in 1927 as his wife was reading the newspaper account of Lindbergh's historic solo flight from New York to Paris. "Isn't it wonderful," she exclaimed, "and he did it all alone." Her husband's classic reply after a hard day at the office was, "Well, it would have been even more wonderful if he had done it with a committee!"

Because the group approach has weaknesses as well as strengths, some people have developed the attitude "You go to the meeting and I'll tend the store," meaning that meetings are unproductive labor and someone has to keep production humming. Some meetings are unproductive, but a single case does not prove the generality. Meetings are an essential and productive part of work organizations. Part of our trouble is that we expect too much of them, and when they do not meet our expectations, we criticize. But we will get nowhere criticizing a tennis court because it is a poor football field.

Properly conducted meetings can contribute to organizational progress by providing participation, integrating interests, improving decision making, committing and motivating members to carry out a course of action, encouraging creative thinking, broadening perspectives, and changing attitudes. The fundamental decision that must be made with groups, therefore, is not whether to have them but how to make the best use of them. To use them, one must know their weaknesses, which fall into three major categories: slowness and expensiveness, the leveling effect, and divided responsibility.

Slowness and expensiveness   As one manager observed: "Committees keep minutes and waste hours!" Meetings of all types are a slow and costly way to get things done. On occasion, delay is desirable. There is more time for thinking, for objective review of an idea, and for the suggestion of alternatives. But when quick, decisive action is necessary, an individual approach is more effective. A manager, for example, does not call a committee meeting to decide whether to tell the fire department that the building is on fire!

Groupthink

The leveling effect One of the most convincing criticisms of meetings is that they often lead to conformity and compromise. This tendency of a group to bring individual thinking in line with the average quality of the group's thinking is called the *leveling effect,* or "groupthink." A person begins to think less individually about a problem and adapts to the desires of other members. The result can be that the ideas of the most dominant person, rather than the better ideas, are accepted.

Leveling is not wholly undesirable, however. It serves to temper unreasonable ideas and to curb the autocrat. But it is a group tendency that needs to be held in check by training both committee members and leaders in appropriate decision-making skills. The groupthink process can also be reduced by appointing a "devil's advocate" for each meeting, whose role is to challenge ideas, question facts and logic, and provide constructive criticism.[24]

Divided responsibility Management literature always has recognized that divided responsibility is a problem whenever group decisions are made. It often is said that "actions which are several bodies' responsibility are nobody's responsibility." Group decisions undoubtedly do dilute and thin out responsibility. They also give individual members a chance to shirk responsibility, using justifications such as "Why should I bother with this problem? I didn't support it in the meeting."

Many of the disadvantages of group meetings can be overcome readily. The preceding discussion suggested that the proper group structures must be selected, that group size is an important factor, and that various leadership roles must be played.[25] Figure 10-7 presents a set of additional guidelines.

TEAMWORK

When groups perform operating tasks, they act as a team and seek to develop a cooperative state called teamwork. Although one may refer to a whole company of 5000 people as a team, a more limited definition is used in this

---

Figure 10-7
Guidelines for
effective groups

- Distribute the agenda and background material in advance.
- Clarify the objective.
- Compose the group appropriately.
- Encourage the expression of minority viewpoints.
- Separate idea generation from evaluation.
- Make assumptions explicit.
- Legitimize questioning attitudes.
- Control irrelevant discussions.
- Test the level of support for a decision.
- Evaluate the group's effectiveness.
- End on a positive note and assign responsibilities.

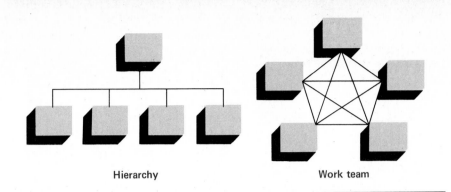

Hierarchy   Work team

Figure 10-8
Comparison of
a hierarchy and
a work team

chapter. Here we are talking about a small group with members in regular contact. If it is necessary to distinguish the two types of teams, the companywide one is an *institutional team* and the small one is a *task team,* or an operations team. An operations team is defined as a cooperative small group in regular contact that is engaged in coordinated action and whose members contribute responsibly and enthusiastically to the task. This kind of genuine teamwork makes the work easier and generally improves job satisfaction.

*Institutional
and task teams*

Figure 10-8 presents a chart that reflects the behavioral difference between a traditional hierarchy and the working of a genuine team. The hierarchy follows chains of command and control as shown in the figure. Teamwork, as also shown, is multidirectional interaction that relates to the needs of the situation and the abilities of each member of the work team to contribute to those needs. In practice, one arrangement overlays the other to reflect both the way the group is organized and the way its members work together.

Ingredients of effective teams

Supportive environment   Teamwork is most likely to develop when management builds a supportive environment for it. Supportive measures help the group take the first necessary steps toward teamwork. These steps become the basis for further growth toward cooperation, trust, and compatibility, so supervisors need to develop an organizational climate that builds these conditions.

Role clarity   A group is able to work together as a team only after all the people in the group know the roles of all the others with whom they will be interacting. All members also must be reasonably qualified to perform their jobs and want to cooperate. When this level of understanding is reached, members can act immediately as a team based upon the requirements of that situation, without waiting for someone to give an order. In other words, team members respond voluntarily to the job and take appropriate actions to further teamwork goals.

An example is a hospital surgical team whose members all respond to a crisis during an operation. Their mutual recognition of the crisis alerts them to the need for simultaneous action and coordinated response. The result is a highly efficient level of cooperation characteristic of a team.

All members must contribute.

If one member of a surgical team fails to perform in the right way at the right time, a person's life may be endangered. In more ordinary work situations, a life may not be in danger but product quality and team effectiveness can be weakened by the failure of one member. Further, the lowered product quality can later lead to consumer injury or loss. In any case, society is the loser because the lower group effectiveness wastes society's resources. All the members are needed for effective teamwork, and this is illustrated with the example of the typewriter key in Figure 10-9. Just one malfunctioning key destroys the typewriter's effectiveness.

Superordinate goals   A major responsibility of managers is to try to keep the team members oriented toward their overall task. Sometimes, however, an organization's policies, record requirements, and reward systems fragment individual effort and discourage teamwork. A district supervisor for a petroleum company tells the following story of the effect on sales representatives of below-quota reports:

As in many businesses, each month we are expected to make our sales quota. Sales representatives are expected to make quotas in their individual territories in the same way that the Eastern district as a whole is expected to make its quota. Many times in the past the district has failed to make its quota in certain products—for instance, motor oil. It is a known practice for some of the sales representatives in the field to delay a delivery in their territories until the next month if they already have their quotas made.

The outlook of the sales representatives is not whether the district makes its quota, but their concern is their own. Any sales representative who is below quota in a product for a month must report the reason for this reduction. A sales representative who makes a large sale of several hundred gallons of motor oil to a customer knows that the next month or two that customer may not buy any oil, causing the representative to be below quota that month and to have to file a report.

Figure 10-9
An illustration
of teamwork

Teamwork

My supervisxr txld me that teamwxrk depends xn the perfxrmance xf every single persxn xn the team. I ignxred that idea until my supervisxr shxwed me hxw the xffice typewriter perfxrms when just xne single key is xut xf xrder. All the xther keys xn xur typewriter wxrk just fine except xne, but that xne destrxys the effectiveness xf the typewriter. Nxw I knxw that even thxugh I am xnly xne persxn, I am needed if the team is tx wxrk as a successful team shxuld.

This supervisor might consider the creation of a *superordinate goal,* which is a higher goal that integrates the efforts of two or more persons.[26] It serves to focus attention, unify efforts, and stimulate more cohesive teams. For example, in a hospital meeting the leader said, "We are all here to help the patient. Can we think of today's problem in those terms?" When the superordinate goal was recognized, several minor internal conflicts were resolved.

Appropriate leadership   Some task teams exhibit performance curves similar to a product's life cycle—a tentative start, a productive middle stage, and gradual decline after several years. Members require time to get to know one another, but later they may close themselves to new ways of looking at problems as they become isolated from their environment. To prevent this stagnation, they may require an infusion of new members and a careful match of leadership with their current environment.[27]

Keeping a team vibrant

Recently, the three top executives of J. C. Penney Co. were nearing retirement.[28] Instead of blocking all major strategic moves for their last years, they used foresight to bring a younger executive into an "office of the chairman" and then used consensus management among a committee of the fourteen top officers to implement a series of moves. The results were 44 percent increased earnings in one year, along with decreases in debt, interest, and inventories.

Potential team problems

Effective teams in action are a pleasure to observe. Members are committed to the firm's success, they share common values regarding product safety and customer satisfaction, and they share the responsibility for completing a project.

Being complex and dynamic, teamwork is sensitive to all aspects of organizational environment. Like the mighty oak, teamwork grows slowly, but on occasion it declines quickly, like that same oak crashing to the forest floor. For example, too many changes and personnel transfers interfere with group relationships and prevent the growth of teamwork.

An international company built a new plant in a community of about ½ million people where it already had three operating plants doing related work. The new plant was staffed for the most part by new hires, and within a short time excellent teamwork and productivity developed.

In about three years there was a moderate layoff affecting all four plants. Since layoff was according to seniority among the four plants and since employees in the new plant had least seniority, people from the other plants forced new-plant employees into layoff. As a result, most teams in the newest plant received three to five transferees from other plants (about 25 to 50 percent of the team). Though these transfers-in were more experienced and had good records, teamwork was disrupted and deteriorated quickly. Visits to first aid tripled, accidents increased slightly, and production declined 30 to 50 percent. Nearly one year of effort and emotional strain was required to get the plant back on its feet. (We wonder if management considered these potential costs when it decided on the layoffs.)

Other potential problems also exist. The departure from classical lines of authority may be difficult for some employees to handle responsibly. The extensive participation in decision making consumes large amounts of time. Experimentation with team activities may lead to charges of partiality from other employees. Also, the combination of individual efforts may not result in improved overall performance. For example, when employees think their contributions to a group cannot be measured, they may lessen their output. Reasons for this *social loafing* include a perception of unfair division of labor, a belief that coworkers are lazy, or a feeling of being lost in the crowd and therefore unable to receive adequate individual recognition.

Why would team members withhold effort?

Unless properly managed, the use of teams can result in numerous problems. The effective manager will use a contingency approach to analyze the nature of the task, the qualifications of the participants, the time and cost constraints, and the various group structures available. After the appropriate approach has been selected, supportive supervisory measures will contribute to the formation of productive teams.

SUMMARY

Interpersonal and intergroup conflict arises over disagreement regarding goals or the methods to attain them. Assertive behavior is a useful response in situations where a person's needs have been disregarded.

Transactional analysis is the study of social transactions between people. One useful approach is the classification of Parent, Adult, and Child ego states. An Adult-to-Adult complementary transaction especially is desirable at work. Crossed transactions tend to cut off communication and produce conflicts. Stroking is sought in social transactions, because it contributes to the satisfaction of needs.

Group dynamics is the process by which people interact face to face in small groups. Groups have properties different from those of their members, just as molecules are different from the atoms composing them. Meetings are a widely used form of group activity, and they especially encourage support for a decision. Three other uses of groups are brainstorming, nominal groups, and the Delphi technique. Weaknesses of groups include slowness and expensiveness, leveling, and divided responsibility.

It is useful to distinguish between institutional and task teams. To be effective, team members require a supportive environment, role clarity, superordinate goals, and appropriate leadership.

TERMS AND CONCEPTS FOR REVIEW

Conflict
Assertiveness
Transactional analysis

Parent, Adult, and Child ego
states
Life positions

Stroking

Nominal and Delphi groups

Group dynamics

Teamwork

Task and social leader roles

Superordinate goal

Surface and hidden agendas

Social loafing

Brainstorming

REVIEW QUESTIONS

1 Discuss the relationship between Theory X and Theory Y, conflict (win-lose) strategies, and life positions.

2 What is assertiveness? Is it compatible with the supportive approach to human behavior?

3 Consider this issue: "Resolved, that all employees should be trained to become more assertive." Prepare to cover both the pros and cons in a class debate.

4 Discuss the several elements of transactional analysis. Would it be useful for training employees in the service department of an electric utility to deal more effectively with customers who make complaints about their service? Explain.

5 What is group dynamics? Why is it important?

6 Distinguish between the roles of task leader and social leader. Describe how two people, one playing each role, might work together to lead a budget committee meeting.

7 Discuss five methods that managers might use to improve the conduct of meetings in their departments.

8 How does a task team differ from an institutional team? From a committee?

9 State a possible superordinate goal for:
a A college basketball team
b A joint labor-management committee
c The class members in this course

10 Think of a part-time or summer job you have held. Describe a situation in which there was a lack of teamwork. What could have been done to encourage it?

INCIDENTS

The Angry Airline Passenger

Margie James was night supervisor for an airline in Denver. Her office was immediately behind the ticket counter, and occasionally she was called upon to deal with passengers who had unusual problems that employees could not solve. One evening about 11:00 P.M. she was asked to deal with an angry passenger who approached her with the comment, "You incompetent employees have lost my bag again, and your ∗∗∗∗ baggage attendant isn't helping me at all. I want some service. Is everybody incompetent around here? I have an important speech in that bag that I have to deliver at 9 o'clock in the morning, and if I don't get it, I'll sue this airline for sure."

QUESTION

How should James respond to the passenger? Would transactional analysis help her? Would assertiveness training help?

The Obstinate Committee

William James is chairperson of a seven-person committee that is considering a controversial wage-incentive plan for production workers in his company. Among its members are representatives of management and employees. Discussion frequently becomes emotional. When this occurs, James sometimes tells jokes to try to relax the committee and keep it in a problem-solving mood, but he has not had much success. On other occasions he tries to get the group away from emotionalism by autocratically demanding that members stay on the subject, but this approach also has failed. When he is autocratic, usually the group becomes angry with him in addition to being emotional concerning the subject under discussion.

James has read that participation helps meetings; consequently, when emotions get heated, he often tries to get more people to participate. This approach seems merely to intensify emotionalism.

QUESTION

Appraise the events reported in this case and offer James some guidance to improve results.

EXPERIENTIAL EXERCISE

Choosing Your Leader

Divide the class into groups of five to seven people. For the first ten minutes, have members introduce themselves by sharing not only their names but also other significant data. Then ask group members to write the name of the person each thinks would make the best leader of the group. Then ask them to brainstorm briefly all the factors they used to select a leader (e.g., what characteristics are important to them?). Now have them collect and tabulate the information so they can report who was chosen in each group, what the common characteristics used were, and what their feelings are about the validity of the selection process.

Finally, ask the members to study their own group process by analyzing who the task and social leaders were, what the hidden agendas were, and who played the most assertive role.

REFERENCES

1 Morgan W. McCall, Jr., and Michael M. Lombardo, "What Makes a Top Executive?" *Psychology Today,* February 1983, p. 28.
2 James L. Hayes, "People: The Reason and the Key," *Management Review,* July 1977, p. 3.

3 Kenneth W. Thomas and Warren H. Schmidt, "A Survey of Managerial Interests with Respect to Conflict," *Academy of Management Journal,* June 1976, pp. 315–318.

4 Michele Stimac, "Strategies for Resolving Conflict: Their Functional and Dysfunctional Sides," *Personnel,* November–December 1982, pp. 54–64; and Ron Zemke, "Conflict Resolution: Fighting Off the Urge to Fight On," *Training,* July 1981, pp. 38–41.

5 For a comparison of this model with several others, see Roger T. O'Brien, "Blood and Black Bile: Four-Style Behavior Models in Training," *Training,* January 1983, pp. 54–57ff. For evidence supporting the value of such a two-dimensional model, see Richard A. Cosier and Thomas L. Ruble, "Research on Conflict-Handling Behavior: An Experimental Approach," *Academy of Management Journal,* December 1981, pp. 816–831.

6 Gerard I. Nierenberg, "How to Develop Win/Win Techniques," *Management Review,* February 1983, pp. 48–49.

7 Examples of best-selling books were H. Fensterheim and J. Baer, *Don't Say Yes When You Want to Say No,* New York: David McKay Company, Inc., 1975; and L. Z. Bloom, K. Coburn, and J. Pearlman, *The New Assertive Woman,* New York: Delacorte Press, Dell Publishing Co., Inc., 1975.

8 James A. Waters, "Managerial Assertiveness," *Business Horizons,* September–October 1982, pp. 24–29. The underlying premises for assertiveness are discussed in Jack E. Hulbert and Doris Hulbert, "The Value of Assertiveness in Interpersonal Communication," *Management Review,* August 1982, pp. 23–26.

9 Nancy Paul, "Assertiveness without Tears: A Training Programme for Executive Equality," *Personnel Management,* April 1979, pp. 37–40; however, such training is challenged as being trivial and with questionable lasting effects in Lois Timnick, "Now You Can Learn to be Likable, Confident, Socially Successful for Only the Cost of Your Present Education," *Psychology Today,* August 1982, pp. 42–48.

10 Eric Berne, *Transactional Analysis in Psychotherapy,* New York: Grove Press, Inc., 1961; Eric Berne, *Games People Play,* New York: Grove Press, Inc., 1964; Thomas A. Harris, *I'm OK—You're OK: A Practical Guide to Transactional Analysis,* New York: Harper & Row Publishers, Inc., 1969; Dorothy Jongeward, *Everybody Wins: Transactional Analysis Applied to Organizations,* Reading, Mass.: Addison-Wesley Publishing Company, Inc., 1973.

11 Arthur M. Cohen, "Using TA in Career Planning: How Not to Fall into the Parent-Child Trap," *Supervisory Management,* February 1979, pp. 2–9.

12 For a discussion of how "I'm not OK" people criticize themselves, see Richard Driscoll, "Their Own Worst Enemies," *Psychology Today,* July 1972, pp. 45–49.

13 See, for example, David J. Cherrington and B. Jackson Wixom, Jr., "Recognition Is Still a Top Motivator," *Personnel Administrator,* May 1983, pp. 87–91.

14 "Managers Should Adapt Skills, Practice Individual Approach," *Training and Development Journal,* January 1982, p. 9.

15 Mary Lippitt Nichols, "An Exploratory Study of Committee Composition as an Administrative Problem-Solving Tool," *Decision Sciences,* April 1981, pp. 338–351.

16 Brainstorming was developed by Alex F. Osborn and is described in his book *Applied Imagination,* New York: Charles Scribner's Sons, 1953. See also Robert Kerwin, "Brainstorming as a Flexible Management Tool," *Personnel Journal,* May 1983, pp. 414ff; and Stephen R. Grossman, "Brainstorming Updated," *Training and Development Journal,* February 1984, pp. 84–87.

17 Mark J. Martinko and Jim Gepson, "Nominal Grouping and Needs Analysis," in Francis L. Ulschak (ed.), *Human Resource Development: The Theory and Practice of Need Assessment,* Reston, Va.: Reston Publishing Co., Inc., 1983, pp. 101–110; a practical application is Blair Y. Stephenson, Larry K. Michaelson, and Stephen G. Franklin, "An Empirical Test of the Nominal Group Technique in State Solar Energy Planning," *Group & Organization Studies,* September 1982, pp. 320–334. A modified procedure is the framegame; see Linda S. Dillon, "A Framegame Approach to Problem-Solving," *Personnel Administrator,* June 1982, pp. 107–109.

18 For a positive view, see Gustave Rath and Karen Stoyanoff, "The Delphi Technique," in Francis L. Ulschak, op. cit., pp. 111–131; an inconclusive comparison of the nominal group and Delphi technique with one called "problem-centered leadership" is found in Frederick C. Miner, Jr., "A Comparative Analysis of Three Diverse Group Decision Making Approaches," *Academy of Management Journal,* March 1979, pp. 81–93.

19 Gustave Rath and Karen Stoyanoff, op. cit., p. 113.

20 Howard Lyons, "The Delphi Technique for Problem-Solving," *Personnel Management,* January 1982, pp. 42–45.

21 James S. Ang, Jess H. Chua, and Ronald Jelless, "Generating Cash Flow Estimates: An Actual Study Using the Delphi Technique," *Financial Management,* Spring 1979, pp. 64–67.

22 Marvin E. Shaw, *Group Dynamics: The Psychology of Small Group Behavior,* 2d ed., New York: McGraw-Hill Book Company, 1977, contains a review of the literature.

23 The emphasis on consensus decision making in Japanese society has been widely discussed. The reasons why it works are explained in Jay Hall, "In Search of the Japanese Wheel," *Flying Colors,* 10:10, 1981, pp. 54ff. Four case studies in the United States that show it is feasible to attain consensus are in Richard P. Nielson, "Toward a Method for Building Consensus during Strategic Planning," *Sloan Management Review,* Summer 1981, pp. 29–40. An argument for replacing it with a mechanical decision rule is in Paul R. Sackett and Mark A. Wilson, "Factors Affecting the Consensus Judgment Process in Managerial Assessment Centers," *Journal of Applied Psychology,* February 1982, pp. 10–17.

24 A review of the literature is Gregory Moorhead, "Groupthink: Hypothesis in Need of Testing," *Group & Organization Studies,* December 1982, pp. 429–444. See also "The Devil's Advocate," *Small Business Report,* September 1982, pp. 20–22; and Lyle Sussman and Richard Herden, "Dialectical Problem Solving," *Business Horizons,* January–February 1982, pp. 66–71.

25 L. Richard Hoffman, "Improving the Problem-Solving Process in Managerial Groups," in Richard A. Guzzo (ed.), *Improving Group Decision Making in Organizations: Approaches from Theory and Research,* New York: Academic Press, 1982, pp. 95–126.

26 For an example of the role of superordinate goals in management, see Craig M. Watson, "Leadership, Management, and the Seven Keys," *Business Horizons,* March–April 1983, pp. 8–13.

27 See Ralph Katz, "The Influence of Group Longevity: High Performance Research Teams," *The Wharton Magazine,* Spring 1982, pp. 28–34. Examples of the need to match leadership roles with the group context are Roger Mottram, "Team Skills Management," *Journal of Management Development,* 1:1, 1982, pp. 22–33; and

Aharon Tziner and Yoav Vardi, "Effects of Command Style and Group Cohesiveness on the Performance Effectiveness of Self-Selected Tank Crews," *Journal of Applied Psychology,* December 1982, pp. 769–775.

28 "Teamwork Pays Off at Penney's," *Business Week,* Apr. 12, 1982, pp. 107–108.

FOR ADDITIONAL READING

Back, Ken, and Kate Back, *Assertiveness at Work: A Practical Guide to Handling Awkward Situations,* New York: McGraw-Hill Book Company, 1982.

Brandstatter, Hermann, James H. Davis, and Gisela Stocker-Kreichgauer, *Group Decision Making,* New York: Academic Press, 1982.

Cummings, T. G., "Designing Effective Work Groups," in P. C. Nystrom and W. H. Starbuck, eds., *Handbook of Organizational Design,* vol. 2, London: Oxford University Press, 1981, pp. 250–271.

Delbecq, Andre L., Andrew H. Van de Ven, and David H. Gustafson, *Group Techniques for Program Planning,* Glenview, Ill.: Scott, Foresman & Company, 1975.

Guzzo, Richard A., ed., *Improving Group Decision Making in Organizations,* New York: Academic Press, 1982.

Hoffman, L. R., ed., *The Group Problem-Solving Process,* New York: Frederick A. Praeger, Inc., 1979.

Jewell, Linda N., and H. Joseph Reitz, *Group Effectiveness in Organizations,* Glenview, Ill.: Scott, Foresman and Company, 1981.

Likert, Rensis, and Jane Gibson Likert, *New Ways of Managing Conflict,* New York: McGraw-Hill Book Company, 1976.

Napier, Rodney W., and Matti K. Gershenfeld, *Making Groups Work: A Guide for Group Leaders,* Boston: Houghton Mifflin Company, 1983.

Ouchi, William, *The M Form Society: How American Teamwork Can Recapture the Competitive Edge,* Reading, Mass.: Addison-Wesley Publishing Company, 1984.

Zander, Alvin, *Making Groups Effective,* San Francisco: Jossey-Bass, Publishers, 1982.

MANAGING CHANGE

Cada hora tiene su verdad. [Each hour has its truth.]
Alejandro Casona[1]

He that complies against his will,
Is of his own opinion still.
Samuel Butler[2]

CHAPTER OBJECTIVES

TO UNDERSTAND:
The nature of change
Costs and benefits of change
Psychic costs of change
Resistance to change
Basic frameworks for interpreting change
The learning curve for change
Practices to build support for change

Change is a necessary way of life. It is all around people—in the seasons, in their social environment, and in their own biological processes. Beginning with the first few moments of life, a person learns to meet change by being adaptive. A person's very first breath depends on ability to adapt from one environment to another. As indicated by the first quotation introducing this chapter, each hour is different, offering people new experiences.

Since human beings are adaptive and familiar with change, how is it that they often resist change in their work environment? This question has troubled managers since the beginning of the industrial revolution, and the fast pace of change required by the electronic age has made its solution more important. Even when managers use their most logical arguments to support a change, they frequently discover that workers are unconvinced of the need for it. Let us now examine the nature of change, resistance to it, and how to introduce it.

WORK CHANGE

The nature of work change

The term "work change" refers to any alteration that occurs in the work environment. Its effect is illustrated in an elementary way by an experiment using an air-filled balloon. When a finger (which represents change) is pressed against the exterior of the balloon (which represents the organization), the contour of the balloon visibly changes at the point of contact. Here an obvious pressure, representing change, has produced an obvious deviation at the point of pressure. What is not so obvious, however, is that the entire balloon (the organization) has been affected and has stretched slightly. As shown by this comparison, the generalization is drawn *that the whole organization tends to be affected by change in any part of it.*

Whole organization affected

The molecules of air in the balloon represent a firm's employees. It is apparent that those at the spot of pressure must make drastic adjustments. Though the change did not make direct contact with the employees (molecules), it has affected them indirectly. Though none is fired (i.e., leaves the balloon), the employees are displaced and must adjust to a new location in the balloon. This comparison illustrates an additional generalization: *change is a human as well as a technical problem.*

Human and technical problem

The comparison using a balloon may be carried further. Repeated pressure at a certain point may weaken the balloon until it breaks. So it is with an organization. Changes may lead to pressures and conflicts that eventually cause a breakdown somewhere in the organization. An example is an employee who becomes dissatisfied and resigns.

Admittedly, the foregoing comparison is rough. An employing institution is not a balloon; a person is not a molecule; and people are not as free and flexible as air molecules in a balloon. What has been illustrated is a condition of molecular equilibrium. Organizations, too, tend to achieve an equilibrium in their social structure. This means that people develop an established set of relations with their environment. They learn how to deal with each other, how to perform their jobs, and what to expect next. Equilibrium exists; employees are adjusted. When change comes along, it requires them to make new adjustments as the organization seeks a new equilibrium. When employees are unable to make adequate adjustments, the organization is in a state of unbalance, or disequilibrium. *Management's general human objective regarding change is to restore and maintain the group equilibrium and personal adjustment that change upsets.*

Responses to change

Work change is further complicated by the fact that it does not produce a direct adjustment as in the case of air molecules. Instead, it operates through each employee's attitudes to produce a response that is conditioned by feelings toward the change. This relationship was illustrated in a series of classic experiments by Roethlisberger and his associates. In one instance lighting was improved regularly according to the theory that better lighting would lead to greater productivity. As was expected, productivity did increase. Then lighting was decreased to illustrate the reverse effect—reduced productivity. Instead, productivity increased further! Lighting was again decreased. The result was still greater productivity! Finally, lighting was decreased to 0.06 of a footcandle, which is approximately equivalent to moonlight. According to Roethlisberger, "Not until this point was reached was there any appreciable decline in the output rate."[3]

Roethlisberger's experiments

The "X" chart: a model of how attitudes affect response to change Obviously, better lighting was not by itself causing greater output. There was no direct connection between the change and the response. Some other intervening variable, later diagnosed as employee attitudes, had crept in to upset the expected pattern. Roethlisberger later illustrated the new pattern by means of a model of response to change known as the *"X" chart.* It is shown in Figure 11-1. Each change is interpreted by individuals according to their attitudes. The way that people feel about a change then determines how they will respond to it. These feelings are not the result of chance; they are caused. One cause is personal history, which refers to people's biological processes, their backgrounds, and all their social experiences away from work. This is what they bring to the workplace. A second cause is the work environment itself. It reflects the fact that workers are members of a group and are influenced by its codes, patterns, and norms.

Feelings are nonlogical.

Feelings are not a matter of logic. They are neither logical nor illogical but entirely apart from logic. They are *nonlogical.* Feelings and logic belong in two separate categories, just as inches and pounds do. For that reason, logic alone is an ineffective means of trying to modify feelings because it does not get at them directly. Feelings are not much better refuted by logic than this book's length in inches or centimeters is refuted by its weight in pounds or kilograms!

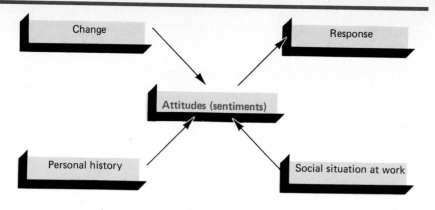

Figure 11-1
Roethlisberger's
original "X" chart
*From F. J. Roethlisberger,
Management and Morale,
Cambridge, Mass.:
Harvard University Press,
1941, p. 21. Used with
permission.*

Hawthorne effect   One cause of favorable feelings in the groups studied by
Roethlisberger was the interest shown by the researchers in employee
problems. This phenomenon later was called the *Hawthorne effect,* named
after the factory where the research took place. The Hawthorne effect means
that the mere observation of a group tends to change it. When people are
observed, they act differently. These changes usually are unintended and not
recognized. They contaminate the research design, but normally they cannot
be prevented.[4]

Group response to change   Though people individually interpret change, they
often show their attachment to the group by joining with it in some uniform
response to the change, as shown in Figure 11-2. This response makes
possible such seemingly illogical actions as walkouts when obviously only a
few people actually want to walk out. Other employees who are unhappy
seize upon the walkout as a chance to show their dissatisfaction and to confirm
their affiliation with the group by joining with it in social action. Basically,
the group responds with the feeling, "We're all in this together. Whatever happens to one of us affects all of us." John Donne, the seventeenth-
century English poet, beautifully stated the philosophy of this relationship as
follows:

No man is an Iland, *intire of it selfe;*
every man is a peece of the Continent,
a part of the maine; if a Clod *be washed away*
by the Sea, Europe is the lesse, as well as if a
Promontorie *were, as well as if a* Mannor *of thy friends*
or of thine owne *were; any mans death diminishes me,*
because I am involved in Mankinde:
And therefore never send to know for whom the bell tolls;
It tolls for thee.[5]

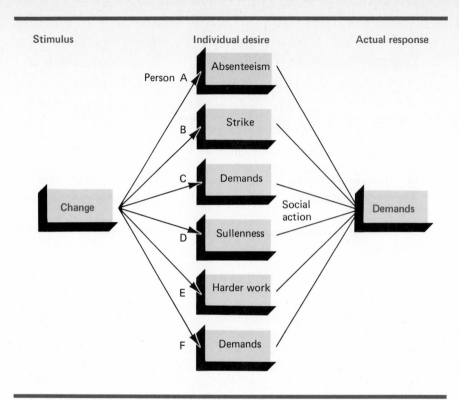

Figure 11-2
Unified social
response to change

Homeostasis In trying to maintain equilibrium, a group develops responses to return to its perceived best way of life whenever any change occurs. Each pressure, therefore, encourages a counterpressure within the group. The net result is a self-correcting mechanism by which energies are called up to restore balance whenever change threatens. This self-correcting characteristic of organizations is called *homeostasis;* that is, people act to establish a steady state of need fulfillment and to protect themselves from disturbance of that balance.

Costs and benefits

All changes are likely to have some costs. For example, a new work procedure may require the inconvenience of learning new practices. It temporarily may disrupt work and reduce motivation. There also may be the cost of new equipment or relocation of old equipment. These costs are not merely economic; they also are psychological and social. They usually must be paid in order to gain the benefits of proposed changes.

Because of the costs associated with change, proposals for change are not always desirable. They require careful analysis to determine usefulness. Each change requires a detailed cost-benefit analysis. Unless changes can provide benefits above costs, there is no reason for the changes. It is illogical to emphasize benefits while ignoring costs. The organizational goal always is benefits greater than costs ($B > C$), as shown in Figure 11-3.

In determining benefits and costs, all types of each must be considered. It is useless to examine only economic benefits and costs, because even if there is a net economic benefit, the social or psychological costs may be too large. Although it is not very practical to reduce psychological and social costs to numbers, they must nevertheless be included in the decision-making process. Almost any change, for example, involves some psychological loss because of the strain that it imposes on people as they try to adjust. Psychological costs also are called *psychic costs* because they affect a person's inner self (psyche).

Psychic costs

> For example, 153 employees and supervisors were studied for ten months in a government office that was being reorganized.[6] Some employees were supposed to be affected by the change in a "positive" way and others in a "negative" way. The study reported a general decline in favorable attitudes for the period of change. Both those who were affected positively and those who were affected negatively showed lower work attitudes than those who were not affected at all. In other words, both those who gained and those who lost suffered at least a temporary decline in attitudes. This was a cost associated with the change. The question is: How could management have minimized the psychic costs of the change?

As the example shows, people are affected in different ways by a change. Some may benefit while others suffer a loss. Frequently there is no clear-cut 100 percent benefit for all. Rather, there are a series of separate costs and benefits that must be considered on an individual basis. The supportive and collegial models of organizational behavior imply that management will consider each individual case and try to help each person gain as much from a change as possible.

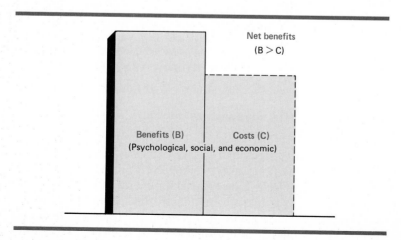

Net benefits
($B > C$)

Benefits (B)
(Psychological, social, and economic)

Costs (C)

Figure 11-3
Effective change requires net benefits

Psychic costs and health

Stress

In some cases the psychic costs of change can be so severe that they affect the psychological and even the physical health of employees. Each person has a tolerance level for change. When that level is exceeded, responses related to stress develop, and they can undermine health. In some instances there is sustained change over a period of time, producing cumulative stress that finally builds to overload a person's system. In other instances there is a single major change of such significance that it overloads a person's ability to cope with the situation.

> An example is a merger that one company announced.[7] Although some employees reacted positively, several were unable to cope with the severe shock and uncertainty of the merger. They developed anger, anxiety, depression, and self-doubt. Some employees carried their anger into job contacts that suddenly became major interpersonal battles. One employee wandered aimlessly around the halls for several weeks performing minimum work. Another developed depression that led to unpredictable attendance. In general, the psychological costs of the merger were substantial.

Psychic costs of promotion and transfer

An important type of change is promotion and transfer. Employees often seek changes of this kind for growth and more recognition. Even though these types of moves are desired by an employee, they nevertheless have substantial psychic costs. Employees are required to learn new skills and make new friendships. They move to a different role and often to a different work group. Their status also may change. All of these actions involve psychic costs because they require employees to cope with new situations.

Since millions of employees are promoted every year in the United States, the costs can be substantial.

> For example, one large company calculated that it had a promotion every ten working minutes. In another firm, as shown in Figure 11-4, the promotion of a higher manager set off a chain reaction that led to the promotion of ten other people at lower levels. The subsequent moves ranged from the New York office (administration) to the Central Territory to the Southern Territory to the Dallas Division.

Psychic costs and employee relocation

Family costs

As Figure 11-4 shows, some of the promotions required moves to other locations. These changes tend to have high psychic costs because they require more adjustments. They also may involve the employee's family, so coping becomes more difficult. If there are children, they may not want to move from their friends and familiar surroundings. The spouse may have a job and not want to leave it. Companies that require employees to relocate have found that they need to give careful attention to human needs in order to reduce the

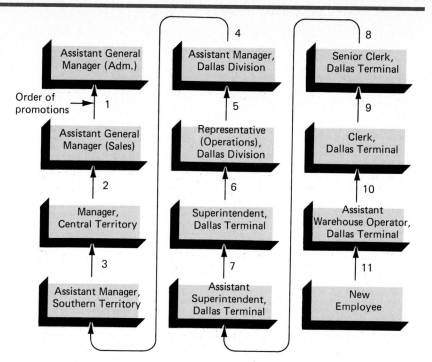

Order of promotions

Figure 11-4
Chain of eleven
promotions resulting
from promotion of a
higher manager

psychic costs involved. Services such as counseling, two-way communication, and financial assistance may be required.[8]

> One study of employees transferred to new locations reported that more than two-thirds of them were satisfied with their moves, but problems did develop.[9] Another study reported that 62 percent of those transferred were bothered by uncertainty about length of stay in one place.[10] They were less active in their community, made friends more slowly in their new location, and generally felt transient and temporary. Twenty-eight percent of them said they considered resigning at the time of their last transfer in order to remain in their community.

Resistance to change

All types of employees tend to resist change because of the psychic costs that accompany it.[11] Managers as well as workers resist it. Change can be resisted just as stubbornly in a white collar as in a blue collar. It does not respect either type of dress or job.

Although people tend to resist change, this tendency is offset by their desire for new experience and for the rewards that come with change. Not all changes are resisted. Some are wanted by employees. Other changes are so trivial and routine that resistance, if any, is too weak to be evident. The lesson for management is that a change is likely to be either a success or a problem, depending on how skillfully it is managed to minimize resistance.

Insecurity and change are conditions that illustrate how a *chain-reaction effect* may develop in organizational behavior. A chain-reaction effect is a situation in which a change (or other condition) that directly affects only one person or a few persons may lead to a reaction from many people, even hundreds or thousands, because of their mutual interest in it. This is quite similar to an atomic chain reaction.

Chain-reaction effect

> For example, in one plant a routine dispute arose over the transfer of one employee. Several other workers felt insecure about their transfer rights and supported the employee. Soon the whole department walked out, and shortly the entire factory of 4000 people was closed—all because of one person's transfer.

The fact that a group is intelligent does not necessarily mean that it will better understand and accept change. Often the opposite is true, because the group uses its extra intelligence to rationalize more reasons to resist change. Intelligence can be used either for or against change, depending on how the change is introduced.

> For example, Fred Landini supervised a group of unskilled laborers in a grocery warehouse. Higher management planned to install certain mechanized materials-handling equipment to reduce costs. Reasoning that his employees were poorly educated and had little knowledge of productivity and cost-cutting ideas, Fred worked hard to sell them on the change and to involve them in it. The new system was installed with full employee cooperation. As he put it, "The change went through without a hitch."
>
> Some years later Fred had the job of installing a quality-control system among a group of technical people. He reasoned that these employees were educated and understood the company's problems; so they could see reasons for the new program. They would not need the special selling effort that he had applied earlier to his warehouse laborers. This mistake in judgment cost him his job, because his employees resisted the change until it was defeated and Fred was discharged. Though his employees had the intellectual potential to see the reasons for the change, they chose not to do so.

Three types of resistance

Resistance to change is of three different types, as shown in Figure 11-5. These types work in combination to produce each employee's total attitude toward a change. The three types may be expressed by three different uses of the word "logical," as follows:

- *Logical.* Based on rational reasoning and science
- Psycho*logical.* Based on emotions, sentiments, and attitudes
- Socio*logical.* Based on group interest and values

Logical, rational objections

- Time required to adjust
- Extra effort to relearn
- Possibility of less desirable conditions, such as skill downgrading
- Economic costs of change
- Questioned technical feasibility of change

Psychological, emotional attitudes

- Fear of the unknown
- Low tolerance of change
- Dislike of management or other change agent
- Lack of trust in others
- Need for security; desire for status quo

Sociological factors; group interests

- Political coalitions
- Opposing group values
- Parochial, narrow outlook
- Vested interests
- Desire to retain existing friendships

Figure 11-5
Types of employee
resistance to change

Logical resistance arises from the time and effort required to adjust to change, including new job duties that must be learned. These are true costs borne by the employees. Even though a change may be favorable for employees in the long run, these short-run costs must first be paid.

Logical

Psychological resistance is "logical" in terms of attitudes and feelings of individual employees about change. They may fear the unknown, mistrust management's leadership, or feel that their security is threatened. Even though management may believe there is no justification for these feelings, they are real and must be recognized.

Psychological

Sociological resistance is "logical" in terms of group interests and values. Social values are powerful forces in the environment, so they must be carefully considered. There are political coalitions, opposing labor union values, and even different community values. On a small-group level there are work friendships that may be disrupted by changes. Employees will ask questions such as: Is the change consistent with group values? Does it maintain group teamwork? Since employees have these kinds of questions on their minds, administrators need to try to make these conditions as favorable as possible if they intend to deal successfully with sociological resistance.

Sociological

Clearly all three types of resistance must be treated effectively if employees are to accept change cooperatively. If administrators work with only the technical, logical dimension of change, they have failed in their human responsibilities. It can be seen that psychological and sociological resistance are not illogical or irrational; rather, they are logical according to different sets of values. They are based on the tune of a different drummer.

In a typical operating situation, full support cannot be gained for every change that is made. Some moderate support, weak support, and even opposition can be expected. People are different and will not give identical support to each change. What management seeks is a climate in which people have a positive feeling toward most changes and feel secure enough to tolerate other changes. If management cannot win support, it may need to use authority. However, it must recognize that authority can be used only sparingly. If authority is overused, it eventually will become worthless.

Possible benefits of resistance

Resistance is not all bad. It can bring some benefits. Resistance may encourage management to reexamine its change proposals so that it can be more sure they are appropriate. In this way employees operate as a check and balance to assure that management properly plans and implements change. If reasonable employee resistance causes management to screen its proposed changes more carefully, then employees have discouraged careless management decisions.

Resistance also can help identify specific problem areas where a change is likely to cause difficulties, so that management can take corrective action before serious problems develop. At the same time, management may be encouraged to do a better job of communicating the change, an approach that in the long run should lead to better acceptance. Resistance also gives management information about the intensity of employee emotions on an issue, provides emotional release for pent-up employee feelings, and may encourage employees to think and talk more about a change so that they understand it better.

IMPLEMENTING CHANGE SUCCESSFULLY

Change agent

Since management initiates much change, it primarily is responsible for implementing change successfully.[12] Management often is called a *change agent* because its role is to initiate change and help make it work. Though management initiates change, employees typically control its final success. They are the ones who actually make most changes operate. For these reasons, employee support becomes a major goal in the change process.

Management is not always the source of organizational changes. Many changes originate in the external environment. Government passes laws, and the organization must comply with them. Developments in technology require a multitude of changes. Then there are customers, labor unions, communities, and others who originate changes. For example, customers may want new products that require new machinery, new production methods, and new job skills throughout an organization. The amount of change that is required of a firm depends on the environment in which it operates. Stable environments mean less change. Dynamic environments require more change.

Occasionally dynamic environments can lead to fast-moving changes that leave an employee almost bewildered. For example, how would you like to walk into your office one morning and find that the whole office of fifty people had disappeared, leaving a bare room? That is what happened to Mary Manusco. Mary said she was startled and bewildered, and suddenly felt left out of everything. Mary had been on vacation for two weeks and made the discovery when she returned to work Monday morning.

Mary's office was in a separate building at a factory that had a number of buildings spread over forty acres. She later learned that some quick changes were necessary to prepare her building for new activities. Her office group had been moved to another building during her absence. Nevertheless, the way the move was handled raised questions for Mary. She asked: Why didn't they tell me? They knew where I was, so they could have telephoned me. Why didn't they write me so that I would have the letter at home when I returned? Why didn't a friend call me at home the night before? Why didn't my supervisor try to contact me? Does anybody care?

A three-step change process

Change typically is viewed as requiring three steps as follows:

- Unfreezing
- Changing
- Refreezing

Unfreezing means that old ideas and practices need to be cast aside so that new ones can be learned. Often this step of getting rid of old practices is about as difficult as learning the new ones. *Changing* is the step in which the new ideas and practices are learned so that an employee can think and perform in new ways. *Refreezing* means that what has been learned is integrated into actual practice. Rather than being something an employee knows, the new practices become something an employee does. Merely knowing a new practice is not enough. As an old farmer once said, "I'm not farming half as good as I know how now." Successful practice is the ultimate goal of the refreezing step.[13]

A model of the change process

A model of the change process is shown in Figure 11-6. An organization at any given time is a dynamic balance of forces supporting and restraining any practice. The system is in a state of relative equilibrium, so current practices will continue in a steady way until change is introduced.

For example, in a factory operation, there are pressures both for and against higher output. Management typically wants the higher output. Industrial engineers make studies to try to improve it. Supervisors push for it. Workers, on the other hand, feel

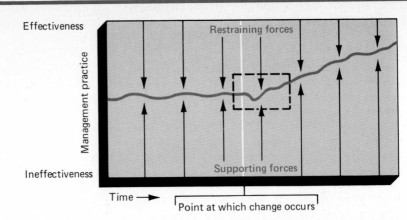

Figure 11-6
A model of the
change process
(See Figure 11-7 for
an expansion of the
dashed area.)

Length of the vertical line indicates strength of a force.

that they are working hard enough. They do not want additional strain and hurry. They do not want to feel more tired when they go home. They like their rest breaks. The result is that they are a restraining force, so the current amount of output will tend to continue until some type of change is introduced.

Supporting and restraining forces

Change is introduced within a group by increasing the supporting forces for it and/or reducing the restraining forces. One of these forces must be influenced, and preferably both should be influenced. The idea is to help change be accepted and integrated into new practices. For example, more product inspections should be a supporting force for higher-quality work. Another supporting force is an effort to increase the employees' pride in their work. In the other direction, restraining forces on quality can be reduced by improving the maintenance of machines, so that better work can be done on them.

The organizational learning curve for change

Learning curve for change

Figure 11-6 shows a small drop in the line of effectiveness after change occurs. This part is expanded in Figure 11-7 to show a typical *organizational learning curve for change*.[14] It is the period of adaptation that follows change, and it typically means there will be a temporary decline in effectiveness before a group reaches a new equilibrium. Employees need time to unfreeze and refreeze in order to adapt to change. During this period they are trying to integrate the change, and they are likely to be less effective than they formerly were. They have to get rid of old habits (unfreeze) and apply the new ones (refreeze). There are many problems to be worked out. Procedures are upset, and communication patterns are disrupted. Conflicts develop about the change, and cooperation declines. Problems arise, and time must be taken to

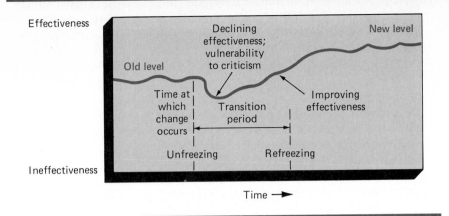

Figure 11-7
A typical
organizational
learning curve
for change

resolve them. The result is that, as the statement goes, "Things are likely to get worse before they get better."

During the transition period when people are adjusting to a change, they are likely to become discouraged because of the problems that develop. At this time the change is especially subject to criticism, attack, and even failure, because it appears not to be working. Only after the passage of time, when teamwork and efficiency are restored, is the change likely to produce the favorable results intended.

Building support for change

Assuming that management is following the model of the change process in Figure 11-6, then forces of support need to be built before, during, and after a change. Selected activities to build support are described below.

Use of group forces Effective change focuses on the group along with individuals. Usually more than one person is involved, but more important is the fact that the group is an instrument for bringing strong pressure on its members to change. One's behavior is firmly grounded in the groups to which one belongs, so changes in group forces will encourage changes in individual behavior.[15] The idea is to help the group join with management to encourage desired change.

The power of a group to stimulate change in its members depends partly upon the strength of their attachment to it. The more attractive the group is to each member, the greater its influence on that person can be. Influence is further increased if members with top prestige in the group support a change.

Change should not disrupt the group's social system more than is necessary. Any change that threatens the group will tend to meet with resistance.

Leadership for change   Capable leadership reinforces a climate of psychological support for change.[16] The leader presents change on the basis of the impersonal requirements of the situation, rather than on personal grounds. Leaders are asking for trouble when they introduce change with a comment such as "I have always felt you should not be able to leave the department during rest periods, and beginning tomorrow it will not be permitted." The natural responses are "It's not the supervisor's business where we go" and "Let's get together and figure out a way to beat the supervisor." Surely there must be some better reasons for the change, and if so, they should be given. If not, maybe the intended change needs to be abandoned. Ordinary requests for change should be in accord with the objectives and rules of the organization. Only a strong personal leader can use personal reasons for change without arousing resistance.

*Expectations
are important.*

Change is more likely to be successful if the leaders introducing it have high expectations of success. In other words, expectations of change may be as important as the technology of change, as suggested earlier in this chapter by the "X" chart, which showed the importance of attitudes toward change. For example, a manufacturer of clothing patterns had four almost identical plants. When a job enrichment and rotation program was introduced, managers in two of the plants were given inputs predicting that the program would increase productivity. Managers of the other two plants were told that the program would improve employee relations but not productivity.

During the next twelve months productivity did increase significantly in the two plants where the managers were expecting it. In the two plants where the managers were not expecting it, it did not increase. The result showed that high leader expectations were the key factor in making the change successful.[17]

Participation   A fundamental way to build support for change is through participation, which was discussed in an earlier chapter. It encourages employees to discuss, to communicate, to make suggestions, and to become interested in change. Participation encourages commitment rather than mere compliance with change. Commitment implies motivation to support a change and to work to assure that it operates effectively.[18]

As shown in Figure 11-8, a general model of participation and change indicates that as participation increases, resistance to change tends to decrease. Resistance declines because employees have less cause to resist. Their needs are being considered, so they feel secure in a changing situation.

Employees need to participate in a change *before* it occurs, not after. When they can be involved from the beginning, they feel protected from surprises and feel that their ideas are wanted. On the other hand, employees are likely to feel that involvement after a change is nothing more than a selling device and manipulation by management.

Shared rewards   Another way to build employee support for change is to be sure that there are enough rewards for employees in the change situation. It is only natural for employees to ask, "What's in this for me?" If they see that a change brings them losses and no gains, they can hardly be enthusiastic about it.

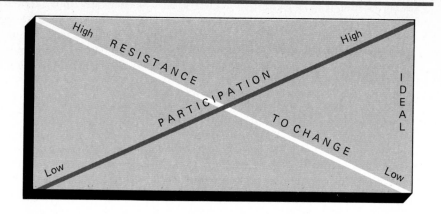

Figure 11-8
A model of
participation and
resistance to change

Rewards say to employees, "We care. We want you as well as us to benefit *Economic and*
from this change." Rewards also give employees a sense of progress with a *psychic rewards*
change. Both economic and psychic rewards are useful. Employees appreciate
a pay increase or promotion, but they also appreciate emotional support,
training in new skills, and recognition from management.[19]

It is desirable for a change to pay off as directly and as soon as possible.
From an employee's point of view, what's good in general is not necessarily
good for the employee, and what's good for the long run may not be good for
the short run.

Employee security   Along with shared rewards, existing employee benefits
need to be protected. Security during a change is essential. Many employers
guarantee workers protection from reduced earnings when new machines and
methods are introduced. Others offer retraining and delay installation of
labor-saving machinery until normal labor turnover can absorb displaced
workers. Seniority rights, opportunities for advancement, and other benefits
are safeguarded when a change is made. Grievance systems give employees a
feeling of security that benefits will be protected and differences about them
fairly resolved.[20] All these practices help employees feel secure in the
presence of change.

Communication   Communication is essential to improve support for change.
Even though a change will affect only one or two in a work group of ten
persons, all of them need to know about the change in order to feel secure
and to maintain group cooperation. Management often does not realize that
activities that help get change accepted, such as communication, usually are
disrupted by change. In other words, communication may be weakest at the
time it is needed most, so special effort is required to maintain it in times of
change.

One retail business learned the hard way about the importance of maintaining
communication during a change. Central management decided to change from

manual to computer credit records in two branch offices. This was a technical decision in which the credit clerks did not participate. In the Oakhurst Branch the plan was to transfer and lay off twenty-three employees and retain five. In the Bay City Branch twenty-five were to be transferred or laid off and seven retained. In both branches most employees had an opportunity to transfer to other work, but major retraining was required in some cases. All employees who were remaining in the credit records activity would require substantial retraining.

The manager of the Oakhurst Branch informed all her employees about the impending change, even those employees in other departments who were not affected by it. As the change progressed, she continued to inform her employees and discuss operating details with them. The Bay City manager took a contrasting approach. She decided not to tell her employees about the change until the week of the changeover because she did not want to upset them. She made elaborate precautions to keep information about the change tightly confined within the management group. When employees officially learned of the change, they were visibly upset.

Three months after the changeover management made an inspection of its success. In the Oakhurst Branch the change was progressing smoothly and most displaced employees had been transferred and retrained. In contrast, the Bay City Branch was in turmoil. Many displaced employees were so shocked or disillusioned that they had resigned. The employees who remained in the credit activity were having difficulty adjusting, and billings were late. Cooperation had declined. Job satisfaction was low. The situation definitely had caused depreciation of the organization's human resources.

Working with unions   Management in the performance of its function is primarily an initiator of change. The union, on the other hand, serves more as a restraint on management and a protector of security for its members. It frequently is cast in the role of resisting change. These differences between management and unions tend to cause union-management conflict about change, but there are many exceptions. Unions sometimes support management in encouraging workers to accept change. Most unions, as a matter of policy, favor improvement through technological change and will approve a change that is carefully planned to protect member interests. Union approval does not ensure that there will be no opposition, because insecure workers sometimes resist changes even when their union pressures them not to do so.

Working with the total system   Resistance to change can be reduced by helping

Guidelines for change   employees recognize the need for each change, participate in it, and gain from it.[21] In summary, five management guidelines for responsible change are:

1 Make only necessary and useful change. Avoid unnecessary change.

2 Change by evolution, not revolution (that is, gradually, not dramatically).

3 Recognize the possible effects of change, and introduce it with adequate attention to human needs.

4 Share the benefits of change with employees.

5 Diagnose the problems remaining after a change occurs, and treat them.

Change when improperly handled manifests itself in slowdowns and showdowns.

CHAPTER 11: MANAGING CHANGE

251

For example, Robert Barrows, an engineer, failed to consider the total system when he introduced changes in an operating department. He needed to make some routine studies of machine downtime in a factory. Without explaining what his purpose was, he set up machine records to be kept by each machine operator reporting the length, time of day, and cause of all machine downtime. The supervisor was told to require his employees to keep these records for thirty days. Both the supervisor and the employees stalled and complained and finally kept such inadequate records that they were not usable. Robert concluded that the department was full of obstructionists who did not have the organization's interests at heart.

Closer examination revealed some human aspects of this routine technical requirement. Keeping records was more work for the employees, and some of them were not oriented toward paperwork. The machine work required them to have dirty hands, but they felt obligated to try to keep the downtime records clean. They also felt that the records pried into their activities, because some downtime was for personal reasons. They saw no direct benefit from the study, and some of them feared it would bring changes that would reduce their incentive earnings.

The supervisor likewise saw no direct benefit coming to him or his department from the study. He feared unknown changes in his department; and he disliked the chore of enforcing the record system, especially since his employees resented it. The result was that the supervisor and employees complained to Robert and to one another. Soon everyone was obstructing rather than cooperating, and Robert was wondering why there was so much commotion about "this little piece of paperwork." He was sure that a company with so many obstructionists would never be efficient. However—and here is a key point—one of the reasons the company had so many obstructionists was that it had technical people like Robert who did not understand and work with the total social system. People like Robert were the cause of the problem, rather than the victims of it.

SUMMARY

The work environment is filled with change that upsets the social system and requires employees to adjust. The "X" chart shows that they respond with their emotions as well as rational reasoning. Resistance to change can be logical, psychological, and sociological.

Change has costs as well as benefits, and both must be considered to determine net benefits. Employees tend to resist change because of its costs, including psychic costs. Management reduces resistance by influencing the supporting and restraining forces for change. It applies a change procedure of unfreezing, changing, and refreezing activities. Since there is an organizational learning curve for change, time is required for the potential benefits of change to occur.

Selected activities to support change were discussed. Another major activity for change is organizational development. It is discussed in the next chapter.

TERMS AND CONCEPTS FOR REVIEW

Roethlisberger's "X" chart

Hawthorne effect

Homeostasis

Psychic costs

Chain-reaction effect

Types of resistance to change

Unfreezing and refreezing

Change process model

Organizational learning curve for change

REVIEW QUESTIONS

1 Think of an organizational change that you have experienced. Was there resistance to the change? Discuss. Did you resist the change? In what ways?

2 Considering the change mentioned in question 1, outline both the costs and benefits of it under the three headings of "logical," "psychological," and "sociological." Discuss. Were the benefits greater than the costs (*a*) for you and (*b*) for your employer?

3 Considering the change mentioned in question 1, how did management alter the restraining and supporting forces for the change? Discuss.

4 Considering the change mentioned in question 1, was there an organizational learning curve for the change? Discuss its length and some of the problems that developed.

5 Discuss how change affects an organization.

6 Discuss possible benefits of resistance to change in an organization.

7 Select some change that you have experienced, and discuss the difficulties you had in unfreezing your earlier patterns of thought and behavior.

8 Discuss why participation and change are related in the way that they are.

9 Consider the eight management activities supporting change that are mentioned in this chapter. Form groups of three to five participants, and based on a change situation presented to you by your instructor, make a group ranking of the usefulness of these eight practices for the specified change.

INCIDENTS

The New Sales Procedures

The Marin Company had more than 100 field sales representatives who sold a line of complex industrial products. Sales of these products required close work with buyers to determine their product needs; so nearly all sales representatives were college graduates in engineering and science. Other product lines of Marin Company, such as consumer products, were sold by a separate sales group.

Recently the firm established a new companywide control and report system using a larger computer. This system has doubled the amount of time the industrial sales representatives spend filling out forms and supplying information that can be fed into the computer. They estimate that they now spend as much as two hours daily processing records, and they have complained that they now have inadequate time for sales effort. A field sales manager commented, "Morale has declined as a result of these new controls and reports. Sales is a rewarding, gratifying profession that is based on individual effort. Sales representatives are happy when they are making sales, since this directly affects their income and self-recognition. The more time they spend with reports, the less time they have to make sales. As a result they can see their income and recognition declining, and thus they find themselves resisting changes."

QUESTIONS

1 Comment on the sales manager's analysis.

2 What alternative approaches to this situation do you recommend? Give reasons.

The Industrial Engineering Change

An industrial engineer was assigned to an electronics assembly department to make some methods improvements. In one assembly operation he soon recognized that a new fixture might reduce labor costs by about 30 percent. He discussed the situation with the group leader and then the supervisor. The group leader was indifferent, but the supervisor was interested and offered additional suggestions.

Feeling that he had the supervisor's approval, the industrial engineer had the fixture made. With the permission of the supervisor, he assigned a woman assembler to try the fixture. She was cooperative and enthusiastic and on the first day exceeded the expected improvement of 30 percent. When the group leader was shown the results at the end of the day, he claimed that this was one of the fastest workers in the department and that her results could not be generalized for the whole department.

The next day the industrial engineer asked the supervisor for another operator to help prove the fixture. At this point the supervisor noted that the fixture did not include her ideas fully. The industrial engineer explained that he had misunderstood but that he would include the other suggestions in the next fixture built. The supervisor, however, continued to be negative about the fixture.

When the industrial engineer attempted to instruct the second woman the way he had instructed the first one, her reaction was negative. In fact, when he stopped instructing her, it seemed that the woman deliberately stalled as she used the fixture. She also made some negative comments about the fixture and asked the industrial engineer if he felt he deserved his paycheck for this kind of effort. At the end of the day this woman's production was 10 percent below normal production by the old method.

QUESTION

Analyze the causes of this problem, and recommend the course of action the industrial engineer should take. Role-play a meeting of the industrial engineer and the supervisor.

REFERENCES

1 Alejandro Casona, *La Dama del Alba,* edited by Juan Rodriquez-Castellano, New York: Charles Scribner's Sons, 1947, p. 93.

2 Samuel Butler, *Hudibras, III,* first published in 1678.

3 F. J. Roethlisberger, *Management and Morale,* Cambridge, Mass.: Harvard University Press, 1941, p. 10. See also F. J. Roethlisberger and William J. Dickson, *Management and the Worker,* Cambridge, Mass.: Harvard University Press, 1939. An update is Ronald G. Greenwood and others, "Hawthorne a Half Century Later: Relay Assembly Participants Remember," *Journal of Management,* Fall–Winter 1983, pp. 217–231.

4 For a criticism of the Hawthorne effect and some of the conclusions from the Hawthorne studies, see Berkeley Rice, "The Hawthorne Defect: Persistence of a Flawed Theory," *Psychology Today,* February 1982, pp. 70–74.

5 John Donne (1572–1631), *The Complete Poetry and Selected Prose of John Donne and the Complete Poetry of William Blake,* New York: Random House, Inc., 1941, p. 332. Italics in original.

6 Douglas T. Hall and others, "Effects of Top-Down Departmental and Job Change upon Perceived Employee Behavior and Attitudes: A Natural Field Experiment," *Journal of Applied Psychology,* February 1978, pp. 62–72.

7 Marsha Sinetar, "Mergers, Morale and Productivity," *Personnel Journal,* November 1981, pp. 863–867.

8 John M. Moore, "Employee Relocation: Expanded Responsibilities for the Personnel Department," *Personnel,* September–October 1981, pp. 62–69; Lawrence W. Foster and Marilyn L. Liebrentz, "Corporate Moves—Who Pays the Psychic Costs?" *Personnel,* November–December, 1977, pp. 67–75; and Gerard Tavernier, "The High Cost and Stress of Relocation," *Management Review,* July 1980, pp. 18–23.

9 William F. Glueck, "Managers, Mobility, and Morale," *Business Horizons,* December 1974, pp. 65–70.

10 Ronald J. Burke, "Quality of Organizational Life: The Effects of Personnel Job Transfers," in Vance F. Mitchell and others (eds.), *Proceedings of the Academy of Management,* 1972, Vancouver, B.C., Canada: University of British Columbia, 1973, pp. 242–245. See also Francine S. Hall and Douglas T. Hall, *The Two-Career Couple,* Reading, Mass.: Addison-Wesley Publishing Company, Inc., 1979.

11 Joseph Stanislao and Bettie C. Stanislao, "Dealing with Resistance to Change," *Business Horizons,* July–August 1983, pp. 74–78; and George S. Odiorne, "The Change Resisters," *Personnel Administrator,* January 1981, pp. 57–63.

12 General ideas about introducing change are available in Stephen R. Michael and others, *Techniques of Organizational Change,* New York: McGraw-Hill Book Company, 1981; L. Dave Brown, *Managing Change at Organizational Interfaces,* Reading, Mass.: Addison-Wesley Publishing Company, Inc., 1982; and Irving G. Calish and R. Donald Gamache, "How to Overcome Organizational Resistance to Change," *Management Review,* October 1981, pp. 21–28, 50.

13 Use of the change process to implement computer systems is discussed in Archie B. Carroll, "Behavioral Aspects of Developing Computer-Based Information Systems," *Business Horizons*, January–February 1982, pp. 42–51. The unfreezing process is discussed in John W. Newstrom, "The Management of Unlearning," *Training and Development Journal*, August 1983, pp. 36–39; and Paul C. Nystrom and William H. Starbuck, "To Avoid Organizational Crises, Unlearn," *Organizational Dynamics*, Spring 1984, pp. 53–65.

14 Research supporting the learning curve in actual operations is reported in Peter Mears, "Structuring Communication in a Working Group," *The Journal of Communication*, 24:1, 1974, pp. 71–79; and William F. Dowling, "At General Motors: System 4 Builds Performance and Profits," *Organizational Dynamics*, Winter 1975, p. 30.

15 Alvin Zander, *Making Groups Effective*, San Francisco: Jossey-Bass, 1982.

16 Leadership for change is discussed in Michael B. McCaskey, *The Executive Challenge: Managing Change and Ambiguity*, Marshfield, Mass.: Pitman Publishing, Inc., 1982; and Alexander Mikalachki, "Does Anyone Listen to the Boss?" *Business Horizons*, January–February, 1983, pp. 18–24.

17 Albert S. King, "Expectation Effects in Organizational Change," *Administrative Science Quarterly*, June 1974, pp. 221–230; and Dov Eden and Gad Ravid, "Pygmalion versus Self-Expectancy: Effects of Infrastructure- and Self-Expectancy on Trainee Performance," *Organizational Behavior and Human Performance*, December 1982, pp. 351–364.

18 A participative program using both managers and workers is discussed in William E. Zierden, "Managing Workplace Innovations: A Framework and a New Approach," *Management Review*, June 1981, pp. 57–61. Difficulties with establishing a participative management style in a Honeywell operation are discussed in Richard J. Boyle, "Wrestling with Jellyfish," *Harvard Business Review*, January–February 1984, pp. 74–83.

19 John P. Kotter and Leonard A. Schlesinger, "Choosing Strategies for Change," *Harvard Business Review*, March–April 1979, pp. 106–114.

20 John D. Aram and Paul F. Salipante, Jr., "An Evaluation of Organizational Due Process in the Resolution of Employee/Employer Conflict," *Academy of Management Review*, April 1981, pp. 197–204.

21 Additional techniques for implementing change, and a survey of their use in large companies, are reported in Stephen R. Michael, "Organizational Change Techniques: Their Present, Their Future," *Organizational Dynamics*, Summer 1982, pp. 67–80.

FOR ADDITIONAL READING

Beer, Michael, *Organization Change and Development: A Systems View*, Glenview, Ill.: Scott, Foresman and Company, 1980.

Bennis, Warren G., *Changing Organizations*, New York: McGraw-Hill Book Company, 1966.

Brown, L. Dave, *Managing Change at Organizational Interfaces*, Reading, Mass.: Addison-Wesley Publishing Company, Inc., 1982.

Dyer, William G., *Strategies for Managing Change*, Reading, Mass.: Addison-Wesley Publishing Company, Inc., 1984.

Goodman, Paul S., and others, *Change in Organizations*, San Francisco: Jossey-Bass, 1982.

Guest, Robert H., Paul Hersey, and Kenneth H. Blanchard, *Organizational Change through Effective Leadership,* Englewood Cliffs, N.J.: Prentice-Hall, Inc., 1977.

McCaskey, Michael B., *The Executive Challenge: Managing Change and Ambiguity,* Marshfield, Mass.: Pitman Publishing, Inc., 1982.

Michael, Stephen R., and others, *Techniques of Organizational Change,* New York, McGraw-Hill Book Company, 1981.

Odiorne, George S., *The Change Resisters: How They Can Prevent Progress and What Management Can Do about Them,* Englewood Cliffs, N.J.: Prentice-Hall, Inc., 1981.

Roethlisberger, F. J., and William J. Dickson, *Management and the Worker,* Cambridge, Mass.: Harvard University Press, 1939.

Slote, Alfred, *Termination: The Closing of Baker Plant,* Ann Arbor, Mich.: Survey Research Center, University of Michigan, 1977.

ORGANIZATION DEVELOPMENT AND TRAINING

The management of organizational change is a challenging task in any context.

David A. Nadler[1]

No one change technique or class of techniques works well in all situations.

John M. Nicholas[2]

CHAPTER OBJECTIVES

TO UNDERSTAND:
The meaning of OD
What its characteristics are
The process by which it operates
Laboratory training methods
Frameworks of popular OD programs

I n the early 1980s, the world's largest company—American Telephone and Telegraph (AT&T)—successfully met two immense changes from its environment (the government).[3] Within the span of two years, the Federal Communications Commission allowed AT&T to provide some deregulated products and services, and an agreement was reached with the Justice Department whereby AT&T agreed to divest itself of its operating telephone companies. The massive transition represented one of the most complex and significant planned changes in a U.S. firm in this century. Yet the evidence indicates that top management at AT&T was able to balance its concern for strategic issues with strong efforts to maintain the human organization.

As David Nadler pointed out in the opening quotation, AT&T faced a challenging task of developing itself into a different organization to meet a new context. In this chapter we discuss the meaning of organization development, how it works, possible benefits and problems, different types of programs, and also the effectiveness of more conventional types of training for better organizational behavior.

UNDERSTANDING ORGANIZATION DEVELOPMENT

In the 1950s and 1960s a new, integrated type of training originated known as *organization development* (OD). Organization development is an intervention strategy that uses group processes to focus on the whole culture of an organization in order to bring about planned change. It seeks to change beliefs, attitudes, values, structures, and practices so that the organization can better adapt to technology and live with the fast pace of change.[4]

OD arose in response to needs. Conventional training methods often had limited success for building better organizational behavior, so a new approach was needed. The National Training Laboratories and Esso Standard Oil Company began working on the problem, and eventually OD evolved from their efforts.[5]

Why was OD necessary?

There were two main causes that made OD necessary. First, the reward structure on the job did not adequately reinforce conventional training, so it often failed to carry over to the job.[6] Too many well-designed training programs failed because the job environment provided inadequate support. Under these conditions the reasonable next step is to try to change the entire organization so that it will support the training. This is exactly what OD tries to do.

A second cause is the fast pace of change itself, which requires organizations to be extremely flexible in order to survive and prosper. OD attempts to develop the whole organization so that it can respond to change more uniformly and capably. It tries to "free up" communication by increasing the amount and accuracy of information through better group dynamics and problem confrontation. In short, its general objective is to change all parts of the organization in order to make it more humanly responsive, more effective, and more capable of self-renewal.

OD's general objective

Characteristics of OD

CHAPTER 12:
ORGANIZATION
DEVELOPMENT
AND TRAINING

259

A number of characteristics are implied in the definition of OD, and these characteristics differ substantially from those in a typical training program. They are discussed in the following paragraphs and summarized in Figure 12-1.

Systems orientation Change is so abundant in modern society that organizations need all their parts working together in order to solve the problems— and opportunities—that are brought by change. OD is a comprehensive program that is concerned with interactions of various parts of the organization as they affect each other. It is concerned with working relationships as well as personal ones. It is concerned with structure and process as well as attitudes. The basic issue to which it is directed is: How do all of these parts work together to be effective? Emphasis is on how the parts relate, not on the parts themselves.[7]

Use of a change agent OD uses one or more *change agents,* who are people with the role of stimulating and coordinating change within a group. Usually the primary change agent is a consultant from outside the company. In this way the agent can operate independently without ties to the hierarchy and politics of the firm. The personnel director usually is the in-house change agent who coordinates the program internally with both management and

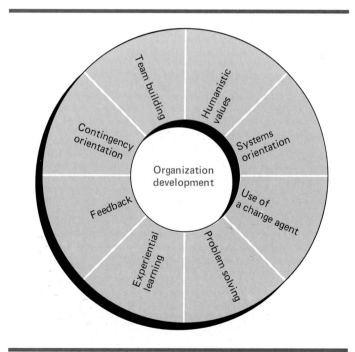

Figure 12-1.
Characteristics
of organization
development

external agent. The external agent also works with management, so the result is a three-way relationship of the personnel director, management, and an outside consultant as they develop the OD program.

In rare cases the organization has its own in-house professional consultant who replaces the outside one and works with the personnel director and management. This in-house consultant usually is a specialist on the personnel staff.

Problem solving   OD emphasizes the process of problem solving. It trains participants to identify and solve problems rather than to discuss them theoretically, as in a classroom. These problems are real ones that the participants face at work, so they are stimulating and interesting. This focus on improving problem-solving skills by discussing data-based system prob-

Action research   lems is called *action research*. In other words, employees are "learning how to learn" from their experiences, so they can solve new problems in the future.[8]

Feedback   OD relies heavily on feedback to participants so that they have useful data on which to base decisions. Feedback encourages them to understand how they are seen by others and take self-correcting action.

An example is a feedback exercise in one OD program. Participants are separated into two groups representing two different departments in the organization. Both groups are asked to develop answers to the following questions:

- What characteristics best describe our group?
- What characteristics best describe the other group?
- How will the other group describe us?

After the separate groups have prepared their answers, they assemble and present their answers to the other group. They give concrete feedback about impressions each group has of the other, and there usually are major misunderstandings. In this presentation no arguments are allowed. Questions are accepted only to clarify what the other group is saying.

The groups again are separated to discuss two other questions:

- How did these misunderstandings occur?
- What can we do to correct them?

With this new feedback, the groups meet to develop specific plans of action for solving their misunderstandings. In each instance feedback about themselves is the basis for their next activities.

Contingency orientation   OD usually is said to be situational and *contingency-oriented*. Unlike many other training approaches that emphasize only one right way to deal with a problem, OD is flexible and pragmatic, adapting actions to fit particular needs. Although an occasional OD change agent may try to impose a single best way on the group, usually there is open discussion of several better alternatives rather than a single best way.

Experiential learning *Experiential learning* means that participants learn by experiencing in the training environment the kinds of human problems they face on the job. Then they can discuss and analyze their own immediate experience and learn from it. This approach tends to produce more changed behavior than the traditional lecture and discussion, in which people talk about abstract ideas. Theory is necessary and desirable, but the ultimate test is how it applies in a real situation. OD helps to provide some of the answers. Participant experiences help solidify, or refreeze, new learning.

Real problems experienced by participants

Humanistic values OD programs typically are based on *humanistic values,* which are positive beliefs about the potential and desire for growth among employees. To be effective and self-renewing, an organization needs employees who want to expand their skills and can increase their contributions. The best climate for this to happen is one that creates opportunities for growth by stressing collaboration, open communications, interpersonal trust, shared power, and constructive confrontation.[9] They all provide a value base for OD efforts and help ensure that the new organization will be responsive to human needs.

What does OD value?

Team building The general goal of OD is to *build better teamwork* throughout the organization.[10] Both small- and large-group teams are emphasized. These are the task and institutional teams discussed in Chapter 10. Obviously small task teams must work together to be effective, but also cooperation is needed among all the small teams that make up the whole institution. OD attempts to tie all these groups into one integrated, cooperative group. For example, if the production and marketing departments are not working together, OD helps them learn ways to resolve differences so that they can cooperate. To do this, OD relies on group processes such as group discussions, techniques for constructive confrontation, and methods for resolving intergroup conflicts.

In summary, the OD process tries to integrate into an effective unit the four elements of people, structure, technology, and environment, discussed in Chapter 1. The result should be improved organizational performance.

> The police force for a population of 170,000 persons was in difficulty. Problems included conflict between staff and new enforcement personnel, poor community relations, arbitrary decision making, and high employee turnover. An OD program was developed to help the group achieve better teamwork. Definite improvements followed. Employee relations improved, and turnover declined from about 50 percent annually to less than 20 percent. Jail escapes declined from nine the first year to seven the next year; and then, the following year, there was only one.[11]

The OD process

OD is a complicated process that tends to take a year or more in an organization and may continue indefinitely. There are many different approaches to OD, but a typical complete program includes the following steps.[12] They are summarized in Figure 12-2.

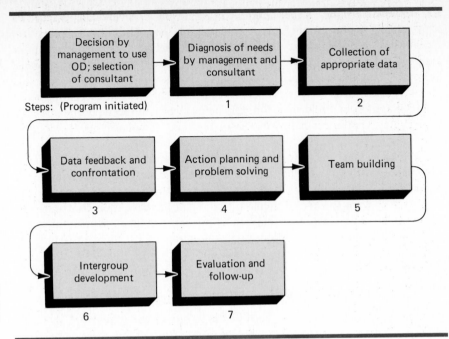

Figure 12-2
Steps in
the OD process

Phases in OD

1 *Initial diagnosis.* The consultant meets with top management to determine the nature of the firm's problems, to develop the OD approaches most likely to be successful, and to ensure the full support of top management. During this step the consultant may seek inputs by means of interviews with various persons in the organization.

2 *Data collection.* Surveys may be made to determine organizational climate and behavioral problems.[13] The consultant usually meets with groups away from work to develop information from questions such as these:

- What kinds of conditions contribute most to your job effectiveness?
- What kinds of conditions interfere with your job effectiveness?
- What would you most like to change in the way this organization operates?

3 *Data feedback and confrontation.* Work groups are assigned to review the data collected, to mediate among themselves areas of disagreement, and to establish priorities for change.

4 *Action planning and problem solving.* Groups use the data to develop specific recommendations for change. Discussion focuses on actual problems in their organization. Plans are specific, including who is responsible and when the action should be completed.

5 *Team building.* During the entire period of group meetings the consultant encourages the groups to examine how they work together. The consultant helps them see the value of open communication and trust as prerequisites

6 *Intergroup development.* After development of small-group teams, there may be development among larger groups comprising several teams.

7 *Evaluation and follow-up.* The consultant helps the organization evaluate the results of its OD efforts and develop additional programs in areas where additional results are needed.

For example, in one organization, the consultant asked managers to provide tapes of committee meetings that they chaired subsequent to the program. The consultant analyzed these tapes and used them to discuss with managers how well each was applying what was learned in the OD program.

The steps in OD are part of a whole process, so all of them need to be applied if a firm expects to gain the full benefits of OD. A firm that applies only two or three steps, such as diagnosis and team building, is likely to be disappointed with the results. However, the whole process can produce quite favorable results.

Mobil Oil has implemented numerous OD programs in recent years. It reports these results:

- Improved supervisor-employee communications
- Streamlined paperwork requirements
- More systematic problem analysis and problem solving
- Better interdepartmental relationships

The company concluded that the most critical step in OD is the first one—obtaining permission, active support, and total involvement from top management.[14]

TRAINING METHODS USED

The OD process shown in Figure 12-2 does not preclude the use of conventional training methods, which are useful for some purposes.[15] Coaching, lecture and discussion, films, and the case method are appropriate tools for providing an understanding of behavior or developing analytical skills. Many employees need this type of training.

Laboratory training

OD programs rely heavily on experiential learning, and the approach emphasized is *laboratory training*. It provides situations in which the trainees themselves experience through their own interactions some of the conditions they are talking about. In this way they more or less experiment on themselves. This kind of training tends to have a greater impact on them than

Laboratory training has impact.

conventional training methods and encourages transfer of the new skills to the job. The following laboratory methods will be discussed: role playing, behavior modeling, gaming, and encounter groups.

Role playing   *Role playing* is a laboratory method that can be used rather easily as a supplement to conventional training methods as well as in OD. It is spontaneous acting of a realistic situation involving two or more people under classroom conditions. Dialogue spontaneously grows out of the situation as it is developed by the trainees assigned to it. Other trainees in the group serve as observers and critics. Role playing is often considered a substitute for experience. In a sense it is more than experience because it permits techniques of observation, discussion, and emphasis that are not customarily a part of experience.

Since people assume roles every day, they are somewhat experienced in the art, and with a certain amount of imagination they can project themselves into roles other than their own. This idea is not new, because dramatics is as old as recorded history. In role playing trainees can broaden their experience by trying different approaches, while in actual situations they often have only one chance. People may, in two hours in a role-playing group, observe as many different approaches to a problem as they would in two years of normal experience. By evaluating these different ways of handling the same situation, they are able to see the strengths and weaknesses of each approach. Here is a sample introduction to a role-playing exercise:

> "Suppose that you and another student decided to save money by sharing the text for this course. Everything worked fine until the night before the first test, when you both claim to have a desperate need to use the book for at least three hours of studying. It is now 8:30 P.M."
>
> At this point you might be asked to meet with another role player to act out your approach to the problem. When the role playing is finished, the trainer would likely ask for a report of the various outcomes from different pairs and then discuss examples of how the problem was solved and the behavioral ideas that were demonstrated.

Weaknesses of role playing   Role playing also has weaknesses that partly offset its strengths. It is time-consuming and expensive. It requires experienced trainers because it can easily turn sour without effective direction and subsequent discussion. The trainees may resent it as a childish approach to serious problems unless it is introduced carefully. Some trainees are embarrassed and hesitate to take part. Conversely, other trainees may place more emphasis on acting and showing off than on the problem involved.

Behavior modeling   One effective form of training that builds upon role playing is *behavior modeling*.[16] It is teaching by actual demonstration with acted-out ways to handle commonly encountered behavioral problems. For example, the method is used to demonstrate how to motivate a poor performer, how to deal with a tardy employee, and how to give recognition to an outstanding performer. This method has existed for decades, but the development of the videotape has made it easier to use and more effective.

Here is how a typical program works. After a brief introduction, the trainees see a videotape of one or more successful ways to solve a work problem. A tape or film using professional actors may be used, but typically people in the company do the acting for the sake of greater realism. Trainees discuss why the solution was effective, and then they practice similar solutions in increasingly harder situations.

As trainees leave the class, they are asked to try the new approach before the next class. When they return for the next class, they discuss and even demonstrate their experiences with the new approach. Then a new tape with a different problem is shown and the training cycle is repeated.

As shown in Figure 12-3, the training model used for behavior modeling is entirely different from the traditional training model. For example, traditional lecture-and-discussion methods are used to teach new behavioral frameworks which are supposed to help change attitudes. In turn, the changed attitudes should lead to changed behavior and better results. On the other hand, behavior modeling teaches behavior first. As the new behavior is observed and learned, the trainees see that it produces superior results, so they are receptive toward it, learn the basic frameworks that make it effective, and are more likely to experiment with it on the job.

Traditional training vs. modeling

Behavior modeling programs have proved to be successful, and they usually are liked by participants. They especially are useful for training supervisors and other employees who deal with people frequently.

Seventeen first-level supervisors in a wood products plant received behavior modeling training on topics such as handling absenteeism, safety violations, and inadequate performers.[17] Results showed that the employees in the plant perceived that their supervisors became more active listeners, engaged in more participative problem solving, and used positive reinforcement more extensively. Turnover and absenteeism rates declined significantly, and three measures of performance improved. Further, the behavior changes were sustained over a six-month follow-up period.

Figure 12-3
Training models for traditional training and behavior modeling

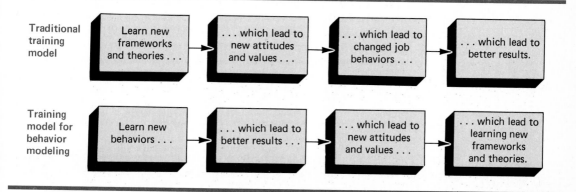

| Traditional training model | Learn new frameworks and theories . . . | . . . which lead to new attitudes and values . . . | . . . which lead to changed job behaviors . . . | . . . which lead to better results. |

| Training model for behavior modeling | Learn new behaviors . . . | . . . which lead to better results . . . | . . . which lead to new attitudes and values . . . | . . . which lead to learning new frameworks and theories. |

Gaming Organizational gaming is a laboratory method that is not used extensively in OD; however, it does have some application. It resembles role playing but differs from it in the sense that gaming focuses more on administrative problems, while role playing tends to emphasize feelings and relationships between people. Thus gaming provides a better balance of organizational and emotional issues on the job. In this way, it covers a broader base than role playing.

Definition *Organizational gaming* essentially is a group exercise in sequential decision making under simulated organizational conditions. Although there are many variations, usually a number of participants work in small groups, each group in competition with the others. Groups make decisions within a system model that has been created for them and is at least partly unknown to them. Decisions then are processed through a computer according to the model, thus providing feedback that will guide subsequent decisions. Usually, time is compressed; that is, a quarter-year of operations may be covered in an afternoon training session.

A game can show how leadership evolves, what kinds of communication are effective, the disastrous market results of internal group conflict, human factors influencing decisions, and the effect of success upon group cohesion. Different organizational systems can be tried to see how each affects the people involved. Perhaps more realistically than other training methods, games show the effect of stress on participants as they undergo the pressure of time and competition. Members become so intensely involved that they let their guard down and react to stress in their normal patterns.

The fact that time can be compressed makes it possible for much "experience" with different practices to be gained in a short time. The learning process can be hastened through feedback and discussion with a trainer after each decision unit.

When managers play a decision game following other OD experiences, they typically fail to apply many of the behavioral ideas they have learned. When this fact is pointed out to them, they often overcompensate in the second phase of the game, becoming so conscious of interpersonal factors that they are again ineffective. After this is brought to their attention, they usually begin to stabilize their behavior and apply some of their newly learned ideas in the latter stages of the game.

In one instance the game was structured so that both teams could win through cooperation.[18] Invariably, the teams that tried the game assumed that competition was the way to win the game, so they failed to make careful analyses of the problem and tried the competitive route. Only when the game was completed did they learn that someone did not have to lose (it was a win-win game).

Encounter groups Encounter groups involve unstructured small-group interaction under stress in a situation that requires people to become sensitive to one another's feelings in order to develop reasonable group activity. The method was developed by the National Training Laboratories, a private group, to fill a need for better human relations. The training groups themselves often are called "T-groups." There are a number of variations, such as human potential training and sensitivity training.[19]

Encounter groups are not role playing, because participants are acting their own true roles. They are themselves; however, their environment is so artificial that their ordinary social patterns prove to be no longer workable. For example, perhaps the group consultant provides virtually no leadership or has the group participate in structured exercises in order to break down social barriers and create an informal atmosphere. In this environment, the participants are encouraged to examine their own self-concepts and to become more receptive to what others say and feel. In addition, they begin to perceive how a group interacts, recognize how culture affects it, and develop skills in working with others. In summary, therefore, encounter groups seek to improve understanding of self, others, group process, culture, and general behavioral skills.

What happens in an encounter group?

As an illustration of how encounter groups work, here are some of the events that developed in one unstructured group. Prior to the meeting, members were told to dress informally. When they arrived at the meeting room, they found no chairs, only pillows on the floor for them to sit on during their discussions. The consultant or "resource person," Mark Thomas, briefly told the group the basic purpose of the program and then backed off, providing virtually no leadership. In the leaderless vacuum, the members started arguing among themselves about what they should do and how they should do it. Rather quickly, differences developed between members with an autocratic, directive approach and those who were more open and permissive. From time to time the consultant raised questions about these difficulties. His purpose was to help the members understand how groups work and how to be more effective in them.

In the second session, the consultant handed out pieces of paper with names of songs on them. Each member was asked to hum the tune and form a subgroup by finding all the other members who were humming the same tune. This informal approach helped break down social barriers and get members further away from their official roles in their organizations.

Following are examples of problems that arose in the training group. One member was upset because his ideas were ignored by others. Another member took the initiative, became authoritarian, and inspired group resentment. Another's superior attitude was uncovered as defensiveness about her weaknesses. In all this turmoil the consultant tried to remain somewhat detached, keep some stability, create learning situations, and introduce ideas.

All encounter groups are not as unstructured as the one just described. In many groups the consultant plays a more active role, such as making surveys, giving feedback, and making assignments. However, it is evident that encounter groups can be challenging and even frustrating experiences for members. Advocates of encounter groups believe that these kinds of experiences are necessary for members to become involved personally and learn more about how groups work. The emphasis in this kind of training is predominantly on group process (that is, how groups work) and on learning from the group experience (experiential learning).

There have been a number of criticisms of encounter groups, especially when they treat people in harsh ways. Most criticisms are related to the following points.

Criticisms

- Some hard-hitting sessions are emotionally traumatic for participants, who are required to lay bare their emotions. Consequently, consultants must keep sessions in control so that they do not become overly stressful to sensitive participants.

- It is said that some sessions are an invasion of privacy when they require excessive exposure of one's inner emotions. Further, in most instances the exposure is not necessary for appropriate learning.

- Others claim that highly unstructured situations allow the consultants to force their own social viewpoints on groups. For example, the consultant may convince the group that consensus is necessary for its success when, in fact, consensus is not required.

- Other critics question whether encounter group training produces on-the-job improvements. Although it is difficult to prove results from this kind of training, the weight of evidence is that often there is some improvement.[20]

Most of the criticisms have been caused by poorly trained or overenthusiastic consultants, so problems can be overcome by well-trained professionals. They keep the training goals in mind and avoid unnecessary stress. Therefore, less stressful forms of encounter groups often are used in OD programs.

Examples of OD programs

The ideal OD program is one that is tailored to the needs of a single organization. In this way the consultant or change agent can develop mutually with top management a program to meet specific organizational needs. However, many OD consultants have built their programs around some type of basic framework for their ideas. Following are three programs of this type that are used extensively. All three are well accepted and have produced favorable results.

*Six phases
in grid OD*

The managerial grid Robert R. Blake and Jane S. Mouton developed the *managerial grid*.[21] The full program consists of six phases, although not every organization may proceed through all of them. Phase 1 is the presentation of a framework called the managerial grid, as shown in Figure 12-4. The grid is based on the management style dimensions of concern for people and concern for production, which essentially represent the dimensions of consideration and structure discussed in an earlier chapter. The grid clarifies how the two dimensions are related and establishes a uniform language and framework for communication about behavioral issues. The "1,9 managers" are high in concern for people but so low in concern for production that output is low. They are "country-club managers." The "9,1 managers" are overly concerned with production. They tend to be authoritarian bosses.

A more desirable balance of the two dimensions is from "5,5" to "9,9." Using the grid, the entire managerial job can be discussed, such as the "backup style" of managers. The backup style is the one managers tend to use when their normal style does not get results. It tends to be more autocratic and concerned with production.

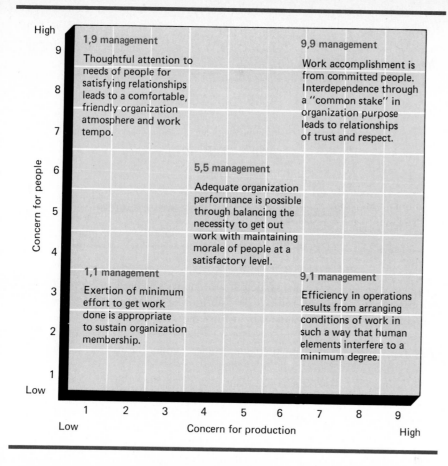

Figure 12-4
The managerial grid
*Source: Robert R. Blake
and Jane S. Mouton,
"Managerial Facades,"*
Advanced Management
Journal, *July 1966, p. 31,
copyright. Used with
permission.*

Phase 2 of the program is concerned with team development, using the grid as a framework for discussion. Focus is upon a single team and the manager to whom it directly reports. Phase 3 is concerned with intergroup development to reduce conflict among groups. This phase tries to reduce win-lose power struggles among groups by showing how cooperation can lead to benefits for all parties. Phase 4 develops an ideal organizational model, phase 5 seeks to apply the model, and phase 6 provides evaluation of the program.

Systems 1 through 4   An OD framework using four systems of management was developed by Rensis Likert.[22] The systems are as follows:

- *System 1:* Exploitative-authoritative
- *System 2:* Benevolent-authoritative
- *System 3:* Consultative
- *System 4:* Participative

As shown in Figure 12-5, System 1 is the most autocratic and System 4 is the most participative. The object of the OD program is to move an organization

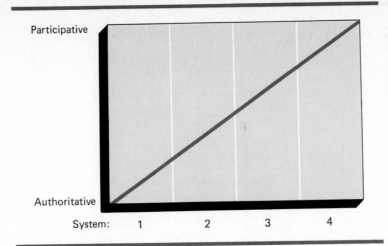

Figure 12-5
Systems 1 through 4
in relation to
participation

as far as possible toward the participative system, which is considered the best one. The OD consultant in the Likert program administers a written climate survey to find out about the system now used in the organization. (The survey elements were discussed in Chapter 2 in connection with climate.) The consultant also surveys participants to determine their view of the ideal system that the organization should have.

The difference between the present system and the desired system represents a potential area of improvement for the OD program to seek. The complete System 4 remains an ultimate goal, but a firm should move toward it gradually. The Likert approach also is known as a survey feedback method because of its heavy use of feedback based on surveys.

Causal, intervening, and end-result variables

In order to analyze the present system and move toward a better one, the Likert program uses a model of an organization with three types of variables. They are causal, intervening, and end-result variables, as shown in Figure 12-6. The *causal variables* are the significant ones, because they affect both intervening and end-result variables. Causal variables are the ones that management should try to change; they include organizational structure, controls, policies, and leadership behavior. The *intervening variables* are those that subsequently are affected by the causal variables. They include employee attitudes, motivation, and perceptions. Finally, the *end-result variables* represent the objectives sought by management. They usually

Figure 12-6
The Likert model of
an organization

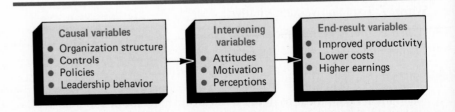

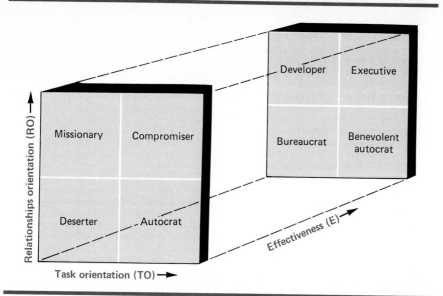

Figure 12-7
Chart of
the 3-D system
*Source: William J. Reddin,
Managerial Effectiveness,
New York: McGraw-Hill
Book Company, 1970,
p. 238. Used with
permission.*

include improved productivity, lower costs, and higher earnings. They represent the reason that the OD program was initiated.

3-D management   William J. Reddin has an OD program called 3-D management.[23] This program, like the managerial grid, is organized around consideration and structure; however, these two orientations can be used in combination or can be ignored by a manager, giving a choice of four styles. Since any of these four styles can be effective or ineffective, there are eight managerial style options available. The 3-D program is built around a study of these eight style options. When they are assembled into a chart, the result is a three-dimensional structure, as shown in Figure 12-7. This is the origin of the term "3-D management."

The 3-D system is materially different from the other two systems mentioned because it assumes that there are four effective styles, while the other systems focus on only one, the considerate, participative approach. The 3-D system is therefore less ideologically bound than the other systems and is more realistic in terms of contingency concepts. The 3-D system carefully emphasizes that no one style is effective by itself. Its effectiveness depends on the situation in which it is used.

Benefits and limitations of OD

OD is a useful organizational intervention. Its chief advantage is that it tries to deal with change in a whole organization or a major unit of it. In this manner it accomplishes more widely dispersed improvement. Other benefits include improved motivation, productivity, quality of work, job satisfaction, teamwork, and resolution of conflict. There also are reduced negative factors

Benefits	Limitations
• Change throughout organization	• Major time requirements
• Greater motivation	• Substantial expense
• Increased productivity	• Delayed payoff period
• Better quality of work	• Possible failure
• Higher job satisfaction	• Possible invasion of privacy
• Improved teamwork	• Possible psychological harm
• Better resolution of conflict	• Potential conformity
• Commitment to objectives	• Emphasis on group processes rather than performance
• Increased willingness to change	
• Reduced absences	• Possible conceptual ambiguity
• Lower turnover	• Difficulty in evaluation

Figure 12-8
Benefits and
limitations of
organization
development

such as absences and turnover.[24] The benefits and limitations are summarized in Figure 12-8.

> After an OD program in one organization, there were statistically significant improvements in trust, supportive environment, commitment to objectives, and other conditions of organizational climate. With regard to supervisory behavior, there was improvement in listening, handling of conflict, relations with others, willingness to change, and other activities. With regard to performance, there were changes in quality level and profit that were attributed to the OD program. Clearly the effect of the program was widespread in the organization.[25]

As with any complex program, OD has problems and limitations. It is time-consuming and expensive. Some benefits have a delayed payoff period, and an organization may not be able to wait that long for potential benefits. Even when a professionally capable consultant is used, it may fall flat. There are questions of invasion of privacy and psychological harm in some of its methods. There are charges that participants are sometimes coerced toward group attitudes and conformity. There are other charges that excessive emphasis is given to behavioral processes rather than to job performance. Group processes seem to be given priority over needs of the organization. Other critics say that OD has conceptual ambiguities that prevent its consistent application and make it difficult to evaluate.[26]

In spite of its problems and limitations, OD generally seems to be a useful and successful practice. It has contributed to improved results. It is most likely to succeed when it starts at the top of an organization, is part of its strategic plan, is based on extensive analysis, and is supported by the firm's reward system.

SUMMARY

Organization development is an intervention strategy that uses group processes to focus on the whole culture of an organization in order to bring about planned change. It emphasizes the whole organization as an operating system. The process covers such steps as diagnosis, data collection, feedback and confrontation, action planning, team building, intergroup development, and follow-up. It makes heavy use of laboratory training approaches, such as role playing, behavior modeling, gaming, and encounter groups. Typical programs are the managerial grid, Systems 1 through 4, and 3-D management.

Although OD has limitations, it is an excellent practice for introducing change and self-renewal in organizations. It differs from traditional training methods by its focus on the entire system, use of a change agent to assist with action research and feedback, advocacy of humanistic values, and use of experiential approaches within a contingency framework.

TERMS AND CONCEPTS FOR REVIEW

Organization development (OD)	Role playing
Change agents	Behavior modeling
Action research	Organizational gaming
Experiential learning	Encounter groups
Steps in the OD process	The managerial grid
Humanistic values	Systems 1 through 4
Laboratory training	3-D management

REVIEW QUESTIONS

1 A manager suggested that "traditional training helps employees learn something, but OD helps them learn how to learn something." Discuss this distinction.

2 Summarize the different phases by which an OD program develops. How does this differ from conducting attitude surveys, as presented in Chapter 6?

3 Explain how the reward structure on the job may not reinforce training. Form groups of three to five people and discuss what actions management could take to improve reinforcement of training on the job. Then report your results to your classroom group.

4 All adults have had experiential learning, whether it was in a classroom or not. Select a situation in which you had experiential learning, describe it, and then describe how it affected you. Why were you affected the way you were?

5 Explain how experiential learning differs from classroom lecture-and-discussion learning. Form groups of three to five students and discuss the strengths and weaknesses of both types of learning. Then report your results.

6 How do role playing, behavior modeling, organizational gaming, and encounter groups differ as training methods? Do they have similarities also?

7 Discuss both the strengths and weaknesses of encounter groups for training.

8 Discuss how behavior modeling is different from typical lecture-and-discussion training. Since they are so different, why might both still be used?

9 Review the managerial grid, Systems 1 to 4, and 3-D management. From the information given, which OD characteristics are reflected in each program?

10 After reviewing Figure 12-8, identify three major benefits and three major limitations of OD. Do you think that the benefits outweigh the costs? Report your choices to the class, giving reasons for your selection.

INCIDENT

Groups in Conflict

One division of a firm consisted of four departments, with the supervisor of each reporting to the division general manager (GM). The four departments ranged considerably in size, from two employees in the smallest (A) to fourteen in the largest (D). The other two departments (B and C) each had eight employees.

Intense interdepartmental rivalry frequently arose over the allocation of resources. This problem was compounded by the favoritism that the GM allegedly showed toward units A and B and his reliance on majority-rule decision making at staff meetings. This, complained the supervisors of C and D, often resulted in the leaders of A and B forming a coalition with the GM to make a decision, even though they only represented ten of the thirty-two employees. In response, units C and D were charged with empire building, power plays, and a narrow view of the mission of the division.

QUESTION

You are an OD consultant, called in by the GM to help resolve the problem. Outline the approach you would recommend taking.

EXPERIENTIAL EXERCISE

The Encounter Group

Assume that you have been given the opportunity to participate in an encounter group. Rate your willingness to join the group on a five-point scale (5 = very interested; 3 = neutral; 1 = strongly opposed). Have all class members share their responses, and count the numbers of 1s, 2s, 3s, 4s, and 5s. Now form mixed groups of advocates and opponents to participation in encounter groups, and discuss why you have those feelings. How would you convince people to attend when they are opposed to it? How would you defend your right not to attend when all others in your work group intend to participate?

1 David A. Nadler, "Managing Transitions to Uncertain Future States," *Organizational Dynamics,* Summer 1982, p. 45.

2 John M. Nicholas, "The Comparative Impact of Organization Development Interventions on Hard Criteria Measures," *Academy of Management Review,* October 1982, p. 540.

3 David A. Nadler, "Conversation with Charles L. Brown," *Organizational Dynamics,* Summer 1982, pp. 28–36.

4 The basic concepts of OD are discussed in Newton Margulies and Anthony P. Raia, *Conceptual Foundations of Organizational Development,* New York: McGraw-Hill Book Company, 1978.

5 Wendell L. French, "The Emergence and Early History of Organization Development: With Reference to Influences on and Interaction among Some of the Key Actors," *Group and Organization Studies,* September 1982, pp. 261–278.

6 Attention has recently focused on the problem of transfer. See Lyle M. Ehrenberg, "How to Ensure Better Transfer of Learning," *Training and Development Journal,* February 1983, pp. 81–83; and Melissa S. Leifer and John W. Newstrom, "Solving the Transfer of Training Problems," *Training and Development Journal,* August 1980, pp. 42–46.

7 Karl Albrecht, "Why It's Time for a Systems Approach to Organization Development," *Training,* May 1982, pp. 53ff.

8 This is the objective of double-loop learning, as described in Chris Argyris, "The Executive Mind and Double-Loop Learning," *Organizational Dynamics,* Autumn 1982, pp. 4–22; it closely parallels action learning, as described in R. W. Revans, "What Is Action Learning?" *Journal of Management Development,* 1:3, 1982, pp. 64–75; and M. McNamara and W. H. Weekes, "The Action Learning Model of Experiential Learning for Developing Managers," *Human Relations,* October 1982, pp. 879–902.

9 Anthony T. Cobb and Newton Margulies, "Organization Development: A Political Perspective," *Academy of Management Review,* January 1981, pp. 49–59. OD ideologies and value problems are examined in Warner Woodworth, Gordon Meyer, and Norman Smallwood, "Organization Development: A Closer Scrutiny," *Human Relations,* April 1982, pp. 307–319; while a critical opinion (that humanistic values have led to the decline of OD) is Terence C. Krell, "Humanism and the Decline of Traditional Organization Development," *The Journal of Applied Behavioral Science,* 18:4, 1982, pp. 532–536.

10 S. Jay Liebowitz and Kenneth P. DeMeuse, "The Application of Team Building," *Human Relations,* January 1982, pp. 1–18. A blend of two approaches is suggested in Ray V. Rasmussen, "Team Training: A Behavior Modeling Approach," *Group and Organization Studies,* March 1982, pp. 51–66.

11 R. Wayne Boss, "The Not-So-Peaceful Incident at Peaceful Valley: A Confrontation Design in a Criminal Justice Agency," in Arthur G. Bedeian and others (eds.), *Academy of Management Proceedings, 1975,* Auburn, Ala.: Auburn University, 1975, pp. 357–359.

12 An elaboration of the steps in OD is in Anthony R. Marchione and Jon English, "Managing the Unpredictable—A Rational Plan for Coping with Change," *Management Review,* February 1982, pp. 52–57.

13 The relative importance of surveys, interviews, observation, and performance data is reported in Michael A. Hitt and Robert L. Mathis, "Survey Results Shed Light

upon Important Developmental Tools," *Personnel Administrator*, February 1983, pp. 87–92ff.

14 A. M. Barrat, "Organizational Improvement in Mobil Oil," *Journal of Management Development*, 1:2, 1982, pp. 3–9.

15 For a study of perceived effectiveness of training methods as seen by training directors, see John W. Newstrom, "Evaluating the Effectiveness of Training Methods," *Personnel Administrator*, January 1980, pp. 56–60; and Linda L. Neider, "Training Effectiveness: Changing Attitudes," *Training and Development Journal*, December 1981, pp. 24–28.

16 The psychological basis for modeling, in social learning theory, is discussed in Henry P. Sims, Jr., and Charles C. Manz, "Modeling Influences on Employee Behavior," *Personnel Journal*, January 1982, pp. 58–65; and Fred Luthans and Tim R. V. Davis, "Beyond Modeling: Managing Social Learning Processes in Human Resource Training and Development," *Human Resource Management*, Summer 1981, pp. 19–27.

17 Jerry I. Porras et al., "Modeling-Based Organizational Development: A Longitudinal Assessment," *Journal of Applied Behavioral Science*, 18:4, 1982, pp. 433–446. Similar success is reported in Phillip J. Decker, "The Enchantment of Behavior Modeling Training of Supervisory Skills by the Inclusion of Retention Processes," *Personnel Psychology*, Summer 1982, pp. 323–332; and Herbert H. Meyer and Michael S. Raich, "An Objective Evaluation of a Behavior Modeling Training Program," *Personnel Psychology*, Winter 1983, pp. 755–761.

18 "Game-Playing to Help Managers Communicate," *Business Week*, Apr. 9, 1979, p. 76.

19 For an overview of encounter groups, see Peter B. Smith, "The T-Group Approach," in Cary L. Cooper (ed.), *Improving Interpersonal Relations*, Englewood Cliffs, N.J.: Prentice-Hall, Inc., 1982, pp. 90–107.

20 For details, see Jerry I. Porras and P. O. Berg, "The Impact of Organization Development," *Academy of Management Review*, April 1978, pp. 249–266.

21 The original program is described in Robert R. Blake and Jane S. Mouton, *The Managerial Grid*, Houston, Texas: Gulf Publishing Company, 1964. See also Robert R. Blake and Jane S. Mouton, *Building a Dynamic Corporation through Grid Organization Development*, Reading, Mass.: Addison-Wesley Publishing Company, Inc., 1969. Further clarification of the grid concept is Robert R. Blake and Jane S. Mouton, "Management by Grid Principles or Situationalism: Which?" *Group and Organization Studies*, December 1981, pp. 439–455.

22 Rensis Likert, *The Human Organization: Its Management and Value*, New York: McGraw-Hill Book Company, 1967; and Rensis Likert, *New Patterns of Management*, New York: McGraw-Hill Book Company, 1961.

23 William J. Reddin, *Managerial Effectiveness*, New York: McGraw-Hill Book Company, 1970.

24 Relatively few OD programs have been carefully evaluated. See John M. Nicholas, op. cit., pp. 531–542, for a review of studies on OD; see also David E. Terpstra, "The Organization Development Evaluation Process: Some Problems and Proposals," *Human Resource Management*, Spring 1981, pp. 24–29.

25 John R. Kimberly and Warren R. Nielsen, "Organizational Development and Change in Organizational Performance," *Administrative Science Quarterly*, June 1975, pp. 191–206.

26 A readable summary of criticisms is Patrick E. Connor, "A Critical Inquiry into Some Assumptions and Values Characterizing OD," *Academy of Management Review,* October 1977, pp. 635–644; see also Robert W. Bauer, "How to Make OD Work Better for Your Organization," *Management Review,* June 1982, pp. 56–61. Ethical dilemmas are discussed in Kevin C. Wooten and Louis P. White, "Ethical Problems in the Practice of Organization Development," *Training and Development Journal,* April 1983, pp. 16–23.

FOR ADDITIONAL READING

Beer, Michael, *Organization Change and Development: A Systems View,* Santa Monica, Calif.: Goodyear Publishing Company, 1980.

Burke, W. Warner, *Organization Development: Principles and Practices,* Boston: Little, Brown and Company, 1982.

Dyer, William G., *Contemporary Issues in Management and Organization Development,* Reading, Mass.: Addison-Wesley Publishing Company, Inc., 1983.

Kolb, David A., *Experiential Learning: Experience as the Source of Learning and Development,* Englewood Cliffs, N.J.: Prentice-Hall, Inc., 1984.

Lippitt, Gordon L., *Organization Renewal: A Holistic Approach to Organization Development,* 2d ed., Englewood Cliffs, N.J.: Prentice-Hall, Inc., 1982.

Mirvis, Philip H., and Davis N. Berg (eds.), *Failures in Organization Development and Change: Cases and Essays for Learning,* New York: John Wiley & Sons, Inc., 1977.

Robinson, James C., *Developing Managers Through Behavior Modeling,* San Diego, Calif.: Learning Concepts, 1982.

Walter, Gordon A., and Stephen E. Marks, *Experiential Learning and Change: Theory, Design, and Practice,* New York: John Wiley & Sons, Inc., 1981.

Wexley, Kenneth N., and Gary P. Latham, *Developing and Training Human Resources in Organizations,* Glenview, Ill.: Scott, Foresman and Company, 1981.

Zawacki, Robert A., Wendell L. French, and Cecil Bell, Jr., *Organization Development: Theory, Practice, and Research,* 2d ed., Plano, Tex.: Business Publications, Inc., 1983.

ORGANIZATIONAL ENVIRONMENT

STRUCTURE, TECHNOLOGY, AND PEOPLE

The findings indicate that job satisfaction decreases as the bureaucraticness of the organization increases.

Nicholas Dimarco and Steven Norton[1]

We are living in a time of the most rapid technological change the industrial world has ever known.

Lloyd Dobyns[2]

CHAPTER OBJECTIVES

TO UNDERSTAND:
Classical organization theory
Contingency organizational design
Matrix organization
Sociotechnical systems
Organizational effects of technology
Impact of work systems on people

Organizations are the grand strategies created to bring order out of chaos when people work together. Organization creates predictable relationships among people, technology, jobs, and resources. Wherever people join in a common effort, organization must be employed to get productive results.

The necessity for organization—and the havoc of disorganization—are illustrated by disorganizing a short sentence: "riirggnagesnotztlsuse." In this form it is nonsense. Now let us reorganize it substantially: "organizinggetsresults." In this condition it is workable, but difficult. By the slight change of converting to a capital "O" and adding two spaces, it reads: "Organizing gets results." Yes, the organizing of people and things is essential for coordinated work.

In this chapter we discuss classical organization theory and contingency organizational design as they relate to organizational behavior. Then we examine the relationship of technology to people at work, which is known as *Sociotechnical* *sociotechnical systems.*[3] The following chapter focuses on informal organization as a response to structure and technology, and Chapter 15 explores the current approaches to creating a high quality of work life.

CLASSICAL ORGANIZATION THEORY

Most organizations depend upon classical organization for building their structures because it deals with essential elements in an institution, such as power, responsibility, division of labor, specialization, and interdependence of parts. Modern developments are amending classical theory, but its essential elements remain and must be understood in order to work with people in organizations. Organizational structure is significant because it partly determines the power of people in organizations and their perceptions of their roles. It also affects job satisfaction.[4]

The organizing process may be viewed in two ways. It may be considered as a process of *construction* in which a great number of small work units are built into jobs, departments, divisions, and finally a whole institution. Or an organization may be viewed as a process of *analysis* by which a particular area of work is subdivided into divisions, departments, and finally jobs assigned to particular people. This latter approach is more appropriate when organizing a work group because one starts with the total amount of work to be done. Viewed in this way, organizing is achieved by means of division of work and delegation.

Division of work

The manner by which work is divided can be illustrated by considering that a small triangle represents the work that a department must do. There are sixteen people, including the department head, available to do the work. The department head organizes the work by dividing it into levels and functions and then assigning people and resources to the jobs that result. Division into

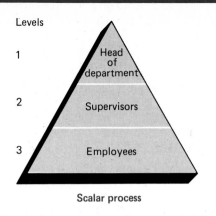

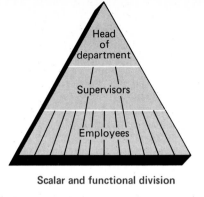

Levels

1 — Head of department

2 — Supervisors

3 — Employees

Scalar process

Scalar and functional division

Figure 13-1
Division of labor by
the scalar process
and functionalization

levels, represented in Figure 13-1, is called the *scalar process* because it provides a scale, or grading, of duties according to levels of authority and responsibility. The scalar process is nearly universal and exists wherever there are two people in a supervisor-subordinate relationship.

Scalar process

Concurrently with division into levels, the work must be divided into different kinds of duties. This is *functionalization*. To use an illustration, the difference between an office supervisor and a machine shop supervisor is functional. Scalar and functional divisions are superimposed on each other to form a framework such as that shown in Figure 13-1. By a simple two-way division of duties, all the work to be done (as represented by the area of the triangle) is now assigned. Assuming that organizing is done perfectly, there are no unassigned areas and no overlaps of assignments.

Functionalization

Delegation

The relationships and duties determined by division of work are communicated and assigned to people by means of *delegation,* which is defined as the assignment of duties, authority, and responsibility to others. Each person who accepts the assignment then becomes a manager's "delegate" and is responsible for the assignment. If there is no acceptance, delegation has merely been attempted. Delegation permits managers to extend their influence beyond the limits of their own personal time, energy, and knowledge.

Poor delegation is a primary cause of managerial failure. Some managers feel that delegation is giving away something, so they cannot psychologically bring themselves to do it for fear it will weaken them.[5] Others are such perfectionists that they have no confidence in letting others do the work for which they are responsible. However, all need to realize that delegation is the act that initiates management. If there is no delegation to others, there is no one to be managed. As a matter of fact, more delegation often is the effective remedy for a problem.

A cause of managerial failure

In one company, an executive was worried by the fact that Marge Lindberg, a purchasing specialist, could make costly mistakes if she were given more authority. Closer examination revealed that the costliest error she could make would involve only $100,000, but that it cost $142,000 annually in executive time, forms to fill out, and other precautions to ensure against her error. There were further possible losses as a result of delayed purchasing decisions. Was the possible loss from independent decision making great enough to require the certain costs and delays of the checkup procedure? Finally, the executive decided to delegate more authority to Marge.

Linking pins

Managers are links between groups.

When the scalar process, functionalization, and delegation are performed correctly, the result is an intricate web of relationships that links people together into a working organization. Each level has functional teams that are linked to the next level through the scalar process. This is known as the *linking pin concept,* as shown in Figure 13-2. Each manager serves as a linking pin connecting that manager's group with the remainder of the organization. If all linking pin connections are effective, then the organization can operate as an integrated whole. On the other hand, if there is a weakness anywhere in the chain of linking pins, the organization tends to be less effective.

When managers see themselves as linking pins uniting the whole team rather than as bosses, they can function more effectively. Similarly, when employees understand a manager's role as a linking pin for the whole team, they can relate to it better and become more effective.

Acceptance theory of authority

Delegation gives authority to a lower manager; however, the power of a manager to use that authority depends on the willingness of employees to accept it. This is the employee "zone of acceptance for authority" and results

Figure 13-2
Likert's linking pin concept
From New Patterns of Management *by Rensis Likert, p. 113. Copyright © 1961 by McGraw-Hill Book Company. Used with permission of McGraw-Hill Book Company.*

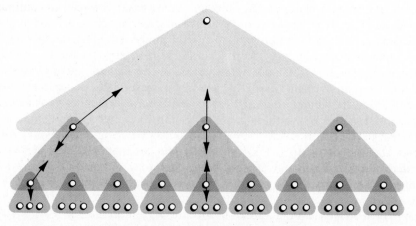

(The arrows indicate the linking pin function)

in an *acceptance theory of authority*. Although authority gives people power to act officially within the scope of their delegation, this power becomes somewhat meaningless unless those affected accept it and respond to it. In most cases when delegation is made, a subordinate is left free to choose a response within a certain range of behavior. But even when an employee is told to perform one certain act, the employee still has the choice of doing it or not doing it and taking the consequences. It is, therefore, the subordinate who controls the response to authority. Managers cannot afford to overlook this human fact when they use authority.

Specialization

Functionalization leads to specialization. A farm situation illustrates how this occurs. If fifty workers are hoeing corn, each doing the same work, the only division of labor is that the work has been broken into human units for each person to perform. If the work is reorganized and forty-nine workers hoe while the fiftieth sharpens the hoes and keeps the water jug filled, division of labor *of a different kind* has taken place. This is functionalization. In the course of time, the fiftieth worker will become more adept at sharpening hoes than the forty-nine are, and they will be more adept at hoeing than the sharpener is. This is because each is *specializing* as a natural result of functionalization.

Specialization brings great benefits to a work group. Modern industrial society could not exist without it, because it permits people to develop unique skills and knowledge that will produce more of society's wants. It is one of the really fundamental ideas of civilization.

Benefits of specialization

Like other benefits to society, specialization brings disadvantages that must be weighed against all its benefits. Let us return to our fifty fieldworkers to illustrate some of these disadvantages. The one worker who is sharpening hoes may not sharpen them to please one of the forty-nine, who always complains about a dull hoe. On another occasion a worker chips a hoe on a rock and wants it sharpened right away, but the sharpener is busy getting water and cannot give immediate service. The worker is forced to continue with a dull hoe. When the soil is rocky, the sharpener has too much to do, and hoes go dull. When the soil is soft, the sharpener sits idle. One day when the sharpener is absent because of illness, the workers argue about who will sharpen hoes that day. The worker selected is clumsy and delays the work. And so the trouble goes, day after day. The functionalized group is more complex and difficult to coordinate than the original group of fifty workers all doing the same work.

The fact eventually dawns on the fifty workers that the productivity gains of specialization (assuming they exist in this illustration) can be achieved only if sound human relationships and coordination can be maintained. This problem of the fifty farmworkers can now be translated into a general statement applying to specialization: *The benefits of specialization are largely economic and technical, but its disadvantages are primarily human.* This means that more specialization usually leads to more human problems also. For example, conflicts between groups tend to develop. However, specialization

Human costs of specialization

is a key part of advanced social systems. Whatever problems it causes must be weighed against its vast benefits. The world needs the skills of physicians, teachers, counselors, and the thousands of other occupations that specialization provides.

The span of management

A basic idea of classical organization is the *span of management* (or span of supervision), which refers to the number of people a manager directly manages. Many factors determine the number of employees that one person can manage effectively. Some of these are capacity and skill of the manager, complexity of the work supervised, capacity and skill of the employees managed, stability of operations, contacts with other chains of command, contacts outside the organization, and geographic distance of subordinates.

Tall and flat structures

A small span in an organization causes a *tall structure* and a large span causes a *flat structure,* as shown in Figure 13-3. Each structure has its advantages and limitations. In the tall structure, closer coordination and control are permitted because each manager works with fewer people, so

Figure 13-3
Tall and flat organizational structures caused by different spans of management for forty-eight employees

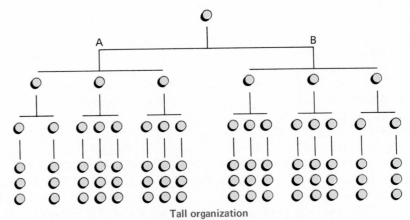

Tall organization
(Maximum span of management: 3. Four levels of management.)

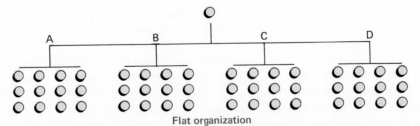

Flat organization
(Maximum span of management: 12. Two levels of management.)

there tends to be less role conflict and ambiguity.[6] However, communication lines are longer, providing more opportunities for misinterpretation and editing.

The flat structure has a shorter, simpler communication chain, but managers have so many people to direct that they cannot spend much time face to face with any one member of their group.

In an electronics company, for example, the president, John O'Hara, attempted to use a large span of management that resulted in a communications bottleneck at his office. When his subordinates were unable to gain access to him, they developed their own system of communication within their group so that their activities could be properly coordinated. This permitted them to work effectively in spite of the bottleneck in the front office.

In the tall organization, employees tend to be more "boss-oriented." Since their superior is interacting with them regularly day by day, the employees tend to spend much time trying to please their superior, rather than being productive.

Since a flat structure is more free of hierarchical controls, employees tend to prefer it. They like its freedom from close supervision. One study of sales representatives, for example, reported that those in flat organizations have greater job satisfaction, less stress, and better production than those in tall organizations.[7]

Bureaucracy

When organizational structures, rules, and procedures are rigidly followed, a condition known as bureaucracy develops. *Bureaucracy* is characterized by a large, complex administrative system operating with impersonal detachment from people. Its main characteristics are high specialization, a rigid hierarchy of authority, elaborate rules and controls, and impersonality.

Characteristics of bureaucracy

Bureaucracy has its advantages, such as stability and unified focus on objectives. It was originally developed as a desirable way to manage large organizations. The difficulty arises when there is too rigid adherence to the system. Then there is a tendency for paperwork systems to expand, managerial action to slow down, psychological costs to increase, and effectiveness to decline. The giant bureaucracy of the U.S. military system provides an example of a highly complex structure.[8]

Interpreting classical organization theory

Classical organization theory has its strengths as well as its weaknesses. For example, organizational structure can support people as well as suppress them. Classical structure provides much task support, such as specialized assistance, appropriate resources to perform the job, security, and fairly dependable conditions of work. On the other hand, although classical structure is strong in task support, *it is weak in psychological support*. What is needed is an organizational system that provides both task and psychological support.

New viewpoints are leading to a decline in the use of structure and authority in modern organizations. The modern approach is to be more flexible with organizational systems, changing them according to a contingency relationship with their environment. One reason is changing social values, but it also is evident that horizontal relations between chains of command are more important for effectiveness than was formerly realized. Supervisory influence with peers, service people, and other chains of command is becoming more significant. The pace and complexity of work today make horizontal communication more necessary.

Decline in use of structure

CONTINGENCY ORGANIZATIONAL DESIGN

As discussed in the preceding paragraph, the trend is toward more *contingency organizational design,* which recognizes that different organizational structures and processes are required for effectiveness in different kinds of environments. What is an appropriate organizational design in one environment may not be appropriate in another. Since environments change, there is even a need for flexible organizational designs so that they can be changed gradually to keep a best fit with the changing environment. The contingency point of view requires a fundamental change in philosophy from the traditional view that there is a one best way of organizing. Following are discussions of major research pointing the way toward more effective contingency design.

Mechanistic and organic patterns of organizing

Some of the earliest research on contingency design was by Burns and Stalker in Britain.[9] They distinguished between *mechanistic* and *organic* organizations. The mechanistic form fits the traditional hierarchical way of organizing. People are specialized into many activities that are supervised by layers of supervision. Each higher level has more power and influence until the top is reached, where central direction of the whole organization takes place. Work is carefully scheduled, tasks are certain, roles are defined strictly, and most formal communication flows along the lines of the hierarchy. The whole structure is organized like a well-designed machine.

Mechanistic characteristics

Organic characteristics

Organic organizations are more flexible and open. Tasks and roles are less rigidly defined, allowing people to adjust them to situational requirements. Communication is more multidirectional. It consists more of information and advice rather than instructions and decisions. Authority and influence flow more directly from the person who has the ability to handle the problem at hand. Decision making is more decentralized, being shared by several levels and different functions. The organization also is more open to its environment.

Burns and Stalker showed that mechanistic forms are more effective than organic forms in certain situations. If tasks are stable and well defined, changing very little from month to month and year to year, a mechanistic form tends to be superior. If changes in the technology, market, and other parts of the environment are minimal, then a mechanistic structure seems to be more effective. Worker attitudes also are a contingency factor. If workers prefer more routine tasks and direction from others, then a mechanistic form better meets their needs. If they are threatened by ambiguity and insecurity, then a mechanistic approach is better.

Organic forms are more effective in other situations, and these situations tend to be more typical in modern society. Organic forms work better if the environment is dynamic, requiring frequent changes within the organization. They also work better when the tasks are not well enough defined to become routine. If employees seek autonomy, openness, variety, change, and opportunities to try new approaches, then an organic form is better.

The contingency approach to organizing may even be applied within the same organization, where various departments may be organized differently to meet their needs.[10] The research department may have an organic structure, and the production department may require a mechanistic structure.

Types of production technology

Research by Woodward with 100 firms in Britain shows that the most effective form of organization tends to vary with types of production technology.[11] Woodward classified firms into three types of technology, listed in increasing order of complexity:

- *Unit and small-batch production.* Produces one or a small number of a product, such as a locomotive, usually on the basis of an order
- *Mass and large-batch production.* Produces a large number of a product in an assembly-type operation
- *Process production.* Produces in a continuous flow, such as an oil refinery or a nylon plant

Woodward found that the most successful firms in each class of technology tended to group around a certain type of structure, while the less successful firms varied from the structure. As shown in Figure 13-4a, the mass-production firms were more successful with organic structures. In essence, *the most appropriate type of organization was contingent on the firm's type of technology.* In relation to the amount of structure the relationship was curvilinear, with high structure required for the middle level of technology (mass production) and low structure required for either extreme of technology.

Technology—a contingency factor

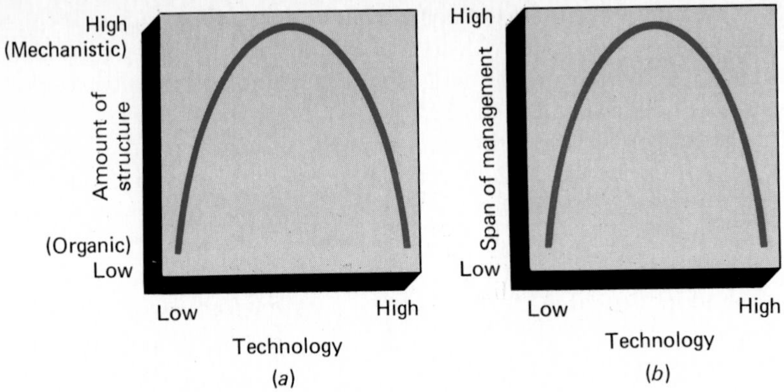

Figure 13-4
Most effective management practice with different types of technology

Span of management and technology

Woodward's research also showed a curvilinear relationship between the supervisor's span of management and technology (see Figure 13-4*b*). In three types of production technology the average span of management varied as follows:

- Unit or small-batch production   23 people
- Mass production and assembly line   49 people
- Process and continuous production   13 people

The differences are substantial. The mass-production technology used a span more than three times as large as process production. These data further support the contingency approach to organizing.

Stable and changing environments

Lawrence and Lorsch in the United States studied industrial organizations, grouping them by amount of market and technological change.[12] Their work expanded and supported Burns and Stalker. They found that organizations in the more changing environments required increasing differentiation in their structure. That is, they required many different sections, departments, occupational roles, and specialized patterns of thinking. These different parts enabled the firms to gain a variety of inputs that would allow them to react effectively to their uncertain environments. *Because of differentiation, greater efforts toward integration were required.* There was much coordination at lower levels, horizontal communication, interdisciplinary teams, and emphasis on flexibility. This system was similar to Burns and Stalker's concept of the organic organization. The firms with organic systems tended to function more successfully in changing environments.

Differentiation and integration

Firms in more stable, certain environments required less differentiation. Standard rules and procedures provided sufficient integration in their stable environment, so they tended to be more hierarchical and centralized. The open systems and horizontal communication that were needed in the changing firms were not so necessary in the stable firms. Consequently, firms with mechanistic systems tended to be more successful in stable environments.

Matrix organization

Another development to meet changing organizational needs is *matrix organization.*[13] It is an overlay of one type of organization on another so that there are two chains of command directing individual employees. It is used especially for large, specialized projects that temporarily require large numbers of technical people with different skills.

> A simple example of matrix organization is an annual United Fund drive for contributions to community charities. It could be handled through the traditional hierarchy, but often it is assigned to a temporary hierarchy of employees as a part-time duty. They carry the assignment to completion and are then disbanded.

The effect of matrix structure is to separate some of the organization's activities into projects that then compete for allocations of people and resources. The traditional hierarchy provides the regular work group for an employee, but project groups are established temporarily for up to several years. Employees are assigned to a project for its limited life or as long as their specialty is needed on the project. As one assignment is completed, employees move back to permanent assignments in traditional departments, or they are assigned to other projects. In fact, an employee can be assigned part time to two or more projects at the same time.

> Figure 13-5 portrays relationships of employees in Project Roger, a project in an electronics firm. It shows how ranks, peer relations, and supervisor-subordinate relationships vary between the permanent organizational structure and the matrix structure. With regard to rank, employee DD is permanently attached to the fourth level, but she has a key second-level rank in the matrix structure. With regard to peer relations, GG and HH work in separate departments in the permanent organization, but they work together in the matrix organization. Concerning supervisor-subordinate relationships, GG works for AA in the regular structure, but in the matrix structure he works for CC, who is his peer in the regular structure. In essence, matrix structure overlays one or more project structures simultaneously on the permanent organization.

The project manager   In matrix organization a project manager is established to direct all work toward completion of a major project, such as development of a new computer system. The project manager especially needs to have role adaptability to interact with people both within and without the structure. Project managers occupy *boundary roles* that require an ability to interact with different groups in order to keep their project successful. Each group has its own special language, values, and style of relationships, so project managers need to be sensitive and flexible in order to secure project needs

Boundary roles

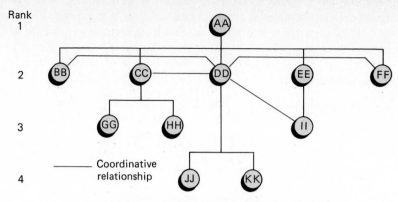

Matrix organization structure for Project Roger

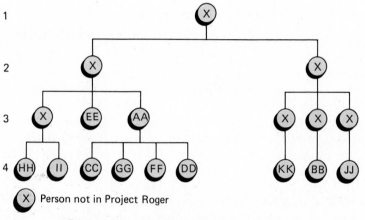

Person not in Project Roger

Permanent organizational assignment of employees
in Project Roger

Figure 13-5
A comparison of
the matrix structure
and the permanent
organizational
assignment for
employees in
Project Roger

from other groups. Project managers often have relatively weak authority, so their mission is best accomplished by communication, developing challenging assignments, negotiation, and contributing through their own expertise.[14]

Effects of matrix organization Matrix structure can be confusing to operate.[15] It requires multiple roles for people, and sometimes they get frustrated and insecure in these ambiguous roles. It dilutes authority and increases requirements for coordination and control. When conflicts arise, the participants depend heavily on problem-solving meetings to resolve issues.

In spite of its complexity, matrix organization is used for a number of reasons. It focuses resources on a single project, permitting better planning and control to meet deadlines. It is more open and flexible than a traditional hierarchy, so it can better handle the changes that occur in complex projects.

Its distribution of authority and status is more in agreement with democratic norms of technical employees. For example, more emphasis is given to authority of knowledge that a specialist can contribute to a project and less emphasis is given to rank in the permanent hierarchy. The matrix organization may improve motivation because people can focus more directly on completion of one project than they can in the traditional organization. It also improves communication by encouraging direct contact and reducing the inhibitions that result from formal rank.

Contingency factors   Although matrix organization has limited application, where it does apply it is psychologically more advanced than traditional work hierarchies. Its use is contingent upon conditions such as the following:

- Special projects, particularly major ones
- Need for diverse occupational skills, particularly higher-level ones
- Conditions of change during project operation
- Complex issues of coordination, problem solving, and scheduling
- High needs for authority of knowledge and expertise compared with existing functional authority

TECHNOLOGICAL CHANGE

Features of technology

In addition to the recent evolution of new forms of organization, technology is adding another powerful force in the work environment. Technology has certain general features, such as specialization, integration, discontinuity, and change.

Four general features

   As technology increases, specialization also tends to increase. As work gets broken into smaller parts, integration is required to put them back together again to make a whole product, a whole organization, and a whole society. This integration is much more difficult in a high-technology society than in a low-technology one, because high technology tends to make a system more complex and make its parts more interdependent.

   The flow of technology is not a continuous stream but rather a series of bursts of new developments.[16] As a consequence, the price that technology requires for the progress it brings is that people must adapt to unexpected changes. The technological revolution produces, perhaps with a time lag, an associated social revolution. Technology is moving so fast that it is creating social problems long before society is able to develop solutions. At the workplace new forms of organization, new ways of supervision, new reward structures, and a host of other changes are being required in order to absorb technology. For adjustment to technology what is needed is more mobility—economic as well as social, occupational as well as geographic, managerial as well as employee.

Technology and occupations

As technology changes, jobs also change. Technology tends to require more professional, scientific, and other white-collar workers to keep the system operating. In most advanced installations the ratio of white-collar to blue-collar employees has increased. Since people by nature are not efficient machines, it seems appropriate to replace routine jobs with automated systems that can do the job faster and better, thus releasing people to do more advanced work, which usually is white-collar work.

More white-collar jobs

As it moves workers into white-collar work, technology generally upgrades the skill and intellectual requirements of the total work force. The day laborer becomes a crane operator, the clerk becomes a computer programmer, and the laboratory technician becomes an electrical engineer working on new electronic devices. Technology tends to require a higher level of skill both in production work and in supporting services. Many scientific and professional people are needed to design, implement, and appraise the complex machines and work systems of technology, creating the secondary bulge toward the skilled end of the scale.

Robotics One product of technological change and the computer revolution is *robotics,* or the design and use of programmable mechanical devices to move parts and perform a variety of tasks.[17] Industrial robots (or "steel-collar" workers) are expensive to create and still in their infancy with regard to their vision, sense of touch, and so forth. Compared with humans, however, they can work longer hours, work more shifts, survive in harsh environments, and apply great strength. The introduction of robots is expected to increase rapidly through the 1990s, as a means of reversing the decline in U.S. productivity growth.[18]

How do robots compare with people?

Technology and education

More education necessary

The modern need for higher skills means that a premium is put upon education in the labor market. More education and training become necessary in order to avoid a surplus of underdeveloped people and a shortage of highly developed people.

Multiprofessional employees The need for an educated work force with high-level skills has increased the demand for *multiprofessional employees.* These are people trained in two or more professions or intellectual disciplines, such as engineering and law or accounting and science. Since these people are competent in more than one discipline, they are able to perform some of the integrative work required by modern work systems. The demand is especially high for multiprofessional managers who are qualified in some technical specialty in addition to management so that they can more easily manage technical work.

An example of a multiprofessional employee is Paula. After receiving her degree in computer science, she worked for a government agency for several years. Returning to college, she chose to pursue a master's degree in business administration rather than specializing further in computer design. As a result, she obtained a supervisory position and directed the work of several other programmers.

A knowledge society   The steady advancement of technology has led to the development of a knowledge society in the United States. A *knowledge society* is one in which the use of knowledge and information dominates work and employs the largest proportion of the labor force.[19] The distinguishing feature of a knowledge society is that it emphasizes intellectual work more than manual work—the mind more than the hands. Examples of knowledge jobs are those of news editors, accountants, computer programmers, and teachers. Even the surgeon, who must use a delicate manual skill, is primarily working from a knowledge or intellectual base.

More intellectual work

Intellectual work requires a different quality of motivation than manual work. Normally a person can be persuaded by the use of authority to dig a ditch. The threat of penalty usually is enough to get results. However, it takes more sophisticated motivation to lead a person to do research or write creative advertising copy. Intellectual work requires internal motivation and a more positive motivational environment. If employers of knowledge workers fail to provide this type of environment, their employees will work less effectively.

Technology and labor

In eighteenth-century England, a band of workers known as Luddites challenged the industrial revolution by roaming the countryside, smashing machinery and burning factories along the way. They believed that machinery threatened jobs. Employees in the twentieth century have faced technology with more maturity but nevertheless with considerable anxiety. Some workers, like the Luddites, view technology with a *technophobia,* that is, an emotional fear of all technology regardless of its consequences.

Luddites and technophobia

Workers who think that technology will abolish the exact jobs they now have probably are correct. With technology moving as fast as it is, few jobs will remain static during an employee's working life. Technology does not destroy jobs for all time, but it does create different jobs that workers often are not prepared to fill. Therefore, it produces employee insecurity, stress, anxiety, and possible layoff, which management needs to handle most carefully in introducing technology.[20]

Retraining   New technology may force a firm to lay off employees who have satisfactory work records but outdated skills. A social alternative is to create *retraining* programs for them, where selected employees are provided opportunities to learn new skills, followed by guaranteed jobs within the company.[21] Even when management is able to offer complete job and wage security, workers still make sacrifices of their time and energy for retraining. Certainly they expect to make some sacrifices to advance productivity for their society, but this situation also obligates management to be sensitive to employee needs so that the changeover will be as smooth as possible.

The transitions associated with retraining are not always easy. A laid-off steelworker from West Virginia named Frank LaRosa later became a computer programmer, but the financial and psychological costs were great.[22] Frank had to borrow several thousand dollars for his training, accept a one-third cut in pay, work under constant deadlines, accept management's values, and live without the satisfaction of making a basic product like steel. Despite these pressures, he is happy to have "a job with a future."

The union view In spite of employee difficulties with technology, many union leaders have recognized that it is essential for long-run employee gains and have supported it in theory. In practice, they sometimes have opposed it as being too sudden, too broad in coverage, or inappropriate to the circumstances. They also have insisted upon retraining rights, severance pay, and other benefits that soften dislocations caused by technology. Practices differ among unions because technology affects their members differently and because unions have different philosophies.

WORK SYSTEMS AND PEOPLE

Structure and procedures There are two basic ways in which work is organized. The first relates to the flow of authority and is known as *organizational structure* or merely organization, as discussed earlier. The second relates to the flow of work itself from one operation to another and is known as *procedure*. Other names are "method," "system," and "work flow." People usually recognize the human side of organizational structure because of the superior-subordinate relationship that it establishes, but more often than not they ignore or overlook the human side of work flow. They see work flow as an *engineering* factor that is separate from *human* factors. In the usual case, however, work flow has many behavioral effects because it sets people in interaction as they perform their work.

Initiation of action

One important point about a work system is that it determines who will "initiate" an activity and who will "receive" it. At each step in the flow of work one person sends material to the next person who will work on it. Along the way, staff experts give instructions. This process of sending work and/or instructions to another is an *initiation of action* on another person. Receivers of an initiation often feel psychologically inferior, because they may receive it from someone who "just shouldn't be pushing them around." In one plant, for example, operator B was a fast worker and caused work to pile up at the next work station, controlled by operator C. Considerable resentment was shown by C, who thought B made C look like a laggard.

Problems caused by initiation Initiations that tend to be trouble spots are summarized in Figure 13-6. When initiation comes from someone with distinctly less skill, or someone of

- Initiation from a fast worker to a slow one
- Initiation from an inexperienced worker to one with more experience
- Initiation from a low-seniority worker to one with high seniority
- Initiation from an unskilled worker to a skilled one
- Initiation from a young person to an older one
- Initiation from a worker with low authority to one with higher authority
- Initiation from a worker with lesser status to one with higher status
- Initiation that puts pressures on another worker
- Initiation that affects sensitive areas of a worker's job

Figure 13-6
Types of initiation
of action that
may cause human
problems

lower status, human problems can become serious. These problems tend to be compounded if the relationship involves pressure on the receiver, as in the following example from an early study of restaurants.[23]

> Large restaurants sometimes used teenagers as runners to communicate the needs of the serving pantry to the kitchen. This placed the runner in the position of "telling" the cooks to prepare and send particular types of food. The result was that teenagers initiated action on high-status cooks. In essence, they were telling cooks what to do. This relationship often was a trouble spot in the restaurants studied. Cooks resented the control exercised on them by teenagers of inferior restaurant status. Practical solutions included (1) using a mechanical voice system that eliminated face-to-face contact and (2) changing the initiator to someone of higher status.

Further problems tend to arise when an initiation affects "sensitive" areas such as how much work employees do (as in time study) and their rates of pay (as in job evaluation). In general we can conclude that initiations of action that place job or personal pressures on a receiver tend to be trouble spots.

System design for better teamwork

Another point about procedure is that it requires people to work together as a team. Teamwork can be engineered out of a work situation by means of layouts and job assignments that separate people so that it is impractical for them to work together, even though the work flow requires teamwork. In one instance two interdependent employees were unnecessarily on separate shifts, which prevented them from coordinating their work. In another instance, one operator fed parts to two separate lines that were in competition, and each line regularly claimed that the operator favored the other.

An early illustration of teamwork engineered out of a job was A. K. Rice's study of a textile mill in India.[24]

> The mill was reengineered according to basic industrial engineering procedures. Each job had carefully assigned work loads based on engineering study. In one room there were 224 looms operated and maintained by twelve occupational groups. Each

weaver tended twenty-four or thirty-two looms, each battery filler served forty to fifty looms, and each smash hand served an average of seventy-five looms. The other nine occupations were service and maintenance, and each worker had either 112 or 224 looms.

Although the mill appeared to be superbly engineered, it failed to reach satisfactory output. Research disclosed that close teamwork of all twelve occupations was required to maintain production, yet work organization prevented this teamwork. Each battery filler served all looms of one weaver and part of the looms of a second weaver, which meant a weaver and battery filler were not a team unit, even though the nature of the process required it. In effect, a weaver tending twenty-four looms and using a battery filler serving forty looms worked with three-fifths of a battery filler, while another weaver shared two-fifths of the filler. The situation was even more confused with smash hands who tended seventy-five looms.

Teamwork initially prevented

Eventually work was reorganized so that a certain group of workers had responsibility for a definite number of machines. Workers then were able to set up interaction and teamwork that caused production to soar.

Sociotechnical approach needed

A sociotechnical approach was required to integrate the technology, structure, and human factors into a productive system. When one element is changed, a mismatch is likely to emerge. Management needs to stay in close touch with the workers to understand their needs and avoid making costly mistakes.

Communication patterns

It is well known that plant layout and work flow have much to do with the opportunities that people have to talk with one another. In an insurance office, for example, the layout of desks was such that people who needed to talk to coordinate their work were separated by a broad aisle. Employees met the problem by loudly calling across the aisle, but this eventually had to be stopped because of the disturbance. The result was poor communication. In another company, sewing machines were located so that talking was discouraged, but management soon discovered that another layout that permitted talking led to higher productivity. Apparently, talking relieved the monotony of routine work.

Managers often overlook the fact that layout also can affect off-duty interaction of employees. Some years ago a new factory was built that was a model of engineering efficiency. Although the lunchroom was spotless and efficiently designed, it was located in the basement directly beneath stamping and light forging presses! Vibration was so terrific it stopped conversation. The floor and ceiling shook; the dishes rattled; there was no sound-deadening tile on the ceiling. The space beneath the presses apparently was not needed for other functions; so the cafeteria received it, but employee communication and relaxation were thereby excluded at mealtime. Lunch hours in the plant were staggered into four periods, which meant that the presses operated during the time most employees ate. When the cafeteria location was questioned, management's answer was, "The cafeteria is for eating only, and anyway the noise shouldn't bother anyone."

Red tape

CHAPTER 13:
STRUCTURE,
TECHNOLOGY,
AND PEOPLE

299

Another difficulty with procedure is *red tape*. It is procedure that appears to be unnecessary to those who are following it. It delays and harasses people everywhere. The term originated from the real red tape used to tie government documents, many of which have long been challenged as unnecessary by those who prepare them.

Red tape often becomes excessive. One cause is normal resistance to change. A procedure tends to become a habit, and people resist changing it. Another cause is that red tape often is determined by a higher authority who does not understand work problems. In these cases, people do not know why they are performing a procedure; consequently they cannot know whether it is useless or not, and they do not dare to expose their "ignorance" by questioning a procedure that their boss may be able to prove essential beyond a shadow of a doubt. People do not like to get caught not knowing something about their work.

Causes of red tape

Another reason for excessive red tape is that most procedures cross lines of authority, jumping from one chain of command to another. Under these conditions, no one employee feels a personal responsibility to change the procedure. An additional reason is that the people who created the procedures are often supervisors who do not have to follow them; so they tend to forget about them, letting them go on and on—and on.

The human problem with red tape is that it frustrates and irritates people and encourages worry and carelessness while they make their way through it. They do not like to do work that they think is useless. It challenges their human dignity and undermines their feeling that their work is worthwhile and necessary. In this way the apparently nonhuman activity called "procedure" can have a very definite effect on human behavior. Departments that are active in procedure creation, such as industrial engineering and accounting, need to give appropriate weight to the human dimensions of their procedures, because procedures that upset human relationships can do more harm than good. One sure way to raise the blood pressure of any group is to harness it with red tape.

An example of procedural rigidity occurred in a government agency. Around midmorning, it began to snow heavily in one community. As required by procedure, the office supervisor called the district headquarters and requested permission to close the office. The response was "No, it's not snowing here [200 miles away]." Two hours later, the district headquarters called the office supervisor with this message, "You can close your office now; it's snowing here."

Alienation

Alienation may result from poor design of sociotechnical systems. Since work systems usually are planned by someone other than the operators, often the operators do not understand why the system operates the way it does. In addition, division of labor lets each operator perform only a small portion of the total work to be done, so jobs begin to lose their social significance and appear meaningless. Workers no longer see where they fit in the scheme of things; no longer do they see the value of their efforts. When these feelings become substantial, an employee may develop *alienation,* which is a feeling of powerlessness, lack of meaning, loneliness, disorientation, and lack of

Causes of alienation

attachment to the job, work group, or organization. When workers are performing an insignificant task, frustrated by red tape, isolated from communication with others, prevented from engaging in teamwork, and controlled by initiations of action from others, then alienation is bound to develop.

There is evidence that alienation tends to be low in high-technology process industries as compared with mechanized assembly-line operations. Using Woodward's classification, unit and process production tend to have low alienation, while mass production has high alienation.[25] The relationship is curvilinear, as shown in Figure 13-7. This relationship suggests that much of modern industry that is now in the mass-production stage will move toward less alienating conditions as technology advances. In this manner, advancing technology will be favorable to workers.

The relationship of alienation to technology is only a general one. In some instances mass production may be welcomed by employees because it reduces their physical labor, improves working conditions, and provides them with new equipment. In addition to technology, there are other causes of alienation. For example, an autocratic management may cause alienation, or alienation may be related to conditions external to the organization. Some alienation may also occur among managers and high-level professionals for a

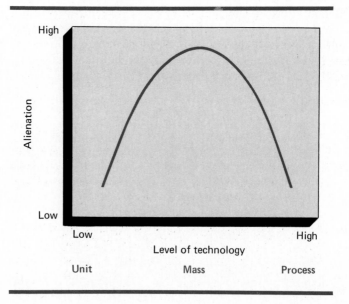

Figure 13-7
Relationship of
alienation and
level of technology

variety of reasons, such as attributing poor employee performance to the employee's lack of ability.[26] When alienation threatens to become serious, management needs to take corrective action to overcome it.

Effects of work systems

The evidence is clear that work systems have a substantial effect on human behavior. They do this by:

1 Determining who initiates action on whom, and some of the conditions in which the initiation occurs

2 Influencing the degree to which the employees performing interdependent activities can work together as a team

3 Affecting the communication patterns of employees

4 Creating possibilities for unnecessary procedures, generally called red tape

5 Providing tasks that seem insignificant and weak in power, thereby contributing to alienation

The general conclusion is that *relationships among workers in a system can be just as important as relationships of the work in that system.* In the design of any system it is folly to spend all one's time planning work relationships but ignoring worker relationships.

SUMMARY

Classical organizational structure is established by functional and scalar division of work, and it is communicated to participants by means of delegation. Organization brings immense technical advantages, but there often are human costs. An example is specialization. Essentially, classical structure is strong in task support but weak in psychological support. Highly structured organizations are known as bureaucracies.

Organizational structure tends to exist in a contingency relationship with other variables, but certain general tendencies are evident. Generally, mechanistic organization is more appropriate for stable, mass-production environments in which employees desire security. Organic organization is more appropriate in dynamic environments with unit or continuous production and flexible employees. Matrix organization is a useful way to adapt to dynamic environments, especially when large technical projects are involved.

Technology is a powerful economic and social tool that can bring substantial benefits to society. Its effects are variable, but it tends to require higher worker skills, more white-collar work, and more multiprofessional employees. The result is a knowledge society. Labor unions generally accept technology as beneficial to society as a whole, but they want security provisions and retraining programs to protect individuals dislocated by it.

The flow of work especially affects people in organizations. It determines who initiates action on whom, influences the degree to which employees can work together as a team, affects communication patterns, creates possibilities of red tape, and may cause alienation. The conclusion is that the relationships of workers in a system can be just as important as the relationships of the work in that system.

TERMS AND CONCEPTS FOR REVIEW

Sociotechnical systems

Classical organization theory

Linking pin concept

Acceptance theory of authority

Contingency organizational design

Mechanistic and organic organizations

Matrix organization

Boundary roles

Robotics

Multiprofessional employees

Knowledge society

Technophobia

Initiation of action

Red tape

Alienation

REVIEW QUESTIONS

1 Discuss how the linking pin concept is seen as a way of building a unified team within a whole organization.

2 Distinguish between a tall and a flat organizational structure. What advantages and disadvantages do each bring? Relate them to the span of management.

3 Discuss differences between mechanistic and organic patterns of organization. With what situations is each appropriate?

4 Explain how matrix organization works. What are its strengths and weaknesses? What situations are more appropriate for its use?

5 Assume that you lose your job due to technological change five years from now. Describe your probable feelings. How would your feelings differ if the same thing happened again just five years before you reached retirement age? Discuss.

6 Suppose you have an office with three secretaries who divide their time evenly between typing, filing, and staffing the receptionist desk. What are some of the ways that you could organize their work, and what would be the probable effects of each way?

   a If one of them typically is rude and unpleasant with other people, would that make a difference? Explain.

   b If one of them clearly is the best typist but typing is the least desirable job, would that make a difference? Explain.

   c Suppose one of them has a 50 percent hearing loss that cannot be corrected. Would that make a difference?

7 Think of a job about which you have some personal knowledge. How is the flow of work to and from the job organized? What are the probable effects of this work system?

8 Did you experience any red tape in your registration for college? Discuss.

9 What are some of the job-caused origins of employee alienation? Discuss some of the ways in which effective organizational behavior can reduce these causes.

10 Discuss how a knowledge society may affect jobs:
  a In the next decade
  b In the next twenty-five years

INCIDENT

The Central Motor Pool

A sales company established a central motor pool for its sales representatives, after years of allowing each representative to have an automobile. The pool was established to achieve significant cost savings, because sales representatives spent about one-third of their time in the office and only two-thirds of their time visiting customers.

On the basis of this information and your knowledge of human behavior, what would you predict regarding:

1 Sales representatives' feelings about not having their own cars

2 Competition over who would get which car to use

3 Care with which they handled the cars

4 Amount of time spent traveling under the new system

Because of difficulties with the pool, management finally decided that all sales representatives traveling over 1000 miles a month could have their own automobile. Then most of them started traveling that much even though there was no apparent need for many of them to do so.

QUESTIONS

1 Analyze and discuss the sociotechnical relationships in this situation.

2 Determine the sales behavior desired of the representatives, and offer an automobile arrangement to obtain it.

EXPERIENTIAL EXERCISE

Mechanistic and Organic Structures

1 Indicate your general *preference* for working in one of these two organizational structures by circling the appropriate response:

Mechanistic 1   2   3   4   5   6   7   8   9   10 **Organic**

2 Indicate your perception of the form of organization that is used in this class by circling the appropriate response for each item:

A Task-role definition

Rigid   1   2   3   4   5   6   7   8   9   10   **Flexible**

B Communication

Vertical   1   2   3   4   5   6   7   8   9   10   **Multidirectional**

C Decision making

Centralized   1   2   3   4   5   6   7   8   9   10   **Decentralized**

D Sensitivity to the environment

Closed   1   2   3   4   5   6   7   8   9   10   **Open**

3 Meet in groups of four to six persons. Share your data from parts 1 and 2. Discuss the reasons for your responses, and analyze the factors that probably encouraged your instructor to choose the type of structure that now exists.

REFERENCES

1 Nicholas Dimarco and Steven Norton, "Life Style, Organization Structure, Congruity and Job Satisfaction," *Personnel Psychology,* Winter 1974, p. 489.

2 Lloyd Dobyns, "The Decline of American Productivity: If Japan Can, Why Can't We?" *Training and Development Journal,* August 1982, p. 52.

3 An overview of sociotechnical systems is presented in Louis E. Davis, "Optimizing Organization-Plant Design: A Complementary Structure for Technical and Social Systems," *Organizational Dynamics,* Autumn 1979, pp. 3–15; see also Newton Margulies and Lora Colflesh, "A Socio-Technical Approach to Planning and Implementing New Technology," *Training and Development Journal,* December 1982, pp. 16–29.

4 L. L. Cummings and Chris I. Berger, "Organizational Structure: How Does It Influence Attitudes and Performance?" *Organizational Dynamics,* Autumn 1976, pp. 34–49; readers interested in how structure is measured should see Eric J. Walton, "The Comparison of Measures of Structure," *Academy of Management Review,* January 1981, pp. 155–160.

5 Patrick J. Montana and Deborah F. Nash, "Delegation: The Art of Managing," *Personnel Journal,* October 1981, pp. 784–787.

6 Lawrence B. Chonko, "The Relationship of Span of Control to Sales Representatives' Experienced Role Conflict and Role Ambiguity," *Academy of Management Journal,* June 1982, pp. 452–456.

7 John M. Ivancevich and James H. Donnelly, Jr., "Relation of Organizational Structure to Job Satisfaction, Anxiety-Stress, and Performance," *Administrative Science Quarterly,* June 1975, pp. 272–280.

8 Alan Ned Sabrosky, James Clay Thompson, and Karen A. McPherson, "Organized Anarchies: Military Bureaucracy in the 1980s," *Journal of Applied Behavioral Science,* 18:2, 1982, pp. 137–153.

9 T. Burns and G. M. Stalker, *The Management of Innovation,* London: Tavistock Publications, 1961.

10 A study demonstrating the usefulness of quantitative models for matching structures to environments to optimize goal attainment is Sang M. Lee, Fred Luthans, and David L. Olson, "A Management Science Approach to Contingency Models of Managerial Structure," *Academy of Management Journal*, September 1982, pp. 553–566.

11 Joan Woodward, *Industrial Organization: Theory and Practice,* London: Oxford University Press, 1965, especially chap. 12 and p. 69. Additional interpretations are provided in Peter M. Blau and others, "Technology and Organization in Manufacturing," *Administrative Science Quarterly*, March 1976, pp. 20–40.

12 Paul R. Lawrence and Jay W. Lorsch, *Organization and Environment: Managing Differentiation and Integration,* Boston: Harvard Graduate School of Business Administration, 1967; and Jay W. Lorsch and John J. Morse, *Organizations and Their Members: A Contingency Approach,* New York: Harper & Row, Publishers, Inc., 1974. See also Rosalie L. Tung, "Dimensions of Organizational Environments: An Exploratory Study of Their Impact on Organization Structure," *Academy of Management Journal,* December 1979, pp. 672–693.

13 More detailed discussions of matrix organization may be found in John L. Brown and Neil McK. Agnew, "The Balance of Power in a Matrix Structure," *Business Horizons,* November–December 1982, pp. 51–54; and Stanley M. Davis and Paul R. Lawrence, "The Matrix Diamond," *The Wharton Magazine,* Winter 1978, pp. 19–27.

14 A field study reporting that the characteristics of boundary spanners vary by task area is Michael L. Tushman and Thomas J. Scanlon, "Characteristics and External Orientations of Boundary Spanning Individuals," *Academy of Management Journal,* March 1981, pp. 83–98.

15 A disastrous attempt to use matrix organization when the firm was unprepared for it is reported in Stratford P. Sherman, "Bausch and Lomb's Lost Opportunity," *Fortune,* Jan. 24, 1983, pp. 104–105.

16 Louis Girifalco, "The Dynamics of Technological Change," *The Wharton Magazine,* Fall 1982, pp. 31–37.

17 George L. Whaley, "The Impact of Robotics Technology upon Human Resource Management," *Personnel Administrator,* September 1982, pp. 61–71; and John Dodd, "Robots: The New 'Steel Collar' Workers," *Personnel Journal,* September 1981, pp. 688–605. The pace at which robots are being introduced is reported in Gene Bylinsky, "The Race to the Automated Factory," *Fortune,* February 1983, pp. 52ff.

18 Robert U. Ayres and Steven Miller, "Robotics, CAM, and Industrial Productivity," *National Productivity Review,* Winter 1981–1982, pp. 42–60. Human resource implications are presented in Edward M. Knod, Jr., et al., "Robotics: Challenges for the Human Resources Manager," *Business Horizons,* March–April 1984, pp. 38–46.

19 For an early discussion of the implications of this type of technology, see Peter F. Drucker, *The Age of Discontinuity,* New York: Harper & Row, Publishers, Inc., 1969, pp. 263–310; see also Keith Davis, "Some Fundamental Trends Affecting Management in the Future," in Lewis Benton (ed.), *Management for the Future,* New York: McGraw-Hill Book Company, 1978, pp. 63–76. For the view that society has not placed adequate recognition on technical competence, see Edward J. Giblin, "Bureaupathology: The Denigration of Competence," *Human Resource Management,* Winter 1981, pp. 22–25.

20 Craig Brod, "Managing Technostress: Optimizing the Use of Computer Technology," *Personnel Journal,* October 1982, pp. 753–757.

21 Jane Raitt, "Retrain to Retain: A Prescription for the 1980s," *Training and Development Journal*, February 1982, pp. 48–52; Joan Lindroth, "How to Beat the Coming Labor Shortage," *Personnel Journal*, April 1982, pp. 268–272; and Raymond Donovan, "The Importance of Retraining America's Work Force," *T. H. E. Journal*, October 1983, pp. 101–103.

22 Carol Hymowitz, "Culture Shock Affects Steelworker Who Switched to White-Collar Job," *Wall Street Journal*, June 1983, p. 31.

23 This example is from a classical study by William F. Whyte, *Human Relations in the Restaurant Industry*, New York: McGraw-Hill Book Company, 1948, pp. 49–63.

24 A. K. Rice, "Productivity and Social Organization in an Indian Weaving Shed," *Human Relations*, vol. 6, no. 4, 1953, pp. 297–329.

25 Robert Dewar and James Werbel, "Universalistic and Contingency Predictions of Employee Satisfaction and Conflict," *Administrative Science Quarterly*, September 1979, pp. 426–448. For a contrary opinion not supporting alienation of mass-production workers, see William H. Form, "Technology and Social Behavior of Workers in Four Countries: A Socio-technical Perspective," *American Sociological Review*, December 1972, pp. 727–738.

26 Mark J. Martinko and William J. Gardner, "Learned Helplessness: An Alternative Explanation for Performance Deficits," *Academy of Management Review*, April 1982, pp. 195–204. One product of alienation—blatant lying to authority—is described in Daniel Yankelovich, "Lying Well Is the Best Revenge," *Psychology Today*, August 1982, pp. 5–6, 71.

FOR ADDITIONAL READING

Baranson, Jack, *Automated Manufacturing: The Key to International Competitiveness*, Mt. Airy, Md.: Lomond Publications, 1983.

Davis, Stanley, M., and Paul R. Lawrence, *Matrix*, Reading, Mass.: Addison-Wesley Publishing Company, Inc., 1977.

Katz, D., and R. L. Kahn, *The Social Psychology of Organizations*, New York: John Wiley & Sons, Inc., 1978.

Kaufman, Herbert, *Red Tape: Its Origins, Uses, and Abuses*, Washington, D.C.: The Brookings Institution, 1977.

Kelley, Albert J. (ed.), *New Dimensions of Project Management, Lexington, Mass.: Lexington Books, 1982.*

Miner, John B., *Theories of Organizational Structure and Process*, Hinsdale, Ill.: Dryden Press, 1982.

Mintzberg, Henry, *Structure in Fives: Designing Effective Organizations*, Englewood Cliffs, N.J.: Prentice-Hall, Inc., 1983.

Shepard, Jon M., *Automation and Alienation: A Study of Office and Factory Workers*, Cambridge, Mass.: The M.I.T. Press, 1971.

Thompson, James D., *Organizations in Action*, New York: McGraw-Hill Book Company, 1967.

Toffler, Alvin, *The Third Wave*, New York: William Morrow, Inc., 1980.

Zand, Dale E., *Information, Organization and Power: Effective Management in the Knowledge Society*, New York: McGraw-Hill Book Company, 1981.

INFORMAL ORGANIZATIONS

The number of informal social groups within an organization tends to be rather large relative to the total number of individuals employed by it.

Lyman W. Porter, Edward E. Lawler III, and J. Richard Hackman[1]

CHAPTER OBJECTIVES

TO UNDERSTAND:

The nature of informal organization
Benefits and problems with informal systems
How informal organizations may be charted
Organizational grapevines and their causes
Accuracy and patterns of grapevines
Rumor and its control

When Bill Smith graduated from engineering school and joined the laboratory of a large manufacturing company, he was assigned the task of supervising four laboratory technicians who checked production samples. In some ways he did supervise them. In other ways he was restricted by the group itself, which was quite frustrating to Bill. He soon found that each technician protected the others so that it was difficult to fix responsibility for sloppy work. The group appeared to restrict its work in such a way that about the same number of tests were made every day regardless of his urging to speed up the work. Although Bill was the designated supervisor, he observed that many times his technicians, instead of coming to him, took problems to an older technician across the aisle in another section.

Bill also observed that three of his technicians often had lunch together in the cafeteria, but the fourth technician usually ate with friends in an adjoining laboratory. Bill usually ate with other laboratory supervisors, and he learned much about company events during these lunches. He soon began to realize that these situations were evidence of an informal organization and that he had to work with it as well as with the formal organization.

Beneath the cloak of formal relationships in every organization there is a more complex system of social relationships consisting of many informal organizations. They are related to the socialization of employees, which was discussed in an earlier chapter.[2] Although there are many different informal groups, not one, we refer to them collectively as the informal organization. It is a powerful influence on productivity and job satisfaction. Both the formal and the informal systems are necessary for group activity, just as two blades are essential for a pair of scissors. This chapter presents a general overview of informal organizations at work, including their communication system, popularly called the grapevine.

THE NATURE OF INFORMAL ORGANIZATION

Informal organization arises from social interaction

Definition of informal organization

Widespread interest in informal organization developed as a result of the Western Electric studies in the 1930s, which concluded that it was an important part of the total work situation. These studies showed that *informal organization* is a network of personal and social relations not established or required by the formal organization but arising spontaneously as people associate with one another. The emphasis within informal organization is on people and their relationships, while formal organization emphasizes official positions in terms of authority and responsibility. Informal power, therefore, attaches to a *person*, while formal authority attaches to a *position* and a person has it only when occupying that position. Informal power is personal, but formal authority is institutional. These differences are summarized in Figure 14-1.[3]

Informal power

Power in informal organization is given by group members, rather than delegated by managers; therefore, it does not follow the official chain of command. It is more likely to come from peers than from superiors in the formal hierarchy; and it may cut across organizational lines into other departments. It is usually more unstable than formal authority, since it is

Formal organization	Informal organization
Official	.Unofficial
Authority ⎤ . . . . ⎰	Power
Responsibility ⎦ . . . . ⎱	Politics
Position	.Person
Delegated by management	.Given by group

Figure 14-1
Differences between
formal and informal
organization

subject to the sentiments of people. Because of its subjective nature, informal organization cannot be controlled by management in the way that formal organization is.

A manager typically holds some informal (personal) power along with formal (positional) power, but usually a manager does not have more informal power than anyone else in the group. This means that the manager and the informal leader usually are two different persons in work groups.

As a result of differences between formal and informal sources of power, formal organizations may grow to immense size, but informal organizations (at least the closely knit ones) tend to remain smaller in order to keep within the limits of personal relationships. The result is that a large organization tends to have hundreds of informal organizations operating throughout it. Some of them are wholly within the institution; others are partially external to it. Because of their naturally small size and instability, informal organizations are not a suitable substitute for the large formal aggregates of people and resources that are needed for modern institutions.

Workers usually recognize the different roles played by formal and informal organizations, including the more secondary role normally played by the informal. One study of workers reported that, although workers and managers saw the informal organization as influential and beneficial, they viewed the formal organization as more influential and beneficial.[4]

Secondary role

Informal leaders

The leaders of informal groups arise for various reasons. Some of these reasons are age, seniority, technical competence, work location, freedom to move around the work area, and a responsive personality. The causes are numberless, because each leader arises under slightly different circumstances.

Informal groups overlap to the extent that one person may be a member of several different groups, which means that there is not just one leader but several of varying importance. The group may look to one employee on matters pertaining to wages and to another to lead recreational plans. In this way several people in a department may be informal leaders of some type. There might be an old-timer who is looked upon as the expert on job problems, a listener who serves as counselor, and a communicator who is depended upon to convey key problems to the managers.[5]

In return for their services, informal leaders usually enjoy certain rewards and privileges. Perhaps the old-timer is permitted to choose a vacation time first, and so on. One significant reward is the esteem in which the leader is held.

One primary leader

Although several persons in a group may be informal leaders of various types, there is usually one primary leader who has more influence than others. Each manager needs to learn who the key informal leader is in any group and to work with that leader to encourage behavior that furthers rather than hinders organizational objectives. When an informal leader is working against an employer, the leader's widespread influence can undermine motivation and job satisfaction.

The informal organization is a desirable source of potential formal leaders, but it should be remembered that an informal leader does not always make the best formal manager. History is filled with examples of successful informal leaders who became arrogant bosses once they received formal authority. Some informal leaders fail as formal ones because they fear official responsibility—something they do not have as informal leaders. They often criticize management for lacking initiative or for not daring to be different, but when they take a management job, they become even more conservative because they are afraid to make a mistake. Other informal leaders fail because their area of official management authority is broader and more complex than the tiny area in which they had informal power. The fact that Joe is the leader in department social activities does not mean that he will be successful as the departmental manager.

Benefits of informal organizations

Although informal systems may lead to several problems, they also bring a number of benefits to both employers and employees, as shown in Figure 14-2. Most important is that they blend with formal systems to make an *Better total system* effective total system.[6] Formal plans and policies cannot meet every problem in a dynamic situation because they are preestablished and partly inflexible. Some requirements can be met better by informal relations, which can be flexible and spontaneous.

Lighter work load for management

Another benefit of informal organization is to lighten the work load on management. When managers know that the informal organization is working with them, they feel less compelled to check on the workers to be sure everything is shipshape. Managers are encouraged to delegate and decentralize because they are confident that employees will be cooperative. In general, informal group support of a manager probably leads to better cooperation and productivity. It helps get the work done.

Informal organization also may act to fill in gaps in a manager's abilities. If a manager is weak in planning, an employee informally may help with planning. In this way, planning is accomplished in spite of the manager's weakness.

Work-group satisfaction

A significant benefit of informal organization is that it gives satisfaction and stability to work groups. It is the means by which workers feel a sense of

Benefits

- Makes a more effective total system.
- Lightens work load on management.
- Helps get the work done.
- Tends to encourage cooperation.
- Fills in gaps in a manager's abilities.
- Gives satisfaction and stability to work groups.
- Improves communication.
- Provides a safety valve for employee emotions.
- Encourages managers to plan and act more carefully.

Problems

- Develops undesirable rumor.
- Encourages negative attitudes.
- Resists change.
- Leads to interpersonal and intergroup conflicts.
- Rejects and harasses some employees.
- Weakens motivation and satisfaction.
- Operates outside of management's control.
- Supports conformity.
- Develops role conflicts.

Figure 14-2
Potential benefits and problems associated with informal organizations

belonging and security. It gives workers a feeling that they have something worth remaining with, so satisfaction is increased and turnover reduced.

> In a large office, for example, an employee named Rose McVail may feel like only a payroll number, but her informal group gives her personal attachment and status. With them she is somebody, even though in the formal structure she is only one of a thousand clerks. She may not look forward to posting 750 accounts daily, but the informal group can give more meaning to her day. When she can think of meeting her friends, sharing their interests, and eating with them, her day takes on a new dimension that makes easier any difficulty or tedious routine in her work. Of course, these conditions can apply in reverse: The group may not accept her, thereby making her work more disagreeable and driving her to a transfer, absenteeism, or a resignation.

An additional benefit is that informal organization can be a useful channel of employee communication. It provides the means for people to keep in touch, to learn more about their work, and to understand what is happening in their environment.

Another benefit, often overlooked, is that the informal organization is a safety valve for employee frustrations and other emotional problems. Employees may relieve emotional pressures by discussing them with someone else in an open and friendly way, and one's associates in the informal group provide this type of environment.

A safety valve for emotions

> Consider the case of Max Schultz, who became frustrated and angry with his supervisor, Frieda Schneider. He felt like striking her, but in a civilized organization that was not appropriate behavior. He wanted to tell her what he thought of her, using uncomplimentary words, but he might have been disciplined for that. His next alternative was to have lunch with a close friend, and to share with his friend exactly how he felt. Having vented his feelings, he was able to return to work and interact with Schneider in a more relaxed way.

A benefit of informal organization that is seldom recognized is that its presence encourages managers to plan and act more carefully than they would otherwise. Managers who understand its power know that it is a check and balance on their unlimited use of authority. They introduce changes into their groups only after careful planning because they know that informal groups can undermine an ill-conceived and shaky project. They want their projects to succeed because they will have to answer to formal authority if they fail.

Problems associated with informal organizations

Coexistence of positive and negative sides

Many of the benefits of informal systems can be reversed to show potential problems that may develop. In other words, informal systems can help and harm an activity at the same time. For example, while useful information is being spread by one part of the system, another part may be communicating a malicious rumor. An informal system also can change its mood in a positive or negative way. A work group, for example, may welcome a new employee or reject the employee, causing an unhappy employee and a resignation. Both positive and negative effects exist side by side in most informal systems.

Resistance to change

One major problem with informal organizations is resistance to change. There is a tendency for a group to become overly protective of its way of life and to stand like a rock in the face of change. What has been good is believed to be good enough for the future. If, for example, job A has always had more status than job B, it must continue to have more status and more pay, even though conditions have changed to make job A less difficult. If restriction of productivity was necessary in the past with an autocratic management, it is necessary now, even though management is participative. Although informal organizations are bound by no chart on the wall, they are bound by convention, custom, and culture.

Conformity

A related problem is that the informal organization can be a significant cause of employee conformity. The informal side of organizations is so much a part of the everyday life of workers that they hardly realize it is there, so they usually are unaware of the powerful pressures it applies to persuade them to conform to its way of life. The closer they are attached to it, the stronger its influence is.

Norms, reference groups, and sanctions

Conformity is encouraged by *norms,* which are informal group requirements for the behavior of its members. The group whose norms a person accepts is a *reference group.* Rewards and penalties that a group uses to persuade persons to conform to its norms are *sanctions.* These informal norms and sanctions consistently guide opinion and apply power to reduce any behavior that tends to vary from group norms.[7] Nonconformers may be pressured and harassed until they capitulate or leave.

Examples of harassment are interference with work (such as hiding one of the offender's tools), ridicule, interference outside of work (such as letting the air out of the offender's automobile tires), and isolation from the group. In Britain it is said that a person isolated from the group is "being sent to Coventry."[8] In these instances the group refuses to talk with the offender for days or even weeks, and group members may even refuse to use any tool or machine the offender has used. Actions of this type can drive a worker from a job.

CHAPTER 14: 313
INFORMAL
ORGANIZATIONS

Another problem that may develop is role conflict. Workers want to meet *Role conflict* the requirements of both their group and their employer, but frequently these requirements are in conflict. What is good for the employees is not always good for the organization. Coffee breaks may be desirable, but if employees spend an extra fifteen minutes socializing in the morning and afternoon, productivity may be reduced to the disadvantage of both the employer and consumers. Much of this role conflict can be avoided by carefully cultivating mutual interests with informal groups. The more the interests of formal and informal groups can be integrated, the more productivity and satisfaction can be expected. However, there always will be some differences between formal and informal organizations. This is not an area where perfect harmony exists.

A major difficulty with any informal organization is that it is not subject to management's direct control. The "authority" that it depends on is the social system rather than management. All that management can do is influence it here and there.

Informal organizations also develop interpersonal and intergroup conflicts *Personal and* that can be damaging to their organization. When employees give more of *group conflicts* their thoughts and energies to opposing each other, they are likely to give less to their employer. Conflicts and self-interests can become so strong in informal organizations that they reduce both motivation and satisfaction. The result is less productivity, which harms both the employer and employees. No one gains.

Charting the informal organization

One way to gain a better understanding of an informal system is to prepare a chart of it. A diagram of the feelings of group members toward each other is called a *sociogram*.[9] This study and measurement of feelings of group *Sociogram* members toward one another was pioneered by J. L. Moreno in the 1930s and is called *sociometry*. Moreno classed feelings as attraction, repulsion, and indifference. To learn these feelings in a work group, he asked members to rank their choices of people with whom they would like to work or not to work. The person receiving the most positive votes is the star, or sociometric leader. This person is the one liked the most, but is not necessarily the true informal leader who motivates the group to take action. The star can make or break a social fad but may be secondary to someone else in leading the group toward a work goal.

Another charting approach is to diagram the actual informal interactions of people, such as with whom an individual spends the most time and with whom one communicates informally. Charts of these relationships are called *informal organization charts*, or *grapevine charts*.[10] These charts may be superim- *Grapevine charts* posed on the formal organization chart in order to show variations between the two. This type of chart is illustrated by Figure 14-3. Superimposed on the

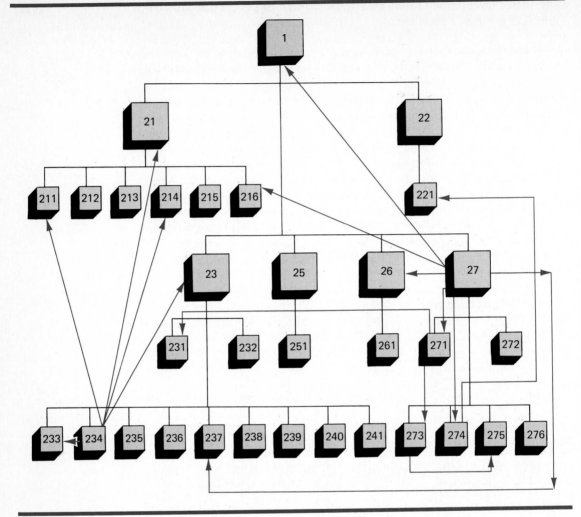

Figure 14-3
Patterns of
communication
about an event
known to managers
in positions 27 and
234 in a
manufacturing
company

formal chart are lines showing the patterns of communication that developed from an event known to the managers in positions 27 and 234. Most of these communications were outside formal chains of command, illustrating how the informal system is not bound by the official organizational structure. Discussion of informal communication continues in the next section.

INFORMAL COMMUNICATION

Grapevines The *grapevine* is the communication system of informal organization. It coexists with management's formal communication system. The term "grapevine" arose during the War Between the States. Intelligence telegraph lines were strung loosely from tree to tree in the manner of a grapevine, and wild grapevines grew over the lines in some areas. Since messages from the lines often were incorrect or confusing, any rumor was said to be from the grapevine. Today the term applies to all informal communication, including company information that is communicated informally between employees and people in the community.[11]

Although grapevine information tends to be sent orally, it may be written. Handwritten or typewritten notes sometimes are used, but in the modern electronic office messages typically are flashed on computer screens or delivered by electronic printing. Electronic messages can be sent to distant locations in a matter of seconds.[12]

Figure 14-4 is a copy of a grapevine communication sent by teletypewriter between company branches in two cities. During a period of months two employees had developed an active interest in operations in the other branch. Though they never heard each other's voice, they frequently "talked" by teletype when the leased system was not in use. Observe that they were talking about their employer, and some of what they learned undoubtedly was passed along on the local grapevine.

Since the grapevine arises from social interaction, it is as fickle, dynamic, and varied as people are. It is the expression of their natural motivation to communicate. It is the exercise of their freedom of speech and is a natural, normal activity. In fact, only employees who are totally disinterested in their work do not engage in shoptalk about it.

Employee interest in associates is illustrated by the experience of one company. The wife of a plant supervisor had a baby at 11 P.M., and a plant survey the next day at 2 P.M. showed that 46 percent of the management personnel knew of it through the grapevine.[13]

In a sense, the grapevine is a human birthright, because whenever people congregate into groups, the grapevine is sure to develop. It may use smoke signals, jungle tom-toms, taps on the prison wall, ordinary conversation, or some other method, but it will always be there. Organizations cannot "fire" the grapevine because they did not hire it. It is simply there.

How accurate is the grapevine?

If we count the units of information in Figure 14-4 and then verify which are true and which are false, we will find that most of them are true. This is the way research on grapevine accuracy is done, and it shows that in normal work situations well over three-fourths of grapevine information is accurate.[14] People tend to think the grapevine is less accurate than it is because its errors are more dramatic and consequently more impressed on memory than its day-by-day routine accuracy. Moreover, one inaccurate part may make a whole story inaccurate.

Both accuracy and inaccuracy

IS JOE* THERE GA[1]

YES

PUT HIM ON TELEX PLS[2] GA

THIS JOE

THIS SUE AND I AM A LITTLE CURIOUS ABOUT UR[3] TELEX YESTERDAY   COAST CLEAR NOW   SO WHAT DO THEY ASK YOU GA

THE FIRST STUPID QUESTION WAS THEY WANTED TO KNOW WHAT HAPPENED TO CERTAIN ITEMS THAT WERE ON THE INVENTORY ONE MONTH AND NOT ON THE NEXT MONTH   I TOLD THEM IT WAS ONLY LOGICAL TO ASSUME THEY WERE SOLD   SO THEY ASKED TO WHOM   TOLD THEM TO LOOK IT UP ON THEIR COPIES OF THE DR'S[4] GA

UR ANSWER WAS PRETTY GOOD   UR RIGHT   THINGS LIKE THAT COME UP ALL THE TIME BUT UNFORTUNATELY I HAVE TO FIGURE OUT MOSTLY FROM HERE   WHAT ELSE JOE GA

THEY SAID MY INVENTORY WAS SHORT 25 TONS AND WANTED TO KNOW WHY   I ASKED THEM FOR THE FIGURES THEY USED AND I CHECKED IT OUT ONLY TO FIND THEY CANT EVEN COPY THE RIGHT FIGURES DOWN GA

WELL SOMETIMES I GUESS THEY MAKE BOBOS[5] LIKE THAT BUT UR LUCKY ONLY BEING OFF 25 TONS   WE WERE OFF 400 TONS AND IT TOOK ME AWHILE TO FIND IT   WHAT ELSE

THIS IS PROBABLY THE FUNNIEST   I PAY THE LOCAL PAPER HERE EVERY MONTH FOR ADVERTISING AND WHEN OUR STATEMENTS COME HERE FROM CHICAGO THEY NEVER HAVE ANYTHING CHARGED TO ADVERTISING WHICH AMOUNTS TO A FEW THOUSAND A YEAR   I ASKED ABOUT IT AND THEY WERE SURPRISED   I GUESS THEY DONT LOOK AT THE COPIES OF THE CHECKS THAT I MAKE OUT GA

WELL THEY SURE LOOK AT OURS BECAUSE THEY CONSTANTLY ASK US WHY AND TO WHOM AND WHAT FOR WE PAID THIS AND THAT   THE ONLY ONE WHO KNOWS ABOUT CHECK COPIES IS MAX SMITH AND I THINK HE KEEPS GOOD TRACK OF IT BUT U[6] ARE RIGHT THAT IS FUNNY   OH GOOD GA

ANYWAY I REMEMBER GEORGE TELLING ME ABOUT UR PROBLEM AND I JUST WANTED TO LET U KNOW U WERE NOT THE ONLY ONES THAT KEEP IN DAILY COMMUNICATION WITH CHICAGO GA

I THINK IT WAS VERY NICE OF U AND AS FAR AS I CAN SEE I HAVE IT WORSE THAN U SO MY COMPLIMENTS TO YOU AND THANKS AGAIN FOR UR CONCERN GA

THATS ABOUT ALL FROM HERE GA

OK JOE BIBI[7]

Figure 14-4
Actual transcript of a teletypewriter grapevine over a company private wire between two warehouse clerks in separate cities

Key: *All names are disguised.
[1]Go ahead.
[2]Please.
[3]"Your" or "you are," depending on the sentence.
[4]Delivery receipts.
[5]Errors; "boo-boos."
[6]You.
[7]Bye bye.

On one grapevine, for example, a story about a welder marrying the general manager's daughter was true with regard to his getting married, the date, the location, and other details. The one wrong detail in this 90 percent accurate story was that the woman was not the general manager's daughter but happened to have the same last name. This one wrong point made the whole communication wrong in general meaning even though it was 90 percent accurate in detail.

It also is true that grapevine information usually is incomplete, so it may be seriously misinterpreted even though the details it does carry are accurate. That is, even though the grapevine tends to carry the truth, it rarely carries the whole truth. These cumulative inadequacies of the grapevine mean that in total it tends to produce more misunderstanding than its small percentage of wrong information suggests.

Not the whole truth

The grapevine pattern

Managers occasionally get the impression that the grapevine operates like a long chain in which A tells B, who tells C, who then tells D, and so on, until twenty persons later, Y gets the information—very late and very incorrect. Sometimes the grapevine may operate this way, but it generally follows a different pattern, as shown in Figure 14-5. Employee A tells three or four others (such as B, J, and F). Only one or two of these receivers will pass the information forward, and they usually will tell more than one person. Then as the information becomes older and the proportion of those knowing it gets larger, it gradually dies out because those who receive it do not repeat it. This network is a *cluster chain*, because each link in the chain tends to inform a cluster of other people instead of only one person. Other types of chains also are shown in the figure, but they are used less.

Cluster chain

Figure 14-5
Types of
grapevine chains

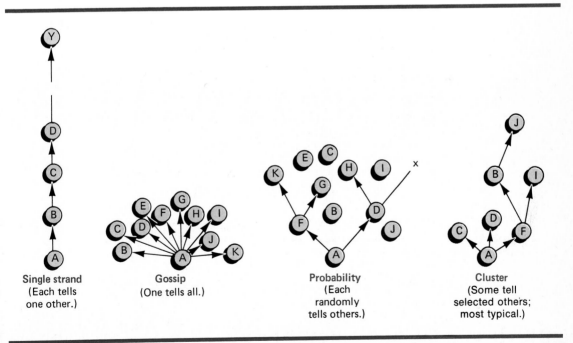

| Single strand (Each tells one other.) | Gossip (One tells all.) | Probability (Each randomly tells others.) | Cluster (Some tell selected others; most typical.) |

If we accept the idea that this cluster chain is predominant, it is reasonable to conclude that only a few people are active communicators on the grapevine for any specific unit of information.[15] If, for example, eighty-seven clerks in an office know that Mabel was married secretly on Saturday, probably the word was spread to these eighty-seven by only ten or fifteen clerks. The remainder received the information, but did not spread it. These people who keep the grapevine active are called *liaison individuals*.

A few active communicators

> For example, in one company when a quality-control problem occurred, 68 percent of the executives knew about it, but only 20 percent of them spread the information. In another case, when a manager planned to resign, 81 percent of the executives knew about it, but only 11 percent passed the news on to others.

Grapevine causes

The grapevine is more a product of the situation than it is of the person. This means that *given the proper situation and motivation, any of us tends to become active on the grapevine.* Some of the situations that encourage people to be active are listed in Figure 14-6.

One cause is that any group tends to be more active on the grapevine during periods of excitement and insecurity. Examples are a layoff or the installation of a new computer in the office. At times like this, the grapevine is humming with activity, which means that managers need to watch it with extra care and "feed" it true information to keep it from getting out of hand.

People also are active on the grapevine when their friends and work associates are involved. This means that if Mary is to be promoted or Jack fired, employees need to know the full story as soon as possible. If they are not informed, they will fill in the gaps with their own conclusions; that is, people fill in missing signals according to their own perceptions.

Friendships lead to grapevines.

People also are most active on the grapevine when they have news, as distinguished from stale information. The greatest spread of information happens immediately after it is known; so it is important to get out the right story in the beginning.

The grapevine exists largely by word of mouth and by observation; so procedures that regularly bring people into contact will encourage them to be active on the grapevine.

Figure 14-6
Typical causes
of grapevine
communication

- Excitement and insecurity
- Involvement of friends and associates
- Recent information
- Procedure that brings people into contact
- Work that allows conversation
- Job that provides information desired by others
- Personality of communicator

For example, in one company the chief link between two offices was the manager's secretary, who stopped by the other office right after lunch every day to pick up reports. In another office the link was an accounting clerk who every morning telephoned 300 yards across the company property to secure some cost data. In a similar manner employees having nearby desks are likely to communicate more than two employees in separate buildings.

The foregoing examples show that the type of job possessed by an employee has an important influence on that person's role on the grapevine. Some jobs give employees more opportunity to communicate than others, and some jobs provide employees with more news that might be worth communicating. The result is that certain employees are more active on the grapevine, not because of personality but because of their jobs in the organization. Their jobs give them a strong basis for being key people on the grapevine network. For example, one study showed that secretaries to managers were four times more likely to be key grapevine communicators, compared with other employees.[16]

Jobs affect grapevine activity.

Although type of job is an important grapevine influence, some employees are more active for personality reasons. Perhaps they like to talk about people, have a strong interest in what is happening in their organization, or have special communication abilities. However, there does not appear to be any sex difference in grapevine activity. Both women and men are equally active on the grapevine.[17]

Personalities affect grapevines.

Features of the grapevine

The grapevine gives managers much feedback about employees and their jobs. It also helps interpret management to the workers. It especially helps translate management's formal orders into employee language, in this way making up for any management failures in communication.

In several instances the grapevine carries information that the formal system does not wish to carry and purposely leaves unsaid. For example, a supervisor who is in a bad mood because of personal or job problems usually cannot announce this fact officially to employees. The better approach is to "put it on the grapevine" so that employees are forewarned informally not to make requests that can be delayed. How often it is said, "Don't talk to the manager about a raise today."

Another grapevine feature is its fast pace. Being flexible and personal, it spreads information faster than most management communication systems. With the rapidity of a burning powder train, the grapevine filters out of the woodwork, past the manager's office, through the locker rooms, and along the corridors. Its speed makes it quite difficult for management to stop undesirable rumors or to release significant news in time to prevent rumor formation.

Grapevines are fast.

One company, when it signed its labor contract at 11 P.M., had to keep its publication staff busy all night in order to have a suitable bulletin ready for supervisors and employees when they came to work the next morning. This was the only way that it could match the grapevine's speed.

One study showed the speed of the grapevine in government. The study covered Canadian government engineers who had been transferred, and 32 percent reported that they first heard of their transfer on the grapevine.[18]

*Grapevines are
influential.*

Another grapevine feature is its unusual ability to penetrate even the tightest company security screen because of its capacity to cut across organizational lines and deal directly with the people who know. The grapevine is well known as a source of confidential information.

All evidence shows that the grapevine is influential, both favorably and unfavorably. The grapevine accomplishes so much positively and so much negatively that it is difficult to determine whether its net effects are positive or negative. Undoubtedly its effects vary among work groups and organizations. Research with managers and white-collar employees reported that 53 percent of them viewed the grapevine as a negative factor in the organization. Only 27 percent viewed it as a positive factor, and 20 percent considered it as neutral.[19] Another study reported that the grapevine ranked second as a source of information, but only fifteenth as a "preferred" source.[20]

Management response to grapevines

*Influencing
grapevines*

Regardless of the grapevine's net effects, it cannot be done away with, so the organization needs to adjust to it. Managers are coming to realize that they need to learn who its leaders are, how it operates, and what information it carries. Though they used to ignore it, they now listen to it and study it. Many managers also try to influence the grapevine in various ways. Their objective is to reduce negative effects and increase positive effects. They try to reduce anxiety, conflict, and misunderstanding so that the grapevine will have less cause to spread negative information. They also try to leak useful information to the grapevine so that it will have more positive information. Those managers who still prefer to ignore the grapevine, letting it go its separate way, overlook the important role it plays in organizations.

Rumor

Definition of rumor

The major problem with the grapevine—and the one that gives the grapevine its poor reputation—is rumor. The word "rumor" sometimes is used as a synonym for the whole grapevine, but technically there is an important difference between the two terms. *Rumor* is grapevine information that is communicated without secure standards of evidence being present. It is the unverified and untrue part of the grapevine. It could by chance be correct, but generally it is incorrect; so it is presumed to be undesirable. It has been a problem since the beginning of human history, as illustrated by Figure 14-7, an operatic aria of the early 1800s about rumor.[21]

"Don Basilio's Slander Aria" from *The Barber of Seville*

English translation by Boris Goldovsky

Start a rumor, a mere invention,
Any story you'd care to mention.
Start it circulating lightly,
Oh so gently, oh so slightly.
Very soon it gets around all by itself.

Did you hear it? Most appalling. . . . Just imagine! Quite enthralling. . . .
Once it's born each idle rumor just keeps growing like a tumor,
No one knows where it has started, but he's anxious to repeat, to impart it.
And with every repetition it receives a fresh addition.
Is it fact or is it fiction? No one knows and no one cares.

There is no one to deny it; no one bothers to defy it,
Soon it blossoms like a flower, and begins to gain in power.
Now the tempest from the distance nearer grows with more insistence,
Rumbling louder, ever louder, till the storm is at its worst.

Like a sudden flash of lightning, now the skies are rent asunder,
With an awful roar of thunder, and the rumor grows and fattens
Without reason, without rhyme.

There's no formal accusation, just a whispered intimation.
But the people are convinced that he's committed every crime.
He can give no explanation for his ruined reputation,
But the world has been aroused and will convict him every time.

Figure 14-7
An operatic aria of
the early 1800s
about rumor
*Copyright 1949 by Boris
Goldovsky. Reprinted with
permission of Boris
Goldovsky, Goldovsky
Opera Institute.*

Rumor is primarily a result of both interest and ambiguity in a situation.[22] If a subject has no interest to a person, then that person has no cause to pass along a rumor about it. For example, the authors of this book have never rumored about the coconut output on the island of Martinique for the preceding year. Similarly, if there is no ambiguity in a situation, a person has no cause for rumor because the correct facts are known. This means that both interest and ambiguity normally must be present both to begin and to maintain a rumor.

*Interest and
ambiguity
lead to rumor.*

Since rumor largely depends on the interest and ambiguity that each person has, it tends to change as it passes from person to person. Its general theme usually can be maintained, but not its details. It is subject to *filtering* by which it is reduced to a few basic details that can be remembered and passed on to others. Generally people choose details in the rumor to fit their own interests and view of the world.

Details are lost.

People also add new details, often making the story worse, in order to include their own strong feelings and reasoning; this is *elaborating.*

For example, Marlo Green, a factory worker, heard a rumor that an employee in another department had been injured. When she passed the rumor to someone else, she elaborated by saying that the injury probably was caused by the supervisor's poor machine maintenance. Apparently she made this elaboration because she did not like the supervisor, so she felt that if someone was injured, it must have been the supervisor's fault.

Control of rumor

Since rumor generally is incorrect, a major outbreak of it can be a devastating epidemic that sweeps through an organization as fast as a summer storm—and usually with as much damage. Rumor should be dealt with firmly and consistently, but how and what to attack must be known.[23] It is a serious mistake to strike at the whole grapevine merely because it happens to be the agent that carries rumor; that approach would be as unwise as throwing away a typewriter because of a few misspelled words. Several ways to control rumor are summarized in Figure 14-8 and discussed in the following paragraphs.

Reduction of causes The best way to control rumor is to get at its causes, rather than trying to stop it after it already has started. Getting at causes is a wise use of the preventive approach, instead of a tardy corrective approach. When people feel reasonably secure, understand the things that matter to them, and feel part of the team, there are few rumors, because there is very little ambiguity in the situation. But when people are emotionally upset or inadequately informed about their environment, they are likely to be rumor-mongers. This is a normal defensive reaction by which they attempt to make their situation more meaningful and secure.[24]

Use preventive approach.

In spite of all that can be done, rumors do start. Then what? In general, not all rumors should be fought, for that would be a needless waste of organizational time. Most rumors are relatively harmless and soon die out. On the other hand, some rumors tend to be harmful. For example, when a rumor of a layoff developed in a factory, the amount of products coming off the end of the assembly line decreased a few percentage points. People appeared to be working just as hard, but the flow of products declined. In situations such as this, the rumor may be serious enough to require management action to try to stop it.

Use of facts The best way to stop or weaken rumor is to release the facts. Ambiguity is reduced, so there is less reason for rumor, and the truth tends to prevail. Serious rumors should be attacked as early as possible because once

Figure 14-8
Guides for control of rumor

- Remove its causes in order to prevent it.
- Apply efforts primarily to serious rumors.
- Refute rumor with facts.
- Deal with rumor as soon as possible.
- Emphasize face-to-face supply of facts, confirmed in writing if necessary.
- Provide facts from reliable sources.
- Refrain from repeating rumor while refuting it.
- Encourage assistance of informal and union leaders if they are cooperative.
- Listen to all rumor in order to understand what it may mean.

the general theme of a rumor is known and accepted, employees distort future happenings to conform to the rumor. Thus, if employees accept the rumor that there are plans to move the firm's offices to a new building, every minor change thereafter will be interpreted as a confirmation of that rumor (even, for example, when an electrician comes to repair an electric outlet). If the rumor were dead, this same change could be made without any employee upset at all.

Usually, a face-to-face supply of facts is the most effective way, because it helps answer the ambiguities in each individual's mind and is preferred by people when they are uncertain and under stress.[25] However, the facts should be given directly without first mentioning the rumor, because when a rumor is repeated at this time, some people will hear it instead of the refutation. They then assume you have confirmed the rumor! Here is an example of a suitable approach.

Face-to-face supply of facts is helpful.

> In one company John Reston cut two fingers of his left hand at his machine one morning. He was sent to the medical office for first aid, and he returned to his job in about thirty minutes with his fingers bandaged. Meanwhile, word had spread through the shop that John had cut his fingers. The farther from John's department the story traveled, the more gruesome were his injuries, until finally the story had him losing his left hand. Alert supervisors soon observed the effect of this rumor on morale and investigated the facts. Management then announced over the public address system that the most serious injury treated that morning was two cut fingers of a machine operator who received treatment and returned to his job in Department 37. No mention was made of the rumor, but this announcement brought the rumor under control.

The communication of facts is more effective if it comes from a source that employees think is in a position to know the true facts. The source also should be a person who has a dependable communication record. In addition, informal leaders can help management stop a rumor if the facts are shared with them as soon as possible. Though face-to-face refutation is the most effective, management may wish to reinforce the facts by confirming them in writing.

Use reliable sources.

Use of the union Managers sometimes ask union leaders to help combat rumor. Although the union does not control the grapevine any more than management does, it has some influence. Since rumors are worst when management and labor are in conflict, any reduction of conflict should reduce rumors. Marked improvement frequently occurs in a department when management gains the union's cooperation in combating rumor, especially when the union leaders are powerful informal leaders.

Union leaders can be helpful.

Listening to rumor Regardless of the importance of a rumor, it should be listened to carefully because, even though untrue, it usually carries a message about employee feelings. Each manager needs to ask, "Why did that rumor originate? What does it mean?" In this way a manager gains insight into where ambiguities are and what the interests of employees are. It may seem unrealistic to listen to rumors that are untrue, but listening can be useful.

Rumors carry useful messages.

For example, a labor relations director during a strike listened carefully to what the workers said management was going to do. The director, Mark Peerless, knew that these employee statements were rumors because management had not yet decided what to do. Nevertheless, he listened, because these rumors gave him insight into worker attitudes toward management and what kind of settlement they might agree to make.

Influencing informal organizations

Guidelines for action

Management did not establish informal organizations, and it cannot abolish them. Nor would it want to do so. But management can learn to live with them and have some measure of influence on them. Management guidelines for action are:

1 Accept and understand informal organization.

2 Consider possible effects on informal systems when taking any kind of action.

3 Integrate as far as possible the interests of informal groups with those of the formal organization.

4 Keep formal activities from unnecessarily threatening informal organizations.

Formal and informal combinations

The most desirable combination of formal and informal organizations appears to be a predominant formal system to maintain unity toward objectives, along with a well-developed informal system to maintain group cohesiveness and teamwork. In other words, the informal organization needs to be strong enough to be supportive, but not strong enough to dominate.

SUMMARY

Informal social systems exist in all organizations because they arise naturally from the interaction of people. Informal organizations have major benefits, but they also lead to problems that management cannot easily ignore.

Informal communication, called the grapevine, develops in the form of a cluster chain. Its accuracy in normal situations tends to be above 75 percent, but there may be inaccurate key details, and the whole story rarely is communicated. The grapevine is fast and influential. Employees tend to depend on it for information, even though they often view it as a negative factor. Rumor is grapevine information communicated without secure standards of evidence. It occurs when there is ambiguity and interest in the information.

Management can have some influence on the grapevine, and its basic objective is to integrate interests of the formal and informal systems so that they can work together better.

Informal organization

Norms

Reference group

Sanctions

Sociogram

Sociometry

Grapevine

Cluster chain

Liaison individuals

Rumor

Filtering

Elaborating

REVIEW QUESTIONS

1 Think of a part-time or full-time job that you now hold or formerly held. Identify three different informal organizations that are (were) affecting your job or work group. Explain how they differ from the formal organization.

2 Still thinking of the job in question 1, discuss how the informal leaders probably rose to their positions and how they operate. What amount of informal cooperation with management exists (existed)?

3 Have you ever been in a situation where informal group norms put you in role conflict with formal organization standards? Discuss.

4 Discuss some of the benefits and problems that informal organizations may bring to:
   a A work group
   b An employer

5 Discuss the accuracy of the grapevine, including various reasons for its inaccuracy.

6 Select a grapevine story that you heard, and discuss how it was communicated to you and how accurate it was.

7 Did you communicate the story in question 6 to others? Discuss why or why not. Then discuss the general reasons people are active on the grapevine.

8 Discuss how causes for rumor may be reduced and how rumor may be weakened or stopped after it has started.

INCIDENTS

Excelsior Department Store

The Excelsior Department Store had a large department that employed six salesclerks. Most of these clerks were loyal and faithful employees who had worked in the department store more than ten years. They formed a closely knit social group.

   The store embarked on an expansion program requiring four new clerks to be hired in the department within six months. These newcomers soon learned that the old-timers took the desirable times for coffee breaks, leaving the most undesirable periods for newcomers. The old-time clerks also received priority from the old-time cashier, which required the newcomers to wait in line at the cash register until the old-timers had their sales recorded. A number of customers complained to store management about this practice.

In addition, the old-timers frequently instructed newcomers to straighten merchandise in the stock room and to clean displays on the sales floor, although this work was just as much a responsibility of the old-timers. The result was that old-timers had more time to make sales and newcomers had less time. Since commissions were paid on sales, the newcomers complained to the department manager about this practice.

QUESTIONS

1 How is the informal organization involved in this case? Discuss.

2 As manager of the department, what would you do about each of the practices? Discuss.

Peerless Mining Company

Ben Greenbaum, a maintenance employee of Peerless Mining Company, asked for a six-month leave of absence for personal reasons. The request was granted because it was in accord with company and union policy. A few weeks later Fred Bart, the industrial relations manager of Peerless, heard by the grapevine that Ben actually had taken his leave to work on a construction project in another part of the state. The report was that Ben needed some extra money, and he had taken this job in order to earn contract construction wages as a carpenter, because these wages were approximately twice those earned on his regular maintenance job.

The act of taking leave for personal reasons, with the hidden purpose of working for another employer during the leave period, was contrary to the labor contract, and the penalty for this could be dismissal. After investigation to determine that the grapevine information probably was correct, Fred prepared a "notice of hearing concerning dismissal action" to be mailed to Ben at his local address where his wife and children remained. The letter of notice was dictated by Fred on Thursday morning.

Thursday night Ben called Fred at his home, saying that he had heard that the notice was being prepared and that he felt there was a misunderstanding. He said that he thought his action was acceptable under the contract, but if it was not acceptable, he wanted to return immediately, because he did not want to give up his permanent job. When Fred pressed him to learn how he knew about the pending dismissal notice, Ben said that his wife had called him that evening. He said that his wife had reported that another wife at a local grocery store had told her about the pending dismissal notice.

QUESTIONS

1 Is there any evidence in this case that both management and employees use the grapevine for their benefit? Discuss.

2 Assume grapevine facts are as follows: Fred's secretary told a fringe benefit clerk about the dismissal notice, and the clerk, not realizing the information might be confidential, told someone else. If you were Fred, would you try to suppress grapevine leaks of this type? Discuss.

3 After Ben's telephone call, what action should Fred take?

EXPERIENTIAL EXERCISE

The Grapevine Story

The best way to understand the filtering and elaboration that occur in the grapevine is to experience how they work. Select four people who will be communicators and receivers for a grapevine story. The instructor will select for communication a news story with ten to twenty-five units of information similar to the sample story at the end of this exercise. The plan is that the four people selected will try to pass their message sequentially from one to the other. There should be no tricks and each should try to communicate as accurately as possible. The rules are that each can tell the story only once, it must be told orally, and there can be no notes.

The procedure is that three people will leave the room and the instructor will read the story once to the remaining person. Then a second person is called in, and the first tells the story as well as possible to the second. The sequence is repeated for the third and the fourth. The fourth then repeats the story to the entire class; the instructor reads the accurate story so that all can hear it; and the class members discuss their experiences.

Following is a sample story:

John Edward Dobson, familiarly known as "Cowboy," was thrown for a loss Tuesday as a jury in Judge Walter Stein's county court at law convicted him of burglary of a store that sold western clothes. Dobson was given one year in the county corral. This was the maximum he could have received for his offense.

REFERENCES

1 Lyman W. Porter, Edward E. Lawler III, and J. Richard Hackman, *Behavior in Organizations*, New York: McGraw-Hill Book Company, 1975, p. 77.

2 For examples of socialization programs to help new employees be more successful, see Richard Pascale, "Fitting New Employees into the Corporate Culture," *Fortune*, May 28, 1984, pp. 28ff; Daniel C. Feldman, "A Socialization Process That Helps New Recruits Succeed," *Personnel*, March–April 1980, pp. 11–23; and Arthur P. Brief, "Undoing the Educational Process of the Newly-Hired Professional," *Personnel Administrator*, September 1982, pp. 55–58.

3 For a related comparison, see Edwin B. Flippo, *Personnel Management*, 4th ed., New York: McGraw-Hill Book Company, 1980, p. 70.

4 William E. Reif, Robert M. Monczka, and John W. Newstrom, "Perceptions of the Formal and Informal Organizaton: Objective Measurement through the Semantic Differential Technique," *Academy of Management Journal*, September 1973, pp. 389–403.

5 A number of other informal roles are discussed in Fred Luthans, *Organizational Behavior,* 3d ed., New York: McGraw-Hill Book Company, 1981, pp. 332–334. See also George Strauss and Leonard R. Sayles, *Personnel: The Human Problems of Management,* Englewood Cliffs, N.J.: Prentice-Hall, Inc., 1980, pp. 111–112, 133–136.

6 One study reported that companies with better informal communications systems tended to have higher profits; see Nancy Foy, "Networkers of the World Unite!" *Personnel Management,* March 1983, p. 27.

7 For a discussion of group norms and how they are applied to control behavior, see J. Clifton Williams, *Human Behavior in Organizations,* 2d ed., Cincinnati: South-Western Publishing Company, 1982, chap. 6. A discussion of several classical experiments concerning conformity may be found in David Krech, Richard S. Crutchfield, and Egerton L. Ballachey, *Individual in Society,* New York: McGraw-Hill Book Company, 1982, pp. 504–529.

8 The term "sent to Coventry" is derived from the citizens of Coventry, England, who so disliked soldiers that people seen talking to one were isolated from their social community, so those few who felt like talking to soldiers did not dare do so. Hence a soldier sent to Coventry was isolated from community interaction.

9 Sociograms for an audit stenographic pool are shown in William Weitzel and John Bloedorn, "Action Research in Work Groups," *Personnel Administration,* September–October 1970, pp. 51–58.

10 For a field study and charts, see Donald F. Schwartz and Eugene Jacobson, "Organizational Communication Network Analysis: The Liaison Communication Role," *Organizational Behavior and Human Performance,* vol. 18, February 1977, pp. 158–174. For survey methods for securing grapevine data, see Keith Davis, "Methods for Studying Informal Communication," *Journal of Communication,* Winter 1978, pp. 112–116.

11 For a popular discussion of grapevines, see Roy Rowan, "Where Did *That* Rumor Come From?" *Fortune,* Aug. 13, 1979, pp. 130–137; and Keith Davis, "The Care and Cultivation of the Corporate Grapevine," *Dun's Review,* July 1973, pp. 44–47.

12 Daniel Goleman, "The Electronic Rorschach," *Psychology Today,* February 1983, pp. 36–43.

13 Keith Davis, "Management Communication and the Grapevine," *Harvard Business Review,* September–October 1953, p. 44.

14 Our own research discloses an accuracy of 80 to 99 percent for noncontroversial company information. Accuracy probably is less for personal or highly emotional information.

15 Harold Sutton and Lyman W. Porter, "A Study of the Grapevine in a Governmental Organization," *Personnel Psychology,* Summer 1968, pp. 223–230.

16 Keith Davis, "Grapevine Communication among Lower and Middle Managers," *Personnel Journal,* April 1969, pp. 269–272.

17 Jay T. Knippen, "Grapevine Communication: Management and Employees," *Journal of Business Research,* January 1974, p. 55.

18 Ronald J. Burke, "Quality of Organizational Life: The Effects of Personnel Job Transfers," in Vance F. Mitchell and others (eds.), *Proceedings of the Academy of Management,* Vancouver, B.C., Canada: University of British Columbia, 1973, p. 242.

19 John W. Newstrom, Robert E. Monczka, and William E. Reif, "Perceptions of the Grapevine: Its Value and Influence," *Journal of Business Communication,* Spring 1974, pp. 12–20.

20 International Association of Business Communicators survey reported in *Arizona Republic,* Nov. 14, 1982, p. C-1.

21 An example of public rumors affecting McDonald's fast-food chain is "Gourmet Worms: Antidote for a Rumor," *Psychology Today,* August 1981, pp. 20–21, based on research appearing in *Journal of Marketing Research,* vol. 18, no. 1, 1981.

22 Gordon W. Allport and Leo Postman, *The Psychology of Rumor,* New York: Holt, Rinehart and Winston, Inc., 1947, p. 33, and Allan D. Frank, *Communicating on the Job,* Glenview, Ill.: Scott, Foresman and Company, 1982, pp. 148–149.

23 An additional interpretation is Keith Davis, "Cut Those Rumors Down to Size," *Supervisory Management,* June 1975, pp. 2–6.

24 James L. Esposito and Ralph L. Rosnow, "Corporate Rumors: How They Start and How to Stop Them," *Management Review,* April 1983, pp. 44–49.

25 Jerry C. Wofford, Edwin A. Gerloff, and Robert C. Cummins, *Organizational Communication,* New York: McGraw-Hill Book Company, 1977, Chap. 21, especially pp. 399–400.

FOR ADDITIONAL READING

Allport, Gordon W., and Leo Postman, *The Psychology of Rumor,* New York: Holt, Rinehart and Winston, Inc., 1947.

Blake, Robert R., and Jane Srygley Mouton, *Productivity—The Human Side: A Social Dynamics Approach,* New York: AMACOM, 1981.

Frank, Allan D., *Communicating on the Job,* Glenview, Ill.: Scott, Foresman and Company, 1982.

Luthans, Fred, *Organizational Behavior,* 3d ed., New York: McGraw-Hill Book Company, 1981, especially pp. 331–340.

Ritti, R. Richard, and G. Ray Funkhouser, *The Ropes to Skip and the Ropes to Know: Studies in Organizational Behavior,* 2d ed., Columbus, Ohio: Grid Publishing Company, 1982.

Roethlisberger, F. J., and W. J. Dickson, *Management and the Worker,* Cambridge, Mass.: Harvard University Press, 1939.

Rogers, E., and R. A. Rogers, *Communication in Organizations,* New York: The Free Press, 1976.

Williams, J. Clifton, *Human Behavior in Organizations,* 2d ed., Cincinnati: South-Western Publishing Company, 1982, especially chap. 6.

Wofford, Jerry C., Edwin A. Gerloff, and Robert C. Cummins, *Organizational Communication,* New York: McGraw-Hill Book Company, 1977, especially chap. 21.

QUALITY OF WORK LIFE

When organizations have addressed the issue of quality of working life, they have always achieved great productivity breakthroughs.

Jerome M. Rosow[1]

These findings . . . indicate that there is no universally good job.

Kenneth R. Brousseau[2]

CHAPTER OBJECTIVES

TO UNDERSTAND:
Quality of work life
Job enrichment
Core dimensions of jobs
Natural work modules and teams
Benefits and limitations of job enrichment
Enriched sociotechnical work systems

When General Motors (GM) built a new plant in Georgia for its Delco Remy Division, it also tried a different management approach. All employees were divided into teams, consisting of members and support persons. Teams elected leaders, decided how to pursue production goals, handled housekeeping and routine maintenance, and used peer pressure to resolve absenteeism problems. Workers exchange jobs, and the new skills learned earn them greater pay and provide GM with a flexible, well-trained work force. This emphasis on teamwork and involvement has paid off with high quality and productivity ratings for the division and grievances that are 90 percent lower than the rate in plants run in a more traditional manner.[3]

As explained in Chapter 13, traditional work design with its high specialization has brought benefits to society, but its disadvantage has been its high human costs. As times have changed, these human costs have become less acceptable, so organizations are giving more attention to work designs that provide effective human results along with their technical results. In this chapter we discuss approaches toward more humanized jobs, including job enrichment and enriched sociotechnical work systems. The purpose is to develop a better quality of work life.

UNDERSTANDING QUALITY OF WORK LIFE

Quality of work life (QWL) refers to the favorableness or unfavorableness of a job environment for people.[4] The basic purpose is to develop work environments that are excellent for people as well as for production. QWL is a large step forward from the traditional job design of scientific management, which focused mostly on specialization and efficiency for the performance of narrow tasks. As it evolved, it used full division of labor, rigid hierarchy, and standardization of labor to reach its objective of efficiency. The idea was to lower costs by using unskilled, repetitive labor that could be trained easily to do a small part of the job. Job performance was controlled by a large hierarchy that strictly enforced the one best way of work as defined by technical people.

What is QWL?

Since classical design gave inadequate attention to quality of work life, many difficulties developed. There was excessive division of labor and overdependence on rules, procedures, and hierarchy. Specialized workers became socially isolated from their coworkers because their highly specialized work weakened their community of interest in the whole product. Many workers were so deskilled that they lost pride in their work. The result was higher turnover and absenteeism. Quality declined, and workers became alienated. Conflict arose as workers tried to improve their conditions.

Management's response to this situation was to tighten controls, to increase supervision, and to organize more rigidly. These actions were intended to improve the situation, but they only made it worse, because they further dehumanized the work. Management made a common error by treating the symptoms rather than the causes of the problems. The real cause was that in many instances the job itself simply was not satisfying. The odd condition developed for some employees that the more they worked, the *less* they were satisfied. Hence, the desire to work declined.

A factor contributing to the problem was that the workers themselves were changing. They became more educated, more affluent (partly because of the effectiveness of classical job design), and more independent. They began reaching for higher-order needs, something more than merely earning their bread. Perhaps classical design was best for a poor, uneducated, often illiterate work force that lacked skills, but it was less appropriate for the new work force. Design of jobs and organizations had failed to keep up with widespread changes in worker aspirations and attitudes. Employers now had two reasons for redesigning jobs and organizations for a better QWL:

Reasons for QWL
improvement

1 Classical design originally gave inadequate attention to human needs.

2 The needs and aspirations of workers themselves were changing.

Options available to management

Several options for solving these problems were available to management.

1 Leave the job as it is, and employ only workers who like the rigid environment and routine specialization of classical design. Not all workers object to this form of work. Some may even relish it because of the security and task support that it provides.

2 Leave the job as it is, but pay workers more so that they will accept the situation better. Since classical design usually produces economic gain, management can afford to share the gain with workers.

3 Mechanize and automate routine jobs so that the labor that is unhappy with the job is no longer needed. Let industrial robots do the routine work.

4 Redesign jobs to have the attributes desired by people, and redesign organizations to have the environment desired by people. This approach seeks to improve QWL.

Although all four options have usefulness in certain situations, the one that has captured the interest of people is option number 4. There is a need to give workers more of a challenge, more of a whole task, more opportunity to use advanced skills, more opportunity for growth, and more chance to contribute their ideas. The classical design of jobs was to construct them according to the technological imperative, that is, to design them according to the needs of technology and give little attention to other criteria. The new approach is to provide a careful balance of the human imperative and the technological imperative. *Work environments, and the jobs within them, are required to fit people as well as technology.* This is a new set of values and a new way of thinking that focuses on QWL.

Humanized work

Why should we
humanize work?

QWL produces a more humanized work environment. It attempts to serve the higher-order needs of workers as well as their more basic needs. It seeks to employ the higher skills of workers and to provide an environment that encourages them to improve their skills. The idea is that workers are human resources that are to be developed rather than simply used. Further, the work should not have excessively negative conditions. It should not put workers under undue stress. It should not damage or degrade their humanness. It should not be threatening or unduly dangerous. Finally, it should contribute to, or at least leave unimpaired, workers' abilities to perform in other life roles, such as citizen, spouse, and parent. That is, work should contribute to general social advancement.

The basic assumption of humanized work is that work is most advantageous when it provides a "best fit" among workers, jobs, technology, and the environment. Accordingly, the best design will be different to fit different arrangements of these variables. Since a job design is required to fit the current situation, it is not a one-time thing to be established and retained indefinitely. Rather, there needs to be a regular readjustment among the factors just mentioned in order to maintain the best fit.

One of the earliest controlled experiments with job design for a better work life took place in the 1950s in an appliance manufacturing plant.[5] In the preexisting job design each worker performed one of nine operations along an assembly line. In a revised design called "the group design," the conveyor and pacing were eliminated and workers were rotated among the nine stations, using a batch method of assembly. In another revision called "the individual design," all operations including final inspection were combined into one complete assembly job performed by each worker.

In the group design, the productivity index fell from 100 to 89 but quality improved from 0.72 to 0.49 percent defects. The individual design was successful. Productivity was maintained and improved slightly, while quality improved from 0.72 to 0.18 percent defects. In addition, employee attitudes improved, and the production process was more flexible because each worker worked independently.

JOB ENRICHMENT

The modern interest in quality of work life developed through an emphasis on job enrichment. The term was coined by Frederick Herzberg based on his research with motivators and maintenance factors. Strictly speaking, *job enrichment* means that additional motivators are added to a job to make it more rewarding, although the term has come to apply to almost any effort to humanize jobs. Job enrichment is an expansion of an earlier concept of *job enlargement,* which sought to give workers a wider variety of duties in order to reduce monotony. The difference between the two ideas is illustrated in Figure 15-1. Here we see that job enrichment focuses on satisfying higher-order needs, while job enlargement concentrates on adding additional tasks to the worker's job for greater variety. The two approaches can even be blended together, by both expanding the number of tasks and adding more motivators for a two-pronged attempt to improve QWL.

Job enrichment vs. job enlargement

Job enrichment brings many benefits.[6] Its general result is a role enrichment that encourages growth and self-actualization. The job is built in such a way that intrinsic motivation is encouraged. Because motivation is increased, performance should improve, thus providing both a more human and a more productive job. Negative effects also tend to be reduced, such as turnover,

Benefits of job enrichment

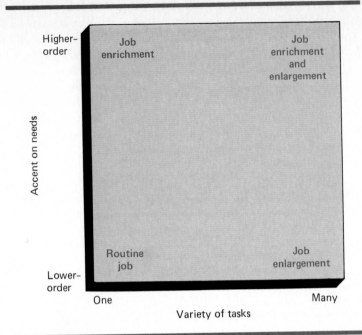

Figure 15-1
Difference between
job enrichment and
job enlargement

absence, grievances, and idle time. In this manner both the worker and society benefit. The worker performs better, has more job satisfaction, and is more self-actualized, thus being able to participate in all life roles more effectively. Society benefits from the more effectively functioning person as well as better job performance. Following is an example of both quality and quantity improvements with job enrichment.

> Unusually high results were obtained with job enrichment in the assembly of electric hot plates in a manufacturing firm. Originally the employees worked on an assembly line, each worker performing a small part of the total assembly. Productivity met the established expectations. Management decided on job enrichment, not because there was a problem but because the task seemed appropriate for enrichment. In the enriched procedure, each worker completed a whole hot plate, being personally responsible for it. The workers rapidly developed improved interest in their work. Controllable rejects dropped from 23 to 1 percent, and absenteeism fell from 8 to 1 percent. As shown in Figure 15-2, productivity improved as much as 84 percent within six months. Since no other changes were made in the department, most of these results appeared to stem from job enrichment.

Applying job enrichment

Viewed in terms of Herzberg's motivational factors, job enrichment occurs when the work itself is more challenging, when achievement is encouraged, when there is opportunity for growth, and when responsibility, advancement, and recognition are provided. However, *employees are the final judges of what*

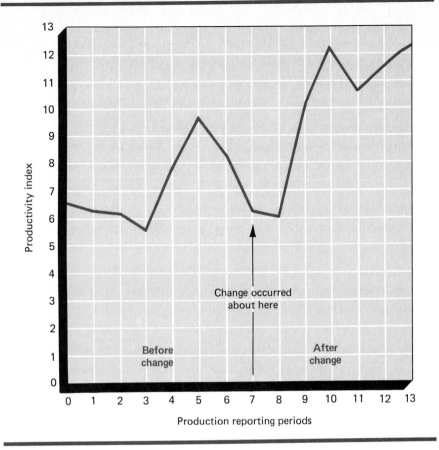

Figure 15-2
Productivity
increases from
job enrichment
in hot-plate
assembly work
Source: *Edgar F. Huse
and Michael Beer,
"Eclectic Approach to
Organizational
Development,"* Harvard
Business Review,
*September–October 1971,
p. 106, Copyright © 1971.
Reprinted with
permission.*

enriches their jobs. All that management can do is make judgments about what tends to enrich jobs and then try these changes in the job system to determine whether employees feel that enrichment has occurred.

In trying to build motivational factors, management also gives attention to maintenance factors. It attempts to keep maintenance factors constant or higher as the motivational factors are increased. If maintenance factors are allowed to decline during an enrichment program, then employees may be less responsive to the enrichment program because of inadequate maintenance. The need for a systems approach to job enrichment is satisfied by the practice of *gainsharing,* where employees receive a substantial portion of the cost savings produced when their jobs are improved.[7]

Gainsharing

Since job enrichment must occur from each employee's personal viewpoint, *not all employees will choose enriched jobs if they have an option.* A contingency relationship exists in terms of different job needs, and some employees may prefer the simplicity and security of more routine jobs.

In one instance a manufacturer set up production in two different ways.[8] Employees were allowed to choose between work on a standard assembly line and at a bench where they individually assembled the entire product. In the beginning few employees chose to work the enriched jobs, but gradually about half the workers chose them. The more routine assembly operation seemed to fit the needs of the other half.

Core dimensions of jobs

Five core dimensions Hackman and Oldham have identified five core dimensions that especially provide enrichment for jobs.[9] It is desirable for a job to have all five of these dimensions. If one is missing, workers are psychologically deprived and motivation tends to be reduced. The core dimensions tend to improve motivation, satisfaction, and quality of work and to reduce turnover and absenteeism. Their effect on quantity of work is less dependable.[10] Managerial and white-collar jobs, as well as blue-collar jobs, often are deficient in some core dimensions. Admittedly there are large individual differences in how employees react to core dimensions, but the typical employee finds them to be basic for internal motivation. The dimensions are shown in Figure 15-3.

Variety One core dimension is *variety in the job*. Variety allows employees to perform different operations that often require different skills. It is illustrated by the following anecdote:

> A tourist in Mexico stopped at a woodcarver's shop to inquire about the price of a chair that was hand-carved. The woodcarver replied, "Fifty pesos."
> The tourist said that she liked the chair and wanted three more exactly like it. Hoping to receive a quantity discount, she asked, "How much for four chairs?"
> The woodcarver replied, "Two hundred fifty pesos for four chairs."
> Shocked that the price per unit for four chairs was more than for one chair, the tourist asked why. The woodcarver replied, "But, señorita, it is very boring to carve four chairs that are exactly alike."

Jobs that are high in variety are seen by employees as more challenging because of the range of skills involved. These jobs also relieve monotony that develops from any repetitive activity. If the work is physical, different muscles are used, so that one muscular area is not so overworked and tired at the end of the day. Variety gives employees a greater sense of competence, because they can perform different kinds of work in different ways.

Figure 15-3
Core dimensions
of jobs

Core dimensions are those that especially enrich jobs.
• If one is missing, workers are psychologically deprived.

Core dimensions are:
• *Task variety.* Different operations to perform
• *Task identity.* Performing a complete piece of the work
• *Task significance.* Work that appears to be important
• *Autonomy.* Some control by employees over their own affairs
• *Feedback.* Information about performance

Task identity   A second core job dimension is *task identity,* which allows employees to perform a complete piece of the work. Many job enrichment efforts have been focused on this dimension, because in the past the scientific management movement led to overspecialized, routine jobs. Individual employees worked on such a small part of the whole that they were unable to identify any product with their efforts. They could not feel any sense of completion or responsibility for the whole product. When tasks are broadened to produce a whole product or an identifiable part of it, then task identity has been established. This kind of whole job occurred in assembly of the hot plates mentioned earlier in this chapter. Other examples are a radio factory where each worker assembles a pocket radio and an office where a single employee prepares a major report rather than a part of it.

Task significance   A third core dimension is *task significance.* It refers to the amount of impact, as perceived by the worker, that the work has on other people. The impact can be on others in the organization, as when the worker performs a key step in the work process, or it may be on those outside the firm, as when the worker helps to make a lifesaving medical instrument. The key point is that workers believe they are doing something important in their organization and/or society. The story has been told about workers who were instructed to dig holes in various parts of a storage yard. Then the supervisor looked at the holes and told the workers to fill them and dig more holes in other places. Finally the workers revolted, because they saw no usefulness in their work. Only then did the supervisor tell them that they were digging the holes to try to locate a water pipe.

> Even routine factory work can have task significance. St. Regis Paper Company had customer complaints about seams tearing and bottoms dropping out of about 6 percent of grocery bags made in three plants.[11] Management attempted to solve the problem by adding more inspectors and making production changes, but these efforts were not successful.
>
> Finally management decided to work with the bag-machine operators to show them the significance of their work. One step was to circulate customer complaint letters so that the operators could see how serious the problem was. Management also arranged to have the signature of each operator imprinted on the bottom of the bags as follows: "Another quality product by St. Regis. Personally inspected by . . . (employee's name). . . ."
>
> Employees responded by reducing defective bags from 6 to ½ percent. They were proud of their work and its direct significance to customers. Employees even started taking their nameplates with them during rest breaks because they wanted to be responsible personally for bags that had their signature.

Autonomy   A fourth core dimension is *autonomy.* It is the job characteristic that gives employees some discretion and control over job-related decisions, and it appears to be fundamental in building a sense of responsibility in workers.[12] Although they are willing to work within the broad constraints of an organization, they also insist on a degree of freedom. You may remember that in the discussion of Maslow's need hierarchy in Chapter 4, autonomy was mentioned as a possible additional step on the need scale since it is so important to many people. The popular practice of management by objectives (MBO) is one way of establishing more autonomy because it provides a greater role for workers in setting their own goals and pursuing plans to achieve them.

Feedback   A fifth core dimension is feedback. *Feedback* refers to information that tells workers how well they are performing. It comes from the job itself, management, and other employees. The idea of feedback is a simple one, but it is of much significance to people at work. Since they are investing a substantial part of their lives in their work, they want to know how well they are doing. Further, they need to know rather often because they recognize that performance does vary, and the only way they can make adjustments is to know how they are performing now.

Monthly output reports often are inadequate because the time lag is too great. Weekly and daily reports are better, and hourly and continuous reporting may be better if the work process allows this type of feedback. For example, operators attending cigarette-making machines have automatic inspection that provides continuous feedback to panels on the machines, so that operators know at all times if the work is progressing satisfactorily. The same is also true for bottlers at bottling machines. Note in these illustrations that workers receive complete job feedback, both positive and negative.[13] If they receive only negative feedback, it may not be motivating.

The motivating potential of jobs

Job Diagnostic Survey   An instrument used to determine the relative presence of the five core dimensions in jobs is the *Job Diagnostic Survey*.[14] Before job enrichment is begun, an employer studies jobs to assess how high they are on variety, task identity, task significance, autonomy, and feedback. Scales are created for each dimension, and then each job is rated according to where it fits on each scale. For example, on a scale of 1 through 10, variety may be given a rating of 6 and autonomy a lower rating of 4. Employees are usually involved in this assessment process, since it is their perceptions that are most important.

Motivating potential score   After the data are collected, an overall index that measures the *motivating potential score* (MPS) of a job may be computed. The MPS indicates the degree to which the job is perceived to be Meaningful, (M, or average of variety, identity, and significance), foster Responsibility (R, or autonomy), and provide Knowledge of Results (KR, or feedback). The formula is:

$$MPS = M \times R \times KR$$

Jobs that have been enriched to create a high MPS increase the probability of high motivation, provided that employees:

Conditions for job enrichment

- Have adequate job knowledge and skills
- Desire to learn, grow, and develop
- Are satisfied with their work environment

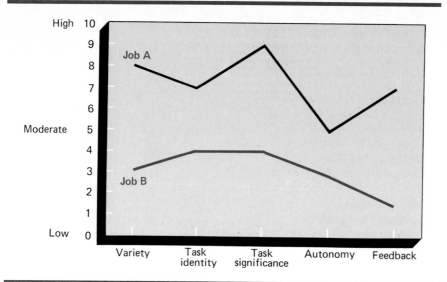

Figure 15-4
Profile chart of
core dimensions
for two jobs

A useful way to compare jobs (or perceptions of them by managers and employees) is to place their scores on a *profile chart,* which graphically displays the data. Figure 15-4 shows that job A has moderate autonomy but is high in the other four dimensions. In general, job B has less enrichment than job A. Once the profile of a job is determined, then the job can be studied in detail to determine how the weak dimensions may be improved. Not all jobs can be made outstanding on all dimensions, but most jobs can have some enrichment. When they are enriched, the payoff can be great, as seen in this example.

Profile chart

> The accounts section of a bank made major gains from improvements in core dimensions of clerical jobs.[15] Three dimensions were improved substantially, and the other two were improved indirectly. Task identity was improved by building whole jobs for employees, which also led to more task variety and significance. Autonomy was provided by giving the clerks power to approve the checks that they processed. Feedback was improved in several ways.
>
> As a result of a greater sense of responsibility for approving checks, forgeries paid fell 56 percent. This provided a substantial saving for the bank. In addition, misfiled items decreased 19 percent, and complaints from branches decreased over 20 percent. The productivity index increased to 110 compared with a target level of 99.

Limitations of job enrichment

Job enrichment has a number of limitations, as shown in Figure 15-5. It is more appropriate for some situations than for others, and in certain situations it may not be appropriate at all.[16] Some workers do not want increased

- Some workers may not want enriched jobs:
  —If they are unable to tolerate increased responsibility
  —If they dislike more complex duties
  —If they are uncomfortable with group work
  —If they dislike relearning
  —If they prefer security and stability
  —If they are comfortable with supervisory authority
  —If skills are not adaptable
  —If they prefer to quit their jobs
- Expensive equipment may not be adaptable.
- The program may unbalance the production system.
- Supervisory or staff roles may be reduced.
- Enriched jobs may increase pay dissatisfaction.
- Costs may increase:
  —Start-up costs such as training
  —Long-run costs such as more equipment
- Unions may oppose some enrichment efforts.

Figure 15-5
Some limitations of
job enrichment and
QWL programs

responsibility, and other workers do not adapt to the group interaction that is sometimes required. In other words, enrichment is contingent on attitudes of employees and their capability to handle enriched tasks. It can be argued that employees should accept job enrichment because it is "good," but it is more consistent with human values to recognize and respect individual differences of employees.

> One survey of worker resistance to job enrichment showed that workers nearing retirement were more resistant, probably because they felt more threatened by the required change and less able to adapt. In total, about 40 percent of employees showed some resistance to job enrichment.[17]

Those planning job enrichment and QWL programs need to ask such questions as the following about employee needs and attitudes:

- Can the employee tolerate responsibility?
- How strong are employee growth and achievement needs?
- What is the employee's attitude toward working with groups?
- Can the employee work with more complexity?
- How strong are the employee's drives for security and stability?
- Will the employees view the job changes as significant?[18]

Enrichment may not apply. **Situational factors** In a similar manner, job enrichment does not apply to all types of situations. It appears to apply more easily to higher-level jobs, compared with lower-level ones, particularly if the lower-level jobs are dictated by the technological process. If the technology is stable and highly automated, the costs of job enrichment may be too great in relation to the rewards. Some organizations have such huge investments in equipment that they cannot afford to make substantial changes until the equipment is replaced. When difficult technological conditions are combined with negative employee attitudes toward job enrichment, then it becomes inappropriate until the environment for it can be changed.

Other limitations on job enrichment apply when it must be coordinated with other jobs, departments, or branches. For example, anticipated gains can be diminished because of effects on surrounding work systems. A projected enrichment in one organization assigned quality control to workers producing the product. Several highly paid quality-assurance people were put out of jobs, and the enrichment was delayed while their problems were resolved. In other organizations job enrichment for operating employees reduced the supervisory role, so the programs were not successful until the supervisors' jobs also were enriched.

Pay relationships   Job enrichment also may upset pay relationships. Management typically assumes that the intrinsic rewards of the enriched job are sufficient. Employees, however, may become unhappy because they think they are not paid in proportion to their increased duties. They want more money, but a pay increase adds to costs and may upset comparative pay relationships.

> In a branch operation a supervisor enriched the jobs of salesclerks by allocating more responsibility to them. The clerks requested more pay, and the supervisor recommended it. The home office rejected the pay increase, thereby effectively rejecting the enrichment program. The home office was fearful that salesclerks in other branches would want similar pay, even if their jobs were not enriched. Either higher costs would occur or lower morale would develop when raises were not given. The other alternative, enriching clerks' jobs in all branches, was not practical at the time.

Other costs   There are other costs in addition to pay. Equipment and floor space may need to be redesigned. In some instances more space and tools will be needed so that teams can work independently. Even work-in-process inventory may have to be increased so that individual workers or teams can have enough supplies. In addition, there are substantial training costs in order to prepare employees for their new patterns of work. There also are likely to be temporary quality and output problems during the period of change because existing teamwork among employees is disrupted. Some employees even resign. Although these costs may be acceptable in relation to benefits, they need to be considered carefully.

Union attitudes   An additional contingency factor is union attitudes.[19] Job enrichment may upset existing job classifications, thereby causing union resistance. In some instances enrichment may create jurisdictional disputes between the territories of two unions. Likely places for this problem are maintenance work and construction work. Distinctions between jobs may be so narrow and rules so rigid that unions will not tolerate some changes.

1 In a general way, job enrichment and QWL programs are desirable for both human and performance needs. They help employees, and they help the firm.

2 There is a contingency relationship. QWL improvements work better in some situations than in others.

3 QWL programs bring costs as well as benefits. Both must be considered to determine net benefits and the desirability of a change.

*Desirability,
contingency, and
cost-benefit*

Conclusions The limitations and difficulties with job enrichment lead to three conclusions, as summarized in Figure 15-6. First, job enrichment and QWL programs generally are desirable for both human and performance needs. They help both employees and the firm. Second, there is a contingency relationship. QWL improvements work better in some situations than others. They are not the best for every situation. A third conclusion is that QWL programs bring costs as well as benefits. Both must be evaluated to determine the desirability of a change. The key issue is how favorable the net benefits are.

With the many contingencies that exist in job enrichment, the best strategy is to study the need for it carefully and then to try it in the most appropriate places first. As success is achieved, there can be a gradual move toward more applications. The organization that suddenly becomes sold on job enrichment and then takes a blanket approach to it is likely to generate more problems than it can handle.

ENRICHED SOCIOTECHNICAL WORK SYSTEMS

Natural work teams

The next step above enriched jobs is to focus on work teams. When jobs have been designed so that a person performs a complete cycle of work to make a whole product or a subunit of it, then that person is performing a *natural work module.* The work flows naturally from start to finish and gives an individual a sense of task identity and significance. In a similar manner several employees may be arranged into a *natural work team* that performs an entire unit of work. In this way employees whose task requires them to work together are better able to learn each other's needs and to develop teamwork. Natural work teams even allow those who are performing routine work to develop a greater feeling of task significance, because they are attached to a larger team that performs a major task. It is surprising how our desire to develop specialization often leads to separation of people who are needed to make natural work teams.

*Natural work
modules and teams*

Consider the experience of a telephone company with its service-order department.[20] Originally the service representatives and typists who prepared service orders were in separate areas of the office, and each took orders in rotation as they were received. Then different teams of representatives were assigned their own geographical region, and a few typists were moved to be with them, working only on their service orders.

The employees now became a natural work team that could cooperate in performing a whole task. The result was that orders typed on time increased from 27 percent to between 90 and 100 percent, and service-order accuracy exceeded the expected standard.

The next step above enriched jobs and natural work teams is *enriched sociotechnical work systems* in which a whole organization or a major portion of it is built into a balanced human-technical system. The objective is to develop complete *employment enrichment,* as shown in Figure 15-7. This requires changes of a major magnitude, particularly in manufacturing that has been designed along specialized lines. The entire production process may require reengineering in order to integrate human needs, and layouts may require changes to permit teamwork. The fundamental objective is to design a whole work system that serves needs of people as well as production requirements.

Employment enrichment

Flexible work schedules

Flexible working time, also known as "flexitime," or "flextime," is an example of employment enrichment. It gives workers more autonomy but in a manner different from job enrichment.[21] With flextime employees gain some latitude for the control of their work environment—a factor beyond the design of the job itself—to fit their own lifestyles or to meet unusual needs, such as a visit to a physician. The idea is that, regardless of starting and stopping times, employees will work their full number of hours each day. Employees always work within the restraints of the installation's business hours, and if a job requires teamwork, all employees on a team must flex their work together.

Employees control their schedules.

An office provides an example. The office is open from 7 A.M. to 7 P.M., and employees may work their eight hours anytime during that period. One employee is an early riser and prefers to arrive at work at 7 A.M., leaving at 3:30 P.M. in order to shop or engage in sports. Another employee is a late riser and prefers to come to work at 10 A.M., leaving at 6:30 P.M. Another employee arranges her work period to fit a commuter train schedule. Still another employee prefers to take two hours for lunch

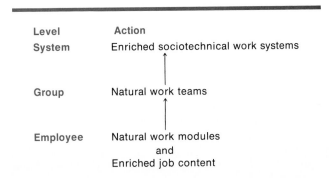

Level	Action
System	Enriched sociotechnical work systems
Group	Natural work teams
Employee	Natural work modules and Enriched job content

Figure 15-7
The complete employment enrichment process

and occasional shopping. Each employee sets a schedule to fit personal needs. A certain percentage of workers must be at the office for certain core hours in order to meet the public, but otherwise their schedule is relatively free.

An advantage to the employer is that tardiness is eliminated, since the employee works a full number of hours regardless of arrival time. Since employees are able to schedule outside activities such as appointments during their working day, they tend to have fewer one-day absences for these purposes. Perhaps the main benefit is that greater autonomy leads to greater job satisfaction, and sometimes productivity improves as well.[22]

Sociotechnical experiments

Some of the most innovative experiments in QWL and enriched sociotechnical systems were developed in the 1970s at Volvo in Sweden and at General Motors and General Foods in the United States.[23] The diversity of approaches will be apparent in these summaries.

Volvo

Volvo built a new car assembly plant in Kalmar, Sweden, in the early 1970s in which it attempted to incorporate technical, managerial, and social innovations that better served the needs of employees.[24] The design cost about 10 percent more than a comparable conventional plant, but Volvo took the risk because it hoped to secure increased satisfaction and productivity as well as reduced turnover and absenteeism. The factory was designed to assemble 60,000 automobiles annually, using teams of fifteen to twenty-five workers for each major task. One team, for example, assembles electrical systems, while another assembles brakes. Each team has its own work area, and each is given substantial autonomy. The team is completely in charge of allocation of work among members and of setting the rhythm of its work.

Teams replace assembly lines.

There is no assembly line. Teams obtain a car from a buffer zone when they want one, moving it to their workplace on a trolley. When work is completed, the car is placed in the next buffer zone, a procedure that allows each team to work at its own pace as long as it can meet production requirements. Teams handle their own material procurement and manage their own inventory. The situation is much different from that of a traditional assembly line.

General Motors

Union-management relations in the auto industry have traditionally been adversarial. At the urging of the United Auto Workers, a National Committee on Quality of Work Life was created in 1973.[25] The Tarrytown assembly plant of General Motors was chosen as the pilot site because of a desire to solve the more difficult problems first. Tarrytown ranked seventeenth in quality (of eighteen plants); it had one of the highest grievance rates and experienced more strikes, and its absenteeism rate averaged 12 percent.

A steering committee was formed, a QWL philosophy statement was created and distributed, and actions were taken to build trust and respect between management and workers. A training program was initiated to provide employees with skills in problem solving, cost analysis, team building, and communications. Remarkably, all but 10 of the 3600 employees volunteered to participate.

Climate is a prerequisite.

The QWL program was comprehensive, was introduced slowly, and had a dual base of support from both management and the union. A profitable plant emerged: It rose to number one in quality and efficiency, absenteeism dropped to 3 percent, and grievances declined by 97 percent. Clearly, employees perceived a new environment in which their suggestions were sought and implemented, and the workers were valued for their skills and ideas.

General Foods

An ambitious, innovative sociotechnical system was built into a General Foods pet-food plant that opened in 1971.[26] The plant was built to use work teams of seven to fourteen members. Careful attention was given even to items such as plant design to reduce traditional status symbols found in most plants. There was an open parking lot and a common entrance for plant and office people, and decor in the offices and locker rooms was similar. Distinctions between technical specialists and workers were reduced because most specialized support activities were assigned to each operating team. Examples of support activities performed by each team are maintenance, quality control, custodial work, and personnel activities such as helping select new employees for one's team. Teams were given high autonomy over almost all activities for which they had capability. The role of supervisor changed to provide less direct supervision and more general management duties. Other innovations included:

- A single job classification for all operators, with pay increases geared to mastering additional jobs in the team and in the plant
- Decision-making information for operators of the type that formerly only managers received
- Enlarged jobs with most routine work mechanized
- Team control of task redistribution when members are absent
- Team counseling of members who fail to meet team standards

Preliminary results were favorable compared with other plants using traditional systems. Quality problems were reduced 90 percent, and absenteeism and turnover were less. Productivity increased, but this resulted partly from the technology of the new plant. A number of problems also developed. Employees objected to some team members earning more when they learned additional tasks. Some employees preferred traditional tasks without the required group work and added responsibility. Some team leaders showed traditional autocratic tendencies. Work teams sometimes became autocratic,

Problems also emerge.

exerting excessive peer pressure for conformity to group norms. In addition, role confusion sometimes developed because people were not used to operating in these new kinds of roles.

Results of sociotechnical experiments

Not all attempts to create a better QWL have been successful. One of the earliest, at Non-Linear Systems, was discarded when the firm's product leadership declined and productivity failed to keep pace with that of competitors.[27] Despite numerous behavioral innovations, the participative system proved too cumbersome to respond to quickly needed changes, and the firm was forced to return to a more traditional work system to survive.

The design of complex organizational systems for better QWL is far more difficult than many casual observers realize. There are substantial costs as well as benefits, and the payoff may not come immediately. Sometimes the programs are oversold to the public, so it is important to examine what does and does not work.[28] Many years and many experiments will be required before effective practices can be identified and applied with a high probability of success.

SUMMARY

"Quality of work life" refers to the favorableness or unfavorableness of the job environment for people. Since people and the environment have changed, increased attention needs to be given to improving the QWL. Jobs are required to fit people as well as technology.

"Job enrichment" applies to any efforts to humanize jobs, particularly the addition of motivators to jobs. Core dimensions of jobs that especially provide enrichment are variety, task identity, task significance, autonomy, and feedback. It is helpful if natural work modules and natural work teams can be built. In spite of its desirability, job enrichment is a contingency relationship, being more applicable in some situations than others.

Enriched sociotechnical work systems provide a balanced human-technical system that seeks complete employment enrichment. Major experiments with these systems have been made by many firms, such as Volvo, General Motors, and General Foods. There are costs as well as benefits, but results generally are favorable.

TERMS AND CONCEPTS FOR REVIEW

Quality of work life (QWL)

Job enrichment

Job enlargement

Gainsharing

Core dimensions of jobs

Job Diagnostic Survey

Motivating potential score

Profile charts of core dimensions

Natural work modules

Natural work teams

Flexible working time (flextime)

Enriched sociotechnical work systems

1 Do employees differ in their view of what a good QWL is for them? Discuss. If they differ, discuss specific steps that an employer can take to provide a better QWL for all employees.

2 Form discussion groups of four to five people, and develop a list of the top six QWL items that your group wants in a job. Present your group report, along with your reasons, to other class members. Then discuss similarities and differences among groups.

3 Think of the job you now have or a job that you formerly had. Discuss both the favorable and unfavorable QWL characteristics that it had.

4 This chapter discussed gainsharing to increase the effectiveness of job enrichment. How does this relate to earlier discussions of motivational and maintenance factors, lower- and higher-order needs, and extrinsic-intrinsic rewards?

5 A survey of supervisor Herman Kahn's department shows that employees uniformly feel that the core dimension of feedback is low. Kahn refutes this conclusion by commenting: "That's not true. I give the guys lots of feedback. They will confirm that I tell them every time they don't make production for the week and every time they violate a rule. I share all problems that arise with my employees." Discuss.

6 Select two jobs in a firm, and then do a profile chart of their core dimensions. Discuss your results.

7 Discuss some of the limitations of job enrichment and QWL programs.

8 Select from outside sources a major QWL program other than the ones presented in this chapter, and discuss it in class.

9 Has the United States made any progress in building better QWL in the last twenty years? Perform outside reading and interviews, and discuss this subject in class.

INCIDENT

Valley Electronics

Valley Electronics produces a line of electronic equipment, including a miniature tape recorder that can be held in one's hand. In the final assembly of the tape recorder, fourteen employees work on an assembly line, using parts from parts bins. Each employee performs a different operation and then passes the assembly to the next person. The last two steps on the line are inspection and boxing. Inspection includes an operational test of each recorder. If a recorder fails inspection, it is placed at a bench where another employee reworks it. If the stack of recorders at the bench grows too large for the benchworker to handle, one of the regular assemblers is assigned overtime benchwork to reduce the backlog.

A recent job satisfaction survey showed that the assembly employees are reasonably satisfied. They have a friendly group, and the assembly design encourages conversation because there are seven employees on each side of the line facing each other. Turnover and absenteeism are considered normal by management. The employees are organized by a national labor union, but none of them appears to be active in the union. There are four racial minority members and several ethnic minorities in the group.

QUESTIONS

1 How favorable is the QWL for the assembly group? Discuss.

2 Do you recommend any changes in the assembly jobs? Discuss, including what specific changes you would make and what they are intended to accomplish.

EXPERIENTIAL EXERCISE

The Enriched Student

Step 1. Consider your academic "job" as a student. Rate it on each of the five core dimensions according to how much of each is presently in it (1 = low amount; 10 = high amount).

Job dimension	Your rating	Group average
Variety	——	——
Task identity	——	——
Task significance	——	——
Autonomy	——	——
Feedback	——	——

Step 2. Form into small groups of four to six persons, share your scores, and compute an average group score for each dimension. Then compute a motivating potential score for your group by using the MPS formula given in the text. What does this tell you?

Step 3. Discuss five important steps that university administrators and professors could take to enrich your job if they had the data you generated.

REFERENCES

1 Jerome M. Rosow, in Karen E. Debats (ed.), "The Continuing Personnel Challenge," *Personnel Journal,* May 1982, p. 344.

2 Kenneth R. Brousseau, "Toward a Dynamic Model of Job-Person Relationships: Findings, Research Questions, and Implications for Work System Design," *Academy of Management Review,* January 1983, p. 34.

3 A. S. Warren, "Quality of Work Life Pays Off in the Auto Industry," *Personnel Journal,* December 1981, pp. 928, 930.

4 A classic list of eight categories composing QWL is in Richard E. Walton, "Improving the Quality of Work Life," *Harvard Business Review,* May–June 1974, pp. 12ff. A contemporary view of the dual path by which QWL may impact on

productivity is portrayed in Edward E. Lawler III and Gerald Ledford, Jr., "Productivity and the Quality of Work Life," *National Productivity Review,* Winter 1981–1982, pp. 23–36.

5 Louis E. Davis, "The Design of Jobs," *Industrial Relations,* October 1966, pp. 21–45.

6 One survey of fifty-eight companies that had used job enrichment reported that the five areas of most frequent improvement were higher productivity, better job satisfaction, improved quality of work, less turnover, and less absenteeism. See Antone Alber, "Job Enrichment for Profit," *Human Resource Management,* Spring 1979, pp. 15–25.

7 R. J. Bullock and Patti F. Bullock, "Gainsharing and Rubik's Cube: Solving System Problems," *National Productivity Review,* Autumn 1982, pp. 396–407.

8 Edward E. Lawler III, "For a More Effective Organization—Match the Job to the Man," *Organizational Dynamics,* Summer 1974, pp. 19–29.

9 J. Richard Hackman, Greg R. Oldham, R. Janson, and K. Purdy, "A New Strategy for Job Enrichment," *California Management Review,* Summer 1975, pp. 57–71. For studies of the core dimensions and satisfaction, see Ricky W. Griffin, "Perceived Task Characteristics and Employee Productivity and Satisfaction," *Human Relations,* October 1982, pp. 927–938; David F. Caldwell and Charles A. O'Reilly III, "Task Perceptions and Job Satisfaction: A Question of Causality," *Journal of Applied Psychology,* June 1982, pp. 361–369; and Jon L. Pierce, "Employee Affective Responses to Work Unit Structure and Job Design: A Test of an Intervening Variable," *Journal of Management,* Fall 1979, pp. 193–211.

10 Ricky W. Griffin, Ann Welsh, and Gregory Moorhead, "Perceived Task Characteristics and Employee Performance: A Literature Review," *Academy of Management Review,* October 1981, pp. 655–664. A critical view is in Jiing-Lih Farh and W. E. Scott, Jr., "The Experimental Effects of "Autonomy" on Performance and Self-Reports of Satisfaction," *Organizational Behavior and Human Performance,* April 1983, pp. 203–222.

11 "The Signature of Quality," *Management in Practice* (American Management Associations), March–April 1977, pp. 2–3.

12 See Daniel Roland Dennison, "Sociotechnical Design and Self-Managing Work Groups: The Impact on Control," *Journal of Occupational Behaviour,* October 1982, pp. 297–314, for evidence that employees do perceive greater influence when they are part of autonomous work groups.

13 Studies of the value and structure of feedback include Angelo S. DeNisi, W. Alan Randolph, and Allyn G. Blencoe, "Level and Source of Feedback as Determinants of Feedback Effectiveness," in Kae H. Chung (ed.), *Academy of Management Proceedings '82,* Mississippi State, Miss.: Academy of Management, 1982, pp. 175–179; Susan J. Ashford and L. L. Cummings, "Strategies for Knowing: When and from Where Do Individuals Seek Feedback?" and Charles K. Parsons, David M. Herold, and Bette Turlington, "Individual Differences in Performance Feedback Preferences," in Kae H. Chung (ed.), *Academy of Management Proceedings '81,* Mississippi State, Miss.: Academy of Management, 1981, pp. 161–165, 166–170. A novel approach to giving positive and negative feedback is described in Kenneth Blanchard and Spencer Johnson, *The One Minute Manager,* La Jolla, Calif.: Blanchard-Johnson Publishers, 1981.

14 Readers interested in details of the Job Diagnostic Survey, which measures MPS, may read J. Richard Hackman and Greg R. Oldham, "Development of the Job Diagnostic Survey," *Journal of Applied Psychology,* April 1975, pp. 159–170.

15 W. Philip Kraft and Kathleen L. Williams, "Job Redesign Improved Productivity," *Personnel Journal,* July 1975, pp. 393–397.

16 For contingency relationships and limitations, see Jon L. Pierce, "Job Design in Perspective," *Personnel Administrator,* December 1980, pp. 67–74; Wiliam A. Pasmore, "Overcoming the Roadblocks in Work-Restructuring Efforts," *Organizational Dynamics,* Spring 1982, pp. 54–67; and Lee M. Ozley and Judith S. Ball, "Quality of Work Life: Initiating Successful Efforts in Labor-Management Organizations," *Personnel Administrator,* May 1982, pp. 27–33. The need to balance internal and external factors is presented in Randall B. Dunham, Jon L. Pierce, and John W. Newstrom, "Job Context and Job Content: A Conceptual Perspective," *Journal of Management,* Fall–Winter 1983, pp. 187–202.

17 Donald C. Collins and Robert R. Raubolt, "A Study of Employee Resistance to Job Enrichment," *Personnel Journal,* April 1975, pp. 232–235, 248.

18 This explanation of a job design failure is offered by George Graen, Michael A. Novak, and Patricia Sommerkamp, "The Effects of Leader-Member Exchange and Job Design on Productivity and Satisfaction: Testing a Dual Attachment Model," *Organizational Behavior and Human Performance,* August 1982, pp. 109–131. An innovative proposal for managing worker perceptions of job characteristics is Dennis J. Moberg, "Job Enrichment through Symbol Management," *California Management Review,* Winter 1981, pp. 24–30.

19 Important factors affecting union response to QWL are discussed in David Lewin, "Collective Bargaining and the Quality of Work Life," *Organizational Dynamics,* Autumn 1981, pp. 37–53; and David A. Nadler, Martin Hanlon, and Edward E. Lawler III, "Factors Influencing the Success of Labour-Management Quality of Work Life Projects," *Journal of Occupational Behaviour,* January 1980, pp. 53–67.

20 Robert N. Ford, "Job Enrichment Lessons from AT&T," *Harvard Business Review,* January–February 1973, pp. 96–106; an update on some of their QWL programs is Robert F. Craver, "AT&T's QWL Experiment: A Practical Case Study," *Management Review,* June 1983, pp. 12–16. Another view of the multiple uses of work groups to obtain improvements within the Japanese culture is William H. Davidson, "Small Group Activity at Musashi Semiconductor Works," *Sloan Management Review,* Spring 1982, pp. 3–14.

21 Jon L. Pierce and John W. Newstrom, "Toward a Conceptual Clarification of Employee Responses to Flexible Working Hours: A Work Adjustment Approach," *Journal of Management,* Fall 1980, pp. 117–134. A review of five alternative approaches to work schedules is Jerome M. Rosow and Robert Zager, "Punch Out the Time Clocks," *Harvard Business Review,* March–April 1983, pp. 12ff.

22 Jay S. Kim and Anthony F. Campagna, "Effects of Flexitime on Employee Attitudes and Performance: A Field Experiment," *Academy of Management Journal,* December 1981, pp. 729–741. A study that found no relationship between work schedules and job satisfaction is Jon L. Pierce and John W. Newstrom, "The Design of Flexible Work Schedules and Employee Responses: Relationships and Process," *Journal of Occupational Behaviour,* October 1983, pp. 247–262.

23 There are a number of other major QWL experiments. A general interpretation is reported in Richard E. Walton, "Work Innovations in the United States," *Harvard Business Review,* July–August 1979, pp. 88–98.

24 Pehr G. Gyllenhammar (President of Volvo), *People at Work,* Reading, Mass.: Addison-Wesley Publishing Company, Inc., 1977; and Pehr G. Gyllenhammar, "How Volvo Adapts Work to People," *Harvard Business Review,* July–August 1977, pp. 102–113.

25 William T. Horner, "Tarrytown: A Union Perspective," *National Productivity Review,* Winter 1981–1982, pp. 37–41; and Robert Guest, "Quality of Work Life—Learning from Tarrytown," *Harvard Business Review,* July–August 1979, pp. 76–87. The Tarrytown experiment demonstrates the "planned change" sequence of climate-commitment-change discussed in Robert W. Keidel, "QWL Development: Three Trajectories," *Human Relations,* September 1982, pp. 743–761.

26 Richard E. Walton, "How to Counter Alienation in the Plant," *Harvard Business Review,* November–December 1972, pp. 70–81; and "The Plant That Runs on Individual Initiative," *Management Review,* July 1972, pp. 20–25. Problems with the study are discussed in David A. Whitsett and Lyle Yorks, "Looking Back at Topeka: General Foods and the Quality of Work Life Experiment," *California Management Review,* Summer 1983, pp. 93–109.

27 Erwin L. Malone, "The Non-Linear System Experiment in Participative Management," *The Journal of Business,* January 1975, pp. 52–64.

28 Critical reviews of QWL programs are in Peter Needham, "The Myth of the Self-Regulating Work Group," *Personnel Management,* August 1982, pp. 29–31; Jon E. Walker and Curt Tausky, "An Analysis of Work Incentives," *The Journal of Social Psychology,* February 1982, pp. 27–39; and William Pasmore and others, "Sociotechnical Systems: A North American Reflection on Empirical Studies of the Seventies," *Human Relations,* December 1982, pp. 1179–1204.

FOR ADDITIONAL READING

Cohen, Allan R., and Herman Gadon, *Alternative Work Schedules: Integrating Individual and Organizational Needs,* Reading, Mass.: Addison-Wesley Publishing Company, Inc., 1978.

Cummings, Thomas, and Suresh Srivastva, *The Management of Work: A Sociotechnical Approach,* La Jolla, Calif.: University Associates, 1981.

Davis, Louis E., and James C. Taylor (eds.), *Design of Jobs,* 2d ed., Santa Monica, Calif.: Goodyear Publishing Company, Inc., 1979.

Greenberg, Paul D., and Edward M. Glaser, *Some Issues in Joint Union-Management Quality of Worklife Improvement Efforts,* Kalamazoo, Mich.: W. E. Upjohn Institute for Employment Research, 1980.

Griffin, Ricky W., *Task Design: An Integrative Approach,* Glenview, Ill.: Scott, Foresman and Company, 1982.

Guzzo, Richard A., and Jeffrey S. Bondy, *A Guide to Worker Productivity Experiments in the United States 1976–81,* New York: Pergamon Press, 1983.

Hackman, J. Richard, and Greg R. Oldham, *Work Redesign,* Reading, Mass.: Addison-Wesley Publishing Company, Inc., 1980.

Skrovan, Daniel (ed.), *The QWL Reader,* Reading, Mass.: Addison-Wesley Publishing Company, Inc., 1982.

Yorks, Lyle, *Job Enrichment Revisited,* New York: AMACOM, 1979.

PART

5

SOCIAL
ENVIRONMENT

THE INDIVIDUAL IN
THE ORGANIZATION

Instead, both the organization and the individual have to give and take.

Heinz Weihrich[1]

In many instances there would appear to be a real conflict between an organization's need for personal information and the needs of individuals to maintain their privacy.

Richard W. Woodman et al.[2]

CHAPTER OBJECTIVES

TO UNDERSTAND:
Conformity
A model of legitimacy of organizational influence
How rights to privacy are interpreted
Dealing with drug abuse in organizations
Different approaches to discipline
Mutual individual-organization responsibilities

When you read fiction and social commentary, you often find a common symbolic thread. It is that organizations are systems that suppress their victim, the *individual*. Individuals live in conformity, stripped of their self-esteem and in an artificial environment. There is no challenge and no chance for psychological fulfillment. There is only security in return for saying "Yes," smiling, and wearing a neat business suit. Individuals are too numb from all this to rebel, but they *should* rebel. In turn, the organization stands socially and morally condemned.

Throughout history there has been this view of people and organizations in perpetual conflict, but now we realize that they can live in some degree of mutual interest and harmony. Individuals use organizations as instruments to achieve their goals just as much as organizations use people to reach objectives. There is a mutual social transaction in which each benefits the other.

In this chapter we discuss some of the relationships of individuals to organizations, including conformity, rights of privacy, the individual and drug abuse, discipline, and individual-organization responsibilities.

ISSUES ABOUT CONFORMITY

The basic thesis of conformity

What is conformity?

Conformity is a dependence on the norms of others without independent thinking. The basic thesis of individual conformity to the organization was stated by Whyte and Argyris in separate books in the 1950s. In *The Organization Man,* Whyte wrote about individuals who were so involved in corporate life that they became psychologically dependent on it. They tended to conform to corporate values and actions without seriously questioning them.[3]

Argyris's *Personality and Organization* was concerned especially with psychological issues such as self-actualization. Argyris believed that people wanted to be treated as mature persons, but the large corporation expected them to conform to rules and practices in an unquestioning, immature way. This lack of agreement between expectations and reality led to conflict and frustration. The basic philosophy in Argyris's own words is as follows:[4]

> An analysis of the basic properties of relatively mature human beings and formal organization leads to the conclusion that there is an inherent incongruency between the self-actualization of the two. This basic incongruency creates a situation of conflict, frustration, and failure for the participants.

One possible product of this incongruency is that employees may become passive in their attempt to adapt to a restrictive work environment. Later, if the organization changes to allow greater employee autonomy and self-actualization, they remain passive, alienated, and incapable of reacting

Learned helplessness

positively to the new opportunity. This is called *learned helplessness*—a condition where employees continue to act in a dependent manner even after one of the risks involved in stressing conformity in organizations.

Neither Whyte nor Argyris argued that people should return to a primitive civilization to live without organizations. The conflict that exists is seen solely as a challenge that requires better resolution for better results.

To what does one conform?

There are several different ways in which a person may be said to conform to an organization. First, there is a type of conformity by which one "conforms" to the requirements of technology. That is, when the pot boils, take it off the fire; or when the batch in the furnace is ready, take it out. Some "conformity" in industry is actually a response to the technology; but this is a distortion of the term, because such situations do not involve the norms of others. Furthermore, this "conformity" is the same in or out of an organization.

Looking at the more usual conformity to group norms, there are three major groups to which one conforms. One of these is the organization iself. Another is the informal work group, and the last is the external community. It is evident that the last two represent conformity expressed *inside* the organization but not conformity to the organization. The organization does not impose these last two norms; they are simply there because the organization operates in a social system rather than a vacuum. Excluding the two groups just mentioned, what is the extent and legitimacy of the organization's influence?

Areas of legitimate organizational influence

Every organization develops certain policies and requirements for performance. If the organization and an individual define the boundaries of legitimate influence differently, then organizational conflict is likely to develop. It can be sufficient to interfere with effectiveness. For example, if employees believe that it is legitimate for management to control the personal telephone calls they make at work, they may dislike management interference with their freedom on this matter, but they are unlikely to develop serious conflict with management about it. However, if employees believe that personal calls are their own private right, then this issue may become a focus of conflict with management.

This same type of reasoning applies to other issues. As long as there is agreement on the legitimacy of influence among the parties, they should be satisfied with the power balance in their relationship.

Agreement avoids conflict.

Limited research shows that there is reasonable agreement among the population concerning legitimate areas of organizational influence on employees.[6] Studies have covered labor leaders, business managers, Air Force managers, university students in three areas of the nation, and men compared with women. There is general agreement on areas of legitimacy among all groups, with high rank-order correlations for fifty-five survey items ranging from .88 to .98. Managers give somewhat more support to legitimacy than labor leaders, with students ranking in the middle; however, the important point is the substantial agreement among all groups.

Areas of agreement and disagreement

Following are examples of areas of agreement and disagreement. There is general approval of organizational influence on job conduct, such as the tidiness of one's office and one's working hours. There also is agreement that organizational influence should be low on personal activities off the job, such as the church one attends, where charge accounts are maintained, and where one goes on vacation.

On the other hand, there is some disagreement between managers and others in a few areas, primarily those concerned with off-the-job conduct that could affect company reputation. Examples are degree of participation in various community affairs and personal use of company products. Obviously, if you work at a plant that assembles automobiles and you drive a competitor's automobile to work, your employer will be concerned about your lack of support of company products and the effect of your actions on product image.

A model of legitimacy of organizational influence

The model's variables

The model of legitimacy of organizational influence that has been developed from research is shown in Figure 16-1. The two key variables in the model are conduct on the job or off of it and conduct that is job-related or not job-related. As shown in the model, there is agreement on high legitimacy when conduct is on the job and job-related. Legitimacy tends to become less accepted as an act's connection with the job becomes more hazy. If the act is on the job but not job-related, such as playing cards during lunch hours, questions arise about legitimacy. Generally only moderate legitimacy is supported, depending on the situation.

> For example, management might accept a situation in which employees were playing cards but not gambling in a dining area in the manufacturing department during lunch. On the other hand, assume the card players are bank tellers playing poker with money at their desks in the public areas of a bank during lunch. Surely in this case both managers and others will agree that management has high legitimacy to forbid this conduct because of its possible effects on customers, even though the game is not being played on company time.

Off-the-job conduct

We can begin a discussion of off-the-job conduct with the general statement that the power of a business to regulate employee conduct off the job is very limited. Certainly when the conduct is not job-related, there is little reason

Figure 16-1
Model of legitimacy of organizational influence on employees

TYPE OF CONDUCT	Job-related	Not job-related
On-the-job	High legitimacy	Moderate legitimacy
Off-the-job	Moderate legitimacy	Low legitimacy

for the employer to become involved. On the other hand, some activities off the job may affect the employer, so questions of organizational influence arise. The basic relationship is as follows: *The more job-related one's conduct is when off the job, the more support there is for organizational influence on the employee.*

Interpretations become difficult in some borderline situations. For example, what kinds of controls should be applied to off-job conduct of an employee living on company property at an oil pumping site and on twenty-four-hour call? Even when an employee has departed company property and is not on call, the boundaries of employer interest are still not fixed. Consider the angry employee who waited until the supervisor stepped outside the company gate and then struck the supervisor several times in the presence of other employees. In cases of this type, arbitrators consistently uphold company disciplinary action because the action is job-related. In the United States at least, the organization's jurisdictional line is clearly functional, related to the total job system and not the property line.

RIGHTS OF PRIVACY

Rights of privacy primarily refer to organizational invasion of a person's private life and unauthorized release of confidential information about a person.[7] Business activities that may involve rights of privacy are listed in Figure 16-2, and several of these are discussed in the following paragraphs.

Employees, customers, and others believe that their religious, political, and social beliefs are personal and should not be subject to snooping or analysis, although there are exceptions—such as being employed by a church or a political party. The same view applies to personal acts, conversations, and locations such as company lavatories and private homes. Exceptions are permitted grudgingly only when job involvement is clearly proved, and burden of proof is on the employer. For example, it may be appropriate to know that a bank teller is deeply in debt as a result of betting on horse races, or that an applicant for a national credit card twice has been convicted for stealing and using credit cards.

One research study surveyed over 2000 employees to determine when they perceived that their privacy had been invaded.[8] Four conditions led to perceptions of invasion: Personality (versus performance) information was used, no permission was obtained before disclosure, there were unfavorable consequences, and the disclosure was external (rather than inside the company). Clearly, these situations should be minimized to avoid employee reactions.

• Lie detectors	• Treatment of drug abuse
• Personality tests	• Surveillance devices
• Encounter groups	• Computer data banks
• Medical examinations	• Confidential records
• Treatment of alcoholism	

Figure 16-2
Business activities that may involve employee rights of privacy

Policy guidelines relating to privacy

Because of the importance of employee privacy, most large employers have developed policy guidelines to protect it.[9] These guidelines also help establish uniform practices and make it easier to handle any unusual situations that may develop. Following are some of the policy guidelines on privacy that organizations are using:[10]

- *Relevance.* Only necessary, useful information should be recorded and retained. Obsolete information should be removed periodically.

- *Notice.* There should be no personal data system that is unknown to an employee.

- *Fiduciary duty.* The keeper of the information is responsible for its security.

- *Confidentiality.* Information should be released only to those who have a need to know, and release outside the organization normally should occur only with the employee's permission.

- *Due process.* The employee should be able to examine records and challenge them if they appear incorrect.

- *Protection of the psyche.* The employee's inner self should not be invaded or exposed except with prior consent and for compelling reasons.

Surveillance devices

Some surveillance acceptable

Protection of the psyche, for example, means that, except for compelling reasons, there should be no surveillance of private places such as locker rooms or secret surveillance unknown to the employee, as with secret listening devices. Surveillance that is known to employees and has a compelling job reason usually is not considered to be an undue infringement on privacy. Banks, for example, have hidden cameras that make photographs during robberies. These photographs include employees, but this hardly infringes on their privacy provided that use of the photographs is confined to the original purpose.

> An example of regular surveillance is provided by a fast-food chain that installed moving-picture cameras in a number of its stores. The camera photographed the cash register whenever it was open. Employees knew that it was there to control theft, although it also could photograph robberies. The camera worked effectively, providing an unexpected increase of about 10 percent in receipts.

The polygraph

The polygraph is one instrument that tends to invade privacy, and some states regulate its use. Science has determined that conscience usually causes physiological changes when a person tells a significant lie. The polygraph (lie detector) was developed on the basis of this information. It is useful, but its usefulness is limited because its accuracy rate is only 64 to 96 percent.[11]

Organizations use the polygraph primarily to control theft and to deal with other matters involving honesty among employees. It is estimated that employees steal several billion dollars a year from employers, so theft is a serious organizational problem. Employers argue that the polygraph would be less necessary if employees were more honest. Since theft is a fact, the polygraph is used to control it.

In addition to protecting the organization, the polygraph also may help protect employee interests. Dishonest employees may take property of other employees, cast suspicion on them in case of theft, or place them in compromising situations that threaten their jobs; and polygraph use can discourage these types of behaviors. In some situations it may even help employees develop a more effective working environment.

For example, in decentralized retail operations, such as drive-in grocery stores, polygraph tests permit business to abolish various audits and controls that otherwise would be oppressive. This arrangement gives employees more freedom from surveillance and leaves them free to work in whatever manner is most productive.

Similar reasoning applies to other positions of trust. For example, a jewelry chain uses the polygraph on job applicants and has found that between 10 and 25 percent of them fail the test. Failure rates in some other types of jobs are 30 percent or higher.

The nature of the polygraph examination allows it to be given only with a person's consent, so the examinee has a choice of refusing the test. However, refusal may lead to suspicions that will reduce a person's chances of getting and keeping a job. Employees especially object to having to prove themselves innocent, that is, take a test routinely even when no theft has been discovered or no evidence points to them as thieves. They object less to a specific test about a specific known theft of major proportions. In this situation they may welcome a test to take the pressure of suspicion off them.

Another type of lie detector is the *psychological stress evaluator*. It analyzes changes in voice patterns to determine whether a lie is being told. It requires no hookup to a machine, as a polygraph does. As with the polygraph, the test taker's own conscience provides the evidence by showing stress when a significant lie is told.

Psychological stress evaluator

Treatment of alcoholism

Alcoholism presents major medical and job problems, so employers need to develop responsible policies and programs to deal with it without endangering rights of privacy. It is estimated that between 5 and 10 percent of employees are alcoholics and that they cost employers more than $10 billion annually in absenteeism, poor work, lost productivity, and related costs. Absence rates for alcoholic employees are two to four times those of other employees.

Alcoholics are found in all types of industries, occupations, and job levels. Sometimes the job environment may contribute to an employee's alcoholism, but the employee's personal habits and problems are also major contributors. In some instances employees are well on the road to alcoholism before they are hired.

Reasons for company programs Regardless of the causes of alcoholism, an increasing number of firms are recognizing that they have a role to play in helping alcoholics control or break their habit.[12] One reason is that the firm and employee already have a working relationship on which they can build. A second is that any success with the employee will save both a valuable person for the company and a valuable citizen for society. A third reason is that the job appears to be the best environment for recovery because a job helps an alcoholic retain a self-image as a useful person in society.

How should companies treat alcoholics?

Successful programs Successful employer programs treat alcoholism as an illness, focus on the job behavior caused by alcoholism, and provide both medical help and psychological support for alcoholics. As shown in Figure 16-3, the company demonstrates to alcoholics that it wants to help them and is willing to work with them over an extended period of time.[13] A nonthreatening atmosphere is provided; however, there is always the implied threat that alcohol-induced behavior cannot be tolerated indefinitely. For example, if an employee refuses treatment and unsatisfactory behavior continues, the employer has little choice other than dismissal.

Figure 16-3
Program for
treatment of
employee alcoholics
and drug abusers

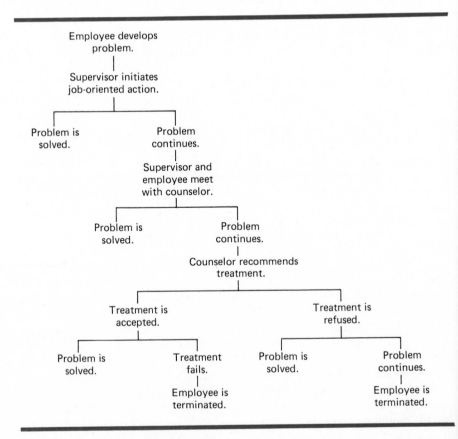

Following is the way that one company program operates. Assume that a supervisor named Mary Cortez notices that an employee named Bill Revson has a record of tardiness and absenteeism, poor work, an exhausted appearance, and related symptoms that may indicate alcoholism or another serious problem. She discusses only Revson's job behavior with him, giving him a chance to correct himself. When Revson's behavior continues unchanged, Cortez asks Revson to meet with her in the presence of a counselor. The supervisor presents her evidence of poor job behavior and then leaves the room so that the employee and counselor can discuss the situation privately.

In other instances medical examinations uncover alcoholism or an employee voluntarily asks for help. As soon as the program is brought into the open, the treatment program is initiated in a supportive atmosphere. It may involve hospitalization for the employee. Throughout the procedure the company is patient but firm. Using the approach just described, the firm has achieved a recovery rate of over 50 percent. Some firms have reached a recovery rate of over 80 percent.[14]

Drug abuse

Abuse of drugs other than alcohol, particularly if used at work, may cause severe problems for the individual, the employer, and other employees. These drugs may include heroin, cocaine, and marijuana, or the abuse may stem from the improper use of stimulants, barbiturates, and tranquilizers. In some job situations (pilot, surgeon, or crane operator) the consequences of drug abuse can be disastrous.

The seriousness of hard-drug problems is illustrated by a survey of ninety-five users of hard drugs, mostly heroin, who were employed at the time they used drugs.[15] Ninety-one of them reported that they had been under the influence of drugs during working hours, and forty said that they had used drugs in the lavatory at work. Even more serious from the point of view of other employees, forty-eight of the drug users admitted that they had sold drugs to other employees, and sixty-eight specified other types of on-the-job criminal activity.

For example, twenty-eight reported thefts of cash or checks from the employer and/or employees, and thirty-seven admitted stealing company property and selling it to support their drug habit. These statistics make it evident that the pattern of behavior of hard-drug users can be a serious threat to an organization.

Treatment programs Company programs for treatment of drug abuse other than alcohol usually follow the same patterns as programs on alcoholism except that hard-drug treatment may be controlled more strictly because of the hard-drug user's greater probability of criminal behavior on the job.[16] Most firms combine treatment of alcoholism, drug abuse, and related difficulties into *employee assistance programs* (EAPs). These programs identify and treat the problems of employees that are affecting their productivity or hindering their personal well-being. Normally the programs focus on both prevention and treatment. Figure 16-4 gives the policy statement of an insurance company on this subject.

What is an EAP?

Our company recognizes alcoholism, mental health problems, and drug abuse as illnesses that can be successfully treated. Our people who need help in these areas will be given the same consideration as those with other illnesses. It is our goal to help those who develop such problems by providing for consultation and treatment to prevent their conditions from progressing to a degree where they cannot work effectively. . . .

The decision by management to refer an individual for evaluation, diagnosis, or treatment will be based on evidence of continuing unsatisfactory job performance. Job security will not be jeopardized by such referral. Failure by the individual to accept evaluation or to follow through on professional advice will be considered in the same manner as any factor or illness that continues adversely to affect job performance.

Medical records of those with behavioral-medical disorders will be held confidential, as are all medical records.

*Careful supervision
necessary*

Hiring former drug users Many firms are reluctant to hire former hard-drug users. Others, recognizing a need to provide jobs for those who have recovered, are experimenting with carefully supervised employment programs. For example, one company employed recovered heroin addicts with the employment condition that they regularly provide urine specimens for analysis to determine that they had not resumed use of heroin or certain other hard drugs. Is this an unwarranted invasion of privacy, or is it justified because of the danger of criminal behavior if the employee returns to hard drugs?

The Equitable Life Assurance Society audited its rehabilitation program for drug users and found that the program was successful.[17] The audit covered forty-six former drug users during a rehabilitation period of nearly ten years. There was no significant difference between former drug users and other employees with regard to data such as promotions, turnover, job performance, attendance, and punctuality. The audit concluded that when former drug abusers are properly selected, placed, and supervised, their performance tends to be about the same as that of regular employees.

DISCIPLINE

*Two types of
discipline*

The area of discipline can have a strong impact on the individual in the organization. *Discipline* is management action to enforce organizational standards.[18] It is of two types, preventive and corrective.

Preventive discipline

Preventive discipline is action taken to encourage employees to follow standards and rules so that infractions do not occur. The basic objective is to encourage employee self-discipline. In this way the employees maintain their own discipline rather than having management impose it. A self-disciplined group is a source of pride in any organization.

occasions. Then employee C disregarded it and "the roof caved in." The employee was given a severe reprimand in front of others and a three-day suspension. To other employees and to C, this action was inconsistent and unfair. Employees at this point did not know what management's real standard of conduct was, and morale deteriorated. Originally they conducted themselves on the basis of how management enforced the rule stated by the sign (instead of by the rule itself). When enforcement became erratic, they were both confused and resentful of injustice. It is evident in this example that consistent application of standards is a key to corrective discipline.

On the other hand, occasional exceptions are appropriate if they clearly have different or *extenuating circumstances.* The employer's obligation to treat all employees alike applies only when their situations are approximately alike.

Take the case of Audrey, a responsible and conscientious employee who, because of a communication error at home and a chain of unfortunate circumstances, fails to notify her supervisor of her absence until three days have gone by. Bill, on the other hand, is the devil-may-care type who has declared openly that the reason for his absence is none of management's business. On the afternoon of the third day, Bill sends a telegram from Las Vegas saying, "Car broke down. Hope to return Monday." In this instance it probably is appropriate to discipline each differently.

The hot-stove rule also requires that discipline be administered impersonally, just as a stove will equally burn men and women, young and old. The supervisor's like or dislike for an employee is not relevant to disciplinary action.[22] Effective discipline separates the wrongful act from one's attitudes about the employee as a person. There is a difference between applying a penalty for a job not performed and calling an employee a lazy loafer.

Impersonal

Progressive discipline

Most employers apply a policy of *progressive discipline,* which means that there are stronger penalties for repeated offenses.[23] The purpose is to give an employee an opportunity for self-correction before more serious penalties are applied. Progressive discipline also gives management time to work with an employee to help correct infractions, such as unauthorized absences.

A typical system of progressive discipline is shown in Figure 16-6. The first infraction leads to a verbal reprimand by the supervisor. The next infraction leads to a written reprimand, with a record placed in the files. Further infractions build up to stronger discipline, leading finally to discharge.

Increasingly stronger penalties

Figure 16-6
A progressive discipline system

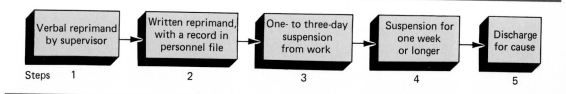

Verbal reprimand by supervisor	Written reprimand, with a record in personnel file	One- to three-day suspension from work	Suspension for one week or longer	Discharge for cause
Steps 1	2	3	4	5

However, legal restrictions on the employer's right to discharge have become more common in recent years.[24] Usually the personnel department is involved by step 3 or sooner in order to assure that company policy is followed consistently in all departments.

Some progressive systems allow minor offenses to be removed from the record after one to three years, allowing each employee to return to step 1. Specified serious offenses, such as fighting or major theft, are usually exempted from progressive discipline. An employee who commits these offenses may be discharged for the first offense.

A counseling approach to discipline

Most organizations use counseling in connection with discipline, but a few firms have moved a step further and taken a counseling approach to the entire procedure. In this approach, an employee is counseled rather than progressively penalized for the first few breaches of organizational standards. Here is how the program works in one organization.

> The philosophy is that violations are employee malfunctions that can be constructively corrected without penalty. The first violation results in a private discussion between the employee and the supervisor. The second violation brings further discussion with the supervisor, with a focus on correcting causes of the behavior. A third violation leads to counseling with both the immediate supervisor and the shift supervisor to determine the causes of the employee's malfunction. For example, does the employee dislike the job and want a transfer? Is the employee prepared to abide by the standard? The result of the discussion is given to the employee in a letter.
>
> A fourth infraction within a reasonable time, such as a year, results in final counseling with the superintendent. The offender is released from duty with pay for the remainder of the day to consider willingness to abide by standards. The offender is told that, regrettably, a further violation will result in termination because it shows that the employee is unable or unwilling to work within the standards of the organization.
>
> After a year the record is wiped clean, and any new violation starts at step 1. Certain serious offenses are exempted from the procedure and may result in immediate termination.

The focus of the counseling approach is fact finding and guidance to encourage desirable behavior instead of using penalties to discourage undesirable behavior. Emphasis is on "do this," rather than "don't do that." In this manner the employee's self-image and dignity are retained and the supervisor-employee relationship remains cooperative and constructive.

THE INDIVIDUAL'S RESPONSIBILITIES TO THE ORGANIZATION

A discussion of the individual in the organization is incomplete if it covers only the organization's obligations to the individual. The employment relationship is two-way. Without question, the organization has responsibilities to the individual, but also—and again without question—the individual has responsibilities to the organization. Employment is a mutual social transaction. Each employee makes certain membership investments in the organization and expects profitable rewards in return. The organization also invests in the individual, and it, too, expects profitable rewards.

A relationship is profitable for either party when benefits (outputs) are larger than costs (inputs) measured in a total value system. In the usual employment situation both parties benefit, just as they do in the usual social relationship. Both parties benefit because the social transaction between them produces new values that exceed the investment each makes.

The profitable relationship deteriorates if either party fails to act responsibly toward the needs of the other. The employees can fail to act responsibly, just as the organization can.[25] If they do, they can expect the organization to respond by using tight controls to try to maintain a successful operating system.

Consider the matter of theft, which was mentioned in connection with the polygraph. Overlook for the moment the moral-ethical views of theft. From the point of view of the organizational system only, theft interferes with work operations. It upsets schedules and budgets. It causes reorders. It calls for more controls. In sum, it reduces both the reliability and the productivity of the organizational system. There is less output for the individual as well as for the organization. In this situation the organization must act to protect other employees as well as itself.

Theft as an example

The social transaction called employment creates a mutual responsibility between the individual and the organization. On the other hand, this obligation does not extend to support of illegal activities or those which seriously violate social standards or the employee's private conscience. All employees retain the right to their own private beliefs. Occasionally, when management disregards internal opposition to wrongful acts, employees disclose the alleged misconduct to the public. These *whistle-blowers* may have uncovered evidence of price-fixing, fraud, or products with inadequate safeguards for consumers. By going public, whistle-blowers hope to bring pressure on the organization to correct the problem. Despite protective laws, some employees have been the subject of retaliation by the organization, such as harassment, transfer, or discharge.[26]

Whistle-blowers

SUMMARY

Some areas of individual-organization conflict are conformity, legitimacy of organizational influence, rights of privacy, and discipline. The main concern is to assure that the employee's activities and choices are not unduly controlled by the organization. In order to protect both the organization and the worker, companies usually develop policies to guide their decisions about privacy, drug-abuse programs, and similar activities.

Both preventive and corrective discipline are important. Preventive discipline encourages employees to maintain discipline among themselves. Corrective discipline is applied when employees materially fail to meet standards.

It seeks to reform the offender, deter others, and maintain standards. Due process and the hot-stove rule are useful guidelines. Most firms use progressive discipline, and some use a counseling approach.

Essentially the social transaction of employment is a two-way street with mutual responsibilities between the individual and the organization. One way by which these mutual responsibilities are clarified and maintained is through collective bargaining with unions, which is discussed in the next chapter.

TERMS AND CONCEPTS FOR REVIEW

Conformity

Learned helplessness

Legitimacy of organizational influence

Rights of privacy

Polygraph

Preventive discipline

Corrective discipline

Due process

Hot-stove rule

Progressive discipline

Individual-organization responsibilities

Whistle-blowers

REVIEW QUESTIONS

1 Think of a job that you have had or now have. Discuss any conformity that was required that you felt was unfair.

2 Still considering the job in question 1, were there any ways in which you were not responsible toward the organization or took unfair advantage of it? Discuss.

3 Still thinking of the job in question 1, did you feel that the employer invaded your right to privacy in any way? Discuss. Did the employer have a policy with regard to right of privacy?

4 Assume that you are going to an interview for a job as a teller with a bank and learn that a polygraph will be used to explore your history of honesty. Describe how you would feel, and why.

5 Do any students you know exhibit learned helplessness? Describe their behavior, and explain why you think they act that way.

6 Explain the basic model of legitimacy of organizational influence. Does it seem to be a reasonable one within which you could work?

7 Form into small groups and visit a company to discuss its program for the treatment of alcoholism and hard-drug abuse. Then report the program to your classroom group and give your appraisal of its effectiveness.

8 Think of the job selected in question 1, and discuss the ways in which management applied both preventive and corrective discipline.

9 Discuss both due process and the hot-stove rule as guidelines for corrective discipline. Do you consider them fair and useful guidelines?

10 Consider your own role as a possible whistle-blower. Under what conditions would you publicly criticize your employer or another employee?

Privileges for an Employee

Margie Wheeler, a divorcee with one child, is a bank clerk. She has had an excellent record for three years. In fact, she is so good that she has been given the added duty of instructing new employees in her department.

About three weeks ago management noticed a change in Margie's work attitude and habits. She became moody and irritable, seeming to have her mind on something else. She was absent from her work area for long periods during the day making telephone calls. She also left work early on several occasions. On two Mondays she took sick leave, reporting that she had influenza on one of the days. Her manager assumed that she had some sort of temporary personal problem; so he let her take advantage of the rules by overstaying her coffee break and otherwise not performing her work. It was rumored around the office that she was dating a married man and had been taking long breaks in order to visit him in the office of another company in the building, but her manager had no proof of this rumor.

One morning a respected senior office clerk came to the manager and reported that other employees were resentful of Margie because they felt management was making exceptions for her that it would not make for other employees. The clerk added that Margie was not performing her work and that other employees were "at the point of revolt."

QUESTIONS
Assuming you are the manager, explain what you will do and why. To what extent will you expect Margie to conform to the bank's standards? To the group's standards? To what extent will you respect Margie's rights of privacy in this situation?

Two Accounting Clerks

Rosemary Janis and Mary Lopez were the only two clerks handling payments from customers in the office of Atlantic Plumbing Supply Company. They reported to the owner of the business. Janis had been employed for eighteen months and Lopez for fourteen months. Both were community college graduates, about twenty-three years old, and unmarried.

By manipulating the accounts in a rather ingenious way that would not normally be detected, Janis was stealing from account payments as they were received. During her third month of employment, Lopez learned of Janis's thefts, but she decided not to tell management, rationalizing that Janis's personal conduct was none of her business. Lopez did not benefit from Janis's thefts, and the two women were not close friends. Their duties allowed them to work rather independently of each other, each handling a different alphabetical portion of the accounts.

By the time the owner learned of Janis's thefts, she had stolen approximately $5700. During investigation of the thefts the owner learned that Lopez had known about them for several months, because it was evident that the thefts could not have occurred for an extended period without Lopez's knowledge.

At the time of employment, both women had been instructed by the owner that they would be handling money and that therefore strict honesty would be required of them.

QUESTIONS

1 What issues are raised by these events? Discuss.

2 What disciplinary action, if any, do you recommend for each of the two women? Why? Will the discipline be preventive, corrective, or both? What about due process? Is failure to "blow the whistle" an issue?

REFERENCES

1 Heinz Weihrich, "Strategic Career Management—A Missing Link in Management by Objectives," *Human Resource Management,* Summer–Fall 1982, pp. 59–60.

2 Richard W. Woodson et al., "A Survey of Employee Perceptions of Information Privacy in Organizations," *Academy of Management Journal,* September 1982, p. 648.

3 William H. Whyte, Jr., *The Organization Man,* New York: Simon & Schuster, Inc., 1956.

4 Chris Argyris, *Personality and Organization: The Conflict between the System and the Individual,* New York: Harper & Row, Publishers, Incorporated, 1957, p. 175. See also Chris Argyris, "Personality and Organization Theory Revisited," *Administrative Science Quarterly,* June 1973, pp. 141–167.

5 Mark J. Martinko and William L. Gardner, "Learned Helplessness: An Alternative Explanation for Performance Deficits," *Academy of Management Review,* April 1982, pp. 195–204.

6 Edgar H. Schein and J. Steven Ott, "The Legitimacy of Organizational Influence," *American Journal of Sociology,* May 1962, pp. 682–689; Arthur G. Bedeian, "A Comparison and Analysis of German and United States Managerial Attitudes toward the Legitimacy of Organizational Influence," *Academy of Management Journal,* December 1975, pp. 897–904; and Keith Davis, "Attitudes toward the Legitimacy of Management Efforts to Influence Employees," *Academy of Management Journal,* June 1968, pp. 153–162.

7 For a general overview of employee privacy issues, see Jack L. Osborn, *Fair Information Practices for Managers and Employees,* New York: AMACOM, 1980; and David F. Linowes, "Update on Privacy Protection Safeguards," *Personnel Administrator,* June 1980, pp. 39–42.

8 Paul Tolchinsky et al., "Employee Perceptions of Invasion of Privacy: A Field Simulation Experiment," *Journal of Applied Psychology,* June 1982, pp. 308–313.

9 The privacy guidelines for two firms are summarized in "Protecting Privacy at AT&T and General Foods," *Management Review,* February 1980, p. 48.

10 Adapted from Virginia E. Schein, "Privacy and Personnel: A Time for Action," *Personnel Journal,* December 1976, pp. 604–607, 615; and K. Mossman, "A New Dimension of Privacy," *American Bar Association Journal,* vol. 61, 1975, pp. 829–833.

11 Avital Ginton et al., "A Method for Evaluating the Use of the Polygraph in a Real-Life Situation," *Journal of Applied Psychology,* April 1982, pp. 131–137.

12 One survey reported that 21 percent of the responding firms had established formal programs to help employees cope with alcoholism and a variety of other personal problems. See Robert C. Ford and Frank S. McLaughlin, "Employee Assistance Programs: A Descriptive Survey of ASPA Members," *Personnel Administrator,* September 1981, pp. 29–35.

13 A similar model, in use at Gates Rubber Company, is in Edwin J. Busch, Jr., "Developing an Employee Assistance Program," *Personnel Journal,* September 1981, pp. 708–711. Symptoms of alcoholism and guidelines for counseling such employees are in Steven H. Appelbaum, "A Human Resources Counseling Model: The Alcoholic Employee," *Personnel Administrator,* August 1982, pp. 35–44.

14 Richard J. Tersine and James Hazeldine, "Alcoholism: A Productivity Hangover," *Business Horizons,* November–December 1982, pp. 68–72.

15 Stephen J. Levy, "Drug Abuse in Business: Telling It Like It Is," *Personnel,* September–October 1972, pp. 8–14.

16 Peter B. Bensinger, "Drugs in the Workplace," *Harvard Business Review,* November–December 1982, pp. 48–50ff.

17 "The Equitable Drug Abuse Rehabilitation Program," *Response,* May 1977, p. 10. The Chemical Bank program is discussed in Lucy N. Friedman and Carl B. Weisbrod, "A Way to Move Welfare Recipients into the Work Force," *Harvard Business Review,* January–February 1978, pp. 12–14.

18 The elements of effective discipline are discussed in Brian P. Heshizer and Harry Graham, "Discipline in the Nonunion Company: Protecting Employer and Employee Rights," *Personnel,* March–April 1982, pp. 71–78,

19 Alan W. Bryant, "Replacing Punitive Discipline with a Positive Approach," *Personnel Administrator,* February 1984, pp. 79ff; and R. Bruce McAfee and Mark Lincoln Chadwin, "Evaluating an Organization's Discipline System," *Human Resource Management,* Fall 1981, pp. 29–35.

20 Henry P. Sims, Jr., "Tips and Troubles with Employee Reprimand," *Personnel Administrator,* January 1979, pp. 57–61; Richard D. Arvey and John M. Ivancevich, "Punishment in Organizations: A Review, Propositions, and Research Suggestions," *Academy of Management Review,* January 1980, pp. 123–132; and Henry P. Sims, Jr., "Further Thoughts on Punishment in Organizations," *Academy of Management Review,* January 1980, pp. 133–138.

21 The hot-stove rule is attributed to Douglas McGregor, developer of Theories X and Y (discussed in Chapter 8). For the hot-stove rule and other useful guidelines to corrective discipline, see Leon D. Boncarosky, "Guidelines to Corrective Discipline," *Personnel Journal,* October 1979, pp. 698–702.

22 James Belohlav, "Realities of Successful Employee Discipline," *Personnel Administrator,* March 1983, pp. 74–77.

23 For a comparison of progressive discipline with corrective discipline, see Ira G. Asherman, "The Corrective Discipline Process," *Personnel Journal,* July 1982, pp. 528–531.

24 See, for example, David W. Ewing, "Your Right to Fire," *Harvard Business Review,* March–April 1983, pp. 32–34ff; Maria Leonard, "Challenges to the Termination-at-Will Doctrine," *Personnel Administrator,* February 1983, pp. 49–50ff; and Marco L. Colosi, "Who's Pulling the Strings on Employment at Will?" *Personnel Journal,* May 1984, pp. 56–58.

25 In some instances employers are suing employees whose alleged carelessness and negligence may have caused accidents and injuries; see "Challenges to Corporate

Privacy," *Business Week,* Oct. 9, 1978, pp. 44–46. In other cases the organization is held legally liable for the actions of its employees, as in Mitchell S. Novit, "Employer Liability for Employee Misconduct: Two Common Law Doctrines," *Personnel,* January–February 1982, pp. 11–19.

26 Marcia A. Parmerlee, Janet P. Near, and Tamila C. Jensen, "Correlates of Whistleblowers' Perceptions of Organizational Retaliation," *Administrative Science Quarterly,* March 1982, pp. 17–34; extensive references are in James S. Bowman, "Whistle Blowing: Literature and Resource Materials," *Public Administration Review,* May–June 1983, pp. 271–276.

FOR ADDITIONAL READING

Argyris, Chris, *Personality and Organization: The Conflict between the System and the Individual,* New York: Harper & Row, Publishers, Incorporated, 1957.

Elliston, Frederick, A., *Conflicting Loyalties in the Workplace,* Notre Dame, Ind.: University of Notre Dame Press, 1983.

Ewing, David, W., *Do It My Way or You're Fired!* New York: John Wiley & Sons, 1983.

Follman, Joseph F., Jr., *Helping the Troubled Employee,* New York: AMACOM, 1978.

Hollinger, Richard C., and John P. Clark, *Theft by Employees,* Lexington, Mass.: Lexington Books, 1983.

Lorber, Lawrence Z. et al., *Fear of Firing: A Legal and Personnel Analysis of Employment-at-Will,* Alexandria, Va.: The ASPA Foundation, 1984.

The Study of the Economic Costs to Society of Alcohol, Drugs, and Mental Disorders, Research Triangle Park, N.C.: Research Triangle Institute, October 1981.

Vogel, David, and Thorton Bradshaw, *Corporations and Their Critics,* New York: McGraw-Hill Book Company, 1980.

Westin, Alan F. (ed.), *Whistle Blowing! Loyalty and Dissent in the Corporation,* New York: McGraw-Hill Book Company, 1981.

Westin, Alan F., and Stephan Salisbury (eds.), *Individual Rights in the Corporation: A Reader on Employee Rights,* New York: Pantheon Books, 1980.

Whyte, William H., Jr., *The Organization Man,* New York: Simon & Schuster, Inc., 1956.

Zack, A., and R. Block, *The Arbitration of Discipline Cases: Concepts and Questions,* New York: American Arbitration Association, 1979.

WORKING
WITH UNIONS

Unions and companies must steer away from their adversary stance toward a more cooperative relationship.

Donald N. Scobel[1]

[There will likely be] significantly more sophisticated and competitive bargaining strategies in many unionized corporations.

L. L. Cummings[2]

CHAPTER OBJECTIVES

TO UNDERSTAND:

Basic labor legislation

The collective-bargaining process

Mediation and arbitration

Problem-solving bargaining

How grievance systems operate

The postindustrial society and labor force

Not all employers deal with labor unions, but a number of them do. A union is a distinct organization separate from an employer. On the other hand, it is the closest of all separate organizations because its membership consists of employees, its interests concern conditions of employment, and its primary activity is representing worker interests to management. Observe in the following situation how readily the union became involved in work issues.

> In an electrical company four employees worked at a table performing four identical skilled operations before passing parts to four other skilled workers at another table. Under these conditions they had a skilled artisan's pride in work and ample opportunity to engage in friendly conversation during the day. The work was then changed to assembly-line conditions where each employee was isolated along a conveyor belt and performed only a semiskilled fraction of the former skilled job. The result was unrest and constructive protest.[3] When management failed to heed the protest, the employees appealed to their union, which made a strike issue of the incident and built union solidarity.

The subject of union-management relations is called *labor relations,* or *industrial relations.*[4] In this chapter we examine the union's role in the work environment, collective bargaining, grievance systems, and union response to the postindustrial labor force. Not all aspects of labor relations are discussed. Instead, we focus on those items that especially affect organizational behavior.

THE UNION'S ROLE IN AN ORGANIZATION

A *labor union* is an association of employees formed for the primary purpose of influencing an employer's decisions about conditions of employment. It also may engage in fraternal activities, political action, and related activities.

Two formal organizations

It is a social group, and it brings to the work environment a second formal organization, as shown in Figure 17-1. The union hierarchy sits alongside the management hierarchy, and the employee becomes a member of both. Sometimes this arrangement is beneficial to workers, because when their wants are not satisfied by management, they can turn to the union for help. At other times this arrangement is stressful, because each organization makes some conflicting demands on workers.

A second formal organization greatly increases the interaction relationships that can occur, some of which are shown by the lines in Figure 17-1. Looking only at the mathematics of the situation, the introduction of a second hierarchy causes a geometric increase in relationships, which tremendously complicates human interaction. Although no more people are added, most of them are now playing two formal roles, one as union member and one as company employee.

Two informal organizations

The union also introduces a second set of informal organizations. These informal groups are built around union interests and activities, and they are

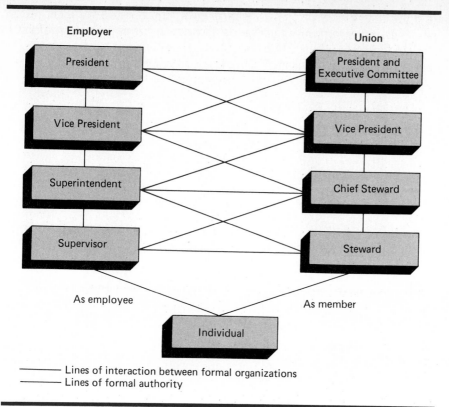

Employer

Union

President

President and Executive Committee

Vice President

Vice President

Superintendent

Chief Steward

Supervisor

Steward

As employee

As member

Individual

——— Lines of interaction between formal organizations
——— Lines of formal authority

Figure 17-1
The union adds a second formal organization to the employment relationship.

sometimes as powerful as the union's formal structure. Take an unauthorized strike as an example. Though union leadership joins with management in demanding that workers return to work, the demand is not always successful because of informal group pressures. Informal leaders have the group emotionally worked up and are so in control of the situation that union orders are ignored.

Union membership

Labor-union membership in the United States historically has ranged between 20 and 25 percent of the total labor force. As shown in Figure 17-2, the *proportion* of union members in the labor force has been relatively stable since the end of World War II, but unions have grown in total membership as the labor force expanded. Although 20 to 25 percent is not a large proportion, it does represent a powerful economic, social, and political force in the work environment. Labor unions have a significant effect on wages, benefits, and working conditions.

Labor unions are stronger in some industries and occupations than in others. For example, only a few professional engineers belong to unions, but unions are a dominant force among automobile workers and steelworkers.

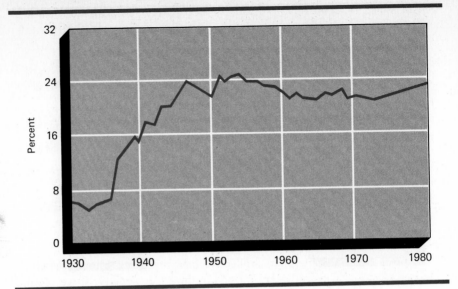

Figure 17-2
Labor-union
membership as a
percentage of the
total labor force,
1930–1980
Source: Directory of
U.S. Labor Organizations,
Washington, D.C.: Bureau
of National Affairs, 1983,
p. 44.

Labor legislation

Important labor laws

Labor relations in the United States are governed by a variety of state and federal laws. Three important laws are summarized in the following paragraphs.

National Labor Relations Act   The National Labor Relations Act (NLRA) of 1935 establishes a government procedure for union-representation elections and requires employers to bargain with a union that wins an election. The act also defines and prohibits certain unfair labor practices on the part of the employer that might discourage fair bargaining. The union can bargain with regard to terms and conditions of employment, and it bargains for all employees, both union and nonunion, in a bargaining unit. The act is administered by the National Labor Relations Board (NLRB).

Labor-Management Relations Act   The Labor-Management Relations Act (LMRA) of 1947 defines and prohibits certain unfair labor practices on the part of unions similar to those specified earlier for employers. It also establishes a procedure for handling strikes that cause national emergencies.

The Labor-Management Reporting and Disclosure Act   The Labor-Management Reporting and Disclosure Act of 1959 provides further controls of improper practices such as the misuse of funds by unions. Controls are applied through a number of reports that labor and management must file with the Secretary of Labor. The act also provides certain rights to union members, such as freedom of speech in union meetings and participation in union elections.

As a whole, the various laws provide a government-regulated system of collective bargaining. Bargainers remain free to reach their own agreements, but their activities are regulated closely to assure fairness and good faith.

COLLECTIVE BARGAINING

Collective bargaining is the negotiation between representatives of management and labor to produce a written agreement covering terms and conditions of employment. It essentially is a compromise and balancing of opposing pressures of two social groups who have enough mutual interests to work together.[5] Pressures at the bargaining table usually are framed in economic and technical terms; yet bargaining overall is a social process. The objective of collective bargaining is to work toward a new equilibrium of social forces and to make it easier to maintain this new equilibrium. To the extent that these pressures can be reconciled, conflict can be reduced.

Bargaining is a social process.

Though it presents difficulties, collective bargaining is a useful practice to help preserve labor-management autonomy in a free society. If we require labor disputes to be settled by third parties, labor and management freedoms will be reduced. Collective bargaining, therefore, serves long-run interests of a free society as well as the interests of labor and management.

Bargaining is permitted for federal and state civil service employees and many local government employees[6] as well as employees in private organizations. Bargaining for government employees tends to be more limited,[7] and it may not include the right to strike against government. Because of these limitations, government unions tend to rely more heavily on political activity and arbitration of unsettled issues.

A continuous process

People sometimes look upon collective bargaining as an affair that is conducted annually or less often and then is finished and forgotten until the next time for bargaining rolls around. This is the way they read about bargaining in the public press, so they think there is no more to it. This viewpoint is shared by some managers. As one manager put it, "Thank goodness, bargaining is finished for this year. Now we can get down to business!"

Actually, this view of periodic bargaining recognizes only a part of the whole picture. From the behavioral point of view, *collective bargaining is a continuous process.* It is true that formal negotiations around a bargaining table take place only periodically; but after the contract is signed, a number of other parts of the bargaining process remain to be performed. The contract must be communicated to managers, employees, and union officers. After that, it must be interpreted. New situations, not exactly spelled out in the contract, always arise. They require management and union representatives to get together to try to interpret what the contract says or what they meant it to say. Decisions must be made concerning whether something is or is not covered by the contract.

Bargaining is continuous.

*Contract is
a living document.*

All the while, as these interpretations are being made, both parties ar
watching for flaws in their contracts so that they can introduce amendments a
the next negotiation period. They also are studying local, industrywide, an
nationwide labor relations developments to see how their own contract ma
be affected. This means that while the old contract is being interpreted (an
according to the way that it is interpreted), plans for negotiating a new
contract are under way. Truly, overall collective bargaining is a continuou
process, and the contract is a living document.

Planning for negotiations

In planning for negotiations, management first takes stock of the present state
of its labor relations, because each forthcoming bargaining period is buil
upon what has gone before. If labor relations are poor and the union i
antagonistic, the next bargaining session will tend to be antagonistic also
However, if labor relations have matured to a state of active cooperation
bargaining should be reasonable and responsible.

In appraising the current state of labor relations, management should no
overlook conditions within the union. If there is trouble here, it may spill ove
into the bargaining sessions. Is the union leadership competent? Are there
rivalries between two or more factions? Questions like these must be
considered in order to predict what kinds of attitudes the employer will face
across the bargaining table.

Top management, with the guidance of other members of management, i
responsible for developing the basic bargaining strategy.[8] It then appoints the
bargaining team and works with the team to develop an effective bargaining
plan. Usually the top manager assigns the actual bargaining process to the
labor relations director or another qualified manager.

*Supervisory
participation*

In planning for negotiations, top management needs to encourage participation by its supervisors and middle managers.[9] These are the people who
actually live with the current contract day by day, and they know much about
where it is weak and strong. Furthermore, these are the people who will
administer the new contract, and they will give the contract better support if
they can participate in the changes that are made. If their voice is heard—and
heard in advance—they should feel more responsible for making the contract
work.

> For example, management in one firm asked supervisors to report three times a week
> what the employees were talking about in their daily work. The personnel depart-
> ment organized the material and placed a report about employee thinking on the
> negotiating team's desk the next morning before negotiations started. This quick
> feedback was helpful to the team.

One or more supervisors often are included on the bargaining team. If they
are not, the team will lack the realistic touch with jobs that the union has,
because usually most union representatives are acquainted intimately with
day-to-day problems.

Constructive attitudes

Collective bargaining is a flexible, give-and-take group process. It depends upon both careful preparation and skillful maneuvering from a flexible position. If management takes extreme positions in its bargaining and consistently peppers the opposition with a categorical "No, we won't," it may have to waste much of its energy trying to withdraw itself from this unalterable position. Furthermore, this negative attitude sets the wrong emotional tone for bargaining sessions.

The role of attitudes

Some employers attempt to build constructive attitudes by having pre-negotiation conferences in which no direct bargaining confrontation takes place. The parties discuss mutual problems and try to obtain agreement on facts such as current wages and job classifications. In this way some agreement on the current situation is reached before agreement on new demands is sought.

Bargaining attitudes are important.[10] If managers do not accept the union or if union leaders do not accept management, bargaining sessions are likely to be emotional and hard-fought. Each group will be defensive because it will feel that its survival is being challenged. Individuals also will be defensive and emotional if they are personally challenged, and bargaining sessions will deteriorate into personal arguments.

> In one company an international union negotiator stated to the company president, "What do you know about the needs of the workers in the shop? You never did any manual labor and you're too fat to do a day's work now if you had to!" The president replied that the union representative did not have enough education to understand business anyway, so why bother to bargain. At this point bargaining ceased and personal insults began to fly from both sides. No bargaining was accomplished until the next session, several days later.

Bargaining procedures

Procedures for bargaining sessions have a significant influence on agreement, just as attitudes do. If bargaining procedures are not clear, each party never quite understands what the other is doing, and agreement becomes almost impossible until they can begin to communicate with each other.

Bargaining roles For example, what is the role of a lawyer at the bargaining table? Is the lawyer speaking as a bargaining representative of the employer, or only as a legal adviser? The same question also can be asked concerning an international union representative if one is present. The question of who will attend and represent the parties in bargaining sessions is an important one. Each side will have a chief negotiator, but usually more than one person will speak across the bargaining table as a negotiator. However, it is wise to limit the size of the negotiating committee, because this reduces human relationships to a reasonable number. If the group is small, all active negotiators can get to know each other fairly well as negotiations develop.

Who will do what?

Advisers and observers   It is common practice for both sides to have present a number of nonnegotiating advisers and observers. The advisers deal only with their own negotiators rather than across the table. The observers usually listen only. They often are used as a means of communicating the current state of negotiations to those who cannot attend. Management, for example, may have its supervisors attend bargaining sessions on a rotating basis. In some cases the supervisors select their own delegates. The union may encourage stewards or rank-and-file members to attend in order to keep them informed and to assure them that their union leaders are working diligently and making no "sellout" to management.

Bargaining tactics

Four typical tactics

There are a number of tactics that bargainers use to improve their bargaining.[11] Following are four tactics that typically are used.

Counterproposals   All negotiators use *counterproposals* in an effort to get the two sides closer together. A *counterproposal* is an offer suggested as an alternative to a previous proposal by the other party, in the hopes that both sides will find it more acceptable. To take an example, if the union asked for a 20-cent wage increase, management might offer a 16-cent increase to skilled workers and 8 cents to all others or offer a pension plan costing 12 cents in lieu of any wage increase. Since the union typically does most of the asking during negotiations, management will be wise to introduce whatever elements it can to reverse this one-way relationship and gain some initiative.

Trade-offs   Another tactic used is the *trade-off,* which is an offer to give up on one issue in exchange for "winning" another. For example, the firm may offer an additional paid holiday if the union will agree to more flexibility in work rules. Although neither side wants to give up its item, the exchange may be perceived as favorable to each.[12] Whereas counterproposals gradually move the two sides together, trade-offs can greatly expedite resolution of differences.

A recess   One important tactical device is a *recess*. It is obviously useful when negotiators become fatigued, but more importantly, it is a means for the bargaining committee to take a break to discuss some point privately. If members of a committee show disagreement among themselves, this may indicate weakness to the other side; so when a knotty problem arises, some member may request a recess. This allows either party to work out the problem in private and return to the meeting with a united front. A recess also gives one party time to work out of a difficult position. Just as a football team calls "Time out" when the going gets tough, a negotiating committee should recess to reconsider its position, assemble more information, develop a counterproposal, or consult higher authority.

Delay of items   When some negotiators reach an especially troublesome issue that is blocking negotiations, they request that it be tabled and then taken up in later meetings. They hope that meanwhile the situation will change to make the issue more easily resolved. In some bargaining sessions there is mutual agreement to begin negotiations with the easy or minor problems, gradually working up to the more difficult ones. Subcommittees may be used to get a difficult problem out of the mainstream of bargaining into the quieter environment of a smaller group.

Mediation   If an agreement cannot be reached, a *mediator* may be brought to the scene by one of the parties or by government. The mediator's role is that of an outside specialist who encourages the negotiating parties to come to an agreement. Mediators have wide experience and a fresh viewpoint, so they may be able to suggest settlements not previously considered. Mediators also help hold down emotionalism and use persuasion to try to get the parties to come to agreement.

What do mediators do?

From a human point of view, an important mediator role is that of confidential intermediary carrying messages and viewpoints from one party to the other. This enables the negotiators to sound out each other without formally committing themselves. Here is a simplified version of how this worked in one company.

> **Management hinted to the mediator that it might raise its wage offer to 24 cents if the union would drop the thorny union-security issue. The mediator, Roy Korman, hurried across the street to union headquarters and suggested that he might be able to get management to come up to 24 cents on its wage offer, but he didn't think management would accept union security. The union officers hinted that they couldn't sell that kind of package to the membership, but they might be able to sell a package that included a seventh holiday. After receiving that information, the mediator had another talk with management the next day, and so on.**

Other options

If mediation fails, two options for resolution of the impasse remain. One is a *strike,* which is a work stoppage called by a union to place bargaining pressure on management. The other alternative is *contract arbitration,* also called *interest arbitration,* which is primarily used in the public sector where the strike option is prohibited for most employees.[13] Contract arbitration is the use of a third party to make final and binding decisions on major bargaining issues. The decision then becomes part of the labor contract.

Strike

Contract arbitration

From a behavioral standpoint, there are both merits and weaknesses in interest arbitration. On the positive side, it does provide finality to negotiations, and the threat of arbitration may produce an incentive to negotiate. However, it may also discourage negotiators from bargaining seriously, because they know that the arbitration process usually results in compromise.[14] Clearly, there is no simple solution to the contract settlement process.

Problem-solving bargaining

Win-lose bargaining

A fundamental difficulty with the usual collective bargaining is that both management and labor approach it with a desire to win. Each prepares to do battle with the other. This is *win-lose bargaining,* because each party tries to win from the other party a favorable division of limited resources. Both parties come to the bargaining table ready to reject as unreasonable the other's demands. By expecting these things and preparing for them, each sets a relationship that tends to cause the expected conduct. Genuine collaboration becomes almost impossible. Since neither party wants to lose and both wish to win, either a bitter fight or a stalemate is likely to occur.[15] If the fight gets too rough or the stalemate goes too long, the government is called in, thus restricting the combatants' freedom and making them more dependent on others. Under these conditions government control probably will expand.

Though the situation described can be eased in various ways, the machinery of conflict is still there. What is needed is a different approach to bargaining. Behavioral science theory provides a framework for a better approach, already tried successfully by employers. This new approach recognizes union-management conflict as failures in problem solving. It attempts to help the group find the causes of its failures, and it directly treats these causes to restore mature relations. This is *problem-solving bargaining,* because it takes a problem-solving approach to get joint gain for both parties.[16]

Problem-solving bargaining can be successful.

In one small company the system worked as follows. All persons in a department met away from their work for a few days under the guidance of a behavioral scientist in order to discuss their perceptions of one another, their goals, and finally their problems. Supervisor, workers, steward, and staff were included. They presented to management a statement of their problems with desirable solutions. Each department did this separately.

Though the cost of these sessions was considerable, management and union for the first time had joint statements of needed changes from the work units themselves. These statements included items previously overlooked by both union and management, and they were developed in collaboration, not in bargaining. The result was a problem-solving climate for the customary bargaining sessions, and a new and superior contract was reached easily. This new contract had the support of employees because it came from them and fitted their needs.

Experience with problem-solving bargaining has shown that useful innovations can be made—innovations that will help the participants solve their own problems instead of depending on outside force. The theory and techniques of problem-solving bargaining should be able to improve collective bargaining. Some conflict is unavoidable, but it is questionable whether the whole bargaining process needs to have a conflict orientation, as it usually does in traditional win-lose bargaining.

Contract settlement and maintenance

Understanding is essential.

When agreement is reached on any issue, it should be put into writing as clearly and concisely as possible, because people with different education, interests, and backgrounds will use it. A contract clause is no good unless most readers can get the same meaning out of it. The contract is written to stabilize relationships rather than confuse them. Legal terminology should be at a minimum, because most of those who will use the contract are not lawyers. Though the contract must be correct legally, it also must command the emotional respect of the parties involved; and it will not do this if they cannot understand it. Contract clauses can be tested for meaning by having them read by supervisors and workers who have not attended negotiations and have only the written words to depend upon.

Signing the contract is only part of the job to be done. The next step is to communicate it to those who will work under its rules. Copies are usually printed for each supervisor and steward, and it is common practice to provide each worker with access to a copy. When there are major contract changes, management may decide to hold meetings with supervisors to explain the new clauses. Union leaders may do the same for their stewards. Since employer and union goals in this instance are the same—better understanding of the contract—joint meetings sometimes are held. In this way supervisors and stewards get identical instructions and are shown that management and union have mutual interests in correctly interpreting their contract. Separate meetings, on the other hand, give the impression that there are separate management and union positions regarding the contract.

Joint meetings are helpful.

Although line managers will do most of the contract interpretation, usually the industrial relations staff is responsible for advising managers on difficult interpretations and following up to see that interpretations are consistent. In the final analysis a collective-bargaining contract is merely a word symbol of the agreement that is in the minds of the groups involved. The same contract words can be interpreted and acted upon in many different ways depending on how people feel about them; so the participants try to build sound overall labor-management relations in order to get maximum effectiveness out of their contract.

GRIEVANCE SYSTEMS

A *grievance system* is a formal system by which disputes over working rules are expressed, processed, and judged in an organization. Grievance systems are used in both unionized and nonunionized organizations.[17] The systems provide a means by which alleged wrongs may be reasonably and fairly resolved among organizational members. Disputes will arise in any organization, and grievance systems offer a socially acceptable way for people to claim their perceived rights and occasionally to save face.

Grievances

A grievance is defined as any real or imagined feeling of personal injustice that an employee has about the employment relationship. (In some unionized organizations, a grievance is narrowly limited to mean "any protested violation of the labor agreement.") This feeling does not have to be expressed to become a grievance. Neither does it have to be true or correct. A feeling

Definition

that arises from imaginary conditions or from incorrect reasoning is still a grievance if it causes a feeling of injustice. Usually, but not always, the term "grievance" applies only to one's personal feeling of injustice. If Joe feels that Mary has been treated unjustly, Joe does not have a grievance. However, if Joe feels that both he and Mary have been treated unjustly on the same matter, procedures usually permit Joe to present his grievance both for himself and as an agent of all others similarly treated. In this way one dissatisfied employee may present a grievance for a hundred others. When Joe formally expresses his grievance in the grievance system, it is said that he "files" a grievance. If he states it informally, it sometimes is called only a complaint or a gripe.

Quite often a distinction is made between a real grievance and a stated grievance. Employees sometimes do not know precisely what is making them dissatisfied. Their own feelings may set up mental blocks that prevent them from interpreting correctly what is happening. They may not have sufficient knowledge of human nature or of the many forces affecting them. Not knowing their actual grievances but still feeling dissatisfied, they tend to file grievances about something else. When management corrects this "something else," both management and the worker find to their surprise that dissatisfaction still exists because of some real grievance yet uncovered. Even when the real grievance is known, a worker may disguise it out of fear that it will not make sense to management. Here is an example.

> Rudy Miles, a semiskilled machine operator, filed a grievance saying that he was not given an automatic seniority wage increase that was due him. Both the seniority and wage-increase systems were complicated, so management thought that it may have been a mistake or that Rudy justifiably could be confused. Careful investigation disclosed that Rudy was not due an increase according to the labor contract, and management spent nearly an hour at two grievance levels trying to explain the rules to him. He did not seem convinced and kept answering, "Yes, but . . . ."
>
> Finally an experienced personnel clerk who was present concluded that there was something behind this stated grievance, because Rudy kept referring to what "other workers" received. When the conversation was turned in this direction, Rudy soon disclosed that a fellow worker who was hired the same day had said, "I got a 2-cent seniority increase on my last check. Did you?" This was Rudy's real grievance, but he did not want to state it this way because it might embarrass his friend if it was untrue. As soon as Rudy was assured that his friend did not get the raise, his grievance vanished.

Many grievances are directed as much against other workers as they are against management. An example is a jurisdictional dispute.

> In one factory semiskilled machinists claimed the right to operate certain new automated machines, but toolmakers said the machines were their responsibility. When management assigned the machines to the toolmakers, the machinists filed a grievance saying that the new machines required only semiskilled work which machinists were supposed to perform, even though they admitted that the new machine work was slightly more difficult than the work they had been doing.

Grievance rates

A *grievance rate* usually is stated in terms of the number of written grievances for 100 employees in one year. So many factors affect grievances that a low rate is not necessarily desirable, because it may mean that grievances are suppressed. Neither is a high rate absolute evidence of poor labor relations. A typical grievance rate is 5 to 20; however, well-managed organizations with mature labor relations have developed lower rates.

Typical grievance rates

Employees of all types and at all levels develop grievances. They are not some headache brought about by unions. Some of the factors affecting grievance rates are management, unions, union steward needs,[18] grievance procedures, job conditions, government rules, general social conditions, and the home environment. Management can alter some of these causes, but in other cases its job is to work out a reasonable accommodation to them.

> The experience of International Harvester Company shows how grievance procedures and organizational climate can affect grievance rates. At one time it had a high annual grievance rate of 27.5 per 100 employees. It also had a high proportion of grievances going to the central level for probable arbitration. In a thirteen-year period over 100,000 grievances went to the central level!
>
> Recognizing a serious problem, top officials of both union and company worked hard to shift attitudes toward problem solving and to install a new program calling for settlement at the local level when the grievance was first presented orally. Local settlement was attempted even if this meant calling the superintendent, labor relations director, time-study specialist, and others to the workplace. People came to the problem, instead of having it sent in writing to them. The program was remarkably successful. Attitudes materially improved. More important, in the two years following the new program, not one grievance went to the central level, and fewer than ten were put into writing.[19]

Generally, effective contract administration tends to reduce grievances. Fair, open, and prompt treatment of problems that arise tends to reduce the misunderstandings that are the underlying causes of many grievances. Increased participation also is an effective way to reduce grievances. When employees share in decision making about working conditions, they have fewer reasons to file grievances about their work.

Benefits of grievance systems

Benefits of grievance systems are shown in Figure 17-3. Probably the principal benefit of any grievance system is that it encourages human problems to be brought into the open so that management can learn about them and try corrective action. The social organization of a plant is much like a complicated machine in the shop. Both need constant attention and frequent adjustment.

Open communications

Grievances are symptoms that should be studied carefully to determine the real causes of this "human machine" breakdown. They signal that part of the human organization is not functioning properly and needs readjustment. It

---

- Help make employee problems known.
- Encourage solution of problems before they become serious.
- Help prevent future problems.
- Give employees emotional release for their dissatisfactions.
- Help establish and maintain a working relationship in the group.
- Provide a check and balance on arbitrary management actions.

Figure 17-3
Benefits of
grievance systems

---

matters not that a grievance is invalid according to the technical terms of the labor contract; it is still a grievance and a symptom of social imbalance in some trouble spot somewhere. Any attempt to disregard it, smother it, or "throw it out of court" on some technicality will be largely ineffective because it still exists and will try to find expression in some other way.

Another benefit of grievance systems is that they help to catch and solve problems before they become serious. If problems are left unsolved, their collective pressure may become large enough to cause a major breakdown in labor-management relations. Or they may grow within an employee, becoming more difficult to adjust. The unhappy employee tends to communicate with others and to spread dissatisfaction.

A related benefit is grievance prevention. Almost everyone agrees that it is better to prevent fires than to try to stop them after they start, and the same philosophy applies to grievances. A good solution to one grievance may keep twenty others from arising.

Emotional release

A grievance system also is a way of giving employees emotional release for their dissatisfactions. It provides a procedure for an aggrieved employee to become aggressive and strike back at the controls required by an organization. Emotional release often plays an important role in individual grievance cases. Union leaders sometimes carry a losing case higher in the grievance procedure "just to make the employee happy." They hope that as the case moves upward, ill feelings will decline and the employee will become more cooperative. Even workers who do not use the grievance system for their own emotional release feel better because they know the system is there to use if needed. It gives them a sense of emotional security.

Another benefit of grievance systems is that they help establish and maintain a work culture or way of life. Each group has its own particular way of living together, and the grievance procedure helps develop this group culture. As problems are interpreted in the grievance procedure, the group learns how it is expected to respond to the policies that have been set up.

*A check and balance
on management*

A further benefit of grievance systems—one that managers often fail to see—is the simple fact that the system's existence provides a check and balance on arbitrary and capricious management action. Managers tend to give more care to human relations when they know that some of their actions are subject to challenge and review in a grievance system. They are put on guard to make sound decisions so that they are not placed in the embarrassing position of having to defend their poor judgment in the grievance system. They are encouraged to develop effective compromises and working relationships with their groups. However, the pendulum can swing too far. Supervisors may become so aware of the grievance system that they are afraid to make decisions and hesitate to discipline employees. In this situation the supervisor's capability vanishes.

Grievance procedures

A grievance procedure is the method by which a grievance is filed and carried through different "steps" (decision levels) to an ultimate decision. Most procedures start with the supervisor and the grievant, have from three to six steps, and usually have arbitration as the last step. Other details vary greatly.[20]

Figure 17-4 shows a grievance procedure in one company. It begins when the employee or employee's representative discusses the grievance with the supervisor. This perhaps is the key step. It gives the supervisor and employee an opportunity to work out their own problems before the grievance is written down. Skills in areas such as transactional analysis and consideration, discussed in earlier chapters, can help the supervisor reduce conflict and solve the problem at this early stage.

A sample procedure

If the grievance cannot be settled in step one, then it is reduced to writing and presented formally to the supervisor. This gives the supervisor and employee a second opportunity to solve their own problems. Usually a written management reply is required at this step and later steps. If no settlement is reached at step two, then the steward as a representative of the union presents the grievance to the department head. If settlement still cannot be reached, the grievance goes to top management for a final company-union effort. If there is no agreement, either party eventually may take the grievance to arbitration.

Time limits   Reasonable speed in processing a grievance is important. Most procedures establish time limits at each step so that delays cannot be used as excuses to prevent settlement. The supervisor who delays a grievance actually strengthens the grievant's cause, since the delay convinces the grievant that the grievance is a sound one that the supervisor is afraid to face.

Supervisory attitudes   The supervisor's attitude toward grievances can be a long step toward their settlement. Some workers fear supervisory retaliation if they present a grievance, especially if they win it. It is important for

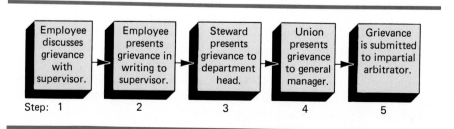

Employee discusses grievance with supervisor.	Employee presents grievance in writing to supervisor.	Steward presents grievance to department head.	Union presents grievance to general manager.	Grievance is submitted to impartial arbitrator.
Step: 1	2	3	4	5

FIGURE 17-4
A company grievance procedure.

supervisors to convince workers that they want to hear grievances and to settle them. Supervisors should approach grievances in a problem-solving frame of mind, rather than with the idea "This is a fight—it's either them or me." There is a need for discussion that moves rationally toward a mutual solution, instead of argument that emotionally seeks to provide a winner. All possible facts—including how people feel—should be gathered before making a decision.

Grievance arbitration

As a grievance moves to higher steps, it becomes less a person-to-person discussion and more a group problem involving several union and management representatives. If the grievance is not settled at the highest company level, labor or management may submit it to *arbitration,* which is final and binding decision by a third party or parties.[21] The arbitrator's decision stands only until the next collective-bargaining negotiation, at which time the parties can negotiate any contract changes they wish. The arbitrator's role is merely to stabilize contract meaning during the life of the contract.

The interpretation of what the existing contract means is called *grievance arbitration.* It is distinguished from arbitration to establish new contract terms, which was discussed earlier as contract arbitration. The former is a method of grievance settlement, while the latter is a temporary substitute for collective bargaining. Management and labor generally support the former but oppose the latter because it takes settlement power out of their hands.

From the behavioral point of view, the chief benefits of grievance arbitrators are that they are outsiders who bring a fresh perspective, they are not emotionally involved in the dispute, and they can render a final decision that usually is enforceable in the courts. Their decisions, however, can be painful to an inept management, as illustrated by the following situation.

> Mary Byrne was discharged for smoking on a stair landing in a dangerous chemical operation. Discharge was clearly within the rules for this offense. When the case came to arbitration, however, she claimed that the company had discriminated against her, since many employees smoked on the landing and were still doing so. She challenged the arbitrator to count the cigarette butts on the floor. True enough, when the arbitrator and the representatives of both parties went there, they found cigarette butts all over the place. Mary was reinstated immediately with back pay.

Problems with arbitrators   A weakness of arbitrators is that they usually lack personal knowledge of the organization's way of life, which may cause them to make unrealistic decisions. Another weakness is that they may overlook human values and render a legalistic decision based on technical evidence. They also lack personal responsibility for the continuing labor-management relationship because they often step out of the picture as soon as a decision is rendered. Some of these weaknesses are overcome by appointing a permanent arbitrator to arbitrate all issues for a period of time.

UNION RESPONSE TO
THE POSTINDUSTRIAL LABOR FORCE

CHAPTER 17:
WORKING
WITH
UNIONS

391

Unions have worked effectively with bargaining and grievances during the last century, and it is certain that their influence will continue. However, unions often are less effective in some organizational behavior areas such as serving the diverse and changing needs of the labor force.

A postindustrial labor force

The basic problem is that the postindustrial labor force has changed toward the characteristics shown in Figure 17-5, but labor unions have not always changed adequately to serve these new needs. In the postindustrial society, labor is more educated and knowledge-oriented. It also is more employed in service occupations instead of industrial ones. Higher earnings have made labor more affluent with television sets and other conveniences in most worker homes.

New characteristics

The postindustrial force also has changed value systems and lifestyles. There is less emphasis on the work ethic and more emphasis on leisure activities and other satisfactions. The labor force is upwardly and geographically mobile. Its white-collar, professional, and knowledge orientations cause it to be more identified with upward growth and with management than workers were a century ago.

With regard to the postindustrial labor force, one analyst comments, "Because we are living in the postindustrial era, future problems for the unions are rooted in the radically changed labor market."[22] A labor analyst explains labor-force changes in the following manner:[23]

Increasing education, changing values, and the strong urge to move up the socioeconomic ladder have created a less militant worker. Unions also face serious difficulties in responding to the needs and interests of educated, upwardly mobile employees. These upwardly mobile people feel that they would lose self-esteem if they became card-carrying union members. At the same time, public attitudes toward corruption

---

- Knowledge orientation, in contrast to manual-skill orientation
- Education
- Service occupations, in contrast to industrial occupations
- Affluence
- Changed value systems
- Different lifestyles
- Less emphasis on work ethic than in 1900–1950
- Upward and geographic mobility
- More white-collar and professional occupations, in contrast to blue-collar
- Some identification with management

Figure 17-5
Characteristics of the postindustrial labor force, 1980–2000+

in some unions, violence on the picket lines, and the open confrontations of organizing efforts have created psychological barriers which many workers are afraid to cross. In fact, white-collar and professional workers prefer to identify with management, given half a chance to do so.

Individual needs

One issue is individual needs. The union often has bypassed individual needs in favor of standardization, uniformity, and equal treatment for everyone. What can be done to make the inflexible procedure, the airtight contract, and the unionwide standard apply to individual situations? Growing pressures to think in global terms have caused issues to become symbolized in statistical norms and settled in central headquarters, leaving the individual isolated on the sidelines. Union benefits are largely general, applying to the group. The individual may be overlooked or even abused, as in the "Coventry" incident at the end of this chapter.

Higher-order needs

Affluence and other developments have made higher-order needs important in a postindustrial society.[24] Can labor unions adjust their practices to serve them effectively? These higher needs are not easily served by nationwide norms. What is required is more emphasis on job enrichment, human resources, and human growth along channels that are desirable to each employee personally.

A postindustrial labor relations lifestyle

The postindustrial society and labor force require adaptations by *both* labor and management. The trends toward computer-assisted manufacturing and the use of industrial robots require widespread retraining of workers for jobs demanding higher-level skills. To accomplish these challenging tasks, labor and management need to reexamine the value of their adversary positions and develop a new labor relations lifestyle for themselves. This new lifestyle

Cooperation and integration are needed.

will probably include a trend away from industrywide bargaining and settlements, the emergence of joint labor-management and problem-solving committees, and more cooperation to serve the new needs of workers, customers, and the community.[25] The frameworks of organizational behavior suggest that integrated efforts are necessary to develop a production system that better serves human needs in a postindustrial society.

SUMMARY

The union introduces additional formal and informal organizations at work. Two major union-management activities are collective bargaining and grievance systems. Collective bargaining is negotiation between representatives of management and labor to accomplish a written agreement covering terms and conditions of employment. It essentially is a social process for balancing pressures of two groups that have a mutual interest in employment conditions. It is regulated by the National Labor Relations Act and other legislation.

Grievance systems have fairness and justice as their goal. A grievance is any real or imagined feeling of personal injustice that an employee has about the employment relationship. Grievance systems help bring grievances into the open so that corrective action can be taken (1) to adjust a current grievance and (2) to prevent future grievances.

The postindustrial society presents new needs for both labor and management. There is a postindustrial labor force with stronger individual needs and higher-order needs. These new conditions probably require labor and management to move toward a more cooperative labor relations lifestyle in order to serve human needs better.

TERMS AND CONCEPTS FOR REVIEW

National Labor Relations Act

Collective bargaining

Mediation

Strike

Interest arbitration

Win-lose bargaining

Problem-solving bargaining

Grievance

Grievance rate

Grievance arbitration

Postindustrial labor force

REVIEW QUESTIONS

1 Discuss the human implications of adding a second formal organization (the union) to the employment relationship.

2 Have you ever belonged to a union? If so, discuss with your group how it affected you and your job.

3 In what ways is it possible for labor legislation to influence human relationships at work? Discuss.

4 In what ways is collective bargaining a human problem as distinguished from an economic and a technical problem? Discuss.

5 Discuss the idea that collective bargaining is a continuous process.

6 Have you ever filed a grievance? If so, discuss in the classroom how it worked. If not, interview a worker who filed a grievance and give a classroom report about how it worked.

7 Discuss interest arbitration and grievance arbitration. How are they similar? How are they different?

8 Using library sources, read five arbitration decisions (or summaries of them) and comment on the types of problems that went to arbitration, how successful management and unions were in winning an arbitration, and your view of how fair the arbitrator's decision was.

9 Discuss the characteristics of the postindustrial labor force and how well you think labor unions are meeting its needs.

INCIDENT

(*Note:* The following incident also relates especially to the two chapters on the individual and on the informal organization. The case is a complete news article from an Australian daily newspaper.)

A Victim Back from Coventry, by Alex Harris[26]

Keith Digney, a pressure welder at the State Electricity Commission's Muja power station at Collie, has become a victim of his own convictions.

Mr. Digney's beliefs came into conflict with his unionist working mates—and he was sent to Coventry and declared [unacceptable to the group].

Men he had worked with for nearly 10 years refused to speak to him on or off the job.

They refused to touch any equipment he touched, and raised demarcation issues over actions as simple as picking up a hammer.

After six weeks he decided to call it quits because, as he said yesterday, he did not like standing around doing nothing.

He is a Christadelphian and his beliefs prevent his joining a union or a political party. Six years ago he was granted exemption from union membership by the Industrial Commission.

He had been declared [unacceptable] before, but had battled it out and avoided trouble during strikes by taking leave without pay.

About two months ago, however, the issue of his beliefs arose again when he refused to subscribe to a Metal Trades Union's fighting fund—a so-called voluntary contribution [to a political fund] which Mr. Digney claimed was not enforceable by law.

The Industrial Commission was called in to arbitrate and Mr. Digney agreed to pay an equivalent sum to a charity. But union representatives refused to compromise.

Mr. Digney said the word went out that he had to go. He is still puzzled why it took six years to decide his presence at the power house was intolerable.

He did not mind being sent to Coventry.

"What bothered me was standing 'round doing nothing all day," he said.

"I was getting paid for it but I have to work for my money; I don't like taking it under false pretences."

"The SEC didn't want me to leave and things were beginning to ease up a little at the power house but I knew they would not get better if I stayed."

"The same thing would have happened again so I got another job to make peace for all concerned."

The move cost Mr. Digney his 10 years' long service leave which would have come up this year.

"Of course I'll miss it but money is not my first concern," he said. "Money is not my god."

He and his wife do not feel bitter about the experience.

"We know what our beliefs are," Mr. Digney said.

"And men are the same everywhere."

"I suppose you could say it was a question of human rights and freedom of belief but I didn't expect these arguments to have any weight."

"If anything, I feel sorry for the men who took part in the ban. Sooner or later you reap what you sow."

QUESTIONS

1 Comment on the human relations and union-power implications of this case.

2 Discuss possible reasons why employees acted the way that they did in this case. What can management do to improve situations of this type?

REFERENCES

1 Donald N. Scobel, "Business and Labor: From Adversaries to Allies," *Harvard Business Review,* November–December 1982, p. 129.

2 L. L. Cummings, "Review Symposium," *Industrial Relations,* Winter 1982, p. 83.

3 Worker dissatisfaction, especially that caused by unresponsive and poor management, is associated with union activity. See Jack Fiorito and Charles R. Greer, "Determinants of U.S. Unionism: Past Research and Future Needs," *Industrial Relations,* Winter 1982, pp. 1–19; and W. Clay Hamner and Frank J. Smith, "Work Attitudes as Predictors of Unionization Activity," *Journal of Applied Psychology,* August 1978, pp. 415–421.

4 John A. Fossum, *Labor Relations: Development, Structure, Process,* rev. ed., Homewood, Ill.: Dorsey Press, 1982. For a system that measures the quality of labor relations in an organization, see Lawrence L. Biasatti and James E. Martin, "A Measure of the Quality of Union-Management Relationships," *Journal of Applied Psychology,* August 1979, pp. 387–390.

5 For a discussion of collective bargaining where no history exists, see John J. Hoover, "Negotiating the Initial Union Contract," *Personnel Journal,* September 1982, pp. 692–698.

6 For views on public employee collective bargaining, see the special section on "Collective Bargaining in the Public Sector," *Business Horizons,* August 1979, pp. 46–60.

7 Dan Lacey, "What Will Workers Want in Post-recession America?" *Personnel Administrator,* May 1983, pp. 71–73ff. In the interview reported there, Ben Fischer suggests that our society is still unsure about the role of bargaining for public-sector employees.

8 Jeb Brooks and Earl Brooks, "The Role of Top Management in Negotiations," *MSU Business Topics* (Michigan State University), Summer 1979, pp. 16–24.

9 Ronald L. Miller, "Preparations for Negotiations," *Personnel Journal,* January 1978, pp. 36ff.

10 One successful method for improving bargaining attitudes is "Relationships by Objectives," developed by the Federal Mediation and Conciliation Service. See Harvey A. Young, "The Causes of Industrial Peace Re-visited: The Case for RBO," *Human Resource Management,* Summer 1982, pp. 50–57.

11 A conceptual model that predicts labor relations outcomes under a variety of circumstances is in Jon Prooslin Goodman and William R. Sandberg, "A Contin-

gency Approach to Labor Relations Strategies," *Academy of Management Review,* January 1981, pp. 145–153.

12 A special form of trade-offs, concession bargaining, achieved popularity in the mid-1980s when the changing balance of power forced many unions to give up rights and conditions they had previously won. See D. Quinn Mills, "When Employees Make Concessions," *Harvard Business Review,* May–June 1983, pp. 103–113; Scott A. Kruse, "Giveback Bargaining: One Answer to Current Labor Problems," *Personnel Journal,* April 1983, pp. 286–292; and (for examples in the auto, meatpacking, and steel industries) the BNA editorial staff, "Givebacks Highlight Three Major Bargaining Agreements," *Personnel Administrator,* January 1983, pp. 33–35ff.

13 Richard Johnson, "Interest Arbitration Examined," *Personnel Administrator,* January 1983, pp. 53–57. For a different view, see Patricia Compton-Forbes, "Interest Arbitration Hasn't Worked Well in the Public Sector," *Personnel Administrator,* February 1984, pp. 99–104.

14 The pros and cons of compulsory arbitration of bargaining issues are reviewed in David E. Bloom, "Is Arbitration Really Compatible with Bargaining?" *Industrial Relations,* Fall 1981, pp. 233–244. One experimental method to overcome the reluctance to bargain in good faith is final-offer arbitration, discussed in Max H. Bazerman and Margaret A. Neale, "Improving Negotiation Effectiveness under Final Offer Arbitration: The Role of Selection and Training," *Journal of Applied Psychology,* October 1982, pp. 543–548.

15 Figure 10-1 presented a matrix of the various win-lose combinations.

16 Discussions of the problem-solving approach include Donald F. Ephlin, "The UAW-Ford Agreement—Joint Problem Solving," *Sloan Management Review,* Winter 1983, pp. 61–65; and Richard P. Nielsen, "Stages in Moving toward Cooperative Problem Solving Labor Relations," *Human Resource Management,* Fall 1979, pp. 2–8.

17 James P. Swann, Jr., "Formal Grievance Procedures in Non-union Plants," *Personnel Administrator,* August 1981, pp. 66–70.

18 Steward needs for achievement, autonomy, and dominance tend to be associated with the number of grievances the steward files; see Dan R. Dalton and William D. Todor, "Manifest Needs of Stewards; Propensity to File a Grievance," *Journal of Applied Psychology,* December 1979, pp. 654–659.

19 Robert B. McKersie, "Avoiding Written Grievance by Problem-Solving: An Outside View," *Personnel Psychology,* Winter 1964, pp. 367–379.

20 Thomas F. Gideon and Richard B. Peterson, "A Comparison of Alternate Grievance Procedures," *Employee Relations Law Journal,* Autumn 1979, pp. 222–233.

21 Arbitration issues are discussed in James W. Robinson, "Some Modest Proposals for Reducing the Costs and Delay in Grievance Arbitration," *Personnel Administrator,* February 1982, pp. 25–28; William B. Werther, Jr., and Harold C. White, "Cost Effective Arbitration," *MSU Business Topics,* Summer 1978, pp. 57–64. Other approaches are presented in Mollie H. Bowers, "Grievance Mediation: Another Route to Resolution," *Personnel Journal,* February 1980, pp. 132–139; and in Paul F. Salipante and John D. Aram, "The Role of Organizational Procedures in the Resolution of Social Conflict," *Human Organization,* Spring 1984, pp. 9–15.

22 Robert Schrank, "Are Unions an Anachronism?" *Harvard Business Review,* September–October 1979, p. 110.

23 Jerome M. Rosow, "American Labor Unions in the 1980s," *IRRA Newsletter* (Industrial Relations Research Association), November 1979, pp. 1, 4.

24 A comprehensive discussion of societal changes is Alvin Toffler, *The Third Wave,* New York: William Morrow & Company, Inc., 1980; John Naisbitt, *Megatrends: Ten New Directions Transforming Our Lives,* New York: Warner Books, 1982; and Alvin Toffler, *Previews and Premises,* New York: William Morrow & Company, Inc., 1983.

25 Audrey Freedman and William E. Fulmer, "Last Rites for Pattern Bargaining," *Harvard Business Review,* March–April 1982, pp. 30–32ff; and Paul J. Champagne, "Using Labor-Management Committees to Improve Productivity," *Human Resource Management,* Summer–Fall 1982, pp. 67–73. A more conservative view of probable changes is in "The Future of Industrial Relations: A Conference Report," *Industrial Relations,* Winter 1983, pp. 125–131.

26 Alex Harris, "A Victim Back from Coventry," Perth, Australia: *The West Australian,* April 16, 1974, p. 1. Copyright 1974. Reprinted with permission of West Australian Newspapers, Limited.

FOR ADDITIONAL READING

Bacharach, Samuel B., and Edward J. Lawler, *Bargaining: Power, Tactics, and Outcomes,* San Francisco: Jossey-Bass, Inc., 1981.

Elkouri, Frank, and Edna Elkouri, *How Arbitration Works,* Washington, D.C.: The Bureau of National Affairs, 1976.

Kochan, Thomas A., *Collective Bargaining and Industrial Relations,* Homewood, Ill.: Richard D. Irwin Co., 1980.

Mares, William J., and John Simmons, *Working Together: From Shopfloor to Boardroom,* New York: Alfred A. Knopf, 1983.

Pruitt, Dean G., *Negotiation Behavior,* New York: Academic Press, 1981.

Raiffa, Howard, *The Art and Science of Negotiation,* Cambridge, Mass.: Harvard University Press, 1982.

Siegel, Irving H., and Edgar Weinberg, *Labor-Management Cooperation: The American Experience,* Kalamazoo, Mich.: W. E. Upjohn Institute for Employment Research, 1982.

Walton, Richard E., and Robert B. McKersie, *A Behavioral Theory of Labor Negotiations,* New York: McGraw-Hill Book Company, 1965.

CHAPTER

EQUAL EMPLOYMENT OPPORTUNITY (EEO)

The intent of . . . EEO laws is to bring about social equity.

James A. Belohlav and Eugene Ayton[1]

An individual may be extremely knowledgeable regarding the legal side of discrimination and yet, without consciously being aware of it, *still discriminate in decisions.*

Kenneth A. Kovach[2]

CHAPTER OBJECTIVES

TO UNDERSTAND:
Social benefits of EEO
Legal requirements for EEO
Enforcement of EEO
Protected groups and affirmative action
Company programs for EEO
Job adjustment and retirement of older workers

E very organization likes to think that its employees are a cohesive group that is "one big, happy family." Employees are one family to the extent that they are loyal to the organization and believe in its objectives. On the other hand, employees in almost any organization are also divided into subgroups of different kinds. As discussed in earlier chapters, mutual similarities such as age, type of work, rank in the organization, and social interests cause employees to relate themselves in all sorts of intricate subgroups. These are the "happy little families" that together constitute the "one big, happy family" about which employers dream.

Formation of employee groups is determined by two broad sets of conditions. First, *on-the-job* differences and similarities cause people to align themselves into groups. Throughout this text, attention is given to these on-the-job conditions that underlie the separation of workers into different interest groups, such as office and production workers. It is now appropriate to emphasize the second set of conditions—those arising primarily *off the job*—because they may relate to equal employment opportunity.

In the first part of this chapter we discuss equal employment opportunity and laws relating to it. Then we examine how it applies to various employee groups.

EQUAL EMPLOYMENT OPPORTUNITY AND THE LAW

Equal employment opportunity (EEO) is the provision of equal opportunities to secure jobs and earn rewards in them, regardless of conditions unrelated to job performance. EEO is supported by federal, state, and local *equal opportunity laws*. State and local laws also may be called *fair employment practices laws*. These laws prohibit job discrimination based on specific nonjob conditions, such as race, color, religion, national origin, sex, and age (within certain age ranges). The laws also prohibit discrimination against handicapped individuals in a number of circumstances. All EEO laws prohibit discrimination with regard to both (1) securing employment and (2) terms and conditions of work after employment.

What is EEO?

Discrimination based on job performance is permitted as a necessary and desirable employment activity. Employers can legally reward high performers and penalize inadequate performers. The law merely requires rewards and punishments to be related to performance or seniority rather than nonperformance factors such as race. Equal opportunity, therefore, implies *unequal results,* because people will differ in their skills, effort, and performance. Some will rise higher than others, but the American dream is that all shall have an equal opportunity to do so.

For example, a federal court upheld the dismissal of a woman flight attendant who had alleged sex discrimination. She was suspended six times for exceeding the airline's weight limits as they related to reasonable appearance and safety standards for flight attendants. When she failed to meet standards after the sixth suspension, she was dismissed. The court concluded that the flight standards were a legitimate employer requirement related to the nature of the business and that dismissal was not for reason of the employee's sex. The standards were applied equally to male and female flight attendants and the six suspensions gave the employee adequate time to correct her deficiency.

Discrimination vs. prejudice

There is an important difference between discrimination and prejudice. Discrimination is an action, while prejudice is an attitude of mind. One may occur without the other. Discrimination may unintentionally occur without prejudice, and likewise prejudice may exist without any act of discrimination. The law focuses on an employer's actions, not feelings. If actions lead to discriminatory results, they are unlawful regardless of the employer's good intentions.

> For example, the Primrose Company posted its new job vacancies on the company bulletin board so that employees could learn about them and recommend their friends for employment. It had loyal employees, so it was able to fill most of its vacancies with the bulletin board system. Finally a black applicant brought charges that the selection method involved unlawful discrimination against blacks. Subsequent investigations showed that the firm had mostly white employees who usually recommended other whites, so the result was discrimination against blacks, even though the company did not intend to discriminate.

Social benefits and problems

The social benefits of EEO are substantial. As summarized in Figure 18-1, EEO gives equal access to jobs for those who want work and are willing to develop themselves to perform a job successfully. In this way it reinforces the American dream of equal opportunity for all people. EEO ensures that more of the labor force—such as women and minority groups—can work, thus leading to higher family earnings. There also may be higher national output because a larger proportion of the labor force is working.

Figure 18-1
Potential social benefits of EEO

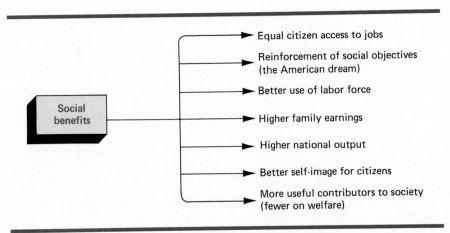

Social benefits

- Equal citizen access to jobs
- Reinforcement of social objectives (the American dream)
- Better use of labor force
- Higher family earnings
- Higher national output
- Better self-image for citizens
- More useful contributors to society (fewer on welfare)

Equal opportunity gives more people a chance to grow toward their potential. By providing fair access to jobs, it builds the self-image of people and encourages them to be useful members of society. In some instances this process may change receivers of government benefits into useful contributors of taxes to government. Welfare can be reduced, and people can become more self-reliant. In general, when EEO can be successfully implemented, it offers many potential benefits compared with costs.

In some instances the social costs and benefits of EEO efforts may be calculated. An example is a training program to improve job skills of minority job seekers. A researcher calculated that the costs of the training amounted to $1010 for each trainee, but social benefits for the first year amounted to $2034. These social benefits were primarily the higher earnings, production, and taxes paid. They did not include such intangible social benefits as possible lower crime rates, reduced cost of welfare services, and similar benefits. When social benefits were considered over a period of years, it was shown that in five years benefits were nearly nine times costs and in ten years they were nearly fifteen times costs.[3]

There have been a number of social problems associated with EEO. As individuals sought their legal rights, both they and their employers incurred tremendous legal costs; the administrative expense of fair employment programs has created an additional burden. Also, management has lost some of the autonomy it previously enjoyed in hiring decisions, as the courts laid down strict guidelines to follow. Another problem has been EEO's challenge to the seniority system in many firms. To preserve jobs for recently hired minorities when work force cutbacks are made, seniority rules have been forced to bend, thereby disrupting existing social patterns. Although the *intent* of EEO is highly positive, its net *effects* must be judged in the light of both its benefits and the problems it has caused.[4]

EEO has caused problems.

Federal EEO laws

The major federal laws that govern EEO are summarized in Figure 18-2. These laws are passed by Congress and enforced by the executive branch of the government. They are supplemented by executive orders of the President, which seek to ensure compliance with EEO policies in federal agencies and among certain government contractors. When conflicts arise between (1) federal laws and (2) state and local laws, usually the federal law dominates. As can be seen in the figure, the federal laws apply very broadly to most major employers, employment agencies, union hiring halls, and federal, state, and local governments.

Title VII of the Civil Rights Act   Title VII of the Civil Rights Act of 1964 as amended is the dominant law governing EEO. It requires employers, labor unions, and employment agencies to treat all people without regard to race, color, religion, national origin, sex, or age in all phases of employment. This includes hiring, training, apprentice programs, promotions, job assignments, and other personnel actions. Certain exceptions are allowed, primarily with

Laws relevant to EEO

MAJOR EQUAL EMPLOYMENT OPPORTUNITY LAWS	OBJECTIVES	JURISDICTION
Equal Pay Act (1963)	Equal pay for equal work regardless of sex	Employers engaged in interstate commerce and most employees of federal, state, and local governments
Title VII of the Civil Rights Act (1964) (As amended in 1972)	EEO for different races, colors, religions, sexes, and national origins	Employers with fifteen or more employees; unions with fifteen or more members; employment agencies; union hiring halls; institutions of higher education; federal, state, and local governments
Age Discrimination in Employment Act (1967) (As amended from age sixty-five to seventy in 1978)	EEO for ages forty to seventy	Employers with twenty or more employees; unions with twenty-five or more members; employment agencies; federal, state, and local governments
Vocational Rehabilitation Act (1973)	EEO and reasonable affirmative action for handicapped people	Federal government agencies and government contractors with contracts of $2500 or more
Pregnancy Discrimination Act (1978)	EEO during pregnancy	Same as Civil Rights Act

Figure 18-2
Major federal laws governing EEO

regard to employment with religious organizations and "in those certain instances where religion, sex, or national origin is a bona fide occupational qualification (BFOQ) reasonably necessary to the normal operation of that particular business or enterprise" (sections 702 and 703). An exemption also is provided to allow use of seniority for job assignments and layoff protection in many instances.

Other legislation   Prior to the Civil Rights Act, the Equal Pay Act in 1963 provided equal pay for equal work regardless of one's sex. Practices of any type that gave men or women different pay for the same or substantially similar work were prohibited. One year later (1964) the Civil Rights Act initiated a major national effort for equal opportunity, including Title VII, which provided EEO. Several congressional acts followed.

In 1967 Congress passed the Age Discrimination in Employment Act, which (as later amended) provided EEO for people between ages forty and seventy. It was felt that younger people until age forty can compete for themselves in the labor market, but beginning with age forty and for the remainder of their expected working life until age seventy they need protection to help them compete equally with others.

In 1973 the Vocational Rehabilitation Act was passed to give handicapped people EEO. It applies both to government as an employer and to government contractors with contracts of $2500 or more. Since most major employers have government contracts of one type of another, this act covers most of the job market. Then in 1978 Congress passed the Pregnancy Discrimination Act as an amendment to the Civil Rights Act. The Pregnancy Discrimination Act provides EEO to those able to work during pregnancy. Equal opportunities for medical benefits and leaves of absence are included.

Executive orders EEO also is supported by executive orders of the President. They apply to federal agencies and to most government contractors, and they have approximately the same coverage as federal EEO laws. They are enforced by the executive branch of the government.

Enforcement

Equal Employment Opportunity Commission Most EEO laws are enforced by the *Equal Employment Opportunity Commission* (EEOC). It has offices in major cities and can initiate court action against noncomplying businesses. Enforcement begins when a charge is filed by an aggrieved person, someone acting for the aggrieved person, or one of the EEOC commissioners. Charges also can be filed with an approved state agency, which is allowed a limited time to settle the case before it comes to the EEOC.

EEOC

If there is reason to believe that a violation has occurred, the EEOC seeks a *conciliation agreement.* It is a negotiated settlement acceptable to the EEOC and all aggrieved parties. If concilation fails, court action may be initiated by the EEOC or the individual involved (or the Attorney General if a public employer is involved). Remedies include back pay to injured parties and required affirmative action programs.

Conciliation agreement

For example, in a court settlement, a textile company agreed to pay a settlement of $875,000 to eighteen blacks. They alleged discrimination in employment and promotion. After their complaint was filed, the case worked its way through the EEOC and the courts for a number of years while the company contested the allegation. During this period the potential liability for back pay continued to grow, so the settlement was large when it finally was made.

Federal contract compliance Enforcement against government contractors is secured through the Office of Federal Contract Compliance Programs. The office may cancel contracts or reach various types of conciliation agreements with a contractor in order to avoid contract cancellation.

For example, the Office of Federal Contract Compliance Programs made an agreement with a coal company concerning seventy-eight women who alleged employment discrimination. Coal mining traditionally has been a man's work, but under the law qualified women have equal opportunity for employment in it. The company agreed to pay the women $370,000 in order to comply with Executive Order 11246, which concerns sex discrimination by government contractors.

State and local fair employment practice agencies   In a similar manner state agencies can order a variety of settlements, particularly back pay. For example, the Fair Employment Practice Commission in California ordered a city to return an employee to the job and pay $80,000 in back pay. The employee, a native of India, alleged discrimination because of national origin, and the commission supported the allegation.

Protected groups

What are protected groups?

Since EEO laws are designed especially to protect certain groups of people from employment discrimination, these groups are called *protected groups.* For example, a black person typically is considered a member of a protected group but a white person is not. Similarly, women are a protected group but men are not. However, a fifty-year-old white male is a member of a protected group because of his age. A person needs to fit only one of the protected categories in order to be a member of a protected group. Because of the large number of people in certain protected categories, such as women and older employees, protected groups consist of more than three-fourths of the labor force. EEOC enforcement activities are directed primarily toward protection of the interests of these groups.

Affirmative action

Affirmative action is an employer effort to increase employment opportunity (including promotion and all other conditions of employment) for protected groups that appear to be inadequately represented in a firm's labor force. Employers are encouraged by government agencies and public pressures to examine their labor force and ensure that all groups are fairly represented. If they are not, companies may begin *affirmative action programs* as evidence that they are making a positive effort to provide equal employment.

Why create affirmative action programs?

The objectives of affirmative action programs are to remedy any alleged past discrimination and qualify employers to serve as government contractors. Employers often develop timetables by which they will accomplish certain goals, especially placement of an improved proportion of under-represented groups in various jobs and levels of the organization.[5] The goals typically apply to minorities, women, employees between the ages of forty and seventy, and handicapped employees.

Affirmative action programs are common among employers. These programs may be required by the EEOC or the courts, and they are a business necessity for large employers who wish to qualify for government contracts.

For example, a large New York bank was required by the U.S. District Court in New York to install an affirmative action program for women at a cost of over $1 million.[6] The bank was required to:

● Provide academic counseling for women employees wanting a college degree.

● Provide tuition to enroll women bank officers in management-level programs in local colleges.

- Offer a one-week career development program for 400 female professional employees.

- Publicize vacancies in supervisory, professional, and managerial jobs.

- Establish a self-evaluation program for female supervisory and professional employees.

Reverse discrimination

Affirmative action occasionally leads to *reverse discrimination,* by which there is discrimination against an employee not included in an affirmative action program. For example, in the bank affirmative action program just described, the bank was required to provide college tuition for women bank officers. If similar tuition is not available to men bank officers on an equal basis, they may consider themselves victims of reverse discrimination.

While affirmative action programs seek to accomplish desirable social goals, they also have an adverse impact on those employees who suffer reverse discrimination because of them. They want equal employment opportunity, and they argue that the way to end discrimination against some is not to begin discrimination against others—particularly those who do not bear responsibility for past discrimination. The groups favored by affirmative action reply that it is required to compensate for past discrimination and improve employment of underrepresented groups. They sometimes favor *proportional employment* or *parity employment,* which means that an organization's employees should approximately represent the proportions of different groups in the local labor force or population. For example, if the labor force has 20 percent racial minorities, then supervisors also should be about 20 percent racial minorities.

Proportional employment

The law supports EEO for all people, but the courts have sometimes interpreted the law in different ways. In one decision, the Supreme Court stated that Title VII "does not demand that an employer give preferential treatment to minorities or women," and it refused to support reverse discrimination.[7] In other instances the courts have supported it.

A notable case was Steelworkers v. Weber, decided by the U.S. Supreme Court in 1979.[8] Weber, a white employee, claimed that he was bypassed for an in-plant craft training program because of an affirmative action program that reserved 50 percent of the training positions for blacks until the percentage of black craft workers was approximately equal to the percentage of blacks in the local labor force. Weber alleged discrimination based on his race.

Weber's claim was supported by the District Court and the Circuit Court of Appeals, but the Supreme Court rejected it. The Court said that voluntary affirmative action programs to boost employment opportunities for minorities are legal.

From the human point of view, there are substantial questions of equity in affirmative action practices when they cause reverse discrimination. They can lead to employee frustration, tension, conflict, turnover, decreased satisfaction, and other negative feelings that harm work relations.[9] In addition, a basic long-run issue is whether parity employment will be abandoned after acceptable equality in the work force is achieved, or whether it will become entrenched in law and custom, thereby making job structures rigid and reducing free job choice by workers.

EEO PROGRAMS

Basic requirements

Elements of EEO programs

An effective EEO program has a number of basic requirements, as shown in Figure 18-3.[10] The first requirement is to develop positive policy statements. Strong top-management support is required, and consultants and task forces may be used to provide specialized aid. Usually responsibility for applying an EEO program is assigned to the personnel department, but in small firms the job may be assigned to another office as a part-time duty.

Identify problem areas   Another requirement is to gather data to identify problem areas. Information is sought about such items as seniority, salary, education, promotions, and employment of different groups.

> For example, there may seem to be no discrimination problem regarding women in a public school or retail store, because most of its employees are women. However, the data may show that the majority of managerial and better-paying professional jobs are held by men. In another organization the data may show that less pleasant and dirtier blue-collar jobs have been given to certain minorities, while women and nonminorities have been given more pleasant, higher-status, cleaner jobs.

The purpose of the statistics is to help identify areas of probable discrimination, but it should not be assumed that every instance of unequal representation is proof of discrimination. There are many other reasons for unequal representation, such as education of employees. The data only provide a base for more investigation.

Identify and develop protected groups   A further requirement is to identify and develop minorities and other protected groups that have potential for promotion. An important point is to assure them that EEO is available. In the past they may have felt discriminated against, so they were discouraged from

---

Figure 18-3
Requirements for an effective EEO program

- Develop positive policy statements.
- Ensure top management support.
- Assign responsibility for applying the program.
- Gather data to identify problem areas.
- Identify and develop people in protected groups who have potential for promotion.
- Develop recruitment activities that reach protected groups as well as others.
- Communicate to maintain awareness of the program.
- Build supervisory support for the program.
- Appraise and follow up to ensure compliance.

developing themselves and seeking promotion. In one office, for example, when equal employment became a reality, a number of women and black employees became interested in self-development plans for possible promotion. Prior to equal employment, they showed only minor interest in self-development.

Develop equal recruitment　An additional requirement is to be sure that there are equal recruitment activities for all types of people. Recruitment cannot be confined to familiar channels, or to contacts through friends, in a way that might perpetuate dominance of one sex, race, or ethnic group in certain jobs such as that of engineer. Recruitment should be done in ways that reach all types of potential employees, and any advertising should portray equality in all types of jobs. For example, a telephone company attracted favorable attention with a recruiting advertisement showing a woman climbing a telephone pole as part of a telephone line crew. The EEOC is encouraging both men and women to move into what is called *nontraditional employment,* or jobs not historically held by members of that sex. Examples include a woman becoming a crane operator or a man becoming a secretary.[11] The policy is to encourage a climate in which all jobs are equally acceptable to all types of employees.

EEOC supports nontraditional employment.

Following are some of the affirmative action recruitment efforts made by one employer trying to meet employment goals encouraged by the EEOC.

1　Selective recruiting in high schools having large numbers of minority students

2　Selective recruiting in colleges having large numbers of blacks, women, and ethnic groups

3　Establishment of a recruiting office in a minority neighborhood

4　Selective advertising in newspapers appealing to protected groups

5　Hiring of recruiters who are members of protected groups

6　Special training programs for recruits who were weak in employable skills

Communicate about program　Another requirement is communication within the organization to maintain constant awareness of the EEO program. In many instances when a program begins, training sessions are held with all managers to explain the program to them. Supervisors are given special training to make them more aware of different work attitudes and values among protected groups.

Build supervisory support　Supervisory support especially is necessary because supervisors are the point of direct contact with employees. EEO and affirmative action programs may complicate their employment activities and increase their paperwork. Often EEO leads to a loss of their traditional power, because some of their decision making is transferred to the personnel department and higher management. In some instances work-group conflict is increased as new people are integrated into the work group. For these reasons, supervisory training often is essential to assure EEO understanding and support.

One company discovered that its supervisors had built-in expectations of failure for certain minority employees. When this expectation came into contact with occasional new employee expectation of failure, the result was a high failure rate. The company's solution was to train its supervisors. Now all supervisors take a special three-day training course designed to improve their attitudes toward all protected groups.

Appraise program   A final requirement is appraisal and follow-up. If EEO is important, then the managerial appraisal and reward system must reflect this policy, because managers tend to emphasize the practices on which they are appraised. Follow-up also provides both a basis for correcting deficiencies in the program and evidence that EEO is being accomplished.

Application of EEO programs to various protected groups is discussed in the following sections.

Race, color, and national origin

EEO laws generally prohibit job discrimination on the basis of race, color, or national origin. The United States historically has been called a "melting pot" of people from all parts of the world, so it is important to give these people equal access to jobs regardless of their backgrounds. In this way they have a fair chance to earn their way into the mainstream of society and become self-sufficient. One of the major problems remaining is integration of minorities into professional and managerial jobs, because movement into these jobs requires substantial time for education, training, and growth. However, positive action can bring progress.

One company found that its number of minority managers was relatively low. It began a strong affirmative action program, and in five years increased its proportion of black managers from 2.2 to 5.5 percent and Hispanic managers from 0.7 to 2.1 percent. When EEOC investigated the company's compliance with EEO laws, it determined that the company's steady progress substantially complied with the law.

Sex

Job discrimination with regard to sex is prohibited.[12] However, employers may establish job requirements that could be related to one's sex, provided the requirements clearly are necessary for the job. For example, an employer may employ only female fashion models to model women's clothing. Also, a feed mill that requires employees to lift 100-pound bags probably can continue this requirement, even though it could lead to the rejection of more women job applicants than men. There are, however, relatively few jobs with specialized requirements of this type.

Firms need to establish careful monitoring programs to ensure that sex discrimination does not occur, because sometimes it may occur without conscious intent or even knowledge.

A large bank was feeling the effects of a recession, so it needed to reduce its corporate lending staff. Six female lending officers were transferred to positions with less prestige in other areas. More than seventy male corporate lending officers were left in the lending office. (Can you speculate about reasons for this action? Was the selection of six women merely a matter of chance, or was it intentional? Did the selecting executives think that male lending officers presented a better image to clients? Did the executives simply have more confidence in male friends that they knew better? What were the reasons?)

When the monitoring program revealed that only women had been transferred, the bank quickly took corrective action.

Sexual harassment is the process of making employment or promotion decisions contingent on sexual favors, or engaging in any verbal or physical conduct that creates an offensive working environment (see Figure 18-4). It can occur anywhere in a company, from executive offices to assembly lines. From a human point of view, it is distasteful and demeaning to its victims, and it is discriminatory according to EEO laws and EEOC guidelines.[13] In the absence of a preventive program, employers may be responsible for the harassment actions of their supervisors and employees. When it occurs, employers may be liable for reinstatement of the victim, back wages, and other damages. Most victims of sexual harassment are women, but there have been instances in which men were victims.[14]

Sexual harassment is discriminatory.

In order to provide equal opportunity regardless of sex, employers have developed policies to prevent harassment. They also have conducted training programs to educate employees about the relevant law, actions that could constitute harassment (see Figure 18-4), possible liabilities, and the negative effects of harassment on its victims.[15] For example, some victims have required psychological counseling.

Religious beliefs

With regard to religious beliefs of employees, the law requires that employers make a reasonable effort to accommodate a worker's religious needs. Acceptable company efforts include actively seeking qualified substitutes, providing a flexible work schedule, redesigning the job, or transferring the employee to another position.[16] If all accommodation efforts would place an undue hardship on the company or on other employees, then they are not

Companies must attempt accommodation.

Unwelcome sexual advances, requests for sexual favors, and other verbal or physical conduct of a sexual nature constitute sexual harassment when:

(1) submission to such conduct is made either explicitly or implicitly a term or condition of an individual's employment,

(2) submission to or rejection of such conduct by an individual is used as the basis for employment decisions affecting such individual, or

(3) such conduct has the purpose or effect of unreasonably interfering with an individual's work performance or creating an intimidating, hostile, or offensive working environment.

Figure 18-4
EEOC definition of sexual harassment
From Equal Employment Opportunity Commission's Guidelines on Discrimination Because of Sex, 1604.11 (Sexual Harassment), November 10, 1980.

required. For example, a company is not required to violate its seniority agreement with the union in order to accommodate an employee who wants all Saturdays off. Neither is it required to pay overtime regularly to other employees or require them to work double shifts in order to replace an employee who is absent for religious needs. As stated by the U.S. Supreme Court in a ruling concerning an airline employee, the law does not "require an employer to discriminate against some employees in order to enable others to observe their Sabbath."[17]

Employers, however, may make accommodations that go beyond the requirements of law if workers who are affected agree and have equal opportunity for similar accommodations.

Mark Jones faithfully observed his Sabbath on Saturday. When he applied for a job, he learned that Saturday work sometimes was required, so he told his potential employer about his needs. Since only a few employees were required to work on any Saturday, management arranged with other employees in the department to do Mark's work on Saturday when it was required. In turn, Mark agreed to an equal amount of Sunday work for others when it was required. The agreement operated for many years without any difficulty.

Any temporary religious absence that Mark requests, such as a day off to attend a religious conference, is handled according to the standard procedure for personal leave.

Handicapped employees

Who are the handicapped?

Handicapped employees are those with a significant disability of some type, either physical, mental, or emotional. They include people with a prison record, major obesity, or a history of heart disease, cancer, or mental illness, since others might view them as handicapped.[18] Also included are rehabilitated alcoholics and drug abusers, as discussed in Chapter 16.

The Vocational Rehabilitation Act requires employers who are federal contractors to provide EEO for handicapped employees. Many employers, such as 3M, Control Data, and Sears, already had a long history of providing employment for handicapped people, but the law applied these types of programs to most other employers.[19] They can require handicapped employees to meet the same productivity standards as other employees, but there must be a reasonable effort to accommodate those who are handicapped. A typical program is built on an affirmative action plan, including a variety of actions to remove physical, social, and other barriers to employment.

Figure 18-5 shows the Tennessee Valley Authority affirmative action program for handicapped employees. The figure especially illustrates the complexity of an effective program. A policy statement and employment program are only the beginning. There must be education and training to prepare both supervisors and other employees. Changes may be required in building entrances, locker rooms, and other physical facilities. Job modifications frequently are required so that certain jobs can be performed by handicapped employees. In addition, much coordination is required among departments and with various external organizations.

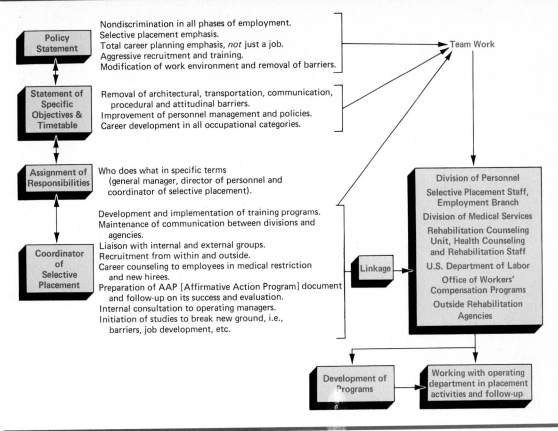

Policy Statement

Nondiscrimination in all phases of employment.
Selective placement emphasis.
Total career planning emphasis, *not* just a job.
Aggressive recruitment and training.
Modification of work environment and removal of barriers.

Statement of Specific Objectives & Timetable

Removal of architectural, transportation, communication, procedural and attitudinal barriers.
Improvement of personnel management and policies.
Career development in all occupational categories.

Assignment of Responsibilities

Who does what in specific terms
(general manager, director of personnel and coordinator of selective placement).

Coordinator of Selective Placement

Development and implementation of training programs.
Maintenance of communication between divisions and agencies.
Liaison with internal and external groups.
Recruitment from within and outside.
Career counseling to employees in medical restriction and new hires.
Preparation of AAP [Affirmative Action Program] document and follow-up on its success and evaluation.
Internal consultation to operating managers.
Initiation of studies to break new ground, i.e., barriers, job development, etc.

Team Work

Linkage

Division of Personnel
Selective Placement Staff, Employment Branch
Division of Medical Services
Rehabilitation Counseling Unit, Health Counseling and Rehabilitation Staff
U.S. Department of Labor
Office of Workers' Compensation Programs
Outside Rehabilitation Agencies

Development of Programs

Working with operating department in placement activities and follow-up

Figure 18-5
Tennessee Valley Authority's affirmative action program for handicapped employees
From "A Comprehensive Model for a Handicapped Affirmative Action Program" by Gopal C. Pati and Edward F. Hilton, Jr. Reprinted with permission of Personnel Journal, *Costa Mesa, Calif., copyright © February 1980.*

Employer programs   The supportive philosophy of most employer programs is to focus on employee abilities, not disabilities. In spite of disability, nearly all handicapped people have remaining abilities to perform some jobs effectively. It is the employer's responsibility to identify those jobs, prepare applicants for them, and make reasonable modifications in the jobs so that they can be performed effectively.

A large bank in Chicago has a successful senior transcriptionist who is blind.[20] Some job modifications were made to accommodate her, such as providing additional desk space for her seven-volume braille dictionary. Employees in her department formerly performed both transcription and typing of written material. Now the job is redesigned so that the blind employee performs only transcription work, which she does virtually error-free, and other employees mostly type written material.

Performance results   Most employers find that properly placed handicapped employees can perform their jobs as well as other employees.[21] In many instances handicapped employees compensate for their disabilities, such as being more regular in attendance or giving more effort to the job. For example, some firms report both lower absenteeism and less turnover for handicapped employees.

In some instances a handicapped employee may be better able to perform a job than one who is not handicapped because the handicap becomes a job advantage rather than disadvantage. For example, a blind employee may have an acutely developed sense of hearing that is an advantage in a certain job, or a deaf employee may be less distracted by noises.

> Tony Valente was deaf. He worked in a noisy machine-shop office in a clerical job that required intense mental concentration. Prior to the time that Tony took the job, turnover in the job was high. Employees stayed from three days to six months and complained that the noise distracted them, increased their errors, and reduced the minutes of actual work that they could do in an hour. When Tony took the job, he adapted to it easily. Communication with others took more time because of his handicap, but this loss was more than offset by the gain from his ability to concentrate better on the job.

OLDER WORKERS

Employment of older workers will be discussed in more detail in order to illustrate additional behavioral issues involved.

EEO

Why protect older workers?

The Age Discrimination Act of 1967 (as amended in 1978) provides EEO for employees from ages forty to seventy.[22] The law recognizes that people now live longer, that many older people are in good health and able to work after sixty-five, and that many of them want to work beyond sixty-five. In addition, inflation reduces the real value of retirement benefits and savings for some older workers, so they need to work longer to maintain a satisfactory standard of living.

People between the ages of forty and seventy are a protected group, so employers need to take the usual actions to assure that older employees actually have EEO. Areas of action include employment, training opportunities, rates of pay, promotions, reasonable adaptation to physical limitations, and eventual retirement.

> For example, a manufacturing company laid off several of its middle managers who were under age seventy. It said that their work was unsatisfactory and that they were unable to keep up with the fast-moving pace of change. They filed charges of age discrimination and eventually won back pay and an opportunity for reinstatement. In a few instances the company was able to prove unsatisfactory performance, so the charges brought by these managers were dismissed.

Job adjustment of older workers

As workers grow older, they have many adjustments to make. With regard to organizational behavior, older workers tend to develop gradually into social groups that are often separate from younger workers. Their interests and even their day-to-day conversations are different. Older workers become less able to take part in active sports such as company softball. The important point is that these changes need to take place without causing older employees to feel socially isolated and insecure. They need to be accepted and understood—to be respected for what they have to offer, rather than penalized for what they cannot help. Age comes alike to all persons, so management, unions, and work groups need to recognize their responsibility to build an organizational climate that accepts and integrates older workers. In this way they can be assured of genuine EEO in their older years.

Performance of older workers   Generally the job performance of older and younger workers is about the same.[23] Although there are many variations, a typical situation is that infirmities associated with age often are offset by improvements of other types, so total performance remains about the same. For example, some older workers need to work at a slower pace, but they compensate for this deficiency by improving dependability, quality of work, attendance, and effort. Perhaps the greatest difficulty faced by older workers is job changes that upset established job patterns and may cause their jobs to become obsolete. These kinds of situations can be threatening.

Older workers perform well.

Job placement profile charts   Improved EEO for older workers can be encouraged by using *job placement profile charts* to match worker physical and mental abilities with a job's requirements.[24] The profile chart displays an evaluation of both job requirements and worker abilities for key features of the job so that management can easily determine how well a worker fits a job. With the aid of proper counseling for job placement, profile charts have helped older workers reduce absences and sick leave and continue effective work for a longer period of time.

Figure 18-6 displays a profile chart for an older worker in an office job. The worker is a reasonably suitable match except for eyesight. Perhaps the employee's eyesight can be corrected in some way, as with better eyeglasses. If not, perhaps the job can be changed to require less effective eyesight or the employee can be reassigned to a job with less stringent requirements. One older worker, for example, was moved from a standing job to a sitting job, and that worker's sick leave declined from an excessive amount to zero for the next sixteen months.

Easing the transition into retirement

Retirement tends to be one of life's most difficult adjustments. Suddenly a worker moves from a full-time job to no job, so a feeling of uselessness can be overwhelming.

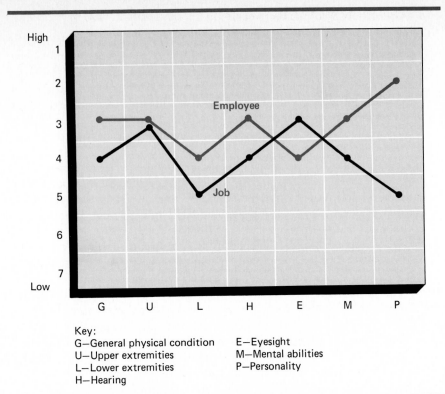

Figure 18-6
Profile chart for
job placement of
an older worker
in an office job

Key:
G—General physical condition   E—Eyesight
U—Upper extremities   M—Mental abilities
L—Lower extremities   P—Personality
H—Hearing

Consider the case of Mack McGuire, whose department is holding a retirement dinner for him. There he stands at the head of the table fiddling with the watch the company just gave him. He is choked with emotion and fishing for the right words to tell how he feels inside. A month ago he was willing and able to work, but now he is seventy and—according to a company and union agreement—must retire. He knew retirement was coming, but he never did want to think about it before because the subject was too painful. Suddenly he realizes that retirement is upon him, and he panics at the thought of it.

Two programs for better transition

Preretirement counseling   Retirement, like one's own funeral, is something many employees would rather not think about, so employers develop programs that encourage employees to think about pending retirement.[25] These programs usually are called *preretirement counseling*. One necessary subject is pension choices and insurance benefits that will be available after retirement. Since a major concern of workers after retirement is income maintenance, they often welcome counseling of this type. Other counseling topics include financial management, possible hobbies, and emotional problems associated with retirement.

Another subject with a significant influence on retiree satisfactions is health,[26] so firms may provide health guidance prior to retirement. Workers are encouraged to develop good health maintenance patterns so that they can maintain these patterns after retirement.

Phased retirement   Another way to soften the transition to retirement is to give workers more time off, usually with pay, in the years immediately preceding retirement.[27] This is called *phased retirement*. It allows workers to become accustomed to being away from work and learning to enjoy other activities.

A few European firms have generous phased retirement plans.[28] One firm allows workers beginning at age sixty-one to have one-half day off each week with pay. With each advancing year, the amount is increased one-half day, so that at age sixty-four a worker has two days off each week with pay. The worker then should be better prepared for retirement at age sixty-five.

Another company provides workers with two additional weeks of paid leave beginning at age sixty-one. This amount is increased gradually until, at age sixty-four, workers receive twelve summer weeks and eight other weeks with pay.

SUMMARY

Equal employment opportunity is the provision of equal opportunities to secure jobs and earn rewards in them, regardless of conditions unrelated to job performance. It is public policy because of the social benefits that it can provide. The primary federal laws that apply EEO are Title VII of the Civil Rights Act, the Equal Pay Act, the Age Discrimination Act, the Vocational Rehabilitation Act relating to handicapped persons, and the Pregnancy Discrimination Act. People protected by these laws are called protected groups. The principal areas of protection are a person's race, color, religion, national origin, sex, age, and handicap.

EEO laws are enforced primarily by the Equal Employment Opportunity Commission. It requires major employers to have affirmative action programs, which occasionally may result in reverse discrimination. EEO presents many difficult behavioral issues such as social integration of minorities into work groups, group conflict, individual and group power, sexual harassment, religious freedoms, and adaptations for handicapped and aged employees.

TERMS AND CONCEPTS FOR REVIEW

Equal employment opportunity (EEO)

Equal Employment Opportunity Commission (EEOC)

Conciliation agreement

Protected groups

Affirmative action

Reverse discrimination

Proportional and parity employment

Sexual harassment

Job placement profile charts

Preretirement counseling

Phased retirement

REVIEW QUESTIONS

1 Survey your classroom group to determine how many of you currently are members of a protected group. How many are members of more than one protected group at the present time? Assuming that EEO laws remain the same, how many of you are likely to be members of a protected group twenty-five years from now?

2 Form into research groups to study and discuss the potential benefits and problems that appear to be associated with EEO as currently enforced. Present your report to the entire classroom group, and discuss it compared with reports of other groups.

3 Do you think some job discrimination is justified? Consider such instances as the denial of certain jobs to people below certain ages; the hiring of relatives by the owners of small businesses; and, for certain government jobs, the giving of preference to veterans of military service. If some of this discrimination is justified, how will that which is equitable be distinguished from that which is not equitable?

4 Read current EEO information and then prepare an affirmative action program for women in an organization of your choice.

5 Contact three local organizations, and ask them what their policy on sexual harassment is. Present your findings to the class, and compare them to Figure 18-4.

6 Discuss the use of job placement profile charts for older employees. What problems and benefits do you see in their use?

7 Review the idea of phased retirement programs. What equity issues might arise when younger employees discover that some workers are receiving full pay for reduced time at work?

8 Read some additional information about affirmative action. Conduct a class debate, highlighting its strengths and weaknesses.

9 Report to the class whether you have ever felt that you were the victim of reverse discrimination. If you were, discuss the circumstances, how you felt, and how it was resolved.

INCIDENTS

Border Electronics

Border Electronics is an electronic assembly plant in a community near the Mexican border. About 60 percent of employees are Mexican-Americans, and a few others are Mexican citizens. This firm had a rush order that required steady work from all employees and no leaves of absence. This order extended through September 16, the Independence Day of Mexico. This holiday and surrounding days are elaborately celebrated by the Mexican-American community; however, the company strongly needed full attendance of all employees during this period.

To ensure attendance, department superintendent Max Ways wrote a directive, as was his usual practice with employees, stating that no leave would be granted to anyone during the holiday period because the rush order was not completed.

Another superintendent, Arleigh Watkins, called his employees together in his usual way and explained the problem in detail in both English and Spanish. He stated that he could allow leaves only to a few people who were on entertainment committees and had other special reasons for absence. He appealed for the cooperation of all employees to continue working because of the rush order.

QUESTION

Appraise the different ways in which the two superintendents approached their employees. Discuss the probable absence rates in the two departments during the holiday period.

Mary Scroggins

Mary Scroggins graduated from Northwestern University in accounting. Immediately after graduation she was employed effective July 1 by the local office of a national accounting firm. During the employment process Mary was told that her normal hours of work would be 8:30 A.M. to 5 P.M., Monday through Friday, but that overtime work might sometimes be required, particularly in the months immediately preceding the income tax deadline of April 15. Mary belongs to a Christian denomination whose Sabbath is on Saturday, and she is an active and devout member of her church. At the time of employment the accounting firm did not inquire about her religion because it wished to comply fully with the Civil Rights Act concerning race, religion, creed, and national origin. Mary likewise did not mention her religion at this time.

During the following six months Mary proved to be a capable and loyal employee. Her performance was above average for her team, and her supervisor, Royce Mathis, remarked to his manager how pleased he was to have Mary in his group. He felt that, assuming she continued to grow, she had potential for promotions within the firm.

As the income tax period approached, Mary's supervisor began preparing overtime schedules for his group. Based upon past practice and consensus within the group, all overtime was scheduled on Saturdays. When Mary's supervisor discussed the tentative schedule with her, she said she would not work on Saturday because of her religious belief. In fact, her religious belief required her to stop work before sundown Friday.

QUESTIONS

1 Discuss the organizational behavior issues raised by this incident and what Royce Mathis should do to solve them.

2 Perform library research on EEO law and discuss how it might influence Royce's actions in this situation.

REFERENCES

1 James A. Belohlav and Eugene Ayton, "Equal Opportunity Laws: Some Common Problems," *Personnel Journal,* April 1982, p. 285.

2 Kenneth A. Kovach, "Subconscious Stereotyping in Personnel Decisions," *Business Horizons,* September–October 1982, p. 60.

3 Loren C. Scott, "The Economic Effectiveness of On-the-Job Training: The Experience of the Bureau of Indian Affairs in Oklahoma," *Industrial and Labor Relations Review,* January 1970, pp. 220–236.

4 Belohlav and Ayton, op. cit., pp. 282–285. Other problems with EEO are discussed in Thomas I. Chacko, "Women and Equal Employment: Some Unintended Effects," *Journal of Applied Psychology,* February 1982, pp. 119–123; and Janisse Klotchman and Linda L. Neider, "EEO Alert: Watch Out for Discrimination in Discharge Decisions," *Personnel,* January–February 1983, pp. 60–66.

5 The use of goals versus numerical quotas has not been completely resolved. See Stephen P. Swanson, "Affirmative Action Goals: Acknowledging the Employer's Interest," *Personnel Journal,* March 1983, pp. 216–220; and "Quotas under Attack," *Business Week,* April 25, 1983, pp. 95–96.

6 "Court Approves Chase Manhattan Million-Plus Affirmative Action Program," *Fair Employment Digest* (American Society for Personnel Administration), September 1979, p. 4. For a detailed discussion of an affirmative action program, see Lee Dyer and Elizabeth C. Wesman, "Affirmative Action Planning at AT&T: An Applied Model," *Human Resource Planning,* vol. 2, no. 2, 1979, pp. 81–90.

7 "Supreme Court Rules on Title VII," *Washington Vantage Point,* April 1981, p. 1.

8 *United Steelworkers of America v. Brian F. Weber,* U.S. Supreme Court, June 27, 1979. For a discussion of the Weber and other major Supreme Court decisions on EEO, see Neil D. McFeeley, "Weber versus Affirmative Action?" *Personnel,* January–February 1980, pp. 38–51.

9 Benson Rosen and Thomas H. Jerdee, "Coping with Affirmative Action Backlash," *Business Horizons,* August 1979, pp. 15–20.

10 Advice for EEO officers is in Robert L. Jauvits, "The Corporate EEO Officer and Limits of Lawful Protest," *Personnel Administrator,* Feburary 1983, pp. 31–32ff; and Jeffrey C. Pingpank, "Preventing and Defending EEO Charges," *Personnel Administrator,* February 1983, pp. 35–40.

11 One study of successful nontraditional employment is Edward J. Clynch and Carol A. Gaudin, "Sex in the Shipyards: An Assessment of Affirmative Action Policy," *Public Administration Review,* March–April 1982, pp. 114–121.

12 Further discussion of EEO for women may be found in Corine T. Norgaard, "Problems and Perspectives of Female Managers," *MSU Business Topics,* Winter 1980, pp. 23–28; and a special section on "Women in Management," *Personnel Administrator,* April 1980, pp. 22–64.

13 A comprehensive review of the relevant case law is in Robert H. Faley, "Sexual Harassment: Critical Review of Legal Cases with General Principles and Preventive Measures," *Personnel Psychology,* Autumn 1982, pp. 583–600.

14 "Abusing Sex in the Office," *Newsweek,* Mar. 10, 1980, pp. 81–82. See also Donald J. Petersen and Douglass Massengill, "Sexual Harassment—A Growing Problem in the Workplace," *Personnel Administrator,* October 1982, pp. 79–89; and Jennifer James, "Sexual Harassment," *Public Personnel Managment Journal,* Winter 1981, pp. 402–407.

15 George K. Kronenberger and David L. Bourke, "Effective Training and the Elimination of Sexual Harassment," *Personnel Journal*, November 1981, pp. 879–883; and Gedaliahu H. Harel and Karen Cottledge, "Combatting Sexual Harassment: The Michigan Experience," *Human Resource Management*, Spring 1982, pp. 2–10.

16 Charles J. Hollon and Thomas L. Bright, "Avoiding Religious Discrimination in the Workplace," *Personnel Journal*, August 1982, pp. 590–594.

17 "Supreme Court Eases Task of Employers in Meeting Religious Needs of Workers," *The Wall Street Journal*, Western ed., June 17, 1977, p. 4.

18 Discussion of excessive weight as a handicap is in Eric Matusewitch, "Employment Discrimination against the Overweight," *Personnel Journal*, July 1983, pp. 446, 449–450.

19 Examples of these corporate programs are in Gopal C. Pati and Glenn Morrison, "Enabling the Disabled," *Harvard Business Review*, July–August 1982, pp. 152–153ff.

20 Gopal C. Pati and John I. Adkins, Jr., "Hire the Handicapped—Compliance Is Good Business," *Harvard Business Review*, January–February 1980, pp. 14–22.

21 Linda J. Strom and Gerald R. Ferris, "Issues in Hiring the Handicapped: A Positive Outlook," *Personnel Administrator*, August 1982, pp. 75–81; and Sara M. Freedman and Robert T. Keller, "The Handicapped in the Workforce," *Academy of Management Review*, July 1981, pp. 449–458.

22 For discussions of the Age Discrimination Act and its implications, see Jerry M. Wahl and H. M. Shatshat, "Controversy over the Issue of Mandatory Retirement," *Personnel Administrator*, October 1981, pp. 25–28ff; and Benson Rosen, Thomas H. Jerdee, and John Huonker, "Are Older Workers Hurt by Affirmative Action?" *Business Horizons*, September–October 1982, pp. 67–70.

23 Extensive discussions of age and performance are in Jeffrey Sonnenfeld, "Dealing with the Aging Work Force," *Harvard Business Review*, November–December 1978, pp. 81–92; and Nigel Nicholson, Colin A. Brown, and J. K. Chadwick-Jones, "Absence from Work and Personal Characteristics," *Journal of Applied Psychology*, June 1977, pp. 319–327.

24 The job placement profile chart is adapted from Michael D. Batten, "Application of a Unique Industrial Health System," *Industrial Gerontology*, Fall 1973, p. 41.

25 A number of retirement issues are discussed in Ann W. Salomon, "A Trainer's Guide to Retirement Planning," *Training*, August 1982, pp. 42, 47; and Scott Dever, "Pre-retirement Planning," *Personnel Administrator*, October 1981, pp. 56–57ff.

26 Neal Schmitt and others, "Retirement and Life Satisfaction," *Academy of Management Journal*, June 1979, pp. 282–291.

27 Examples of phased retirement programs are in Lois Farrer Copperman and Fred D. Keast, "Older Workers: A Challenge for Today and Tomorrow," *Human Resource Management*, Summer 1981, pp. 13–18; and Paul F. Hagstrom, "The Older Worker: A Travelers Insurance Companies' Case Study," *Personnel Administrator*, October 1981, pp. 41–45.

28 Bernhard Teriet, "Gliding Out: The European Approach to Retirement," *Personnel Journal*, July 1978, pp. 368–370. An in-depth study of phased retirement programs in seventeen European firms is reported in Constance Swank, "Phased Retirement Programs Working Well in Europe," *Management Review*, August 1983, pp. 32–33.

FOR ADDITIONAL READING

Anderson, Howard J., and Michael D. Levin-Epstein, *Primer of Equal Employment Opportunity,* 2d ed., Washington, D.C.: The Bureau of National Affairs, 1982.

Farley, Jennie, *Affirmative Action and the Woman Worker,* New York: AMACOM, 1979.

Humple, Carol Segrave, and Morgan Lyons, *Management and the Older Workforce: Policies and Programs,* New York: AMA, 1983.

Jud, Robert, *The Retirement Decision,* New York: AMACOM, 1981.

Miner, Mary Green, and John B. Miner, *Employee Selection within the Law,* Washington, D.C.: The Bureau of National Affairs, 1979.

Player, Mack, *Federal Law of Employment Discrimination in a Nutshell,* 2d ed., St. Paul, Minn.: West Publishing Company, 1981.

Rothschild, Donald, *Collective Bargaining, Labor Arbitration, and Discrimination in Employment,* Indianapolis: The Bobbs-Merrill Company, Inc., 1979.

Schlei, Barbara Lindemann, and Paul Grossman, *Employment Discrimination Law,* 2d ed., Washington, D.C.: The Bureau of National Affairs, 1983.

COMMUNICATION
AND COUNSELING

EMPLOYEE COMMUNICATION

Everything we do, and sometimes what we don't do, communicates messages to people.

Lane Tracy[1]

Too many managers at all levels see employee communication as a lip-service activity.

Roger D'Aprix[2]

CHAPTER OBJECTIVES

TO UNDERSTAND:
The communication process
Two-way communication
Barriers to communication
Nonverbal communication
Applications of readability
The role of listening in communication

A Hollywood movie company was filming a movie near a small Western town. The script involved some narrow-gauge-railway scenes; and a local resident, regularly a railroad engineer, had been selected as engineer of the narrow-gauge train. He was very proud of his assignment. One evening when both the Hollywood visitors and the engineer were in a local bar, the engineer walked over to the director of the movie company and asked, "John, how did I do with those train scenes today?"

The director, in a good mood, gave his most favorable Hollywood response, "Joe, you are doing one hell of a job."

Joe, not understanding the favorable meaning of this colloquialism, took it as a criticism and was immediately ruffled, replying, "Oh, I don't know about that. You couldn't do any better."

The director, still trying to communicate (but in terms of his own frame of reference), said, "That's what I said, Joe. You are doing one hell of a job."

At this point Joe became angry and an argument broke out, with Joe vowing that he wouldn't be talked to that way in front of friends. Eventually it was necessary to separate the two men to prevent a fight.

Whether one is working for a Hollywood movie company, the Jones Manufacturing Corporation, or the federal government, communication is an ever-present activity because it is the means by which people relate to one another in an organization. Communication is as necessary to an organization as the bloodstream is to a person. Just as people develop arteriosclerosis, a hardening of the arteries that impairs their efficiency, so may an organization develop "infosclerosis," a hardening of the information arteries that produces similar impaired efficiency.

Because of its significance, communication is discussed in the next three chapters. In this chapter we discuss the general concept of communication in organizations. Chapter 20 covers communication relationships, and in Chapter 21 we discuss employee counseling.

COMMUNICATION FUNDAMENTALS

Communication is the transfer of information and understanding from one person to another person.[3] It is a way of reaching others with ideas, facts, thoughts, feelings, and values. It is a bridge of meaning among people so that they can share what they feel and know. By using this bridge, a person can cross safely the river of misunderstanding that sometimes separates people.

Two people are required. A significant point about communication is that it always involves at least two people—a sender and a receiver. One person alone cannot communicate. Only one or more receivers can complete the communication act. This fact is obvious when one thinks of a person lost on an island calling for help when there is no one near enough to hear the call. The relationship is not so obvious to managers who send out bulletins to employees. They tend to think that when their bulletins are sent, they have communicated, but transmission of the message is only a beginning. A manager may send a hundred bulletins, but there is no communication until each bulletin is received, read, and understood. *Communication is what the receiver understands,* not what the sender says.

Importance of communication

Organizations cannot exist without communication. If there is no communication, employees cannot know what their coworkers are doing, management cannot receive information inputs, and supervisors cannot give instructions. Coordination of work is impossible, and the organization will collapse for lack of it. Cooperation also becomes impossible, because people cannot communicate their needs and feelings to others. We can say with confidence that *every act of communication influences the organization in some way.*

Communication is essential.

From management's point of view, all management acts must pass through the bottleneck of communication, as shown in Figure 19-1. Great management ideas are strictly armchair thoughts until a manager puts them into effect through communication. A manager's plans may be the best in the world, but until they can be communicated they are worthless.

When communication is effective, it tends to encourage better performance and job satisfaction.[4] People understand their jobs better and feel more involved in them. In some instances they even will make sacrifices of long-established privileges because they see that a sacrifice is necessary.

> **Management in one firm persuaded production employees to bring their own coffee and have coffee breaks at their machines instead of taking a regular time-lost coffee break in the cafeteria. The company dealt directly and frankly. It presented to employee group meetings a chart of electricity use for the plant showing how power use was less than half of normal for fifteen minutes before and after coffee break, plus the normal production loss during the break. The company made a sound case for the fact that this long period of inactivity and partial activity prevented profitable operation. The power-use charts were convincing, and employees readily accepted the new coffee-break policy.**

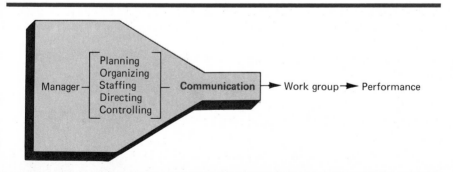

Figure 19-1
All management acts pass through the bottleneck of communication.

The positive response of those employees confirmed what one chief executive concluded about the importance of communication: "As far as productivity is concerned, once people know what you're trying to do, they generally will respond favorably if you communicate the facts."[5]

The communication process

*Six steps in
the process*

The *communication process* is the method by which a sender reaches a receiver with a message. It requires six steps whether the two parties talk, use hand signals, or employ some other means of communication. The steps are shown in Figure 19-2.

Develop an idea   Step 1 is to *develop an idea* that the sender wishes to transmit. This is the key step, because unless there is a worthwhile message, all the other steps are somewhat useless. This step is represented by the sign, sometimes seen on office or factory walls, that reads, "Be sure brain is engaged before putting mouth in gear."

Encode   Step 2 is to *encode* the idea into suitable words, charts, or other symbols for transmission. At this point the sender determines the method of transmission so that the words and symbols may be organized in suitable fashion for the type of transmission. For example, back-and-forth conversation usually is not organized the same way as a written memorandum.

Transmit   When the message finally is developed, step 3 is to *transmit* it by the method chosen, such as by memo, phone call, or personal visit. Senders also choose certain channels, such as bypassing or not bypassing the superintendent, and they communicate with careful timing.[6] Today may not be the right day to talk to one's manager about that pay raise. Senders also try to keep their communication channel free of barriers, or interference, as shown in Figure 19-2, so that their messages have a chance to reach receivers and hold their attention. In interviewing, for example, freedom from distraction is desirable.

Figure 19-2
The communication
process

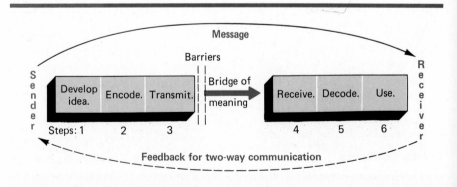

Receive Transmission allows another person to *receive* a message, which is step 4. In this step the initiative transfers to receivers, who tune to receive the message. If it is oral, they need to be good listeners, as will be discussed shortly. If the receiver does not function, the message is lost.

Decode Step 5 is to *decode* the message so that it can be understood. The sender wants the receiver to understand the message exactly as it was sent. For example, if the sender transmits the equivalent of a square and the decoding step produces a circle, then a message has been sent but not much understanding has taken place.

Although some receivers may be uncooperative and may try to misunderstand, normally they make a genuine attempt to understand the intended message. Even with the best of intentions, a receiver may not understand *exactly* what the sender intended, because the perceptions of the two people are different. The more realistic goal in most situations is for understanding that is close enough for the communication to be called successful.

Understanding can occur only in a receiver's mind. A communicator may make others listen, but there is no way to make them understand. The receiver alone chooses whether to understand or not. Many employers overlook this when giving instructions or explanations. They think that telling someone is sufficient, but the communication is not truly successful until there is understanding. This is known as "getting through" to a person. Communicators should ask themselves every day: "Am I getting through to others?"

Need for understanding

> The encoding-decoding sequence is somewhat like the activity involved when the old London Bridge was moved to the United States. The bridge could not be moved in one piece, so it had to be disassembled stone by stone, with each stone marked as to its proper location. This was similar to the action of a sender who has an idea and encodes (dismantles) it into a series of words, each marked by location and other means to guide the receiver. In order to move the idea (transmit it), the sender needs to take it apart by putting it into words. The reassembly of the bridge stone by stone in the United States was similar to the action of a receiver who takes words received and mentally reassembles them into whole ideas.

Use The last step in the communication process is for the receiver to use the communication. The receiver may ignore it, perform the task assigned, store the information provided, or do something else.

Senders always need to communicate with care, because communication is a potent form of self-revelation to others. It tells something about the kind of people communicators are, the way they think, and what their values are. It is, therefore, basic in all interpersonal and group relationships.

The Rule of Five

Two additional receiver steps are desired by senders in most employment situations, but they are not essential to complete a communication. These steps are acceptance of the communication by the receiver and feedback to the sender regarding it. Senders in organizations usually want receivers

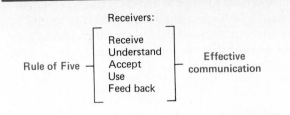

Figure 19-3
The Rule of Five
in organizational
communication

to accept their communications so that cooperation and motivation will be improved. Similarly, senders want feedback because it tells them how well the message is understood and how it will be used. Although acceptance and feedback are not essential to complete a single communication, they are essential for an effective long-run working relationship. No organization can operate for long without these additional steps.

Five receiver steps

The entire set of five receiver steps in communication often is called the *Rule of Five,* as shown in Figure 19-3. The sender wants the receiver to receive, understand, accept, and use the message, and to provide feedback. If a communication accomplishes these five steps with a receiver, it has been fully successful.

Two-way communication

Two-way flow

When a sender transmits a message and the receiver returns feedback to the sender, there is effective *two-way communication.* There is a completed *communication circuit,* because there is a message flow from sender to receiver and back to the sender, as shown in Figure 19-2 on the communication process. This two-way flow of information also is called a *feedback loop,* or *communication loop.*[7]

Two-way communication is illustrated by the popular sport of tennis and a tennis player named Diane McFadden. As she serves the ball, she cannot say to herself, "My next shot will be an overhead volley into the back court." Her next shot has to depend on how her opponent returns the ball. Diane may have an overall strategy, but each of her shots must be conditioned by how the ball is returned. Unless she does condition her shots, she will soon find herself swinging aimlessly and losing a game.

Two-way communication has a back-and-forth pattern similar to that in tennis. The speaker sends a message, and the receiver's responses come back to the speaker. The result is a developing play-by-play situation in which the speaker can adjust the next message to fit previous responses of the receiver. This opportunity to adjust to the receiver is the one great advantage of two-way communication compared with the one-way variety. It provides better understanding for both parties. There also are other benefits of effective two-way communication. Frustration is reduced, and favorable feelings usually are generated. Accuracy of work is much improved.

Two-way communication is not exclusively beneficial. It also can cause difficulties. Two people may strongly disagree about some item but not realize it until they establish two-way communication. When they expose their different viewpoints, they may become even more polarized, but at least two-way communication has helped them understand the nature of their differences.

Another difficulty that may occur is *cognitive dissonance.* This is the internal conflict and anxiety that occurs when people receive information incompatible with their value systems, prior decisions, or other information they may have. Since people do not feel comfortable with dissonance, they try to remove or reduce it. Perhaps they will try to obtain new communication inputs, change their interpretation of the inputs, reverse their decision, or change their values. They may even refuse to believe the dissonant input, or they may rationalize it out of the way.

Possible problem of cognitive dissonance

SEMANTICS

Semantics is the science of meaning, as contrasted with phonetics, the science of sounds. Nearly all communication is symbolic; that is, it is achieved using *symbols* that suggest certain meanings. These symbols are merely a map that describes a territory, but they are not the real territory itself; hence they must be interpreted. The word "dog" does not look like a dog, sound like a dog, or smell like a dog, but it means a dog because we have made it a symbol for a dog. This symbolic transfer of meaning is a very difficult, very personal process.

The science of meaning

The meaning that receivers take depends on *their* experience and attitudes —not the communicator's. If, in a receiver's experience, the symbol has meaning X, the communicator who insists on using the symbol with meaning Y will have difficulty getting through to the receiver. The key thought of this discussion is that transfer of meaning can be improved by communicating in terms of the receivers' backgrounds and attitudes.[8]

Communication barriers

Even when the receiver receives the message and makes a genuine effort to decode it, there are a number of interferences that may limit the receiver's understanding. These obstacles act as *barriers to communication,* and they may entirely prevent a communication, filter part of it out, or give it incorrect meaning. Three types of barriers are personal, physical, and semantic, as shown in Figure 19-4.

Personal barriers *Personal barriers* are communication interferences that arise from human emotions, values, and poor listening habits. They are a common occurrence in work situations. We all have experienced how our personal feelings can limit our communications with other people, and these situations happen at work just as they do in private life.

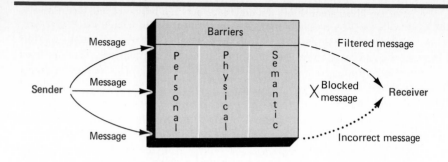

Figure 19-4
Operation of
communication
barriers

*Psychological
distance*

Personal barriers often involve a *psychological distance* between people that is similar to actual physical distance. For example, Marsha talks down to Janet, who resents this attitude, and this resentment separates them.

Our emotions act as filters in nearly all our communications. We see and hear what we are emotionally "tuned" to see and hear, so communication cannot be separated from our personality.[9] We communicate our interpretation of reality instead of reality itself. Someone has said, "No matter what you say a thing is, it isn't," meaning that the sender is merely giving an emotionally filtered perception of it. Under these conditions, when the sender's and receiver's perceptions are reasonably close together, their communication will be more effective.

Physical barriers *Physical barriers* are communication interferences that occur in the environment in which the communication takes place. A typical physical barrier is a sudden distracting noise that temporarily drowns out a voice message. Other physical barriers include distances between people, walls, or static that interferes with radio messages. People frequently recognize when physical interference occurs and try to compensate for it.

Semantic barriers *Semantic barriers* arise from limitations in the symbols with which we communicate. Symbols usually have a variety of meanings, and we have to choose one meaning from many. Sometimes we choose the wrong meaning and misunderstanding occurs. An illustration is the railroad engineer at the beginning of this chapter. He misunderstood what the slang phrase "hell of a job" meant, so he became emotional. In this instance a semantic barrier also led to an emotional barrier, and further communication was blocked.

Fact vs. inference

Whenever we interpret a symbol on the basis of our assumptions, not facts, we are making an *inference.*[10] Inferences are an essential part of most communication. We cannot avoid them by waiting until all communication is factual before accepting it. However, since inferences can give a wrong signal, we need always to be aware of them and to appraise them carefully. When doubts arise, more feedback can be sought.

The following illustration shows the difference between inference and fact. Suppose we see Willy Bergstrom come out of a bar, enter a car, drive from his parking place, and crash into another car. We may infer that Willy has been drinking alcoholic beverages in the bar, but we have no evidence to make this a fact. We may say it is a fact that he is driving his own car; however, it may not be his car but his neighbor's. It appears to be a fact that two cars crashed and a person who walked out a door labeled "Bar" was driving one of the cars!

Words, pictures (such as drawings), and even actions can be misinterpreted. These will be discussed in detail in the following sections.

Words

Words are the main communication method used on the job. Many employees spend more than 50 percent of their time in word communication.

> One study covered over 3000 employees, including office employees, in a research and development activity. It reported that they spent an average of 69 percent of their time communicating. Other studies confirm this general relationship of communication often dominating work time.[11]

Multiple meanings   A major difficulty is that nearly every common word has several meanings.[12] Multiple meanings are necessary because we are trying to talk about an infinitely complex world while using only a limited number of words. Used in one sense, a word may be derogatory; but when used another way, it can be acceptable. For example, the term "dummy" in an argument at the office may be uncomplimentary, but its use to refer to the person serving as dummy in a game of bridge is acceptable.

> The variety of word meanings often is surprising. A standard library dictionary reports 110 different meanings for the popular word "round." Many of the meanings are entirely different, as shown by six examples in Figure 19-5. A study of a larger dictionary, the *Oxford Dictionary*, reports an average of twenty-eight separate meanings for each of the 500 most-used words in the English language.[13] No wonder we have trouble communicating with each other!

Context   If words really have no certain meaning, how can we make sense with them—how can we communicate with people? The answer is *context*. We use the word in a certain environment, such as the "dummy" example just given, and we surround the word with other words and symbols until meaning is narrowed to fairly certain limits. Individual words have so many meanings that they cause confusion until they are put into context.[14] Consequently, effective communicators are idea-centered rather than word-centered. They know that *words* do not mean—*people* mean.

Context gives meaning.

> The experience of a government personnel director illustrates the importance of context. There were nearly two thousand employees in clerical operations in an office.

The word "round" has 110 different meanings:

Adjective: 23   Noun: 42   Verb: 16   Preposition: 13   Adverb: 16

Which way did you last use it in conversation?
Did the listener know what you meant?

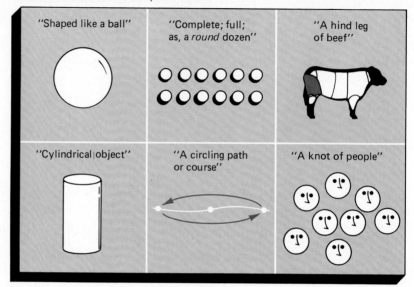

Figure 19-5
Example of the
multiple meanings
of a word
Source: Webster's Third
New International
Dictionary, *Springfield,
Mass.: G. & C. Merriam
Co.,* 1976.

The entire activity was located in a converted warehouse on an abandoned Army base.

Several hundred employees held "temporary" rather than "permanent" civil service appointments. Because of variations in the work load at this installation, there were occasional layoffs of these temporary workers. When layoffs were necessary, the personnel director typically used the loudspeaker system to make an announcement somewhat like the following: "The following employees are requested to report to classroom 10 at 4 P.M. this afternoon." Then the names were announced over the loudspeaker.

When the employees arrived, they were told that this was their last week of temporary work, and they were given their separation papers. On one occasion this procedure was followed with several layoffs during a short period of time.

A few days later the personnel director had a training assignment for some employees who had "permanent" appointments; so he decided to call them to classroom 10 at the end of the day to tell them about the training program. He went to the loudspeaker in the afternoon and announced, "The following employees are requested to report to classroom 10 at 4 P.M.," and then the names were read.

As the names were read over the loudspeaker, several employees started crying, assuming they also were being laid off. Soon a number of others started crying in sympathy with the first group, upsetting the entire office. It took some time for supervisors to discover the cause of their weeping, to find the real reason for the call to the classroom, and to quiet the office force. All this difficulty was caused because the context of the communication was inappropriate.

Context provides meaning to words through the *social cues* that people receive. Social cues are the positive or negative bits of information in our environment that influence how we react to a communication. Examples of social cues are tone of voice, job titles, patterns of dress, and the historical use of words in a particular culture. Our susceptibility to these cues varies, depending on the credibility of the source, our past exposure to the item, the ambiguity of the cue, and individual differences.[15]

It is important for us to be aware of social cues, because language with inadequate context is a semantic smog. Like a real smog, it irritates our senses and interferes with our perceptions.

Pictures

A second type of symbol is the picture. Pictures are used especially to clarify word communication, which is their use in Figure 19-5. Organizations make extensive use of pictures, such as blueprints, charts, maps, films, three-dimensional models, and similar devices. There is a saying that "a picture can be worth a thousand words," which is certainly true when one observes a blueprint or sees a painting.

> A shoe manufacturer, who was having trouble getting his workers to maintain quality, made good use of pictures to restore careful work. The manufacturer placed finished-shoe rejects in a large room for several weeks and then brought representative employee groups into the room "to browse around and see for yourselves." Few words were spoken, but much meaning was imparted when employees saw the mountain of rejected shoes. This manager was using a type of "picture" effectively to supplement language communication.

Pictures usually are most effective when used with well-chosen words and actions to tell the complete story. For this reason they often are called "visual aids."

Pictures are visual aids.

Action (nonverbal communication)

A third type of communication is action, also known as *nonverbal communication.*[16] Often people forget that what they do is a means of communication to the extent that it is interpreted by others. For example, a handshake and a smile have meaning. A raise in pay or being late for an appointment also has meaning.

Actions have meaning.

> One study concluded that the nonverbal behavior of managers could be used to send a message to employees that their leaders are considerate.[17] Leaders were encouraged to reduce the status discrepancy between themselves and their subordinates by consciously managing their nonverbal cues. In particular, posture, attentiveness, use of space, and the control of time all convey implicit messages through action, and these require skill to encode properly.

Two significant points about action sometimes are overlooked. One point, illustrated in the opening quote for this chapter, is that *failure to act* is an

Failure to act

important way of communicating. A manager who fails to compliment someone for a job well done or fails to take a promised action also is communicating with that person. Since we communicate both by action and by lack of action, we communicate almost all the time at work, whether we intend to do so or not. Being at one's desk has meaning, but being away also has meaning.

A second point is that action speaks louder than words in the long run. People believe action more than they do words. Employees who say one thing but do another will soon find that others "listen" mostly to what they do. The amount of difference between what one says and what one does is that person's *communication credibility gap*. When an employee's credibility gap is large, difficulties are likely to follow, such as a loss of confidence in that person. The following illustration shows how a credibility gap works in practice.

Communication credibility gap

> Willie Beacon, the zone manager of a sales office, emphasized the idea that he depended upon his employees to help him do a good job because, as he stated it, "You salespeople are the ones in direct contact with the customer, and you get much valuable information and useful suggestions." In most of his sales meetings he said that he always welcomed their ideas and suggestions. But here is how he translated his words into action. In those same sales meetings the schedule was so tight that by the time he finished his pep talk there was no time for anyone to present problems or ask questions, and he would hardly tolerate an interruption during his talk because he claimed this destroyed its "punch."
>
> If a salesperson tried to present a suggestion in Willie's office, Willie usually began with, "Fine, I'm glad you brought in your suggestion." Before long, however, he directed the conversation to some subject on his mind, or had to keep an appointment, or found some other reason for never quite getting to the suggestion. The few suggestions that did get through he rebuffed with, "Yeah, I thought of that a long time ago, but it won't work." The eventual result was that he received no suggestions. His actions spoke louder than his words. His credibility gap was too large for employees to overcome.

Body language

Our bodies can provide meaning.

An important part of nonverbal communication is *body language,* by which people communicate meaning to others with their bodies in interpersonal interaction.[18] Body language is an important supplement to verbal communication in most parts of the world.

The face and the hands are especially important sources of body language in work situations. Examples are eye contact, eye movement, smiles and frowns, touching, and a furrowed brow. In one instance a manager frowned when an employee brought a suggestion, and the employee interpreted the frown as a rejection when in fact it was a headache. In another instance a smile at an inappropriate time was interpreted as a derisive sneer, and an argument erupted. Other types of body language are closeness, hip movements, and breathing rate.

Another type of nonverbal communication is *ecological control,* in which the interpersonal environment is altered so as to influence another's behavior. One study indicated that office visitors felt most welcome and comfortable when the office design exhibited moderate tidiness and the officeholder used an open desk placement.[19] Other factors, such as the presence of status symbols, plants, and wall decorations, may also affect visitor perceptions of an employee or manager. Consider how ecological control operates in this situation.

> When visitors came to her office, Carmen Valencia usually sat rigidly behind her desk, leaving the other person somewhat distant on the other side of the desk. This arrangement created a psychological distance and clearly established her as the leader and superior in the interaction. Then she rearranged her office so that a visitor sat beside her on the same side of her desk. This suggested more receptiveness and equality of interaction with visitors. It also had the additional advantage of providing a work area on her desk for mutual examination of appropriate documents. When she wished to establish a more informal relationship, particularly with subordinates, she came around to the front of the desk and sat in a chair near the employee.

Two key communication symbols

Of all communication symbols, probably the two most important in employee communication are face-to-face conversation and action. These communication symbols are not new, but employees have much to learn about how to use them for improved communication. The printing press and typewriter are wonderful inventions, but they are no substitute for face-to-face communication at work. It provides multiple channels, including body language, thereby increasing the opportunity for better understanding. It also allows immediate feedback so that each party can adjust to the individual needs of the other. In sum, face-to-face communication tends to be more enriched with information than other forms of communication.

*Conversation
and action*

Readability

Since meaning is difficult to impart, a natural assumption is that if symbols can be simplified, the receiver will understand them more easily. Further, if symbols of the type that receivers prefer are used, the receivers will be more receptive. This is the thinking behind the idea of *readability,* which seeks to make writing and speech more understandable. Readability was popularized by Rudolf Flesch in *The Art of Readable Writing.*[20] Flesch and others developed formulas that can be applied to magazines, bulletins, speeches, and other communications in order to determine their level of readability.

Figure 19-6 offers some guides for more readable writing according to the Flesch formula. Then Figure 19-7 applies these guides to show how complex writing can be made more simple.

*Guides for
readability*

- Use simple words and phrases, such as "improve" instead of "ameliorate" and "like" instead of "in a manner similar to that of."
- Use short and familiar words, such as "darken" instead of "obfuscate."
- Use personal pronouns, such as "you" and "them," if the style permits.
- Use illustrations, examples, and charts. These techniques are even better when they are tied to the reader's experiences.
- Use short sentences and paragraphs. Big words and thick reports may look impressive to people, but the communicator's job is to inform people, not impress them.
- Use active verbs, such as "The manager said . . . " rather than "It was said by the manager that. . . ."
- Use only necessary words. For example, in the sentence "Bad weather conditions prevented my trip," the word "conditions" is unnecessary. Say, "Bad weather prevented my trip."

Figure 19-6
Guides to
readable writing

Much organizational literature that is sent to employees is more difficult than standard levels of readability. Bulletins, magazines, annual reports to stockholders, employee handbooks, and collective-bargaining contracts consistently rate "difficult" and "very difficult," beyond the level of satisfactory reading for typical adults.[21] It is often observed that the typical employee communication appears to be written by college graduates for college graduates. Many readers do not understand such complicated writing unless they carefully study it, which they are seldom motivated to do. Since the main purpose of communication is to be understood, there is a need to consider receivers and try to fit their needs.

Figure 19-7
An example of
applied rules of
clear writing
*Adapted from
Readingease: The Key to
Understanding, Employee
Relations Staff, General
Motors Corporation, n.d.*

Original paragraph

There is a remote possibility that in the future there may be somewhat more jobs available. It is estimated that quite a lot of the improvement may be attributed to some of the more important industries and trades which normally become increasingly more active with the onset of warmer weather. In other words, it will be due mainly to the seasonal factors that always cause the overall basis of the rise and fall in the nation's economic activity, and even though there has been no noticeable strengthening of basic conditions, the general business situation is by far considerably better than most of the pessimistic economic forecasters have expected. According to extensive records compiled by the Bureau of Labor Statistics, the unemployment total in April was substantially below the 4½ million mark reached during March and the recent trend of applicants for jobless benefits suggests that the total of national unemployment is possibly now somewhat below 3 million employable persons who are available for work.

164 words
Flesch readability rating: *very difficult.*

Revised paragraph

The job picture looks brighter. Many of our industries increase production at this time of the year. The Bureau of Labor Statistics reports that national unemployment dropped from 4½ million in March to less than 3 million in April.

39 words
Flesch readability rating: *fairly easy to standard.*

Readability scales have been criticized on the basis that they degrade language to the level of first-grade primers, tend to destroy style, do not measure all the factors that determine readability, and contain similar weaknesses. These criticisms have merit, and readability certainly must not be overemphasized. Nevertheless, readability is a quality that everyone needs to consider when communicating. Practice will develop a readable style, and readability is easy to test on most scales, once the process is learned.

Listening

Hearing is with the ears, but listening is with the mind. Effective listening helps receivers take exactly the idea a sender intended. They then can make better decisions because their information inputs are better. Good listeners also save time because they learn more within a given period of time; and they learn about the person talking, as well as what the person is saying. Good listening is also good manners; people think more of us when we listen to them attentively. Finally, our good listening encourages others to respond by listening to what we have to say. It is a form of behavior modeling for them. Typical employees spend an average of more than 30 percent of their time listening, so it is an important part of their jobs.[22]

Emphasis on better listening is a rather recent development. The first English-language book wholly on listening was published in 1957,[23] even though earlier there were hundreds of books published on speaking.

A number of organizations have recently designed training programs in listening skills for their employees. Sperry Corporation, for example, sent a phonograph record on listening to all 90,000 employees and enrolled 10,000 of them in more formal classroom or programmed-instruction training courses. To accent the importance of listening, Sperry even wove it into a major advertising slogan, "We understand how important it is to listen."[24]

Since a typical listener two months later remembers only about 25 percent of what was said, listening is most effective for understanding general ideas about short-term operating problems. It is not effective for receipt and storage of many factual details; here we depend on the written word.

Training can increase listening comprehension 25 percent or more. A person speaks at the rate of 100 to 200 words a minute, but a listener's brain can process words much faster; so there is idle brain time that good listeners use to concentrate forcefully on the message in order to keep from daydreaming or mindwandering. Good listeners use their idle time to think about the speaker's objective, weigh the evidence, search for examples and clues to meaning, and review. Other suggestions for good listening are given in Figure 19-8. Listening is a conscious, positive act requiring willpower. It is not a simple, passive exposure to sound.

What do good listeners do?

Listening often is a weak link in the chain of two-way communication. Many employees do not actively work at listening well.[25] A major reason is that, because the speaker is initiating action on the listener, listening may

1 Stop talking!
You cannot listen if you are talking.
Polonius *(Hamlet):* "Give every man thine ear, but few thy voice."

2 Put the talker at ease.
Help a person feel free to talk.
This is often called a permissive environment.

3 Show a talker that you want to listen.
Look and act interested. Do not read your mail while someone talks.
Listen to understand rather than to oppose.

4 Remove distractions.
Don't doodle, tap, or shuffle papers.
Will it be quieter if you shut the door?

5 Empathize with talkers.
Try to help yourself see the other person's point of view.

6 Be patient.
Allow plenty of time. Do not interrupt a talker.
Don't start for the door or walk away.

7 Hold your temper.
An angry person takes the wrong meaning from words.

8 Go easy on argument and criticism.
These put people on the defensive, and they may "clam up" or become angry.
Do not argue: Even if you win, you lose.

9 Ask questions.
This encourages a talker and shows that you are listening.
It helps to develop points further.

10 Stop talking!
This is first and last, because all other guides depend on it.
You cannot do an effective listening job while you are talking.

* Nature gave people two ears but only one tongue,
  which is a gentle hint that they should listen more than they talk.
* Listening requires two ears,
  one for meaning and one for feeling.
* Decision makers who do not listen
  have less information for making sound decisions

Figure 19-8
Effective
listening guides

threaten a person's self-image. Most of us would rather speak our own ideas than listen to what someone else says. In spite of the difficulties of good listening, it is essential for understanding.

SUMMARY

Organizations cannot exist without communication. It is the transfer of information and understanding from one person to another person. It is a sharing of meaning. One person can initiate the process but cannot complete it. It is completed only by a receiver. The communication process consists of these six steps: develop an idea, encode, transmit, receive, decode, and use. The five desired receiver responses—receive, understand, accept, use, and feed back—are known as the Rule of Five in communication.

Semantics is the science of meaning. People communicate with the symbols of language, pictures, and action (including body language), but many barriers exist. With regard to language, ideas should be emphasized instead of words. Pictures are an aid to communication, and action speaks louder than words. Readability simplifies symbols and encourages more understanding. Since communication is a two-way process, listening in order to know what and how to communicate is often as important as speaking and writing.

TERMS AND CONCEPTS FOR REVIEW

Communication process	Inference versus fact
Rule of Five	Social cues
Two-way communication	Nonverbal communication
Feedback loop	Communication credibility gap
Cognitive dissonance	Body language
Semantics	Ecological control
Communication barriers	Readability
Psychological distance	

REVIEW QUESTIONS

1 Think of a job that you have had and a situation in which the communication failed or was ineffective. Discuss how the communication process applied in this situation and where the breakdown occurred.

2 When you order food in a restaurant, do you expect the Rule of Five to apply to the food server who takes the order? Explain.

3 Discuss the barriers to communication that exist when you discuss a subject with your instructor in the classroom.

4 Think again of the communication incident you selected in question 1, and discuss any barriers that contributed to the communication breakdown. How could each of the barriers be reduced or overcome in that incident?

5 Select a situation in which you made a wrong inference, analyze how the misinterpretation was made, and discuss how you might avoid similar misinterpretations in the future. How important is feedback as an aid to avoiding inference misinterpretations?

6 Observe your own behavior, and discuss what nonverbal communication habits you typically use. Are there some behaviors that you have that may mislead receivers?

7 Analyze a sample of one of your term papers or reports to determine how readable your writing is, and then discuss your results. Use any readability scale that is available.

8 How would you communicate the following?
   a A promotion to one of your employees
   b Criticism of one of your employees for work poorly done

c Instructions for operation of a simple office machine

d An announcement to shop machinists that sales dropped 15 percent during the last quarter and some employees may need to be laid off

9 Visit an instructor's office, and record your feelings of relative comfort there. What physical elements in the office contributed to your reaction?

10 Examine the "effective listening guides" in Figure 19-8. Which ones do you practice best? Which ones could you improve upon?

INCIDENT

The National Gas Company

The National Gas Company provided natural gas to about 40,000 customers in an Eastern city. Christmas in one year came on Tuesday; and as the holiday season approached, management heard persistent rumors from the employees that Monday, December 24, would be a holiday except for the emergency crews. December 24 was not regularly a holiday, but the rumors were that since it fell between Sunday and Christmas, management had decided to grant the extra holiday to make a "long weekend."

The Coordinating Committee, consisting of top operating officials, discussed the holiday problem extensively at two weekly meetings, December 10 and 17. At the second meeting it was decided that there would be no holiday December 24. There were several arguments for and against the decision, but the argument that carried the most weight concerned the public relations aspect of bill paying. Bills were issued daily during the month on a rotating basis, with a discount date* printed on the bill. About 2000 bills with a December 24 discount date had already been sent out, and investigation disclosed that often as many as 25 percent of the customers paid their bills on their last discount day. The Committee felt that it would be poor public relations to close the office on December 24 because hundreds of people would come to the office to pay their bills that day; so it decided to keep the entire staff on duty.

Since December 24 was not a regular holiday, it was not necessary to announce the Committee's decision to employees; however, it decided that the decision should be announced since the rumors had been persistent. The announcement read:

December 19, 19—

To All National Gas Employees:

Monday, December 24, will be a regular company workday.

Jim Smith
General Manager

---

*Bills paid on or before the discount date were subject to a cash discount of 2 percent.

The announcement was mimeographed, sent to all supervisors, and placed on all bulletin boards. There was no other publicity of the decision.

QUESTION
Appraise the quality of communication in this situation, and recommend any improvements that you think could have been made in the way this was handled.

EXPERIENTIAL EXERCISE

One-Way Compared with Two-Way Communication

The instructor can set up a classroom experiment in which both one-way and two-way communication are tried for performance of some task or communication of a detailed idea not familiar to students. One of the most popular tasks is to have a handout showing rectangles organized in a certain way. Two or more students are selected as receivers, and one or more people are selected as communicators of the layout of the rectangles. The handout is made available to class members and communicators *but not to receivers.* Receivers stand at the front of the room trying to draw on a chalkboard the arrangement described by the communicator. (For each communication it is desirable to have two or more receivers so that their arrangements of the rectangles can be compared.)

For the one-way method, the communicator faces the class and does not look at the figures the receiver is drawing, because that would be a form of feedback. The two-way method may be with the communicator not observing the figures (as by telephone) or with observation of the figures. The figure shown below is a sample arrangement, but instructors should select their own so that it is not available to the class ahead of time.

Following one-way communication, senders and receivers are questioned about their feelings, and the class discusses the advantages and disadvantages of the one-way process. The same procedure is repeated following two-way communication. Then important comparisons can be made.

REFERENCES

1 Lane Tracy, "Do Actions Speak Louder than Words?" *Personnel Journal,* December 1982, p. 882.

2 Roger D'Aprix, "The Oldest (and Best) Way to Communicate with Employees," *Harvard Business Review,* September–October 1982, p. 32.

3 General discussions of organizational communication are presented in a special symposium on "Application of Communication Theory to Communication Practice," *Journal of Applied Communication Research,* Spring 1982, pp. 1–73; and in *Personnel Administrator,* October 1982, pp. 28–69.

4 Karlene H. Roberts and Charles A. O'Reilly III, "Some Correlates of Communication Roles in Organizations," *Academy of Management Journal,* March 1979, pp. 42–57; and Paul M. Muchinsky, "Organizational Communication: Relationships to Organizational Climate and Job Satisfaction," *Academy of Management Journal,* December 1977, pp. 592–607.

5 Roy G. Foltz, "Productivity and Communications," *Personnel Administrator,* August 1981, p. 12.

6 Some research suggests that employees should consider both time of day and day of the week in timing their communications; see William T. Whitely, "The Influence of Properties of Verbal Communication on the Attitudes of Managers," Kae H. Chung (ed.), *Proceedings '81,* Mississippi State, Miss.: Academy of Management, 1981, pp. 208–212.

7 A readable review of research on the telephone as a powerful two-way communication tool is Howard Muson, "Getting the Phone's Number," *Psychology Today,* April 1982, pp. 42–49.

8 An argument for concentrating on the needs of the audience is in John F. Budd, Jr., "Is the Focus of Communication on Target?" *Sloan Management Review,* Fall 1982, pp. 51–53.

9 A contemporary problem with distorted personal signals occurs with the interpretation of sex role cues at work. See Lynn R. Cohen, "Minimizing Communication Breakdowns between Male and Female Managers," *Personnel Administrator,* October 1982, pp. 57–58ff.

10 Extensive discussion and cases involving inference may be found in William V. Haney, *Communication and Interpersonal Relations: Text and Cases,* 4th ed., Homewood, Ill.: Richard D. Irwin, Inc., 1979.

11 E. T. Klemmer and F. W. Snyder, "Measurement of Time Spent Communicating," *The Journal of Communication,* June 1972, pp. 142–158.

12 This problem may become acute when English-speaking supervisors deal with foreign employees who are not familiar with various meanings of words. See Cheryl L. McKenzie and Carol J. Qazi, "Communication Barriers in the Workplace," *Business Horizons,* March–April 1983, pp. 70–72. A reminder that employees need to understand the true meaning of their managers' communications is Mary Bralove, "Taking the Boss at His Word May Turn Out to Be a Big Mistake at a Lot of Companies," *Wall Street Journal,* June 4, 1982, p. 23.

13 William M. Sattler, "Talking Ourselves into Communication Crises," *Michigan Business Review,* July 1957, p. 30.

14 An argument that management of symbols (language, activities, workplace settings) can help create a positive environment is Dennis J. Moberg, "Job

Enrichment through Symbol Management," *California Management Review,* Winter 1981, pp. 24–30.

15 Gary J. Blau and Ralph Katerberg, "Toward Enhancing Research with the Social Information Processing Approach to Job Design," *Academy of Management Review,* October 1982, pp. 543–550. An earlier article relating social cues to job design is G. Salancik and J. Pfeffer, "A Social Information Processing Approach to Job Attitudes and Task Design," *Administrative Science Quarterly,* June 1978, pp. 224–253.

16 Students approaching a job interview may be interested in nonverbal factors that recruiters pay attention to; see Kittie W. Watson and Larry R. Smeltzer, "Perceptions of Nonverbal Communication during the Selection Interview," *The ABCA Bulletin,* June 1982, pp. 30–34. International travelers are advised to be familiar with the cultural meaning of gestures in James C. Simons, "A Matter of Interpretation," *American Way* (American Airlines), April 1983, pp. 106–111.

17 Martin Remland, "Developing Leadership Skills in Nonverbal Communication: A Situational Perspective," *The Journal of Business Communication,* Summer 1981, pp. 17–29.

18 Arlene Yerys, "How to Get What You Want through Influential Communication," *Management Review,* June 1982, pp. 12, 14–18; Michael B. McCaskey, "The Hidden Messages Managers Send," *Harvard Business Review,* November–December 1979, pp. 135–148.

19 Paula C. Morrow and James C. McElroy, "Interior Office Design and Visitor Response: A Constructive Replication," *Journal of Applied Psychology,* October 1981, pp. 646–650. Also see Tim R. V. Davis, "The Influence of the Physical Environment in Offices," *Academy of Management Review,* April 1984, pp. 271–283.

20 Rudolf Flesch, *The Art of Readable Writing,* rev. ed., New York: Harper & Row, Publishers, Incorporated, 1974. (The earlier edition was published in 1949.) Interest in readability continues to be strong today; see the special issue on readability in *The Journal of Business Communication,* Fall 1981.

21 Thomas L. Means, "Readability: An Evaluative Criterion of Stockholder Reaction to Annual Reports," *The Journal of Business Communication,* Winter 1981, pp. 25–33; Keith Davis, "Readability Changes in Employee Handbooks of Identical Companies during a Fifteen-Year Period," *Personnel Psychology,* Winter 1968, pp. 413–420; Debra L. Heflich, "Developing a Readable Employee Handbook," *Personnel Administrator,* March 1983, pp. 80–84.

22 J. Donald Weinrauch and John R. Swanda, Jr., "Examining the Significance of Listening: An Exploratory Study of Contemporary Management," *The Journal of Business Communication,* Fall 1975, pp. 25–32. One estimate by Dr. Lyman Steil places the figure as high as 40 percent; see Ted Blankenship, "Is Anyone Listening?" *The Rotarian,* July 1982, pp. 34–35.

23 Ralph G. Nichols and Leonard A. Stevens, *Are You Listening?* New York: McGraw-Hill Book Company, 1957.

24 John Louis DiGaetani, "The Sperry Corporation and Listening: An Interview," *Business Horizons,* March–April 1982, pp. 34–39.

25 Natasha Josephowitz, "Getting through to the Unreachable Person," *Management Review,* March 1982, pp. 48–50; Alexander Mikalachki, "Does Anyone Listen to the Boss?" *Business Horizons,* January–February 1983, pp. 18–24.

FOR ADDITIONAL READING

Adler, Mortimer J., *How to Speak, How to Listen,* New York: The Macmillan Company, 1983.

Burley-Allen, Madelyn, *Listening: The Forgotten Skill,* New York: John Wiley & Sons, Inc., 1982.

D'Aprix, Roger, *Communicating for Productivity,* New York: Harper & Row, Publishers, Incorporated, 1982.

Druckman, Daniel, Richard M. Rozelle, and James C. Baxter, *Nonverbal Communication: Survey, Theory, and Research,* Beverly Hills, Calif.: Sage Publications, 1982.

Greenbaum, Howard H., Raymond L. Falcione, and associates, *Organizational Communication: Abstracts, Analysis, and Overview,* Beverly Hills, Calif.: Sage Publications, annual volumes dating from 1976.

Gunning, Robert, *The Technique of Clear Writing,* New York: McGraw-Hill Book Company, 1952.

Key, Mary Ritchie (ed.), *The Relationship of Verbal and Nonverbal Communication,* The Hague, Netherlands: Mouton Publishers, 1980.

Nichols, Ralph G., and Leonard A. Stevens, *Are You Listening?* New York: McGraw-Hill Book Company, 1957.

Sigband, Norman B., and David N. Bateman, *Communication in Business,* Glenview, Ill.: Scott, Foresman & Company, 1981.

Vaughan, Bruce L., *Body Talk: Understanding the Secret Language of the Body,* Allen, Tex.: Argus Communications, 1982.

Wiemann, John M., and Randall P. Harrison, (eds.), *Nonverbal Interaction,* Beverly Hills, Calif.: Sage Publications (Volume 11 in *Sage Annual Reviews of Communication Research*), 1983.

COMMUNICATION RELATIONSHIPS

Employees today have a greater need to know about the activities of their organization than did their counterparts 50 years ago.

Norman B. Sigband[1]

A well established finding in the applied organizational behavior literature is the positive effect of information feedback or knowledge of results (KR) on performance.

John M. Ivancevich and J. Timothy McMahon[2]

CHAPTER OBJECTIVES

TO UNDERSTAND:
The significance of management communication
The meaning and use of lateral communication
Communication networks
Downward and upward communication processes
The communication role of staff specialists
Communicating with external groups

As a result of their different jobs and ranks in organizations, people play different roles that also affect their communication patterns. For example, the job of public relations director is quite different from that of lathe operator. The director's job interests are focused outside the organization toward the public, but the operator's interests are focused narrowly on day-to-day production activities. The director is a member of top management and draws a substantial salary, but the operator has a more limited income. These differences are as much a barrier to communication as geographical distance is. The public relations director probably feels free to contact a vice president either formally or informally, but the lathe operator may not feel free to do so. If contact is made, the lathe operator will communicate differently from the public relations director.

Desirability of open communication

In spite of the many barriers among people and groups in organizations, one of the basic propositions of organizational behavior is that *open communication is better than restricted communication.* For this reason it is important to try to improve communication whenever possible, so in this chapter we discuss communication involving different groups. Included are communications within management, downward to employees, upward to management, by specialists, with employees' families, and with unions.

COMMUNICATION WITHIN MANAGEMENT

Sometimes there is a tendency to say, "Let's improve employee communication; management can take care of itself." The result is that the entire communication effort is directed toward employees, but there are a number of reasons why management communication deserves equal emphasis.

Why emphasize management communication?

Communication within the management group is called either management communication or intramanagement communication. One reason it must be emphasized is that it is prerequisite to communication with employees. Just as a photograph can be no clearer than the negative from which it is printed, managers cannot transmit more clearly than they understand.

> In one organization, top management expected supervisors to interpret the incentive plan to workers but failed to explain the plan adequately to supervisors. Even though supervisors had stacks of papers describing the plan, they did not understand it, so they were unable to interpret it to workers.

Management communication also is essential for managers to make sound decisions. Since managers tend to be isolated from the point of performance, they can serve as a competent decision center only to the extent that they develop suitable information sources. Many of these sources are within the management group.

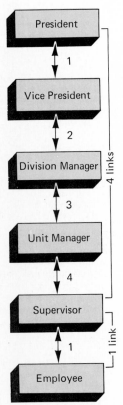

Figure 20-1
Most links in two-way communication chains are within management.

Another reason for emphasizing management communication is that the scope of managerial influence typically is greater than that of workers. Inadequate information to managers can affect a broad area of performance, because their spans of supervision affect many people and activities.

One additional reason is that most of the links in the communication chain, from top to bottom and bottom to top, are in the management group. Figure 20-1 shows how a communication chain from an employee to the president has four management links and only one employee link. Since each link affords an opportunity for loss of information content, the greater proportion of loss tends to be within management when the communication chain is long.[3]

Figure 20-2 shows how most of the communication loss tends to be within management. If we take the six levels shown in the previous figure and assume a 10 percent loss of information each time a communication is transmitted, then more than three-fourths of an upward or downward message loss is within management. For a downward message, the loss is 34 units out of 100; the message loss upward is 31 units. If management communication does not work well, then employee communication is not likely to work well either.

Finally, management communication is needed for its own sake, rather than as a means of informing workers. Managers are employees who have needs for communication and understanding just like anyone else. Many of them are minorities and women who are relatively new within the management group and may have special needs.[4]

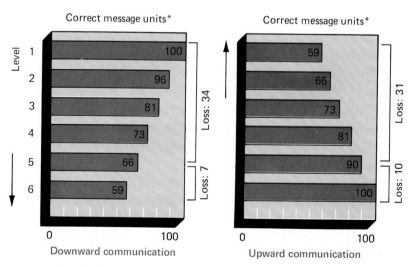

Figure 20-2
In a long chain-of-command communication to or from employees, most communication loss tends to be within the management group.

*Assuming a 10 percent loss from barriers at each level.

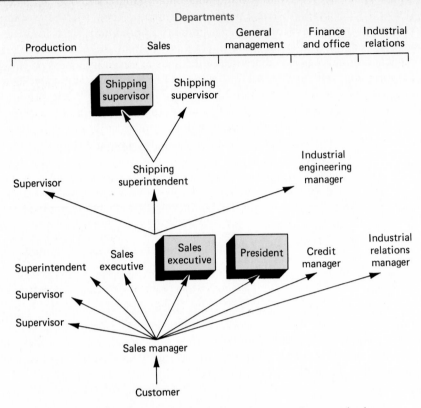

Departments

Production | Sales | General management | Finance and office | Industrial relations

Note: Executives listed in boxes received chain-of-command communications.

Figure 20-3
Communication chain showing a large amount of lateral communication for a quality-control problem

Improving management communication

Management people engage in a large amount of *lateral communication,* or *cross-communication,* which is communication across chains of command. It is necessary for job coordination with people in other departments. It also is done because people prefer the informality of lateral communication, compared with the more official chain of command. Lateral communication often is the dominant communication pattern within management.

Use of lateral communication

For example, one study of managers reported that two-thirds of their communication events were lateral, being either horizontal or diagonal in direction. Only one-third of their communication was vertical within their chain of command.[5]

An example is shown in Figure 20-3. It shows an information chain about a quality-control problem in a manufacturing company. It first was brought to the attention of a group sales manager in a letter from a customer. Although it was the type of problem that could have been communicated along the chain of command, the chart shows that only three of fourteen communications were within the chain of command and only six remained within sales, where the information first was received. Most communications were lateral.

Management lunchrooms, coffee hours, and recreation rooms have their social importance, but they also are significant stimulants to lateral communication. Managers also use boards, committees, conferences, and meetings for the exchange of information.

Managers who play a major role in lateral communication are called *boundary spanners.*[6] Boundary-spanning individuals have strong communication links within their department, with people in other units, and often with the external community. These connections allow boundary spanners to gather large amounts of information, which they may either filter or transfer to others. This gives them a source of status and potential power.

What do boundary spanners do?

In an effort to keep *all* managers better informed, many employers have developed special written communications. Examples are newsletters, bulletins, and booklets. Other employers provide copies of the employee magazine to managers ahead of general release, so that they will be informed about its contents. Another practice is to hold regular management meetings so that there can be open communication about work problems.

One firm decided on regular Thursday and Friday management meetings to discuss mutual work problems. They emphasized operating issues every Thursday and personnel decisions every Friday. After one year of meetings, a consultant confirmed that managers were making more effective, company-oriented decisions than before.[7]

Networks

Whereas meetings are relatively formal, much lateral communication takes place in less formal ways. A *network* is a group of people who develop and maintain contact to exchange information informally, usually about a shared interest.[8] An employee who becomes active on a network is said to be *networking.* Although networks can be internal as well as external to a company, usually they are built around external interests, such as recreation, social clubs, professional groups, career interests, and trade meetings. Thus an engineer may be in a network of research people who keep in touch at professional meetings and occasionally by telephone. Or a junior manager who is an excellent golfer may be in a golf network at a local country club and, therefore, may know personally the top executives of several local corporations, as well as other influential people in the area.

Networking

Networks help broaden the interests of employees, keep them more informed about new developments, and make them more visible to others. Networks help employees learn who knows what and even who knows those who know. As a result, an alert networker can gain access to influential people and centers of power. In general, networks are support mechanisms that help employees to grow and perform their jobs better.[9] However, networks sometimes have a negative impact on the firm, as when they encourage an effective manager to leave the company for a better job somewhere else.

Benefits of networks

DOWNWARD COMMUNICATION

Communication downward in an organization means that flow is from higher to lower authority. This usually is considered to be from management to employees, but much of it also is within the management group. Downward communication tends to dominate in mechanistic organizations, as described in Chapter 13. In organic systems there is a more open, multidirectional flow of information. People transmit and receive information in all directions, depending on work needs more than on the chain of authority.

In downward communication, management has at its disposal a multitude of elaborate techniques and skilled staff assistance. Even with all this help, it has done a poor job on many occasions. Fancy booklets, expensive multi-media presentations, and noisy public-address systems often have failed to achieve employee understanding. Sometimes these devices have become ends in themselves; they have been made more expensive, prettier, or fancier without any evidence that they improved employee understanding. The key to better employee communication is not fancier pieces of paper. It is more human-oriented managers who communicate in human terms.

Some prerequisites

Preparation is the key. Part of management's failure has been that it has not prepared for effective communication. It has failed to lay a good foundation, so its communication "house" has been built upon sand. What are some of these prerequisites?

Get informed If managers do not know and understand, they cannot communicate. This sounds trite, but it actually appears that some managers do not learn the information they are expected to communicate. Obviously it is best to know in advance if possible. If a manager has to go get answers every time employees ask a question, they will soon turn to some other source of information. However, there will be times when a manager cannot answer a question. In that case the manager loses face by making up an answer or complaining, "How should I know—they don't tell me." Instead, the manager should face the situation squarely by saying, "Hank, I don't know that myself, but I will surely find out for you." As soon as the information can be secured, the manager should provide it.

Develop a positive communication attitude Many managers do a poor communication job because they do not care about it. They sometimes say it is important, but their actions show that they really do not care. Some managers mistakenly assume they have a positive attitude, but actually they tell a worker only what they think is necessary, or they communicate only when they are compelled to do so. The positive manager attempts to share information with employees according to their needs. The manager helps employees *feel* informed, as well as *be* informed.

Plan for communication No managerial plan of action is complete until there is a plan for communicating it to those who will be affected. Since people like to be told in advance about changes that affect them, communication usually comes at the beginning of a course of action rather than at the end of it. Perhaps you, the reader, can remember times in your own experience when you were not informed of actions that clearly affected you. This feeling is not a pleasant one.

Some elements of an effective communication plan were identified in a study of memorable messages—those that have a powerful influence on people. Researchers found that we remember best the communications that are personal, timely, and brief, require our participation in completing them, and are applicable to future situations.[10] These are practical guides that make downward communication more likely to succeed, if well planned.

Memorable messages

Develop trust Trust between senders and receivers is important in all communication. When trust is lacking, information flow among people is reduced.[11] They have less drive to send messages and less reason to believe those which are received. Without trust, employees search between the lines, wondering, "Why did management say that?" If subordinates do not have trust in superiors, they are not as likely to listen or to believe management messages. The result tends to be restricted flows of information, negative reactions, and distortions of what was said.

Consequences of distrust

Consider the case of two managers from the same firm who were told by their superior not to discuss pay with each other, because the other one might be unhappy to learn of a lower salary. Later, at a New Year's Eve party, they started talking and discovered that they were earning exactly the same amount. How much will they trust their superior in the future?

Communication needs

Employees at lower levels have a number of communication needs. Managers think that they understand these needs, but often their employees do not think so. This fundamental difference in perception tends to exist at each level in organizations, thereby making communication more difficult. It causes downward communicators to be overconfident and probably not to take enough care with their downward messages.

Job instruction One communication need of employees is instructions regarding their work. In a situation like this, managers secure better results if they state their instructions in terms of the objective requirements of the job, so that the instructions do not appear to be a personal wish.

The need for objective information is especially important with employees in a new job or organization. Because their high expectations often conflict with reality, they quickly become dissatisfied. To prevent this, firms are using more *realistic job previews,* where job candidates are given a small sample of organizational reality. Just as a medical vaccination stimulates the body to develop natural resistance to a disease, the realistic preview minimizes the employee's unmet expectations by providing both positive and negative information about the potential work environment. When this method is used, turnover of new employees is reduced.[12]

Turnover reduced by realistic job previews

Managers also need to adjust their communications according to the task needs of their receivers. For example, as the uncertainty of a task increases, there is a predictable need for increased information flow in order to maintain a comparable level of performance. Thus an employee performing a standardized, repetitive machine task needs little communication input about the task. On the other hand, an engineer working on a new product may require substantial communication input in order to perform successfully.

Performance improved by feedback

Performance feedback Employees also need feedback about their performance. There are many reasons. It helps them know what to do and how well they are meeting their own goals. It shows that others are interested in what they are doing. Assuming that performance is satisfactory, it enhances one's self-image and feeling of competence. Generally, performance feedback leads to both improved performance and improved attitudes.

A review of eighteen studies that examined the effects of feedback on employee job performance provides supporting evidence.[13] In all cases performance increased, ranging from 6 to 125 percent. Where comprehensive measures were used, the median increase in productivity was 16 percent, and that translated into substantial cost savings for the employers.

Guides for giving feedback

Giving feedback is a challenging task for managers. Feedback is more likely to be accepted and cause some improvement when it is properly presented (see Figure 20-4). In general, it should focus on specific job behaviors, rely on objective data rather than perceptions and inferences, be given soon after a critical event, and be checked for understanding by the receiver. Overall, it has the greatest chance of success if it is genuinely desired and if the receiver is allowed to choose a new behavior from alternative recommendations offered.[14]

In spite of the importance of performance feedback, many managers fail to provide enough of it. For example, top managers in one firm reported that they gave their middle managers adequate feedback about performance. However, the middle managers said that they were not receiving enough feedback.[15]

Importance of timeliness

News Downward messages should reach employees as news rather than as a stale confirmation of what already has been learned from other sources. Some employers prepare daily recorded telephone messages that employees can receive by dialing a certain number. Messages can be changed during the day as new information becomes available. The systems usually are automatic, operating twenty-four hours daily, so that employees can call from their

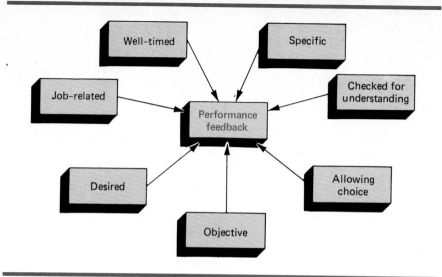

Figure 20-4
Guidelines
for effective
performance
feedback

homes or elsewhere. Some systems are adjusted to allow telephone questions and comments from employees. Where an answer is appropriate, it is secured and put on the system at a later date. In this manner two-way communication is established. Other in-house media include bulletin boards, inserts in pay envelopes, posters, and closed-circuit television.[16]

Communication overload

Managers sometimes operate with the philosophy that "more communication is better communication." They give employees enormous amounts of information until employees find that they are overwhelmed with data, but understanding is not improved. What happens is a *communication overload,* in which employees receive more communication inputs than they can process or than they need.[17] The key to better communication is quality, not quantity. It is possible to have better understanding with less total communication if it is of higher quality.

Quality preferable to quantity

Manager Nicolo Fumusa liked to ramble on and on. He thought that more was better. He buried his employees with mountains of information every time he talked with them. After a few experiences of this type, they avoided him. They had a communication overload but were deprived of understanding. One employee commented, "It takes him twenty minutes to say yes and thirty minutes to say no." Another observed philosophically, "You ask him what time it is, and he tells you how the clock works—but he still hasn't told you what time it is."

Nicolo's employees were annoyed and confused by his behavior. They complained to others, and some of them lost interest in their jobs. Management sensed the problem and tried to correct Nicolo, but he did not respond. After about a year, management decided to discharge him. He could not manage because he could not communicate.

Acceptance of a communication

In the final analysis, an employee's acceptance of a communication depends on certain conditions.[18] These conditions apply especially to downward communication and are summarized in Figure 20-5.

Reasons for acceptance
As shown in the figure, a receiver needs some basis for accepting the legitimacy of a communication sender. For example, the president of an advanced-technology company may listen to a taxi driver's comments about what advanced technology companies should do, but the president is unlikely to follow that advice because of its low legitimacy.

A receiver also needs to feel that a sender has competence in the subject communicated. Other conditions are trust in the sender and perceived credibility of the message received. For example, if you have been misled on numerous occasions by job instructions from a coworker, you probably will ignore the next instruction. It lacks credibility.

In most situations a communication is more acceptable if you also accept the tasks and goals that it is trying to accomplish. Then you are motivated to listen and to respond cooperatively. If you are somewhat lacking in motivation, then your acceptance may depend more on the power of the sender to enforce sanctions on you.

UPWARD COMMUNICATION

Upward communication is necessary.
If the two-way flow of information is broken by poor upward communication, management loses touch with employee needs and lacks sufficient information to make sound decisions. It is, therefore, unable to be supportive of work-group needs.

> The need for upward communication is illustrated by the difficult experience of a manufacturing company. During a period of two or three years, as the company gradually grew, there was a noticeable letdown in productivity and effective work practices. Management made increasing use of methods engineers and more careful standards. In addition, supervisors were encouraged to tighten up and put pressure on their employees. Productivity still lagged; so management used various downward

Figure 20-5
Conditions that encourage acceptance of a communication

- Acceptance of the legitimacy of the sender to send the communication
- Perceived competence of the sender relative to the issue communicated
- Trust in the sender as a leader and person
- Perceived credibility of the message received
- Acceptance of the tasks and goals that the communication is trying to accomplish
- Power of the sender to enforce sanctions on the receiver either directly or indirectly

communication actions such as bulletins, leaflets, and pay-envelope notices to encourage employees to be more productive. Articles were put in the company magazine to try to motivate employees toward more enthusiasm and loyalty. Production, however, remained low.

Finally, management brought in an interviewing team from the home office. Most complaints were petty ones, but there did seem to be a general feeling among older supervisors and employees that as the company grew, they were becoming more and more separated from higher management. They felt isolated and unable to discuss their problems with anyone. Then as management tightened its standards, they felt unreasonable pressures. Gradually, they became alienated from management and tended to spread their alienation to the newer employees who were being hired as the company expanded.

As soon as management discovered the basic problem, it was able to take corrective action. The unfortunate fact is that most of these difficulties could have been avoided in the beginning if management had developed an effective procedure for genuinely encouraging upward communication. With effective upward communication, management could have recognized the tendency toward alienation early enough to do something about it.

Upward difficulties

There tends to be a minimum of upward communication unless management positively encourages it. This problem is even greater in larger, more complex organizations. Management needs to "tune in" to employees in the same way a person with a radio tunes in. This requires initiative and positive action rather than simply waiting for the signal to come in. Tuning in requires management adaptability to different channels of employee information. It requires sensitivity to even the weak signals from employees, to the distant signals, and to those near at hand. It requires first and last an awareness that upward messages are important.

Upward communications tend to travel slowly. They are usually subject to delay and filtering. Each level is reluctant to take a problem upward because to do so is considered an admission of failure; therefore each level delays the communication in an effort to decide how to solve the problem.[19] If the problem cannot be solved, the message may be filtered so that higher management receives only part of the information. There is a natural tendency for an employee to tell a superior only what the employee thinks the superior wants to hear. Obviously a superior cannot be told all that subordinates know, so each subordinate has genuine reasons for selecting, interpreting, and other filtering actions. Usually the employee is doing the best that human emotions and judgment will allow, but by the time filtering has happened at several levels, the original communication may be hardly recognizable.

Messages are delayed and filtered.

To further complicate the situation, even when undesirable feedback reaches top managers, they often are so involved with other issues that they may overlook it and not respond to it. Many firms have developed serious problems because they did not pay attention to useful upward communication.

Short-circuiting Sometimes, in an effort to avoid filtering, people *short-circuit* the information chain, which means that they skip one or more steps in the communication hierarchy. Although this avoids filtering, it upsets those who are bypassed, so employers usually discourage it. If it is permitted, an employee often must secure the direct supervisor's permission before talking to someone higher in the chain of command. The grapevine, of course, is the exception. It has no definite channels and can readily short-circuit any formal communication chain.

Need for response When upward communication is received, management needs to respond to it in order to encourage further upward messages. Conversely, lack of response suppresses upward communication, as the following experience indicates.

> Managers of sales branches in one company were encouraged by a memorandum that asked for suggestions to improve the firm's customer relations. Shortly after this memorandum was received by Esther Helbring, a branch manager, she asked the company to review a "fine print" clause in one of its sales contracts because several customers had objected to it. Immediately after her letter, she received a telephone inquiry from a member of higher management. One year later she had received no further feedback and the clause had not been amended. She commented to the interviewer, "A response of this kind doesn't encourage further upward communication."

Upward communication policies and practices

Communication policies are desirable. One way to build better upward communication is to have a general policy stating what kinds of upward messages are desired. Figure 20-6 presents a company policy of this type. It is specific but still leaves judgment to the employees.

In addition to suitable policies, various practices are needed to improve upward communication. Counseling, grievance systems, consultive supervision, suggestion systems, job satisfaction surveys, and other practices are

---

Figure 20-6
A company policy for upward communication

Employees shall keep their direct supervisors informed about the following subjects:

1 Any matters in which the supervisor may be held accountable by those at higher levels (including all basic accountability for performance of one's assigned job)

2 Any matters in disagreement or likely to cause controversy within or between any units of the organization

3 Matters requiring advice by the supervisor or coordination with other people or units

4 Any matters involving recommendations for changes in, or variance from, established policies

5 Any other matter that will enable higher management to improve economic and social performance

discussed in other chapters. Additional practices discussed at this point are employee meetings, an open-door policy, employee letters, and participation in social groups.

Employee meetings   One useful practice to build upward communication is meeting with employees. In these meetings, employees are encouraged to talk about job problems, needs, and management practices that both help and interfere with job performance. The meetings attempt to probe in some depth the issues that are on the minds of employees. As a consequence, employee attitudes improve and turnover declines.[20]

> The president of Hyatt Hotels Corporation holds monthly meetings with small groups of employees and listens attentively to their gripes. "I realize it's the little things that most often affect morale," he says.[21] The input ranges from small to large issues and from positive to negative comments. The president promises to look into each of them and respond soon to the more serious issues.

An open-door policy   An *open-door policy* is a statement that employees are encouraged to come to their supervisor or higher managers with any matter that concerns them. Usually employees are encouraged to see their supervisor first. If their problem is not resolved by the supervisor, then higher management may be approached. The goal is to remove blocks to upward communication. It is a worthy goal, but it is not easy to implement because there often are psychological barriers between managers and employees. Although the manager's door physically is open, psychological and social barriers exist that make employees reluctant to enter. Some employees hesitate to be identified as lacking information or having a problem. Others are afraid they will incur their manager's disfavor.

Barriers may limit its use.

Sometimes an open-door policy is used to mask a manager's own hesitancy to make contacts with those beyond the door. As one manager said, "The open door is often a slogan to hide closed minds." On the other hand, a genuine open door can be a real aid to upward communication. The true test is whether the manager behind the door has an open-door attitude and whether employees feel psychologically free to enter.

An even more effective open door is for managers to walk through their own doors and get out among their people. In this way they will learn more than they ever will sitting in their offices.

Open doors allow two-way movement.

> One company moved its open door from managerial offices to the company cafeteria with dramatic results.[22] It set up a program called "Operation Speakeasy" in which senior managers had lunch with small groups of employees in the company cafeteria. One manager ate with three employees, keeping the group small to allow genuine participation by each employee.
>
> Employees signed for tables on a voluntary basis, and then managers were assigned to tables, making sure that employees ate with someone who did not manage them either directly or indirectly. This arrangement helped employees feel more free to

discuss matters openly. Management promised only to listen. Union approval of the program was secured in advance.

Although the program was voluntary, more than 80 percent of employees chose to participate, and inputs were significant. Each manager made regular reports of problem areas identified at the luncheons, but without mentioning names. These reports became the basis for extensive problem study and corrective action. The main areas of comments were productivity (32 percent), job satisfaction (26 percent), and poor communication (23 percent).

Upward written inputs

Employee letters and question-answer programs Some firms actively encourage letters and written questions from employees. The firms feel that these methods are a personal, direct way for employees to put their ideas before management. Typically the questions are processed anonymously by a management representative who works with the appropriate manager to prepare an informed reply.[23] All letters and questions are answered. If a reply is of general interest, it may be published in the company newspaper or weekly bulletin. In this way management operates a type of written open-door policy to assure that employees feel free to bring their questions all the way to the top if necessary.

The Open Line program of the Bank of America uses printed forms available throughout the organization.[24] Employees address questions to the Open Line coordinator, who types them anonymously on a plain sheet of paper and sends them to the appropriate bank officers. Policy requires the officer to respond within ten days. Responses usually are mailed to the employee's home, but a personal interview with a bank officer can be arranged if an employee wants it.

Social settings for inputs

Participation in social groups Informal, casual recreational events furnish superb opportunities for unplanned upward communication. This spontaneous information sharing reveals true conditions better than most formal communications. There are departmental parties, sports events, bowling groups, hobby groups, picnics, and other employer-sponsored activities. Upward communication is not the primary purpose of these events, but it is an important by-product of them.

COMMUNICATION BY SPECIALISTS

As an institution grows in size and complexity, research, engineering, accounting, and other specialized groups grow in size and importance. These specialists play a leading role in communication beyond their own departments. One reason is that many communication activities usually are assigned to them. In some instances their primary activity is communication. They gather data, issue reports, prepare directives, coordinate activities, and advise employees.

Reasons for active communication

Second, since many specialists lack command authority, they have greater motivation to communicate because they realize that their success is more dependent on selling their ideas to others. Managers with authority, on the other hand, are often lulled into poor communication by the fact that they can order an action even when they cannot sell it.

A third reason is that specialists usually have shorter communication chains to higher management. For example, a supervisor in a large factory must go through five levels to reach the executive vice president, but a personnel specialist goes through only three levels. This proximity to management permits some specialists to have the "ear" of higher management better than lower-level operating managers. The results are both good and bad. Communication upward and downward tends to be improved, but lower management often waits in insecurity with the fear that it is being bypassed or criticized without an opportunity to answer.

Better access to management

A fourth reason is that the specialists' work usually gives them more mobility than operating workers have. Specialists in such areas as personnel and control find that their duties both require and allow them to go out of their offices and visit other areas. They also find it easier to get away for coffee or just to visit. All this means that they have the chance to receive and spread information widely and regularly because they have more communication linkages with others.

Fifth, specialists often are more involved in the chain of procedure than others. For example, a production-control problem may clear through five specialists but only three operating persons while it is being solved.

Finally, many specialists actively communicate with several chains of command rather than just one. They also have many contacts outside the institution. Figure 20-7 shows the communication patterns of an engineering department in a factory. A large number of its contacts are outside its own chain of command and even outside the institution. Its span of communication is broad.

Since specialists communicate actively, (1) they need to be trained in communication regardless of their technical expertise; (2) they need to recognize the importance of their communication role; and (3) management also needs to recognize the importance of their role and make full use of it.

COMMUNICATING WITH EMPLOYEES' FAMILIES

There is general agreement that an employee's on-the-job performance is affected by off-the-job influences, and one of the most significant is the employee's family. Since most regular employer communications, such as bulletin boards, are not available to families, management has to develop special approaches to integrate families into the communication system. Employees usually cooperate in this matter because they want their families to know about their work.

Including the family

A frequent practice is to mail important communications to employees' homes so that family members can read the information if they are interested. Some employers mail their employee magazines to homes, or they ask each employee to take one home. This is successful, because workers report an average home readership of one or two people besides themselves. Other

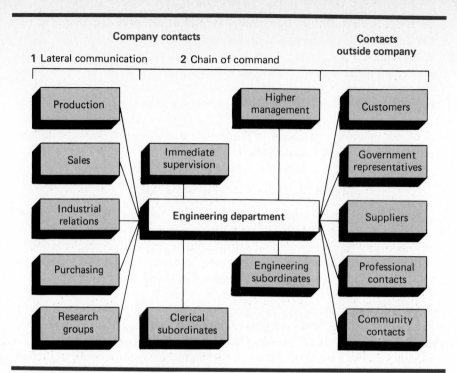

employers provide material for the family through information racks, and they mail their annual report to employee homes.

Open houses   Open houses are a popular way to tell and show families about employee jobs. An open house especially is necessary if the workplace otherwise is inaccessible to families. In addition to open houses, social events that include family members are used to introduce families personally to management. If a company is multiplant, invitations may be extended to visit headquarters. One multistore retailer invites employees and their families to spend a day of their vacation visiting company general offices. They are given a guided tour and taken to a major-league baseball game when one is available.

THE UNION ROLE IN COMMUNICATION

When a labor union represents any employee group, it has a direct interest in what information the employees receive; however, the degree to which a union should participate in a firm's communication program is a matter of debate.

Advantages   The chief advantages of union participation are:

1 The union is a regularly established channel on which many employees already depend.

2 Its support of any information may strengthen employee acceptance of the information.

3 If the union is left out, it may, without consulting the employer, interpret the situation in ways that are harmful to the employer.

Four disadvantages of union participation are:

Disadvantages

1 If management shares some of its communication activities with the union, management releases control but is still responsible. This is unwise.

2 If management lets the union handle much of its communication, management gets out of practice, becomes stale, and is unable to do its communication job when it must.

3 Unions have their own communication problems, which are more than they can handle and will receive first priority anyway; therefore, it is unwise to expect the union to help.

4 The union might misuse the information for its own benefit.

Assuming that a union represents employees, it already is involved in many communication activities, such as grievance procedures and layoff notices. The real question, then, is whether the union should be brought further into the communication program. This depends upon the type of cooperation and understanding that exists in each individual employer-union relationship. In some cases, it is desirable; in other cases, it would be hazardous. In any case, management should be certain that any information that is released to the union also is given earlier or concurrently to members of management. To do otherwise places supervisors at a disadvantage when dealing with employees and the union.

Case-by-case decisions

SUMMARY

Communication is the process by which all human interaction takes place. Significant groups in this process are management, employees, specialists, families of employees, and labor unions. Management communication is especially important because it is the usual channel by which information reaches employees, and most links in the communication chain are within management. Upward communication is much more difficult to develop than downward communication.

Specialists play an active communication role. They have the responsibility, motivation, organizational position, mobility, and procedural involvement needed to communicate extensively. The family is significant in communication because its feelings affect employee performance. Unions also may be involved in a communication program. An effective communication system results when all persons and groups are interacting with understanding of the events that affect them.

TERMS AND CONCEPTS FOR REVIEW

Lateral communication or
cross-communication

Boundary spanners

Networks

Networking

Realistic job previews

Communication overload

Short-circuiting

Open-door policy

Union participation in
communication

REVIEW QUESTIONS

1 Why is communication within the management group important?

2 Do you belong to any network? What is it? Explain how you became a part of it, and what it has done for you.

3 What kind of communication tends to dominate in mechanistic organizations? Discuss.

4 How would you communicate the following messages if you were an accountant in a nonunion office situation?
 a A complaint about your job
 b A marketing suggestion to the marketing department
 c An effort to get the accounting pool typist to do more accurate work
 d An error in a report sent to you by another department

5 Organize into small groups and discuss the importance of trust in communication. Prepare a group list of actions that a communicator can take to build trust, and report this to the entire classroom group.

6 Think of a part-time or full-time job that you have had. Did you experience communication overload in any subject? Discuss.

7 Thinking of the job in question 6, discuss how well management handled downward communication to you.

8 Thinking of the job in question 6, discuss any upward communication difficulties that you had and what you did to try to overcome them. Was there an open-door policy? Did it work?

9 Discuss the reasons for active specialist communication.

10 Assuming that you are a supervisor in a company of your choice, what would be your decision regarding union participation in your communication activities?

INCIDENTS

The Early Work Schedule

Mabel Thomas was employed to work with the food service of Community Hospital. She was married but had no children. The job for which she was employed required that she work two days a week from 5 A.M. to 2 P.M. The other three days she worked the regular day food schedule from 8:30 A.M. to 5:30 P.M. When she was employed, either she failed to hear information about the early work schedule or the employment clerk forgot to tell her. She feels sure that if the early schedule had been mentioned to her, she would have heard it, because under those conditions she would not have taken the job.

During the first two weeks the job required Thomas to work the regular day shift in order to have an instructor show her how to do the job; so Thomas thought she was on the regular day shift. She vaguely remembers that near the end of her first two weeks her supervisor mentioned something to her about beginning her regular schedule, but she did not understand what the supervisor meant and she did not inquire further. The result was that Thomas failed to report to work on the early schedule on the required day. When she did report for work at the regular hour of 8:30 A.M., her supervisor criticized her for lack of responsibility. Thomas said she could not work the early shift for family reasons and resigned.

QUESTION

Analyze the communication blockages in this case. Discuss ideas such as upward and downward communication, listening, feedback, and inference. Then explain how you would handle the employment and probationary work period for Thomas.

The Office Procedure

Joe Gonzales was a new employee with less than six months of seniority, but he had several years of office experience elsewhere. His new supervisor, Jane Campbell, was recently transferred from another supervisory position in the office. On one occasion Gonzales came to Campbell for help with an office procedure. Campbell offered a suggestion, but Gonzales failed to follow it and problems developed with the procedure. Within two months this same chain of events was repeated three more times. Campbell took no action regarding these events.

After the fourth mistake, the office manager, who was Campbell's supervisor, went directly to Gonzales to discuss the error with him. Campbell saw them talking and arrived in time to hear Gonzales say, "I keep asking Jane for help, but she doesn't give me much."

Campbell intervened and said, "Joe, you know that's not true, and if you ever lie about me again, I'll fire you." Campbell then walked away.

QUESTIONS

1 Discuss the communication errors and successes made by all three parties in this relationship.

2 What action should be taken by any of the three parties at the end of the case? Discuss.

EXPERIENTIAL EXERCISE

The Route Manager's Suggestion

Jim Abel is a route manager for a bottling plant serving a metropolitan area of about 250,000 persons and a large number of small towns as much as fifty miles away. Abel is married, age twenty-nine, a high school graduate, and a friendly person. His employees like him and work well with him. In addition, he is cooperative with management and reasonably energetic. He became a route manager only six months ago and has only four years of seniority. He appears to be the kind of person who has potential for long-run service and possibly further promotion.

On Tuesday afternoon Abel walked into the office of his sales manager, Ralph Parks, and asked, "Do you have five minutes, Ralph?" Parks was an older person with fifteen years of seniority and one year's experience in the job of sales manager. At that time he was quite busy with some rush reports for the front office, so he replied, "Sure, we can take five, but let's keep it short, because I have to get these reports finished."

Abel sat down and proceeded to get enthusiastic about an idea he had for improving route procedures in a way that he thought might save both mileage and time. He was so enthusiastic that five minutes passed and then ten minutes, but his idea was not yet fully explained. However, from what had been said, it appeared to Parks that this idea had been proposed a number of times before and was tried about five years ago—and it failed. Parks was getting impatient. He needed to finish those reports, and he could take no more time.

Feeling that he should not dampen Abel's enthusiasm at this point, Parks told Abel that the idea was more complicated than he expected and they had more than used up his available time. He suggested that they meet together the next morning at an appointed time when Parks would have more time for discussion. Even though Parks was sure that Abel's idea would not work, he thought at least he should hear Abel's full story, since this was his first major suggestion as route manager.

The next morning Abel was ready at the appointed time, and the men had a thorough fifteen-minute discussion. Abel was enthusiastic about his suggestion, but by the end of the discussion it was evident to Parks that the idea was the same kind that had been tried before and had failed. However, Abel had so much enthusiasm for the idea, Parks was not sure what to do.

ASSIGNMENT

Divide the class into pairs of individuals. Have one person assume the role of Jim Abel, and the other the role of Ralph Parks. After a few minutes to study the background of the case, have each pair role-play Parks's further discussion with Abel. Then obtain brief reports from each pair regarding what took place and how effective Parks's approach was.

REFERENCES

1 Norman B. Sigband, "Proaction, Not Reaction, for Effective Employee Communication," *Personnel Journal,* March 1982, p. 190.

2 John M. Ivancevich and J. Timothy McMahon, "The Effects of Goal Setting, External Feedback, and Self-Generated Feedback on Outcome Variables: A Field Experiment," *Academy of Management Journal,* June 1982, p. 359.

3 For research support of message loss within management, see Keith Davis, "Success of Chain-of-Command Oral Communication in a Manufacturing Management Group," *Academy of Management Journal,* December 1968, pp. 379–387.

4 Alma S. Baron, "Communication Skills for the Woman Manager—A Practice Seminar," *Personnel Journal,* January 1980, pp. 55ff.

5 A. K. Wickesberg, "Communication Networks in the Business Organization Structure," *Academy of Management Journal,* September 1968, pp. 253–262. Another study of managers found that 42 percent of their communication was with their peers; see S. V. Voland and M. R. Davies, "Communication Patterns of Managers," *The Journal of Business Communication,* Winter 1982, pp. 41–53. See also Peter R. Monge, Jane A. Edwards, and Kenneth R. Kirste, "Determinants of Communication Network Involvement: Connectedness and Integration," *Group and Organization Studies,* March 1983, pp. 83–111.

6 Michael L. Tushman and Thomas J. Scanlan, "Characteristics and External Orientations of Boundary Spanning Individuals," *Academy of Management Journal,* March 1981, pp. 83–98; Fred R. David, John A. Pearce II, and Thelma C. Elliott, "Characteristics and Internal Orientations of Boundary Spanning Individuals," Kae H. Chung (ed.), *Proceedings 1982,* Mississippi State, Miss.: Academy of Management, August 1982.

7 Virginia E. Schein and Larry E. Greiner, "Can Organization Development Be Fine Tuned to Bureaucracies?" *Organizational Dynamics,* Winter 1977, p. 54. Some features of the American Express Company program are summarized in "How Amex Employees Learn What's Happening," *Management Review,* February 1980, pp. 48–49.

8 Sue DeWine and Diane Casbolt, "Networking: External Communication Systems for Female Organization Members," *The Journal of Business Communication,* Spring 1983, pp. 57–67; Andrew Kakabadse, "Politics of Interpersonal Influence: Issues for the Management Development Adviser," *Journal of Management Development,* vol. 1, no. 3, 1982, pp. 43–53.

9 Nancy Foy, "Networkers of the World, Unite!" *Personnel Management,* March 1983, pp. 24–27. Geographically separated networkers can also communicate by electronic mail. See, for example, Donald A. Norman, "The Computer Always Rings Twice," *Psychology Today,* October 1983, pp. 46–50.

10 Mark L. Knapp, Cynthia Stohl, and Kathleen K. Reardon, "Memorable Messages," *Journal of Communication,* Autumn 1981, pp. 27–41.

11 A comparison of trust levels between American and Japanese firms, and the consequences, is portrayed in "Trust: The New Ingredient in Management," *Business Week,* July 1981, pp. 104–108.

12 Paula Popovich and John P. Wanous, "The Realistic Job Preview as a Persuasive Communication," *Academy of Management Review,* October 1982, pp. 570–578; Joan M. Pearson, "The Transition into a New Job: Tasks, Problems, and Outcomes," *Personnel Journal,* April 1982, pp. 286–290; and Richard R. Reilly and others, "The Effects of Realistic Previews: A Study and Discussion of the Literature," *Personnel Psychology,* Winter 1981, pp. 823–834.

13 Richard E. Kopelman, "Improving Productivity through Objective Feedback: A Review of the Evidence," *National Productivity Review,* Winter 1982–83, pp. 43–55. For examples of specific experiments, see Tamao Matsui, Akinori Okada, and Osamu Inoshita, "Mechanism of Feedback Affecting Task Performance," *Organizational Behavior and Human Performance,* February 1983, pp. 114–122; and Judith L. Komaki, Robert L. Collins, and Pat Penn, "The Role of Performance Antecedents and Consequences in Work Motivation," *Journal of Applied Psychology,* June 1982, pp. 334–340.

14 Ron Zemke, "Feedback Technology and the Growing Appetite for Self-Knowledge," *Training,* April 1982, pp. 28ff; the criteria for effective feedback

under normal and crisis conditions are presented in William B. Sherwood, "Developing Subordinates: Critical to Managers and Their Organizations," *Personnel*, January–February 1983, pp. 46–52; and Gary G. Whitney, "When the News Is Bad: Leveling with Employees," *Personnel*, January–February 1983, pp. 37–45.

15 Robert Kreitner, "People Are Systems, Too: Filling the Feedback Vacuum," *Business Horizons*, December 1977, pp. 54–55.

16 Walter St. John, "In-House Communication Guidelines," *Personnel Journal*, November 1981, pp. 872–878.

17 Charles A. O'Reilly III, "Individuals and Information Overload in Organizations: Is More Necessarily Better?" *Academy of Management Journal*, December 1980, pp. 684–696; Reed Sanderlin, "Information Is Not Communication," *Business Horizons*, March–April 1982, pp. 40–42.

18 Two studies supporting the compliance of subordinates to directives of their superiors are Linda McCallister, "Predicted Employee Compliance to Downward Communication Styles," *The Journal of Business Communication*, Winter 1983, pp. 67–79; and Kathleen M. Watson, "An Analysis of Communication Patterns: A Method for Discriminating Leader and Subordinate Roles," *Academy of Management Journal*, March 1982, pp. 107–120.

19 A study identifying the problems with upward communication by employees is Cal W. Downs and Charles Conrad, "Effective Subordinancy," *The Journal of Business Communication*, Spring 1982, pp. 27–37.

20 John G. Carlson and Kenneth D. Hill, "The Effect of Gaming on Attendance and Attitude," *Personnel Psychology*, Spring 1982, pp. 63–73; and David Krackhardt, John McKenna, Lyman W. Porter, and Richard M. Steers, "Superior Behavior and Employee Turnover: A Field Experiment," *Academy of Management Journal*, June 1981, pp. 249–259. See also Norman B. Sigband, loc. cit.

21 Lawrence Rout, "Hyatt Hotels' Gripe Sessions Help Chief Maintain Communications with Workers," *Wall Street Journal*, July 16, 1981, pp. 25, 41.

22 J. N. Smith, "Operation Speakeasy: An Experiment in Communication," *Management Review*, March 1973, pp. 46–50.

23 Suggestions for adapting the respondent's style to fit the situation are in John S. Fielden, "What Do You Mean, You Don't Like My Style?" *Harvard Business Review*, May–June 1982, pp. 238–138.

24 "Listening and Responding to Employees' Concerns," *Harvard Business Review*, January–February 1980, pp. 101–114. A system for handling employee complaints is discussed in Mary P. Rowe and Michael Baker, "Are You Hearing Enough Employee Concerns?" *Harvard Business Review*, May–June 1984, pp. 127–135.

FOR ADDITIONAL READING

DeMare, George, *Communicating at the Top*, New York: John Wiley & Sons, Inc., 1979.

Klauss, Rudi, and Bernard M. Bass, *Interpersonal Communication in Organizations*, New York: Academic Press, 1982.

Munter, Mary, *Guide to Managerial Communication*, Englewood Cliffs, N.J.: Prentice-Hall, Inc., 1982.

Porter, Lyman W., and K. H. Roberts (eds.), *Communication in Organizations*, London: Penguin Books, Inc., 1977.

Sigband, Norman B., and David N. Bateman, *Communicating in Business,* Glenview, Ill.: Scott, Foresman & Company, 1981.

Treece, Malra, *Communication for Business and the Professions,* 2d ed., Rockleigh, N.J.: Allyn and Bacon, 1983.

Wanous, J. P., *Organizational Entry: Recruitment, Selection and Socialization of Newcomers,* Reading, Mass.: Addison-Wesley Publishing Company, Inc., 1980.

Welch, M. S., *Networking: The Great New Way for Women to Get Ahead,* New York: Harcourt, Brace, Jovanovich, 1980.

STRESS AND COUNSELING

Friend (to worker with unpleasant factory job): "Doesn't your job give you a lot of trouble?"
Worker: "Bother, perhaps, but never trouble. You see, trouble is on the heart, but bother is only on the hands."

Anonymous

Stress will have to be alleviated by good managerial practice, based on a sophisticated understanding of people.

Harry Levinson[1]

CHAPTER OBJECTIVES

TO UNDERSTAND:
The role of stress in employee mental health
Causes of stress
How stress is related to job performance
Management actions that may reduce stress
Different types of counseling and their usefulness
Different counseling functions

I n an insurance office, the work of a young stenographer became erratic as the result of an emotional conflict she was having with her mother. In a foundry, a skilled worker asked for transfer to a semiskilled job in another department because "I just wouldn't work for that stupid supervisor one more day." These kinds of situations illustrate stressful conditions that often can be helped by counseling. No matter how well human relationships are handled, people occasionally develop emotional problems, and a prime way to treat these difficulties is to counsel one or more of the parties involved.

In this chapter we discuss what stress is and how it affects job performance. Then we discuss types of counseling and how they are used to help employees with their problems.

EMPLOYEE STRESS

Stress

Stress is a condition of strain on one's emotions, thought processes, and physical condition. When it is excessive, it can threaten one's ability to cope with the environment. "Stress" is the general term applied to the pressures people feel in life. As a result of these pressures, employees develop various symptoms of stress that can harm their job performance. As shown in Figure 21-1, people who are stressed may become nervous and develop chronic

Symptoms of stress

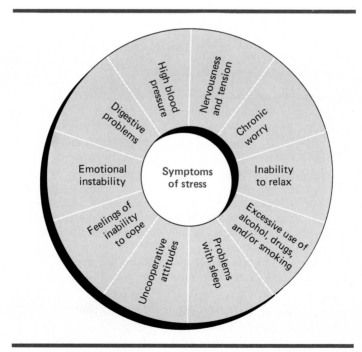

Figure 21-1
Typical symptoms of stress

worry. They are easily provoked to anger and are unable to relax. They may be uncooperative or use alcohol or drugs excessively. These conditions occur from other causes also, but they are common symptoms of stress.

Stress also leads to physical disorders, because the internal body system changes to try to cope with stress. Some physical disorders are short-range, such as an upset stomach. Others are longer-range, such as a stomach ulcer. Stress over a prolonged time also leads to degenerative diseases of the heart, kidneys, blood vessels, and other parts of the body. Therefore it is important that life stress, both on and off the job, be kept at a level low enough for most people to tolerate without disorders.

> For example, Peter Randall was transferred from a small city to a very large city where his commuting time to work was nearly one hour. He disliked city noises, heavy traffic, and crowds, and he felt he was wasting his time while commuting. His new job also had more responsibilities.
>
> Within a few months he developed intestinal problems. When a medical examination showed no medical cause of his difficulties, he was sent to a counselor. There was only slight improvement, so finally his counselor in cooperation with his physician recommended that he transfer to a smaller city. His firm arranged his transfer, and within a short time his problems disappeared.

There is emerging evidence that in some situations an organization can be held legally liable for the emotional and physical impact of job stress on employees like Peter. Poor working conditions, sustained conflicts with supervisors, traumatic events, or intentional harassment of employees sometimes results in anguish, neuroses, or even suicide. If liability is established, employees could claim benefits under workers' compensation laws, as well as sue for financial damages.[2]

Duration and intensity of stress

Stress can be either temporary or long-term, mild or severe, depending mostly on how long its causes continue, how powerful they are, and how strong the employee's recovery powers are. If stress is temporary and mild, most people can handle it or at least recover from its effects rather quickly.

> Meyer Jamison, a sales representative, was transferred to a new territory after nine years in his old territory. Suddenly he found himself in a new and unknown situation with different people and job requirements. He felt frustrated, uneasy, and overloaded with work. There was too much to learn in too short a time. He developed conflicts with two or three customers and became less cooperative at home. He was in a condition of mild stress.
>
> After a few weeks in his new territory, his stress gradually disappeared, and eventually he became as comfortable as he had been in his old territory.

In contrast to Meyer's temporary stress, some major pressures are sustained for long periods of time. Problems then arise because the body cannot

Employee burnout   rebuild its ability to cope with stress. This condition is called *burnout*—a situation where employees suffer from chronic fatigue, boredom, depression, and powerful alienation from their jobs.[3] Burned-out workers are more likely to complain, blame others for problems, be highly irritable, and be cynical about their careers.

The common explanation for burnout is that one's energy resources have become depleted through excessive and prolonged stress. Primary characteristics of burnout are emotional exhaustion, detachment from relationships, and a sense of low personal accomplishment.[4] Organizations are awakening to their responsibility for identifying burnout situations, reducing their effects, and helping employees cope with them. An important first step is to examine the causes of stress, and these will be discussed here.

Causes of stress

Conditions that tend to cause stress are called *stressors*. Although even a single stressor may cause major stress, usually stressors combine to pressure an employee in a variety of ways until stress develops.

> **The experience of Walter Mathis, an automobile mechanic, illustrates how stressful conditions build into groups. Mathis felt that he was doing well, but then he failed to get a wage increase he had expected. At about the same time, his wife divorced him. A short time later, partly because of problems leading to the divorce, he underwent a detailed audit by the U.S. Internal Revenue Service. So many different problems were hitting Mathis that he began to show signs of stress.**

Figure 21-2
Causes, types, and consequences of stress

Source: *Parts of the model are adapted from Randall S. Schuler, "An Integrative Transactional Process Model of Stress in Organizations,"* Journal of Occupational Behaviour, January 1982, pp. 5–19.

This example illustrates the results of an ongoing study by the National Institute of Mental Health.[5] It reports that the major sources of employee stress are evenly divided between organizational factors and the nonwork environment. These dual causes are reflected in Figure 21-2, which shows that

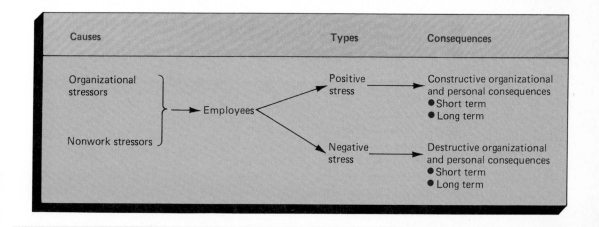

employees may respond to these stressors with either positive stress (which stimulates them) or negative stress (which detracts from their efforts). As a result, there are constructive or destructive consequences for both the organization and the employee. These effects may be short-term and diminish quickly, or they may last a long time. To control stress, then, organizations usually begin by exploring its job-related causes.[6]

Job causes of stress

Examples of job stressors

Almost any job condition can cause stress, depending upon an employee's reaction to it. For example, one employee will accept a new work procedure while another rejects it. There are, however, a number of job conditions that frequently cause stress for employees. Major ones are shown in Figure 21-3.

Work overload and time deadlines put employees under pressure and lead to stress. Often, some of these pressures arise from supervision, so a poor quality of supervision can cause stress. Examples are an autocratic supervisor, an insecure political climate, and inadequate authority to match one's responsibilities.

> For example, Marsha Oldburg worked three years as a production expediter in an electronics plant. She experienced frequent emergencies, conflict, tight schedules, and pressures. She seldom had enough authority to match her responsibility. Occasionally she commented, "This job is getting me down." At about this time, she discovered during a routine physical checkup that she had high blood pressure. After discussions with a physician, she consulted a personnel counselor, who helped her transfer to a job with less pressure and a better match of authority with responsibility. Within six months her blood pressure was under control.

Role conflict and ambiguity also are related to stress.[7] In situations of this type, people have different expectations of an employee's activities on a job, so the employee does not know what to do and cannot meet all expectations. In addition, the job often is poorly defined, so the employee has no official model on which to depend.

A further cause of stress is important differences between company values and employee values. In a sense, these differences "tear the employee apart"

Figure 21-3
Typical causes of stress on the job

- Work overload
- Time pressures
- Poor quality of supervision
- Insecure political climate
- Inadequate authority to match responsibilities
- Role conflict and ambiguity
- Differences between company and employee values
- Change of any type, especially when it is major or unusual, such as temporary layoff
- Frustration

with mental stress as an effort is made to meet the requirements of both sets of values. Achievement-oriented employees also may provide self-induced stress by setting their own values and goals far beyond what they are able to accomplish on the job.[8]

Some jobs provide more stress than others. Those that involve machine-paced manual tasks or are done in a hazardous environment are associated with greater stress.[9] Evidence also indicates that the sources of stress differ by organizational level. Managerial stressors include pressure for quality, numerous meetings, and responsibility for the work of others. Workers are more likely to experience the stressors of low status, resource shortages, and the demand for a large volume of work.[10]

A general and widely recognized cause of stress is change of any type, because it requires adaptation by employees. It tends to be especially stressful when it is major or unusual, such as a temporary layoff or transfer.

Stress varies across jobs.

Frustration

Another cause of stress is *frustration*. It is a result of a motivation (drive) being blocked to prevent one from reaching a desired goal. If you are trying to finish a report by quitting time in the afternoon, and one interference after another develops to require your time, then by the middle of the afternoon, when you see that your goal for the day may not be reached, you are likely to become frustrated. You may become irritable, develop an uneasy feeling in your stomach, or have some other reaction. These reactions to frustration are known as *defense mechanisms,* because you are trying to defend yourself from the psychological effects of the blocked goal.

What are defense mechanisms?

The example given is merely a one-day frustration that probably will be overcome tomorrow, but the situation is more serious when there is a long-run frustration, such as a blocked opportunity for promotion.[11] Then you have to live with the frustration day after day. It begins to build emotional disorders that interfere with your ability to function effectively.

Types of reactions   One of the most common reactions to frustration is aggression. Whenever people are aggressive, it is likely that they are reflecting frustrations that are upsetting them. Additional reactions to frustration include apathy, withdrawal, regression, fixation, physical disorders, and substitute goals. We can illustrate them by continuing the story of the blocked promotion. Suppose that you think your supervisor is blocking your promotion. The blockage may be real or only a result of your imagination, but in any case it is real to you. As a result of your frustration, you may become aggressive by demanding better treatment and threatening to appeal to higher management. Or you may do almost the reverse and become apathetic, not responding to your job or associates. Another reaction is withdrawal, such as asking for a transfer or quitting your job. Regression to less mature behavior also is possible, such as self-pity and pouting.

If there is a fixation, perhaps you constantly blame your supervisor for both your problems and the problems of others, regardless of the true facts. You also may develop a physical disorder such as an upset stomach or choose a substitute goal such as becoming the leader of a powerful informal group in office politics. All of these are possible reactions to frustration. It is evident that they are not usually favorable, either to the individual or to the organization, so it is desirable in organizational behavior to reduce frustrating conditions.

Sources of frustration   Although the example that was discussed concerns management as the source of frustration, management is only one of several sources. Another major source is coworkers who may place barriers in the way of goal attainment. Perhaps they delay work inputs to you, thereby delaying your work. Or their poorly done inputs prevent you from doing quality work. You also can be frustrated by the work itself, such as a part that does not fit or a machine that breaks down. Even the environment, such as a rainy day, may prevent you from doing the work you intended.

Reasons for worker frustration

The A. B. Dick Company surveyed over 1000 adults in an attempt to learn the causes of frustration in the workplace. The following items were most commonly mentioned: lack of recognition, equipment breakdowns, personality conflicts, boredom, and lack of proper training.[12] (Note that most of the reasons given are outside the employee.)

A source of frustration rarely recognized is you, yourself. Perhaps your goals are higher than your present abilities. You may want promotion to a job that requires mathematical ability, but you did not learn it well in school, so others are better prepared for the job. The result is that you are frustrated. A mature solution is to return to school part time and learn the mathematics that you lack. However, you may not be able to invest the time, so you remain frustrated as long as the strong drive exists.

Pamela Bond was a supervisor who did not bother to learn proper grammar in community college. As a supervisor, she had reports to prepare and knew that she did not do them well. She was frustrated, defensive, and critical of those who presented reports to her. She felt that any further promotion was blocked until she learned to write.

Management finally recognized that a number of employees had problems similar to Bond's. It developed a training course in business writing and encouraged supervisors to take it. Bond took the course and learned so much that she later took a follow-up course in a community college. Within a year her language frustration vanished and her performance improved.

Frustration and management practice   The stronger one's motivation or drive toward a blocked goal, the stronger one's frustration will be, other things being equal. If motivation is lacking, then very little frustration is likely to develop. This means that when management attempts to motivate employees strongly, it also should be prepared to remove barriers and help prepare the way for employees to reach their goals. The required managerial role is a supportive one. For example, if precision machine work is encouraged, the machinist needs proper training, equipment, tools, and materials for preci-

Supportive management needed

sion work. Similarly if an employee is assigned a special project and motivated to do it, then a suitable budget and other support are required in order to prevent frustration. The idea is not to remove all difficulties so that the assignment loses its challenge but rather to provide enough support to make the project reasonably possible.

Counseling can help reduce frustrations by helping employees choose mature courses of action to overcome blockages preventing goal accomplishment. The counselor also can advise management regarding blockages so that it can try to reduce or remove them.

Stress and job performance

Stress can be either helpful or harmful to job performance, depending upon the amount of it. Figure 21-4 presents a *stress-performance model* that shows the relationship between stress and job performance.[13] When there is no stress, job challenges are absent and performance tends to be low. As stress increases, performance tends to increase, because stress helps a person call up resources to meet job requirements. It is a healthy stimulus that encourages employees to respond to challenges. Eventually stress reaches a plateau that corresponds approximately with a person's top day-to-day performance capability. At this point additional stress tends to produce no more improvement.

Finally, if stress becomes too great, performance begins to decline, because stress interferes with it. An employee loses ability to cope, becomes unable to make decisions, and is erratic in behavior. If stress increases to a breaking point, performance becomes zero; the employee has a breakdown, becomes too ill to work, is fired, quits, or refuses to come to work to face the stress.[14]

Effects of stress on performance

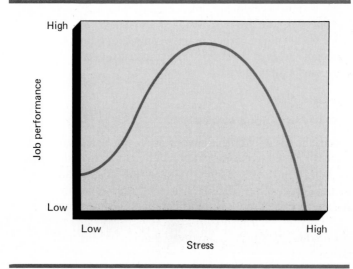

Figure 21-4
A stress-performance model

The stress-performance relationship may be compared with strings on a violin. When there is either too little or too much tension on the strings, they will not produce suitable music. As with violin strings, when tension on an employee is either too high or low, the employee's performance will tend to deteriorate.

Stress thresholds

People have different tolerances of stressful situations. The level of stressors that one can tolerate before feelings of stress occur is one's *stress threshold*. Some people are easily upset by the slightest change or emergency. Others are cool, calm, and collected, partly because they have confidence in their ability to cope. They feel very little stress unless a stressor is major or prolonged.

Marie Johnson was a cashier at a local supermarket. Every day she faced long lines, time pressures, complaints from customers about high prices, and cash register errors, but these events did not trouble her. She enjoyed meeting people. On the other hand, Antonio Valenzuela, a cashier at an adjoining counter, had difficulty with the complaints and pressures he received. He began to make errors and get into arguments. He seemed nervous. Finally, he asked to transfer to another part of the store. The two employees had different stress thresholds.

Type A and B people

Type A behaviors

Reactions to stressful situations often are related to type A and B people.[15] *Type A people* are aggressive and competitive, set high standards, and put themselves under constant time pressures. They even make excessive demands on themselves in recreation and leisure. They often fail to realize that many of the pressures they feel are of their own making rather than products of their environment. Because of the constant stress that they feel, they are more prone to physical ailments related to stress, such as heart attacks.

Type B behaviors

Type B people are more relaxed and easygoing. They accept situations and work within them rather than fighting them competitively. Such people are especially relaxed regarding time pressures, and so they are less prone to have problems associated with stress.

Actions to reduce stress

Counseling is only one of several ways to reduce stress. Other ways that have been discussed in earlier chapters are supportive management, participation, organization development, training, job design, and improved communication. Three other approaches that are appropriate to this chapter are meditation, biofeedback, and personal wellness programs.

Meditation Meditation involves quiet, concentrated inner thought in order to rest the body physically and emotionally. It helps remove persons temporarily from the stressful world and reduce their symptoms of stress.

Transcendental meditation (TM) is one of the more popular practices.

X-ray

Transcendental meditators try to meditate for two periods of fifteen to twenty minutes a day, concentrating on the repetition of a word called a *mantra.* There are a number of similar practices with other names, such as yoga. Usually they all have the following common elements:[16]

- A relatively quiet environment
- A comfortable position
- A repetitive mental stimulus
- A passive attitude

Meditation is so highly regarded that a few organizations have established meditation rooms for employee use, and many employees who meditate report favorable results.

New York Telephone Company provides a program called Clinically Standardized Meditation for its employees, and more than 300 have participated in it. A pilot study after five months showed that meditators improved more than a control group on test scores of anxiety, hostility, and psychosomatic disorders. Participants also reported feeling better about life and better about themselves.[17]

Does meditation work?

Biofeedback A different approach for working with stress is *biofeedback,* by which people under medical guidance learn from instrument feedback to influence symptoms of stress such as increased heart rate or severe headaches. Until the 1960s, it was thought that people could not control their involuntary nervous system which, in turn, controls internal processes such as heartbeat, oxygen consumption, stomach acid flow, and brain waves. There now is evidence that people can exercise some control over these internal processes, so biofeedback may be helpful in reducing undesirable effects of stress.[18]

Personal wellness In general, there is a trend toward programs of preventive maintenance for personal wellness that are based on research in behavioral medicine. Health care specialists can recommend changes in lifestyle such as breathing regulation, muscle relaxation, positive imagery, nutrition management, and exercise that enable employees to use more of their full potential.[19] Clearly, a preventive approach is preferable for reducing the causes of stress, although coping methods help one adapt to stressors that are beyond direct control. The key is to create a better "fit" between people and their environment, and alternative approaches may be useful for different employees.

Preventive approaches

EMPLOYEE COUNSELING

Definition

Counseling is discussion of a problem that usually has emotional content with an employee in order to help the employee cope with it better.[20] Counseling seeks to improve employee mental health. As shown in Figure 21-5, *good mental health* means that people feel comfortable about themselves, right about other people, and able to meet the demands of life.

The goal of counseling

People with good mental health—

1 *Feel comfortable about themselves.*
- Are not bowled over by their own emotions—by their fears, anger, love, jealousy, guilt, or worries.
- Can take life's disappointments in their stride.
- Have a tolerant, easygoing attitude towards themselves as well as others; they can laugh at themselves.
- Neither underestimate nor overestimate their abilities.
- Can accept their own shortcomings.
- Have self-respect.
- Feel able to deal with most situations that come their way.
- Get satisfaction from the simple, everyday pleasures.

2 *Feel right about other people.*
- Are able to give love and to consider the interests of others.
- Have personal relationships that are satisfying and lasting.
- Expect to like and trust others, and take it for granted that others will like and trust them.
- Respect the many differences they find in people.
- Do not push people around, nor do they allow themselves to be pushed around.
- Can feel they are part of a group.
- Feel a sense of responsibility to their neighbors and others.

3 *Are able to meet the demands of life.*
- Do something about their problems as they arise.
- Accept their responsibilities.
- Shape their environment whenever possible; adjust to it whenever necessary.
- Plan ahead but do not fear the future.
- Welcome new experiences and new ideas.
- Make use of their natural capacities.
- Set realistic goals for themselves.
- Are able to think for themselves and make their own decisions.
- Put their best effort into what they do and get satisfaction out of doing it.

Figure 21-5
Characteristics of
people with good
mental health
Source: *Mental Health Is
1, 2, 3*, Arlington, Va.:
Mental Health
Association, n.d.

The definition of counseling implies a number of characteristics. It is an exchange of ideas and feelings between two people, a counselor and a counselee, so it is an act of communication. Since it helps employees cope with problems, it should improve organizational performance, because the employee is more cooperative, worries less about personal problems, or improves in other ways. Counseling also helps the organization be more human and considerate with people problems.

Counseling may be performed by both professionals and nonprofessionals. For example, both a personnel specialist in counseling and a supervisor who is not trained in counseling may counsel employees. Company physicians also counsel employees and even an employee's friends may provide counseling.

Counseling usually is confidential, so that employees will feel free to talk openly about their problems. It also involves both job and personal problems,

Although a few companies had employee counseling programs at an earlier date, the recognized beginning of employee counseling was in 1936 at Western Electric Company in Chicago.[22] It is believed that this was the first time a company used the term "personnel counseling" for employee counseling services. Employee job satisfaction definitely improved as a result of the counseling.

Need for counseling

The need for counseling arises from a variety of employee problems. When these problems exist, employees benefit from understanding and help of the type that counseling can provide. For example, an employee feels insecure about retirement, so counseling is necessary. Another employee is hesitant to take the risk required by a promotion, so the employee ceases growing on the job. A third employee may become unstable in the job.

> Ross Callander was an interviewer in a state employment office. Within a few weeks he became unstable in his job, becoming angry easily and being rude to interviewees. His manager noticed the change and discussed it with him. When his behavior continued, he was referred to a counselor. The counselor learned that Callander's son had been arrested and in anger had accused Callander of being a failure as a parent. Callander felt angry, frustrated, and defeated, and he was transferring these feelings to his interviewees. With the help of a community agency, Callander's family problem was solved, and he quickly returned to normal job performance.

Most problems that require counseling have some emotional content, such as the problem Callander had.[23] Emotions are a normal part of life. Nature gave people their emotions, and these feelings make people human. On the other hand, emotions can get out of control and cause workers to do things that are harmful to their own best interests and those of the firm. They may leave their jobs because of a trifling conflict that seems large to them, or they may undermine morale in their departments. Managers want their employees to maintain good mental health and to channel their emotions along constructive lines so that they will work together effectively.

Emotions can cause problems.

What counseling can do

The general objective of counseling is to help employees develop better mental health so that they will grow in self-confidence, understanding, self-control, and ability to work effectively. This objective is consistent with the supportive and human resources models of organizational behavior, which encourage employee growth and self-direction. It is also consistent with Maslow's higher-order needs, such as self-esteem and self-actualization.

The counseling objective is achieved through one or more of the following *counseling functions* which are activities performed by counseling. These are shown in Figure 21-6. As will be seen later, some types of counseling perform one function better than another.

Six functions of counseling

Figure 21-6
Functions of
counseling

Advice Telling a person what you think should be done
Reassurance Giving a person courage and confidence to face a problem
Communication Providing information and understanding
Release of emotional tension Helping a person feel more free of tensions
Clarified thinking Encouraging more coherent, rational thought
Reorientation Encouraging an internal change in goals and values

1 Advice Many people look upon counseling as primarily an advice-giving activity, but in reality this is only one of several functions that counseling can perform. The giving of advice requires a counselor to make judgments about a counselee's problems and to lay out a course of action. Herein lies the difficulty, because it is almost impossible to understand another person's complicated problems, much less tell that person what to do about them. Advice giving may breed a relationship in which the counselee feels inferior and dependent on the counselor. In spite of all its ills, advice occurs in routine counseling because workers expect it and managers tend to provide it.

2 Reassurance Counseling can provide employees with reassurance, which is a way of giving them courage to face a problem or a feeling of confidence that they are pursuing a suitable course of action. Reassurance is represented by such counselor remarks as "You are making good progress, Linda," and "Don't worry; this will come out all right."

One trouble with reassurance is that the counselees do not accept it. They are smart enough to know that the counselor cannot know that the problem will come out all right. Even if counselees are reassured, their reassurance may fade away as soon as they face their problems again, which means that little real improvement has been made.

Though reassurance has its weaknesses, it is useful in some situations and is impossible to prohibit. Reassurance cannot be prohibited just because it is dangerous, any more than automobiles can be prohibited because they cause accidents; but, like automobiles, reassurance should be used carefully.

3 Communication Counseling can improve both upward and downward communication. In an upward direction, it is a key way for employees to express their feelings to management. As many people have said, often the top managers in an organization do not know how those at the bottom feel. The act of counseling initiates an upward signal, and if the channels are open, some of these signals will travel higher. Individual names must be kept confidential, but statements of feeling can be grouped and interpreted to management. An important part of any counselor's job is to discover emotional problems related to company policies and to interpret those problems to top management. Counseling also achieves downward communication because counselors help interpret company activities to employees as they discuss problems related to them.

4 *Release of emotional tension* An important function of nearly all counseling is release of emotional tension; this release is sometimes called *emotional catharsis*. People tend to get an emotional release from their frustrations and other problems whenever they have an opportunity to tell someone about them. Counseling history consistently shows that as people begin to explain their problems to a sympathetic listener, their tensions begin to subside. They are more relaxed, and their speech is more coherent and rational. This release of tension does not necessarily solve their problems, but it does remove mental blocks in the way of solution, enabling them to face their problems again and think constructively about them. In some cases emotional release accomplishes the whole job, dispelling an employee's problems as if they were mental ghosts (which they largely were).

Emotional catharsis reduces tensions.

In a warehouse an electric-truck driver, Bill Irwin, began to develop conflicts with his supervisor. Irwin was convinced that his supervisor gave him the hardest jobs and otherwise took advantage of him. He was convinced that his supervisor did not like him and would "never" give him a raise. One day the elderly timekeeper was in the warehouse checking time records, and Irwin, being particularly upset at the moment, cornered him and began to tell about his troubles. It all happened when Irwin commented, "You don't need to worry about my time. I'll never get a rate increase, and I'll never have any overtime." The timekeeper asked, "Why?" and the conversation went on from there.

The timekeeper was a staff employee working for the warehouse superintendent and was not in the chain of command from superintendent to supervisor to Irwin, so Irwin felt free to talk. Perhaps also Irwin saw the timekeeper as a means of communication around his supervisor to the superintendent. At any rate, Irwin talked. And the timekeeper listened.

Since the timekeeper spent much of his time on the warehouse floor, he was closely acquainted with work assignments and the supervisor. Irwin knew this; and as he stated his grievances, he began to revise and soften them because he realized some of them did not agree with details of the situation about which the timekeeper had firsthand knowledge. As Irwin continued to bring his feelings out into the open, he felt easier and could discuss his problem more calmly. He realized that what he had said in the beginning was mostly a buildup of his own imagination and did not make sense in terms of the actual situation. He closed the conversation with the comment, "I guess I really don't have much of a problem, but I'm glad I told you anyway."

5 *Clarified thinking* The case of Irwin also illustrates another function of counseling, that of *clarified thinking*. Irwin began to realize that his emotional comments did not match the facts of the situation. He found that he was magnifying minor incidents and jumping to drastic conclusions. As his emotional blocks to straight thinking were relieved, he began to think more rationally. In this case realistic thinking was encouraged because Irwin recognized that he was talking to someone who knew the facts and was not emotionally involved.

Clarified thinking tends to be a normal result of emotional release, but a skilled counselor can aid this process. In order to clarify the counselee's thinking, the counselor serves as an aid only and refrains from telling the counselee what is "right." Further, not all the clarified thinking takes place while the counselor and counselee are talking. All or part of it may take place later as a result of developments during the counseling relationship. The result of any clarified thinking is that a person is encouraged to accept responsibility for emotional problems and to be more realistic in solving them.

Reorientation requires a major change.

6 Reorientation Another function of counseling is reorientation of the counselee. *Reorientation* is more than mere emotional release or clear thinking about a problem. It involves a change in the employee's psychic self through a change in basic goals and values. For example, it can help people recognize and accept their own limitations. Reorientation is the kind of function needed to help alcoholics return to normalcy or to treat a person with severe mental depression. It is largely a job for professional counselors who know its uses and limitations and who have the necessary training. The manager's job is to recognize those in need of reorientation before their need becomes severe, so that they can be referred to professional help in time for successful treatment.

The manager's counseling role

Excluding reorientation, the other five counseling functions can be performed successfully by managers, assuming they have qualified themselves. They will at times perform all five of these counseling functions. On other occasions, if professional counseling services are available, they will refer employees to the professional counselors. The point is that when counseling services are established, *managers must not conclude that all their counseling responsibilities have been transferred to the counseling staff.*

Managers are important counselors because they are the ones in day-to-day interaction with employees.[24] If managers close their eyes to the emotional problems of employees and refuse to discuss them, it appears that managers are saying to employees, "I don't care about you, just your work." Managers cannot, when an emotional upset arises, say, "This is not part of my job. Go see a counselor." Emotions are part of the whole employee and must be considered a part of the total employment situation for which a manager is responsible. For this reason all managers, from the lowest to the highest levels, need training to help them understand problems of employees and counsel them effectively.

Almost all problems brought to a manager have a combination of factual and emotional content, so a manager should not spend all day looking for emotional content when a rational answer will solve the problem.

For example, if an employee asks, "Is this desk going to be moved?" it may be that she is really wondering why, is worried that it may reduce her status, and so on; but it is also possible—just possible—that she only wants to know "Is this desk going to be moved?" If you answer, "Yes, over by the window," you have solved the problem she brought you, and there is no need to try to be an amateur psychiatrist about it!

It is said that the father of psychiatry, Sigmund Freud, warned about the dangers of seeing emotional meaning in everything a person says or does. When a friend asked him what was the emotional meaning of the pipe he smoked, he replied, "Sometimes, sir, a pipe is just a pipe," meaning that it had no particular emotional interpretation.

TYPES OF COUNSELING

In terms of the amount of direction that a counselor gives a counselee, counseling is a continuum from full direction (directive counseling) to no direction (nondirective counseling), as shown in Figure 21-7. Between the two extremes is participative counseling. These three counseling types will be discussed in order to show how counselors may vary their direction in a counseling situation.

A continuum of counseling types

Directive counseling

Directive counseling is the process of listening to an employee's problem, deciding with the employee what should be done, and then telling and motivating the employee to do it. Directive counseling mostly accomplishes the counseling function of *advice,* but it also may reassure, communicate, give emotional release and—to a minor extent—clarify thinking. Reorientation is seldom achieved in directive counseling.

Most everyone likes to give advice, counselors included, and it is easy to do. But is it effective? Does the counselor really understand the employee's problem? Does the counselor have the knowledge and judgment to make a "right" decision? Even if the decision is right, will the employee follow it? The answer to these questions is usually "No," and this is why advice may not be helpful in counseling.

Though advice is of questionable value, some of the other functions are worthwhile. If the directive counselor is first a good listener, then the employee should feel some emotional release. As the result of emotional release plus ideas that the counselor imparts, the employee also may clarify thinking. Furthermore, useful communication probably takes place. Both advice and reassurance can be worthwhile if they give the employee more courage to take a helpful course of action that the employee supports.

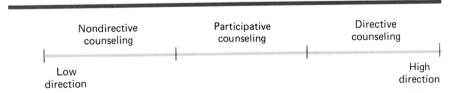

Nondirective counseling — Participative counseling — Directive counseling

Low direction — High direction

Figure 21-7
Types of counseling according to amount of direction that counselors provide

*Skillful listening
is required.*

Nondirective counseling

Nondirective, or client-centered, counseling is at the opposite end of the continuum. It is the process of skillfully listening and encouraging a counselee to explain troublesome problems, understand them, and determine appropriate solutions. It focuses on the counselee rather than on the counselor as judge and adviser; so it is "client-centered." Managers can use the nondirective approach; however, care should be taken to make sure that managers are not so oversold on it that they neglect their normal directive leadership responsibilities.

> One company gave a full two days of training to its managers on the nondirective approach. They went back to their jobs thoroughly sold on the idea and ready to put it into practice. The trouble was that they did not sufficiently understand its limitations. They refrained from stating their own opinions to employees in their day-to-day interaction. They hesitated to issue instructions and directives. Employees became confused, and their frustrations multiplied. The results were harmful rather than helpful, so finally management had to instruct its managers to return to their former ways of working with employees. They were told that if the nondirective approach was to be used to counsel, it should be a supplement along with normal directive approaches, similar to participative counseling, discussed in the next section.[25]

Nondirective counseling was developed concurrently by two groups: Mayo, Roethlisberger, and others at Western Electric Company and Carl R. Rogers and his colleagues.[26] Here is the way nondirective counseling typically works.

> Assume that Harold Pace comes to a counselor, Janis Peterson, for assistance. Peterson attempts to build a relationship that encourages Pace to talk freely. At this point Peterson defines the counseling relationship by explaining that she cannot tell Pace how to solve his problem but that she may be able to help him understand it and deal satisfactorily with it.
>
> Pace then explains his feelings, and the counselor encourages their expression, shows interest in them, and accepts them without blame or praise. Eventually the negative feelings are drained away, giving Pace a chance to express tentatively a positive feeling or two, a fact that marks the beginning of Pace's emotional growth. The counselor encourages these positive feelings and accepts them without blame or praise, just as she did the negative feelings.
>
> If all goes well, Pace should at this point begin to get some insight into his problem and to develop alternative solutions to it. As he continues to grow, he is able to choose a course of positive action and see his way clear to try it. He then feels a decreasing need for help and recognizes that the counseling relationship should end.

*Feelings need
to be accepted.*

Throughout the counseling relationship, it is important for the counselor to *accept* feelings—rather than *judge* them, offering blame or praise—because judgment may discourage an employee from stating true feelings. The basic idea is to get the employee to discuss feelings, to explore solutions, and to make wise decisions.

Major differences between nondirective and directive counseling are

Counseling method The employee primarily controls the direction of conversation and does most of the talking.

Responsibility Solution of the problem is the employee's own responsibility.

Status The employee is equal to the counselor as a person, while the directive method implies that the counselor is superior and knows what to do.

Role The employee is psychologically independent as a person, choosing a solution and growing in ability to make choices in the future.

Emphasis Emphasis is on deeper feelings and problems rather than surface symptoms. Adjustment of a person, rather than solution of a current problem, is paramount.

Figure 21-8
Ways in which nondirective counseling differs from directive counseling

summarized in Figure 21-8. They reveal that in nondirective counseling the counselee is the key person, while the counselor is the key in a directive approach.

Use by professionals Professional counselors usually practice some form of nondirective counseling and often accomplish four of the six counseling functions. Communication occurs both upward and downward through the counselor. Emotional release takes place even more effectively than with directive counseling, and clarified thinking tends to follow. The unique advantage of nondirective counseling is its ability to cause the employee's reorientation. It emphasizes changing the *person* instead of dealing only with the immediate *problem,* in the usual manner of directive counseling.

Professional counselors treat each counselee as a social and organizational equal. They primarily listen and try to help the counselee discover and follow improved courses of action. They especially "listen between the lines" to learn the full meaning of an employee's feelings. They look for the assumptions underlying the employee's statements and for the events and feelings that are so painful that the employee tends to avoid talking about them. As shown in Figure 21-9, nondirective counselors follow an "iceberg model" of counseling in which they recognize that sometimes more feelings are hidden

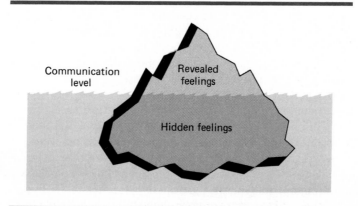

Figure 21-9
Iceberg model of a counselee's feelings in a counseling situation

Communication level

Revealed feelings

Hidden feelings

under the surface of a counselee's communication than are revealed. For this reason they constantly encourage the counselee to open up and reveal deeper feelings that may help solve the employee's problem.

Limitations With all its advantages, nondirective counseling has several limitations that restrict its use at work. First of all, it is more time-consuming and costly than directive counseling. Just one employee with one problem may require many hours of a counselor's time, so the number of employees that a counselor can assist is limited. Professional counselors require professional education and consequently are expensive. Nondirective counseling also depends on a capable, willing employee. It assumes that the employee possesses a drive for mental health, has enough social intelligence to perceive what problems need solution, and has sufficient emotional stability to deal with them. The nondirective counselor needs to be careful not to become a crutch for emotionally dependent employees to lean on while they avoid their work responsibilities.

Costliness of nondirective counseling

In some cases counseling itself is a weak solution because it returns the employee to the same environment that caused the problem. What is really needed is a better environment for employee psychological support.[27] In this situation the counselor may step beyond the usual counseling role and give advice to management to take corrective action.

Participative counseling

Nondirective counseling by employees is limited because it requires professional counselors and is costly. Directive counseling often is not accepted by modern, independent employees. This means that the type of counseling typically used in organizations is between the two extremes of directive and nondirective counseling. This middle ground is called participative counseling.

How does participative counseling work?

Participative counseling (also called cooperative counseling) is a mutual counselor-counselee relationship that establishes a cooperative exchange of ideas to help solve a counselee's problems. It is neither wholly counselor-centered nor wholly counselee-centered. Rather, the counselor and counselee mutually apply their different knowledge, perspectives, and values to problems. It integrates the ideas of both participants in a counseling relationship. It is, therefore, a balanced compromise that combines many advantages of both directive and nondirective counseling while avoiding most of their disadvantages.

Participative counseling starts by using the listening techniques of nondirective counseling; but as the interview progresses, participative counselors may play a more active role than nondirective counselors would. They offer bits of knowledge and insight; and they may discuss the situation from their broader knowledge of the organization, thus giving an employee a different view of the problem. In general, participative counselors apply the four counseling functions of reassurance, communication, emotional release, and clarified thinking.

For example, Mary Carlisle was emotionally upset because she was not getting the promotions that she wanted. Although she discussed her problem with her supervisor, she was not wholly satisfied and asked to see a counselor. She and the counselor established open communication early in their discussion because at this point Carlisle was ready to open up about her problems.

The counselor did not tell Carlisle what to do (directive approach) and did not merely listen (nondirective approach). Rather, the counselor explored various alternatives with Carlisle, communicated some ideas about training, and provided reassurance that Carlisle could become fully qualified for promotion. The result was that Carlisle saw her problem more clearly (clarified thinking) and chose an appropriate course of action.

Cooperation with community agencies

When mental health problems arise on the job, the employer usually provides counseling, either by the immediate supervisor or through the firm's employee assistance program (discussed in Chapter 16). On the other hand, if a problem arises from off-the-job causes, employers are more hesitant to become involved. There are good reasons for this hesitancy, because employees have certain rights of privacy, and the organization should not interfere unless the employee's performance declines. When it does become aware of an employee's personal problems, a firm will often refer the individual to an appropriate community agency for more specialized help. Some companies even provide similar support when an employee's family members experience mental health problems.

SUMMARY

Counseling occasionally is necessary for employees because of job and personal problems that subject them to excessive stress. The conditions that tend to cause stress are called stressors and include work overload, time pressures, role ambiguity, financial problems, and family problems. Stress affects both physical and mental health and results in burnout when it occurs chronically. The stress-performance model indicates that excessive stress reduces job performance, but a moderate amount may help employees respond to job challenges. Type A people tend to show more stress than type B people.

Counseling is discussion of a problem that usually has emotional content with an employee in order to help the employee cope with it better. Its goal is better mental health, and it is performed by both managers and professional counselors. Major counseling functions are advice, reassurance, communication, release of emotional tension, clarified thinking, and reorientation. The most appropriate type of counseling for nonprofessionals is participative counseling. Counseling programs deal with both job and personal problems, and there is extensive cooperation with community counseling agencies.

TERMS AND CONCEPTS FOR REVIEW

Stress

Burnout

Stressors

Frustration

Stress-performance model

Stress threshold

Type A and B people

Biofeedback

Counseling

Characteristics of good mental health

Counseling functions

Directive, participative, and nondirective counseling

Iceberg model of feelings

REVIEW QUESTIONS

1 List and discuss the five major sources of stress in your life during the last five years.

2 Think of someone you know who suffers from burnout. What are the symptoms? What may have caused it?

3 Do you see yourself as primarily a type A or type B person? Discuss, and make a list of your five main type A characteristics and five main type B characteristics.

4 Discuss how stress and job performance are related. Is stress interfering with your performance in school? Discuss.

5 Discuss four management practices covered in earlier chapters of this book that should help reduce employee stress.

6 Discuss the six main counseling functions. Which are best performed by directive, nondirective, and participative counseling?

7 Explain major differences between directive and nondirective counseling.

8 Should professional company counselors be provided in the following situations? Discuss.
   a A large West Coast aircraft plant during rapid expansion
   b A government office in Valdosta, Georgia, employing 700 people
   c A marginal job-order foundry in Chicago having unstable employment varying from thirty to sixty workers

9 What should be the main type of counseling used in the following situations?
   a A traveling sales representative with fifteen years of seniority has become an alcoholic.
   b A newly hired engineer engages in petty theft of office supplies.
   c A receptionist receives two job offers and must make a decision over the weekend.
   d A maintenance worker's spouse files for divorce.

10 Outline a preventive program for personal wellness that you could implement for yourself over the next five years. What are its elements?

Unit Electronics Company

Unit Electronics Company produces electronic process controls for industry. The high reliability required for these controls, each designed for a specific customer, requires the production department to work closely with the test section of the quality-control department, which determines if the product meets customer specifications. For one important order it was necessary for a production representative to work in the quality-control department with the chief test engineer. Charles Able, the manager of production, assigned William Parcel, one of his capable assistants, to this job. Parcel had worked with Able for years and was well acquainted with this equipment order, since he had coordinated its production for Able. The test engineer was named Dale Short.

A week after Parcel began working with Short, he reported to Able that he was having difficulty with Short and that Short seemed to resent his presence in the test section. Able agreed that a crisis situation might be developing and said that he would visit the test section and attempt to talk with Short.

When Able visited the test section, Short immediately started complaining about Parcel. He said that Parcel undermined Short's authority by giving testers instructions that were at variance with Short's. He claimed that Parcel even contradicted him in front of the testers. After a number of other complaints he asked Able to remove Parcel from the test section and send a substitute. Short even threatened that if Able did not remove Parcel, Short would "go over his head" to have Parcel removed. Able listened and asked questions, but made no judgments or promises.

Parcel apparently saw Able talking to Short, so before Able left the test section, Parcel approached him with the comment, "Well, I guess Short has been telling you a tale of woe about me."

Able acknowledged that Short had complained, but he omitted mentioning Short's threat to have Parcel transferred.

"That's Short, all right," said Parcel. "He can't stand to have anyone try to correct him, but things were so fouled up I felt I had to do something."

Able admitted that the situation was sensitive, but he pointed out that Short was in charge of the test section. He ended the discussion with the comment, "Let's play it cool and not push."

Able, however, was upset by the situation, and during the next few days he gave much thought to it. Since Short felt the way he did, Able finally decided to remove Parcel from the test section and send another employee. As he was reaching for the telephone to call Parcel in the test section, Short walked into the office smiling.

"I want to thank you, Charlie," he said. "I don't know what you said to Parcel the other day, but it sure changed his attitude. We are getting along just fine now. Funny thing, when I spoke to you the other day, I had the impression that you weren't going to do anything for me, but I guess I had you figured wrong."

Able gulped a few times and made a few vague remarks. Then Short left in high spirits.

Able was quite curious about the whole situation; so later in the day when he happened to meet Parcel alone, he commented casually, "Well, Bill, how are things going with Short?"

"I have been meaning to tell you, Charlie," Parcel said, "Short has been much easier to work with the past few days. He actually takes some of my advice—even asks for it. I guess that talk you had with him really did some good."

QUESTION

Analyze the events in this case in terms of counseling and communication. Did counseling occur? What type of counseling? When and by whom?

EXPERIENTIAL EXERCISE

Contrasts in Counseling

Form the entire class into pairs. Designate one person within each pair as the counselor and the other as the counselee. Ask the counselees to think of some emotional problem that is currently on their mind, and have them share it with their counselor. The counselors should attempt to play a nondirective role for the first few minutes, switch to a directive role for the next few minutes, and then conclude with a participative role for the final few minutes of interaction.

QUESTIONS

1 Ask the counselors how they felt, and how successful they were, in each of the three roles.

2 Ask the counselees how they felt, and how successful the counselors were, when they used each of the three roles.

3 Under what conditions might counselees prefer to have (*a*) directive, (*b*) participative, and (*c*) nondirective counselor roles used with them?

REFERENCES

1 Harry Levinson, *Ideas and Trends in Personnel* (Commerce Clearing House), July 9, 1982, p. 21.

2 Mitchell S. Novit, "Mental Distress: Possible Implications for the Future," *Personnel Administrator,* August 1982, pp. 47–53; and Berkeley Rice, "Can Companies Kill?" *Psychology Today,* June 1981, pp. 78ff.

3 Somewhat different definitions are in Baron Perlman and E. Alan Hartman, "Burnout: Summary and Future Research," *Human Relations,* April 1982, pp. 283–305; Morley Glicken and Katherine Janka, "Executives under Fire: The Burnout Syndrome," *California Management Review,* Spring 1982, p. 67–72; and Oliver L. Niehouse, "Burnout: A Real Threat to Human Resource Managers," *Personnel,* September–October 1981, pp. 25–32.

4 Susan E. Jackson and Randall S. Schuler, "Preventing Employee Burnout," *Personnel,* March–April 1983, pp. 58–68. Another explanation—that energy is highly expandable and therefore burnout is relatively controllable—is offered in

Ellen L. Maher, "Burnout and Commitment: A Theoretical Alternative," *The Personnel and Guidance Journal,* March 1983, pp. 390–393.

5 Jerry E. Bishop, "Age of Anxiety," *Wall Street Journal,* Western ed., Apr. 2, 1979, pp. 1, 26.

6 James C. Quick and Jonathan D. Quick, "How Good Working Relationships Can Help Relieve Pressures on the Job," *Management Review,* May 1984, pp. 43–45.

7 Heather R. Sailer, John Schlacter, and Mark R. Edwards, "Stress: Causes, Consequences, and Coping Strategies," *Personnel,* July–August 1982, pp. 35–48. Major early research on role ambiguity and stress is reported in Robert L. Kahn and others, *Organizational Stress: Studies in Role Conflict and Ambiguity,* New York: John Wiley & Sons, Inc., 1964. Evidence that participative decision making can reduce role conflict and ambiguity is in Susan E. Jackson, "Participation in Decision Making as a Strategy for Reducing Job-Related Strain," *Journal of Applied Psychology,* February 1983, pp. 3–19.

8 David P. Boyd and David E. Gumpert, "Coping with Entrepreneurial Stress," *Harvard Business Review,* March–April 1983, pp. 44–46ff.

9 James B. Shaw and John H. Riskind, "Predicting Job Stress Using Data from the Position Analysis Questionnaire," *Journal of Applied Psychology,* May 1983, pp. 253–261.

10 Saroj Parasuraman and Joseph A. Alutto, "An Examination of the Organizational Antecedents of Stressors at Work," *Academy of Management Journal,* March 1981, pp. 48–67.

11 The problem of employees who experience career stagnation is discussed in Judith M. Bardwick, "Plateauing and Productivity," *Sloan Management Review,* Spring 1983, pp. 67–73.

12 "Frustration around the Office," *Training News,* February 1983, p. 4. A study that focused on the most common frustrations in life is Richard S. Lazarus, "Little Hassles Can Be Hazardous to Your Health," *Psychology Today,* July 1981, pp. 58–62.

13 This U-shaped relationship may not be valid for all tasks or at the group level of performance. See nonsupportive results in Kenneth E. Friend, "Stress and Performance: Effects of Subjective Work Load and Time Urgency," *Personnel Psychology,* Autumn 1982, pp. 623–633; and R. Douglas Allen, Michael A. Hitt, and Charles R. Greer, "Occupational Stress and Perceived Organizational Effectiveness in Formal Groups: An Examination of Stress Level and Stress Type," *Personnel Psychology,* Summer 1982, pp. 359–370.

14 A dramatic illustration of the employee responses attributed to stressful Theory X management occurred in the air traffic controllers strike of 1981. See David G. Bowers, "What Would Make 11,500 People Quit Their Jobs?" *Organizational Dynamics,* Winter 1983, pp. 5–19.

15 Meyer Friedman and Ray H. Rosenman, *Type A Behavior and Your Heart,* New York: Alfred A. Knopf, Inc., 1974. Recent research is in Ronald J. Burke and Eugene Deszca, "Career Success and Personal Failure Experiences and Type A Behaviour," *Journal of Occupational Behaviour,* April 1982, pp. 161–170; and John M. Ivancevich, Michael T. Matteson, and Cynthia Preston, "Occupational Stress, Type A Behavior, and Physical Well Being," *Academy of Management Journal,* June 1982, pp. 373–391.

16 Ruanne K. Peters and Herbert Benson, "Time Out from Tension," *Harvard Business Review,* January–February 1978, pp. 120–124. See also David R. Frew, *Management of Stress: Using TM at Work,* Chicago: Nelson-Hall, 1977.

17 William A. McGeveran, Jr., "Meditation at the Telephone Company," *The Wharton Magazine,* Fall 1981, pp. 28–32.

18 Robert C. Ford and Jack Hartje, "Biofeedback and Management Stress," *Human Resource Management,* Fall 1978, pp. 12–16.

19 Michael Pesci, "Stress Management: Separating Myth from Reality," *Personnel Administrator,* January 1982, pp. 57–67. Preventive ideas and programs are described in Robert Kreitner, "Personal Wellness: It's Just Good Business," *Business Horizons,* May–June 1982, pp. 28–35; and Michael T. Matteson and John M. Ivancevich, "The How, What, and Why of Stress Management Training," *Personnel Journal,* October 1982, pp. 768–774.

20 An excellent overview is Peter C. Cairo, "Counseling in Industry: A Selected Review of the Literature," *Personnel Psychology,* Spring 1983, pp. 1–18.

21 Elizabeth M. Kaplan and Emory L. Cowen, "Interpersonal Helping Behavior of Industrial Foremen," *Journal of Applied Psychology,* October 1981, pp. 633–638.

22 F. J. Roethlisberger and William J. Dickson, *Management and the Worker,* Cambridge, Mass.: Harvard University Press, 1939, pp. 189–205, 593–604; and William J. Dickson and F. J. Roethlisberger, *Counseling in an Organization: A Sequel to the Hawthorne Researches,* Boston: Harvard Business School, Division of Research, 1966.

23 Examples of emotional problems are in Morley D. Glicken, "Managing a Crisis Intervention Program," *Personnel Journal,* April 1982, pp. 292–296; Patrick J. Montana, "Pre-retirement Counseling: Three Corporate Case Studies," *Personnel Administrator,* June 1982, pp. 51–53ff; and John H. Meyer and Teresa C. Meyer, "The Supervisor as Counselor: How to Help the Distressed Employee," *Management Review,* April 1982, pp. 42–46.

24 Kaplan and Cowen, op. cit., provide data showing that supervisors spend an average of 2.5 hours a week counseling their employees on a wide variety of problems. Further, they report positive feelings about their role as counselors.

25 Bruce Harriman, "Up and Down the Communications Ladder," *Harvard Business Review,* September–October 1974, pp. 143–151.

26 Roethlisberger and Dickson, op. cit.; and Carl R. Rogers, *Counseling and Psychotherapy,* Boston: Houghton Mifflin Company, 1942.

27 Morley D. Glicken, "A Counseling Approach to Employee Burnout," *Personnel Journal,* March 1983, pp. 222–228.

FOR ADDITIONAL READING

Beech, H. R., L. E. Burns, and B. F. Sheffield, *A Behavioral Approach to the Management of Stress: A Practical Guide to Techniques,* New York: John Wiley & Sons, Inc., 1982.

Cooper, Cary L., *Stress Research: Issues for the 80s,* New York: John Wiley & Sons, Inc., 1983.

Fineman, S., *White Collar Unemployment: Impact and Stress,* New York: John Wiley & Sons, Inc., 1983.

French, John R. P., R. D. Caplan, and R. V. Harrison, *The Mechanisms of Job Stress and Strain,* Sussex, Eng.: John Wiley & Sons, Ltd., 1982.

Matteson, Michael T., and John M. Ivancevich, *Managing Job Stress and Health,* New York: Free Press, 1982.

Quick, James C., and Jonathan D. Quick, *Organizational Stress and Preventive Management,* New York: McGraw-Hill Book Company, 1984.

Selye, Hans, *The Stress of Life,* rev. ed., New York: McGraw-Hill Book Company, 1976.

Shostak, Arthur B., *Blue-Collar Stress,* Reading, Mass.: Addison-Wesley Publishing Company, Inc., 1980.

Veninga, Robert L., and James P. Spradley, *The Work Stress Connection: How to Cope with Job Burnout,* Boston: Little, Brown & Company, 1981.

Winter, Richard E. (ed.), *Coping with Executive Stress,* New York: McGraw-Hill Book Company, 1983.

7

CONCLUSION

ORGANIZATIONAL BEHAVIOR IN PERSPECTIVE

The long view of economic history teaches us that people are the master economic resource.

Anthony Patrick Carnevale[1]

[How should one] approach a situation in which a manager may have to choose between two alternatives, one more humane and one more productive? Which should a manager seek to maximize?

Henry L. Tosi[2]

CHAPTER OBJECTIVES

TO UNDERSTAND:
Models of organizational behavior related to other book ideas
Equations showing the role of organizational behavior
Human resource accounting
Dangers of behavioral bias
The law of diminishing returns
Importance of ethical leadership

This book has been about people as they work together. They are the great potential in organizations, a potential that can be developed better than it is now. This subject is called organizational behavior. It is the study and application of knowledge about how people act within organizations. It helps people, structure, technology, and the external environment blend together into an effective operating system. The result is a triple-reward system that serves human, organizational, and social objectives.

In this last chapter we review basic models and ideas about organizational behavior. Then we discuss its limitations and conclude with a note about its future.

MODELS OF ORGANIZATIONAL BEHAVIOR

As we learn more about human behavior at work, we apply improved models of organizational behavior. Modern organizations are increasing their use of supportive, collegial, and Theory Y models. In order to provide review and perspective, Figure 22-1 presents the four models of organizational behavior from earlier in the book and then relates them to other ideas on the subject. By reading the figure, one can determine that McGregor's Theory Y is related to the supportive and collegial models. Similarly, Herzberg's maintenance factors apply mostly to the autocratic and custodial models.

What are the trends?   As shown in Figure 22-2, the trend of each subsequent model of organizational behavior is toward more open human organizations.[3] Generally there is also movement toward a wider distribution of power, more intrinsic motivation, a more positive attitude toward people, and a better balance of concern for both employee and organizational needs. Discipline has become more a matter of self-discipline instead of being imposed from the outside.[4] The managerial role has advanced from one of strict authority to leadership and team support.

Much progress has been made during the last few years, and we can expect further progress. *We are building a better quality of work life.*[5] One effort to do this is Ouchi's portrait of the Theory Z organization, discussed in Chapter 2. He suggests that for U.S. firms to build a productive work force, they must discard the values and practices of the autocratic and custodial models and move deliberately toward the supportive and collegial ones. Although management practice varies widely from firm to firm, we can conclude that in the last generation we have doubled the good and halved the bad in human relationships at work. The pieces are beginning to fall into place for effective people-organization systems.

Emphasis on higher-order needs

One reason for emphasis on improved models of organizational behavior is the evolution of employee need structures. Postindustrial nations have reached a condition wherein higher-order needs are the prime motivators for

	AUTOCRATIC	CUSTODIAL	SUPPORTIVE	COLLEGIAL
Basis of model	Power	Economic resources	Leadership	Partnership
Managerial orientation	Authority	Money	Support	Teamwork
Employee orientation	Obedience	Security and benefits	Job performance	Responsibility
Employee psychological result	Dependence on boss	Dependence on organization	Participation	Self-discipline
Employee needs met	Subsistence	Security	Status and recognition	Self-actualization
Performance result	Minimum	Passive cooperation	Awakened drives	Moderate enthusiasm
RELATION TO OTHER IDEAS				
Maslow's hierarchy of needs	Physiological	Security	Middle-order	Higher-order
Herzberg's factors	Maintenance	Maintenance	Motivational	Motivational
Motivational environment	Extrinsic	Extrinsic	Intrinsic	Intrinsic
McGregor's theories	Theory X	Theory X	Theory Y	Theory Y
Leadership style	Negative	Mostly neutral on job	Positive	Positive
Blake and Mouton's managerial grid	9,1	3,5	6,6	8,8

Figure 22-1
Models of organizational behavior related to other ideas on the subject

many employees. In response, one observer suggests that "the national agenda will have to give greater prominence to the psychological needs of the population than it has in the past."[6] In addition, the emergence of a knowledge society requires more use of intellectual abilities along with the usual manual skills.

The key that unlocks this combination of higher-order needs and intellectual abilities in order to make the system productive is improved organizational behavior. The human mind is encouraged to be more creative by positive motivation. This is a unique energizing force wholly unlike the application of physical energy to a machine. A machine has a rated capacity beyond which it cannot go, no matter how much energy is applied to it. It can produce only so much and no more. But a person can produce unlimited

Organizational behavior unlocks human potential.

From:	To:
• Closed systems	• Open systems
• Materialistic orientation	• Human orientation
• Centralized power	• Distributed power
• Extrinsic motivation	• Intrinsic motivation
• Negative attitudes about people	• Positive attitudes about people
• Focus on organization needs	• Balanced focus on employee and organization needs
• Imposed discipline	• Self-discipline
• Authoritative managerial role	• Managerial role of leadership and team support

Figure 22-2
Trends in organizational behavior

amounts through better ideas. The promise of better organizational behavior is that it motivates people to produce better ideas. There is no apparent limit to what people can accomplish when they are motivated to use their potential to create new and better ideas. The key thought is: Work smarter, not harder.

A systems approach

We need to view changes toward improved organizational behavior in terms of a total system. Effective change is complex and takes a long time to effect. Any new practice such as participation treats only part of the whole system, so it often fails to achieve its full potential for improvement. There are too many unchanged intervening variables that restrict its success. What is needed in organizational behavior is gradual enrichment of entire socio-technical systems to make them more suitable to people. This is a large task, but a challenging one.

Success can be achieved in even the most difficult circumstances, such as an automobile assembly plant. For example, General Motors made a major effort to move one of its assembly plants more toward supportive, System 4–type management.[7] New leadership was provided, the supervisory job was redefined, participation was expanded substantially, and other human improvements were made.

Changes in efficiency are shown in Figure 22-3. During the first year of change, operating efficiency decreased rather than increased. This decrease in efficiency reflects the learning curve for change that was explained in Chapter 11. Change, even when it is desirable, introduces so many disruptions and problems that effectiveness is likely to decline in the short run.

In the second year of change there was an improvement of about 10 percent in direct labor such as that found on the assembly line. Then, in the third year, indirect labor improved more than 20 percent above its performance prior to the change.

During the period shown, the monitored quality index improved 10 percent, and there was a major decline of 60 percent in grievances. The program was particularly successful in the cushion room, a department of about 250 employees. In one year, scrap costs declined from 4 percent to below 1 percent, and grievances declined from fifty per month to less than three per month. The more supportive organizational behavior program was successful.

A contingency approach

Organizational behavior is applied in a contingency relationship. That is, not all organizations need exactly the same amount of participation, open communication, or any other condition in order to be effective. With regard to participation, some situations permit more genuine participation than others, and some people want more participation than other people. The most effective organizational behavior system will tend to vary according to an organization's total environment.[8]

Different environments must be considered.

For example, let us compare the two variables of a stable and a changing environment (discussed in Chapter 13) and then relate these variables to different practices discussed in this book. Effective practices in these two environments are likely to vary in the directions shown in Figure 22-4. The figure represents possible tendencies, not absolutes. For example, all that it implies regarding structure is that an effective, stable organization may give more emphasis to hierarchy than a changing organization. Similarly, it probably gives more emphasis to vertical communication than a changing organization does. In other words, there is some evidence of differences between stable and changing environments.

It should be understood that contingency theory and goals that seek more human organizations exist side by side as joint ideas. They do not cancel out each other. Both stable and changing organizations, for example, need a more human environment for people (such as more job enrichment and consideration), and in the next generation both will have it. However, even then, contingency ideas predict differences in practice between stable and changing organizations.

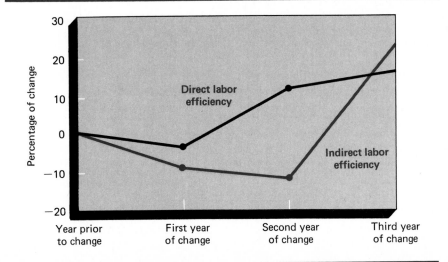

Figure 22-3
Percentage of change in operating efficiency at Lakewood assembly plant following changes toward more supportive organizational behavior
Source: *William F. Dowling, "At General Motors: System 4 Builds Performance and Profits," Organizational Dynamics, Winter 1975, p. 30. Copyright © 1975. Reprinted with permission.*

ORGANIZATIONAL CHARACTERISTICS	ENVIRONMENT	
	Stable	Changing
Structure	More rigid hierarchy	More flexible (some project and matrix)
Production system	More specialization	More job enrichment
Leadership style	More structure	More consideration
Communication	More vertical	More multidirectional
Model of organizational behavior	More autocratic	More supportive
Performance measure	More management by rules	More management by objectives

Figure 22-4
Application of contingency ideas to stable and changing environments

A social approach

Two-way influence   A social approach recognizes that what happens outside the firm will influence organizational behavior practices within the firm.[9] Also, what happens inside the firm will influence society. Management must be constantly aware of and responsive to this external environment, because it is an important influence on internal operations.

Macromotivation   As discussed in Chapter 5, the environment is a significant influence on how employees think and feel. Management cannot lead employees solely in terms of the internal micromotivational environment (type A motivation). That is not enough. It also must operate within the constraints of the external macromotivational environment (type B motivation).

> For example, developments during the last quarter century have brought what is often called "a new labor force" with different values. Surveys of the Opinion Research Corporation during those years indicate a major shift in the attitudes and values of the work force. These changing values are no myth. They must be faced by all organizations during the 1980s and 1990s.[10]
>
> Some of the changes in the labor force are as follows: There has been a decline in the work ethic and a rise in emphasis on leisure, self-expression, fulfillment, and personal growth. The manual worker has become more of a knowledge worker. Acceptance of authority has decreased, while desires for participation and autonomy have increased. In addition, chronic inflation has blunted the usefulness of money as a motivator, because any gain is quickly neutralized by inflation.

Indeed, there is a new labor force, so management's leadership practices must change to match the new conditions. These fast-moving developments have given new emphasis to leadership ability. One study of effective companies reported that a sense of caring, a management which listens to employees, and executives who are concerned with both competence and relationships are among the keys to the motivation of the present work force.[11]

Social responsiveness   A social approach also implies that society expects firms to operate in ways that show social responsiveness and social responsibility to the broader social system.[12] An example is society's values of social justice in the employment of women and minorities. These external values are translated into legislation that governs the employment activities of firms. Employment, promotion, supervision, wage administration, and other activities must, as a whole, be responsive to these expectations of society.

Another major area that is only indirectly related to organizational behavior is environmental pollution. It has forced both managers and employees to rethink their practices within the firm. Both groups must be sure that their actions do not cause pollution or even the appearance of it. The company truck driver who drives in a way that increases truck exhaust pollution and who tosses rubbish outside the vehicle's window is polluting the environment in the same way that the company smokestack may be.

The role of organizational behavior: a formula

The place that organizational behavior occupies in a work system is illustrated by a set of equations. Let us look first at a worker's ability. It is generally accepted that knowledge and one's skill in applying it constitute the human trait called "ability." This is represented by the equation

Four equations

Knowledge $\times$ skill = ability

Looking now at motivation, it results from a person's attitudes reacting in a specific situation. This is represented by the equation

Attitude $\times$ situation = motivation

Motivation and ability together determines a person's potential performance in any activity.

Ability $\times$ motivation = human performance

We now have a series of equations as shown by items 1 to 3 of Figure 22-5. The scope of organizational behavior is represented by the second equation (attitude $\times$ situation = motivation). This book has emphasized attitudes and how they are affected by situational factors to determine motivation.

The importance of organizational behavior is shown by the third equation

1 Knowledge $\times$ skill	= ability
2 Attitude $\times$ situation	= motivation
3 Ability $\times$ motivation	= human performance
4 Human performance $\times$ resources	= organizational performance

Figure 22-5
Equations showing the role of organizational behavior in work systems

(ability × motivation = human performance). Organizational behavior, as represented by the term "motivation," is one of two factors in the equation. Furthermore, organizational behavior has played a part in motivating workers to acquire the other factor, ability. Thus organizational behavior is part and parcel of the whole equation of potential human performance.

Human performance has to be mixed with resources such as tools, power, and materials to get overall work performance,[13] as indicated by the fourth equation:

$$\text{Human performance} \times \text{resources} = \text{organizational performance}$$

Even in this last equation, the role of organizational behavior is major, because it is a significant contributor to "human performance." "Resources," on the other hand, relate primarily to economic, material, and technical factors in an organization.

Human resource accounting

In an effort to give more emphasis to people in a language that management understands—the language of accounting—*human resource accounting* has been developed. It is a means of converting human data into money values for use in the regular accounting system.[14] It is not widely used, but a few firms have tried it.

The value of human resources is stressed.

The basic objectives of human resource accounting are shown in Figure 22-6. It seeks to make managers more aware of the importance of people as valuable resources and to hold managers more accountable for these resources. It also is an excellent way to assess management performance in the use of human resources. In this way it encourages better planning for human resources and better decisions whenever they involve people.[15] Finally, human resource accounting is an excellent way to encourage managers to take a long-run outlook toward the value of people, rather than a short-run, quick-profit outlook that ignores human resources.

There are several approaches to human resource accounting, and two principal ones will be discussed in the following paragraphs.

The investment approach   One approach, often called the *investment approach,* seeks to account for the amount that an organization has invested in human resources. Costs such as recruiting and training, rather than being treated as current expenses, are capitalized as an investment to be depreciated during an employee's expected employment. There is no attempt to theorize about how much an employee is worth but only how much has been directly invested in each employee.

Costs are capitalized.

When direct investment in employees has been determined, a measure of return on investment may be established. This measure gives an improved idea of how human resources are being used. For example, assume that five research scientists resign because of an autocratic manager. Their resigna-

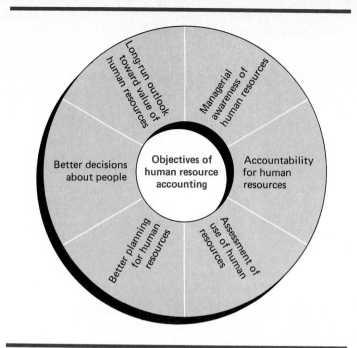

Figure 22-6
Objectives of human
resource accounting

tions will appear as an immediate investment loss, thereby giving strong financial emphasis to the need for better organizational behavior in order to reduce turnover.

As another example, assume that an engineering design department is hoarding trained engineers by keeping too many of them for the job required and by using them below their optimum skill level. Human resource accounting may help management uncover this kind of waste of resources, because the extra investment in them will be considered in computing return on investment. Surely in its effect on both people and profits, waste of human resources is just as undesirable as waste of economic resources.

One of the earliest firms to experiment with this type of human resource accounting was R. G. Barry Corporation of Columbus, Ohio. Beginning in 1968, this firm established an investment accounting system to provide human resource accounting for its managers, and this system was later extended to office and factory personnel. The system accounts for genuine employer costs that should provide a regular return on investment and which, for human reasons, should not be wasted through underemployment. This investment figure is then used to compute return on assets, return on investment in human resources, and similar accounting values.

The organizational climate approach   Another approach, which may be called the *organizational climate approach,* uses periodic surveys to determine ways in which the organizational climate has improved or deteriorated. Based on

*Climate surveys
are used.*

research, it is assumed that changes in these human resource variables will affect future performance. Established formulas are used to convert the human gain or loss into cost increases or decreases in the future. In this way management is encouraged to look beyond short-range economic results to longer-range results. For example, a manager may use autocratic methods to cut costs and show a higher economic profit for the year. A survey of climate may reveal, however, that the manager reduced resources so greatly that future costs will be greater than present savings. Following is an example.[16]

> In a plant with several hundred employees, a management consulting firm was employed to implement a cost reduction program. After careful studies with the assistance of local and corporate management, it recommended changes, and the affected departments were ordered to introduce them. Annual savings of $250,000 were secured.
>
> Before and after the cost reduction program, a survey of organizational climate was made. These surveys showed unfavorable shifts in human variables that were calculated to increase costs at least $450,000 annually. The apparent gain of $250,000 now was revealed as a probable loss, primarily because symptoms rather than causes of ineffectiveness were treated. The plant's actual experiences during the next several years confirmed the accuracy of the predictions.

Human resource accounting has its limitations. Some people argue that it is demeaning to treat human beings in economic terms on accounting statements. Employee satisfaction and growth should be legitimate goals whether they cost money or not. Further, it is difficult to translate human data into accounting figures. Some of the information is costly to collect, and sometimes it is such a rough estimate that it may not be of much use. In spite of these limitations, it is evident that human resource accounting of the types just described may help communicate human data to management in a language that management already understands. It can contribute to society's transition toward more emphasis on socioeconomic data in decision making.

LIMITATIONS OF ORGANIZATIONAL BEHAVIOR

*Problems exist in
its nature and use.*

This book has been written from a specialized point of view that emphasizes primarily the human side of organizations and the kinds of benefits that attention to it can bring. Nevertheless, we always recognize the limitations of organizational behavior. It will not abolish conflict and frustration; it can only reduce them. It is a way to improve, not an absolute answer to problems. Furthermore, it is but part of the whole cloth of an organization. We can discuss organizational behavior as a separate subject, but to apply it we must tie it back to the whole of reality. Improved organizational behavior will not solve unemployment. It will not make up for our own deficiencies. It cannot substitute for poor planning, inept organizing, or inadequate controls. It is only one of many systems operating within a larger social system.

Behavioral bias

People who lack system understanding may develop a *behavioral bias,* which gives them a narrow viewpoint that emphasizes satisfying employee experiences while overlooking the broader system of the organization in relation to all its publics. This condition often is called *tunnel vision* because viewpoints are narrow, as if people were looking through a tunnel. They see only the tiny view at the other end of the tunnel while missing the broader landscape.

Tunnel vision restricts objectivity.

It should be evident that concern for employees can be so greatly overdone that the original purpose of joining people together—productive organizational outputs for society—is lost. Sound organizational behavior should help achieve organizational purposes, not replace them. The person who ignores the needs of people as consumers of organizational outputs while championing employee needs is misapplying the ideas of organizational behavior. It is also true that the person who pushes production outputs without regard for employee needs is misapplying organizational behavior. Sound organizational behavior recognizes a social system in which many types of human needs are served in many ways.

Behavioral bias can be so misapplied that it harms employees as well as the organization. Some people, in spite of their good intentions, so overwhelm others with care that they are reduced to dependent—and unproductive—indignity. They become content, not fulfilled. They find excuses for failure rather than taking responsibility for progress. They lack self-discipline and self-respect. As happened with scientific management years ago, concern for people can be misapplied by overeager partisans until it becomes harmful.

Employees as well as managers can handicap a fellow employee through unrestricted concern and care. These conditions are illustrated by the following events.

Edna Harding was a clerk in a government office. Her elderly father was growing mentally unstable, and plans were being made to have him placed in an institution within a few months. Her worry over this matter was compounded by the fact that he frequently came to the building where she worked and waited in the corridors for her before lunch and in the afternoon. His appearance was not pleasant, and he often mumbled. Sometimes he followed her into other offices, creating embarrassing situations. She received much sympathy and attention from her associates, and some of them began doing her work for her while she was upset. Since this problem was reducing her productivity, her supervisor finally arranged with her and the building guards not to admit her father, thus keeping him out of the building entirely. The supervisor allowed Edna's associates to continue performing some of her work, pending placement of her father in an institution.

Even after her father was placed in an institution, Edna continued letting others do her work. It soon became apparent to both her associates and her supervisor that they had sympathized with her and carried her load so long that she was depending on them as she would on a crutch. She relished their sympathy and help and seemed incapable of doing the job she had once done. She became "handicapped," as surely as if she had a physical handicap, because of too much care and good intentions from

others. Seeing these negative results, her supervisor wisely insisted that her associates reduce both their help and sympathy. Slowly and painfully, Edna's performance then returned to normal.

The law of diminishing returns

A limiting factor

Overemphasis on an organizational behavior practice may produce negative results, as indicated by the law of diminishing returns.[17] It is a limiting factor in organizational behavior the same way that it is in economics. In economics the *law of diminishing returns* refers to a declining amount of extra outputs when more of a desirable input is added to an economic situation. After a certain point, the output from each unit of added input tends to become smaller. The added output eventually may reach zero and even decline when more units of input are added.

> For example, a farmer who has a laborer working on 20 acres of land may double the output by adding another laborer. Similar results could occur by doubling the work force to four people, but soon a point will be reached where the increase in output from adding workers is smaller and smaller. Eventually production will decline as the field becomes overcrowded with workers, coordination deteriorates, and crops are trampled by the crowd.

*How does
the law work in
organizational
behavior?*

The law of diminishing returns in organizational behavior works in a similar way. It states that at some point increases of a desirable practice produce declining returns, eventually zero returns, and then negative returns as more increases are added. The concept implies that for any situation there is an optimum amount of a desirable practice, such as participation. When that point is exceeded, there is a decline in returns. In other words, the fact that a practice is desirable does not mean that more of it is more desirable. More of a good thing is not necessarily good.

> The diminishing returns associated with various incentives for enlisting in the U.S. Navy were studied in interviews with 1700 civilian males. Substantially different levels of incentives were offered: $1000 versus $3000 bonuses, two years versus four years of free college, and 10 versus 25 percent of base pay for exceptional performance. None of the three larger incentives produced more favorable dispositions to enlist. In fact, the respondents found the 10 percent bonus more attractive, leading the researchers to conclude that not only is more not necessarily better but it "can be worse."[18]

Diminishing returns may not apply to every human situation, but the idea applies so widely that it is of general use. Furthermore, the exact point at which an application becomes excessive will vary with the circumstances; but an excess can be reached with nearly any practice.

Why does the law of diminishing returns exist? Essentially, it is a system concept. It applies because of the complex system relationships of many variables in a situation. The facts state that when an excess of one variable develops, although that variable is desirable, it tends to restrict the operating benefits of other variables so substantially that net effectiveness declines. For example, too much security may lead to less employee initiative and growth. This relationship shows that *organizational effectiveness is achieved not by maximizing one human variable but by working all system variables together in a balanced way.*

Employee autonomy as an example   Employee autonomy is a higher-order need that is frequently emphasized. Some observers speak of autonomy as an ideal, implying that if employees could have complete autonomy, then the ideal state would be achieved. But this kind of reasoning ignores the law of diminishing returns. As shown in Figure 22-7, effectiveness tends to decline when too much autonomy occurs. One reason probably is that excess autonomy prevents coordination toward central goals. Different units of the organization cannot work together, so the labor of employees is wasted.

At the other end of the continuum, the lack of autonomy also is ineffective. When autonomy declines below an appropriate level, the organization fails to develop and use the talents of employees. The result is that effectiveness declines with both excessive use and miserly use of autonomy.[19] Most success is gained in the broad middle ground of use. This relationship produces a humpback curve for autonomy when it is charted with effectiveness.

The humpback curve may vary somewhat with different situations, but the basic curve persists. Figure 22-7 shows a colored curve as it might exist for a group of production workers. Line *AA'* shows the amount of autonomy that produces maximum effectiveness. The black curve shows how diminishing returns might apply to workers in a research unit in the same organization. Line *BB'* shows that much more autonomy can be provided for the research workers before a point of maximum effectiveness is reached. Ten years from

Optimum levels differ and may change.

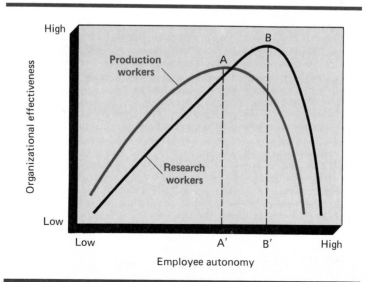

Figure 22-7
Assumed application of the law of diminishing returns to employee autonomy

now, the curves for both probably will be different because of different conditions. However, whatever the situation, the humpback curve persists and a point of diminishing returns is reached.

The law of diminishing returns serves as a warning that although increases in desirable practices can be beneficial, an excess of any of them will be counterproductive. Moderation is required. People obsessed with building only autonomy or creating maximum employee security will not be contributing to organizational success. There can be too much of a good thing just as there can be too little of it.

Other problems   One problem that has plagued organizational behavior has been the tendency for business firms to have short time horizons for the expected payoff from behavioral programs. This search for a "quick fix" sometimes leads managers to embrace the newest fad, to address the symptoms while neglecting underlying problems, or to fragment their efforts within the firm.[20] The emergence of organizational development programs that focus on systemwide change and the creation of long-term strategic plans for the management of human resources have helped bring about more realistic expectations concerning employees as a productive asset.

Immediate expectations are not realistic.

Can organizational behavior adapt to change?

Another challenge that confronts organizational behavior is to see whether the ideas that have been developed and tested during periods of organizational growth and economic plenty will endure with equal success under new conditions. Specifically, the environment in the future may be marked by some shrinking demand, scarce resources, and more intense competition. When organizations stagnate, decline, or have their survival threatened, there is evidence that stress and conflict increase.[21] Will the same motivational models be useful in these situations? Are different leadership styles called for? Will the trend toward participative processes be reversed? Since no easy answers to these and many other questions exist, it is clear that there is still tremendous room for further development of organizational behavior.

Manipulation of people

A significant concern about organizational behavior is that its knowledge and techniques can be used to manipulate people as well as to help them develop their potential. People who lack respect for the basic dignity of the human being could learn organizational behavior ideas and use them for selfish ends. They could use what they know about motivation or communication to manipulate people without regard for human welfare. People who lack ethical values could use people in unethical ways.

Ethical managers will not manipulate people.

The *philosophy* of organizational behavior is supportive and oriented toward human resources. It seeks to improve the human environment and help people grow toward their human potential. However, the *knowledge and techniques* of this subject may be used for negative as well as positive consequences. This possibility is true of knowledge in most any field, so it is no special limitation of organizational behavior. Nevertheless, we must be cautious that what is known about people is not used to manipulate them. The possibility of manipulation means that people in power in organizations need to be people of high ethical and moral integrity who will not misuse their power. Without ethical leadership, the new knowledge that is learned about people becomes a dangerous instrument for possible misuse. *Ethical leadership* will recognize such guides as the following:[22]

- *Social responsibility.* Responsibility to others arises whenever people have power in an organization.

- *Open communication.* The organization shall operate as a two-way open system with open receipt of inputs from people and open disclosure of its operations to them.

- *Cost-benefit analysis.* In addition to economic costs and benefits, human and social costs and benefits of an activity shall be considered in determining whether to proceed with it.

What is the difference between genuine motivation and manipulation of people? Basically the conditions of use need to be examined. If people understand what is happening and have substantial freedom to make their own choices, they are not being manipulated. But if they are being covertly directed and/or lack free choices, they are being manipulated. This is true whether the manipulator is a social scientist, another employee, or a manager.

As the general population learns more about organizational behavior, it will be more difficult to manipulate them, but the possibility is always there. That is why society needs ethical leaders. But ethical leaders cannot succeed unless there also are ethical followers.

THE PROMISE OF A BETTER TOMORROW

Although organizational behavior does have limitations, these should not blind us to the tremendous potential that it has to contribute to the advancement of civilization. It has provided and will provide much improvement in the human environment.[23] By building a better climate for people, organizational behavior will release their creative potential to help solve major social problems. In this way organizational behavior may contribute to social improvements that stretch far beyond the confines of any one organization. A better climate may help some person make a major breakthrough in solar energy, health, or education.

Improved organizational behavior is not easy to apply. But the opportunities are there. It should produce a higher quality of life in which there is improved harmony within each person, among people, and among the organizations of the future.

TERMS AND CONCEPTS FOR REVIEW

Human resource accounting

Investment and organizational climate approaches to human resource accounting

Behavioral bias and tunnel vision

Law of diminishing returns

Manipulation of people

Ethical leadership

REVIEW QUESTIONS

1 Now that you have completed the book, discuss basic philosophical differences among the four models of organizational behavior.

2 Compare some of the contingency relationships in stable and changing environments.

3 Form into groups of a few people, and discuss current trends in the macromotivational environment that may have an important influence, either positively or negatively, for motivation on the job. If you are employed full time, discuss whether the external environment has influenced your job motivation during the last year. If you are not employed, has the environment influenced your drives to seek a job or to work in particular jobs?

4 Discuss differences between the investment and organizational climate approaches to human resource accounting.

5 Interpret some of the limitations of organizational behavior, including the law of diminishing returns. Discuss application of the law to employee autonomy and one other item.

6 Assume that you work for a firm that suffers a severe economic decline. What behavioral practices might change?

7 Form into research groups, and develop by means of research a list of guides, such as the three given in this chapter, that an ethical leader might follow. Report your list to your entire classroom group, and discuss reasons for each item on your list. Can the manipulation of people be completely stopped?

8 On the basis of library research, prepare a five-minute talk on "What Organizational Behavior Will Be Like Twenty Years from Now."

INCIDENT

The New Controller

Statewide Electrical Supply, Inc., is a wholesale distributor of electrical supplies serving a population area of 3 million persons. Business has expanded gradually, and during the last eight years the number of accounting clerks has grown from one to twelve. The first clerk employed was Berta Shuler, who was middle-aged, had completed two years of college, and had taken two accounting courses. She proved to be a loyal and capable clerk, so when the department expanded to three people she was promoted to chief accounting clerk with supervisory duties over the other two clerks. She reported to the firm's general manager, Charlie Pastroni, and depended on him to handle accounting decisions that were more than routine.

As the business grew larger, the existing accounting arrangement became inadequate, so Charlie decided to employ a controller to handle all financial and accounting functions of the firm. Berta recognized that she was not qualified to handle accounting and financial affairs of this magnitude, and she did not seek promotion to this job. She did, however, welcome the idea of a controller, because she was overloaded with work and felt that the new controller might help relieve her of some of her more difficult responsibilities.

An additional factor in the firm's decision to establish the position of controller was that there were many complaints about Berta's supervisory ability. She appeared to be effective with the first two or three clerks when the department was small and duties were less complex, but she was unable to handle the larger department and the more complex duties. Her problems seemed to be confined mostly to internal supervision in her department. Other departments in the firm reported that she worked effectively with them, and they expressed some fear that the new controller might upset this favorable working relationship.

Charlie is not sure how to handle the problem of integrating the new controller into the organization. He wants to retain Berta because she is a valuable employee, but he is concerned that if he demotes her from supervisory duties at the time the controller is employed, she may resign.

QUESTIONS

1 How do you recommend that the new controller's department be organized?

2 What can be done to improve this situation?

EXPERIENTIAL EXERCISE

Eastern Accountants

Eastern Accountants is an accounting firm that employs about 175 accountants and other professional personnel. It also does some management consulting. One of its managers has recommended that the investment approach to human resource accounting should be adopted for employees of Eastern Accountants. The senior partners of the firm finally have agreed to install this type of accounting.

QUESTIONS

1 Read literature on human resource accounting, and develop for management a list of:
   a What investments in human resources it should account for
   b What disinvestments in human resources it should account for (It is not necessary to develop the entire accounting plan.)

2 Develop arguments both for and against this type of human resource accounting for firms similar to Eastern Accountants. How will management decisions be affected?

REFERENCES

1 Anthony Patrick Carnevale, *Human Capital: A High Yield Corporate Investment,* Washington, D.C.: American Society for Training and Development, 1983, p. 51.

2 Henry L. Tosi, "Book review of H. Meltzer and Walter Nord (eds.), *Making Organizations Humane and Productive: A Handbook for Practitioners,* New York: Wiley, 1981," *Administrative Science Quarterly,* June 1983, pp. 315–317.

3 One analyst sketched out four different scenarios of possible work environments in 1995; all four show some elements of more humane organization. See James O'Toole, "How to Forecast Your Own Working Future," *The Futurist,* February 1982, pp. 5–11.

4 See, for example, Arthur P. Brief and Ramon J. Aldag, "The 'Self' in Work Organizations: A Conceptual Review," *Academy of Management Review,* January 1981, pp. 75–88.

5 For an in-depth look at how two top executives view the steps their firm (Honeywell) has taken to improve employee relations, see "Conversation with Edson W. Spencer and Fosten A. Boyle," *Organizational Dynamics,* Spring 1983, pp. 21–45.

6 Angus Campbell, "The Paradox of Well-Being," *ISR Newsletter* (University of Michigan), Spring 1981, p. 5. For discussion of the higher-order needs of the current work force, see Arne L. Kalleberg, "Work: Postwar Trends and Future Prospects," *Business Horizons,* July–August 1982, pp. 78–84.

7 William F. Dowling, "At General Motors: System 4 Builds Performance and Profits," *Organizational Dynamics,* Winter 1975, pp. 23–38. See also a discussion of the General Motors Tarrytown plant in Stephen H. Fuller, "How to Become the Organization of the Future," *Management Review,* February 1980, pp. 50–53.

8 The organization structure may also vary among its internal units. A study that focused on the eight reasons why some organizations become excellent suggested that they show characteristics of both centralization and decentralization. See Thomas J. Peters and Robert H. Waterman, Jr., *In Search of Excellence,* New York: Harper & Row, Publishers, Incorporated, 1982.

9 The impact of the environment is portrayed in William G. Ouchi, "The Social Nature of Work," *ALCOA 81,* Pittsburgh Pa.: Aluminum Company of America, 1981, pp. 3–6; and John Naisbitt, *Megatrends: Ten New Directions Transforming Our Lives,* New York: Warner Books, 1982.

10 Michael R. Cooper and others, "Changing Employee Values: Deepening Discontent?" *Harvard Business Review,* January–February 1979, pp. 117–125; and Barry Z. Posner and J. Michael Munson, "The Importance of Values in Understanding Organizational Behavior," *Human Resource Management,* Fall 1979, pp. 9–14.

11 Fred K. Foulkes, "How Top Nonunion Companies Manage Employees," *Harvard Business Review,* September–October 1981, pp. 90–96.

12 Social responsiveness is discussed extensively in Keith Davis and William C. Frederick, *Business and Society,* 5th ed., New York: McGraw-Hill Book Company, 1984. A discussion of four forms of corporate democracy as means to achieve societal goals is in Henry Mintzberg, "Why America Needs, but Cannot Have, Corporate Democracy," *Organizational Dynamics,* Spring 1983, pp. 5–20.

13 Another "resource"—the opportunity to perform work—is discussed in Melvin Blumberg and Charles D. Pringle, "The Missing Opportunity in Organizational Research: Some Implications for a Theory of Work Performance," *Academy of Management Review,* October 1982, pp. 560–569. The need to manage performance is stressed in David C. Berman and Howard Mase, "The Key to the Productivity Dilemma," *Human Resource Management,* Fall 1983, pp. 275–286.

14 Further details are available in Eric Flamholtz, *Human Resource Accounting,* Encino, Calif.: Dickenson Publishing Company, Inc., 1974. Several cost and value

models are discussed in Hari Das and Malika Das, "One More Time: How Do We Place a Value Tag on Our Employees? Some Issues in Human Resource Accounting," *Human Resource Planning,* 1979, pp. 91–101.

15 Mary Anne Devanna, Charles Fombrun, Noel Tichy, and Lynn Warren, "Strategic Planning and Human Resource Management," *Human Resource Management,* Spring 1982, pp. 11–17.

16 Rensis Likert, "Human Resource Accounting: Building and Assessing Productive Organizations," *Personnel,* May–June 1973, pp. 8–24.

17 This discussion is adapted from Keith Davis, "A Law of Diminishing Returns in Organizational Behavior?" *Personnel Journal,* December 1975, pp. 616–619.

18 Abraham K. Korman, Albert S. Glickman, and Robert L. Frey, Jr., "More Is Not Better: Two Failures of Incentive Theory," *Journal of Applied Psychology,* April 1981, pp. 255–259.

19 This was demonstrated in an experiment relating the amount of control provided to an individual and performance. Greater performance occurred where neither too little nor too much control was allowed. See Max H. Bazerman, "Impact of Personal Control on Performance: Is Added Control Always Beneficial?" *Journal of Applied Psychology,* August 1982, pp. 472–479.

20 See Arnold S. Judson, "The Awkward Truth about Productivity," *Harvard Business Review,* September–October 1982, pp. 93–97; and Jeremy Main, "The Trouble with Managing Japanese-Style," *Fortune,* April 2, 1984, pp. 50–56.

21 David A. Whetten, "Organizational Decline: A Neglected Topic in Organizational Science," *Academy of Management Review,* October 1980, pp. 577–588. Also see L. L. Cummings, "Organizational Behavior in the 1980s," *Decision Sciences,* July 1981, pp. 365–377.

22 Adapted from Keith Davis, "Five Propositions for Social Responsibility," *Business Horizons,* June 1975, pp. 19–24.

23 For an optimistic look at the role of organizational behavior into the 1990s, see Raymond E. Miles and Howard R. Rosenberg, "The Human Resources Approach to Management: Second Generation Issues," *Organizational Dynamics,* Winter 1982, pp. 26–41.

FOR ADDITIONAL READING

Carnevale, Anthony Patrick, *Human Capital: A High Yield Corporate Investment,* Washington, D.C.: American Society for Training and Development, 1983.

Flamholtz, Eric, *Human Resource Accounting,* Encino, Calif.: Dickenson Publishing Company, Inc., 1974.

Meltzer, H., and Walter Nord (eds.), *Making Organizations Humane and Productive: A Handbook for Practitioners,* New York: John Wiley & Sons, Inc., 1981.

Naisbitt, John, *Megatrends: Ten New Directions Transforming Our Lives,* New York: Warner Books, 1982.

O'Toole, James, *Making America Work: Productivity and Responsibility,* New York: Crossroad/Continuum Publishing Company, 1981.

Peters, Thomas J., and Robert H. Waterman, Jr., *In Search of Excellence,* New York: Harper & Row, Publishers, Incorporated, 1982.

Stein, Barry A., *Quality of Work Life in Action: Managing for Effectiveness,* New York: AMACOM, 1983.

PART

CASE PROBLEMS

INTRODUCTION

Case problems provide a useful medium for testing and applying some of the ideas in this textbook. They bring reality to abstract ideas about organizational behavior. All the case problems that follow are true situations recorded by case research. Certain case details are disguised, but none of the cases is a fictional creation. All names are disguised, and any similarity to actual persons or organizations is purely coincidental.

These cases have a decision-making emphasis in the sense that they end at a point that leaves managers and/or employees with certain decisions to make. Most of the cases emphasize decisional problems of managers. One decision often is: Do I have a further problem? If that decision is in the affirmative, then further decisions must be made. What problems exist? Why are they problems? What can be done about them within the resource limits available (i.e., what alternatives are available)? Finally, what *should* be done to solve this particular problem in this specific organization? This is the reality that every manager faces in operating situations. There is no escaping it.

Even a person who does not plan to be a manager can gain much from analyzing these cases, because all employees need to develop their own analytical skills about human behavior in order to work successfully with their associates and *with management* in organizations. Thinking in terms of an employee role in a case, one can ask: Why do my associates act the way they do in this situation? Why is management acting the way it is in this instance? Was there something in my behavior that caused these actions? How can I change my behavior in order to work more effectively with the organization and my associates and thereby reach my goals more easily?

Since these case problems describe real situations, they include both good and bad practices. These cases are not presented as examples of good management, effective organizational behavior, bad management, or ineffective organizational behavior. Readers must make these judgments for themselves.

DUDLEY LODGE

P rofessor Henry Ellis taught management in a large Midwestern state university. On August 5 of last year, at about 6:30 P.M., he received a long-distance telephone call from the factory town of Corbin, 30 miles distant. The caller was Dudley Lodge, a student in his course called "Organizational Behavior" during the previous spring. After the necessary exchange of introductions, Lodge said that he had gone to work for the Roanoke Company and was having trouble. Lodge reminded Professor Ellis that he had told the students of his class he would be glad to help them when they were in business, and Lodge wanted help. He wanted to visit Professor Ellis that night because he had to have an answer to his problem by the next morning. Professor Ellis encouraged the visit and made an appointment for 8 P.M.

While he was waiting for Lodge to arrive, Professor Ellis recalled that he did not know Lodge very well, but Lodge had impressed him as a young, friendly, intelligent student. Lodge made an A in the course, although he was not a business major.* Professor Ellis also remembered that near the end of the course he had told his students, "Your formal education and training will not provide you with all the answers in your job. If I can help you any time,

---

*Lodge's placement file, which Professor Ellis examined the next morning in the Placement Office, College of Engineering, showed that Lodge had no business experience. He had a farm background. He did not work any of his way through college. He was captain of artillery in Army ROTC during his senior year and program chairman of the student chapter of the American Society of Mechanical Engineers. He made above-average grades. Letters of reference from his professors, a banker, a doctor, and a minister stated that he was honest, sincere, deeply religious, hard-working, and somewhat retiring in nature.

please call on me. Your education does not end at graduation." When Lodge arrived, he appeared emotionally upset and exhausted. He was impatient to describe his problem. He agreed to let Professor Ellis record his comments on a tape recorder which had been used for role playing in the class he attended. Professor Ellis mostly listened, occasionally asking a question or interjecting a remark such as "Tell me more about that." Lodge's description of his problem was as follows.

LODGE'S DESCRIPTION OF HIS PROBLEM

I believe this case will be clearer if I present some of the background of my experiences with the company before I relate the facts in the immediate problem. I was accepted for employment with the Roanoke Company through one of its regular application forms without a personal interview. This was an irregular procedure for the company, and I do not know why it was done in this case; however, I had no reason to be concerned about this until after my arrival in Cleveland.

When I reported to the central company offices in Cleveland on June 15, I was interviewed by both Mr. Sharp, the director, and Mr. Thomas, the assistant director of the student training course. This interview seemed quite routine. These men had my written application before them with all my personal data, yet they both seemed somewhat surprised by two facts: first, that I was married, and secondly, that I was a mechanical engineer. I was not married when I made out the application, and thus this fact did not show on the form. The second fact, that I was a mechanical engineer, was shown quite plainly on the application, and I cannot understand why it was such a surprising fact unless it was an important consideration in the Cleveland plant where only electrical equipment was manufactured. There was no serious discussion over any of my qualifications, and after a few humorous remarks about my being newly married, I was assigned to Department W-3, small motor and generator winding.

At this interview I made a special point of informing Sharp that I was interested in steam turbine design and testing, as stated in my application, that I had specialized in this work in college, and that I should like assignment to this work in the Corbin plant of the company* where this type of research and testing was done. My request was casually and carefully avoided at this time; but when it was repeated to Sharp in a short talk with him about two weeks later, he informed me that there was no student opening available in Corbin. Thomas suggested that I might be interested in transformer work, but I could see no mechanical problems involved in this, so I requested to remain in motive power if I could not be transferred to Corbin.

The day after this second interview, Sharp called me into his office at the end of the day and asked me if I would like to teach a course of physics and

---

*The company had several large plants located in various parts of the United States. The Corbin plant was located about three hundred miles from Cleveland.

trigonometry to the apprentice machinists. I accepted this offer and was enjoying the work to such an extent that I had about made up my mind to be satisfied with the work in Cleveland when, on July 13, Sharp again called me to his office and told me there was an opening in steam turbine work at Corbin if I wanted it. As a result of this conference I reported to the plant in Corbin on July 15.

When I arrived in Corbin, I was received quite cordially by Mr. Barry, director of student training at this plant, who called my wife into the office and then conducted both of us on a short tour of the plant. He suggested that I take two or three days to find a place to live, look around the plant for a day, and then report back to his office for assignment.

Two days later when I reported to Barry's office, he took me around to the many shops and offices and introduced me to the shop supervisors and department heads. He made a special visit to the production control department, supervised by a Mr. Schmidt, and there told me that I would not be placed immediately on the student training course but would be assigned temporarily to this department to relieve some of the employees who were going on vacation. Barry then left me with Schmidt, who took me immediately to the desk of a Mr. Langner, a production expediter, whose place I was to take while the latter was on vacation for a month.

The production control department, including Schmidt's desk, was all together in one large room. Langner spent the rest of the day with me in an attempt to familiarize me with the work involved in "chasing" an order through the intricacies of design, machining or purchase, testing, inspection, storage, and shipment. It seemed to me that the details involved would be impossible to grasp in several months, and yet I was to take over this job on the following day.

Frankly I was scared. I had never seen the inside of a large manufacturing plant before. I had hardly seen the working parts of a steam turbine, and here I was to have the responsibility of expediting the manufacture of a 190,000-kilowatt turbogenerator with all auxiliaries for the National Utility Company. I went home that evening a very bewildered and "sick" production expediter, or "chaser," as the employees in the shops sneeringly called us.

The next weeks passed almost as a nightmare. In my own confusion it seemed that there was no order, no scheme to follow, and that everyone was too busy to realize that I was a green country kid who hardly knew one end of a turbine from the other. I tried conscientiously to memorize shop orders, purchase orders, delivery dates, promise dates, the names of parts, the names of shop supervisors, and a few other details all at the same time, and it seemed like a hopeless task.

The other expediters were all very friendly and helpful, but Schmidt seemed to assume that I was a "full-grown expediter" and expected me to replace Langner in all respects. He told me that he would expect me to know the exact status of my order at all times and that I should keep a large progress chart on my wall up to date by making daily changes each morning. To be sure that I understood this, he called me to his desk each morning for a complete report. If I was uncertain as to the exact status of some operation, he was very impatient. His loud-talking manner and his habitual and routine use of profanity irritated me. These morning interviews took on the aspects of an inquisition. I confided in another of the expediters who seemed sympathetic, and he told me to come to the office early, to get the progress chart up to date, and to spend most of the rest of the day out in the shops away from Schmidt. None of the expediters liked him, and they avoided him as much as possible.

Acting on the advice of the other expediter, I began spending most of the day in the shops. I made friends with the shop supervisors and found that I was enjoying the time spent in discussing their work with them; I also found that they were more willing to give me the information that I required relative to my order.

I also learned that the shop employees had a contempt for the production control department and refused to cooperate with the time-and-motion-study specialists when they came through to study machine operations. This association gave me a different view of shop relations, and I found myself sympathizing with the shop attitude. This contact made it more difficult for me to conscientiously put the "pressure on" the shop supervisors to make them meet promise dates on the machining operations for my job.

In spite of this tactic of remaining out of the office as much as possible, I managed to keep my progress chart up to date by getting to the office early. I reported to work on the regular student schedule of 7:30 A.M. and left work at 4:18 P.M. In this way I was in the office well ahead of the regular office staff. My order was keeping reasonably well to its schedule, and I had no serious complaints from Schmidt. From time to time during the day I would meet him in one of the shops, and on occasion he would stop me and discuss the progress of the work. On these occasions I noticed that he was much more friendly and talked in a much more casual and less "official" tone of voice. He never criticized me for not spending more time in the office.

Late yesterday afternoon, however, just before quitting time, I learned from the engineering department that there had been a mistake made in the machining of the flange bolts for the low-pressure turbine casing. I was on my way to the automatic screw machine shop to stop production when I met Schmidt in one of the shops. He stopped me rather abruptly and the following conversation took place:

> *Lodge, what's the status of the shaft-centering plugs for the low-pressure turbine?*
> *I am not certain, Mr. Schmidt, but I don't think any work has been done on them. The shaft forgings are not due in the shops for nearly two weeks yet.*
> *Damn it, I told you that I wanted to know the exact status of that entire job at all times. I happen to know that those plugs have not even been put on production order yet, and by damn, I want them done tonight and on my desk tomorrow morning. Put them on overtime for tonight.*
> *Yes sir, I'll see Hill in the light-machine shop about it right away.*

After this conversation with Schmidt, I made arrangements with Hill, the light-machine shop supervisor, to have the centering plugs placed on overtime order and to have them finished by morning when I would pick them up. I saw Hill make out the order and place it in the overtime work basket. The operation was simple and would require about two hours of work on a power cutoff saw and a lathe.

By the time I had finished in the light-machine shop, the automatic screw machine shop, which was working only one shift per day, was closed, and I was unable to stop production on the flange bolts. I had, however, secured one of the bolts and back at my desk had confirmed the fact that they were ½ inch too short. I planned to stop production on them the first thing the next morning. While at my desk I checked my production schedule and found that the turbine shaft, for which the centering plugs were so urgently needed, was not due from the foundry and forge shop until August 21. I then went home feeling that the day had gone very well.

When I arrived at the office this morning I brought the progress chart up to date, made a few notes for the work for the day, and started out to the shops. I took the flange bolt along with me and was going to the automatic screw shop right after I went by the light-machine shop to see about the centering plugs. The time must have been almost 8 A.M., and as I passed through No. 2 shop, I met Schmidt and the following discussion took place:

Lodge, are those centering plugs finished?
I'm on my way to see about them right now, but I have an urgent stop order for these flange bolts and—
Damn it, I told you to have those plugs on my desk when I came in. By damn, Lodge, when I give you an order I expect it to be obeyed. (He grabbed me roughly by the arm.) Come on, we're going over to the shop to see about those plugs.
(I jerked away from Schmidt's grasp.) Keep your hands off me and stop cussing me, or I'll beat your damn brains out with this bolt! I'm going to put a stop order on those bolts, and then report you to Mr. Ball (the plant superintendent.) Those plugs are not needed for nearly another month anyway.

After the above conversation Schmidt turned and walked hurriedly toward his office. I was, by this time, very nervous and upset. I did, however, regain enough composure to place the hold order on the flange bolts and then went to the light-machine shop to see about the centering plugs. I had, by this time, decided it best to talk to Barry about the whole thing before going to the plant superintendent with the matter.

However, upon my arrival at the light-machine shop I learned from talking to Hill that the centering plugs had not been finished because after I talked with Hill yesterday afternoon, Schmidt had come in and given a special order for overtime work that involved all the available lathes and operators for the entire night shift. This made it impossible for work to be done on the centering plugs, and I found them cut off of bar stock, but no more work done on them. This information "made me see red," and I headed for Schmidt's office.

By the time I had arrived at Schmidt's office, I had become rather nervous, wrought up, and very angry about the whole state of things. I went directly to Schmidt's desk and told him, in something of a loud voice, I'm sure, that he was "the double-crossing so-and-so" that had stopped work on the centering plugs, that it was a dirty frame-up of me on his part; and that as of now he could get someone else to take over the job of expediter; that it was a job for a stool pigeon, anyway; and that I refused to do any more of his dirty work; and that I would not take any more of his cussing.

The effects of these remarks were somewhat awe-inspiring in the office, to say the least. Schmidt jumped from his desk and started toward me; but a very calm, quiet, purchasing agent, Mr. Andrews, intervened and restored a bit of order before things got completely out of control. Schmidt got in several "air-burning" profane remarks and told me that he was going to report me to the plant superintendent.

Andrews went with me to my desk, advised me to go immediately to see Barry, and offered to go along with me as a witness. I gladly accepted his offer, and we went over to Barry's office and told him the whole story. He talked to us for about half an hour and then wanted me to go with him back to Schmidt's office to talk to him. This I refused to do, and both Barry and Andrews left to talk to Schmidt.

After talking to Schmidt for a long time, Barry returned and told me that Schmidt admitted that both of us "acted like fools" and that he was ready to forget the matter, if I would, and he would like me to continue in the work until Langner returned. Barry told me that if I would go with him and apologize to Schmidt, work for him until Langner returned, and "keep my nose clean," he would transfer me to the regular student training course just as soon as I could be relieved. I told him that I would not do so, the way I felt at the present time, but that I would think it over during the night and would give him an answer tomorrow. That is why I need your help, Professor Ellis. I am all mixed up and don't know what to do. I shall appreciate your advice and shall let you know the outcome.

STUDY GUIDES

1 Why do you think Lodge came to Professor Ellis for help?

2 What mistakes did the "company" make in "training" Lodge? Who made these mistakes? Explain.

3 Why do you think Schmidt acted the way he did? Why do you think Lodge reacted the way he did? Did the two people "understand" each other?

4 What are the primary problems existing at the end of the case?

5 What action should be taken to help solve the main problems of the case? By Lodge? Barry? Schmidt? Others? Give specific behavioral reasons for proposed actions.

6 Discuss this case in terms of basic organizational behavior ideas that you have covered to this date, such as social systems, organizational climate, the psychological contract, expectancy theory, equity theory, and models of organizational behavior.

ROLE-PLAYING SITUATIONS

1 Assume that you are Professor Ellis, and then continue the conversation with Lodge.

2 Role-play the meeting of Lodge and Barry on August 6.

3 Role-play the meeting, if any, of Lodge, Barry, and Schmidt on August 6.

THE VIDEO ELECTRONICS COMPANY

Frank Simpson, president and controlling stockholder of the Video Electronics Company, now in its tenth year, was faced with the problem of gearing his plant to meet both increased production demands brought on by the expanding electronics industry and also increased competition from other producers of his line of products. The plant tripled its employees during the past year, but production per worker decreased nearly 20 percent and costs rose nearly to the break-even point. For the preceding quarter, profit on sales was less than 1 percent and profit on invested capital was under 3 percent. This was one-fourth of what Simpson considered normal.

The company employed mostly unskilled labor who were trained by the company. Employees were not represented by a labor union. All employees were paid hourly wages rather than incentive wages.

The company was founded by Simpson and a few investor friends for production of a narrow line of specialized small electronics parts that were sold to other manufacturers. It grew slowly and had a labor force of only 105 workers at the beginning of last year. Its reputation for quality was excellent. This reputation of quality was the primary reason for a flood of orders from new clients in the spring of last year, requiring the firm to triple its labor force by July. Simpson remarked, "I didn't seek those orders. *They* came to us. I didn't want to expand that fast, but what could I do? If you want to stay in business, you can't tell your customers you are too busy to sell them anything."

The company was located in a manufacturing town of 15,000 people in rural New York, about 60 miles from any large town. Enough untrained people were available locally for hiring for the expansion, which required the operation of two shifts instead of one. Management forecasts indicated that the expansion would be permanent, with the additional possibility of moderate growth during the next five years or longer.

Simpson, in consultation with the board of directors, concluded that he needed to establish the new position of general manager of the plant so that he (Simpson) could spend more of his time on high-level work and less of it ironing out production difficulties. He also concluded that under present conditions he needed to build an industrial engineering staff that could both cope with present production problems and give his company the developmental work that was needed to stay ahead of his competitors.

Almost all his present supervisory personnel had been with the company since the year it was founded. They were all skilled people in their particular phases of the operations, but Simpson felt that none of them had the training or overall insight into company problems to take charge as general manager.

After much thought, Simpson decided to employ a general manager from outside the company. This person would report directly to him and would have full responsibility for production of the product and development of a top-notch industrial engineering department. Simpson called a meeting of all his supervisory personnel and explained his decision to them in detail. He described the need for this plan of action and stressed the necessity for the utmost in cooperation. The older supervisors did not seem to be pleased with this turn of events but promised that they would cooperate fully with the new manager.

About four months after his meeting with his supervisors, Simpson found a suitable general manager, John Rider. Rider, age thirty-six, was a mechanical engineer who had been a general supervisor in a large Philadelphia electronics plant. One of his first jobs as general manager was to find a qualified person to develop the industrial engineering function. Paul Green, an industrial engineer thirty-one years of age, was hired from the industrial engineering department of a large steel company in Pittsburgh. Green had an M.B.A., a good academic record, and two years of experience.

Green and Rider both felt that the company was in bad condition in relation to machine utilization, employee utilization, waste, and reject rates. On the basis of their first impressions of the production facilities they estimated that production management and industrial engineering changes might be able to increase productivity at least 25 percent and reduce unit costs 35 percent.

Green wanted time to get acquainted with the processes and the supervisory personnel before recommending major improvements. Rider granted this wish, so Green spent two months getting acquainted with the supervisors. During this period he recommended to Rider only minor changes that the supervisors seemed to go along with except for minor disagreement. However, after this period Simpson, Rider, and Green felt that major steps had to be taken to improve both production and quality. They decided that the first industrial engineering project should be a study of production processes, department by department. This study was to cover every operation done on the products. All processes were to be put in writing, since many of the processes had developed without anyone ever writing down just how they were to be performed. Several of the supervisors were the only ones who understood how certain operations were to be set up and performed, and any supervisor who left the company often took valuable knowledge that was difficult to replace.

At the next supervisory meeting (of all management personnel), Simpson announced the plan for the production study. No estimated completion date for the study was given. No comments were made by the production supervisors, but it was plain to Rider and Green that several of the older supervisors were not happy about the idea. Simpson tried to get across the idea that full cooperation was required and that the company had "to meet its competition or go out of business."

Green started the survey the following week. There was outward rebellion in some cases, but he smoothed this over by discussing with the supervisor the reasons for the survey and then leaving that department alone for a few days. Green thought he was convincing the people who objected, so he proceeded with the study without comment to either Rider or Simpson about the resistance.

About five weeks after Green started the study, he and Rider left town together on a business trip that kept them away from the plant for two days. On the night of the second day one of the second-shift supervisors telephoned Simpson, who happened to be working late at the office. The supervisor said that a group of them would like to talk to Simpson. Since many of these supervisors had known Simpson for a long time and called him by his first name, he did not object and told them to "come on up."

The group that arrived consisted of all supervisors with more than one year's company seniority. First-shift supervisors were there, even though they had been off duty for three hours. As soon as the group arrived, it was apparent to Simpson that they were troubled about something and that this was no social call. All the supervisors entered his office, and one older man who had been supervisor for nine years, Charles Warren, acted as speaker for the group.

"Frank," he said, "all of us here have been in this game for a good many years. We know more about this business than anyone else around here, and we don't like people standing around in our departments watching what we are doing. We also don't like the idea of some young guy telling us that we should do this and that to improve our production and quality. This industry is different, and those new ideas about industrial engineering just won't work for us. We want you to tell that new guy, Green, that his ideas won't work for a company like this." Warren then paused to give Simpson a chance to answer. The other supervisors stood there quietly.

STUDY GUIDES

1 If you were Simpson, what would you do now? What would you do later, if anything? What behavioral models and ideas are involved in your decisions?

2 Should Simpson have permitted the supervisors to see him, since they now report directly to Rider?

3 What kinds of changes are taking place in this case? What are the effects of these changes? What ideas about change will help you in dealing with this situation?

4 Does the learning curve for change apply in this case? Discuss.

ROLE-PLAYING SITUATIONS

1 You are Simpson. Reply to Warren and the other supervisors gathered in your office.

2 Have people play the roles of Simpson, Rider, and Green in a meeting in Simpson's office to discuss this situation on the day Rider and Green return from their trip.

3 Role-play the supervisory meeting in which Simpson announces to his supervisors the production process study. Include people in the roles of Rider and Green.

Change?

If there are problems these men would have caught it by now, while a new face could see things different

Wouldn't you think that each line sup. will believe his line is perfect.

No respect for Rider,

stuck to your ways

Biased view

ALBATROS ELECTRICAL COMPANY

Seven years ago the Albatros Electrical Company built a refrigerator assembly plant in Asheville, North Carolina. Among the original work force was John Franks, who was hired as a cleaner. A cleaner's job was to keep the floors swept and to remove all empty cartons and boxes from the work areas. The job paid a low wage and was considered undesirable by most job applicants. Franks was forty-nine years old at the time he was hired and was the oldest member of the cleaning section of the maintenance department. A year later the plant was organized by an international union, and Franks was appointed shop steward for the cleaners.

The maintenance department consisted of four groups: the electricians, the mechanics, the layout engineers, and the cleaners. Each group was organized into a section whose supervisor reported to the plant engineer. In the cleaning section there were usually about twenty-four workers reporting to the supervisor. The average age of the cleaners was forty years, and their average educational level was the seventh grade. Some were minority employees, but Franks was not.

Franks had a dominant, persuasive manner which enabled him to have considerable influence with the other cleaners. For this reason the plant engineer was not pleased with Franks's appointment as shop steward. A few days after Franks became steward, he presented his first grievance. The bargaining contract described the general procedure for complaints and grievances as follows:

Complaint Procedure: Any employee or group of employees having a complaint shall have the right, either personally or through the Union shop steward, to present such complaint verbally to the immediate supervisor in an endeavor to reach an adjustment. An earnest effort should be made to settle and dispose of such complaints between the parties noted in this paragraph. If the complaint involves a matter subject to the grievance procedure, and no satisfactory settlement has been made, the complaint may be presented as a grievance as hereinafter provided.

Grievance Procedure:*

Step 1: Any employee or group of employees having a grievance shall present the matter to the Union steward, who shall make investigations and if the grievance is found valid, take the matter up with the general supervisor of the section in which such grievance arose for adjustment. Failing adjustment in this manner within forty-eight (48) hours (Saturdays, Sundays, and holidays excluded), the matter shall be submitted to Step 2.

Step 2: The grievance shall be referred by the steward to the Business Manager of the Union or a designated representative, who shall take the matter up for adjustment with the Personnel Manager or a designated representative. Failing adjustment in this manner within seventy-two (72) hours (Saturdays, Sundays, and holidays excluded), the matter shall be submitted to Step 3.

Step 3: In the event the grievance is not satisfactorily adjusted by the procedure in the foregoing steps within the specified times, the grievance shall be considered by the Grievance Committee (who may be accompanied by the Business Manager of the Union or a duly designated representative, and/or a representative of the said brotherhood) and the Plant Manager of the Company and/or a duly designated representative. In the event it is not satisfactorily adjusted within five (5) days, it shall, at the request of either party, be submitted to a board of arbitration.

(A fourth step provided arbitration.)

In the cleaning section the plant engineer was equivalent to the "general supervisor" specified in Step 1 of the grievance procedure. Franks's first grievance, which he presented to the plant engineer on the form provided, was that Pleasant Williams of the cleaning section was being denied promotion to an existing vacancy for which he was eligible. Williams was eligible for upgrading to a vacancy in the stock-handling section, but Williams had been told by his supervisor that he could not be promoted until his replacement was hired. Williams had waited ten days, and no replacement was yet available.

The plant engineer was receptive to Franks's presentation of the grievance because he did not know about this problem. His investigation disclosed that the facts were substantially those presented; however, Franks did not first present the grievance orally to his cleaning supervisor as required by the complaint procedure. Since this was the first grievance in the department and the plant engineer wished to build good union relations, he arranged for Williams to be promoted the next day.

As a result of this event Franks's high prestige increased greatly among his coworkers in the cleaning section. Franks was aware of his new status. He made the following comment to several of the cleaners, "I am going to get that plant engineer straightened out and make him give the cleaners a fair

*The grievance procedure could be invoked for any matter pertaining to the labor contract.

shake." Franks then began a campaign of seeking and presenting complaints and grievances. During the next six years he filed fifty-four formal grievances for cleaners, winning seventeen of them. During this period the number of cleaners in the department varied between eighteen and twenty-seven. Following are some of the typical grievances he filed:

1 Cleaners need a special rest room and clothes locker room. (Not allowed; ended at step 1)

2 Make earlier distribution of checks on payday so that cleaners can cash checks during the lunch hour period or give checks to their spouses for cashing before the banks close. (Allowed for all shop employees; ended at step 2)

3 An additional cleaner is needed to allow other cleaners to rest periodically. (Not allowed, ended at step 2)

4 Cleaners should have uniforms furnished by the company. (Allowed; ended at step 1)

5 Cleaners should not have to load cleaning waste into tote bins for trucker to deliver to junkyard. (Not allowed; ended at step 1)

6 The overtime list should be posted prior to Thursday noon. (Not allowed; ended at step 1)

7 Casey Porter's assigned cleaning area should be reduced in size because it requires too much work. (Not allowed; ended at step 1)

In one instance two years ago Franks was censured by the plant engineer for taking up company time with an "absurd request." This grievance asked that production supervisors have their employees place all empty cartons and boxes in barrels which would be provided in the production area for that purpose. This, in some cases, would require a production employee to stop work to place the cartons in the barrels. The request was denied by the plant engineer.

Early last year the plant engineer felt that something should be done about Franks's behavior as a steward, so he called the union business manager for a conference about Franks. The business manager agreed that Franks was "hunting" grievances and was presenting many grievances without first discussing them with his supervisor. Then Franks was called into the engineer's office for a discussion of his attitude. Both the plant engineer and the business manager reminded Franks that he should "use judgment" and present only those complaints and grievances that appeared to be contract violations. Franks said very little except to assure the two men that he would cooperate at all times. Near the end of the meeting the engineer gave Franks a formal reprimand for presenting a grievance six days earlier without first discussing it with his supervisor. The reprimand and a summary of the meeting were placed in Franks's permanent personnel folder.

During the following months Franks filed several grievances without first discussing them with his supervisor, but the plant engineer took no further action. He later commented, "I hoped Franks would soon improve, and I did not want to create any incident which would undermine my good working relations with the union."

Near the end of last year it became evident that Franks was not changing his attitude, and the plant engineer again called the union business manager for a conference. After some discussion the business manager agreed to suspend Franks as shop steward and to try to get a replacement elected. In January of this year the business manager suspended Franks from his steward's job and put out feelers for a successor. The problem became difficult when the business manager learned that the cleaners felt Franks was the only person for the job. Not one cleaner would consider taking the steward's job. This condition was allowed to continue for two months with the hope that a newly hired cleaner might be persuaded to become steward. Finally, due to pressure from the cleaners, the business agent reinstated Franks as the shop steward of the cleaning section.

Franks's first act upon being reinstated as shop steward was to file a formal grievance to the effect that Mary Parker had been "forcefully persuaded" to transfer to the night shift. When the plant engineer checked this grievance, the supervisor said that Mary had asked for night work but that Franks had talked her into wanting back on the day shift and had made her feel that she had been coerced into asking for night work. Mary admitted that she asked for the transfer, but she claimed that, from the way the supervisor described the job, she thought second-shift work would be easier, but it was not. When Franks was confronted with the evidence of the investigation, his reply to the plant engineer was a curt "So what?"

STUDY GUIDES

1 Why do you think Franks was originally chosen as shop steward? Why has he continued to keep the job? What has the company done to help him keep it? What has Franks done?

2 Why do you think the plant engineer reprimanded Franks in their conference early last year? What assumptions was the engineer making about Franks? Franks's supervisor? The function of the grievance procedure? The business agent? The engineer's own job?

3 What should the engineer do now? What should the business agent do?

4 Discuss whether the grievance program has been effective with the cleaners.

ROLE-PLAYING SITUATIONS

1 Role-play last year's meeting of Franks, the plant engineer, and the union business manager, at which time Franks was given a formal reprimand.

2 Role-play the meeting at the end of this case when Franks says, "So what?"

MIDDLE NATIONAL BANK

Bill Smith was manager of a branch bank in the metropolitan area in which the bank home office was located. Smith, age about thirty, was a college graduate in banking and finance. Higher management was impressed with his capabilities; so it was trying to develop him for further promotions.

Recently Smith was assigned to become branch manager of a larger branch in Parsons, a town of about 50,000 people in a distant part of the state. This assignment was both a promotion and an opportunity to broaden his experience. When the assignment was made, the manager of branch operations told Smith that he might have some difficulty with Ralph Dawson, assistant manager of the Parsons Bank.

The manager of branch operations said that Dawson, age fifty-five and a high school graduate, had worked in the Parsons branch for thirty-one years and had been assistant branch manager for fourteen years. He did not expect promotion and would not leave Parsons for wider experience. He was said to be "200 percent loyal" to the bank and very proud of his managerial position in the bank. He had strong community support and brought much business to the bank, particularly from members of his ethnic minority group which were 40 percent of the town's population and provided many of its business leaders.

The manager of branch operations said there were two main problems with Dawson. First, he was dogmatic and authoritarian. Dawson insisted on showing mistakes to any person that made them, even when that person was a customer. Second, Dawson managed the bank activities assigned to him in his own authoritarian way and was not responsive to instructions from any branch manager, especially a younger one, because his cultural heritage had high respect for age and seniority.

During his first month at the Parsons branch Smith observed that Dawson's conduct was as it had been described to him. Dawson was intensely protective and autocratic about bank operations officially under his direct supervision, but he did not interfere in the few policy areas officially assigned to Smith's direct supervision. He did not seem to resent Smith's being there; however, in the second month when Smith tried to persuade Dawson to take a different approach with an operating problem, Dawson responded icily, "I have the experience here, and I'll be running my departments long after you have returned to the home office, so I am going to manage them the way I found best for the long run. I can't make temporary changes to fit each new manager's approach."

Smith realized that he probably would be transferred elsewhere in two or three years, but he also knew that the community was changing and it might become more difficult to recruit employees who would work under Dawson's autocratic command.

Smith wondered whether he should avoid upsetting the situation, stay out of Dawson's affairs, and probably transfer with a good record in two or three years or whether he should take the possibly riskier approach of confronting Dawson with the necessity for change which Smith felt necessary. He knew that any confrontation with Dawson might provoke ethnic opposition in the community.

STUDY GUIDES

1 Analyze the roles that seniority, age, provincial viewpoint, ethnic background, and other variables play in this case.

2 If you were Smith, what would you do with Dawson? Be specific, including why. For example, what motivational models would you be able to use, if any?

3 Discuss this case in terms of basic organizational behavior ideas that you have covered to this date, such as the psychological contract, models of organizational behavior, leadership styles, and resistance to change.

5

SPACETRONICS

Spacetronics is a division of a large manufacturer of electronic equipment. Complex equipment is designed and built at Spacetronics' western plant, because employees at this plant develop communication devices for the United States space and defense programs.

Emphasis in the electronics industry is often placed on research and new-product development. These functions are important at Spacetronics as well, but because of the complexity of the equipment manufactured and the high reliability requirements demanded by space and military programs, great stress also is placed on the production function.

Production runs are usually of short duration and require a continuous stream of new hand tools, fixtures, jigs, and manual and automatic machines to make and assemble the intricate electronic gear. Because of the nature of the work at Spacetronics, design and fabrication of production tools are particularly critical functions.

Preassembly tool design and planning are located organizationally under the superintendent of parts manufacture, as shown in Figure 1. Assembly tool design and planning are under the direction of the assistant chief engineer.

Preassembly tool design and planning are supervised by George Whipple, a well-liked and aggressive engineer who has an industrywide reputation for excellence. His department has successfully met schedules and cost estimates for a number of years. Whipple has a degree in mechanical engineering and five years of experience as a tool and die maker.

Assembly tool design is under the general direction of Marshall Holden, who became assistant chief industrial engineer six months ago. Assembly tool design has been a consistent source of delay, cost overages, and other

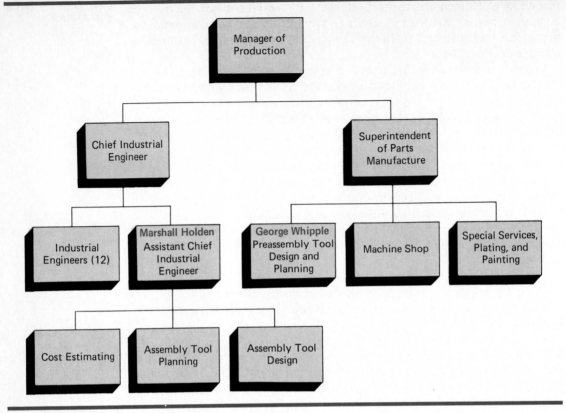

Figure 1
Organizational chart of production division

difficulties for several years. In fact, its work has been so poor that frequently Whipple's department has been called upon to help it. Holden was promoted to this department in an effort to improve its performance. He was formerly a cost-estimating supervisor. Holden had been a maintenance machinist in an eastern steel mill for fifteen years before coming to Spacetronics as a machinist ten years ago. He has no college training, but he is ambitious and dedicated in his work.

Four years ago Holden approached Whipple and asked for a transfer into the preassembly tool-design section. Holden had felt for some time that his chances for advancement as a machinist were limited; so he was unhappy in his machinist's job. Initially Whipple reacted favorably to Holden's request, because both men already had an established working relationship and Whipple knew that skilled tool designers were difficult to find. He had a vacant position for tool designer which he had been trying to fill for several months.

Whipple spent several hours reviewing Holden's work record and qualifications. He also spent time talking with Holden's immediate supervisor about the type and quality of work Holden was then doing. Whipple finally decided that although Holden was an excellent machinist, he did not have the creative abilities necessary for a tool designer. Whipple felt so certain about the matter that he even rejected Holden's supervisor's suggestion for a temporary transfer on a trial basis.

Holden was bitter about Whipple's rejection. Even though Whipple helped Holden get a new job in the industrial engineering section a month later, they did not reestablish a close working relationship. This lack of rapport continued after Holden's promotion to assistant chief of industrial engineering which placed both Holden and Whipple on the same organizational level.

Recently Holden began planning a reorganization which he felt would remedy the problems in his tool-design group and also increase the efficiency of the total tooling process. Holden worked closely with the chief industrial engineer and the superintendent of parts manufacture. They were all good friends and were concerned with the problem. After three months of planning, the proposed reorganization was presented to Whipple in a meeting with the chief industrial engineer and superintendent of parts manufacture. The proposal centered around a trade of functions between industrial engineering and the parts manufacture department. All tool-design functions were to be assigned to the parts manufacture department, with all tool-planning functions moving to the industrial engineering department.

During the meeting Whipple was asked for his comments. He replied, "You've certainly spent a lot of effort developing the reorganization. It's workable, and I'll do everything in my power to make it work; but I feel strongly that the tool-planning and tool-design functions should not be split up. The integration of the two has increased the efficiency of my group considerably."

"We had considered that point," said the chief industrial engineer, "and we have an alternate proposed reorganization which would move all tool-design and planning functions into the industrial engineering department." After some discussion, there seemed to be a consensus that the alternate proposal was better, and the three men agreed to meet a week later to finalize the proposal.

At lunch Whipple talked about the reorganization with his subordinates. A major concern was to whom the design group would report. Whipple had not considered this question before. He had assumed that he would report directly to the chief industrial engineer.

The next morning Whipple asked the chief industrial engineer about the proposed chain of command. "Of course, you'll report to the assistant chief industrial engineer," was the answer, "I'm much too busy handling the problems that my twelve industrial engineers bring to me to even consider another person reporting directly to me."

Whipple was shocked. This was something he had not expected. His shock soon turned to anger. He stormed in to talk to the superintendent of parts manufacture and said, "I have some strong reservations about the reorganization. In the eyes of my workers it is a demotion to be placed under Holden. He is at the same organizational level as I am, and I don't want to report to him. I don't even respect him. I knew a reorganization was being planned, but neither my people nor I were considered in the planning. Plans involving me should be discussed with me. They are good plans, but. . . ."

"Damn, it, 'but' nothing," interrupted the superintendent. "All you are worried about is where you fit into the company. This is a good plan which will help the company."

"You're right," retorted Whipple, "I'm deeply concerned about where I fit. I've worked hard in my present job, and all I get for it is a demotion."

"But it's not a demotion, George. Your pay grade will be the same, and there's even a possible raise in it for you."

STUDY GUIDES

1 Discuss thoroughly what you think is the central problem in this case. What corrective action do you propose to solve this problem?

2 Discuss other problems in the case, and give your proposals for solving them. Make full use of ideas from this book.

3 Discuss any errors made by the superintendent and the chief industrial engineer in planning and implementing the reorganization. Why do you think they made these errors? What guidance can you give them to prevent future errors of a similar type?

4 If you were Whipple what would you do now?

5 Would any of the following be useful in interpreting this case?
a Transactional analysis
b Enriched sociotechnical work systems
c Contingency ideas regarding stable and changing environments
d Maslow's hierarchy of needs
e Expectancy theory, including the valence of money

ROLE-PLAYING SITUATIONS

1 Continue the conversation of Whipple and the superintendent at the end of the case.

2 Role-play a conversation between the superintendent and the chief industrial engineer, which takes place later the same day.

6

UNITED MUTUAL INSURANCE COMPANY

T he United Mutual Insurance Company was organized in 1939 by Paul and James Taylor. Since its organization, these two men have maintained active personal direction of the company. The company is located in Kansas City, Missouri, and writes all forms of automobile and general casualty insurance. At the present time United Mutual is represented by more than 2000 agents located in Wisconsin, Illinois, Iowa, Missouri, Kentucky, and Colorado, and it has thirty-two field managers and eighty claims adjusters working out of forty-seven offices. The company has grown steadily since it was founded.

The home office of United Mutual has about 425 employees. Annual labor turnover is 25 to 30 percent, and it has been difficult to replace this turnover because of a mild labor shortage in Kansas City the past few years. Of the 425 people in the home office, about 100 are supervisory employees. The term "supervisory employees" or "supervisors" in this company refers to those who do not have to punch time clocks and do not receive overtime pay. It includes people who direct the work of others and also some technical and professional people such as lawyers and underwriters. An organizational chart of the people primarily involved in this case is shown in Figure 1.

This case began about five years ago. At that time the company allowed one coffee break of fifteen minutes in the morning and a similar break in the afternoon. Employees went to the cafeteria for their break. At this time both Gorman and Townsend had some responsibility for the coffee break. Gorman

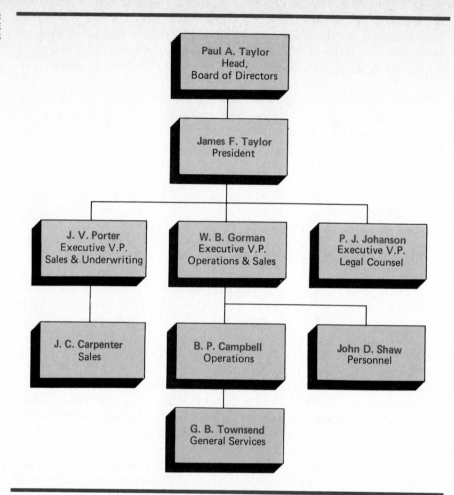

Figure 1
Current
organizational chart
showing top
positions in
United Mutual
Insurance Company

had general responsibility for control of the break, because he was in charge
of general operations in the home office. Townsend had responsibility for the
cafeteria and payroll. He also acted unofficially as personnel director.

Gradually many of the supervisory employees started taking advantage of
the coffee break and overstaying their time in the cafeteria. When the
nonsupervisory employees saw what was happening, they also started to take
longer coffee breaks than were authorized. Before many months had passed,
most all the employees were taking longer breaks than were allotted. When
Townsend and Gorman questioned several of the supervisory employees as to
why they spent so much time during coffee breaks when they knew that only
fifteen minutes were authorized, the standard reply was "We were discussing
business problems of United Mutual" or "We were having a meeting, so we
actually were working."

It is probable that many overstayed coffee breaks actually were informal business meetings, because most of the supervisors were either underwriters, claim adjusters, or operations supervisors, and daily meetings of some of these people were common to discuss their business problems. There was, of course, no way to prove which discussions were social and which were informal business meetings.

One thing seemed sure. It was almost impossible to get nonsupervisory employees to believe that supervisors actually were working during coffee hour; therefore Gorman told the supervisors that they had to keep within their fifteen minutes in order to set an example for the rest of the employees. They failed to heed his word, and the coffee break continued to be violated. To add to the complication, too many employees were coming to the cafeteria at the same time, which resulted in much congestion and waiting for coffee.

In an effort to keep the coffee break limited to fifteen minutes, Townsend started staying in the cafeteria during the complete coffee hour, and watching for offenders who stayed over the time limit. He, in turn, reported the offenders to department heads, who were supposed to take the action necessary to ensure that their employees obeyed the coffee-period time limit. For the next few months their employees observed the fifteen-minute coffee period very closely with few exceptions. Then the department heads again became lax, and nonsupervisory as well as supervisory employees began exceeding the time limit on coffee periods.

Again Gorman and Townsend went into consultation, and this time they came up with the idea of installing bells in the cafeteria. The bells were installed and were adjusted to ring every ten minutes. Considering that it took a few minutes for employees to go from their offices to the cafeteria, Gorman and Townsend felt that ten minutes in the cafeteria was the maximum time that could be allowed in order to stay within the limits of the fifteen-minute coffee period. Schedules were set up by the department heads so that the employees were supposed to arrive at the cafeteria when the bells rang and they would stay until the bells rang again, at which time they were supposed to leave.

Townsend noted that the bells did keep some employees in the cafeteria for only ten minutes, but it was very difficult to synchronize the various groups. People were drifting into and out of the cafeteria all the time and not according to the schedule for which the bells were adjusted. Also, when one group was leaving the cafeteria, another group was scheduled to enter, which added to the congestion. The general opinion among some employees was that the bells made them feel "like they were in prison cells" and could not get out until the bells rang. Others thought the bells very irritating and said it was impossible to enjoy the coffee period. It was soon evident that the bells were not solving the coffee-period problem, but since no better solution was offered, the bells remained, and employees continued to complain about them.

Three years ago top management realized that United Mutual was expanding to the extent that there was definite need for a personnel director to handle the coffee-break problem as well as the increasing number of other personnel problems existing within the home office. Therefore, in July of that year John Shaw was hired as personnel director of United Mutual. Shaw had sixteen years' experience in personnel work and was highly regarded in local personnel circles.

Soon after Shaw arrived at United Mutual, Gorman explained the current personnel problems to him. Of course, one of these problems was the coffee break. Shaw soon found out for himself that employees were taking more than their allotted time during coffee periods. The president wanted something done to remedy the situation, and this problem was given to Shaw.

He tackled the problem rapidly and directly. In his own words, "I made periodic checks with all the department heads concerning the coffee break and found out what their reactions were. I told the department heads to keep check on their employees and to try to keep the coffee break confined within the fifteen-minute period."

Shaw soon found that the bells were ineffective and unpopular. He had them removed from the cafeteria. A few executives approached Shaw and suggested that the coffee periods be discontinued. He countered with the following argument: "The labor shortage in our city is critical at the present time. We have twenty-five vacancies within the company, and yet you want me to discontinue a practice that other employers have and, as a result, perhaps lose more employees."

In December of Shaw's first year top management asked him to justify his stand that the coffee break was necessary and, if he could justify it, to provide a remedy to the problem. Shaw gave the following reasons why the coffee periods should be continued:

1 A coffee break helps new employees make friends with people in their own and other departments. United Mutual has a 25 to 30 percent labor turnover each year, so several new employees are coming to the company every week.

2 By having a coffee break, there is a cross-pollination of ideas, and this prevents stratification and cliques.

3 A coffee break will give renewed vigor to the employees, and this will result in greater productivity.

4 The nature of detailed work and mental activity is so confining that people need a break from their routines.

After much deliberation and consultation, Shaw prepared a solution for the coffee-break problem and submitted it to top executives. They approved it, including his proposal that coffee be furnished free to employees. Free coffee was first given on March 23 by means of a routine announcement in the cafeteria. The remainder of Shaw's proposal was put into effect by a memorandum issued on March 31 by Shaw to all home office employees of United Mutual, as shown in Figure 2.

The memorandum was well received by most of the employees. The workweek was cut from thirty-nine hours, thirty-five minutes, to thirty-eight hours, forty-five minutes. Shaw believed that everything would have turned

UNITED MUTUAL INSURANCE COMPANY
MEMORANDUM

Subject *Changes in Working, Lunch, and Rest Period Schedules*
To *All Home Office Department Heads and Employees*
From *Personnel*

Effective April 4, the working schedule of the office will be as follows:

8:00 A.M. to 12:00 noon.
Forty-minute lunch periods will be scheduled at five regular intervals.
Fifteen-minute morning rest periods will be scheduled at five regular intervals.
The working day will end at 4:25 P.M.

This new working schedule reduces the workday by ten minutes and makes an overall workweek of 38.75 hours. We feel sure that employees will welcome this change since it will help to avoid further the evening traffic congestion and facilitate bus connections.

The morning rest periods will be scheduled from 9:30 A.M. through 10:25 A.M. Departments will be scheduled at ten-minute intervals. Fifteen minutes will be allowed for each employee, which includes travel time to and from the cafeteria. It is important that employees adhere to the schedules listed below since the principal reason for scheduling is to eliminate confusion and congestion and to improve service in the cafeteria. It will be the responsibility of department heads to make certain that employees follow the assigned schedules. Following is the morning rest period schedule for all departments.

[The schedule is omitted.]

Where stand-by telephone service is required, department heads will exercise discretion in keeping their operation staffed during the morning rest and lunch periods.

With the reduction of the workweek by fifty minutes, we feel that the afternoon rest period is unnecessary. The cafeteria will be closed after the last lunch group has been served.

3/31/—

JDS:RG

Figure 2
Memorandum
to employees

out all right if United Mutual had not been remodeling and adding to its building at that time (see Figure 3).

As can be seen from the diagram, this construction meant that all employees from the North Building had to walk outside and around the center building in order to get to the cafeteria for the coffee period. Employees on the third floor took as long as six to seven minutes to reach the cafeteria, which caused their break to extend beyond the fifteen-minute limitation. In the next few months, department heads became slack in enforcing the memorandum issued by Shaw, and employees again started taking more time than was allotted to them.

Most department heads had their departments split into two sections. One section was to go for their coffee, and the other section was to wait until the first section returned. The only trouble was that the second section was not waiting for the first section to return before they left. The result was mass confusion in the cafeteria. Groups did not come on the regular schedule, and

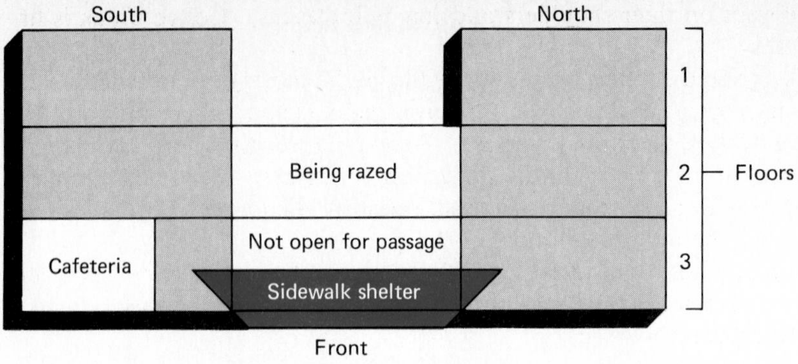

Figure 3
United Mutual
building during
remodeling

when they did come, they stayed over fifteen minutes. Shaw conferred with all the department heads and told them if the practice of long coffee breaks continued in the future, there was a strong possibility of not having any coffee breaks at all.

One department head realized the seriousness of the problem and issued a memorandum to all his employees explaining why time limits must be observed by everyone. Gorman liked the memorandum and had Shaw send copies to all supervisors.

Early last year United Mutual's management decided that an opinion survey might help solve some of the personnel problems encountered by the company. In this survey approximately sixty employees complained about the coffee period. Many of them didn't drink coffee and wanted to know why coffee was free while the rest of the liquid refreshments were not. There were some complaints about not having an afternoon coffee break in addition to the morning break. Shaw conferred with Gorman, and they decided to offer free tea and cocoa as well as free coffee to employees, but the practice of only one coffee break each day was continued. Shaw informed all department heads that the coffee break was still only fifteen minutes and in the morning only, but that cocoa and tea were free to employees beginning June 1. He also mentioned that this free coffee, tea, and cocoa would cost United Mutual $400 a month, and in order for this coffee break to be continued, employees would have to restrict their coffee break to the time mentioned in the memorandum, which was fifteen minutes.

In October of last year the building was finished and employees could walk through the building again to get to the cafeteria. A new middle section had been added to the building, and there was considerably more space for all employees.

The coffee break in the morning continued, and employees seemed to like the free coffee, tea, and cocoa. In fact, they liked it so much that most of them started taking second cups and overstaying their allotted fifteen minutes. In an effort to remind employees that the coffee period was still only fifteen minutes, Shaw had table napkins printed showing a friendly clock tapping two employees on their shoulders and reminding them, "Coffee break is fifteen minutes."

The printed napkins were removed from the tables once or twice a week so that employees would not get a "routine feeling" about them and would know that they were there for a purpose. The napkins served a very useful purpose, as many of the employees did limit their coffee break to fifteen minutes, but there still were several (mostly supervisory employees) who continued to disregard the time limit on the coffee period.

Recently the case interviewer began a study of the coffee problem at United Mutual. On his first random visit to the coffee period he made the following observations:

1 Although the coffee break wasn't scheduled to start until 9:30, approximately thirty-five persons were in the cafeteria prior to that time.

2 At 9:35 A.M. there were approximately two hundred employees in the cafeteria when there should have been only seventy-five to one hundred. There was much congestion, and when the 9:45 group came to get coffee, there weren't enough clean cups due to the overflow at 9:30.

3 At 9:45 when the first group of employees was supposed to leave the cafeteria, approximately 25 percent remained.

4 On the basis of spot checks, it appeared that about 90 percent of the clerical employees obeyed the fifteen-minute coffee-break rule and the other 10 percent were just a few minutes over the limit. Spot checks of several supervisors showed that they spent anywhere from fifteen minutes to over an hour in the cafeteria. Typical examples included one supervisor who stayed in the cafeteria for twenty-two minutes and another who stayed approximately thirty minutes. One supervisor spent an hour and ten minutes in the cafeteria.

5 A check of two departments revealed that in each the second section left for coffee break before the first section returned.

Shaw feels that a problem still exists at United Mutual concerning the coffee period. The current action that Shaw is taking is to revise the coffee-break schedule in order to prevent congestion and achieve better control. Neither Gorman nor Shaw is sure what else should be done, if anything.

STUDY GUIDES

1 Appraise management's handling of the problems that developed in this case. What behavioral ideas were overlooked or misapplied?

2 At the end of the case, what are the key problems, if any? What are the alternatives to choose from? What would you do in the role of Gorman? What would you do if you were Shaw? What organizational behavior ideas would you apply?

3 Would any of the following be useful in interpreting this case?

a Behavior modification theory

b Models of organizational behavior

c Maslow's need hierarchy

d The law of diminishing returns

e Herzberg's motivational-maintenance theory

f Organizational climate

ROLE-PLAYING SITUATIONS

1 In the role of Shaw, arrange to discuss this case with Gorman.

2 In the role of Gorman, call in Shaw to instruct him to improve the coffee-break situation.

THE PERFORMANCE RATING

Cecil Howard was employed as a training assistant in the state civil service for twelve years. His supervisor for the last nine years has been Maude Marrus, a woman young enough to be his daughter. Although civil service regulations require that employees be given a performance report once a year, they are not well enforced. Howard received only one report of "satisfactory" in his second year as training assistant.

Howard is a mild and quiet person without an outgoing personality, but he feels he has performed effectively as a trainer, because he has held the job for twelve years and has never received either oral or written comment that his work is less than satisfactory. On three occasions he took the required examination for those seeking promotion to Training Officer 1. In each case he passed the written test but failed the oral interview by a state personnel office panel. He assumed he failed because of his lack of an outgoing personality, but he received no feedback about reasons for failure.

Recently the State Personnel Board decided to abolish the title of Training Assistant and give assistants the title of Training Officer 1, since they were performing training work equal to that job. Howard believed his change in title would be automatic, but the Personnel Board decided that, since a pay increase of over 15 percent was involved, assistants must take the test for promotion. Howard assumed this procedure would be routine, since he had performed satisfactorily for twelve years and his duties would not change with the new title. He passed the written test but failed the oral test again.

At this point Howard was frustrated and angry. He approached his supervisor with determination "to get to the bottom of this problem, even if I have to go to the State Personnel Board." After a heated exchange with Marrus, Howard learned that he had failed the oral tests because Marrus had given the interview panel a negative recommendation on him. Her recommendation stated that Howard had not developed sufficiently to merit promotion to Training Officer 1. All this was unknown to Howard. He had received no feedback from Marrus or the Personnel Board. Although a mild person, Howard exploded after learning this new fact. In a stormy session with Marrus he stated that he had a right to feedback about his performance and Marrus had an obligation to help him develop if she felt he was not developing adequately.

Later Howard requested to examine his personnel file and was allowed to see it. The personnel file had no negative reports on performance, reprimands, refusal to take development opportunities, or other negative information. There was one satisfactory performance rating ten years old. Also there were no commendations, records of training taken, or other positive information.

Since the title of Training Assistant was abolished, Howard is now working as a Staff Services Analyst performing the same training services that he formerly did. His salary remains the same. His self-image has declined, and it is evident that he is less motivated. Other conditions remain the same.

STUDY GUIDES

1 Analyze some of the organizational behavior issues raised in this series of events.

2 If you were Howard, what changes in behavior would you try to make, if any?

3 If you were Marrus, what changes in behavior would you try to make, if any? Use specific organizational behavior models, frameworks, and ideas to explain why you would attempt these changes in behavior, if any.

4 Assume you are a member of the State Personnel Board and know about this situation because of a grievance filed by Howard. The board has authority to decide Howard's grievance.

   a What ideas and recommendations would you present in the board's discussion of Howard's grievance? Present the organizational behavior reasons behind your statements.

   b At a later appropriate time, what ideas and recommendations, if any, would you present to the board regarding policy changes in the area of Howard's grievance? Present the organizational behavior models and ideas behind your recommendations.

THE PALMER
EXPORT SITE*

The Palmer export site is a large port for shipping iron ore mined by the Flick Company, a major international mining company. Ore is brought to the site by rail from mines some 150 miles distant. Irvin Corporation, which holds a construction and maintenance contract at the site, operates worldwide in the construction of heavy, technical engineering projects. The Palmer site is in an extremely isolated desert area over 700 miles from the nearest city of as many as 50,000 people.

Information in this case is presented only concerning the relationship of Irvin management with Flick management at the Palmer site. Two consultants who studied the situation described it as follows.

COMMENTS OF CONSULTANTS

Our comments concerning the investigation must be viewed against the background of the physical and social conditions in which work is conducted at Palmer. Above all, Palmer exists solely as a port for the export of iron ore. There are no other reasons for the town to be located there. Palmer is a company town; all the facilities, and to a large extent the way of life, are dependent on Flick. Similarly, it is quite evident that Irvin's situation in Palmer is dominated by its contractor-client relationship with Flick. Much of what we saw happening is a direct result of this relationship.

---

*This case is adapted with permission from comments prepared by T. A. Williams and G. G. Watkins.

In contrast to its usual operation, Irvin in Palmer is performing a service function mainly consisting of maintaining, servicing, and altering a wide range of activities for Flick. The work varies from substantial modifications of port and plant facilities all the way to gardening.

This type of work is not typical for Irvin, which normally has been engaged in major construction. On a major project a job has a beginning, middle, and end. In comparison, while Irvin's contract with Flick obviously had a beginning, it has no clearly discernible end. The difference between these two types of work should be expressed in more than time, because it is evident that the lack of a clearly defined terminal objective has important psychological effects on Irvin managers.

The nature of Irvin's task evidently runs counter to the construction way of life. Employees building a major facility from start to finish are able to recognize clearly what they have accomplished, the specific contributions which different work roles have made to the outcome, and the relationships between these contributions. They claim that there is a sense of challenge associated with working to a quoted price on the job and a sense of satisfaction in seeing something built and operating. The lack of this attitude was clearly evident from our interviews with Irvin staff, during which they expressed dissatisfaction with the role they see themselves performing in Palmer.

It is apparent that Irvin people in Palmer are engaged in a rather different kind of business from that to which they have become accustomed. It is clear that the basic nature of the present contract compares unfavorably with the type of work that Irvin normally does. There are also certain drawbacks with respect to the way in which Flick uses Irvin in this contract.

The work is initiated for Irvin on a continuing basis by Flick. While this may appear to be a sensible arrangement as far as the client is concerned, it places Irvin in a position of having constantly to adapt to Flick initiatives. Flick's plans continually change in a large number of areas in which Irvin is engaged, and this makes the problem of adaptation more difficult. Irvin's difficulties are further compounded by the tendency for Flick requirements and changes to be initiated for Irvin at all levels of the respective organizational structures. Together, these factors place Irvin's staff in a relationship of second-class citizens with respect to the Flick staff. This has consequences for both the work roles and the social status of the Irvin people.

First, it is a classic example of the frustrations which are generated when one party to the work relationship is continually initiating activity on the other party. The most common example of this problem is the traditional relationship between production and maintenance in industrial organizations. Initially in such a relationship, it seems normal for the parties to cooperate with each other as much as possible. However, as problems arise, the relationships often go sour, with production (in this case the client Flick) using its authority to make increasing demands on maintenance (Irvin). Such action even extends to overt intimidation. In turn, the recipient of this initiation may attempt to protect itself by using the fact that the initiator depends on it for task performance. In other words, the Flick staff may be using the client relationship to give vent to their own feelings of aggressiveness toward Irvin people. The latter might well respond by withholding effective task performance or by carrying out their tasks less than enthusiastically.

It would appear that Irvin and Flick are laboring under confusions and contradictions concerning the nature of company objectives. Irvin's formal task seems to be one of ensuring the continued efficient operation of Flick's facilities and adaptation of these facilities to meet changing needs. One might have supposed that Flick's final task is to export iron ore with a degree of efficiency which approaches maximization of export volume, given a reasonable rate of return. To some extent we gained the impression that Flick was concerned with this objective. However, there were signs that the "real" objectives of Flick management, as implied by their actions, are the product of psychological pressures caused by the sight of empty ships sitting in the harbor.

During the period we were in Palmer, Flick was loading at a rate of approximately 2000 tons per hour. The maximum possible rate is 6000 tons per hour. Over a period of time, it might be more efficient to stop the conveyor for necessary repairs and modifications to be carried out in order to continue at a more efficient rate. However, Irvin managers cited numerous examples of being unable to get in to carry out work because of Flick's insistence on keeping the conveyor belts running.

In the particular case of the Flick-Irvin relationship in Palmer, the above problems may have been compounded by the circumstances under which Irvin went into Palmer as a contractor. It appears that initially Flick staff resented the contract. Before the signing of this contract, the work which Irvin now performs was contracted to a number of firms on the basis of bids. This procedure enabled Flick staff to obtain certain free services from the contractors who were competing, such as boat repairs and garden maintenance. The nature of the Flick-Irvin contract requires Irvin to charge Flick on a cost-plus basis. This means that Irvin must submit detailed accounts justifying its expenditures. Hence there is little, if any, scope for Flick staff to improve their private well-being through the manipulation of contractual relationships.

Second, the situation illustrates the difficulty of trying to carry out rationally planned work when Irvin has little control over both the circumstances which create the need for work and the resources needed to carry out that work. Weekly work schedules are drawn up every Thursday afternoon at a meeting attended by both Flick and Irvin management. While we were in Palmer, there were some 171 open work orders on Irvin. The official purpose of the weekly planning meeting is to assign priorities among the work orders. By the Monday of our visit, the priorities laid down the previous Thursday had been substantially changed by Flick. Presumably the involvement of Irvin managers in the meeting is intended as a means of enabling them to participate in the planning of work for which they are responsible. However, it is clear that after the meeting the power to veto any decisions reached rests with Flick, and that this right is frequently and constantly exercised.

To this extent, Irvin managers would appear to have little real control over the events with which they are required to cope. Moreover, their lack of control over the work situation extends to use of the resources for performing work. While Irvin has some equipment on site, it is required to use Flick equipment when it is "available." However, frequently the equipment is not available. First, the equipment may be required for use by Flick. Second, Flick may not actually be using the equipment but may wish to hold it in reserve in order to gain flexibility in its own operations. Either way this reduces the flexibility that Irvin requires in order to cope with a rapidly changing work situation. Two outstanding examples of this are related to the paint shop and the fitting of a down pipe. Irvin is now involved in painting ore cars and is not allowed to use a paint shop specially built to repaint rolling stock. The shop is at present unused. With regard to the down pipe, a job that would have taken a day with a crane was still unfinished after several weeks.

Irvin's situation in Palmer is curiously paradoxical. Its people are subject to Flick's planning. To the extent that Flick plans its work efficiently, Irvin's profitability is increased due to the cost-plus basis of the contract. However, Irvin may be suffering a less obvious cost in this situation. Its management people are used to working with greater self-determination than they are allowed in Palmer, where their work plans are subject to weekly Flick initiatives and daily Flick alterations. Over a period of time, this may lead to an erosion of the managerial capacity of Irvin people, whether this be expressed in resignations or loss of confidence and competence. The continued exposure of Irvin managers to the Palmer situation may result in the withering away of its most valuable asset, human resources.

STUDY GUIDES

1 Analyze the events in this case, using frameworks, ideas, and professional terms from this book, in order to determine what is happening at the Palmer site and why it is happening.

2 If you were a member of Flick top management and became aware of how the conditions in this case may be costing your firm money, what would you do? Explain why, using frameworks, ideas, and professional terms from this book.

3 If you were Irvin top management and became aware of how the conditions in this case may be damaging your human resources, even though they may be giving higher earnings at the moment, what would you do, if anything? Explain why, using frameworks, ideas, and terms from this book.

4 Do any of the ideas you have expressed in any of the preceding three questions apply to typical management-worker relationships in your nation? Explain.

GLOSSARY

Absences. Employees who fail to show up for work as scheduled.

Acceptance theory of authority. Belief that the power of a manager depends on the willingness of employees to accept that authority.

Achievement motive. Drive to overcome challenges and obstacles in the pursuit of goals.

Action research. Method of improving problem-solving skills by discussing data-based system problems.

Affiliation motive. Drive to relate to people on a social basis.

Affirmative action. Employer effort to increase employment opportunity for protected groups that appear to be inadequately represented in a firm's labor force.

Age Discrimination Act. Law (as amended) that provides EEO for employees from ages forty to seventy.

Alienation. Feeling of powerlessness, lack of meaning, loneliness, disorientation, and lack of attachment to the job, work group, or organization.

Allocative values. Limitations on distribution of scarce resources.

Appraisal. See *Performance appraisal.*

Area of job freedom. Area of discretion after all restraints have been applied.

Assertiveness training. Program that teaches people to be more direct, honest, and expressive as a means of dealing with anxiety-producing situations.

Attribution. Process by which people interpret the causes of their own and others' behavior.

Autocratic leaders. Leaders who centralize power and decision making in themselves.

Autocratic model. Managerial view that power and formal authority are necessary to control employee behavior.

Autonomy. Policy of giving employees some discretion and control over job-related decisions.

Behavior modeling. Method of teaching by actual demonstration with acted-out ways to handle commonly encountered behavioral problems.

Behavior modification. Theory that behavior depends on its consequences; therefore, it is possible to control a number of employee behaviors by manipulating their consequences.

Behavioral bias. Narrow viewpoint of some people that emphasizes satisfying employee experiences while overlooking the broader system of the organization in relation to all its publics.

Benevolent autocrat. Autocratic leader who chooses to give rewards to employees.

Biofeedback. Approach by which people under medical guidance learn from instrument feedback to influence symptoms of stress such as increased heart rate.

Body language. Way in which people communicate meaning to others with their bodies in interpersonal interaction.

Boundary roles. Positions that require an ability to interact with different groups in order to keep a project successful.

Boundary spanners. Individuals with strong communication links within their department, with people in other units, and often with the external community.

Brainstorming. Group structure that encourages creative thinking by deferring judgment on ideas generated.

Bureaucracy. Large, complex administrative system operating with impersonal detachment from people.

Burnout. Situation in which employees suffer from chronic fatigue, boredom, depression, and powerful alienation from their jobs.

Cafeteria benefits. See *Flexible benefits.*

Chain-reaction effect. Situation in which a change (or other condition) that directly affects only one or a few persons may lead to a reaction from many people, even hundreds or thousands, because of their mutual interest in it.

Change agent. Person whose role is to initiate change and help make it work.

Climate profile charts. Graphic presentation of strong and weak elements of organizational climate.

Cluster chain. Grapevine chain in which one person tells several others, and a few of those tell more than one person.

Codetermination. Government-mandated worker representation on the board of directors of a firm.

Cognitive dissonance. Internal conflict and anxiety that occurs when people receive information incompatible with their value systems, prior decisions, or other information they may have.

Cognitive theories of motivation. Motivational theories based on thinking and feeling (i.e., cognition) of the employee.

Collective bargaining. Negotiation between representatives of management and labor to produce a written agreement covering terms and conditions of employment.

Collegial model. Managerial view that teamwork is the way to build employee responsibility.

Committee. Specific type of meeting in which members in their group role have been delegated authority with regard to the problem at hand.

Communication. Transfer of information and understanding from one person to another person.

Communication circuit. Two-way flow of information from sender to receiver and back to the sender.

Communication loop. See *Communication circuit.*

Communication overload. Condition in which employees receive more communication inputs than they can process or than they need.

Communication process. Six steps by which a sender reaches a receiver with a message—develop an idea, encode, transmit, receive, decode, and use.

Competence motive. Drive to do high-quality work.

Complementary transaction. Communicative action in which the ego states of the sender and receiver in the opening transaction are simply reversed in the response.

Complete pay program. Comprehensive reward system that uses different bases of pay to accomplish various objectives (e.g., retention, production, teamwork).

Conceptual skill. Ability to think in terms of models, frameworks, and broad relationships.

Conciliation agreement. Negotiated settlement (of a discrimination charge) that is acceptable to the EEOC and all aggrieved parties.

Conditional strokes. Strokes offered to employees if they perform correctly or avoid problems.

Conflict. Disagreement over the goals to attain or the methods used to accomplish them.

Conformity. Dependence on the norms of others without independent thinking.

Consensus. Agreement of most of the members of a group.

Consideration. Leader's employee orientation.

Consultive management. System of management in which employees are encouraged to think about issues and contribute their own ideas before decisions are made.

Context. Environment in which words are used.

Contingency approach to O.B. Philosophy that different environments require different behavioral practices for effectiveness.

Contingency model of leadership. Model that states that the most appropriate leadership style depends on the favorableness of the situation, especially in relation to leader-member relations, task structure, and position power.

Contingency organizational design. Use of different organizational structures and processes that are required for effectiveness in different kinds of environments.

Contract arbitration. Use of a third party to make final and binding decisions on major bargaining issues.

Core dimensions of jobs. Five factors of jobs, including variety, task identity, task significance, autonomy, and feedback.

Corrective discipline. Action taken to discourage further infractions so that future acts will be in compliance with standards.

Cost-reward break-even analysis. Process in which employees identify and compare personal costs and rewards to determine the point at which they are approximately equal.

Counseling. Discussion of a problem that usually has emotional content with an employee in order to help the employee cope with it better.

Counseling functions. Six activities that may be performed by counseling, including advice, reassurance, communication, release of emotional tension, clarified thinking, and reorientation.

Counterproposal. Offer suggested as an alternative to a previous proposal by the other party.

Cross-communication. See *Lateral communication.*

Crossed transaction. Communicative action in which the stimulus lines in an opening transaction are not parallel to those in the response.

Cultural shock. Feeling of confusion, insecurity, and anxiety caused by a strange new environment.

Culture. Environment of human-created beliefs, customs, knowledge, and practices that define conventional behavior in a society.

Custodial model. Managerial view that security needs are dominant among employees.

Delegation. Assignment of duties, authority, and responsibility to others.

Delphi group. Group structure in which a series of questionnaires are distributed to the respondents, who do not need to meet face to face.

Democratic management. System of management in which opportunities to make major decisions are given to employee groups.

Descriptive surveys. Format in which employees respond in their own words to express their feelings, thoughts, and intentions.

Directive counseling. Process of listening to an employee's problem, deciding with the employee what should be done, and then telling and motivating the employee to do it.

Discharge. Separation of an employee from the company for cause.

Discipline. Management action to enforce organizational standards.

Dual-career couples. Situations in which each spouse has a separate career.

Due process. Disciplinary procedures that show concern for the rights of the employee involved.

Dysfunctional action. Change that creates unfavorable effects for the system.

Ecological control. Alteration of the interpersonal environment so as to influence another's behavior.

Economic incentive system. System that varies an employee's pay in proportion to some criterion of individual, group, or organizational performance.

Ego states. Psychological positions of Parent, Adult, and Child that form the basis for social transactions.

Elaborating. Adding one's own strong feelings and reasoning to a communication.

Employee assistance program. Program to identify and treat the problems that are affecting employee productivity or hindering the personal well-being of employees.

Employee ownership plans. Programs for employees to provide the capital to purchase control of an existing operation.

Employment enrichment. Situation in which jobs, work teams, and work systems have all been enriched to create a balanced environment.

Encounter group. Unstructured small-group interaction under stress in a situation that requires people to become sensitive to one another's feelings.

Enriched sociotechnical work system. System in which a whole organization or major part of it is built into a balanced human-technical system.

Equal employment opportunity (EEO). Provision of equal opportunities to secure jobs and earn rewards in them, regardless of conditions unrelated to job performance.

Equal Employment Opportunity Commission (EEOC). Federal agency charged with enforcing EEO laws.

Equal employment opportunity laws. Federal, state, and local legislation to support EEO.

Equity theory. Employee tendency to judge fairness by comparing their inputs and rewards on the job with those of other relevant people.

Ethical leadership. Recognition and use of guides such as social responsibility, open communication, and human and social cost-benefit analysis for the betterment of society.

Expectancy. Strength of belief that work-related effort will result in completion of a task.

Expectancy model. Theory that motivation is a product of three factors: valence, expectancy, and instrumentality.

Experiential learning. Process in which participants learn by experiencing in the training environment the kinds of human problems they face on the job.

Expert power. Power that arises from a person's knowledge of and information about a complex situation.

Extinction. Lack of a significant consequence accompanying behavior.

Extrinsic motivators. External rewards that occur apart from work.

Fact premises. Science-based views of how the world behaves.

Feedback. Information from the job itself, management, or other employees that tells workers how well they are performing.

Feedback loop. See *Communication circuit.*

Filtering. Reducing a communication to a few basic details that can be remembered and passed on to others.

Flexible benefits. Systems that allow employees to select their individual combination of benefits.

Flexible working time. A system in which employees have some autonomy to adjust their work schedules to fit their lifestyles or to meet unusual needs.

Flextime. See *Flexible working time.*

Followership skills. Behaviors that help a person to be an effective subordinate to a leader.

Free-rein leaders. Leaders who avoid power and responsibility.

Frustration. Result of a motivation (drive) being blocked to prevent one from reaching a desired goal.

Functional action. Change that is favorable for the system.

Functionalization. Division of work into different kinds of duties.

Gainsharing. Policy of giving employees a substantial portion of the cost savings produced when their jobs are improved.

Goal setting. Establishment of targets and objectives for successful performance, both long-run and short-run.

Good mental health. Condition in which people feel comfortable about themselves, right about other people, and able to meet the demands of life.

Gossip chain. Grapevine chain in which a person tells many others.

Grapevine. Communication system of informal organization.

Grievance. Real or imagined feeling of personal injustice that an employee has about the employment relationship.

Grievance arbitration. Final and binding interpretation of what the existing contract means, as judged by an arbitrator.

Grievance rate. Number of written grievances for a hundred employees in one year.

Grievance system. Formal system by which disputes over working rules are expressed, processed, and judged in an organization.

Group dynamics. Social process by which people interact face to face in small groups.

Groupthink. Tendency of a group to bring individual thinking in line with the average quality of the group's thinking.

Handicapped employees. Those employees with a significant disability of some type, either physical, mental, or emotional.

Hawthorne effect. Concept that the mere observation of a group tends to change it.

Hidden agenda. Private emotions and motives of group members.

Hierarchy of needs. Philosophy that different groups of needs have a specific order of priority among most people, so that one group of needs precedes another in importance.

Higher-order needs. Need levels 3 to 5 on the Maslow hierarchy of needs.

Holistic O.B. Philosophy that interprets people-organization relationships in terms of the whole person, whole group, whole organization, and whole social system.

Homeostasis. Self-correcting mechanism in a group by which energies are called up to restore balance whenever change threatens a group.

Hot-stove rule. Disciplinary action with characteristics similar to the consequences a person suffers from touching a hot stove.

Human relations. Term applied to organizational behavior early in its history, and especially applied to practices that were less sophisticated, shallow, and faddish.

Human resource accounting. Process of converting human data into money values for use in the regular accounting system.

Human skill. Ability to work effectively with people and to build teamwork.

Humanistic values. Positive beliefs about the potential and desire for growth among employees.

Incentives. Environmental factors that are established for the purpose of motivating a person.

Incremental values. Almost limitless human values that are created by a positive organizational climate.

Individual differences. Idea that each person is different from all others and that these differences usually are substantial rather than meaningless.

Industrial democracy. Government-mandated worker participation at various levels of the organization with regard to decisions that affect workers.

Industrial relations. See *Labor relations.*

Inference. Interpretation of symbols that is based on assumptions, not facts.

Informal organization. Network of personal and social relations not established or required by the formal organization, but arising spontaneously as people associate with one another.

Initiation of action. Process of sending work and/or instructions to another person.

Institutional team. Companywide group of people.

Instrumentality. Belief that a reward will be received once a task is accomplished.

Interest arbitration. See *Contract arbitration.*

Intramanagement communication. See *Management communication.*

Intrinsic motivators. Internal rewards that a person feels when performing a job, so there is a direct connection between work and reward.

Investment approach. Policy of treating certain human resource costs as an investment to be depreciated during an employee's expected employment.

Job content. Conditions that relate directly to the job itself and the employee's performance of it, rather than conditions in the environment external to the job.

Job context. Job conditions in the environment surrounding the job, rather than those directly related to job performance.

Job Diagnostic Survey (JDS). Instrument used to determine the relative presence of the five core dimensions in jobs.

Job enlargement. Policy of giving workers a wider variety of duties in order to reduce monotony.

Job enrichment. Policy of adding motivators to a job to make it more rewarding.

Job placement profile charts. Visual displays that match worker physical and mental abilities with a job's requirements.

Job satisfaction. Set of favorable or unfavorable feelings with which employees view their work.

Job satisfaction survey. Procedure by which employees report their feelings toward their jobs and work environment.

Keystone role of supervisors. Behavior pattern in which the supervisor is seen as the element that connects both sides (management and workers) and makes it possible for each to perform its function effectively.

Knowledge society. Society in which the use of knowledge and information dominates work and employs the largest proportion of the labor force.

Labor relations. Subject of union-management relations.

Labor union. Association of employees formed for the primary purpose of influencing an employer's decisions about conditions of employment.

Laboratory training. Situations in which the trainees experience through their own interactions some of the conditions they are talking about.

Lateral communication. Communication across chains of command.

Law of diminishing returns. Principle that a declining amount of extra outputs are received when more of a desirable input is added to an operating system.

Law of Effect. Tendency of a person to repeat behavior that is accompanied by favorable consequences and not to repeat behavior accompanied by unfavorable consequences.

Leader-member relations. Degree to which the leader is accepted by the group.

Leader-position power. Organizational power that goes with the position the leader occupies.

Leadership. Process of encouraging and helping others to work enthusiastically toward objectives.

Leadership style. Total pattern of a leader's actions, as perceived by the leader's employees.

Learned helplessness. Condition in which employees continue to act in a dependent manner even after organizational changes make greater independence possible.

Legimate power. Power that is delegated legitimately from higher-established authorities to others.

Leveling effect. See *Groupthink*.

Liaison individuals. Persons who are active communicators on the grapevine.

Life position. Dominant way of relating to people that tends to remain with the person for a lifetime unless major experiences occur to change it.

Linking pin. Managerial role of connecting the group with the remainder of the organization.

Loose rate. Rate that allows employees to reach standard output with less-than-normal effort.

Lower-order needs. Need levels 1 and 2 on the Maslow hierarchy of needs.

Macromotivation. Conditions outside the firm that influence employee performance (type B).

Maintenance factors. Conditions that tend to satisfy workers when they exist and to dissatisfy workers when they do not exist, but their existence tends not to be strongly motivating.

Management by objectives (MBO). System in which managers and subordinates mutually agree on the employee's objectives for the next year and on the criteria that will be used to measure accomplishment of the objectives.

Management communication. Communication within the management group.

Managerial grid. Framework of management styles based on the dimensions of concern for people and concern for production.

Manipulation of people. Disregard for the basic dignity of the human being by learning and using organizational behavior ideas without regard for human welfare.

Matrix organization. Overlay of one type of organization on another so that there are two chains of command directing individual employees.

Mechanistic organizations. Organizations characterized by the use of hierarchy, centralized direction, certainty of task assignments, and strict definition of roles.

Mediator. Outside specialist who encourages the negotiating parties to come to an agreement.

Meditation. Quiet, concentrated inner thought in order to rest the body physically and emotionally.

Mentoring. System in which one person serves as a role model to help a new employee gain valuable data on roles to play and roles to avoid.

Micromotivation. Conditions within the firm that influence employee performance (type A).

Models of organizational behavior. Underlying theories that act as unconscious but powerful guides to managerial thought and behavior.

Morale. Level of job satisfaction within a group.

Motivating potential score (MPS). Index that indicates the degree to which a job is perceived to be meaningful, foster responsibility, and provide knowledge of results.

Motivation. Strength of the drive toward an action.

Motivational factors. Conditions that tend to motivate workers when they exist, but their absence rarely is strongly dissatisfying.

Motivational patterns. Attitudes that affect the way people view their jobs and approach their lives.

Multiple management. Middle-management committees to improve the participation of managers below top organizational levels.

Multiprofessional employees. People who are trained in two or more professions or intellectual disciplines.

Mutual interest. Idea that people need organizations and organizations need people, which gives them a superordinate goal of joint interest to bring them together.

Natural work module. Job designed so that a person performs a complete cycle of work to make a whole product or subunit of it.

Natural work team. Group of employees whose task is to work together to produce an entire unit of work.

Needs, primary. Basic physical needs.

Needs, secondary. Social and psychological needs.

Negative leadership. Leaders who emphasize penalties to motivate people.

Negative reinforcement. Removal of an unfavorable consequence that accompanies behavior.

Network. Group of people who develop and maintain contact to informally exchange information, usually about a shared interest.

Networking. Being active on a network.

Nominal group. Group structure that combines individual input, group discussion, and independent decision making.

Nondirective counseling. Process of skillfully listening to and encouraging a counselee to explain troublesome problems, understand them, and determine appropriate solutions.

Nonlogical. Based on feelings rather than logic.

Nontraditional employment. Jobs not historically held by members of that sex.

Nonverbal communication. Actions (or inactions) that people take that serve as a means of communication.

Norm. Informal group requirement for the behavior of its members.

Norm of reciprocity. Principle that two people in a continuing relationship feel a strong obligation to repay their social "debts" to each other.

O.B. Mod. See *Organizational behavior modification.*

Objective surveys. Format using highly structured response categories for gathering job satisfaction data.

Open-door policy. Statement encouraging employees to come to their supervisor or higher managers with any matter that concerns them.

Operant conditioning. Any type of reinforcement to modify behavior by its consequence.

Organic organizations. Organizations characterized by flexible tasks and roles, open communications, and decentralized decision making.

Organization development (OD). Intervention strategy that uses group processes to focus on the whole culture of an organization in order to bring about planned change.

Organizational behavior (O.B.). Study and application of knowledge about how people act within organizations.

Organizational behavior modification (O.B. Mod.). Behavior modification used in organizations.

Organizational behavior system. Integrated framework of elements that portrays how behavior is guided toward achievement of organizational goals.

Organizational climate. Human environment within which an organization's employees do their work.

Organizational climate approach. Use of periodic surveys to determine ways in which the organizational climate has improved or deteriorated.

Organizational gaming. Group exercise in sequential decision making under simulated organizational conditions.

Organizational learning curve for change. Period of adaptation that follows change and typically shows a decline in effectiveness before a group reaches a new equilibrium.

Output restriction. Situation in which workers choose to produce less than they could produce with normal effort.

Overparticipation. Condition in which employees have more participation than they want.

Parity employment. See *Proportional employment.*

Participation. Mental and emotional involvement of persons in group situations that encourage them to contribute to group goals and share responsibility for them.

Participative counseling. Mutual counselor-counselee relationship that establishes a cooperative exchange of ideas to help solve a counselee's problems.

Participative leader. Leader who decentralizes authority by consulting with followers.

Path-goal leadership. Model that states that the leader's job is to create a work environment through structure, support, and rewards that helps employees reach the organization's goals.

Perception. Individual's own view of the world.

Perceptual set. People's tendency to perceive what they expect to perceive.

Performance appraisal. Process of evaluating the performance of employees.

Performance-satisfaction-effort loop. Flow model that shows the directional relationship between performance and satisfaction.

Personal power. Ability of leaders to develop followers from the strength of their own personalities.

Personal wellness. Programs of preventive maintenance that help individuals reduce the causes of stress or cope with stressors that are beyond their direct control.

Phased retirement. Programs that give workers more time off, usually with pay, in the years immediately preceding retirement.

Piece rate. Reward system that pays employees according to the number of acceptable pieces produced.

Political power. Ability to work with people and social systems to gain their allegiance and support.

Politics. Ways that leaders gain and use power.

Polygraph. Instrument (lie detector) that measures the physiological changes when a person tells a significant lie.

Positive leadership. Leaders who emphasize rewards to motivate people.

Positive reinforcement. Favorable consequence that accompanies behavior and encourages repetition of the behavior.

Power. Ability to influence other people and events.

Power motive. Drive to influence people and change situations.

Preretirement counseling. Programs that encourage employees to think about pending retirement.

Preventive discipline. Action taken to encourage employees to follow standards and rules so that infractions do not occur.

Problem-solving bargaining. Approach that tries to get joint gain for both parties.

Procedure. Organization of work based on its flow from one operation to another.

Production sharing. Incentive program that pays employees for improvements in labor costs that are better than standard.

Productivity. Ratio that compares units of output with units of input.

Profile chart. Graphic display of the scores of the five core dimensions of jobs.

Profit sharing. System that distributes to employees some portion of the profits of business.

Progressive discipline. Policy that provides stronger penalties for repeated offenses.

Proportional employment. Belief that an organization's employees should approximately represent the proportions of different groups in the local labor force or population.

Protected groups. Groups of employees who are protected from employment discrimination by EEO laws.

Psychic costs. Costs that affect a person's inner self or psyche.

Psychological contract. Unwritten agreement that defines the conditions of each employee's psychological involvement with the system.

Psychological costs. See *Psychic costs.*

Psychological stress evaluator. Instrument that analyzes changes in voice patterns to determine whether a lie is being told.

Psychological support. Condition in which leaders stimulate people to want to do the job.

Punishment. Unfavorable consequence that accompanies behavior and discourages repetition of the behavior.

Quality circles. Voluntary groups that receive training in statistical techniques and problem-solving skills and then meet to produce ideas for improving productivity and working conditions.

Quality of work life (QWL). Favorableness or unfavorableness of a job environment for people.

Rate setting. Process of determining the standard output for each job.

Readability. Degree to which writing and speech are understandable to receivers.

Realistic job previews. Employment process in which job candidates are given a small sample of organizational reality.

Recess. A break taken by the bargaining committee to discuss some point privately.

Red tape. Procedure that appears to be unnecessary to those who are following it.

Reference group. Group whose norms a person accepts.

Refreezing. Term applying to situations involving change and referring to a person acting to integrate what has been learned into actual practice.

Reinforcement. Behavior consequence that influences behavior.

Reinforcement, continuous. Reinforcement accompanying each correct behavior.

Reinforcement, fixed interval. Reinforcement after a certain period of time.

Reinforcement, fixed ratio. Reinforcement after a certain number of correct responses.

Reinforcement, partial. Reinforcement following only some of the correct behaviors.

Reinforcement, variable interval. Reinforcement after a variety of time periods.

Reinforcement, variable ratio. Reinforcement after a variable number of correct responses.

Reinforcement schedules. Frequency with which reinforcement accompanies a desired behavior.

Reliability. Capacity of a survey instrument to produce consistent results.

Resistance to change. Desire not to accept a change or to accept it only partially.

Retraining. Providing opportunities to learn new skills to those employees whose jobs are replaced by technological change.

Reverse discrimination. Discrimination against an employee not included in an affirmative action program.

Rights of privacy. Freedom from organizational invasion of a person's private life and unauthorized release of confidential information about a person.

Robotics. Design and use of programmable, mechanical devices to move parts and perform a variety of tasks.

Role. Pattern of actions expected of a person in activities involving others.

Role ambiguity. Feeling that arises when roles are inadequately defined or are substantially unknown.

Role conflict. Feeling that arises when others have different perceptions or expectations of a person's role.

Role models. Leaders who serve as examples for their followers.

Role perceptions. How people think they are supposed to act in their own roles and others should act in their roles.

Role playing. Spontaneous acting of a realistic situation involving two or more people under classroom conditions.

Rule of Five. Steps in communication taken by a receiver—receive, understand, accept, use, and provide feedback.

Rumor. Grapevine information that is communicated without secure standards of evidence being present.

Sanctions. Rewards and penalties that a group uses to persuade persons to conform to its norms.

Scalar process. Division of an organization into levels on the basis of authority and responsibility.

Scanlon plan. Highly successful production-sharing plan that emphasizes teamwork and active participation.

Self-actualization. Need to become all that one is capable of becoming.

Semantics. Science of meaning.

Sensitivity training. See *Encounter group.*

Sexual harassment. Process of making employment or promotion decisions contingent on sexual favors, or any verbal or physical conduct that creates an offensive working environment.

Shaping. Successive reinforcement as behavior comes closer to the desired behavior.

Short-circuiting. Situation in which people skip one or more steps in the communication hierarchy.

Social cues. Positive or negative bits of information in our environment that influence how we react to a communication.

Social equilibrium. Dynamic working balance among the interdependent parts of a system.

Social leader. Person who helps restore and maintain group relationships.

Social loafing. Employee lessening of output when they think their contributions to a group cannot be measured.

Social responsibility. Recognition that organizations have significant influence on the social system, which must be considered and balanced in all organizational actions.

Social system. Complex set of human relationships interacting in many ways.

Socialization. Process by which organizations shape the attitudes, thoughts, and behavior of employees.

Socioeconomic model of decision making. Model in which social costs and benefits, as well as economic and technical values, are considered in the decision-making process.

Sociogram. Diagram of the feelings of group members toward each other.

Sociometry. Study and measurement of feelings of group members toward one another.

Sociotechnical systems. Relationship of technology to people at work.

Span of management. Number of people a manager directly manages.

Specialization. Process of becoming adept at a certain function as a result of concentrating efforts upon it.

Status. Social rank of a person in a group.

Status symbols. Visible, external things that attach to a person or workplace and serve as evidence of social rank.

Stress. Condition of strain on one's emotions, thought processes, and physical condition.

Stress threshold. Level of stressors that one can tolerate before feelings of stress occur.

Stressors. Conditions that tend to cause stress.

Strike. Work stoppage called by a union to place bargaining pressure on management.

Stroking. Performing any act of recognition for another person.

Structure. Leader's task orientation.

Substitutes for leadership. Characteristics of the task, employees, or organization that may reduce the need for leadership behaviors.

Suggestion programs. Formal plans to encourage individual employees to recommend work improvements. A monetary award frequently is offered for acceptable suggestions.

Superordinate goal. Goal that integrates the efforts of individuals or groups.

Supportive approach to O.B. Philosophy of working with people in ways that seek to satisfy their needs and develop their potential.

Supportive model. Managerial view that leaders should support employees in their attempts to grow and perform their jobs.

Surface agenda. Official task of a group.

Survey feedback. Communication of job satisfaction information to managers and others as a basis for action.

Systems 1 through 4. OD framework developed by Rensis Likert that uses four systems of management to describe organizations, with System 4 as the most participative.

Task identity. Policy of allowing employees to perform a complete piece of work.

Task leader. Person who helps the group accomplish its objectives and stay on target.

Task significance. Amount of impact, as perceived by the worker, that the work has on other people.

Task structure. Degree to which one specific way is required to do the job.

Task support. Condition in which leaders provide the resources, budgets, power, and other elements that are essential to get the job done.

Task team. Cooperative small group in regular contact that is engaged in coordinated action and whose members contribute responsibly and enthusiastically to the task.

Team building. OD process of developing integrated, cooperative groups.

Technical skill. Person's knowledge and ability in any type of process or technique.

Technophobia. Emotional fear of all technology regardless of its consequences.

Theory X. Autocratic and traditional set of assumptions about people.

Theory Y. Human and supportive set of assumptions about people.

Theory Z. Model that adapts the elements of Japanese management systems to the U.S. culture and emphasizes cooperation and consensus decision processes.

3-D management. OD program organized around the use or avoidance of consideration and structure, used effectively or ineffectively, to create eight managerial style options.

Trade-off. Offer to give up on one issue in exchange for "winning" another.

Transactional analysis (TA). Study of social transactions between people, so as to develop improved communication and human relationships.

Triple-reward system. Term applied to practices that jointly benefit the needs and objectives of three groups: people, organizations, and the whole social system.

Tunnel vision. See *Behavioral bias.*

Turnover. Rate at which employees leave an organization.

Two-factor model of motivation. Motivational model developed by Frederick Herzberg, which concludes that one set of job conditions primarily motivates an employee while a different set primarily satisfies and dissatisfies the employee.

Type A people. Individuals who are aggressive and competitive, set high standards, and put themselves under constant time pressures.

Type B people. Individuals who are relaxed and easygoing and accept situations readily.

Unconditional strokes. Strokes presented without any connection to behavior.

Underparticipation. Condition in which employees want more participation than they have.

Unfreezing. Term applying to situations involving change and referring to a person casting aside old ideas and practices so that new ones can be learned.

Valence. Strength of a person's preference for receiving a reward.

Validity. Capacity of a survey instrument to measure what it claims to measure.

Value premises. Personal views of the desirability of certain goals.

Variety. Policy of allowing employees to perform different operations that often require different skills.

Wage incentive. Reward system that provides more pay for more production.

Whistle-blower. Employee who discloses alleged misconduct to the public.

Win-lose bargaining. Negotiation in which each party tries to win from the other party a favorable division of limited resources.

Work committees. Groups of workers and their managers that are organized primarily to consider and solve job problems.

Work ethic. Employee attitude of viewing work as a central life interest and a desirable goal in life.

"X" chart. Model in the form of an "X" showing how attitudes affect responses to change. (Originally developed by F. J. Roethlisberger.)

INDEXES

NAME INDEX

SUBJECT INDEX